Ancient Celtic Place-Names in Europe and Asia Minor

Publications of the Philological Society, 39

Ancient Celtic Place-Names in Europe and Asia Minor

Patrick Sims-Williams

Publications of the Philological Society, 39

Oxford UK & Boston USA

Blackwell Publishing Ltd
9600 Garsington Road, Oxford, OX4 2DQ, UK

and
350 Main Street,
Malden, MA 02148, USA

Library of Congress Cataloging-in-Publication Data

Sims-Williams, Patrick.
Ancient Celtic place-names in Europe and Asia Minor / Patrick Sims-Williams.
p. cm. - (Publications of the Philological Society ; 39)
Includes bibliographical references and index.
ISBN-13: 978-1-4051-4570-1 (alk. paper)
ISBN-10: 1-4051-4570-6 (alk. paper)
1. Names, Geographic–Celtic. 2. Names, Geographic–Europe.
3. Names, Geographic–Turkey. 4. Celtic languages–Etymology–
Names. 5. Linguistic geography. I. Title. II. Series.
PB1093.S56 2006
914.001'4–dc22

2006009956

A catalogue record for this publication is available from the British Library.

Set in Times by SPS (P) Ltd., Chennai, India
Printed and bound in Singapore by
Seng Lee Press Pte Ltd

The publisher's policy is to use permanent paper from mills that operate a sustainable forestry policy, and which has been manufactured from pulp processed using acid-free and elementary chlorine-free practices. Furthermore, the publisher ensures that the text paper and cover board used have met acceptable environmental accreditation standards.

For further information on Blackwell Publishing, visit our website:
http://www.blackwellpublishing.com

Dedicated to the members of the Ptolemy workshops:

*Peter Anreiter
Patrizia de Bernardo Stempel
Javier de Hoz
Alexander Falileyev
Juan Luis García Alonso
Ashwin E. Gohil
Joaquín Gorrochategui
Marialuise Haslinger
Graham R. Isaac
Pierre-Yves Lambert
Eugenio R. Luján
David N. Parsons
Ulrike Roider
Paul Russell
Peter Schrijver
Gregory Toner
Lauran Toorians
Naomi Ward
Stefan Zimmer*

CONTENTS

LIST OF MAPS

PREFACE

I hope that this book will appeal not only to philologists, but also to historians and archaeologists interested in the ancient Celts – here defined as Celtic-speakers. Non-linguists opening the text or index at random should be warned that not all the names mentioned are Celtic. In fact very many are not, and are cited only to be eliminated in the course of the enquiry. Much non-Celtic data had to be cited so as to allow specialists to make their own judgements about my decisions as to what was Celtic and what was not. As a result the book resembles the Centre Pompidou: all the workings are on the outside. This may not be aesthetically pleasing, but it should allow easy maintenance in future.

Anyone wishing to find a quick overview of where I think genuine Celtic place-names are attested in early sources should look at Map 11.1. This has surprises such as Corsica alongside well-known Celtic-speaking regions from Galicia to Galatia. Beyond the area outlined on Map 11.1, I found only a few tantalizing glimpses of arguably Celtic names: a *polis* called *Vobrix* in Morocco, a tributary of the Euphrates called *Sabrina* and a tribe of *Tektosakes* in Central Asia (see Chapter 10).

This study grew out of an interest in the early distribution of the Celtic branch of the Indo-European language family. My fascination with the evidence of place-names in particular goes back to 1999, when the International Joint Activities Fund of the British Academy funded a workshop in the Department of Welsh, University of Wales, Aberystwyth on *Ptolemy: Towards a Linguistic Atlas of the Earliest Celtic Place-Names of Europe* (ed. Parsons & Sims-Williams 2000). The group has gone from strength to strength, and has held further 'Ptolemy' workshops in Innsbruck in 2000, in Madrid in 2002 (ed. De Hoz, Luján & Sims-Williams 2005) and in Munich in 2004. A further one is planned for Salamanca in 2006. Frequent citations indicate my debt to these workshops.

A generous grant for 2001–6 to the Department of Welsh of the University of Wales, Aberystwyth, from the Arts and Humanities Research Council contributed towards the cost of the workshops, and more particularly funded two Ph.D. studentships and a senior research post which was held by Graham Isaac up to 2004 and by Alexander Falileyev from 2005. Dr Isaac's main task was to create comprehensive databases of two of the main sources for Celtic – and non-Celtic – names: the *Antonine Itinerary* (AILR) and Ptolemy's *Geography* (PNPG). These were issued on CD in 2002 and 2004. The Ph.D. studentships were held by Ashwin Gohil, from the University of Utrecht (Dr Gohil also held a Postgraduate

Research Studentship from the University of Wales, Aberystwyth) and Naomi Ward, from the University of Cambridge.

The immense expense of producing a 'linguistic atlas', implied by the subtitle of the 1999 workshop, was obviated by the happy appearance of the large-scale *Barrington Atlas of the Greek and Roman World* in 2000. In this work, which is unlikely to be superseded for many decades, the majority of ancient toponyms appear in their geographical and historical context, and further unlocated ones are listed in its accompanying *Map-by-Map Directory*. Richard J. A. Talbert, its editor, and Tom Elliott, of the Ancient World Mapping Center at the University of North Carolina at Chapel Hill, kindly furnished me with a file of the 20,000 + ancient place-names in the *Atlas*. This made it possible for me to search electronically for Celtic-looking names, as described in Chapters 2–5 below. It soon became apparent that the greatest density of such names occurred in north-western Europe (see Maps 5.1 and 5.2 below). I then concentrated my own research on the areas where the Celtic-looking names were thinning out, with a view to establishing the frontiers of Celtic toponymy in southern and eastern Europe and Asia Minor (see Chapters 6–9 below). The most densely Celtic areas of the Continent were divided between the two Ph.D. students: Ashwin Gohil concentrated on northern France and Germany and Naomi Ward concentrated on central France and northern Iberia. Their work, and some of the material in the present book, will be incorporated into a concise etymological dictionary analysing all the Celtic place-names that are marked on the *Barrington Atlas* maps of Continental Europe and Asia Minor. This work, which is being co-ordinated by Dr Falileyev, will be the final stage of the current Aberystwyth project. A spin-off of the project is a searchable version of the headwords in Holder's massive *Alt-celtischer Sprachschatz*. This was generously begun by a volunteer, Mrs Llinos Dafis, a kind friend of the Department of Welsh, and was completed by Dr Gohil. It may be issued on CD as an appendix to a reprint of Georges Cousin's rare *Additions au 'Alt-celtischer Sprachschatz'*.

I am indebted to all the participants in the 'Ptolemy' workshops for their stimulus and inspiration; to Graham Isaac, Alexander Falileyev and Paul Russell for their comments on sections of this book; to David Williams for fair copies of Map 3.1 and Maps 6.1 to 10.1, and to Gwen Sims-Williams for the outline used in the remaining maps. Readers wishing to extract the full value from these maps should use them in conjunction with the *Barrington Atlas*. For the historical context, I would mention *The Historical Atlas of the Celtic World* by John Haywood, which appeared in 2001, and John T. Koch's *Atlas for Celtic Studies*, which is in preparation. All the material in this present book has been made available for the latter work.

In addition to members of the 'Ptolemy' workshops and other scholars already named, the following have sent essential books and articles: Robert Bedon, Francesco Benozzo, Pierre-Henri Billy, Leonard A. Curchin,

Helmut Humbach, Francesco Prontera, Blanca M. Prósper, Alastair Strang and Francisco Villar. I am very grateful to them all.

Finally, I thank the Philological Society and its Publications Secretary, Dr Paul Rowlett, for accepting a second Celtic book by me in its series, the staff of the Old College Library in Aberystwyth for their patience, and Marged, Gwen and Gwilym for allowing our house to be taken over by maps and atlases.

Department of Welsh
October 2005   *University of Wales, Aberystwyth*

1

INTRODUCTION

1.1 PLACE-NAMES AND ANCIENT LINGUISTIC GEOGRAPHY

Place-names preserve fragments of history. *Stratford-upon-Avon* is an English name containing an English preposition and English syntax, *ford* is an English word, with a well-known Germanic sound change (Indo-European **p* > Germanic **f* by Grimm's Law), *Strat-* (Modern English *street*) is from Old English *strǣt*, a loanword from Latin *strata* 'road', and *Avon* is the Welsh word for 'river', medieval Welsh *avon* – *afon* in Modern Welsh spelling. The Anglo-Saxons gave the name *Stratford* to the settlement where the Roman road crossed a river, and the name of the river was picked up from Celtic-speaking Britons.[1] Thus the name *Stratford-upon-Avon* tells us of Celtic-speakers, Latin-speakers and English-speakers in Warwickshire. In the same way *Nogent sur Avon* in France tells us of Celtic-speaking Gauls in Seine-et-Marne.[2]

Such place-names confirm what we already knew about the history of England and France. In many countries, however, place-names are the only non-archaeological evidence to have survived in bulk from early times. Potentially they have as much to tell us about human history as the DNA we carry in our bodies – in both cases if only we knew how to interrogate them. And, unlike DNA, which has wandered from country to country, place-names are fixed in space.

The toponymy of the landscape can be compared to a palimpsest upon which successive linguistic groups have written their signatures, and continue to do so. Some have supposed that our oldest place-names go back to the end of the last Ice Age;[3] speculation on such matters is best deferred, however, until the layers of the palimpsest written in the last two to three thousand years are identified. Here philologists have two good starting-points. One is that they can easily get back two millennia by consulting Greek and Latin texts. The other is by following the well-established methods for differentiating languages. For example *f* < IE **p* is one feature that makes *ford* Germanic, versus Latin *portus* 'passage' etc., where **p* was retained, or Gaulish *ritu-*, Welsh *rhyd*, Old Cornish *rit*, Old Breton *rit*, 'ford', where IE **p* was lost, as was regular in Celtic.

---

[1] It is still unclear whether **Abona* was actually a name or whether the English name was derived from the common noun **abona* (VEPN s.n. **abonā*). Cf. Smith, 'Survival of Romano-British toponymy', p. 37.

[2] Nègre i, §§ 1012 and 2385; DLG s.vv. *abona* and *nouuios* (and p. 10, n. 4).

[3] Vennemann, 'Linguistic reconstruction', p. 263.

For those who study the early history of the Celts, it is particularly important to establish the distribution of their language in Europe and Asia Minor because modern scholarship is almost unanimous in defining 'the Celts' primarily as 'speakers of Celtic languages'.[4] This linguistic definition is much more precise than any definitions available to historians,[5] archaeologists and art historians[6] from within their own disciplines.

'Celtic languages' means languages which philologists have assigned to the so-called 'Celtic' sub-family of the Indo-European language family on account of various innovations and peculiarities, like the loss of *p above, which these languages share in distinction to the other sub-families, such as Germanic, Greek and Indo-Iranian, which descended independently from Proto-Indo-European.[7] The term 'Celtic languages' does not necessarily mean languages spoken by people who were called, or called themselves, *Celti*, nor languages spoken by people who favoured so-called 'Celtic' art styles such as the 'La Tène' style. Some speakers of Celtic languages certainly called themselves Celts – the phrase *Celtica lingua* is no modern coinage – but others, including the Celtic-speakers of Britain and Ireland,

---

[4] Some of them would have been bilingual or multilingual of course. Some – perhaps most – of them would have acquired Celtic at the expense of other ancestral languages. As a result we cannot expect to correlate linguistic evidence with biological evidence; on that fallacy see Sims-Williams, 'Genetics, linguistics, and prehistory'.

[5] Historians have to depend on ancient writers' use of the ethnic label 'Celts' (*Keltoi, Celti, Celtae*, etc.) and its synonyms or near-synonyms 'Galatians' (*Galatai*) and 'Gauls' (*Galli*). Notoriously, many ancient writers use ethnic terms loosely (cf. Whittaker, *Frontiers*, pp. 212–13), especially from the linguistic point of view, failing to distinguish Celts from Germans, for example, and never referring to the inhabitants of Britain and Ireland as 'Celts'. See Sims-Williams, 'Celtomania and Celtoscepticism'. On whether the terms *Celts, Galatians* and *Gauls* are linguistically Celtic and etymologically identical see ibid. pp. 21–22. In the present work I will accept the linguistic Celticity of these three terms, following the consensus (e.g. GPN, pp. 332–33; Schmidt, 'Sprachreste', p. 15; PNPG Celtic Elements s.v. *gallo-*) and so classify names like *Galli* or *Pagus Gallorum* as linguistically Celtic. The lack of correlation between the linguistic origin of tribal names and the language of the tribes so named is well known (Papazoglu, p. 262), so I do not count the names of 'Celtic' tribes as linguistically Celtic except on etymological grounds. Note that although purists might label *Pagus Gallorum* as Latin (and similarly *Stratford-upon-Avon* as English and *Nogent sur Avon* as French), that would be inappropriate in the present investigation; in the same way, I shall treat hybrid names like *Augustodunum* as Celtic, not Latin. All are relevant to Celtic linguistic geography. In another context a more discriminating approach to hybrid names would be needed; see García Alonso, 'Ptolemy and the expansion of Celtic language(s)', pp. 138–40.

[6] Archaeological discussion of 'the Celts' tends to depend on nineteenth- and twentieth-century definitions of 'Celtic' material 'cultures' which fail to coincide fully either with areas where Celtic speech is attested in inscriptions, for example in Spain and north Italy, or with areas assigned to the Celts by ancient writers. See Sims-Williams, 'Celtomania and Celtoscepticism', pp. 31–32; Collis, *The Celts*, pp. 208–9. Collis reiterates points made in Sims-Williams, 'Degrees of Celticity', about place-name evidence for the distribution of Celtic speech and adds that he is 'highly sceptical how much archaeology can contribute to the debate'.

[7] An introduction to this field from the linguistic standpoint is Ramat & Ramat (eds), *The Indo-European Languages*. Attempts to locate speakers of Proto-Indo-European via biology and archaeology are fraught with methodological problems; see Sims-Williams, 'Genetics, linguistics, and prehistory'; also Day, *Indo-European Origins* (with my review).

seem never to have called themselves Celts before the modern period. Similarly, while Celtic-speakers certainly favoured the La Tène style in some areas, in other parts of ancient Europe Celtic languages co-existed with different styles: for example, the Celtic 'Lepontic' language in north Italy was accompanied by the so-called 'Golasecca' culture and its existence would hardly have been imagined if it were not for the lucky survival of the 'Lepontic' inscriptions.[8]

1.2 THE EXTENT OF CELTIC SPEECH

Inscriptions are the most tangible evidence of ancient Celtic speech, but their distribution is unfortunately restricted, owing to the greater prestige of Greek and Latin as written languages and the limited literacy of Celtic-speakers. Ancient Celtic inscriptions are concentrated in northern Italy, Switzerland, Spain and Gaul.[9] They are completely absent, for example, from Galatia in Asia Minor[10] and from ancient Ireland. No inscriptions in any language survive from Ireland before about the fifth century AD, when we have the first Irish inscriptions, written in the ogam alphabet,[11] while in Britain, apart from some fragments from Roman Bath, the first vernacular Celtic inscription is the one in Old Welsh from Tywyn, c. 800 AD.[12]

Four types of source provide evidence for Celtic speech over a much wider area of ancient Europe and Asia Minor than the surviving inscriptions. One is the Celtic personal names recorded in inscriptions in Latin and Greek from the various provinces of the Roman Empire.[13] Their distribution is significant despite the problem that many people such as soldiers and potters were highly mobile. The second source is the names of Celtic divinities named in Latin and Greek inscriptions.[14] Only a few of these, such as Epona, attained a cult beyond their original locale. The third source is the items of Celtic vocabulary recorded by ancient scholars or surviving as loanwords in other languages, such as the Romance dialects.[15]

---

[8] On the above see Sims-Williams, 'Celtomania and Celtoscepticism'.

[9] For maps see RIG and De Hoz, 'Mediterranean frontier of the Celts'.

[10] Mitchell, *Anatolia*, i, 51.

[11] McManus, *Guide*. For early medieval inscriptions in Irish and other Celtic languages in Britain and Brittany see CIB; they are greatly outnumbered in CIB by inscriptions in Latin but containing Celtic *names*.

[12] Sims-Williams, 'Five languages of Wales', pp. 6–9. In RIG ii/2, the Bath tablets (nos. L-107–8) are regarded as Latin, but see Sims-Williams, 'Common Celtic, Gallo-Brittonic and Insular Celtic', and Schrijver, 'Early Celtic diphthongization', pp. 57–60.

[13] For maps see Mócsy, *A római név mint társadalomtörténeti forrás*, pp. 31–35, and Sims-Williams, 'Five languages of Wales', p. 13. Dr M. E. Raybould and I are preparing a more detailed study of compound names; see section 12.4 below. The best source is now OPEL and the classic studies are KGP and GPN; see also DLG and KPP.

[14] These are the subject of an international project; see De Bernardo Stempel, 'Die sprachliche Analyse'.

[15] For an example of such material see Grzega. Cf. Billy's review of Grzega, p. 358.

Unfortunately vocabulary, unlike toponymy, is always 'on the move'; words can be acquired in one place and turn up later hundreds of miles away. This makes it difficult to extract ancient linguistic geography from vocabulary, and this is also true of the loanwords that appear in toponyms. For example, ancient toponyms containing the element *burg* are limited to the Rhine–Danube area, with the exception of those containing the Latin loanword *burgus* 'tower', which turn up in western Gaul and north Africa. Clearly, once it had been borrowed into Latin, *burgus* could be used anywhere in the Empire and provides no clue to the locality of the language(s) that originally provided the term.[16]

The fourth source, which is the subject of the present study, comprises the Celtic place-names recorded by ancient authors and geographers and occasionally found on inscriptions.[17] While place-names offer many problems, they are at least abundant throughout the Roman Empire and to some extent beyond it – extending even to Ireland, mainly thanks to Ptolemy *c*. AD 150.[18] Moreover, since some of them probably date back many centuries beyond the time when they were first recorded, they are potentially the oldest as well as the most widespread Celtic linguistic records. At least, that seems a reasonable hypothesis. In practice it is not easy to separate out early and late names, chiefly owing to the lack of early sources for most areas;[19] consequently this study presents a chronologically 'flat' picture of Celtic place-names in Antiquity at their widest known extent, with Celtic ethnonyms recorded by early writers like Caesar appearing on equal footing with names of estates recorded in the Late Empire. A few names may be of the 'New York' or 'New South Wales' type, that is names with only a shallow chronological significance. A relevant fact here is the Roman custom of deliberately posting 'ethnic' army units far from home.[20] This may have led to the movement of names. Obvious examples on the Danube frontier are *Asturis* (near Vienna) and *Batavi* (Passau), reflecting the names of units of Astures and Batavi from Spain and the Low Countries.[21] Such place-names are early examples of the process that led to

---

[16] See section 12.3 below.

[17] Under 'place-names' I include river-names, mountain-names, ethnic names, etc., generally without any distinction – the research could perhaps be refined by making these distinctions (see Ch. 12 below, p. 314). The most comprehensive source, Holder (supplemented by Cousin), is uncritical. DLG is more critical but selective and the same applies to the papers in Parsons & Sims-Williams (eds), *Ptolemy* and De Hoz et al. (eds), *New Approaches*.

[18] Many of Ptolemy's names in Ireland cannot be localized exactly, which may partly explain the omission of many of them from *Atlas*. Those that are included are sufficicient to establish Ireland's Celticity *c*. 150 AD, so I have not attempted to enhance the *Barrington* database for Ireland. For detailed discussion see: Toner, 'Identifying Ptolemy's Irish places and tribes'; De Bernardo Stempel, 'Ptolemy's Celtic Italy and Ireland' and 'More on Ptolemy's evidence for Celtic Ireland'; and PNPG.

[19] See section 12.1 below.

[20] Whittaker, *Frontiers*, pp. 223–25.

[21] *Atlas* Map 12 I4 and G4.

places being called *Asturias* in Argentina and *Batavia* in Indonesia (Jakarta), Argentina and the United States of America. Less obvious examples which have been suggested include *Gelduba* on the Rhine in Germany, with its Iberian-looking termination *-uba*, perhaps introduced by the *Cohors prima Vasconum*,[22] and *Durostorum* on the Danube in Bulgaria, perhaps introduced by a unit from Belgic Gaul, where names in *Duro-* are common.[23] Fortunately such names conspicuously fail to fit into their surroundings, and are probably so rare that they do not affect the overall linguistic picture.

1.3 EARLY STUDY OF CELTIC PLACE-NAMES

Although strangely neglected in most modern books on the Celts, the study of Celtic place-names has a long history, perhaps even an unbroken history. Not long after Gaulish had died out, the tract *De Nominibus Gallicis* (also called *Endlicher's Glossary*) attempted to give the meanings of place-name elements like *dunum* 'montem', *are* 'ante', *brio* 'ponte', *nanto* 'valle', *auallo* 'poma' and *doro* 'ostea',[24] and similar translations from *Celtica lingua* or *Gallica lingua* appear in the works of Venantius Fortunatus and Heiric of Auxerre in the sixth century and the ninth.[25] Such explanations were not forgotten on the Continent, and their basic accuracy was confirmed when knowledge of the British language – known from Tacitus, *Agricola*, 11, to be close to Gaulish – became available from the first Welsh dictionaries, notably the *Dictionarium Duplex* of John Davies (1632). Thus Boxhorn, in his posthumous *Origines Gallicae* (1654), connects Gaulish *Allobrogae* with Welsh *bro* 'region', Gaulish *Augustoritum* with Middle Welsh *ryd* 'ford' and so on,[26] and Adrien de Valois, in his *Notitia Galliarum* (1675), interprets *Aballo* as the word for 'apple' *lingua Gallicâ & Brittanicâ* and *Augusto-dunum* as 'mons Augusti', and so on.[27] Scholars in England could draw on Welsh more directly. William Camden had set about learning Welsh in order to analyse Romano-British place-names in his *Britannia* (1586) – where *Camboritum* in Britain and *Augustoritum* in Gaul are already

[22] *Atlas* Map 11G1. Cf. Rasch, Einleitung and §§ V and VIII; Weisgerber, pp. 353–54; Villar, *Indoeuropeos y no indoeuropeos*, pp. 63–68, 141 and 157 (Germanic according to Reichert i, 315, and ii, 519).

[23] *Atlas* Map 22E4. Suggested by Rivet, 'Celtic names and Roman places', p. 13 and n. 30 (for other possibilities see p. 216 below).

[24] Lambert, *Langue gauloise*, pp. 203–4, and 'Gaulois tardif et latin vulgaire', pp. 410–11. A name which the ancients were unable to explain correctly was *Mediolanum*: Dottin, *Langue gauloise*, p. 23; PNRB, p. 4.

[25] Dumville, 'Ekiurid's *Celtica lingua*', p. 89; Sims-Williams, 'Celtic languages', p. 347.

[26] Boxhornius, *Originum Gallicarum Liber*, pp. 36–45 (but he confounded Gallo-Brittonic words with homonyms in other languages).

[27] Valesius, *Notitia Galliarum*, pp. 1 and 61. His importance is noted by Gendron, *Les noms des lieux en France*, p. 19.

explained by the Welsh for 'ford' (*rhyd*) – and in 1687 John Aubrey, who employed a Welsh servant for his conversation,[28] regarded Welsh as the best key to Gaulish place-names:

> The Franks did overrun Gaule and settled the French language: but the old Gallick names of Rivers, Townes &c: (I think) are not so much obliterated/lost as here: & the present French language does retaine many Gallick words: which I have heretofore desired some learned friends of mine of Wales, who were masters of the French tongue, to collect out of the French Dictionary, or French Janua Linguarum: but I could not persuade them to undertake it, though so easie a Taske. Quaere if any one has made a Villare Gallicum? Buxhornius has made a Tentamen for the interpretation of the names of severall Townes, and Rivers in France: for which he deserves praise, but no body can doe it as it should be; but a Welshman, that is master of the French tongue; of which there are many that are. It would be delightfull to curious persons, and Lovers of Antiquity, to unde[r]stand the meaning of antiquated words, now un-intelligib[le] which may give light to many things. This ancient language (that is now crept into Corn[wall] and disesteemed) was heretofore the current Speech over a[ll] Brittaine, & Gaule: from the Orcades and the northern Isles to the Appenine-hills; (nay the very name (Pen) seems yet to speake it.) and to the Pyrenean-hills: and though it be so out of fashion; is in it selfe, as significant & copious as a[ny] of the modern languages, which the learned that understand doe assert.[29]

For all these antiquarians, Irish (Gaelic) lay unnoticed outside the Gallo-Brittonic family, and there it remained for most scholars until Edward Lhuyd's *Archaeologia Britannica* of 1707.[30] An early exception, however, was George Buchanan (d. 1582) in his *Rerum Scoticarum Historia*.[31] Buchanan also made pioneering use of place-names, as John Collis has described:

> He combed through such ancient sources as Ptolemy, Caesar, Strabo, the Antonine Itinerary and *Notitia Dignitatum* looking for correspondences between place-names in Britain and on the Continent. Whereas previous authors might have used the apparent similarity of tribal names to claim links (whence, for instance, the confusion between Cimbri, Cimmerii and Cymry), Buchanan based his argument

---

[28] Piggott, 'William Camden', pp. 201 and 207; PNRB, p. 5; Sims-Williams, 'Celtomania and Celtoscepticism', pp. 12 and 15.

[29] John Aubrey's unpublished 'Villare Anglicanum' (1687), ed. Fellows-Jensen, 'John Aubrey, pioneer onomast?', pp. 104–5. The English name *Pennines* was invented in the eighteenth century: Coates et al., *Celtic Voices*, p. 343.

[30] Sims-Williams, 'Celtomania and Celtoscepticism', p. 15.

[31] Especially Liber II. See Sims-Williams, 'Celtomania and Celtoscepticism', p. 15 and references.

on name-elements whose meaning could be plausibly deduced, and whose occurrence was not confined to one or two cases, but comprised what we would call a statistically significant base. Thus, for example, he lists fifty-two names beginning or ending with the element *dun/dunum* (for which, on the basis of Modern Gaelic *dùn*, he deduced the meaning 'fort'); forty-five names containing *bria/brica/briga* (which he took to mean 'city'); twenty-one with *magus* (which he took as 'home', 'building', 'city'); and thirty-five containing *duro/durum* (taken as meaning 'water'). His conclusion from this body of evidence was that in the pre-Roman period there was a common Gallic language spoken across western Europe, which was also spoken by the earliest inhabitants of Britain, who must therefore have originated in Gaul.[32]

Remarkably, the first three of these elements seem not to have been mapped before Helmut Rix mapped them in 1954, with no reference to Buchanan, and the *duro-* names were not mapped before A. L. F. Rivet in 1980.[33] Obviously Buchanan made mistakes, for example in translating *durum* as 'aqua' (p. 66), perhaps influenced by knowledge of Welsh *dŵr* (really from **dubron*), but his work was by no means inferior to what passed for scholarship among reputable historians as recently as 2003:

> The standard proto-Celtic word for 'river' is reflected in the modern Welsh word *dŵr*, meaning 'water'. It recurs in river names across Europe wherever ancient Celtic settlements were established, and in forms as varied as *Douro* (Portugal), *Dordogne* (France) and *Derwent* (England) – that is, 'White Water'. So it is not unreasonable to suppose that Odra [Oder] may belong to the same series. One should also take note of the curious figure called Odras in Celtic mythology. The prehistoric Celts spurned all forms of writing, but the legend of Odras has survived in Ireland. There, she is presented as a wayward nymph who, having offended the vengeful queen and deity, Morrigan, is changed into a pool of water.[34]

Every single one of these equations is incorrect!

---

[32] Collis, 'George Buchanan and the Celts in Britain', pp. 100–1. (Collis objects to the term 'Celtic' for this language family but does not suggest an alternative. I accept it as not wholly misleading and sanctioned by centuries of usage.) See also MacQueen, 'Renaissance in Scotland', pp. 46–47, and Collis, *The Celts*, pp. 36–40. On the meanings of Buchanan's elements see below, Ch. 4.

[33] Rix, 'Zur Verbreitung' (distribution maps frequently repeated since, e.g. by Piggott, *Ancient Europe*, pp. 172–74, Grzega, pp. 29–31, and Collis, *The Celts*, pp. 130–31); Rivet, 'Celtic names and Roman places', p. 14. Cf. my maps in section 12.1 below.

[34] Davies & Moorhouse, *Microcosm*, p. 43. For Odras (eponym of a river *Odhras*) see Gwynn (ed.), *Metrical Dindshenchas*, iv, pp. 196–201. Cf. Schwarz, *Ortsnamen der Sudetenländer*, pp. 26–27; Skála, 'Ortsnamen', p. 389.

1.4 IDENTIFYING CELTIC PLACE-NAMES

From the point of view of modern philology, place-names can be identified as Celtic, with varying degrees of probability, to the extent to which they include elements which show:

(*i*)   typically Celtic sound changes vis-à-vis the other Indo-European languages, or

(*ii*)   typically Celtic suffixes, inflexions or other morphological features, or

(*iii*) correspondences with words attested in ancient or modern Celtic languages.

Some would add the criterion:

(*iv*)   that the element in question was frequent in what we regard as 'Celtic' regions,

although there is an obvious danger of circularity if this is the *only* criterion.[35]

On the basis of such criteria it has been suggested that place-names could be graded on a 'scale of Celticity'.[36] Although hard to carry out with scientific precision, as an approximation with cumulative value this seems a theoretically reasonable procedure, so long as it is understood what is being implied: a name with a low degree of Celticity must in reality be either Celtic or non-Celtic; its lowish grade is an indication of our own difficulty in classifying it, not an indication that the name has an inherent weak Celticity. This sort of diffident assessment may arise because a Celtic name-element, such as *corn-* 'horn', has not evolved sufficiently from its Proto-Indo-European prototype to be securely assigned to Celtic rather than to another Indo-European language. While one might feel fairly confident of the Celticity of a case of *corn-* in a predominently Germanic area (where *chorn-*, later *horn-*, would be expected in Germanic),[37] one would feel much less certain in a predominently Italic area, where *corn-* could simply be Latin. At other times, a name may show a Celtic sound change but still be dubious because the same sound change occurred in some other Indo-European language. For example, *Boukolion* in western Turkey might be regarded as Celtic on the grounds of the sound change PIE *g^w > Celtic *b* (compare Welsh *bugail* 'cowherd,

---

[35] Vendryes, 'Note', p. 641, complained that Continental Celtic was chiefly known from proper names and yet proper names were explained on the basis of Continental Celtic: 'Il y a là une manière de cercle vicieux.' Since 1955, however, the corpus of non-onomastic Continental Celtic has grown rapidly.

[36] See Sims-Williams, 'Degrees of Celticity', pp. 4–5; De Bernardo Stempel, 'Ptolemy's Celtic Italy and Ireland', p. 84. This type of evaluation was pioneered by García Alonso, 'On the Celticity of some Hispanic place names' (see also Curchin, 'Celticization and Romanization') and has been further discussed in the 'Ptolemy' workshops and by the reviewers of Parsons & Sims-Williams (eds), *Ptolemy*: Billy, and Falileyev, 'Ptolemy revisited'. See also Anreiter, *Die vorrömischen Namen Pannoniens*, pp. 147–48, and Sims-Williams, 'Measuring Celticity', pp. 268–70 and 276.

[37] Unless there is hypercorrection, archaism or Latin influence! See Reichert, *passim*.

shepherd') but, since the same change took place independently in Greek, *Boukolion* could equally well be Greek.[38] Where an element shows more than one Celtic sound change, for instance *ritu-* 'ford', which shows both the loss of *$*p$* and the typical Celtic development of *ri* < IE *$*r̥$*, the probability of the element being anything other than Celtic is greatly reduced. Even in such a case, however, a Devil's advocate could hypothesize the existence of an unknown IE dialect in which both these sound changes had also occurred.[39] While that might seem special pleading, it can hardly be doubted that there were many IE dialects which have left no trace except in toponymy.[40] Fortunately, the cumulative nature of the evidence is helpful: while a completely isolated *ritu-* 'ford' might conceivably be non-Celtic, it would be perverse to doubt the Celticity of a *ritu-* name surrounded by other names showing other Celtic sound changes.

In the present study I have placed most emphasis on criteria (*i*) and (*iii*) for Celticity. Criterion (*ii*) is used less often, partly because the inflections of ancient Celtic names are often distorted in the ancient sources (as we may see when a name is attested in several texts),[41] partly because the Greeks and Romans tended to recycle familiar suffixes when adopting and adapting foreign toponyms,[42] and partly because inflectional features found in Celtic are often shared by other Indo-European languages.[43] The only frequently occurring suffix which seems to be distinctively Celtic is /a:ko-/,[44] and even

---

[38] See below, p. 270. The same applies to places called *Boion*; see below, p. 263.

[39] Summary tables of the main IE sound changes are given by Watkins, 'Proto-Indo-European'.

[40] Scholars of place-names in Asia Minor and the Mediterranean littoral are more alert to such possibilities because they know from other sources of the existence of lost Indo-European dialects (see Woodard (ed.), *Cambridge Encyclopaedia of the World's Ancient Languages*). In the same way, northern Europe presumably had IE dialects other than the well-known Celtic, Germanic, Baltic and so on. On the other hand, there is no advantage in hypothesizing them *praeter necessitatem*. Some of the grander substratum theories (critically described by Mees, 'Stratum and shadow') gratuitously applied labels like 'Ligurian', 'Illyrian' or 'Old European' to names which could satisfactorily be assigned to well-known Indo-European families. It is only constructive to postulate new dialects and languages where there is a reasonable amount of data for them to explain; from this standpoint 'Old European' is still the best contender. For more optimistic views than Mees's, see Bammesberger & Vennemann (eds), *Languages in Prehistoric Europe*.

[41] Examples in Dottin, *Langue gauloise*, pp. 31–32, and Barruol, p. 139.

[42] Katičić, *Ancient Languages of the Balkans*, p. 48, cites *-essos* in *Tartessos* in Spain; cf. De Hoz, 'Sobre algunos problemas', pp. 119–20.

[43] With the completion of the main dictionaries, Celtic word-formation is at last attracting systematic attention (see especially NWÄI), but much remains to be done, especially with place-names.

[44] Russell, 'Suffix', although he cautions that 'we have no means of knowing whether *-ako-* was productive as a native suffix in any of these other languages [Illyrian, Thracian, Dacian, Scythian, etc.]' (p. 164). Establishing the quantity of the *a* is a recurrent problem. In the analyses in AILR and PNPG the *a* is only marked long (using an acute accent rather than macron to aid automatic alphabeticization) where this is reasonably unambiguous. In a paper at the Munich 'Ptolemy' workshop Russell showed that in Ptolemy *-(i)akos* was common in Greece and Asia Minor, that *-akon* was typically Western (presumably Celtic), though not as productive as *-acum* later became, and that *-aka* was found very widely. See also Rubio Orecilla, 'Las formaciones secundarias en -ko- del Celtibérico', and VCIE, pp. 88–89.

this seems to have been absorbed into Gallo-Latin, especially as a proprietorial marker, in names like *Iuliacum* (compare English and American names like *Bournville* and *Jacksonville*, which cannot be used to map French speech).[45] The most one can say is that -*acum* was productive in areas which were probably regarded as Celtic in language. In this study I will draw attention to any areas where the /a:ko-/ is the sole evidence for Celticity.[46]

Criterion (*iv*), unaccompanied by other criteria, has only been allowed for one or two elements which seem securely attested in ancient Celtic toponymy and have a viable Celtic etymology, for example **ocelo-* 'sharpness, promontory', which lacks any descendant in the medieval and modern Celtic languages.[47] This book is arranged in such a way as to enable readers unhappy with criterion (*iv*) to identify and eliminate the effect of such data if they wish.

The danger of circularity arises when an element is labelled 'Celtic' because it occurs in a supposedly 'Celtic' region and is subsequently employed to 'confirm' the region's Celticity. There is a reverse danger, of course, in arguing that an element cannot be Celtic because it occurs in supposedly 'non-Celtic' regions.[48] Most of these problems can be expected to solve themselves once the names of an area are examined in sufficient bulk. They must, however, be examined from a *linguistic* point of view and primarily with reference to what is *actually known* about the Celtic language from ancient inscriptions and the medieval and modern languages. The circularity of labelling names as Celtic or non-Celtic on *geographical* rather than linguistic grounds are well brought out by Fanula Papazoglu:

> From Mursa to Ratiaria there were many place-names along the Danube which are considered Celtic. Holder includes the following in his 'Treasury of ancient Celtic names': *Cornacum, Cuccium, Bononia, Malata, Cusum, Acumincum, Rittium, Burgenae, Taurunum, Singidunum, Tricornium, Vinceia, Vimniacum, Lederata, Picum, Taliatae, Egeta*. Some of these names are certainly Celtic, others may be so. Unfortunately, one who is not a specialist cannot form any definite opinion on this matter, for the place-names of this region have not yet been the subject of special investigation. The majority of the names quoted above are included by Mayer in his lexicon of Illyrian names, but this collection, like Holder's, is

---

[45] See below, p. 307, on -*briga* names.

[46] See especially Ch. 11 below, p. 302

[47] See below, pp. 31–32 and 96–97. See already Buchanan, *Rerum Scoticarum Historia*, p. 68, on *Ocellum*.

[48] Cf. Rostaing, *Essai*, p. 105 (and cf. p. 28 and Dottin, *Langue gauloise*, p. 22): 'Il est exact que le celtique possède le mot *briga* dans son vocabulaire. Mais nous le trouvons dans les régions où les Celtes n'ont jamais pénétré; nous sommes donc autorisés . . . à considérer le mot comme antérieur au celte, *donc pré-indo-européen*.' The last phrase (my italics) introduces a further *non sequitur*; on the vexed subject of the 'substrat . . . méditerranéen, appelé aussi préceltique' compare the more agnostic approach of Fabre, *Noms de lieux du Languedoc*, pp. 30–31.

based rather on geographical principles than on linguistic ones when peripheral areas with a mixed population are in question, so that it leaves the historian in complete perplexity. Of the place-names quoted, *Bononia* and *Singidunum* do not appear in Mayer, or *Vimniacum* (according to P. Skok . . . a Latin name), *Lederata*, *Egeta* and *Taliata*, which were on territory considered to be Thracian. How far all this is uncertain is shown by the following examples: while for Holder *Pincum* is Celtic (II, 1004, where reference is made to the name *Pinci, -acus* in Gaul), for Mayer . . . and Krahe . . . it is Illyrian, and for Detschew . . . Thracian. In the same way, *Egeta* is, according to Holder, I, 1048, Celtic, according to Tomaschek . . . and Detschew . . . Thracian. Krahe . . . has not got *Taurunum*, *Cusum*, *Acumincum*, *Rittium*, while Budimir . . . considers *Cusum* and *Acumincum* to be Illyrian names, and also *Taurunum*.[49]

The fact is that it is dangerous to assume *a priori* that the place-names of any region must be, or cannot be, Celtic. Given what we know about the travels of Celtic mercenaries as far afield as Sicily, Egypt and Libya,[50] the *possibility* of Celtic names in the most unlikely places cannot be ruled out.

A similar point can be made about chronology;[51] the fact that we have no historical information about Celts in Asia Minor before 280 BC does not rule out the possibility that some names attested before that date could *in theory* be Celtic, due to earlier, undocumented migrations.[52] In this book I shall therefore avoid assuming that the presence or absence of Celtic names is intrinsically likely or unlikely anywhere or at any period. In the final analysis, however, the apparent Celticity of a name in Egypt, or of one in Asia Minor before 280, is bound to attract more scrutiny than a similar name in Britain or Gaul!

1.5 PROBLEMS AND OBJECTIONS

The study of ancient Celtic place-names has been neglected. The most eminent Celtic linguists have tended to avoid this often inconclusive subject in favour of elegant grammatical topics of little interest to non-linguists.[53] Rudolf Thurneysen even claimed that:

---

[49] Papazoglu, p. 368 and n. 299. On *Pincus* cf. Duridanov, 'Thrakische und dakische Namen', p. 831.

[50] Freeman, 'Earliest Greek sources on the Celts', pp. 20–21; Collis, *The Celts*, p. 209; below, p. 290 n. 24.

[51] The opposite is well argued, however, by Luján, 'Galatian place names', pp. 255–56.

[52] In fact Sergent, 'Les premiers Celtes d'Anatolie', p. 358, deduced a Celtic arrival as early as the eighth century BC (from very fragile evidence).

[53] 'Revisiting the nasalizing relative clause instead of answering prehistorians' questions', as a noted archaeologist put it in a lecture in Aberystwyth!

The study of place-names is dry, and of interest mostly to those who live in a particular district. The results, as a rule, are likewise far from striking. We learn, perhaps, that the original name of a certain river was 'river' or 'water', or 'the limpid', or 'the red'; or that a locality was called after its owner in Gaulish or in Roman times. All this is jejune enough. . . . It is thus not surprising to find that the scientific study of such names in Germany led few to a deeper knowledge of Celtic philology. In most cases the investigator's purpose was served once he had discovered in a dictionary the meaning of the word he sought. . . . Alfred Holder, the Karlsruhe librarian, who strove to gather every Celtic name or word (known to have existed before the 6th or 7th century of our era) into his valuable work *Altceltischer Sprachschatz*, never came to understand any of the Celtic languages thoroughly. Yet he sacrificed all his holidays, up to his death during the War years, exerpting Celtic words from manuscripts.[54]

Thurneysen does no justice to the wider historical importance of identifying Celtic names. Joseph Vendryes was equally scathing. For him all explanations of place-names (including those of Thurneysen himself) were hypothetical.[55] Hence,

L'onomastique est une science difficile et, chose plus grave, une science dangereuse. Malgré les tentations qu'elle offre, il faut en détourner les novices, car elle est nuisible à la formation de l'esprit; c'est la plus mauvaise initiation aux recherches linguistiques. On ne doit l'aborder qu'avec la prudence que donne une expérience consommée.[56]

Perhaps because of such warnings, very few Celtic specialists have studied place-names other than those of the modern Celtic countries, leaving the matter to specialists in other languages, sometimes with dire results.

It has to be granted that the Celticity of even the most 'obviously' Celtic place-names is a matter of probability rather than absolute certainty. Yet it can be a high probability verging on certainty. For example, *Augustodunum* (Autun) in France is regarded as a definitely Celtic name in the present study. The second element *dunum* corresponds exactly to the word used for a hillfort in Old Irish (*dún*) and, with a regular British vowel-change, in Old Breton (*din*, glossing 'arx'); it frequently occurs in the 'Celtic' areas of the Continent

---

[54] *Gesammelte Schriften*, ii, 273–80 and cf. pp. 281–82. Thurneysen's article, originally published in *Studies* in 1930, is 'particularly disappointing', according to Shaw, 'Background to *Grammatica Celtica*', p. 6. Shaw shows how the great Zeuss came to pure philology via history including place-names (p. 3). On Holder and the damage caused by uncritical reliance on his work cf. Thurneysen's 1891 review; Jackson, 'On some Romano-British place-names', p. 54; Evans, 'Labyrinth of Continental Celtic', pp. 500–1 and 521; Villar, *Indoeuropeos y no indoeuropeos*, p. 66.

[55] Vendryes, 'Note', p. 646 (alluding to Thurneysen's 'Etymologien' of 1932). Compare his review of Ekwall, *English River-Names*: 'Il eût mieux valu renoncer à toute étymologie, hors des cas où l'origine du mot est évidente' (p. 337).

[56] 'Note', p. 649.

and the British Isles; and it is explained as 'hill' in ancient sources such as *De Nominibus Gallicis*: '*Lugduno* desiderato monte : *dunum* enim montem.'[57] Heiric of Auxerre even explains *Augustidunum* (Autun) as meaning 'Augusti mons' in *Celtica lingua*.[58] This seems as good a case for Celticity as one could have. However, a sceptic might still argue that the element *dunum* (whether Indo-European or non-Indo-European) could have been current in other north-western European languages as well,[59] or that medieval scholars like Heiric were merely speculating.[60] It might also be argued that the Romans may have picked up such name-elements in Gaul (and elements such as *-briga* in Spain) and have used them for new formations like *Augustodunum* without much concern for the language of the local population (rather as *-ville* and *-polis* are used in names in the USA), in which case they might not indicate where Celtic was spoken even assuming that *dunum* was an exclusively Celtic word.[61] Finally, one could argue that a simple sequence of three sounds like /duːn/ could recur by coincidence anywhere in the world.[62]

[57] Lambert, *Langue gauloise*, p. 203. In view of its probable etymology 'enclosure' (see Watkins, *Selected Writings*, ii, 751–53), *dunum* did not mean 'hill' originally and in fact in cases like *Caesarodunum* (Tours), 'la hauteur . . . se limite à quelques mètres' (Bedon, 'Hypothèses', p. 259, n. 19). Yet the semantic evolution to 'hill' (< 'hillfort' < 'enclosure') may have happened by the Late Gaulish period, to judge by the probable loanwords, Old English *dun*, Old Dutch *duna*, 'hill' (see Smith, *English Place-Name Elements*, i, 139, as against Gelling & Cole, *Landscape of Place-Names*, p. 164).

[58] *Vita sancti Germani*, 1.353, cited by Dumville, 'Ekiurid's *Celtica lingua*', p. 89, and Bedon, 'Hypothèses', p. 265, n. 92.

[59] As would indeed be the case if Old English *tūn* ('enclosure' > *town*) and its Germanic congeners were *cognates* of the Celtic word rather than *derivatives* as usually supposed (e.g. in LEIA D-223 and by Watkins, *Selected Writings*, ii, 751). In fact Udolph, *Namenkundliche Studien*, pp. 610–11, regards them as possible cognates (similarly Elston, *Earliest Relations between Celts and Germans*, pp. 144–46). Andersson, 'Origin of the *tuna*-names', is non-committal. A possible middle way is to suppose that the Celtic and Germanic words were cognate but that the former influenced the semantic development of the latter. Note that Orel, 'Thracian and Celtic', p. 6, n. 10, and Anreiter, *Die vorrömischen Namen Pannoniens*, p. 178, n. 644, both dismiss L. A. Gindin's theory of a non-Celtic origin for *-dunum* in eastern Europe.

[60] As Vendryes argues, 'Note', pp. 643–44.

[61] Vendryes, 'Note', p. 649, thinks of names like those in *-briga* spreading by a sort of contagion. Rivet, 'Celtic names and Roman places', pp. 4–9, compares modern Soviet names like *Leningrad* and *Stalingrad*, but notes that the second element was adapted to suit local circumstances, whence *Leninakan* and *Stalinabad* in the Caucasus and Central Asian republics (p. 9). In the same way, the distribution of names like *Augustodunum* (rather than *-polis* etc.) may reflect the distribution of Celtic speech, even if they are Roman creations (and Bedon, 'Noms de villes hybrides', p. 44, argues that they are native creations). See also section 12.1 below. Schmidt, in his review of Parsons & Sims-Williams (eds), *Ptolemy*, pp. 275-76, compares hybrid names like *Augustodunum* with hybrid ethnic names like *Ambidrauoi* (Celtic preposition *ambi* 'on either side of' + non-Celtic river-name). In this book I count hybrids as 'Celtic', as noted above, p. 1, n. 5.

[62] See Chapter 3 below. In bilingual areas there will always be a few names which can now be analysed, and perhaps were analysed at the time, according to two different languages. Gorrochategui (e.g. in 'Establishment and analysis', pp. 154 and 161) instances *Andelos* in the Pyrenees which could be either Celtic (cf. *Ux-elo-*) or Basque (cf. *Pompa-elo*), and this example is taken up by Wodtko in her review of Parsons & Sims-Williams (eds), *Ptolemy*, p. 234. Cf. VCIE, p. 437. Such ambiguous names will always be in a minority, so a larger sample of names should usually clarify the overall linguistic situation.

While one must admit the force of such objections in individual instances, the advantage of working with place-names is that they are extremely numerous and so provide a cumulative picture that is unlikely to be confused by individual coincidences and paradoxes. Moreover, although it is true that the comparative etymology of names generally lacks the semantic control available with ordinary words, this is not always the case; for example, place-names containing Celtic *cambo- 'bend' (or containing Germanic cognates like Old English hamm) are often situated at bends of rivers, confirming the etymology.[63] Such examples contradict Meillet's blanket objection: that 'les étymologies de noms propres sont incertaines parce que, des deux données dont la concordance avec des faits d'autres langues établit la valeur, le sens et la forme phonique, on peut utiliser un seul: la forme phonique'.[64]

Vendryes seems to draw a distinction between unique names like Glanum in Provence, whose similarity to medieval Insular Celtic glan 'pure' could be mere coincidence, he claimed, and names which form a series, such as the Gaulish names in -ialum, for which he accepted Thurneysen's comparison with an alleged Welsh iâl 'open space, fair region'.[65] Such a distinction does not appear logical. The fact that an element recurs in a series of names does not really strengthen the probability of its being Celtic; nor can one be sure that identical-looking elements in such a series are always the same element. For example, as Buchanan observed, there is a series of names stretching across Europe in -briga or -briva, sometimes reduced to -bria. Many of these names may be Celtic (*briga 'hill(fort)' or *briwa 'bridge'), but at some point on the map they no doubt give way to names containing Thracian bria, which meant 'polis' according to Strabo.[66]

Maps making linguistic claims from the wide distribution of what appears to be a 'single' element must therefore be regarded with suspicion, since homonyms may be involved.[67] It is much more significant, statistically speaking, when a region, large or small, contains a good number of *different*

---

[63] Davillé, 'Le mot celtique "cambo-"', p. 45 (map); Dodgson, 'Place-names from hām, distinguished from hamm names'; Gelling, Signposts to the Past, p. 114; Gelling & Cole, Landscape of Place-Names, pp. 46–55; Billy, 'Le toponyme chambon'.

[64] Meillet, La méthode comparative, pp. 41–42. Cf. Davies, 'Greek personal names', p. 15: 'Most onomastic work is seen as etymological in nature and consequently flawed, since personal names are even more difficult to etymologize than normal nouns.'

[65] Vendryes, 'Note', pp. 645 and 647–48 (suggesting Glanum might be Ligurian). On **iâl and -ialon see Sims-Williams, 'Welsh Iâl' .

[66] See below, pp. 50, 262, and 269. Buchanan, Rerum Scoticarum Historia, pp. 62–64, equated the Thracian and Celtic elements, following Stephen of Byzantium's interpretation of Broutobria in Spain (Meineke (ed.), Ethnikôn, p. 187); cf. Dottin, Langue gauloise, p. 24, n. 5; De Hoz, 'Sobre algunos problemas', p. 120.

[67] Guyonvarc'h, 'Le nom des Cotini', p. 198, rightly stresses the danger of equating mere homographs or homonyms, but then cuts the Gordian knot too readily by suggesting that Celticity can be established when the majority of occurrences are Celtic or probably Celtic. The maps in this volume disprove this, including the one for Guyonvarc'h's sequence COT in Map 4.5 below.

elements which can all be paralleled in the Celtic lexicon. There may come a point when a region contains so many such *different* elements that the only economical explanation is genuine Celticity rather than an extraordinary series of coincidences.

Here we can return to the unfavourable comparison between onomastics and the etymology of common nouns. Etymologists who try to explain a proper name or a common noun without considering the context are on speculative ground, but if they consider the context their tasks are not so different. It is the nature of the context that differs. If they are looking at a *hapax* in a Gaulish inscription or a line of *Beowulf*, the etymology has to make sense in the context of the whole sentence. Place-names, however, come in the context of regions. They have to make sense in the context of the other names in the same region.

2

A DATABASE APPROACH

2.1 THE *BARRINGTON ATLAS*

Considerations such as those outlined in the preceding chapter lead one inexorably towards the analysis of a large database. The choice of a dataset is a difficult one. It would impractical and in some ways unbalanced to use place-names from all periods, ancient, medieval and modern; for instance, the Celtic element in the corpus would be biased towards the modern Celtic-speaking countries.[1] There are practical advantages in taking particular ancient texts as samples or 'snapshots' and studying them in detail, as has now been done in the case of Ptolemy's *Geography* and the *Antonine Itinerary*;[2] textual and philological problems can be controlled very closely. On the other hand, even such extensive sources as these are uneven in their geographical coverage. In the present work, therefore, I have tried to be more comprehensive, while sacrificing some chronological and philological precision. The source used is the indispensable *Barrington Atlas of the Greek and Roman World*, edited by Richard J. A. Talbert, published in 2000 together with its two-volume *Map-by-Map Directory* and CD-ROM. Without doubt, this work includes the vast majority of extant ancient Celtic toponyms. Its coverage is shown in Map 2.1.

The *Barrington Atlas* is directed at historians and archaeologists, rather than linguists, and this affects the nature of the linguistic research that can easily be done with it. It is generous in its chronological coverage, aiming to include all names and significant variants down to and including the Late Antique period (AD 300–640), and occasionally going still later. Names on the maps are colour-coded for period – Late Antique ones being underlined in orange, for instance – but this coding may refer to the date of the named feature rather than the date of attestation of the name itself, which is what concerns linguists. A few names known from 'earlier or later' sources are given within square brackets; their chronological status also has to be checked where necessary.[3] It is generally difficult to see when names are first attested because the *Map-by-Map Directory* tends to cite secondary rather

---

[1] Sims-Williams, 'Degrees of Celticity', p. 3. See also below, n. 20.
[2] Ibid. pp. 3–4. See Parsons & Sims-Williams (eds), *Ptolemy*; De Hoz et al. (eds), *New Approaches*; AILR; PNPG.
[3] *Atlas*, p. xxv and Map Key.

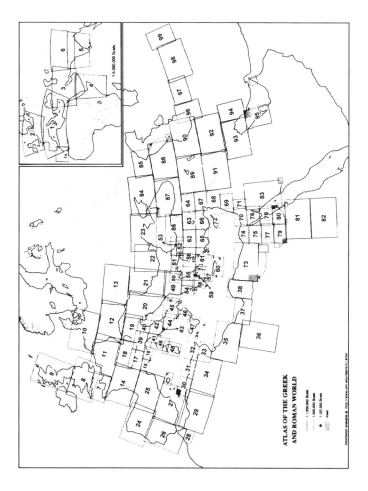

Map 2.1 The structure of the *Barrington Atlas*

than primary sources for the most part.[4] This partly explains why the present work presents a rather timeless picture of ancient Celtic toponymy at its greatest extent rather than a dynamic account of its expansion. A more discriminating approach, using a database differentiating toponyms by date of attestation,[5] might perhaps reveal important developments from period to period; compare the seminal paper by Cox, 'The place-names of the earliest English records', which, by investigating the names chronologically, revealed that several classic types of Old English place-name only emerged after 731. This procedure might not work with ancient Celtic names, however, especially in northern Europe, where the attestation of names is not well spread out chronologically.[6]

The exact spelling of names is obviously more important for the linguist than the historian. The *Atlas* generally offers at least the main variants, and some minor variants are added in the *Map-by-Map Directory*, but the selection is not always ideal; for example, Map 20E4 has *'Cardono'/ Iovia*, but not the more archaic form *Karrodounon* given by Ptolemy.[7] Inverted commas, as in *'Cardono'*, indicate 'Name in its attested form (considered inaccurate)', but the names so marked vary from authentic Vulgar Latin forms, like *Cardono*, to scribal blunders. The *Atlas* uses an asterisk for 'reconstructed name'. Here the degree of reconstruction varies; often it is no more than the provision of a nominative case, but occasionally it is more drastic; for example **Mediolanum* (Map 17, unlocated toponym) is a modern etymology for *Méolans*.[8] A further point to be noted wherever *Barrington* data is cited below is that a question mark after a name (e.g. *Alauna?*) indicates uncertainty about whether it is being applied to the right site, *not* about the correctness of the spelling.

The above remarks are not intended as a criticism of a magnificent *Atlas*, but merely as indications of possible pitfalls when it is used for linguistic purposes for which it was not designed. An exhaustive database of toponyms from all ancient sources in all ancient languages is an almost impossible dream.

---

[4] To give an extreme (and fairly rare) example, for *Condacum* (Kontich) on Map 11 the only reference is to an article by Rapsaet-Charlier in 1975, which only gives the name without specifying her source. One has to go to Gysseling's *Toponymisch Woordenboek* to find it, in *medieval* sources (see below, p. 179). For this and some other references in Europe north of latitude 48 I am indebted to Gohil, *Ancient Celtic and Non-Celtic Place-Names*. Map 14 includes a relatively high number of medieval forms; cf. Sims-Williams, 'Welsh *Iâl*', p. 63, n. 30.

[5] A tall order; for example, a toponym from the *Antonine Itinerary* would have to be dated both according to the supposed original date of that source and the date of the earliest manuscript. Such documentation would take up a lot of space, as can be seen from Gysseling's *Toponymisch Woordenboek*.

[6] See further section 12.1 below. On Cox's paper see Gelling & Cole, *Landscape of Place-Names*, pp. xix–xx.

[7] See Chapter 4, s.v. *carr-*.

[8] See ibid. s.v. *medio-*. On the other hand, *Novioritum* (Niort, Map 14) appears without the asterisk that Holder ii, 793, gives it. On the whole such etymological reconstructions, so characteristic of Holder's collection, are excluded from the *Atlas*; I consider this an advantage.

Unlocated toponyms cannot of course be mapped, but many of them are listed in the *Map-by-Map Directory*, more completely in some areas than others. This is a great boon, as they can be just as relevant for linguistic work as the exactly located names. For instance, many of Ptolemy's names in Ireland are unlocated, but that hardly matters to the linguist interested in the linguistic situation in Ireland as a whole. Where relevant, I have tried to localize the *Atlas*'s 'unlocated' names – generally abbreviated *unl.* – to the nearest one-degree square.[9] It is unfortunate from our point of view that the *Atlas* omits some unlocated names, particularly from Ptolemy, in areas where evidence is sparse, such as beyond the Rhine–Danube frontier.[10] I will draw attention to Celtic ones where relevant but, mindful of statistical considerations, I have not inserted them into the main dataset, for fear of distorting it in favour of Celtic.

The *Barrington Atlas* is convenient for linguistic work because its CD-ROM can be searched for strings of letters.[11] A disadvantage of working with the CD-ROM itself is that such a search cannot skip over modern names of archaeological sites, proper names in the bibliographies and so on, and is therefore rather slow. I have therefore preferred to use a shortened version, restricted to *ancient* names, compiled by the Ancient World Mapping Center in the University of North Carolina, Chapel Hill: the 'AWMC Placename Inventory', or, 'APNI'.[12] Anyone wishing to check the data, however, can find it all on the published CD-ROM.

In the *Atlas* some places naturally appear on more than one map. The APNI, however, aims to give only one reference, so it is possible to estimate the total number of located places, rivers, peoples, etc. with ancient names (some of them with more than one name of course) at about 13,760.[13] The places, etc. with 'unlocated' names total 7,125,[14] so

---

[9] To save space, I have done this silently (but giving the grid reference in *italics*) wherever my reasoning can be verified by following up the secondary literature cited in the *Map-by-Map Directory*. Otherwise I provide references to the sources consulted.

[10] On the decision not to emulate Ptolemy's coverage, and on Map 2 as a late addition to the *Atlas*, see Talbert, 'Cartographic fundamentals', p. 14.

[11] Note, however, that the use of brackets, as in *Kam(br)e* (i.e. *Kambre* with variant *Kame*), will impede electronic searches for e.g. KAMB and KAME. I have tried to cope with this in an ad hoc way by looking manually through all forms containing brackets, but I may have missed some relevant forms.

[12] Further details on http://www.unc.edu/awmc. I have used a version on disc (Version 1.0 beta) kindly provided by Dr Tom Elliott of AWMC in 2001. Located names in Corsica (Map 48C–E) were missing on this beta version but I have included them in all statistics below. The same applies to names in the *unl.*, *cn.* (= coin-legend) and *Av.* (= Avienus) classes from Maps 14–15, 24–27, 53, 94 and 99. Thanks to Naomi Ward for typing out the names from Maps 24–27.

[13] I counted 13,760 from the APNI (adding Corsica), but there are undoubtedly a few duplicates among them, for example *Helinium* at 10A5 and 11E1, *Aquae* at 13B4 and 20D1, or *Trogitis L.* at 65G3 and 66A2. Of course there is deliberate duplication in the case of migrating tribes like the *Langobardi* who are properly listed more than once.

[14] Including those from Maps 14, 15, etc., as just mentioned; note, however, that there is considerable duplication of *unl.* names from map to map, especially in Hispania.

the total corpus examined comes to over 20,000 items, many with more than one name.

Throughout the present work I follow the APNI in privileging only one localization for names of linear features like rivers and mountain ranges that appear on several maps. The *Atlas*'s system of reference for names stretching over more than one map square gives preference to the square nearest 'A1' (= top left = north-west), so that, for example, while the legend *Caucasus Mons* on Map 88 stretches south-eastwards from the B2 square to square E3, the name is indexed under 88B2 only. This system, which I have followed throughout, is inevitably biased towards assigning river-, mountain- and ethnic names to the north-west. I mention this, but do not regard it as a particular problem.

I have translated the *Atlas*'s Map references into longitude and latitude throughout.[15] The longitude and latitude references are based on the longitude on the *western* side of the square and the latitude on the *southern* side of the square – the same system as the United Kingdom's National Grid – so that, for example, +13/42 covers all points in the square bordered by longitude +13 and +14 and latitude 42 and 43. (Plus signs are not needed for latitudes since they are all above the equator.) It is important to note that this system of designating one-degree squares by their south-western corner applies *west* of Greenwich as well as east: for example, a place at −0.3 degrees longitude is counted as −1 and a place at −1.3 is counted as −2. Thus *Londinium* (London), for example, is −1/51.

Most of the *Barrington Atlas* maps have squares which correspond exactly to full degrees. Some maps, however, are on a large scale and have squares corresponding to half degrees and in these cases I have given references to the nearest whole degree. In the case of the small scale maps (such as Map 1, with its 5-degree squares) I have estimated references to 1 degree by eye. Hence all the sketch-maps and analyses in the present work are based on a simple grid with one degree per square. (The coastline is based on satellite images.)[16] Analysing the data by one-degree squares may seem crude and occasionally bizarre, especially along coastlines, but on balance I believe that these squares are preferable to using modern political borders or even the boundaries of Roman provinces or hypothetical ancient ethnic divisions, precisely because they are neutral and beg no questions.[17] A similar problem faced the Human Genome Diversity Project. I agree that 'the Project should have taken the advice of the late Allan Wilson, who wanted samples to be taken according to an

---

[15] Using a concordance carefully compiled by Dr A. Gohil.
[16] Taken from NASA's website.
[17] In some areas it would be possible to group names according to peoples named by Ptolemy and others; this is done, for instance, by J. L. García Alonso in his work on Iberia, and also by Curchin, 'Celticization and Romanization'.

objective grid superimposed across the world, rather than from populations predefined by culture and language'.[18]

The advantages and drawbacks of the *Barrington Atlas* as a corpus can
be seen from Maps 2.2 and 2.3. The figures and corresponding shading
show the number of located places per square in the area covered by the
maps, that is, north of 35 degrees latitude and west of 36+ degrees
longitude.[19] Figures in squares which appear to be wholly in the sea are
names of seas or islands. Where a toponym is given in two or more
forms in the *Atlas*, they are counted as one place for statistical purposes,
not only in cases of slight variants like *Ibericum Mare/Hibericum Mare*
but also in cases like *Britannia/Albion*. Obviously the nature of these two
pairs is quite different, but in many instances it would be less easy to
distinguish between variants and distinct names. In any case, this
procedure should not impair the main aim of Maps 2.2 and 2.3, which is
to show the relative density of names from area to area. The same
applies to the exclusion of all 'unlocated' names, only some of which
could have been included at the level of one degree of accuracy (at the
expense of years of research).

The maps show, first, the importance of the imperial Rhine–Danube
boundary; obviously conclusive work on Celtic toponymy to the north-east
of this line could hardly be attempted without resorting to medieval
evidence.[20] (Ireland also looks badly covered, but this can be repaired
thanks to Ptolemy.) Secondly, the maps show how much higher the density
of named places is in the south than the north. This is very important
statistically. For instance, if the distribution of a string like DUN/DOUN
were completely random, we would expect it to be more common in
the south than the north; whereas, if it is more common in the north than
the south – as is in fact the case – that must be significant.[21] Conversely,
the situation raises more sinister questions for students of so-called

---

[18] Day, *Indo-European Origins*, p. 294. Similarly, Marks, *What it Means to be 98%
Chimpanzee*, pp. 202–3. The long-term instability of such 'populations' was rightly
emphasised in 1995 by Moore, 'The end of a paradigm', pp. 530–31, an optimistically titled
review of Cavalli-Sforza's work. According to M'Charek, *The Human Genome Diversity
Project*, p. 8, cost dictated the rejection of Wilson's proposed 100-mile grid in favour of
linguistic criteria, and the latter choice entailed the close involvement of the 'Professor of
Linguistics [*sic*] Colin Renfrew' (p. 18, n. 37).

[19] I have to omit three toponyms shown north of 59° in the *Atlas*: *Hyperboreios/
Douekaledonios Okeanos* at 2B1 = −7/62; *Thule? Inss.* at 2C1 = −1/61; and *Scadinavia/
Scandza* at 2E1 = +6/62.

[20] That lies outside the scope of this book and would require detailed knowledge of Slavonic,
Hungarian and the other transmitting languages. Note, however, that quite a lot of names
from Ptolemy's Germania Magna are omitted in the *Atlas* (see PNPG) and that these will be
used in Chapter 6 below. The frontier in general is discussed by Whittaker, *Frontiers*. The
Roman sources' geographical bias towards the Empire can be seen from Adams & Laurence
(eds), *Travel and Geography in the Roman Empire*; see also Talbert & Brodersen (eds), *Space
in the Roman World*.

[21] See below, p. 329.

	35	36	37	38	39	40	41	42	43	44	45	46	47	48	49	50	51	52	53	54	55	56	57	58	59	
-10				6	3			2	1																	-10
-9			9	5	6	6	21	33	8																	-9
-8		1	12	3	8	14	14	21	12								2	3		1	1		1			-8
-7		23	26	14	12	7	5	13	6					1			1	5	7	5	4	2	1	1		-7
-6	14	42	31	11	5	7	24	17	9				1	1	1		1	1		1	5	2	1			-6
-5	11	15	38	7	3	4	6	17	9				1	4		2	5	2	3	4	2	4	4			-5
-4	1	4	21	16	5	8	8	19	5			4	3	1	4	10	5	3	13	8	9	4	6			-4
-3	4	7	8	4	3	3	11	16	3		3	8	4	3	4	13	12	11	21	9	1	3		1		-3
-2	12		5	11	1	3	26	15	12	4	4	7	12	3	5	2	10	11	9	16	4		1			-2
-1	15		4	15	13	2	8	12	10	19	17	4	9	3	4	3	7	6	10	2						-1
0	9	4		3	2	7	13	8	24	16	12	13	34	7	6	1	12	4	1							0
1	3	15		3	1	1	17	7	23	33	28	13	18	5	7	9	7	4					1			1
2	1	19		2		23	23	23	6	6	13	7	9	13	7											2
3		17	1	5	1	1	10	24	11	23	13	6	6	11	12	3										3
4	10	21		1	1		35	31	13	11	6	6	6	6	7	8										4
5	27	37					38	24	21	3	4	8	6	9	13	5										5
6	19	40	2				31	34	27	17	4	4	21	18	21	3	1									6
7	18	27	4				21	18	24	5	7	10	9	13	4	2	3	2								7
8	28	38	1	4	21	34	9	16	2	29	36	3	11	13	16	8	1	1	1	2	2	2				8
9	27	13 4	13	1	19	25	27	26	3	38	39	17	8	5	7		1	2	1	2						9
10	23	31	11			1	12	15	21	34	6	11	16	6	1				3			1				10
11	9	3	3				43	19	29	28	26	12	12				2	1	2							11
12		1	20	6		3	10 4	86	41	33	30	13	6	7	4	2		1	2	1		1				12
13	2	2	41	7		7	91	60	38	7	34	22	9	6		2		1								13
14	2	14	51	15		68	64	17		14	26	18	12	10		2										14
15		15	46	42	8	44	49	2	10	22	9	11	1	11		2	2									15
16		1	3	37	26	18	18	4	37	10	12	13	8	15												16
17			1	1	9	25	2	5	21	18	8	7	11	4			1	1	2	1						17
18				5	12			15	3	4	29	14	18	2			1		1	1						18
19				9	26	19	13	3	12	9	1	8	1	1					1							19
20			3	34	74	20	20	4	4	13	2	3	1						2							20
21		12	10 6	10 3	39	26	29	7	11	18	5	2						1		1						21
22	41	49	19 7	14 4	95	55	14	12	16	19	12	1	2		1		1		1	1	2					22
23	60	12	13 5	19 8	34	72	23	14	14	3	4	9	4	1												23
24	59	14	44	33	2	30	11	11	20	5	7								1	1		1		1		24
25	23	32	39	8	11	21	7	11	9	1	2															25
26	14	11	41	72	11 5	60	12	2	3	2		2														26
27		66	11 1	10 4	51	37	24	14	8	10		2	2													27
28		71	51	60	15	35	44		7	24	10	3														28
29	4	89	32	41	13	92	86		2	15	4	1														29
30		31	48	40	31	36	9			5	6	3														30
31		21	23	24	16	18	20			8	4															31
32	15	40	23	19	21	26	17		2	9																32
33	23	45	12	11	11	13	10	5	1	8	4	6	1													33
34	10	20	17	39	9	2	10	1		9	2	1														34
35	14	29	10	19	10	18	14	3		2	4	2	1													35
	35	36	37	38	39	40	41	42	43	44	45	46	47	48	49	50	51	52	53	54	55	56	57	58	59	

Map 2.2   Number of located places etc. per degree square

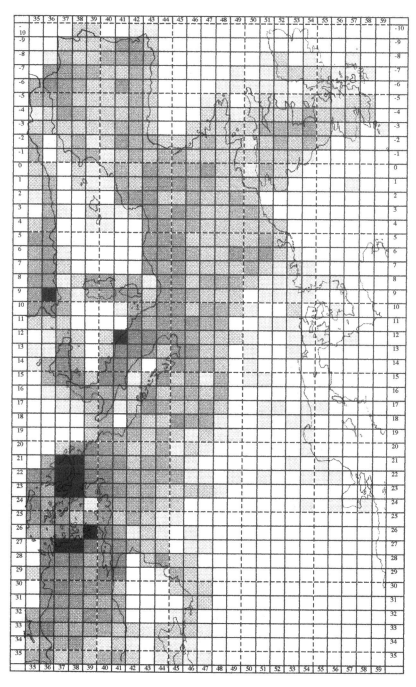

Map 2.3   The same indicated by density of shading

'Mediterranean' names. For example, is the Mediterranean concentration of IPO names[22] really significant or does it simply result from names of all sorts being commoner in the south? An additional problem here is that students of 'Mediterranean' names have tended to be eclectic and incomplete in their collections.[23]

2.2 SELECTING THE CELTIC ELEMENTS TO STUDY

Some Celtic place-name elements are too rare to be usefully mapped, while others are not amenable to electronic identification. The two extremes can be illustrated by *bogio-* on the one hand and *al-* on the other. There is no doubt of the existence of a Celtic element *bogio-*, which is common in personal names and occurs in the ethnic name *Tolistobogioi* in Galatia, Asia Minor (Map 63A1).[24] *Tolistobogioi* is the only name to be found by a search for BOGI, however, and hardly warrants listing or mapping on its own. At the other extreme, a Celtic root *al-* ('nourish' or 'wander'?) may appear in river-names like *Alauna*,[25] but a search for AL (as opposed to ALAUN) would be bound to produce vast quantities of irrelevant data, including cognates from other Indo-European languages and a mass of unrelated names.[26] Between these two extremes, there is no hard and fast rule to predict what is worth searching for. The length of the string is not in itself a reliable guide. For example, BON leads to a fairly coherent group of plausibly Celtic names,[27] but BED leads nowhere, even though the Celtic element *bed-* 'pit, ditch' (Old Welsh *bed* 'grave' < IE *bhedh-* 'dig') may sometimes appear in place-names, for example *Beda* (11G3: *Antonine Itinerary* 372.4) – the old name of Bitburg (north of Trier) – or *B(a)edunia* in Asturia in Spain (24F2: *Antonine Itinerary* 439.7).[28] The string BED is obviously so frequent and widespread that it cannot be regarded as

---

[22] Villar, *Indoeuropeos y no indoeuropeos*, p. 111, and below, section 12.3.

[23] See VCIE, pp. 60–64, on *mal-*.

[24] GPN, pp. 152–53. Sometimes *bogio-* may have developed to *boiio-* etc., although this is debatable (cf. De Bernardo Stempel, 'Ptolemy's Celtic Italy and Ireland', p. 90, and VCIE, pp. 252–54). A search for BOI produces numerous results, mostly irrelevant; cf. below, Chapter 5.3.

[25] DLG s.v. *alaunos*, and Delamarre, 'Gallo-Brittonica', pp. 126-27; for other views see Chapter 4 below, s.v. *alauna*.

[26] The folly of searching for such minimal strings can be seen from Rostaing's *Essai*. For him, following Trombetti, *AL-* indicates 'height' (pp. 41–52). *AR-* is both hydronymic *and* orographic, as in Mount *Ararat* (pp. 56–63)! Research on 'Old European' river-names raises similar problems (see section 12.3 below for *Al-*), but at least restricts itself to a single name-category. For Rostaing, by contrast, a root like *AB-* could refer both to mountains *and* to streams as the latter normally issue from mountains (pp. 29–30)!

[27] See Chapter 4 below, s.v. *bon-*.

[28] Krahe, 'Zu einigen alten Gewässernamen'; Grzega, p. 79; Weisgerber, pp. 353–54; AILR and PNPG Celtic Elements s.v. {beda:-}; García Alonso, 'Lenguas prerromanas', pp. 397–98, and 'Place names of ancient Hispania', pp. 226–27; cf. CPNE, s.n. *beth*.

distinctively Celtic.[29] Vennemann's attempt to link names in *Bed-* and *Bid-* and connect them with Basque *bide* 'road' has not been well received but at least provides an antidote to any pan-Celtic explanation of what may be a very disparate set of toponyms.[30] An awful warning is provided by Rostaing's attempt to derive *bed* 'grave' and everything remotely similar from a pre-Indo-European oronymic-cum-hydronymic root *B—D.[31]

In this study I have taken a pragmatic approach, making a rapid decision on the basis of trial and error as to which Celtic elements are so rare in toponymy (like *Bogio-*) that they would not be worth collecting and which ones contain strings of letters that are so commonplace that they are liable to turn up frequently more or less anywhere by coincidence (**callo-* 'wood' and **calo-* 'call'[32] being instances in addition to **al-* and **bed-*). Anyone wishing to reinstate excluded elements or to include elements not considered by me can modify the data accordingly. I doubt whether the final results would be worth the effort. Nevertheless, this work is arranged in a way intended to make it possible.

Having decided which elements to include, I made detailed lists of names containing the relevant strings and subdivided them into 'formally admissible' and 'formally inadmissible' names (see Chapter 4 below). To give an example, *Abala* in southern Italy, found by the string ABAL, is regarded as 'admissible' as a possible instance of Celtic **abal-* 'apple' (despite its location) whereas the *Gabali* tribe in Gaul is regarded as 'inadmissible' because such a name could not possibly be segmented *G-abali* in Celtic – or indeed in any other language known to me. It is not claimed that *Abala* is genuinely Celtic, of course.

On methodological grounds, having got this far, I did not discard any of my lists even when closer inspection suggested that some of them contained many non-Celtic names. For example, the strings by which I had searched for Celtic **briga* 'hill(-fort)' and **briva* 'bridge' included BRIA, since both elements could evolve phonetically to **bria*. However, while BRIG and BRIV turned out to be distinctively north-western in distribution, BRIA was much more widespread, appearing not only in *Calabria* in Portugal, no doubt from Celtic **-briga*, but also in *Calabria* in Italy (meaning the

---

[29] There are 18 other instances of BED in the *Atlas*, from Portugal to India. One of them is **Bedaium* (i.e. *Bedaio* in TP, *Bidaio* in AI, but *Bedakon* in Ptolemy), on which Anreiter et al., 'The names of the Eastern Alpine Region', p. 117, comment that 'The Celtic origin of this name cannot be proved'. Cf. Rasch, §IVC45; PNPG Comments s.n. *Bédakon*; De Bernardo Stempel, 'Die sprachliche Analyse', p. 47. Some *Bed-* forms may stand for *baed-* (cf. Villar, *Indoeuropeos y no indoeuropeos*, pp. 239–46), on which see Evans, 'Nomina Celtica II', pp. 507–8. See also Falileyev, 'Galatian BEΔOPEΓ'.

[30] Vennemann, 'Pre-Indo-European toponyms'; cf. review by Coates, p. 160. Cf. PNPG Comments s.vv. *Idoúbeda* and and *Ortóspeda*, citing García Alonso, *Península Ibérica*, pp. 185–86.

[31] *Essai*, pp. 75–78.

[32] AILR Celtic Elements s.vv. Compare the very heterogeneous names collected by Rostaing, *Essai*, pp. 117–27, under **K—L*.

'territory of the *Calabri*') and *Mesembria* in Bulgaria (generally supposed to contain the known Thracian word *bria* 'polis').[33] Attention is drawn to such problems as required, but I felt that it would be dangerous silently to change the dataset itself in order to eliminate them.

At first sight names in the 'wrong' place like *Abala* and 'false friends' like *Calabria* and *Mesembria* pose a serious problem (in the absence of external information). In practice, however, they are less common than might be expected, and it would be defeatist to overemphasize the paradoxical nature of one or two spectacular coincidences. While what I call 'Celtic-looking' elements may appear anywhere in the ancient world, it is highly significant that they do not *cluster* in areas where we would not expect to find Celtic languages: in other words, we do not find parts of India or Egypt with clusters of 'Celtic-looking' elements, as opposed to isolated instances, whereas we do find such clusters in Britain, Gaul, Spain and so on. This point is discussed and illustrated in Chapter 3.

[33] Albertos, 'Los topónimos en -*briga*', p. 135; Villar, *Estudios*, p. 157; *Map-by-Map Directory* i, 695; and below, p. 262. On the name *Calabri* see Papazoglu, p. 262.

3

THE LONG ARM OF COINCIDENCE

I know of no reliable statistical approach to the problem of coincidence in proper names, which differ from the rest of the lexicon in that their meaning is generally unknown or conjectural. With ordinary words, it is possible to make calculations on the basis of the average number of sounds in languages and prove, for example, that the phonetic similarity between English *widow* and Latin *vidua*, which both mean 'widow', cannot be due to chance.[1] With proper names there is often no semantic control,[2] even if we limit the comparison to a particular category such as mountain- or river-names. For instance a river *Vidua* might be a personified 'widow' (goddess?) in one place[3] but derive from the Celtic word for a 'forest'[4] in another.

We can never know for certain when two proper names are etymologically the same and when they are different. What we can be sure of is that similar-looking names are bound to turn up by coincidence. Notorious candidates are *Brest* in Belarus as well as Brittany and *Samara* in Gaul and Russia.[5] This explains Vendryes' extreme scepticism about etymologizing place-names.[6] The great advantage of proper names, however, is that they do not occur in isolation but rather in great numbers. When Area X and Area Y share, or fail to share, a large number of different place-names it is unlikely to be due to coincidence. Imagine a group of people travelling by air. If they are told that they are flying over *Brest* they might wonder which country they were crossing. After a few more names, however, they would be able to decide between Brittany and Belarus long before they landed in Paris or Minsk. Much the same applies to similarities between place-names and common nouns. A few similarities could be misleading,[7] but if a good proportion of the names in a region resemble words in a particular language more than those in any other language, the reasonable explanation is that they belong to that language. For this to work well, of course, the language

---

[1] Probability less than one in 100,000 according to Nichols, 'Comparative method', p. 50.
[2] Although see above, p. 14.
[3] O'Rahilly, *Early Irish History and Mythology*, p. 6: '*Vidva* is a good Celtic name, = O. Ir. *fedb*, "widow", W. *gweddw*.' Cf. Pokorny, 'Some Celtic etymologies', p. 135: 'there can be hardly any doubt that the Irish name also belongs to Celt. *vidu-*, "tree", and has nothing to do with a mythical "widow".'
[4] DLG and PNPG Celtic Elements s.v. *uidu-*; Nègre i, §2319.
[5] Cf. Quentel, 'Le nom de Brest', pp. 89-90 ('c'est un peu comme si l'on rapproachait Carnac, dans le Morbihan, et Karnak, en Egypte'), but with an impossible Breton etymology: *bre* [< *brigā] + -st (p. 91) – a Norse etymology (cf. VEPN s.v. *brēost*) seems more likely. On *Samara* see below, p. 32.
[6] See above, p. 12.
[7] Compare Trask, *History of Basque*, pp. 358–415.

has to be a known language, like Latin or Celtic, not an unknown language hypothesized to explain an obscure set of place-names.

The above considerations explain this book's emphasis on percentages and proportions: the Celticity of an area emerges, or fails to emerge, on the basis of cumulative evidence. Isolated Celtic-looking names, in a non-Celtic context, are much harder to assess, though no doubt some legitimate examples occur. The most striking yet plausible candidates I have discovered – *Ouobrix* in Morocco, *Sabrina* in eastern Turkey and *Tektosakes* in Central Asia – are discussed in Chapter 10.

The rest of this chapter focuses on some striking examples of Celtic-looking elements which appear to recur – no doubt by chance – in distant lands. (Further data on them, including references to latitude and longitude, can be found in Chapter 4 below.)

ABAL(L)-

There are two related Celtic stems **abalo-* 'apple' and **aballo-* 'apple-tree', the latter from **abal-no-* with the Celtic sound change /ln/ > /ll/. These are *afal* and *afall(en)* in Welsh. One or other of them is common in French place-names like *Avallon, Avalon* and *Vallon*.[8] There is also a Gaulish potter at Lezoux(?) called *Abalus* and a gloss 'poma' on Gaulish *avallo*.[9] Looking for ancient names beginning *Aball-* we find only two: *Aballava* in Britain (Burgh-by-Sands, Cumberland) and *Aballo* or *Aballone* in Gaul (Avallon, Yonne).[10] Everyone will be happy to call these Celtic; *Aballo* was already classified as Gallo-Brittonic by Adrien de Valois (1675).[11] But when we search for *Abal-* with a single *l*, we find: Pliny's *Abali* tribe in India,[12] and his *Abalus* island (*insulam Abalum*), seen by Pytheas in the North Sea (Helgoland),[13] an unlocated harbour called *Abala* in Bruttii in southern Italy,[14] and a place on the Nile (El Moqren, Sudan?) which Pliny calls *Abale* (according to Priese a corruption of **Al(a)be* i.e. *'Alwā*, perhaps identical

---

[8] LEIA s. *aball*; Nègre i, 139; Holder iii, 470. DLG s.vv. *abalo-, aballo-*, also includes names in *Abul-*. He rejects the theory that the 'apple' word is pre-Indo-European, as does Mees, 'Stratum and shadow', pp. 26–27.

[9] Oswald, *Index of Potters' Stamps*, p. 1; *De Nominibus Gallicis* in Lambert, *Langue gauloise*, p. 203.

[10] Both in PNRB, p. 238. Note also *Amallobriga* (AI) var. *Abulobrica* (Rav.) in Spain (24F3 = −6/41) and bronze *Amallobrigenses*: TIR K-30, p. 47; **Abalobriga* is an easy common denominator, although note the names in *Abul-* in Villar, *Indoeuropeos y no indoeuropeos*, p. 131; cf. VCIE, p. 195, n. 89.

[11] Valesius, *Notitia Galliarum*, p. 1.

[12] 6.67; the *Atlas* locates the *Abali* in South Bihar, following McCrindle, *Ancient India as Described by Megisthenês and Arrian*, p. 138: 'The Abali answer perhaps to the Gvallas or Halvaïs of South Bahâr and of the hills which covered the southern part of the ancient Magadha.'

[13] 37.35 (citing Pytheas); *RGermAlt*, s.n. *Abalus*.

[14] Appian, *Bellum Civile*, 5.112.

with Ptolemy's Ὀρβα).[15] Of course, nobody wants to claim any of these as Celtic, except perhaps the German island, compared with the mythical Isle of Avalon in modern scholarship; but if *Abale* were on the Seine rather than the Nile we would surely say it was Celtic.

C(A)ET

The Celtic word for a wood, **kaito-* (Welsh *coed*), appears in Latin sources both with *ae* and with *e*, so it is necessary to examine examples of the strings CAET and CET (and K(A)ET, KAIT). Most of the 44 resulting names can be eliminated on the grounds of word-formation (names like *Decetia* (Decize, France) and *Sketis* (in Egypt)[16] cannot be *De-cetia* and *S-ketis*!), leaving 13 superficially possible cases. *Caetobriga* (*Kaitobrix*, etc.) in Portugal (Setúbal) is plausibly Celtic,[17] as are *Ketion oros* (Wienerwald, Austria) and *Cetium* (St Pölten, Austria) in Pannonia and Noricum and [*L*]*etoceto* in Britain (> *Llwytgoed* 'grey wood', the Welsh name for Lichfield).[18] Other names with *e* are more doubtful. *Cetaria* and *Ceturgi* in southern Spain could have Celtic **kait-* but equally well some other element; Villar mentions the possibility of Greek *kêtos* for *Cetaria* (which was on the coast) and an 'ibero-pirinaico' *ket-* in the case of *Ceturgi*.[19] *Anicetis* in Britain (only in the *Ravenna Cosmography*) is hard to segment *Ani-cetis* and is more likely to derive from the personal name *Anicetus*.[20] What about another, unlocated *Ketaria* somewhere in western Sicily (Ptolemy 3.4.3, sometimes identified as Tonnara, north-west of Palermo, on the basis of a derivation from Greek *kêtos*),[21] a

[15] Pliny 6.179; Priese, 'Orte des mittleren Niltals in der Überlieferung bis zum Ende des christlichen Mittelalters', p. 496. Priese's Ὀρβα is presumably Ὀρβαδάρου in Müller's edition of Ptolemy, 4.5.6.

[16] Cf. *Scetis* as variant of *Scitis* (Skye, Scotland, PNRB, p. 452), not listed in the *Atlas*.

[17] TIR J-29, p. 49; Albertos, 'Los topónimos en *-briga*', p. 134; Villar, *Estudios*, p. 156.

[18] TIR M-33, pp. 34 and 61; Anreiter, *Die vorrömischen Namen Pannoniens*, pp. 163-64 (*Citium* in TP for *Cetium* is a slightly worrying variant, cf. Rasch §IVC48); PNRB, pp. 387-88. Note that the *Barrington Atlas* does not include the probably Celtic *Vocetium montem* (acc., Tacitus, *Historiae*, 1.68), somewhere in Switzerland (Holder iii, 425; Greule & Müller, 'Keltische Resistenzgebiete', p. 246). Possible derivatives or cognates in eastern Europe are mentioned by Udolph in his review of Anreiter, p. 135.

[19] Villar, *Indoeuropeos y no indoeuropeos*, pp. 284 and 333 and n. 204. On *-urg-* cf. VCIE, pp. 38, 99 and 101. *Cetaria* (modern Getares) is an emendation of *Cetraria*, var. *Cecraria*, in Rav. (TIR J-30, p. 148). The same etymology ('fish ponds'?) has been proposed for *Cetaria* in Sicily (see below) and for a place of the same name, not in the *Atlas*, in Etruria (Müller, p. 393). *Ceturgi* is known from an inscription 11 km north-west of Rute and may be in that vicinity according to Tovar, *Baetica*, p. 123.

[20] PNRB, p. 252; OPEL i, 114. But cf. DLG s.v. *caito-*: '**Ande-ceto-* "Grand-Bois"'.

[21] Map 47. The *Atlas* gives *Ketaria* (see Ptolemy 3.4.3) as a variant name of the town beside *Kytattara* and *Enattara*. Manni, *Geografia fisica e politica della Sicilia antica*, p. 159, identifies this *Ketaria* with modern Tonnara (north-west of Palermo) and cites also *Citarini* from Pliny 3.91 and *Cetarinos* from Cicero. The localization and equations with *Kytattara* and *Enattara* are rejected in Nenci & Vallet (eds), *Bibliografia topografica della colonizzazione greca in Italia e nelle isole tirreniche*, v, 267–68, and vii, 52–53 and 180.

Tamariceto Praesidio in Algeria,[22] the promontory '*Ketia*' (Κητια) in Crete (Cape Vamvakia),[23] Pliny's *Cetae* tribe[24] in Russia (N. Azov), the river *Keteios* at Pergamum (Turkish Kestel Çay)[25] and Ptolemy's promontory *Ketaion* (7.4.5) on the south-east coast of Sri Lanka? If they occurred in Britain, some of these might well be listed as Celtic.[26]

RUTU

There is a peculiarly Brittonic word for 'filthy', Welsh *rhwd* (now meaning 'rust'), which occurs, for example, in the Cornish place-name *Polroad* 'dirty pool'.[27] This has been thought to occur in Britain in the name of the Kentish port, *Rutupiae*/*portus Rutupis*/etc., and perhaps in the place-name *Rutunium* on the river *Rutuna* (> English *Roden*), and also in Liguria in *Rutuba flumen* (Pliny 3.48, Lucan 2.422), now Roya near the French–Italian border, a not impossible location for a Celtic name.[28] But what about Pliny's *portus Rutubis*[29] in Mauretania (Moulay Abdallah, Morocco?)? Does it belong with *Rutuba* in 'an old Mediterranean level of naming'?[30] The topographical similarity between *Rutupis* and *Rutubis* is tantalizing.[31] Is this a maritime word that travelled with sailors and traders? Did the name of the famous British *portus Rutupis* (cf. *Rutupi portus*, var. *Rutubi portus* in Orosius)[32] influence Pliny's spelling of the Mauretanian name, which was perhaps properly *Rusibis*, as in Ptolemy 4.1.2? Or is it just a coincidence?

---

[22] AI 38.8. See n. 26 below.

[23] Halbherr, *Inscriptiones Creticae*, iii, ed. Guarducci, p. 164.

[24] Pliny 6.19.

[25] Radt, *Pergamon*, pp. 18–19; Zgusta, p. 252 (who gives other forms in *Ket-* from Asia Minor which are not in the *Atlas*).

[26] *Tamariceto* is presumably derived from *tamarix* in the same way as *salicetum* 'willow grove' derives from *salix*, but such a name was liable to reinterpretation as containing British *kε:to-* (with open *e* as opposed to the close Latin *e*), as we know from Cormac, who interpreted a place-name *Sailchóit* as containing Cymric *cóit* 'wood' (Welsh *coed*): cf. Stokes, 'On the Bodleian Fragment', p. 205; Loth, 'Bretons insulaires en Irlande', pp. 308-9; and Russell, 'Brittonic words in Irish glossaries', p. 176.

[27] CPNE, p. 203.

[28] Ekwall, *English River-Names*, p. 345; GPN, pp. 466-67; Hamp, 'Roman British *Rutupiae*, Gaulish *Rutuba*', pp. 413–14, and '*Ρουτύπιαι, Rŭtŭpīnus*'; PNRB, pp. 448–50. I cannot find the source of the form *Rotuba* preferred in the *Atlas*.

[29] Pliny 5.9. This is sometimes equated with the *Rhousibis limên* of Ptolemy 4.1.2; see Müller, p. 577, and Desanges, *Pline l'Ancien V, 1–46*, p. 112.

[30] PNRB, p. 449. On these names and *-uba* cf. Villar, *Indoeuropeos y no indoeuropeos*, pp. 150, 156–57 and 160.

[31] If it were not for *Rutuba*, one might risk a guess that *Rutubis* was a Celtic locative plural in *-u-bis*,'at the muds', and was the original form in both Kent and Morocco, in the Kentish case contrasting with *Dubris* (Dover, French *Douvres*) which Hamp, 'Breton *dour zomm, leur zi*', implies to be a (latinized) locative plural 'at the waters'. On the Celtic presence in Morocco, presumably via Iberia, see Ch. 10 below.

[32] PNRB, p. 449; they note that Latin poets frequently used *Rutupinus* as a variant on *Britannicus*.

OCEL

Similar problems are raised by *ocel-, perhaps meaning 'something sharp, a promontory'. Tovar thought it Ligurian, but Hamp and most other scholars think it is Celtic although there is no later Celtic reflex.[33] On either side of the Alpes Graii there is an *Ocelum*[34] and a tribe of *Graioceli*,[35] which geographically could be 'Ligurian'. However, the *Atlas* also has several examples of the string in Hispania: *Castellum Araocelum* (São Cosmado (Mangualde), Portugal);[36] *Ocelum* (Ferro (Covilhã), Portugal?);[37] *Ocelum Duri* (i.e. *Ocelo Duri* AI, *Ocelodorum* Rav., *Octodouron* Ptolemy) (Zamora, Spain?)[38] and nearby *Albocela* (var. *Arboukale*);[39] and four unlocated places: the Cantabrian *polis* of *Okela/Opsikela*,[40] the Vetton *Ocelum*,[41] the Galician *Okelon*[42] and the *Castellum Louciocelum* in the territory of the Interamici.[43] In Britain there is *Cindocellum* (*Ravenna Cosmography*) somewhere in Scotland (probably for *Cintocelum*).[44] (There is also *Tunnocelo* (Notitia Dignitatum) somewhere in north-west England, but this is omitted in the *Barrington Atlas*, which includes only 'Iuliocenon' from the *Ravenna Cosmography*, on the basis of which an original *Itunocelum* is usually reconstructed.)[45] More certain is an *Okel(l)ou Akron* in Ptolemy (2.3.4),

---

[33] Cf. PNRB, p. 246; García Alonso, 'On the Celticity of some Hispanic place names', p. 196; Curchin, 'Five Celtic town-names', pp. 46–47; Hamp, ' Ὄκελον', p. 276 (IE *hek'-* 'sharp'); Luján, 'Ptolemy's *Callaecia*', p. 59.

[34] TIR L-32, p. 100: Chiusa di S. Michele. According to Strabo 5.1.11, this was the start of the Alps and *Keltike*.

[35] Only in Caesar, BG 1.10. See Barruol, p. 318, n. 4.

[36] De Alarcão, *Roman Portugal*, i, 137 and ii/1, 61: the site of a *castellum* called *Araocelum* is deduced from an inscription at São Cosmado: 'C. Caelianus Modestus Castellanis Araocelensibus D.D.'

[37] De Alarcão, *Roman Portugal*, ii/1, 69: a votive altar at Ferro 'Arant[i]a(e) Ocela[e]ca(e) et A[r]antio [O]celaeco' 'proves the existence of a settlement called Ocelum, possibly in this same town of Ferro'. The *Atlas*'s reference to TIR K-30, p. 163, properly belongs under its 24unl. *Ocelum*.

[38] Luján, 'Ptolemy's Callaecia', p. 59; Curchin, 'Five Celtic town-names', pp. 46-47; Prósper, *Lenguas y religiones prerromanas*, p. 109. Cf. PNPG Comments s.n. *Ektódouron*.

[39] García Alonso, 'On the Celticity of the Duero plateau', p. 45. Cf. Villar, *Indoeuropeos y no indoeuropeos*, pp. 229 and 272. A different etymology is suggested by Curchin, 'Celticization and Romanization', pp. 258-59. The spelling *Albocola* on Map 24F3 must be deduced from *Albocolensi* (CIL II 880), cited by Villar (p. 272) and Curchin (p. 259).

[40] Strabo 3.4.3; TIR K-30, p. 163. Strabo says that *Ôpsikella* was founded by *Okela*, whence the suggestion that *Ôpsikella* might be emended to *Okel(l)a*; see edition by Lasserre, pp. 62 and 196.

[41] TIR K-30, p. 163: Ptolemy 2.5.7 (Ὄκελον) and Pliny 4.118 (*Ocelenses*). The star in the *Atlas*'s *Ocelum* must refer to the supplied Latin ending.

[42] Ptolemy 2.6.22; TIR K-29, p. 80.

[43] Ibid. p. 61. For more detailed discussion of *ocelum* in Hispania see Albertos, 'A propósito de algunas divinidades lusitanas', pp. 470–74, Prósper, *Lenguas y religiones prerromanas*, pp. 107–18 and 509, and VCIE, pp. 346–47.

[44] PNRB, p. 308.

[45] Ibid. pp. 380–81. Rivet and Smith also reconstruct an *Alaunocelum* in Scotland (PNRB, p. 246), but this is probably fanciful (cf. review by Coates, p. 70). Neither *Cindocellum* nor *Tunnocelo* is included in my map.

Spurn Head, Yorkshire,[46] which is a striking promontory (see Map 8H1). But what about a topographically perfect *Okēlis* beside the great promontory where Yemen juts into the Red Sea, mentioned by Ptolemy as a peninsula (1.7.4 and 1.5.11) and *emporion* (6.7.7), and a century earlier by the *Periplus Maris Erythraei* (§§ 7 and 25–26) as harbour and staging-post rather than an *emporion*?[47] See *Atlas* Map 4B2.[48] Is this just a coincidence? Artemidorus (*fl.* 104–101 BC) had called the promontory *Akila* (Strabo 16.4.5) and the spelling varies in Pliny: 'ueniuntque . . . *Ocelim* Arabiae . . . Indos autem petentibus utilissimum est ab *Oceli* egredi' (6.104); 'emporium . . . *Acila*, ex quo in Indiam nauigatur (6.152); 'portum Gebbanitarum qui uocatur *Ocilia*' (12.88). Perhaps *Akila* was the older name which was distorted to *Okelis* by Western mariners on account of its topographical similarity to some Western *Okelis*.[49]

SAMAR

There is a string SAMAR well represented not only in the later toponymy of France,[50] where it can obviously be understood as Celtic 'summer(y)' (cf. Old Irish *sam*, Welsh *haf* 'summer'), but also in that of eastern Europe including Russia, where it has attracted many competing etymologies.[51] There are only four ancient European examples of the string, namely *Samarobriva Ambianorum* (Amiens) on the river *Samara* (the Somme) in France, and, in Spain, an unlocated *Samarium* in Galicia (Rav. 307.14),[52] and an unidentified *metallum Samariense* in Baetica (Pliny 34.165). On the latter Schulten rightly comments that in Baetica one can entertain both Celtic comparisons such as *Samara* (the Somme) and Semitic ones such as the *Samaria* in Palestine.[53] Outside Europe, in addition to the famous Biblical *Samaria* (both place and

---

[46] PNRB, p. 429.

[47] Humbach & Ziegler (eds) *Ptolemy: Book* 6, i, 90 (the preceding place is *Pseudokêlis* (cf. Sprenger, *Die alte Geographie Arabiens*, p. 67, §69); Casson, 'The Greek and Latin sources for the southwestern coast of Arabia', pp. 219–20; Robin, 'La Tihāma yéménite avant l'Islam', p. 225 ('on ne sait pas quel est le toponyme dont les Grecs ont tiré Okèlis'); Potts, *Arabian Gulf in Antiquity*, ii, 312; and especially Casson (ed.), *Periplus Maris Erythraei*, pp. 46, 116, 121 and 157–58, quoting an identification with 'the lagoon called Shaykh Sa'īd or Khawr Ghurayrah (12°43′N, 43°28′E)'. On the importance of *Okelis* for Ptolemy see Berggren & Jones, *Ptolemy's Geography*, pp. 65, 78, 138–39 and 175.

[48] Cf. Sims-Williams, 'Measuring Celticity', p. 278, fig. 1.

[49] The difference between *epsilon*, *eta* and *iota* is probably not significant by this date. Is it possible that the name was associated with the transitive and intransitive Greek verb *okéllô* 'to run aground'?

[50] Nègre i, 122; Billy, 'Toponymie française et dialectologie gauloise', pp. 87–88 and 95.

[51] Hengst, 'Eigennamen und Sprachkontakt'.

[52] Tovar, *Tarraconensis*, p. 321.

[53] Schulten, *Landeskunde*, ii, 492. As noted in the edition by Le Bonniec and Gallet de Santerre, pp. 163 and 314, the reading *Samariensi metallo* is not certain. They quote a suggestion that it was in the region of Castulo; I follow this on my map, *faute de mieux*. It is not located in TIR J-30, p. 289.

region, whence also *Castra Samaritanorum* near Sykamina), there is a *Samaria* on the Nile,[54] and even a *Samarabiae* (var. *-briae*) tribe on the Indus in N. Taxila, mentioned only by Pliny.[55] (How far were Pliny and his scribes influenced by knowledge of the Gaulish *Samarobriva/Samarabriva*, which is contracted to *Samarobria* in some sources?)[56] If any of the above oriental names in *Samar-* occurred in Gaul, we would certainly label them Celtic and not regard them as mere homonyms of the Gaulish *Samara*.

CAMB

Cambo- 'crooked' (Old Irish *camb*, Welsh *cam*) is a common name-element in Europe:[57] in the *Atlas* there are thirteen promising examples of CAMB/KAMB in Europe, all in obviously 'Celtic' areas except for *Cambunii montes* (the Pieria mountains) in Macedonia.[58] Outside Europe, however, in addition to Pliny's *Forum Cambusis* in Egypt on the Nile (which merely contains the famous Iranian personal name),[59] we have a city in Mysia called *Cambre* (Pliny 5.126)[60] and a river *Kambyses* (now Jori) in *Kambysênê* (Kambetchan, Azerbaijan).[61] If the river *Kambyses* were recorded in Gaul, it would be taken as Celtic, despite its suffix. The same applies to the two estuaries of the Ganges mentioned by Ptolemy (7.1.18 and 30), *Kambêrichon Stoma* and *Kambouson Stoma*.[62] Indeed, if one ignores non-Celtic-looking suffixes and other problems one could also include the district of

---

[54] Probably in Arsinoites/Krokodeilopolites Nomos: Calderini & Daris, *Dizionario dei nomi geografici e topografici dell'Egitto romano*, iv, 240 and *Supplemento* ii, 183 (Σαμαρία). The *Atlas* also includes *Samarra* on the Tigris, 60m north of Baghdad (91E3), but this is only given in square brackets as a modern form beside "'Sumere'". According to Meyers (ed.), *Oxford Encyclopedia of Archaeology in the Near East*, v, 473, s.n. Samarra, it was 'formally called *Surra man ra'a* "he who sees it is delighted"'.

[55] Pliny 6.78 (variants in André & Filliozat's edition, p. 43).

[56] Holder ii, 1336-37; TIR M-30/31, p. 18. The variant *Samarabriae* appears in MSS R, d and E² of Pliny, which are all from France (Reynolds (ed.), *Texts and Transmission*, pp. 312-13 and 316).

[57] Anreiter et al., 'Eastern Alpine region', p. 121 and n. 24; Nègre i, 241-43.

[58] Livy, 42.53.6, 44.2.6 and 44.2.10. Pauly-Wissowa, s.n. Καμβούνια, derive this from Greek *skambós*, a cognate of Celtic **kambo-* (LEIA C-29), always attested with the sigma, however. It has been supposed that **kambo-* occurred in other Indo-European branches of toponymy, including 'Illyrian': Schwarz, *Ortsnamen der Sudetenländer*, pp. 38-39.

[59] Pliny 6.181; cf. Ptolemy 4.7.5: *Kambusou tamieia*; Calderini & Daris, *Dizionario dei nomi geografici e topografici dell'Egitto romano*, iii, 61; Priese, 'Orte des mittleren Niltals in der Überlieferung bis zum Ende des christlichen Mittelalters', p. 489. According to Pauly-Wissowa, s.n. Καμβύσου Ταμεῖα, the name dates from the campaigns of Cambyses.

[60] *Kam(br)e* in the *Atlas* (56unl), where its implied localization depends on an equation in Pauly-Wissowa with *Kame* which is generally rejected; see Robert, *Villes d'Asie Mineure*, p. 17; Zgusta, p. 217.

[61] Strabo, 11.4.1 and 5 (*Kambusênê*), with note on p. 152 of the edition by Lasserre. Strabo also mentions an unidentified Armenian region of *Kambala* (11.14.8, with note on p. 152), not included in the *Barrington* data.

[62] Berthelot, *L'Asie ancienne centrale et sud-orientale d'après Ptolémée*, p. 307, only discusses their location.

Kambadênê/Kampa(n)da/Sambana in Media (western corruptions of Old Persian *Ka(m)pa(n)da* which had /p/ rather than /b/)[63] and Arrian's *Kambistholoi* tribe in southern Panjab (a corruption of Sanskrit *Kāpiṣṭhala*, attested as the name of the adherents of a Vedic school and also as an ethnonym, but always without an /m/).[64]

GABR

Similarly with the element *gabro*- 'goat' (Old Irish *gabor*, Welsh *gafr*). There are examples in Britain (*Gabrosentum*, *Gabrantouikes*, *Gabrantouikon kolpos*),[65] a *Gabromago* in Austria (Windischgarsten),[66] the *Gabrêta* forest (the Böhmerwald) in Germany,[67] and a *Gabris* in France, now Gièvres.[68] But what about the other *Gabris*, mentioned by Ptolemy in north Media, perhaps Tabriz, and another unlocated *Gabra* in Persia?[69] Only their locations stop them being as Celtic as the French *Gabris*.

CONCLUSION

Thus we see that Celtic-looking strings can be found throughout the ancient world. In most cases, no doubt, this is by sheer coincidence, although other possibilities are the presence of similar cognates in other Indo-European languages, the distortion of exotic names so as to resemble Western ones,[70] and the occasional re-use of Western names by travellers.

At first sight the occurrence of these Celtic-looking strings in India, Persia, Africa and so on is methodologically disturbing. Does it invalidate the use of such strings to identify the Celtic areas of Europe and Asia Minor? In fact not, because the quasi-Celtic elements are nearly always quite isolated from each other in the east and south (see Map 3.1, bearing the scale in mind), unlike the situation in Europe (see Map 3.2), where the majority of examples appear, often in clusters. There are 54 relevant names in the area of Map 3.2 (including 3 unlocated names from the same area

---

[63] Isidore of Charax, *Parthian Stations*, §5, in Schoff, *Parthian Stations*, p. 6, and other sources cited by Pauly-Wissowa, s.n. Καμβαδηνή, and Herzfeld, *Persian Empire*, p. 13.

[64] Arrian, *Anabasis*, 8.4.8; Witzel, 'On the localisation of Vedic texts and schools', pp. 181 and n. 37 and 212; Wirth & von Hinüber (eds), *Arrian: der Alexanderzug, Indische Geschichte*, p. 1095.

[65] PNRB, pp. 363–65.

[66] AI 276.9.

[67] Holder ii, 1510; TIR M-33, p. 39: Strabo 7.1.5; Ptolemy 2.11.3 and 5.

[68] Holder ii, 1510 (TP); *Gabrae* (CAG 41, p. 39, no. 22) is a reconstructed nominative.

[69] Humbach & Ziegler (eds.), *Ptolemy*, 6.2.8 (cf. another *Gabris* at 6.2.10, not in the *Atlas*) and 6.4.6 (= Map 94unl). See also below, p. 79, on *Gabranus*.

[70] Cf. Casson (ed.) *Periplus Maris Erythraei*, pp. 6 and 198 (e.g. an Indian *Abēria* becoming *Ibēria*).

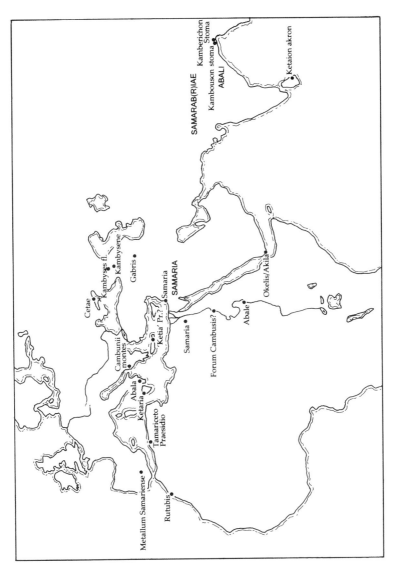

Map 3.1 False friends in the wrong places

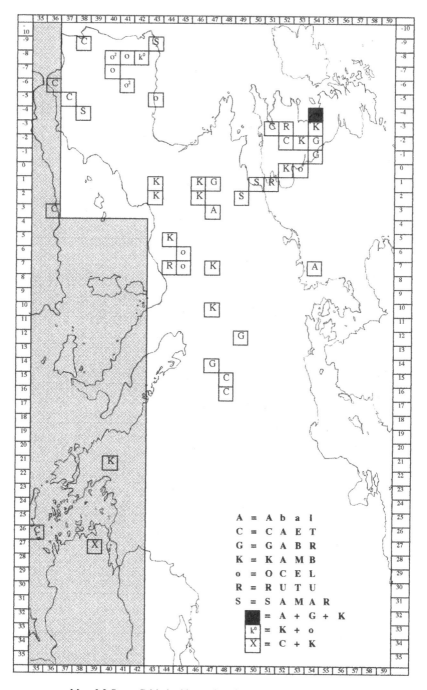

Map 3.2 Some Celtic-looking strings in Europe and the vicinity

which cannot be mapped even at this low level of accuracy: *Abala* in Italy, *Ketaria* in Sicily and *Cindocellum* in Scotland); by contrast, there are only 17 relevant names (including the unlocated Persian *Gabra*) outside the area of Map 3.2 (see Map 3.1). The 54:17 figure (76% to 24%) is not significant, since it must partly reflect the fact that Western names are better attested (74% of all places marked in the *Barrington Atlas* with ancient toponyms occur in the area of Map 3.2).[71] What is more significant is the lack of *clusters* of Celtic-looking elements outside the area of Map 3.2.[72]

The most significant statistic is that most of our Celtic-looking strings are concentrated in north-western Europe, despite the fact that in general far more names are attested from southern Europe, Asia Minor and north Africa. Of the *Atlas*'s 10,168 located toponyms in the area of Map 3.2, 62% occur in the shaded area to the south of the marked line.[73] By contrast, only 8 of our Celtic-looking elements appear south of that line (including the unlocated *Abala* and *Ketaria* in southern Italy and Sicily) versus 46 appearing north of the line (including the unlocated *Cindocellum* in Scotland). If the distribution were purely random we would expect nearer 50 rather than 8 occurrences south of the line. As it is, however, most or all of the 8 southern occurrences seem likely to be due to coincidence. Apart from *Abala*, *Cambunii montes* and *Cambre* they are all examples of the string CET/KET, which no doubt has several sources besides Celtic **kait-*.

The general conclusion to be drawn is that one cannot use isolated 'Celtic' elements to prove the Celticity of an area, but that the presence of a variety of such elements in an area has a definite cumulative value. The more Celtic-looking elements that are mapped, the clearer the divide between areas of Celtic and pseudo-Celtic toponymy will become.

---

[71] That is, 10,168 places, tribes etc. (some with more than one name) versus 13,760 in the whole area mapped in this *Atlas*. The 24% is presumably unusually high, however, because I deliberately chose to examine Celtic elements that seemed to appear outside Europe.

[72] The only cluster outside the north-west is due to Pliny's *Cambre* and *Cetius* in Mysia (5.126) and neither is likely to be Celtic: Zgusta, pp. 217 and 252.

[73] 6,322 places, tribes etc. versus 3,846 north of the line. The percentage given in Sims-Williams, 'Measuring Celticity', p. 275, is to be corrected.

4

SELECTED CELTIC-LOOKING STRINGS AND ELEMENTS

In this chapter I provide a list of Celtic elements and the strings by which they – and irrelevant homographs – may be found in the APNI database. The criteria for selection were explained in Chapter 2. For most linguistic purposes it is normal to work with 'elements', for example considering *wiros* or the stem *wiro-* as the Celtic word for 'man'; but automated searching requires the use of strings, for example VIR, OUIR and UIR (rather than WIRO or VIRO) if relevant forms are not to be missed, such as *viri* 'men' or forms with Latinized case-endings. The obvious disadvantage of searching by strings is the amount of irrelevant data that is collected.

It cannot be overemphasized that the purpose of this chapter is *not* to identify any names as certainly Celtic but rather to *exclude* as 'formally inadmissible' a mass of names which happen to contain relevant strings of letters but cannot reasonably be segmented so as to show the Celtic-looking elements under discussion (for example, *Gabala* is formally inadmissible as an example of *abal-* 'apple' even though it will be found by searching for ABAL).[1] In making a decision as to which names are or are not 'formally admissible' no account has been taken of the geographical location of the name; in each case I asked myself, 'Would this name be regarded as an instance of the Celtic element if it occurred in Britain or Gaul?' A few decisions may be subjective, but these are statistically insignificant in number.[2] I should emphasize, particularly to linguists looking at the data, that I have erred on the side of generosity in counting as 'admissible' forms which seem to have non-Celtic suffixes – because ancient authors tend to assimilate foreign forms to Greek and Latin usage – and even in including names which are more probably Greek or Latin. It seemed methodologically unsound to exclude 'Celtic-looking' names in southern Europe where we have the advantage of knowing a great deal about the other ancient

---

[1] See above, p. 25.

[2] No two linguists would be likely to concur exactly, but the following figures give some idea of the likely level of agreement. Dr G. R. Isaac looked over my first draft of the section from ABAL to RATA (excluding BRIG, DUN, DURO and MAG) and suggested moving up into the 'admissible' class 16 forms which I had already independently moved up in my second draft and a further 7 forms which I moved up in my third draft, following his suggestions. (I did not accept his suggestions with regard to another 4 forms.) Dr Isaac also looked at the second draft of the section from RIG to the end. Here I accepted his suggestions with regard to moving 9 out of 12 forms. Five further changes were adopted from a referee and from Dr A. Falileyev. This level of disagreement is statistically very trivial.

languages in use, when we are not in a position to do the same in northern Europe. Hence, for example, under *cot(t)*- 'old' below I have not excluded some names that are no doubt really to be connected with Greek *kotulê* 'cup' or *kotinos* 'olive tree'. I may not have been wholly consistent, however; for example, under Celtic *corno*- 'horn' I have excluded a number of very obviously Latin names like *Via Cornelia*, feeling that it would be bizarre to admit them. The raw data is all here, however, so that readers of the book can redo the statistics if they wish.

In the following pages, grid references to one-degree squares are added *in italics* where possible for the 'formally admissible' 'unlocated' (*unl*) names that fall within my main area of study (that is, north of latitude 35 and west of longitude + 36), but generally not for those in India, Egypt and so on. To save space, my evidence for these approximate localizations is not given wherever it can be traced via the bibliographical references given in the Barrington *Map-by-Map Directory*. The distribution of most of the better attested 'formally admissible' strings is shown on maps, either in this chapter or in Chapters 3 and 12. There are a few additional locations on the maps, to which attention is always drawn. Squares on the maps in which an example of the string in question occurs are outlined; if there are two or more occurrences in the same square a figure '2' or '3', etc. is added.

No discussion of etymologies is attempted here, but references are given where possible to Old Irish and Modern Welsh cognates to facilitate consultation of the headwords in LEIA and GPC, where basic etymological orientation can be found. References are also given to GPN and to the second edition of DLG, which both contain detailed bibliographical information. Obviously, the other references given could have been expanded indefinitely. In practice, I have given priority to the recent publications arising from the 'Ptolemy' workshops[3] and to G. R. Isaac's discussions in AILR and PNPG.[4] As the arrangement of AILR and PNPG may be not be familiar to all readers, it should be explained that they present the names in the *Antonine Itinerary* and in Ptolemy's *Geography* in Word tables which can be re-sorted alphabetically or numerically on a selected column so as to arrange the material according to various categories, for example: ancient name; modern name; longitude and latitude; province; or linguistic element (prefix(es), lexeme(s), suffix(es)). In addition to printable files of 'Comments', there are printable files of 'Celtic' and 'Possibly Celtic' elements, and it is to these that most reference is made in this chapter. It should be noted that AILR and PNPG use various special conventions, such as the use of acute accents or colons instead of macrons for long vowels, in order to

---

[3] Parsons & Sims-Williams (eds), *Ptolemy*; De Hoz et al. (eds), *New Approaches*.
[4] The AILR data is included unchanged as an appendix on the PNPG CD-ROM, which is available from CMCS Publications, Department of Welsh, University of Wales, Aberystwyth, SY23 2AX. This CD needs only Microsoft Word (PC or Macintosh).

facilitate automated sorting and maximum readability on different computers.

ABAL- 'APPLE' (W AFAL, CF. OI UBULL) AND ABALLO- < *ABAL-NO- 'APPLE TREE' (OI ABALL, W AFALLEN)

AILR Celtic Elements s.v. *aballo-*; DLG s.v. *abalo-* (and p. 431). See Chapter 3 above, with maps.

String ABAL

Formally admissible (6)

9	D6	– 04	54	**Abal**lava
6	E5	+ 84	24	**Abal**i
10	D2	+ 07	54	***Abal**us? Ins.
18	A2	+ 03	47	**Abal**lo
46	*unl*			**Abal**a
82	D4	+ 33	17	**Abal**e

Formally inadmissible[5]

4	*unl*			Ga**bal**a		
5	*unl*			Ga**bal**iba		
6	*unl*			Para**bal**ei		
6	*unl*			Sa**bal**assa		
6	C3	+ 72	32	Akesinos	Sand**abal** fl.	Cantaba
10	E1	+ 08	55	Sa**bal**ingioi?		
11	*unl*			Na**bal**ia fl.		
15	*Av.*	*+ 05*	*43*	Mastr**abal**a		
17	A4	+ 03	44	Anderitum	Civitas Ga**bal**um	
17	A5	+ 03	44	Ga**bal**i		
25	*unl*			Ga**bal**aika		
29	*unl*			Sard**abal**e fl.		
35	C2	+ 10	32	Ta**bal**ati?		
47	*unl*			K**abal**a		
62	A4	+ 28	38	Ta**bal**a		
63	B4	+ 32	38	Ca**bal**lucome		
63	F4	+ 34	38	And**abal**is		
64	D4	+ 36	38	Coduzalaba	Sa**bal**assos?	
65	C3	+ 29	37	K**abal**itis L.		
65	C4	+ 29	36	K**abal**is		
67	C2	+ 36	37	Hierapolis	Kast**abal**a	
68	A3	+ 35	35	Ga**bal**a		
71	*unl*			D**abal**oth		

---

[5] Theoretically, *Andabalis* could perhaps be **ande-* + **abal-*; cf. *ande-* below.

80	G5	+35	24	Cabalsi		
81	*unl*			Tabales		
87	G4	+41	40	Kaballa		
87	*unl*			Sabalia		
88	F4	+47	40	Chabala	Cabala	
90	C2	+47	38	[Sabalan] M.		
90	*unl*			Gabale		
91	B2	+40	35	Gabalein	Nabagata	Gablini?

ABONĀ < *AB-ON- 'RIVER' (OI *ABANN*, W *AFON*)

AILR and PNPG Celtic Elements s.v. *abo-*; DLG s.vv. *abona, abu-* (and p. 431); cf. Stalmaszczyk and Witczak, 'Studies in Indo-European vocabulary', p. 25, n. 3.

String ABON

Formally admissible (3)

8	E3	− 03	51	Abona fl.
8	E3	− 03	51	'Abone'
20	E2	+ 17	47	Arrabona

The first two are a river and place named from it.[6] The third is a place on the river *Arrabo* (TP), called *Arabôn* or *Narabôn* by Ptolemy 2.11.3, 2.14.1, 2.15.1, explained by Anreiter et al., 'Names of the Eastern Alpine region', pp. 130 and 136, as Celtic 'eastern river' (< *are*).[7] They maintain that this and other river-names in -*abôn* in the Balkans point to a Celtic or 'Proto-Balkanic' form with long vowel in contrast with Brittonic *afon*.[8] If this is correct, some of the following 'formally inadmissible' names may be relevant to Celtic after all (although note that *Alabon fl.*, for example, is in Sicily).

Formally inadmissible

4	C3	+45	14	Cerbani	Caeubani	Catapani	Cebb(r)anitae	Gabonita	Gataphani
17	F5	+05	44	Alabonte					
21	C5	+20	44	Oktabon					
23	*unl*			Chabon					
23	*unl*			Erkabon					
26	A3	−10	38	A(qua)bona	Equabona				

---

[6] Cf. VEPN, s.v. and above, p. 1.

[7] See also Anreiter, *Die vorrömischen Namen Pannoniens*, pp. 220–22. GPC links *Arabo* with Welsh *araf* 'slow'; cf. DLG s.v. *aramo-*.

[8] Like *Arrabo*, not all of these are given with -*n* in the *Atlas*, e.g. 21F5 *Rhabo*, on which see below, p. 211, n. 140.

31	*unl*			Strabonianensis Fundus	
47	G4	+ 15	37	Alabon fl.	Alabis fl.
47	*unl*			Alabon	
68	C2	+ 36	35	Rabona?	
75	*unl*			Arabon Kome	
75	*unl*			Ptolemais he ton Arabon	
86	D2	+ 33	41	Abonouteichos	Ionopolis
95	inset	+ 56	25	Asabon M.	
95	inset	+ 56	26	Maketa Pr.	Asabon Pr.

I am assuming that *A(qua)bona*/*Equabona* in Portugal is Latin *aqua bona*, but it could be Celtic.[9] It is *Aquabona* (var. *Equabona* 'horse-river??') in the *Antonine Itinerary* (AI 416.5) but *Abona* in the *Ravenna Cosmography* (Rav. 306.19); cf. TIR J-29, p. 32, and Tovar, *Lusitanien*, pp. 216–17.

ALAUNĀ < *AL-AU-NĀ < ? *AL-AM-NĀ, RIVER-NAME (CF. W RIVER-NAME *ALUN*)

This is definitely Celtic but the etymology is controversial: AILR and PNPG Celtic Elements s.v. *alo-*; PNRB, pp. 243–44; DLG s.v. *alaunos, -a*, and Delamarre, 'Gallo-Brittonica', pp. 126–27; Lambert, 'Welsh Caswallawn', pp. 208–9; Isaac, 'Scotland', p. 190; VCIE, p. 327.

String ALAUN (nothing found under ALOUN and ALAOUN)

Formally admissible (12; but 11 if the third is the same as the fourth, PNRB, pp. 243–44 and 247)

7	E2	– 02	49	Alauna	
8	F2	– 02	52	Alauna?	
8	*unl*			Alauna	
8	*unl*	– 04	50	Alaunos fl.	
9	D4	– 04	56	Alauna	Litana
9	D6	– 04	54	Alauna	Alione
9	F5	– 02	55	Alauna	
9	F5	– 02	55	Alauna fl.	
9	E6	– 03	54	Alone?	Alauna?
16	A2	+ 05	43	Alaunium	
19	E2	+ 12	47	Alaunoi	
25	*cn.*	– 02	41	Alaun	

The last of these is a coin-legend referring to modern Alagón in Spain, *Allobo*/*Alauona* in the Atlas (25D4); see TIR K-30, p. 45 s.n. *Allobone*,

[9] Cf. Villar, 'Celtic language', p. 251.

Alavona, AILR Comments s.n. *Allobone* and VCIE, pp. 327 and 433–35. See **Map 12.21**. On Ptolemy's *Alaunoi* for the Alani see PNPG Comments s.n. *Alaunoí* and below, p. 195.

Formally inadmissible (as probably syncopated from *vellauno-* below; see GPN, p. 276, and DLG s.v.; cf. PNRB, p. 305):

11	E4	+ 04	48	Cata**launi**
11	E4	+ 04	48	Duroca**talaunu**m

ANDE-, INTENSIVE PREFIX (OI *IND-*, W *AN(N)-*)

PNPG Celtic Elements s.v. *ande-, ando-*; GPN, p. 140; DLG s.v. *and-, ande-, ando-* (and p. 431); Hamp, 'Briona AN(N)OKO(M)BOGIOS'; Lambert, '*Lugdunensis*', p. 222.

String And (case-sensitive) plus vowel. This string excludes a few examples with syncope or haplology (GPN, p. 136, n. 10), but *And + consonant* would bring in too many irrelevant names. Note that *Ande-* and *Andi-* are not kept apart in the sources; with *Andecavi* below compare ANDICAVA in RIG iv, no. 24. *Ando-* may be distinct according to Hamp.

Formally admissible (19)

3	*unl*			Anamis fl.	**An**(d)anis fl.	
6	F5	+ 87	23	**And**omatis fl.		
6	*unl*			**And**iseni		
7	D2	– 03	49	**And**ium? Ins.		
8	H4	+ 00	50	**And**eridos	**And**erelium	**And**eritos
11	G3	+ 06	49	**And**ethanna		
11	*unl*	+ *02*	*48*	**And**eritum		
11	*unl*	+ *05*	*47*	**And**esina		
14	E1	– 01	47	**And**ecavi		
14	E1	– 01	47	Iuliomagus	Civitas **And**ecavorum	
14	G2	+ 01	46	***And**ecamulum		
17	A4	+ 03	44	**And**eritum	Civitas Gabalum	
18	C2	+ 05	47	**And**ematunnum		
20	D6	+ 16	43	**And**etrium		
20	F4	+ 18	45	**And**izetes		
25	D3	– 02	42	**And**elos		
25	G3	+ 01	42	**And**osinoi		
63	F4	+ 34	38	**And**abalis		
65	D3	+ 30	37	**And**eda		

Andium and *Andelos* could be formed from *ande-* plus suffix (for the type cf. respectively Lambert, 'Préverbes gaulois suffixés en -*io*', and Gorrochategui, 'Ptolemy's Aquitania and the Ebro valley', p. 151, where an alternative Basque etymology is suggested; see also PNPG Celtic Elements s.v. *ande-* on OI *indel*, Middle Welsh *annel*). A different segmentation is clearly possible in several cases, e.g. *An-dizetes* (KPP, pp. 24–25) and *Andos-inoi* (below, p. 239). See **Map 4.1**.

Formally inadmissible

4	*unl*			**And**idalei	Anti(a)dalei	Ant(h)iadala
5	E3	+80	16	**And**arae	**And**re Indi	
6	*unl*			**And**aka		
15	B1	+03	44	**And**usia		
20	D4	+16	45	**And**autonia		
20	F7	+18	42	**And**erva		
27	*unl*			**And**ura		
32	*unl*			**And**a		
39	H3	+10	45	**And**es		
56	D2	+26	39	**And**iros fl.		
56	E2	+27	39	Astyra?	**And**eira?	
58	B3	+21	37	**And**ania		
58	*unl*			**And**ania		
62	*unl*			**And**aeiton Chorion		
63	A3	+32	38	***And**eira		
68	D2	+37	35	Androna	**And**arna	
81	*unl*			**And**ura		
89	E1	+42	39	**And**aga		
93	E1	+48	32	[Jundishapur]	Veh-**And**iyok-Shapur	Beth Lapat　Bendosaboron

Banno- < *$B(A)ND-NO$- 'HIGH; HEIGHT' (OI BENN, W BAN)

AILR and PNPG Celtic Elements s.v. {banna:}; DLG s.v. *banna, benna*; cf. McCone, *Towards a Relative Chronology*, pp. 50, 73 and 106; Villar, 'Celtic language', pp. 258–59.

String BANN

Formally admissible (6)

8	G1	− 01	53	**Bann**ovallum	
8	F2	− 02	52	**Bann**aventa	
9	E6	− 03	54	**Bann**a	
9	D4	− 04	56	**Bann**atia?	
19	A2	+ 08	47	*Brigo**bann**is	
34	C2	+ 04	35	A**bann**ae?	

The last could theoretically be a compound in **ad-*. See **Map 12.5**.

Formally inadmissible

| 49 | B2 | + 19 | 41 | **Barbann**a fl. |
| 8 | D3 | − 04 | 51 | 'Gobannio' |

BLĀTO- 'FLOUR' / 'FLOWER' (OI *BLÁTH*, W *BLAWD*; CF. OI *MLÁITH*)

AILR Celtic Elements s.v. {bla:to-} ALT1, ALT2; DLG s.v. *blato-*.

String BLAT

Formally admissible (2)

| 9 | D5 | − 04 | 55 | **Blat**obulgium |
| 14 | G2 | + 01 | 46 | **Blat**omagus |

Formally inadmissible

| 87 | | *unl* | | **Ablat**a |

BON- 'BASE, FOUNDATION?' OI *BUN*, W *BÔN*?)

AILR and PNPG Celtic Elements s.v. *bono-*, {bon(n)a:}; DLG s.vv. *bona* and *bouno-*; Anreiter, *Die vorrömischen Namen Pannoniens*, pp. 158–59; Lambert, '*Lugdunensis*', p. 241. A different Celtic etymology for *Bononia* (**bouno-* 'lasting') is suggested by De Bernardo Stempel, 'Gaulish accentuation', p. 24, and 'Ptolemy's Celtic Italy and Ireland', pp. 86, 89, 94 and 107. Cf. KPP, pp. 258–59.The Pannonian *Bononia* principally discussed by Anreiter appears in the *Atlas* only under its alternative name *Malata* (Map 21B4 = + 19/45)[10] and is therefore missing from the list below (but it is included on **Map 12.29**). *Arrabona* also appears under ABON above, which is where it more probably belongs.

---

[10] Cf. TIR L-34, p. 76; PNPG Comments s.n. *Bono:nía*. The famous name *Ratisbon* is not attested early enough to appear in the *Atlas* (see Reinecke, 'Die örtliche Bestimmung' (1924), p. 40).

String BON

Formally admissible (11)

6	*unl*			**Bon**is	
11	A3	+00	49	Iulio**bona**	
11	B2	+01	50	Gesoriacum	**Bon**onia
11	E4	+04	48	Augusto**bona**	
11	H2	+07	50	**Bon**na	
13	B4	+16	48	Mun. Vindo**bona**	
13	B4	+16	48	Vindo**bona**	
20	E2	+17	47	Arra**bona**	
21	E5	+22	44	**Bon**onia	
40	A4	+11	44	Felsina	**Bon**onia
86	D2	+33	41	**Bon**ita	

Formally inadmissible (some of these also appear under ABON above)[11]

2	H2	+22	56	Kar**bon**es
4	*unl*			Kolo**bon** M., Pr.
4	C3	+45	14	Cer**bani** Caeubani Catapani Cebb(r)anitae Ga**bon**ita Gataphani
6	*unl*			Caetri**boni**
8	E3	−03	51	**Abon**a fl.
8	E3	−03	51	'**Abon**e'
11	E2	+04	50	Car**bon**aria Silva
14	H2	+02	46	Cam**bon**um
15	C2	+04	43	Nar**bon**ensis
17	F4	+05	44	Cam**bon**um
17	F5	+05	44	Ala**bon**te
20	B4	+14	45	Al**bon**a
21	C5	+20	44	Okta**bon**
22	*unl*			**Bon**a Mansio
22	*unl*			Kasi**bon**on
23	*unl*			Cha**bon**

[11] I have assumed that names in *-bonon* are inadmissible as *-bona* names. Note, however, that the name listed as 22unl *Kasibonon* (from Procopius, *Buildings*, 4.11.20) is gen. pl. of a Celtic **Kasibona* according to Beševliev, pp. 23–24 and 133–34. He and Duridanov, 'Sprach-spuren', p. 139, connect it with the name of a god *Casebonus* culted near Trun (Trän), Bulgaria (+22/42). *Bona Mansio* is presumably Latin; but is this certain?

23	*unl*			Erkabon		
24	C2	− 09	42	Burbida	Bonisana	
25	H2	+ 02	43	Atax fl.	Narbon? fl.	
25	H2	+ 02	43	Cambone		
25	*unl*			Albonica		
26	A3	−10	38	A(qua)bona	Equabona	
27	*unl*			Valebonga		
28	C4	− 06	34	Baniurae?	Banioubai	Boniuricis
31	*unl*			Strabonianensis Fundus		
32	*unl*			Bonustensis Plebs		
40	C2	+ 12	45	Ostium Carbonaria		
41	*unl*			Bondelia		
44	*unl*			In Monte Carbonario		
46	C4	+ 15	38	Vibonensis Sinus		
47	G4	+ 15	37	Alabon fl.	Alabis fl.	
47	*unl*			Alabon		
49	*unl*			Arbon		
52	F3	+ 29	40	[Libon] M.		
56	*unl*			Ambonium		
61	E1	+ 27	38	*Boneita		
65	B4	+ 29	36	Boubon		
67	F4	+ 37	36	Chalybonitis		
67	*unl*			*Sambon Chorion		
68	C2	+ 36	35	Rabona?		
69	D2	+ 36	33	*Chalybon		
70	C3	+ 33	31	Serbonitis L.		
71	B3	+ 35	31	Dibon		
71	*unl*			Libona		
75	*unl*			Arabon Kome		
75	*unl*			Ptolemais he ton Arabon		
80	B2	+ 32	25	Kastron Thebon		
80	*unl*			Mesthbon		
81	*unl*			Bonchis		
81	*unl*			Bongiana		
82	*unl*			Bonchis		
86	D2	+ 33	41	Abonouteichos	Ionopolis	
87	*unl*			Kamouresarbon		
91	*unl*			Banathsamson	Bonasamson	
95	inset	+ 56	25	Asabon M.		
95	inset	+ 56	26	Maketa Pr.	Asabon Pr.	

BOUD- 'VICTORY' (OI *BÚAID*, W. *BUDD*) AND BODIO- 'YELLOW' (OI *BUIDE*), GROUPED TOGETHER HERE AS NOT ALWAYS DISTINGUISHABLE

AILR and PNPG Celtic Elements s.v. *boudo-, boudi-*; GPN, p. 158 and n. 4; DLG s.vv. *boudi-* and *badios, bodios*; Lambert, '*Lugdunensis*', p. 230. On *Bodotria* (*Boderia* in Ptolemy 2.3.4) see Isaac, 'Scotland', pp. 191 and 210–11.

String BOUD, BOD

Formally admissible (22)

6	unl			**Boud**aia	
7	F2	− 01	49	Baiocasses	**Bod**iocasses
9	C4	− 05	56	**Bod**otria fl.	
9	D4	− 04	56	**Bod**otria? Aestuarium	
11	G4	+ 06	48	Vicus **Bod**atius?	
11	H2	+ 07	50	**Bod**obrica	
12	unl	+ 14	49	Maro**boud**on	
13	unl	+ 17	50	**Boud**origon	
16	B1	+ 06	44	**Bod**iontici	
18	C2	+ 05	47	Sego**bod**ium?	
19	C2	+ 10	47	A**bod**iacum	
22	unl			**Bod**as	
39	C3	+ 08	45	**Bod**incus fl.	
39	C3	+ 08	45	Industria	**Bod**incomagum?
39	F5	+ 09	44	**Bod**etia	
48	A3	+ 08	39	Moli**bod**es Ins.	
55	E3	+ 23	38	**Boud**oros fl.	
55	unl	+ 23	38	**Boud**(e)ion	**Boud**(e)ia
59	A3	+ 23	37	**Boud**oron	
60	B2	+ 24	35	**Boud**roe Inss.	
62	E4	+ 30	38	Beudos (Palaion)	**Boud**eia
63	unl			Touto**bod**iaci	

Abodiacum (*Aboudiakon* in Ptolemy 2.12.4) could be a compound in **ad-* (AILR s.n. *Abuzaco*; PNPG *Alpes*; cf. Russell, 'Suffix', p. 162, and Rasch §IICa, favouring a personal name *Abudius*). *Bodas* (acc. pl.?) is an unidentified place on the Danube in Lower Moesia or Scythia mentioned by Procopius. The *Toutobodiaci* are an unlocated Galatian tribe (Pliny 5.146). The *Atlas* omits Ptolemy's *Boudoris* (Büderich, + 6/51) and *Boudorgis* (Pardubice, + 15/50), both in his Germania Magna (2.11.14; see PNPG and cf. *rīgo-* below); these are included on **Map 12.14**.[12] On Ptolemy's *Bôdinoi* (+ 29/47?) and *Bôdinon oros* (+ 30/50?), see below, p. 195.

Formally inadmissible

9	unl			Cam**bod**unum	
19	C2	+ 10	47	Cam**bod**unum	
51	unl			Rum**bod**ona	
70	F4	+ 34	30	E**bod**a	O**bod**a

BRAUO- 'QUERN' (OI *BRAO*, W *BREUAN*)

AILR Celtic Elements s.v. {bra:uon-}; DLG s.v. *brauon-* (and p. 432); Curchin, 'Five Celtic town-names', p. 46.

---

[12] Cf. De Bernardo Stempel, 'Ptolemy's evidence for Germania Superior', pp. 88 and 90.

String BRAV, BRAU, BRAOU

Formally admissible (2)

9	E6	− 03	54	**Brav**(o)niacum
24	H2	− 04	42	**Brau**on?

Formally inadmissible

4	B2	+ 44	16	Labaetia	Labecia	La**brau**m
9	C6	− 05	54	'**Abraou**annos'? fl.		
61	F3	+ 27	37	La**brau**nda		

BREMO- 'ROAR, LOW' (W *BREFU*)

AILR and PNPG Celtic Elements s.v. *bremo-*; Hamp, '*Bremenio* and Indo-European', and 'Some toponyms of Roman Britain', p. 16.

String BREM

Formally admissible (4)

8	D2	− 04	52	**Brem**ia
8	E1	− 03	53	*****Brem**etennacum Veteranorum
9	E5	− 03	55	**Brem**enium
39	H2	+ 10	45	[**Brem**tonicum]

Formally inadmissible None

BRIG- 'HIGH PLACE, HILLFORT' (OI *BRÍ* < *****BRIG-S*, W *BRE* < *****BRIGĀ*, LOCATIVE *FRY* < *****BRIGĪ*) AND OCCASIONALLY BRĪG- 'POWER, PRESTIGE' (OI *BRÍG*, W *BRI*), GROUPED TOGETHER HERE AS NOT ALWAYS DISTINGUISHABLE

AILR and PNPG Celtic Elements s.v. {briga:-}; DLG s.vv. *briga* (and p. 432) and *brigo-*; Villar, *Estudios*, pp. 153–88; Prósper, *Lenguas y religiones prerromanas*, pp. 357–82 and 514; Hamp, 'British Celtic BRIGE and morphology'; Greule, 'Keltisch *****brig-'.

String BRIG[13] (excluding BRIGANT, q.v.), BRIC, BRIK, BIRIC, BIRIK, BRIA,[14] BRIX, BRIS, BRIZ, BRENSE, BRENSI and word-final -BRI (BREAEG and BRIENSE are not found).

Fuller information about morphology and the above spellings in Hispania is provided by Villar. For variant spellings see also Albertos, 'Los topónimos en -*briga*'. In localizing the 'unl' names in Spain and Portugal I have made much use of her article.

Formally admissible (97 – as '24 *unl* Kontobris', '26 *unl* Arabriga', '26 *unl* Langobriga' and '26 *unl* Talabrica/Talabriga?/Talabara?' are duplicates)

8	*unl*	– 02	50	**Brige**	
9	*unl*	– 03	54	**Brig**a	
11	C3	+ 02	49	Litano**briga**?	
11	H2	+ 07	50	Bodo**bric**a	
12	B3	+ 08	49	*Salio**briga**	
14	E1	– 01	47	Ro**bric**a	
14	E2	– 01	46	**Brig**iosum	**Brio**ssus
14	F1	+ 00	47	**Brigg**ogalus	
14	F1	+ 00	47	**Bric**ca	
15	C1	+ 04	44	***Brig**innum?	
15	E3	+ 05	43	Sego**brig**ii	
16	C2	+ 06	43	***Brig**omagus	
17	H4	+ 06	44	**Brig**ianii	
17	I2	+ 07	45	Are**brig**ium	
18	A1	+ 03	48	Euro**briga**	
19	A2	+ 08	47	***Brig**obannis	
19	E2	+ 12	47	Arto**briga**	
20	F2	+ 18	47	**Brig**etio	
22	E6	+ 27	42	Mesem**bria**	
22	F3	+ 28	45	Alio**brix**	
24	C1	– 09	43	Arta**bris** Sinus	Megas Limen
24	C1	– 09	43	Castellum Avilio**bris**	
24	C1	– 09	43	Phlaouia Lam**bris**	
24	C2	– 09	42	Lans**bric**a	Lais
24	C3	– 09	41	*Tongo**briga**	Tounto**briga**
24	C4	– 09	40	Conim**briga**	Flavia Conim**briga**
24	C4	– 09	40	Lango**briga**	
24	C4	– 09	40	Tala**briga**	
24	D2	– 08	42	Koilio**briga**	
24	D2	– 08	42	Nemeto**briga**	
24	D3	– 08	41	Ara**brig**enses	
24	D3	– 08	41	Calia**briga**	Cala**bria**

---

[13] BRIGG seems to occur in *Briggogalus*, but this precise form may be unattested (cf. Sims-Williams, 'Welsh *Iâl*', p. 58, n. 4); it may be a *brīuo-* name.

[14] On BRIA see p. 14 above and cf. *brīuo-* below.

24	D4	– 08	40	Longo**briga**			
24	D4	– 08	40	Me(i)du**briga**			
24	E4	– 07	40	Miro**briga**	Municipium Val(...)		
24	F2	– 06	42	**Briga**ecini			
24	F2	– 06	42	**Briga**ecium	**Brig**eco		
24	F3	– 06	41	Amallo**briga**	Abulo**brica**		
24	G2	– 05	42	Desso**briga**			
24	G2	– 05	42	Iulio**briga**			
24	G2	– 05	42	Laco**briga**			
24	H1	– 04	43	Portus Victoriae Iulio**brig**ensium			
24	H2	– 04	42	Deo**brig**ula			
24	*unl*	– 09	*41*	Abourica	*Auo**briga**	Avo**brica**	Abo**brica**
24	*unl*	– 09	*43*	Adro**brica**			
24	*unl*	– 08	*41*	Ara**briga**			
24	*unl*	– 09	*41*	Arco**briga**			
24	*unl*	– 09	*40*	Caeilo**brig**oi			
24	*unl*	– 08	*42*	*Calu**briga**			
24	*unl*			Cani**bri**			
24	*unl*	– 07	*43*	Castellum Ercorio**bris**			
24	*unl*	– 09	*41*	Castellum Letio**bris**			
24	*unl*	– 08	*42*	Castellum Tala**briga**			
24	*unl*	– 09	*41*	Elaeneo**briga**			
24	*unl*			Konto**bris**			
24	*unl*	– 08	*39*	Kottaio**briga**			
24	*unl*			Lambria**ca**			
24	*unl*	– 05	*43*	Tono**brica**	Tenobrica?		
24	*unl*	– 09	*41*	*Vala**briga**			
25	B2	– 04	43	Flavio**briga**	Portus Amanum		
25	C3	– 03	42	Deo**briga**	Sobo**brica**?		
25	C4	– 03	41	Arco**briga**			
25	D4	– 02	41	Augusto**briga**	Augusto**brica**		
25	D4	– 02	41	Nerto**briga**			
25	*cn.*	– 03	*39*	Seko**birikes**			
26	A2	– 10	39	Iera**briga**	Lera**briga**		
26	A2	– 10	39	Londo**bris** Ins.			
26	B3	– 09	38	Caeto**briga**			
26	B4	– 09	37	Lac(c)o**briga**			
26	B4	– 09	37	Miro**briga**	Miro**briga** Celtica	Municipium Flavium Miro**brig**ensium	
26	D2	– 07	39	*Tongo**briga**			
26	D3	– 07	38	Nerto**briga** Concordia Iulia			
26	D4	– 07	37	Turo**briga**			
26	E2	– 06	39	Augusto**briga**			
26	E3	– 06	38	Bruto**briga**			
26	E3	– 06	38	Miro**briga**			
26	*unl*			Ara**briga**			
26	*unl*	– 09	*38*	Arco**briga**			
26	*unl*	– 09	*41*	Avo**briga**	Abo**brica**		
26	*unl*			Bruto**briga**			
26	*unl*	– 08	*38*	Burrulo**briga**			
26	*unl*	– 08	*39*	Deo**briga**			
26	*unl*	– 07	*39*	Ebero**briga**			
26	*unl*			Konto**bris**			
26	*unl*			Lango**briga**			

26	unl	− 09	38	Meribriga	Merobriga	
26	unl	− 08	39	Montobrica	Montobriga	Mundobriga
26	unl			Perbriga		
26	unl			Talabrica	Talabriga?	Talabara?
27	A2	− 05	39	Caesarobriga		
27	C2	− 03	39	Segobriga		
28	unl	− 06	34	Ouobrix		
51	F3	+ 25	40	Mesambria		
52	C2	+ 28	41	Sely(m)bria	Eudoxiopolis	
61	unl	+ 27	37	Thymbria		
62	unl	+ 28	38	Bria		
63	D1	+ 33	39	Ecobrogis	Eccobriga	
63	E4	+ 34	38	Salambriai	Salaberina	
69	C4	+ 35	32	Sennabris	Ginnabris	
71	B2	+ 35	31	Bethennabris		
91	unl			Mambri		

Note that '24 *unl* Kontobris' duplicates '26 *unl* Kontobris', an unidentified Lusitanian (or Celtiberian?) city mentioned by Diodorus Siculus, 33.24 (Tovar, *Lusitanien*, p. 270; TIR J-29, p. 67), that '26 *unl* Arabriga' duplicates '24 *unl* Arabriga', that '26 *unl* Langobriga' duplicates '24C4 Langobriga' and that '26 *unl* Talabrica/Talabriga?/Talabara?' duplicates '24C4 Talabriga'. '26 *unl* Perbriga' (Rav. 316.8) may duplicate '26A2 Ierebriga' (TIR J-29, p. 126). The *Brutobriga* located on Map 26E3 at Villanueva de la Serena (cf. Albertos, no. 20, and TIR J-30, p. 113) is distinct from '26 *unl* Brutobriga', an unidentified place in Conventus Scallabitanus (see Curchin, *Magistrates*, pp. 169 and 272). The two places called *Avobriga* (24unl and 26unl) seem to have been fairly close but distinct (Albertos, nos. 16–17). The *Sekobirikes* (25cn.) are here assigned to *Segobriga* (27C2) (see TIR K-30, p. 210). '24 *unl* Lambriaca' is possibly identical with '24C1 Phlaouia [*Flavia*] Lambris' (Albertos, no. 48; Villar, *Estudios*, pp. 174–75; PNPG Comments s.n. *Phlaouía Lambris*). *Canibri* (24unl) was somewhere on the north coast of Spain (TIR K-30, p. 80). On *Ouobrix* (28unl) in north Africa see Chapter 10 below. *Bria* (62unl) is localized by Zgusta, pp. 127–28 (s.n. *Bríana*), in the area of Map 62C5. *Eccobriga* also appears as *Ecobrogis* under BROG below. An additional *Artobriga* (+ 11/48 ?), not in the *Atlas*, occurs in Ptolemy 2.12.4 (see p. 186 below) and is included on **Map 12.1** below. A possible further addition is *Sarabris* (Ptolemy 2.6.49), if this is not an error for *Sarabis*, *Sabaris*, or similar (see AILR Comments s.n. *Sibarim* and PNPG Comments s.n. *Sarabrís*; Map 24F3 = −6/41).

Formally inadmissible (on *Rubricatum* 'reddened' cf. PNPG Comments s.n. *Rhoubríkata*)

2	E2	+ 08	56	Chersonesos Kimbrike
6	unl			Brisari
6	unl			Salobriasae

6	*unl*			Sugam**bri**			
8	I3	+01	51	Portus Du**bris**			
11	G1	+06	51	Sugam**bri**			
11	G3	+06	49	Eru**bris** fl.			
11	H4	+07	48	**Bris**igavi			
11	H4	+07	48	(Mons) **Bris**iacus	**Bris**iacus		
12	D3	+10	49	**Biric**iana			
14	F1	+00	47	**Brix**is			
14	G1	+01	47	Ga**bris**	*Ga**brae**		
14	G3	+01	45	Ca**bria**necum			
14	H4	+02	44	Trio**bris** fl.			
18	C3	+05	46	Pons Du**bris**			
19	D3	+11	46	**Brix**enetes?			
20	*unl*			Cim**bria**nis			
22	*unl*			Castris Ru**bris**			
22	*unl*			Cim**bria**nae			
22	*unl*			Hymauparou**bri**			
22	*unl*			*Maskio**brias**			
23	*unl*			Hy**bris**tes fl.			
24	F1	− 06	43	Boreios	Gallicus	Canta**bric**us Oceanus	
25	F2	+00	43	Ono**bris**ates			
25	H2	+02	43	*Ru**bres**sus? L.	Ru**bren**sis? L.		
25	G4	+01	41	Ru**bric**atum fl.			
25	H4	+02	41	Ru**bric**atum?			
26	D5	− 07	36	Na**bris**sa			
32	B3	+08	36	Rou**brik**atos? fl.			
36	C4	+13	27	De**dris**?	**Debris**	De**cri** Oppidum	
39	G2	+10	45	**Brix**ia			
39	H4	+10	44	**Brix**ellum			
41	*unl*			Sca**bris**			
42	D1	+12	43	Um**bria**	Um**bri**		
45	G3	+17	40	Cala**bria**	Cala**bri**		
47	F4	+14	37	**Brik**inniai?			
48	B3	+09	39	Custodia Ru**brien**sis			
48	B3	+09	39	*Ru**bren**ses			
51	E3	+25	40	**Bria**ntike	**Bria**ntae	Gallaike	Priantae
56	C3	+26	39	**Bris**a Pr.			
62	D2	+30	39	Tem**bris** fl.			
65	D2	+30	37	Tym**bria**nassos			
65	F2	+31	37	Tim**bria**da			
87	*unl*			E**bria**pa			
87	*unl*	+*36*	*45*	Kim**brik**e? kome	Kim**merik**e? kome		
94	*unl*			**Bris**oana			
94	*unl*			**Brix**a			
94	*unl*			**Briz**ana			
90	*unl*			Ga**bris**			

Instances of *-bris* in river-names, *-bri* in ethnonyms and *-bria* in district-names have been placed in the above 'inadmissible' list on semantic grounds. So have instances of non-final *brix-* on the grounds that the nominative **brig-s* would not occur medially; however, some such instances of (-)*brix-* may derive from *brig-* + sigmatic suffix (cf. Anreiter, *Breonen*, p. 137; De Bernardo Stempel, 'Ptolemy's Celtic Italy and Ireland', pp. 92 and 106, and 'Additions to Ptolemy's evidence for Celtic Italy'; DLG s.v. *briga*; PNPG Possibly Celtic Elements s.v. *brixo-*).

BRIGANT- 'HIGH PERSON/PLACE' (OI *BRIGIT*, W *BRAINT*)

AILR and PNPG Celtic Elements s.v. *brigant-*; DLG s.v. *brigantion*; Hamp, 'British Celtic BRIGE and morphology' (differently De Bernardo Stempel, 'More on Ptolemy's evidence for Celtic Ireland', p. 99).

String BRIGANT[15]

Formally admissible (7)

8	A2	− 07	52	**Brigant**es		
9	E6	− 03	54	**Brigant**es		
17	G2	+ 06	45	**Brigant**io		
17	H4	+ 06	44	**Brigant**io		
19	B2	+ 09	47	**Brigant**inus L.	Ven(non)etus L.	
19	B2	+ 09	47	**Brigant**ium	**Brigant**ii	
24	C1	− 09	43	(Flavium) **Brigant**ium	**Brigant**ium	Portus Magnus?

See **Map 4.2**

Formally inadmissible None

BRĪUO-, BRĪUĀ 'BRIDGE' (OBSOLETE IN INSULAR CELTIC ?CF. OI *BRÚ* 'BRINK' AND *BRÁ* 'EYEBROW')

AILR and PNPG Celtic Elements s.v. *breuo-*, {bri:uo-}, {briua:-}; DLG s.v. *briua* (and p. 432); Evans, 'Celts and Germans', p. 245; Zimmer, '*A uo penn*', p. 207; Lambert, '*Lugdunensis*', pp. 215–16.

String BRIV, BREV, BRIOU (BREOU not found), BRIO, BRIA[16]

Formally admissible (20)

8	G2	− 01	52	Duro**briv**ae
8	G3	− 01	51	Duroco**briv**is
8	H3	+ 00	51	Duro**briv**ae
11	C3	+ 02	49	**Briv**a Isarae
11	C3	+ 02	49	Samaro**briv**a Ambianorum

---

[15] Since BRIA was included beside BRIGA above, one might search for BRIANT beside BRIGANT. However, the only form would be 51E3 *Briantike/Briantae* around Mesambria in Thrace (see the 'Formally inadmissible' list above). This has been derived from Thracian *bria*: cf. TIR K-35, I, p. 22.

[16] On BRIA see p. 14 above and cf. *brig-* above.

11	*unl*	+ *00*	*49*	Breviodurum	
14	F1	+ 00	47	*Briotreidis?	
14	G3	+ 01	45	Briva (Curretia)	
14	H1	+ 02	47	Brivas	
14	H1	+ 02	47	Brivodurum	
17	A3	+ 03	45	Brivas	
17	E2	+ 05	45	*Brioratis	
22	E6	+ 27	42	Mesembria	
24	C2	– 09	42	Brevis	
24	*unl*			Aliobr(i)o	
51	F3	+ 25	40	Mesambria	
52	C2	+ 28	41	Sely(m)bria	Eudoxiopolis
61	*unl*	+ *27*	*37*	Thymbria	
62	*unl*	+ *29*	*38*	Bria	
63	E4	+ 34	*38*	Salambriai	Salaberina

Breviodurum (i.e. *Brevodorum*, var. *Briuodor*, *Breviodorum* in AI 385.2) is also attested as *Brevoduro* (TP) (TIR M-31, p. 56; TIR M-30/31, p. 31). The *e* here and in *Brevis* may be a transmissional error. On *Bria* (62unl) see s.v. *brig-* above. *Aliobr(i)o* is very uncertain (see Tovar, *Tarraconensis*, p. 293). See **Map 12.6**.

Formally inadmissible

5	*unl*			Sibrion			
6	*unl*	+ *73*	*33*	Samarab(r)iae			
6	*unl*			Salobriasae			
14	E2			Brigiosum	Briossus		
14	F3			C(...)o	*Calambrio		
14	G3	+ 01	45	Cabrianecum			
20	*unl*			Cimbrianis			
22	*unl*			Cimbrianae			
22	*unl*			*Maskiobrias			
24	D3	– 08	41	Caliabriga	Calabria		
24	*unl*			Lambriaca			
42	D1	+ 12	43	Umbria	Umbri		
45	G3	+ 17	40	Calabria	Calabri		
51	E3	+ 25	40	Briantike	Briantae	Gallaike	Priantae
56	C2			Thymbrios fl.			
62	*unl*			Tembrion (Chorion)			
62	*unl*			Thymbrion			
65	A2	+ 28	37	Brioula			
65	D2	+ 30	37	Tymbrianassos			
65	F2	+ 31	37	Timbriada			
66	D4			*Imbrioga			
74	*unl*			Chabriou kome			
87	*unl*			Ebriapa			

Instances of *-bria* in ethnonyms (on *Samarab(r)iae*, cf. p. 33 above) and in district-names have been placed in the above 'inadmissible' list on semantic grounds.

BROC(C)O- 'BADGER' (OI *BROCC*, W *BROCH*)

AILR and PNPG Celtic Elements s.v. *broc(c)o-*; DLG s.v. *broccos*.

String BROC, BROK

Formally admissible (3)

9	E5	− 03	55	*Brocolitia
9	E6	− 03	54	Brocavum
11	H4	+ 07	48	Brocomagus

Formally inadmissible

8	*unl*			Bibroci	
25	I3	+ 03	42	Sambroka fl.	
53	B2	+ 29	41	Proochthoi	Brochthoi
69	C2	+ 35	33	Brochoi	

BROG- 'COUNTRY' (OI *MRUIG*, W *BRO*)

AILR and PNPG Celtic Elements s.v. *brog-*; GPN, pp. 159–60; DLG s.v. *brog(i)-* (and p. 432).

String BROG

Formally admissible (5 – the two instances of *Petobrogen* are the same place in Galatia)

14	F4	+ 00	44	Nitiobroges	
14	*unl*			Antobroges	
17	E3	+ 05	45	Allobroges	
62	*unl*			Petobrogen	
63	D1	+ 33	39	Ecobrogis	Eccobriga
86	C3	+ 32	40	'Petobrogen'	

The *Antobroges* (var. *Antebroges*) were a people in Aquitania named by Pliny 4.109, but often emended to *Nitiobroges* (see Mayhoff's note, p. 353). *Ecobrogis* also appears under *Eccobriga* s.v. BRIG above.

Formally inadmissible None

CAITO- 'FOREST' (W *COED*)

AILR and PNPG Celtic Elements s.v. *caeto-*, {ce:to-}; DLG s.v. *caito-* (cf. review by Falileyev, p. 284). See Chapter 3 above, with maps.

Strings CAET, KAIT, CET, KET (CAIT, KAET not found)

Formally admissible (13)

5	*unl*			**Ket**aion Akron		
8	F2	− 02	52	*Letocetum		
8	*unl*	− *03*	*51*	Ani**cet**is		
12	I4	+ 15	48	**Cet**ium		
13	B4	+ 16	48	**Ket**ion Oros		
26	B3	− 09	38	**Caet**obriga		
26	E5	− 06	36	**Cet**aria		
26	*unl*	− *05*	*37*	**Cet**urgi		
30	*unl*	+ *03*	*36*	Tamari**cet**o Praesidium		
47	*unl*			Kytattara	Enattara	**Ket**aria
56	E3	+ 27	39	**Ket**eios fl.		
60	F2	+ 26	35	'**Ket**ia'? Pr.		
84	*unl*	+ *38*	*47*	**Cet**ae		

Ketaria was in western Sicily (see above, p. 29, n. 21).

Formally inadmissible

3	G4	+ 57	26	Maka	Ma**ket**a
3	*unl*			'**Cet**rora'	
6	*unl*			**Caet**riboni	
14	I2	+ 03	46	De**cet**ia	
15	C1	+ 04	44	U**cet**ia	
25	B3	− 04	42	Der**cet**ius M.	
25	H3	+ 02	42	Indigetes	Indi**cet**es
25	G4	+ 01	41	La**cet**ani	
25	*cn.*			Ark(r)eturki	
37	E2	+ 19	30	Ma**ket**ai?	
40	B1	+ 11	45	Vi**cet**ia	
44	*unl*			E**cet**ra	
44	*unl*			Pi**ket**ia	
45	E3	+ 16	40	Peu**cet**ii	
47	*unl*			El**ket**ion	
47	*unl*			Hel**ket**ion	
52	F4	+ 29	40	*Plo**ket**ta	
55	*unl*			Cer**cet**ius M.	
56	F5	+ 27	38	Tro**ket**ta	

59	B2	+23	38	**Ket**tos?	
61	F3	+27	37	Chal**ket**or	
61	D2	+26	37	Ker**ket**eus M.	
61	E4	+27	36	Lak(e)ter Pr.	
62	*unl*			Malkaitenoi	
66	B3	+32	36	**K**(i)**et**is	Cietae
74	C3	+30	30	S**ket**is	
75	D2	+30	29	Ker**ket**hoeris?	
75	D2	+30	29	Per**ket**haut	Philagris?
75	*unl*			Ker**ket**hyris	
77	*unl*			Ker**ket**hoeris	
77	*unl*			Teker**ket**hothis	
84	D4	+38	44	Ker**ket**ai	
84	*unl*			Ker**ket**is Kolpos	
91	*unl*			Rakoukaitha	
95	inset	+56	26	Ma**ket**a Pr.	Asabon Pr.

CAMBO- 'CROOKED' (OI *CAMB*, *CAMM*, W *CAM*)

AILR and PNPG Celtic Elements s.v. *cambo-*; GPN, p. 322; DLG s.v. *cambo-*. See Chapter 3 above, with maps, also p. 14, n. 63.

String CAMB, KAMB

Formally admissible (19)

6	F5	+87	22	**Kamb**ouson Stoma	
6	G5	+90	22	**Kamb**erichon Stoma	
8	H2	+00	52	'**Camb**orico'?	
9	E6	−03	54	*****Camb**oglanna	
9	*unl*	*−02*	*53*	**Camb**odunum	
9	D6	−04	54	Mori**kamb**e *Eischusis	
14	G2	+01	46	**Camb**iovicenses?	
14	H2	+02	46	**Camb**onum	
17	F4	+05	44	**Camb**onum	
18	E2	+07	47	**Camb**ete	
19	C2	+10	47	**Camb**odunum	
24	*unl*	*−08*	*42*	**Kamb**aiton	
25	G2	+01	43	**Camb**olectri	
25	H2	+02	43	**Camb**one	
50	A4	+21	40	**Camb**unii M.	
56	*unl*	*+27*	*39*	**Kam**(br)e	
81	B3	+31	22	Forum **Camb**usis?	
88	D3	+45	41	**Kamb**ysene	
88	D3	+45	41	**Kamb**yses fl.	

Formally inadmissible

6	C3	+72	30	**Kamb**istholoi		
24	*unl*			**Camb**racum		
92	C2	+47	34	**Kamb**adene	Kampa(n)da	Sambana

CAMULO- (NAME OF A GOD;[17] ? OI *cumal(l)*)

AILR and PNPG Celtic Elements s.v. *camulo-*; GPN, p. 161; DLG s.v. *camulos*.

String CAMUL, KAMUL, KAMOUL (CAMOUL not found)

Formally admissible (5)

8	F1	− 02	53	**Camul**odonum?	
8	H3	+ 00	51	Col. **Camul**odunum	
9	*unl*	− 04	*55*	**Camul**ossesa Praesidium	
14	G2	+ 01	46	*Ande**camul**um	
63	G3	+ 35	38	**Kamoul**ianai	Iustinianoupolis Nova

Formally inadmissible

89	E3	+ 42	37	**Kamul**, Mon.

CARNO- 'PEAK, TUMULUS, CAIRN' (OI *carn*, W *carn*)

AILR and PNPG Celtic Elements s.v. *carno-*; DLG s.v. *carnitu* (cf. *carnon*); De Bernardo Stempel, *Vertretung*, pp. 151–52; Nussbaum, *Head and Horn*, pp. 5–6; Lambert, '*Lugdunensis*', p. 227. Cf. Bonfante, 'Il problema dei Taurisci e dei Carni', pp. 19–21; Anreiter et al., 'Names of the Eastern Alpine region', p. 122.

String CARN, KARN

Formally admissible (23)

4	B2	+ 44	16	**Karn**a	**Carn**us	**Karn**ana			
6	A4	+ 63	25	Asthala	Solis?	Karmina? Ins.	**Karn**ine Ins.	Nosala Ins.	Nymph-arum Cubile
6	*unl*			Cartana	**Karn**asa	Tetrogonis			
6	*unl*			**Karn**asa					
9	B3	− 06	57	**Karn**onakai					
11	B4	+ 01	48	**Carn**utes					
13	B4	+ 16	48	**Carn**untum					

---

[17] Maier, 'Is Lug to be identified with Mercury?', p. 128, and 'Carlisle und Colchester', suggests that *Camulus* may be a personal name here.

13	B4	+ 16	48	Col. **Carn**untum	Col. Septimia Aurelia Antoniniana		
14	E1	– 01	47	***Carn**ona			
19	F3	+ 13	46	Alpes **Carn**icae			
19	F3	+ 13	46	**Carn**i			
19	F3	+ 13	46	Iulium **Carn**icum			
20	B3	+ 14	46	**Carn**ium			
54	C4	+ 20	38	**Karn**os Ins.			
54	C4	+ 20	38	A**carn**ania			
58	B3	+ 21	37	**Karn**asion			
58	C3	+ 22	37	**Karn**ion fl.			
58	*unl*	+ 22	*37*	**Karn**eates M.			
58	*unl*	+ 22	*36*	**Karn**ion			
61	E3	+ 27	37	Hali**carn**assus			
64	D2	+ 36	39	**Karn**alis	Komaralis		
68	A4	+ 35	34	**Carn**e	**Karn**os		
69	D4	+ 36	32	**Karn**aia	Astaroth?		

See **Map 12.15**.

Formally inadmissible

21		*unl*		**Scarn**iunga fl.

CARR- 'CART, CHARIOT' (OI *CARR*, W *CAR*)

PNPG Celtic Elements s.v. *carro-*; GPN, pp. 63, n. 2, and 163; DLG s.v. *carros*; De Bernardo Stempel, 'Ptolemy's Celtic Italy and Ireland', pp. 93–94.[18]

String CARR, KARR

Formally admissible (7)

23	*unl*	+ 25	*48*	**Karr**odounon			
24	*unl*			**Carr**inensis Ager			
26	E4	– 06	37	**Carr**uca			
31	*unl*	+*07*	*36*	Capraria	**Carr**aria?		
39	B3	+ 07	45	**Carr**eum Potentia	**Karr**ea		
83	C5	+ 37	26	**Carr**ei	Cariati		
95	A3	+ 48	26	Gerra?	**Carr**a?	Gerraioi	**Carr**ei

[18] They refer to *Karraka* on which see below, Ch. 7, p. 200, and Ch. 8, n. 23.

Pliny's *Carrinensis Ager* (2.231) may be connected with the *rio Carrión* in Cantabria but this is uncertain (Tovar, *Tarraconensis*, p. 370). The above unlocated *Karrodounon* (Ptolemy 3.5.15) was on the river *Tyras* (Dniester) beside Dacia (Müller, p. 434; see below, p. 194). The *Atlas* does not include three other examples of *Karrodounon* in Ptolemy: one in Pannonia (2.14.4, 2.15.1), only listed as '*Cardono*' /*Iovia* [Map 20E4 = +17/45], the second in Germania Magna (2.11.14), now Krapkowice/Krappitz in Poland [i.e. Map 13C2 = +17/50] and the third in Vindelicia (2.12.4 [Müller] = 2.12.5 [Cuntz]), perhaps a place called Karnberg near Wasserburg am Inn [i.e. in the area of Map 12F4 = +12/48].[19] See Anreiter, *Die vorrömischen Namen Pannoniens*, pp. 162–63. A further relevant name may be *Cardena* from the *Ravenna Cosmography* (11H2 = +7/50), attested as *Karadona* in 836.[20] The *Atlas* omits *Karraka* (Ptolemy 3.1.28), apparently in the Brixia region (+10/45).[21] All these are included on **Map 12.26**.

Formally inadmissible

50	unl			**Karra**bia	
55	C2	+22	39	*****Ekarr**a	Acharrae
58	unl			A**karr**a	
67	H3	+38	36	**Carr**hae	
94	unl			An**karra**kan	

CASSI- 'TIN? BRONZE? SPLENDID? CURL?' (OI *CAS*, OW *CASCORD*, LATER *COSGORDD*)

AILR and PNPG Celtic Elements s.v. *cassi-*; GPN, pp. 170–71; DLG s.v. *cassi-, -casses*; Delamarre, 'Gallo-Brittonica', p. 127; Lambert, '*Lugdunensis*', p. 231; De Hoz, 'Narbonensis', pp. 180–81.

String CASS, KASS

(Some examples of CAS, such as *Casinomagus* under *mag-* below, may be relevant, but the string CAS would bring in innumerable irrelevant forms. Note also *Kasibonon*, discussed in a footnote to *bon-* above.)

---

[19] See Müller, p. 284. Cf. PNPG Comments s.n. *Karródounon*. Possibly, however, *Parrodunum* in the *Atlas* (12E4 = +11/48), from ND, Oc. XXXV.28, is a corrupt form of this *Karrodounon*. See Seeck's note, p. 201, n. 10, and Cousin, p. 448.

[20] Greule and Kleiber, 'Moseltal', p. 158; see also Gohil, *Ancient Celtic and Non-Celtic Place-Names*, p. 103, citing Gysseling's *Toponymisch Woordenboek*, p. 553. The first part, however, is always *Cara-* or *Car-*, never **Carro-*.

[21] PNPG, *Italia*. This name can also be compared with W *carrog* 'torrent'; see below, p. 226.

Formally admissible (21)

4	B2	+43	16	Casani	Gasani	**Kass**anitai
5	*unl*			**Kass**ida		
7	F2	− 01	49	Vidu**casses**		
7	F2	− 01	49	Baio**casses**	Bodio**casses**	
8	*unl*	*+00*	*51*	**Cass**i		
11	A3	+00	49	Velio**casses**		
11	B4	+01	48	Duro**casses**		
11	D4	+03	48	Tri**casses**		
14	F3	+00	45	**Cas**(s)inomagus		
14	G4	+01	44	**Cass**iaco		
19	*unl*	*+ 10*	*47*	**Cass**iliacum		
25	*Av*	*+00*	*40*	**Cass**ae Herronesi		
26	*Av*	− 06	36	Argentarius M.	**Cass**ius M.	
42	C4	+12	42	Forum **Cass**ii		
47	*unl*			**Cass**itana Massa		
51	B4	+23	40	Ass(er)a?	Asseros	**Cass**era
52	G3	+30	40	*****Kass**a		
62	*unl*	*+ 30*	*39*	**Kass**enoi		
67	C4	+36	36	Oro**kass**ias Oros		
68	A2	+35	35	**Cas**(s)ius M.		
68	B2	+36	35	**Kass**iotis		

Avienus' *Cassius M.* is here identified with the Cerro de Asperillo (= *Cappa* in the *Atlas* Map 26E5), following the *communis opinio* in Murphy's edition (p. 57). (*Map-by-Map Directory* i, 437, identifies it with *Argentarius M.* = Sierra del Pinar.) *Forum Cassii* is on the Via Cassia which is said to be named after a member of the gens *Cassius* (Lewis & Short, *Latin Dictionary*, s.n. *Cassius*); however, *Cassius* is included in GPN, p. 170, so it seems safer not to exclude these names at this stage (cf. KPP, p. 262). *Cassitana Massa* was somewhere in Sicily. See **Map 4.3**.

Formally inadmissible

25	H2	+02	43	Car**cas**(s)o	Col. Iulia	Car**cas**um Volcarum Tectosagarum
50	D4	+23	40	Poteidaia	**Kass**andreia	
54	A2	+19	39	**Kass**iope		
54	A2	+19	39	**Kass**iope Pr.		
54	C3	+20	39	**Kass**ope		
54	C3	+20	39	**Kass**opia		

CATU- 'BATTLE, ARMY' (OI *CATH*, W *CAD*)

AILR and PNPG Celtic Elements s.v. *catu-*; GPN, p. 174; DLG s.v. *catu-* (and pp. 432–33).

String CATU, KATOU (KATU, CATOU not found)

Formally admissible (8)[22]

8	G3	−01	51	**Catu**vellauni
11	D3	+03	49	**Catu**siacum?
11	F1	+05	51	**Catu**alium
11	F4	+05	48	**Catu**ricis
15	F2	+05	43	**Catu**iacia
17	G4	+06	44	**Catu**riges
17	G4	+06	44	**Catu**rigomagus
19	E3	+12	46	**Catu**brini

See **Map 12.7**.

Formally inadmissible

7	E3	− 02	48	Ingena	Abrincas	Civitas Abrin**catu**m	Legedia	Abrin**catu**i
25	G4	+01	41	Rubri**catu**m fl.				
25	H4	+02	41	Rubri**catu**m?				
27	B4	− 04	37	Agatucci?	A**catu**cci			
31	G2	+07	37	Ta**catu**a				
37	E2	+19	30	Ma**katou**tai				
91	*unl*			*Va**catu**m				

Cʟᴏᴜɴ- 'ᴍᴇᴀᴅᴏᴡ' (OI *cʟúᴀɪɴ*, W *ᴄʟᴜɴ*)

AILR and PNPG Celtic Elements s.v. {clu:no-}; DLG s.v. *clunia* < *clounia*.

String CLUN, KLOUN (CLOUN, KLUN not found)

Formally admissible (3)

19	B2	+09	47	**Clun**ia
25	B4	− 04	41	Col. **Clun**ia (Sulpicia)
48	D2	+09	42	**Kloun**ion

Formally inadmissible None

Cᴏᴍ-ᴘʟ(ᴇ)ᴜ-ᴛ- 'ᴄᴏɴꜰʟᴜᴇɴᴄᴇ' (ɴᴏᴛ ɪɴ Iɴꜱᴜʟᴀʀ Cᴇʟᴛɪᴄ)

---

[22] *Catuiacia* is also attested as *Catuiaca* (var. *Catuluca* etc.); see Barruol, pp. 74–75, and DLG, p. 432. AILR Comments s.n. is incorrect.

AILR and PNPG Celtic Elements s.v. *pleu-*, *plu-* 'flow'; García Alonso, 'On the Celticity of the Duero plateau', pp. 33–34; Gorrochategui, 'En torno a la clasificación del Lusitano', p. 82; Villar, 'Celtic language', p. 255. As these authorities point out, Celtic retention of IE **p* is not irregular in this position.

String COMPL (KOMPL not found)

Formally admissible (2)

24	E3	−07	41	**Compl**eutica
25	B5	−04	40	**Compl**utum

Formally admissible None

CON-DAT-E 'CONFLUENCE' (NOT IN INSULAR CELTIC)

AILR and PNPG Celtic Elements s.v. *dati-*; DLG s.v. *condate*; Lambert, '*Lugdunensis*', p. 243.

String CONDAT (KONDAT not found)

Formally admissible (11)

8	E1	− 03	53	**Condat**e		
7	E3	− 02	48	**Condat**e Redonum	Civitas Riedunum	R(i)edones
11	A4	+ 00	48	**Condat**e		
11	C4	+ 02	48	**Condat**e		
14	E3	− 01	45	**Condat**e		
14	F1	+ 00	47	*****Condat**e		
14	H1	+ 02	47	**Condat**e		
14	E4	− 01	44	**Condat**is		
17	B4	+ 03	44	**Condat**e		
17	F2	+ 05	45	**Condat**e		
25	I1	+ 03	44	**Condat**omagus?		

See **Map 12.8**.

Formally inadmissible None

CORIO- 'WARBAND' (OI *CUIRE*, W *CORDD*)

AILR and PNPG Celtic Elements s.v. *corio-*; PNRB, pp. 317–19; GPN, p. 339, n. 3; DLG s.v. *corios*; Evans, 'Celts and Germans', pp. 243–44; Hamp, '*Coria* and *Curia*'.

String CORIO, KORIO, CORIA, KORIA[23]

Formally admissible (13)

4	*unl*			**Coria**	Boanum	
7	D3	− 03	48	Fanum Martis	Civitas **Corio**solitum	**Corio**solitae
7	E2	− 02	49	**Coria**llum		
8	A2	− 07	52	**Korio**ndoi		
9	E6	− 03	54	****Corio**sopitum	Coria	
9	*unl*	*− 05*	*55*	**Koria**		
9	*unl*	*− 03*	*55*	**Corio**nototae		
11	F2	+ 05	50	**Corio**vallum	Cortovallium	
14	A1	− 05	47	**Corio**solites	**Corio**sopites	
15	*unl*	*+ 04*	*43*	****Corio**ssedum		
44	*unl*	*+ 12*	*41*	**Corio**li		
60	C2	+ 24	35	**Korio**n		
89	B1	+ 39	39	**Koria**ia?	Garine?	

See **Map 12.9**.[24]

Formally inadmissible

24	*unl*		Castellum Er**cori**obris	
63	*unl*		Las**koria**	Lassora

Corno- 'horn (OI *corn*, W *corn*)

AILR and PNPG Celtic Elements s.v. *corno*-; De Bernardo Stempel, *Vertretung*, pp. 151–52; Sims-Williams, 'Degrees of Celticity', p. 9 (rejecting a Latin derivation, with L. S. Joseph); cf. DLG s.v. *carnon*. According to Nussbaum, *Head and Horn*, p. 5, n. 9, names like *Cornovii* 'are not demonstrably related to the IE words for "horn"'; but the correlation with 'horns' of land seems more than coincidental (*pace* PNRB, p. 325).

---

[23] These strings leave out *Petrucorii* (14F3 = + 0/45), *Tricorii* (17F4 = + 5/44), and *Vertamo-corii* (17E4 = + 5/44); these are included on **Map 12.9**.

[24] Cf. preceding note.

String CORN, KORN

Formally admissible (17)

4	*unl*			**Corn**an		
8	E2	− 03	52	**Corn**ovii		
8	F3	− 02	51	Duro**corn**ovium		
9	D2	− 04	58	**Korn**aouioi	**Korn**abioi	**Korn**ouboi
14	G4	+ 01	44	**Corn**ucio		
20	F4	+ 18	45	**Corn**acates		
20	G4	+ 19	45	**Corn**acum		
21	C5	+ 20	44	Tri**corn**(i)enses		
21	C5	+ 20	44	Tri**corn**ium		
42	*unl*	*+ 12*	*42*	**Corn**etus Campus		
48	A2	+ 08	40	**Corn**us		
48	A2	+ 08	40	**Korn**ensioi 'Aichilensioi'		
58	*unl*	*+ 23*	*37*	**Korn**iata M.		
63	F1	+ 34	39	**Corn**iaspa		
64	H4	+ 38	38	**Korn**e		
66	A1	+ 32	37	**Korn**a?		
72	C3	+ 33	34	**Korn**os?		

See **Map 12.16**.[25]

Formally inadmissible (some clearly Latin, cf. p. 39 above)

32	F2	+ 10	37	Castra **Corn**eli(ana)?
38	B3	+ 20	30	**Corn**iclanum
40	B4	+ 11	44	Forum **Corn**elii
40	C3	+ 12	44	**Corn**iculani
43	C1	+ 12	42	**Corn**iculum
44	B1	+ 12	42	S. **Corn**elia, Mon.
44	*unl*			Via **Corn**elia
45	B1	+ 15	41	**Corn**eli
45	B2	+ 15	41	Ligures **Corn**eliani?

CORTO- 'ROUND?, SHORT?, WICKER?' (NOT IN INSULAR CELTIC)

AILR and PNPG Celtic Elements s.v. *corto*-; KPP, p. 227; cf. Villar, *Indoeuropeos y no indoeuropeos*, pp. 301 and 304–5.

Corticata /*Kortikata* may be distinct but still Celtic (cf. Celtiberian *kortika*, if its *k* = /k/, although cf. references in MLH v/1, pp. 197–99, also De Bernardo Stempel, 'Celtib. *karvo gortika*'. See De Hoz, 'From Ptolemy to the ethnic and linguistic reality', p. 20. Yet derivation from Latin *cortex* 'cork' remains plausible (e.g. De Bernardo Stempel, 'Ptolemy's Celtic Italy and Ireland', p. 93, n. 15).

[25] Cf. VCIE, pp. 85 and 123–25.

String CORT, KORT

Formally admissible (13)

11	D2	+ 03	50	**Cort**oriacum	
11	E3	+ 04	49	Duro**cort**orum	
11	F2	+ 05	50	Coriovallum	**Cort**ovallium
14	E3	– 01	45	**Cort**erate	
22	*unl*			'Zetnou**kortou**'	
24	C2	– 09	42	**Cort**icata Ins.	
25	C4	– 03	41	*****Cort**ona	
26	D4	– 07	37	**Kort**ikata	
42	B2	+ 11	43	**Cort**ona	
42	*unl*			**Cort**uosa	
47	*unl*	+ *13*	*37*	**Kort**yga	
81	C2	+ 72	23	**Kort**ia	**Corte**
82	B3	+ 31	18	**Cort**um	

See **Map 4.4.** *Zetnoukortou* (Procopius, *Buildings*, 4.6.32) was in Dacia Ripensis. *Cortuosa* (Livy 6.4.9) was in southern Etruria.

Formally inadmissible None

Cot(t)- 'old' (Old Cornish *coth*, Breton *coz*), ?originally 'curved, hump(backed), hillock' (cf. Catalan *cot* 'hill', Spanish *cueto*)

AILR and PNPG Possibly Celtic Elements s.v. *cotto-* and *cottaeo-* respectively; DLG s.v. *cottos*; GPN, p. 187; De Bernardo Stempel, 'Ptolemy's Celtic Italy and Ireland', p. 95; Guyonvarc'h, 'Le nom des Cotini'; KPP, pp. 191–92. A different explanation of *Cotini* is proposed by Anreiter, *Die vorrömischen Namen Pannoniens*, p. 212 (that it is a Pannonian cognate of English *cot* 'hut', etc., cf. IEW, pp. 393–94 and 586–87), while Falileyev, 'Place-names and ethnic groups in north-western Dacia', p. 35, doubts the Celticity of *Kotensioi* and compares Thraco-Dacian anthroponyms such as *Cotis*, *Cotus* and *Cotiso*.

Ancient writers associated the *Alpes Cottiae* and *Cotti(i) Regnum* with an eponymous King *Cottius* (Nissen, *Italische Landeskunde*, ii/1, pp. 148–49; Holder i, 1144–48; Barruol, p. 88), and Tovar, *Lusitanien*, p. 270, mentions that Hübner (in Pauly-Wissowa iv, 1677) thought that *Kottaiobriga* was probably named from Aurelius *Cotta* (*Cottaius* would be more likely). This is not really a problem for us if these personal names in *Cott-* are Celtic, as argued by Guyonvarc'h.

String COT, KOT

Formally admissible (31)[26]

5	D5	+71	08	Cottonara	Kottanarike		
5	D5	+71	08	Kottiara	Cotiara		
5	E3	+80	15	Kottis			
5	E3	+82	17	Kottobora			
6	*unl*			Kottobara			
6	*unl*			Pharnacotis fl.			
7	G2	+00	49	Caracoticum			
9	*unl*			Atecotti			
13	E3	+19	49	Cotini			
17	H4	+06	44	Alpes Cottiae			
17	H5	+06	44	Cotti Regnum			
17	H4	+06	44	Druantium	*Alpis Cottia	Summae Alpes	Alpis Iulia
22	*unl*	*+24*	*45*	Kotensioi			
24	*unl*	*− 08*	*39*	Kottaiobriga			
25	*unl*			Cottion			
26	D5	− 07	36	Cotinussa Ins.	Gaditana Ins.		
26	*unl*	*− 05*	*38*	Kotinai	Oleastron		
28	C2	− 06	35	Cottae?	Kotes	Gytte	
55	G3	+24	38	Kotylaion			
55	F3	+23	38	Kotylaion M.			
56	D2	+26	39	Kotylos M.			
58	B3	+21	37	Kotilion M.			
58	D4	+22	36	Kotyrta			
58	*unl*	*+21*	*37*	Kotilon			
62	C3	+29	39	Kotiaeion			
65	G3	+31	37	Kotenna			
84	*unl*	*+38*	*47*	Cotobacchi			
87	C4	+37	40	Kotyora			
88	A2	+42	42	Kotais	Kytaia		
88	*unl*			Kotomana			
89	G2	+44	38	Kotor(odz)			

The *Atecotti* 'very old ones' (cf. *Senones*) were in Britain or Ireland (PNRB, p. 259; Rance, 'Attacotti', with preposterous etymology; Freeman, 'Who were the Atecotti?'). Ptolemy 3.8.3 puts the *Kotensioi* in the same area as *Bouridauensioi* (around Buridava, Map 22B3) so I adopt this as an approximate location. On *Kottaiobriga* (in the area of Map 26) see Albertos, 'Los topónimos en -briga', no. 34, and Tovar, *Lusitanien*, p. 270. Ptolemy's co-ordinates (2.5.7) put it south-west of *Lancia oppidana*. On the location of *Kotinai* see below, p. 230. The name *Cottion* appears in

---

[26] As noted above (p. 39), some of these are probably Greek. 7G2 *Caracoticum* is a mistake from TIR M-31, p. 100, for *Caracotinum* as in TIR M-30/31, p. 57; it is probably to be segmented *Caraco-tinum*, without **cot-*. See AILR s.n. *Caracotino* and Comments s.n.; KPP, pp. 158–59.

Sidonius, *Carmina* 24.75 ('Hinc tu Cottion ibis'); his kinsman Avitus lived there (*Epistulae* iii.1). It may belong in the Auvergne (Map 14) rather than the area of Map 25; Holder i, 1144, places it between Clermont-Ferrand and Narbonne. Note that *Cuttiae* in Italy (39D3 = +8/45) is sometimes *Cottiae* in the sources (see p. 197 below); it is included on my **Map 4.5**.

Formally inadmissible[27]

9	*unl*			Mar**c**otaxon		
14	F2	+00	46	Lo**cote**iacus	Lo**c**o**c**iacum	
33	D1	+09	35	Ma**cot**a		
44	F4	+14	40	Bos**cot**recase		
45	*unl*			Leu**cot**hea		
48	A2	+08	40	Fundus **Cot**ronianus		
50	D2	+23	41	S**kot**oussa		
51	H4	+26	40	Palaiper**kote**		
51	H4	+26	40	Per**kote**	Per**k**ope	
52	E4	+29	40	Ei**kote**		
52	F4	+29	40	Sar**kot**yle		
55	D2	+22	39	S**kot**oussa		
55	*unl*			A**kot**ieis		
55	*unl*			S**kot**essa		
58	D3	+22	37	S**kot**itas	S**kot**ina	
58	*unl*			S**kot**ane		
59	B2	+23	38	**Kot**hokidai?		
61	*unl*			Leu**kot**hea spring		
64	*unl*			No**cot**esso		
65	G4	+31	36	Leu**c**olla Pr.	Leu**kot**heion? Pr.	
66	A3	+32	36	Ano **Kot**radis		
66	A3	+32	36	Klima **Kot**radon		
67	B3	+35	36	*Kir**kot**a		
67	H1	+38	37	La**cot**ena		
69	B4	+35	32	Legio	Capor**cot**ani	Maximianopolis
75	*unl*			Tychinne**kot**is		
79	*unl*			Pmoun T**kot**o		
86	D3	+33	40	I**kot**arion?		
87	A4	+35	40	S**kot**ios		
88	B3	+43	41	Leu**kot**hea		

Dᴇʀᴠᴏ- 'ᴏᴀᴋ' (OI *ᴅᴀᴜʀ*, W *ᴅᴇʀᴡᴇɴ*)

AILR Celtic Elements s.v. *deruo-* (cf. PNPG Celtic Elements s.v *dario-*, *daro-*, and Possibly Celtic Elements s.v. *dru-*); DLG s.v. *deruos, derua, deruenton*.[28]

---

[27] Note, however, that Guyonvarc'h, 'Le nom des Cotini', p. 201, argues that some names in *Cotr-* are relevant.

[28] A different analysis is suggested by Kitson, 'River-names', pp. 77–81 and 94.

String DERV, DEROU

Formally admissible (7)

8	*unl*	– 04	50	*Derventio fl.	
9	D6	– 04	54	Derventio	
9	E6	– 03	54	Dorvantium fl.	[Derventio] fl.
9	G6	– 01	54	Derventio	
9	G7	– 01	53	[Derventio] fl.	
14	H2	+ 02	46	Derventum	
94	*unl*			Derousiaioi	

The last name, *Derousiaioi*, is from Persia. For the others see **Map 12.10**.

Formally inadmissible

20	F7	+ 18	42	Anderva	
65	E5	+ 30	36	Siderous Pr.	
65	E5	+ 30	36	Siderous Limen	Posidarisous?
87	*unl*			Tzacher	**Sideroun**

In theory *Anderva* might be analysed *an(de)- + derv-*, but the form of the name is uncertain (*Anderba* in Rav., *Sanderva* in TP, and probably *Andarva* in AI 338.7).

DĒVO-, DĪVO- 'GOD' (OI *DÍA*, W *DUW*)

AILR and PNPG Celtic Elements s.v. {de:uo-}, {di:uo-}; GPN, p. 192; DLG s.v. *deuos*; Isaac, 'Scotland', pp. 191–92. Cf. VCIE, p. 457.

    Some spellings with *div-* are probably due to Latin influence and some may actually be Latin rather than Celtic. Cf. GPN, p. 191, Gorrochategui, 'Ptolemy's Aquitania and the Ebro Valley', p. 144, and Lambert, 'Remarks', p. 166.

String DEV, DIV, Deo (case-sensitive),[29] DEOU, DIOU

Some examples of *Dio-* such as *Diolindum* are presumably Celtic (see under second element) and might have been included, except for the fact that the string DIO or Dio would bring in too many ambiguous and irrelevant names. A full study of Celtic names of this type would have to take *Dio-* names into account and evaluate them as Celtic or Greek etc. according to the second element.

---

[29] *Deoueltos* in Ptolemy 3.11.7 (*Deultum* in the Atlas, 22E6) is not a *Deo-* name judging by the Latin forms cited by Müller, p. 482.

Formally admissible (20 – although note that PNRB, pp. 335–36, emends *Deventia* to *De[r]ventia*, perhaps the river Dart; cf. **Derventio fl.* above under *dervo-*)

4	B2	+ 41	17	**Dev**ade Inss.	
4	*unl*			**Div**itia	
5	C3	+ 74	19	**Deo**palli	
5	C4	+ 72	11	**Div**ae	
8	E1	– 03	53	**Dev**a	
8	*unl*			**Dev**entia Statio	
8	*unl*			**Dev**ionisso	
9	C5	– 05	55	**Deo**ua fl.	
9	E3	– 03	57	**Deo**ua fl.	
9	*unl*	*– 03*	*57*	**Deo**uana	
11	B4	+ 01	48	**Div**odurum?	
11	G3	+ 06	49	**Div**odurum	Mettis
14	G4	+ 01	44	**Div**ona	Civitas Cadurcorum
18	C2	+ 05	47	Castrum **Div**ionense	*Dibio
22	*unl*			**Deo**niana	
24	G1	– 05	43	**Dev**ales? fl.	
24	H2	– 04	42	**Deo**brigula	
25	C2	– 03	43	**Deo**ua fl.	
25	C3	– 03	42	**Deo**briga	Sobobrica?
26	*unl*	*– 08*	*39*	**Deo**briga	

Devionisso was in south-western Britain (PNRB, pp. 337–38). *Deoniana* was in Moesia II (for which see *Atlas* Map 102: Thrakike 5). The *Atlas* omits *Dêouona* (Ptolemy 2.11.14) in Bavaria (+ 10/49 ?); it is included on **Map 12.22**.

Formally inadmissible (some clearly Latin)

2	G3	+ 17	54	Vi**div**arii		
5	inset	+ 80	07	Palaeogoni	Seren**div**ae	
11	G2	+ 06	50	Castellum **Div**itia		
14	D1	– 02	47	Civitas Namnetum	Kon**deou**inkon?	'Portunamnetu'
24	*unl*			**Deo**rum Inss.		
27	E2	– 01	39	U**div**a? fl.	Uduba fl.	
29	E1	– 01	35	Portus **Div**inus		
52	A2	+ 27	41	Berg(o)ule	Arka**diou**polis	
60	*unl*			A**diou**nos		
65	*unl*			*Gor**diou**teichos		
77	*unl*			Topos Apa Klau**diou**		
80	*unl*			Isi**diou** Oros		
86	B3	+ 31	40	Gor**diou**kome	Iuliopolis	
86	*unl*			Ho**diou**polis		
89	C3	+ 40	37	Sar**deou**a	'Sardebar'	

Dubro- 'water' (OI *dobur*, W *dŵr*)

AILR Celtic Elements s.v. *dubro-*; DLG s.v. *dubron*

String DUBR (DOUBR not found)

Formally admissible (3)

8	I3	+01	51	Portus **Dubr**is
18	C3	+05	46	Pons **Dubr**is
25	H3	+02	42	Verno**dubr**um fl.

Formally inadmissible

24	D4	−08	40	Me(i)**dubr**iga

Dumno- 'deep, world' (OI *domun, domain*, W *dwfn, (An)nwn*)

AILR and PNPG Celtic Elements s.v. *dumno-*; GPN, p. 197; DLG s.v. *dubnos, dumnos.*

String DUMN (DUBN, DOUMN, DOUBN not found)

Formally admissible (5)[30]

8	C4	− 05	50	**Dumn**onii
9	A2	− 07	58	**Dumn**a Ins.
11	H3	+07	49	**Dumn**issus
14	E3	− 01	45	**Dumn**itonus
17	C1	+04	46	Ro**dumn**a

Formally inadmissible None

Dūno- 'enclosure, fort' (OI *dún*, W *din*)

---

[30] Possibly some forms in *-dun-* like *Riduna Ins.* (see below s.v. *dūno-*) belong here.

AILR and PNPG Celtic Elements s.v. {duːno-}; DLG s.v. *dunon*; Watkins, *Selected Writings*, ii, 751–53; Anreiter, *Die vorrömischen Namen Pannoniens*, p. 178, n. 644.[31]

String DUN, DOUN

Formally admissible (55 – as the two instances of *Vellaunodunum* are duplicates)

7	F3	− 01	48	Noio**doun**on Diablintum		
7	G3	+ 00	48	Noio**doun**on	Nu Dionnum	
8	C3	− 05	51	*Mori**dun**um		
8	E1	− 03	53	Rigo**doun**on?		
8	F3	− 02	51	Sorvio**dun**um		
8	G2	− 01	52	Margi**dun**um		
8	H2	+ 00	52	Brano**dun**um		
8	H3	+ 00	51	Col. Camulo**dun**um		
8	*unl*	*− 03*	*50*	**Doun**ion		
8	*unl*	*− 07*	*52*	**Doun**on		
8	*unl*	*+ 01*	*51*	**Dun**(...)		
8	*unl*	*− 04*	*50*	Mori**dun**um		
9	D2	− 04	58	*Tarou**edoun**on	Orkas Akra	
9	E6	− 03	54	Uxelo**du**(**nu**)m		
9	F6	− 02	54	**Doun**on Kolpos		
9	F6	− 02	54	Sege**dun**um		
9	*unl*	*− 02*	*53*	Cambo**dun**um		
9	*unl*	*− 02*	*54*	Lugun**duno**		
10	A4	+ 04	52	Lug**dun**um		
11	B4	+ 01	48	**Dun**ense Castrum		
11	C4	+ 02	48	Metlosedum	Mello**dun**um	
11	D3	+ 03	49	Novio**dun**um?		
11	F3	+ 05	49	Virio**dun**um	Verio**dun**um	
11	*unl*	*+ 02*	*47*	Vellauno**dun**um		
12	B3	+ 08	49	Lopo**dun**um		
12	E4	+ 11	48	Parro**dun**um		
13	*unl*	*+ 16*	*49*	Melio**doun**on		
13	*unl*	*+ 16*	*49*	Ebouro**doun**on		
14	F1	+ 00	47	Caesaro**dun**um	Civitas Turonorum	
14	G1	+ 01	47	Novio**dun**um		
14	H2	+ 02	46	Acito**dun**um		
14	H2	+ 02	46	*Exoli**dun**um		
14	H4	+ 02	44	Sego**dun**um	'Eto**doun**on'	Civitas Rutenorum
14	H4	+ 02	44	Uxello**dun**um		
14	I1	+ 03	47	Novio**dun**um?	Nevirnum?	'Ebirno'
14	*unl*	*+ 02*	*47*	Vellauno**dun**um		
15	C2	+ 04	43	*Aran**dun**um		
17	C2	+ 04	45	Lug**dun**ensis		

---

[31] Cf. above, p. 12.

17	D2	+ 04	45	Col. Lugdunum	Col. Copia Claudia Augusta Lugdunum
17	G4	+ 06	44	Eburodunum	Ebrudunum
18	B3	+ 04	46	Augustodunum	
18	D3	+ 06	46	Col. Iulia Equestris	Noviodunum
18	D3	+ 06	46	Eburodunensis L.	
18	D3	+ 06	46	Eburodunum	
18	D3	+ 06	46	Minnodunum	Minodum
19	C2	+ 10	47	Cambodunum	
20	C4	+ 15	45	Neviodunum	
21	C5	+ 20	44	Singidunum	
22	F3	+ 28	45	Noviodunum	
23	*unl*	*+ 25*	*48*	Karrodounon	
24	D3	− 08	41	Caladunum	
25	F2	+ 00	43	Lugdunum Convenarum	
25	H3	+ 02	42	Sebendounon?	Beseldunum
26	*unl*	*− 06*	*37*	Arialdunum	
26	*unl*			Esttledunum	
48	B2	+ 09	40	'Luguidunec'	Castra Felicia?

Vellaunodunum is here identified with Montargis (Bedon, *Les villes des trois Gaules*, p. 40, n. 114). On '23 *unl* Karrodounon' and other places of the same name, partly omitted by the *Atlas*, see above under *carr-*. They are included on my **Map 12.2**. *Caladunum* is a peculiar formation but is paralleled in France by Châlons < medieval *Caladunno* (Luján, 'Ptolemy's *Callaecia*', pp. 59–60). *Arialdunum* (Pliny 3.10) was in the Conventus Astigitanus; on its location see TIR J-30, pp. 87 and 154. *Esttledunum* was perhaps in the same *conventus* according to *Map-by-Map Directory* i, 434 (cf. Tovar, *Baetica*, p. 138). See, however, De Hoz, 'From Ptolemy to the ethnic and linguistic reality', p. 20, and Sims-Williams, 'Welsh *Iâl*', p. 62. Note that '12 *unl* Bragodurum' (under *duro-* below) may really be a *-dunum* name. Names in Germania Magna in Ptolemy which are omitted from the *Atlas* include *Segodounon* (2.11.14) around + 8/50, *Taro(u)dounon* (2.11.15) i.e. Kirchzarten (+ 7/47), *Lougidounon* (2.11.13) i.e. Legnica/Liegnitz (+ 16/51) and *Dounoi* (2.11.10) around + 18/51.[32] All these are included on **Map 12.2**. Note also an unlocated Scordiscan *polis* of *Kapedounon* (Strabo 7.5.12) in Moesia Superior, below, Chapter 7, n. 153.

[32] On *Dounoi* see PNPG Comments s.n.

Formally inadmissible[33]

5	C3	+ 70	15	**Doun**ga	
7	D2	– 03	49	Ri**duna** Ins.	
14	C1	– 03	47	Vin**dun**it(t)a Ins.	
14	G2	+ 01	46	I**dun**um	
16	*unl*			A**dun**icates	
18	E3	+ 07	46	*Se**dun**um	Seduni
19	*unl*			Sin**duni**	
24	C2	– 09	42	Castellum Mei**dun**ium	
24	F2	– 06	42	B(a)e**dun**ia	
24	F2	– 06	42	Be**dun**ienses	
30	*unl*			Mo**doun**ga	
48	A2	+ 08	40	Bu**dun**tini	
49	F1	+ 23	42	**Doun**ax M.	
55	D3	+ 22	38	Rho**doun**tia	
62	*unl*			Kour**doun**eis	
65	D3	+ 30	37	Sibi**doun**da	

DURO- 'GATED FORT?, YARD, FORUM?' (CF. OI *dor*, W *dôr*)

AILR and PNPG Celtic Elements s.v. *duro-*; DLG s.v. *duron* (cf. *duorico-*); Hamp, 'Morphologic criteria', pp. 177–78. Cf. Vendryes, 'L'étymologie du gaulois *dumias*', p. 465.

A distinction between names in *Duro-* (mostly Belgic?) and *-duro* has been suggested (Rivet, 'Celtic names and Roman places', p. 13). Since *-duro-* can occur as *-doro-* (cf. Philipon, 'Le gaulois *dŭros*', pp. 74–75; Falileyev, ''Ολόδορις', p. 265), DOR is also searched for here.[34]

String DURO, DURU, DOURO (DOURU not found), DOR

---

[33] *Idunum* (Dun-le-Palestel?) cannot be segmented *I-dunum* regularly but the *I-* in 'Castrum . . . Idunum nomine' (Holder ii, 27) could be a miscopying of *.i. = id est*; Nègre i §2410 cites the form *Dunus* from A.D. 987. On *Riduna Ins.* cf. above, n. 30.

[34] The strings used do not allow for the unlikely possibility that various rivers called *Duria* and *Durius* are relevant. On them see Schwarz, *Ortsnamen der Sudetenländer*, pp. 28–29, and De Bernardo Stempel, 'More on Ptolemy's evidence for Celtic Ireland', p. 96. On other *Dur*-names see Evans, 'Nomina Celtica II', pp. 501–4.

Formally admissible (50 – since '32 *unl* Audurus Fundus' duplicates '31 *unl* Audurus')[35]

7	F2	– 01	49	Augusto**durum**	Baiocas	
8	E4	– 03	50	**Duro**triges		
8	F3	– 02	51	**Duro**cornovium		
8	G2	– 01	52	**Duro**brivae		
8	G2	– 01	52	**Duro**vigutum		
8	G2	– 01	52	Lacto**dorum**		
8	G3	– 01	51	**Duro**cobrivis		
8	H2	+ 00	52	**Duro**liponte		
8	H3	+ 00	51	**Duro**brivae		
8	H3	+ 00	51	**Duro**litum		
8	I3	+ 00	51	*****Duro**vernum		
10	B5	+ 05	51	Batavo**durum**	Noviomagus	(Ulpia) Batavi Noviomagus
11	B4	+ 01	48	Divo**durum**?		
11	B4	+ 01	48	**Duro**casses		
11	C2	+ 02	50	**Duro**(i)coregum		
11	C4	+ 02	48	*Nemeto**durum**		
11	D2	+ 03	50	**Duro**num		
11	E3	+ 04	49	**Duro**cortorum		
11	E4	+ 04	48	**Duro**catalaunum		
11	F1	+ 05	51	Teu**durum**?		
11	F3	+ 05	49	Iblio**durum**?		
11	G3	+ 06	49	Divo**durum**	Mettis	
11	*unl*	*+ 00*	*49*	Brevio**durum**		
12	E4	+ 11	48	Venaxamo**durum**		
12	F4	+ 12	48	Sorvio**durum**		
12	G4	+ 13	48	Boio**durum**	Boiotro	
12	*unl*	*+ 09*	*48*	Brago**durum**		
14	F2	+ 00	46	Iciodo**ro**		
14	G3	+ 01	45	**Duro**tincum?		
14	H1	+ 02	47	Brivo**durum**		
14	H2	+ 02	45	Erno**dorum**		
14	I1	+ 03	47	Autessio**durum**	Civitas Autissio**dor**ensis	
14	I3	+ 03	45	*Icio**dorum**		
17	G3	+ 06	45	**Duro**tincum	**Duro**tingum	
17	G4	+ 06	44	Icto**durus**		
17	I1	+ 07	46	Octo**durus**	Forum Claudii Vallensium	
18	D2	+ 06	47	Epamanduo**durum**		
18	E2	+ 07	47	Salo**durum**		
18	*unl*	*+ 06*	*47*	Vetatu**duro**		
19	A2	+ 08	47	Vitu**durum**		
22	E4	+ 27	44	**Duro**storum		
24	*unl*	*– 06*	*41*	Okto**douron**		

[35] *Teudurum* (AI 375.6) is uncertain, as Ptolemy (2.11.13) has *Teuderion*. But on *-dero-* for *-duro-* see Philipon, 'Le gaulois *dŭros*', pp. 74–75.

25	H4	+02	41	Ilduro	
25	*unl*	*– 03*	*41*	Mutudurum	
31	*unl*	*+07*	*36*	Audurus	
32	*unl*	*+07*	*36*	Audurus Fundus	
44	*unl*	*+14*	*41*	Duronia	
55	E3	+23	38	Boudoros fl.	
59	A3	+23	37	Boudoron	
91	*unl*	*+44*	*33*	Douros fl.	
93	C3	+46	30	Dur-Yakin?	**Duru**(m)?

In the case of *Bragodurum* in southern Germany (in Ptolemy, 2.12.3), Cuntz (p. 71, cf. p. 161) hesitates between the variants -δουρον and -δουνον (Müller, p. 281). Ptolemy's *Oktodouron* (24unl) is assumed to be the same as *Ocelum Duri* (see above, p. 31). *Mutudurum*, a Celtiberian *civitas* mentioned by Sallust, is located approximately only. *Duronia* (Livy 10.39.4) was in Samnium and is located approximately.[36] Note that *Boudoros fl.* and *Boudoron* also appear under *boud-* above, with a different analysis. It is not serious supposed that *Audurus* near Hippo Regius contains Celtic *Au-* (as in *Aulerci*), but that is how it might be analysed if it occurred in Gaul. A name missing from the *Atlas* is *Gauauodouron* (Ptolemy 2.13.3) at +13/48 (see PNPG *Alpes* and Comments s.n. on its form and location); it is included on **Map 12.4**. On whether or not Ptolemy's *Gan(n)oduron* (2.9.10) is identical with *Salodurum* above see PNPG Comments s.n. (cf. Celtic Elements s.v. *gando-*), and De Bernardo Stempel, 'Ptolemy's evidence for Germania Superior', pp. 81 and 91–92.

Formally inadmissible (not including 12 names containing Greek *Theodora*, *Theodoros*, etc.)

6	*unl*			**Dor**is**dor**sigi	
8	*unl*			'Mo**donn**os' fl.	[Mo**dor**nus] fl.
9	*unl*			Ta**dor**iton	
13	*unl*			Bou**dor**igon	
24	*unl*			Vicus Bae**dor**us	
26	*unl*			Bae**dor**us	
26	*unl*			Vicus Bae**dor**us	
34	*unl*			Siud**duru**si P(rae)sidium)	
50	C3	+22	40	Echei**dor**os fl.	
58	*unl*			Chely**dor**ea M.	
58	*unl*			Inous Hy**dor**	
62	*unl*			A**dor**eus M.	
65	D5	+30	36	Moron Hy**dor**	

---

[36] Cf. Nissen, *Italische Landeskunde*, ii/2, pp. 679, n. 5, and 980. *Duronia* is properly marked as *modern* name at 44F2 = +14/41. The village was 'Civitavecchia' until renamed in 1875, owing to a speculative identification with Livy's *Duronia* (Oakley, *Hill-Forts of the Samnites*, p. 93, n. 425).

70	G2	+ 35	31	**A**do**r**a
75	D2	+ 30	29	Metro**dor**on
75	*unl*			Metro**dor**ou Epoikion
77	*unl*			Dio**dor**ou
77	*unl*			Isi**dor**ou
84	*unl*			Uti**dor**si
94	*unl*			**Dor**a

EBURO- 'YEW' (OI *I(U)BAR*, W *EFWR*)

AILR and PNPG Celtic Elements s.v. *eburo-*; DLG s.v. *eburos* (and p. 434).

String EBUR, EBOUR

Formally admissible (14, excluding *Ebura Cerialis* – see below)

9	F7	– 02	53	**Ebur**acum	
9	*unl*			**Ebur**o *Castellum	
11	A4	+ 00	48	**Ebur**ovices	
11	B3	+ 01	49	Mediolanum Aulercorum	**Ebur**ovicum
11	G2	+ 06	50	**Ebur**ones	
13	*unl*	*+ 16*	*49*	**Ebour**odounon	
17	G4	+ 06	44	**Ebur**odunum	Ebrudunum
18	A1	+ 03	48	**Ebur**obriga	
18	D3	+ 06	46	**Ebur**odunensis L.	
18	D3	+ 06	46	**Ebur**odunum	
25	H2	+ 02	43	Hebromagus	**Ebur**omagus
26	A2	– 10	39	**Ebur**obrittium	
26	*unl*			**Ebur**a Cerialis	
27	B4	– 04	37	**Ebur**a	Cerialis
45	B3	+ 15	40	**Ebur**um	

Eburo *Castellum* was in southern Scotland or Northumberland (PNRB, p. 358). '26 *unl* Ebura Cerialis' is a duplicate of the 27B4 entry, *Ebura quae* (= 'or') *Cerialis* (Pliny 3.10). The correct reading of Pliny, however, is *Ebora*, which is doubtfully relevant. Cf. TIR J-30, p. 170.[37] Besides 13unl *Ebourodounon* (2.11.15), Ptolemy has an *Ebouron* (2.11.14) in the same vicinity (near Brno?, + 16/49) and this is also included on **Map 12.23**.

---

[37] Here *Ebora* for *Ebura* agrees with the editions by Zehnacker (p. 37) and Bejarano (*Hispania Antigua*, p. 23). Note also the otherwise unknown *Ebora* in Ptolemy 2.6.62 (at approximately –1/41); this is clearly Celtic according to Tovar, *Tarraconensis*, p. 420, but note that one of the two other places called *Ebora* in the *Atlas* (26C3 and 26D5) is also recorded as *Aipora*. Cf. De Hoz, 'From Ptolemy to the ethnic and linguistic reality', p. 20, n. 18, and Villar, 'Celtic language', pp. 263–66.

Formally inadmissible

91	*unl*				Theboura

Essedo- 'chariot' (cf. W *asedd*)

AILR Celtic Elements s.v. *essedo-*; DLG s.v. *essedon*.

String ESSED, ESED

Formally admissible (3)

8	F2	– 02	52	Manduessedum	
19	B3	+ 09	46	*Tarvessedum	
85	*unl*			Issedones	Essedones

Formally inadmissible

25	*unl*				Beseda

Gabro- 'goat' (OI *gabor*, W *gafr*)

AILR and PNPG Celtic Elements s.v. *gabro-*; DLG s.v. *gabros*. See Chapter 3 above, with maps.

String GABR

Formally admissible (8)

9	D6	−04	54	Gabrosentum	
9	F6	−02	54	Gabrantouikes	
9	G6	−01	54	Gabrantouikon Kolpos	
12	F3	+ 12	49	Gabreta? Hyle	
14	G1	+ 01	47	Gabris	*Gabrae
20	B2	+ 14	47	'Gabromago'	
90	*unl*	+ 46	37	Gabris	
94	*unl*			Gabra	

A form perhaps to be added is a river-name *Gabranus* near Histria in Scythia Minor (22F4 = + 28/44); see Duridanov, 'Sprachspuren', p. 137, and Falileyev, '*Tylis*', p. 111. Duridanov's parallel from Holder i, 1510 (*Gabranus*), is a false friend, however, being a Latinization of OI *Gabrán* < *Gabragnas*. Falileyev, 'Celtic presence in Dobrudja', is sceptical; he stresses the lack of Celtic *river*-names in the east in general and the non-Celtic onomastic landcape of this area in particular, and he notes the occurrence of *Gabr-* in Baltic river-names.

Formally inadmissible

27	A4	−05	37	**Igabrum**	Egabrum	Municipium Iulium

Ico- '?' (NOT IN INSULAR CELTIC?)

AILR and PNPG Celtic Elements s.v. *ico-*; GPN, pp. 351–52; DLG s.v. *ico-*.

String Ico, Iko (case-sensitive, to avoid a vast quantity of irrelevant material)

Note that this string excludes names such as *Iceni* [Map 8H2 = +0/52] which are probably relevant. Compare also *Iciodoro* s.v. *duro-* above, and see below, p. 185, on *Iciniacum*.

Formally admissible (7)

11	G2	+06	50	**Ico**rigium			
17	G3	+06	45	Ucennii	**Iko**nioi		
27	*unl*	− 01	38	**Ico**sitani			
30	F3	+03	36	**Ico**sium			
55	F2	+23	39	**Iko**s			
66	B1	+32	37	**Ico**nium	Claudi**co**nium	Col. Iulia	Col. Aelia
						Augusta Equestris?	Hadriana Augusta
86	D3	+33	40	**Iko**tarion?			

The *Icositani*, whom the *Atlas* places in Spain 'near Ilici?' (followed here), were more likely the people of *Icosium* in north Africa. See below, p. 232.

Formally inadmissible None

Iscā 'FISH, WATER' (CF. OI *íASC*, ?AND W RIVER-NAME *WYSG*)[38]

AILR and PNPG Celtic Elements s.v. {isca:-}.

---

[38] On *Wysg* cf. CIB, p. 193, n. 1183. If related, it would be from the full grade *eisk-. This may occur in *Eiskadia* below, a form only found in Appian, *Iberike*, 68.290, in conjunction with *Gemella* (26unl) and *Obulcula* (26E4), and regarded as a corruption or mistake for *Astigi Vetus* (Pliny 3.12) or for *Nescania*; see Tovar, *Baetica*, pp. 113, 133 and 138; Goukowsky (ed.), *Appien: Histoire romain*, ii, p. 131, n. 388.

String ISCA, ISKA

Formally admissible (5)

8	D4	− 04	50	**Isca**	
8	D4	− 04	50	**Iska** fl.	
8	E3	− 03	51	**Isca**	
8	E3	− 03	51	**Isca** fl.	
93	*unl*			Ioukara	**Iska**ra

Formally inadmissible

2	G3	+ 17	54	Goth**isca**ndza	
6	*unl*			**Piska**	
19	D2	+ 11	47	Isin**isca**	
20	F3	+ 18	46	Al**isca**	
21	F7	+ 23	42	Scret**isca**	
22	B5	+ 24	43	Secur**isca**	
22	D4	+ 26	44	Transmar**isca**	
22	*unl*			Din**iska**rta	
22	*unl*			Tib**iska**	
25	D4	− 02	41	Contrebia (Bela**isca**)	
25	*unl*			B**isca**rgis	
25	*cn.*			Ka**iska**ta	
26	*unl*			Astigi Vetus?	E**iska**dia?
33	F2	+ 10	35	Ov**isca**e?	
38	*unl*			Palaeb**isca**	
42	B4	+ 11	42	Grav**isca**e	
62	*unl*			M**iska**mos	
87	E4	+ 39	40	Sed**isca**	Solonenica?

Lanc- 'lance??' (cf. lang- below) (W *llanc* ?)

AILR Celtic Elements s.v. *lanci-* and PNPG Celtic Elements s.vv. *lanco-* and *laco-*; DLG s.v. *lancia*; García Alonso, 'On the Celticity of the Duero plateau', p. 37. On *lank/lang* see MLH v/1, pp. 215–16.

String LANC, LANK

Formally admissible (7 – since '26 *unl* Lancienses Transcudani' duplicates the 24D4 entry)

24	D4	– 08	40	**Lanc**ienses Transcudani		
24	E4	– 07	40	**Lanc**ienses Oppidani		
24	F2	– 06	42	**Lanc**ia	**Lanc**e	**Lanc**ienses
24	*unl*	*– 07*	*40*	**Lank**ia Oppidana		
25	B4	– 04	41	Segortia **Lank**a		
26	*unl*			**Lanc**ienses Transcudani		
58	*unl*	*+ 22*	*37*	**Lank**ia		
62	C4	*+ 29*	*38*	*****Lank**ena		

Formally inadmissible

5	D5	+ 76	08	**Elank**oros	Alcon?	
12	*unl*			K**olank**oron		
13	*unl*			K**olank**oron		
47	*unl*			P**alank**aios fl.		
58	D1	+ 22	38	Aigip**lank**tos M.	Geran(e)ia M.	Geranion M.
65	D3	+ 30	37	[*****Praedium **Planc**ianum]		
87	*unl*			Me**lanch**lainoi		

LANG- 'LANCE??' (CF. LANC- ABOVE)

AILR Celtic Elements s.v. *lango-* (cf. PNPG Celtic Elements s.v. *laco-*); MLH v/1, pp. 215–16; Gorrochategui, 'Establishment and analysis', pp. 164–65. Cf. DLG s.v. *longo-*.

String LANG

Formally admissible[39] (6 – since '26 *unl* Langobriga' duplicates the 24C4 entry)

10	G3	+ 10	53	**Lang**obardi
13	B4	+ 16	48	**Lang**obardi
24	C4	– 09	40	**Lang**obriga
26	*unl*			**Lang**obriga
39	D5	+ 08	44	**Lang**enses
39	D3	+ 08	45	**Lang**obardi
58	*unl*	*+ 21*	*37*	**Lang**on

[39] As *passim*, it is not being claimed that all these 'admissible' forms actually *are* Celtic (e.g. *Langobardi*, on whom see p. 185 below)!

Formally inadmissible

4	B2	+ 44	19	Malangitai	
4	*unl*			Phalangis M.	
5	D4	+ 78	12	Malanga	
5	E4	+ 80	14	Melange	
42	*unl*			Plangenses	
58	C2	+ 22	37	Melangeia	

LĒMO- 'ELM' (W *LLWYF*, IR. PLACE-NAME *LÍAMAIN*; CF. OI *LEM*)[40]

AILR and PNPG Celtic Elements s.v. {le:mo-}; PNPG Possibly Celtic Elements s.v. *limo-*; DLG s.v. *lemo-, limo-*; Isaac, 'Scotland', pp. 196–97.

String Lem (case-sensitive)

Formally admissible (8)

2	F3	+ 13	53	Lemovii?	
8	H3	+ 00	51	Lemana fl.	
8	I3	+ 00	51	Portus Lemanis	
9	B5	− 06	55	Lemannonios Kolpos	
14	F3	+ 00	45	Lemovices	
17	F2	+ 05	45	Lemincum	
18	D3	+ 06	46	Lemannus L.	Lausonius L.
24	D2	− 08	42	Lemavi	

See **Map 4.6**

---

[40] Sims-Williams, review of PNRB, pp. 91–93. The Insular Celtic forms *llwyf* ~ *lem* might seem to imply Celtic /e:/ < IE **ei* ~ /i/ < **i*, but this is uncertain (see Hamp, 'On notable trees', De Bernardo Stempel, *Vertretung*, pp. 124–25, and Anreiter, *Die vorrömischen Namen Pannoniens*, p. 77) and anyway it is not clear how far variation between *e* and *i* in Continental forms would reflect this ablaut, if at all. Cf. Gorrochategui, 'Ptolemy's Aquitania and the Ebro valley', p. 150. My string Lem leaves out the *Lim-* forms, and may bring in names with more than one quantity. (The string Lim would bring in innumerable irrelevant forms.)

Formally inadmissible

29	C1	− 03	35	Lemnis?
34	C2	+ 04	35	Lemellef
53	B2	+ 29	41	Lembos Pr.
56	A2	+ 25	39	Lemnos Ins.

LINDO- 'LAKE' (OI *LIND*, W *LLYN*)

AILR and PNPG Celtic Elements s.v. *lindo*-; DLG s.v. *lindon*; Hamp, 'Morphologic criteria', p. 178.

String LIND

Formally admissible (5)

8	G1	− 01	53	Col. **Lind**um	
8	E4	− 03	50	**Lind**inis	
9	C4	− 05	56	**Lind**on?	
14	F4	+ 00	44	Dio**lind**um?	
60	G3	+ 28	36	**Lind**os	**Lind**ia

Formally inadmissible

2	H3	+ 21	53	Ga**lind**ai		
4	*unl*			Pa**lind**romos Pr.		
5	D4	+ 77	10	Ka**lind**oia		
6	D3	+ 76	32	Ky**lind**rene Chora		
6	D5	+ 79	22	Pou**lind**ai	Agriophagi	
6	F4	+ 86	26	Maroundai	Mo**lind**ae	
20	F6	+ 18	43	G**lind**itiones		
50	D3	+ 23	40	Ka**lind**oia	A**lind**oia	Tripoiai
56	F5	+ 27	38	*Se**lind**a		
56	*unl*			Si**lind**ion		
61	F2	+ 27	37	A**lind**a	Alexandria ad Latmum	
62	G5	+ 31	38	*Sei**lind**a		
65	C2	+ 29	37	Au**lind**enos? L.		

LITANO- 'BROAD' (OI *LETHAN*, W *LLYDAN*)

AILR Celtic Elements s.v. *litano*-; GPN, p. 216; DLG s.v. *litanos* (and p. 435); Hamp, '*llydan*'.

String LITAN

Formally admissible (9 – since '24 *unl* Cibilitani' duplicates the 26B4 entry)

9	D4	– 04	56	Alauna	**Litan**a
9	*unl*	*– 05*	*56*	**Litan**omago	
11	C3	+ 02	49	**Litan**obriga?	
24	*unl*			Cibi**litan**i	
26	B4	– 09	37	Cibi**litan**i	
31	E4	+ 06	36	Castellum Arsaca**litan**um	
32	D4	+ 09	36	Pagus Assa**litan**us	
32	E4	+ 09	36	*Civitas Siva**litan**a	
32	*unl*	*+ 10*	*36*	Vo**litan**a Plebs	
48	A2	+ 08	40	Giddi**litan**i	

Formally inadmissible

15	D3	+ 04	43	Gradus Massi**litan**orum		
27	C4	– 03	37	*Tagili	Respublica Tagi**litan**a	
28	C5	– 06	34	Volubilis	Volubi**litan**i	Ouoloubilianoi
30	*unl*			Barzufu**litan**i		
31	E4	+ 06	36	*Uzelis	Respublica Uze**litan**orum	
31	G4	+ 07	36	Aquae Thibi**litan**ae		
32	F3	+ 10	36	Pagus Mercurialis?	Mede**litan**orum	
32	*unl*			Meg(a)lopo**litan**a Plebs		
35	C2	+ 10	32	Tripo**litan**a		
38	B1	+ 20	32	Pentapolis	Regio Pentapo**litan**a	
47	*unl*			Her**litan**a		
47	*unl*			Seme**litan**i		
48	A3	+ 08	39	Aquae Calidae Neapo**litan**orum	Hydata Neapo**litan**a	
48	A3	+ 08	39	Neapolis	Neapo**litan**i	
48	B3	+ 09	39	Cara**litan**um Pr.	Karalis Akra	
48	B3	+ 09	39	Kara**litan**os Kolpos		
62	D5	+ 30	38	Metropo**litan**us Campus		

Respublica Tagilitana is not admissible as it is a derivative of **Tagili* (= *Tagilit*, Punic *tglt*, in TIR J-30, pp. 311–12); similarly *Caralitanum Pr.* derives from the attested *Karalis*. On the other hand, while *Cibilitani* may well derive from **Cibilis*, the latter is not actually attested (see below, p. 225). Obviously, however, forms like *Cibilitani* are suspicious.

LUGU- (NAME OF THE GOD?)[41] (OI *LUG*, W *LLEU*, *LLEU*; CF. OI *LUIGE*, W *LLW*)

AILR and PNPG Celtic Elements s.v. *lugu-*; GPN, p. 221; DLG s.v. *lugus*; Ahlqvist, 'Two ethnic names in Ptolemy'; Tovar, 'The god *Lugus* in Spain'; MLH v/1, pp. 235–36; Lambert, '*Lugdunensis*', pp. 244–45. (For a homonym see Anreiter, *Die vorrömischen Namen Pannoniens*, pp. 216–17, on *Lugio* and *Lougeon Helos*.)

String LUG, LOUG

Formally admissible (16)

2	G3	+17	52	**Lug**ii	
9	D2	−04	58	**Loug**oi	
9	E6	−03	54	**Lugu**valium	
9	*unl*	*−02*	*54*	**Lugu**nduno	
10	A4	+04	52	**Lug**dunum	
17	C2	+04	45	**Lug**dunensis	
17	D2	+04	45	Col. **Lug**dunum	Col. Copia Claudia Augusta **Lug**dunum
20	B4	+14	45	**Loug**eon Helos	
20	F3	+18	46	**Lug**io	Florentia
24	D2	−08	42	**Loug**ei	
24	E2	−07	42	**Lug**goni	
24	F1	−06	43	**Lug**goni	
24	*unl*	*−06*	*43*	**Lug**iso	
25	F2	+00	43	**Lug**dunum Convenarum	
48	B2	+09	40	'**Lugu**idunec'	Castra Felicia?
48	B2	+09	40	Portus **Lugu**idonis	

The two instances of *Luggoni* are not duplicates; TIR K-30, p. 143, notes that there were two groups of them (also that Tovar preferred the form *Luggones*). There seems to be a haplological syncope < **Lugugon-* (see PNPG Comments s.n. *Louggóno:n* and Celtic Elements s.v. *gono-*). The name *Lugiso* may be connected (TIR K-29, p. 70). A name from Ptolemy's Germania Magna, omitted from the *Atlas*, is *Lougidounon* (2.11.13) i.e. Legnica/Liegnitz (+16/51); this is included on **Map 12.24**.

Formally inadmissible

11	B3	+01	49	Catos**lug**i	
25	E3	−01	42	Aspal**lug**a	
27	B3	−04	38	I**lug**o	
91	E4	+43	33	Misiche	Peroz-Shapur Anbar Pumbedita Pal**lug**htha Bersabora

---

[41] Questioned by Maier, 'Is Lug to be identified with Mercury?', and 'Carlisle und Colchester'. See also Wilkinson, '**Lanum* and *Lugudunum*'.

Mag- 'field, plain' (OI *mag*, W *ma*, *-fa*; cf. W *maes*)

AILR and PNPG Celtic Elements s.v. *magos*, *mages-*; PNRB, pp. 287–88 and 406–7; DLG s.v. *magos*.

This seems not to occur as the first element of compound names (*Magio-* 'great?' being distinct: AILR Celtic Elements and DLG s.v. and KPP, p. 197). Most examples of the simplex are doubtful, but see PNRB, pp. 406–7, on *Magia* in Switzerland, now *Maienfeld*, a nice tautology. Isaac notes that 'the Celtic *s*-stem *magos, **mages-* is typically represented as an *o*-stem in Latin and Greek sources' (AILR Celtic Elements s.v.). The string MAGES is not found at all.

String MAG or MAGG plus vowel[42]

Formally admissible (68)

7	G3	+ 00	48	Noviomagus Lexoviorum			
8	F3	− 02	51	*Leucomagus			
8	G4	− 01	50	Noviomagus			
8	H3	+ 00	51	Caesaromagus			
8	H3	+ 00	51	Noviomagus			
8	*unl*	*+ 01*	*52*	*Sitomagus			
9	D6	− 04	54	**Mag**is?			
9	*unl*	− *05*	*56*	Litano**mag**o			
9	*unl*			Ouako**mag**oi			
10	B5	+ 05	51	Batavodurum	Novio**mag**us	(Ulpia) Novio**mag**us	Batavi
11	B2	+ 01	50	Linto**mag**us?			
11	B3	+ 01	49	Roto**mag**us			
11	C3	+ 02	49	Augusto**mag**us	Castrum de Silvanectis		
11	C3	+ 02	49	Caesaro**mag**us			
11	C3	+ 02	49	Novio**mag**us			
11	C3	+ 02	49	Ratu**mag**us Silvanectum?	Ratum(...)?		
11	E3	+ 04	49	Novio**mag**us			
11	F3	+ 05	49	Moso**mag**us			
11	F4	+ 05	48	Novio**mag**us			
11	G1	+ 06	51	Durno**mag**us			
11	G2	+ 06	50	Marco**mag**us?			
11	G3	+ 06	49	Novio**mag**us Treverorum			

---

[42] Some forms in MAC may belong here, e.g. 14E4 *Salomacus* (cf. Holder ii, 1318, and AILR at AI 457.1). Cf. PNRB, p. 287. The string MAG + consonant brings in irrelevant names, although some instances of *Magnis* may still be Celtic (cf. W *maen* 'stone'; see AILR and PNPG Celtic Elements s.v. *magno-* and PNRB, pp. 407–8.

11	G3	+06	49	Vicus Contio**magus**		
11	H2	+07	50	Rigo**magus**		
11	H4	+07	48	Broco**magus**		
11	I3	+08	49	Borbeto**magus**		
11	I3	+08	49	Novio**magus**	Nemetae	
11	*unl*	*+01*	*49*	Ritu**magus**		
14	E1	−01	47	Iulio**magus**	Civitas Andecavorum	
14	E3	−01	45	Nouio**magos**		
14	E3	−01	45	'Sermanico**mago**'?		
14	F1	+00	47	*Ciso**magus**		
14	F1	+00	47	Roto**magus**?		
14	F1	+00	47	*Mantoloma(g)**um**		
14	F2	+00	46	*Torno**magus**?		
14	F3	+00	45	Cas(s)ino**magus**		
14	G2	+01	46	*Argento**magus**		
14	G2	+01	46	Blato**magus**		
14	G2	+01	46	Claudio**magus**		
14	H2	+02	46	Aquae Neri	*Nerio**magus**	
14	H2	+02	46	*Nogeo**magus**		
14	H4	+02	44	Caranto**magus**		
14	I3	+03	45	*Rico**magus**		
16	C2	+06	43	*Brigo**magus**		
17	A2	+03	45	*Bilio**magus**		
17	B3	+03	45	Icid**mago**		
17	D5	+04	44	Noio**magos**	Col. Augusta Tricastinorum	Tricastini
17	D5	+04	44	Seno**magos**		
17	E5	+05	44	Noio**magos**		
17	F2	+05	45	Venetoni**magus**		
17	G4	+06	44	Caturigo**magus**		
17	H3	+06	45	Scingo**magus**		
17	H5	+06	44	Rigo**magus**		
18	*unl*	*+06*	*46*	Viro**magus**	Uro**mago**	
19	A2	+08	47	Iulio**magus**		
19	B2	+09	47	**Mag**ia		
20	B2	+14	47	'Gabro**mago**'		
25	F2	+00	43	Casino**magus**		
25	G2	+01	43	Sosto**magus**	Sexto**magus**	
25	H2	+02	43	Hebro**magus**	Eburo**magus**	
25	I1	+03	44	Condato**magus**?		
27	inset	+04	39	**Mago**		
39	C3	+08	45	Industria	Bodinco**magum**?	
39	C3	+08	45	Rigo**magus**		
39	E3	+09	45	'Comeli **magus**'	'Camelio**magus**'	
47	*unl*	*+15*	*37*	**Mag**ea Fons		
67	*unl*	*+36*	*36*	**Mag**ia Vicus		
94	*unl*			**Mag**oi		

The *Ouakomagoi* were somewhere in Scotland (see PNRB, pp. 484–85, where an entry *Maromago* in the *Ravenna Cosmography* is equated with **Vacomagi*, which is why *Maromago* does not appear in the *Barrington* data). The *Atlas* omits *Drousomagos* in Ptolemy 2.12.3; PNPG suggests

+ 8/47 ? for it (see also Comments s.n.) and this is where it is placed on **Map 12.3**.

Formally inadmissible (putting names beginning *Mag(g)-* separately at the end)

5	*unl*			Ar**mag**ara		
5	*unl*			Bra**mag**ara		
5	*unl*			Ta**mag**is		
6	B4	+ 65	25	Ka**mig**ara	Ca**mag**ora?	
6	C3	+ 70	30	Assakanoi	As**mag**i	Assoi Assakia
6	*unl*			Chonna**mag**ara		
6	*unl*			Sar**mag**ana		
13	B4	+ 16	48	Co**mag**ena		
20	A4	+ 13	45	Hu**mag**um		
24	D2	+ 16	47	Ta**mag**ani		
67	D2	+ 36	37	Com**mag**ene		
67	E3	+ 37	36	Ciliza	Ur**mag**iganti	
71	*unl*			Sa**mag**a	Samoga	
4	*unl*			**Mag**on Ins.		
4	*unl*			**Mag**usum		
5	F2	+ 86	20	**Mag**aris		
6	F4	+ 85	25	**Mag**on fl.		
6	*unl*			**Mag**arsus fl.		
8	G3	– 01	51	**Mag**iovinium		
8	*unl*			**Mag**antia Ins.		
15	B2	+ 03	43	**Mag**alona		
24	G2	– 05	42	Civitas **Magg**aviensium		
25	C3	– 03	42	*Tritium **Mag**allum		
63	C1	+ 33	39	**Mag**aba M.	Mordiacus M.	
65	D2	+ 30	37	*****Mag**astara		
65	E4	+ 30	36	**Mag**ydos		
66	G3	+ 35	36	**Mag**arsa	Antiochia ad Pyramum **Mag**arsos	
68	C2	+ 36	35	*****Mag**arataricha		
69	C2	+ 35	33	**Mag**oras fl.		
75	*unl*			**Mag**ais		
81	*unl*			**Mag**adale Parva		
81	*unl*			**Mag**assa		
82	*unl*			**Mag**ada		
87	C4	+ 37	40	**Mag**abula		
89	*unl*			Matoustana	*****Mag**ustana	
91	*unl*			**Mag**(o)uda		

MANDU- 'YOUNG ANIMAL' (OI *MENN*, W *MYN*) OR 'MINDED' (W *MYNNAF*)?

AILR and PNPG Celtic Elements s.v. *mandu-*; GPN, p. 223; DLG s.v. *mandus*.

String MANDU (not found under MANDOU)

Formally admissible (6)

8	F2	− 02	52	**Mandu**essedum		
11	D3	+ 03	49	Augusta Viro**mandu**orum		
11	D3	+ 03	49	Viro**mandu**i		
18	B2	+ 04	47	**Mandu**bii		
18	D2	+ 06	47	Epa**mandu**odurum		
45	G4	+ 17	40	**Mandu**ria	Mandonion	Amandrinum

Formally inadmissible None

MANT- 'PATH' (W *MATHRU*, OI *MEN*)

AILR and PNPG Celtic Elements s.v. *manto/u-*; LEIA M-36; DLG s.v. *mantalon* (and p. 436); Delamarre, 'Gallo-Brittonica', pp. 128–29.

String MANT

Formally admissible (20 – since the 35unl entry duplicates the following *Garamantes* entry, assuming the emendation of Pliny's *Amantes* etc. (5.34) is correct; cf. Desanges' edition, p. 376, and Desanges, *Catalogue*, pp. 76–77)

5	*unl*			**Mant**itour	
6	C3	+ 72	34	Mala**mant**os? fl.	
11	*unl*	*+ 02*	*48*	Petro**mant**ulum	Petrum Viaco
14	F1	+ 00	47	*****Mant**oloma(g)um	
17	G2	+ 06	45	**Mant**ala	
20	F2	+ 18	47	Kela**mant**ia	
21	*unl*	*+ 18*	*46*	Cara**mant**esium Vicus	
24	F4	− 06	40	Sal**mant**ica	
24	G4	− 05	40	**Mant**ua	
35	*unl*			*****Amant**es (Garamantes?)	
36	C4	+ 13	27	Gara**mant**es	
36	C5	+ 13	26	Fauces Gara**mant**icae	
38	D1	+ 22	32	Ma(ra)ndis?	Ari**mant**os Kome?
39	H3	+ 10	45	**Mant**ua	
48	D2	+ 09	42	**Mant**inon	
51	B2	+ 23	41	Odo**mant**es	Odo**mant**ike
58	C2	+ 22	37	**Mant**ineia	Antigoneia
62	C3	+ 29	39	**Mant**alos	
73	E2	+ 27	31	Lada**mant**ia	Leoda**mant**ium
86	C3	+ 32	40	**Mant**ineion	
89	*unl*			Odo**mant**is	

See **Map 12.27**.

Formally inadmissible (including examples of Greek *manteion* 'oracle')[43]

4	*unl*			**Mant**eion Artemidos				
6	A3	+ 62	30	Erymandros fl.	Cymander? fl.	Ebimaris fl.	Etymandros fl.	Ethy**mant**us fl.
21	B4	+ 19	45	A**mant**ini				
23	*unl*			**Mant**hion Pedion				
25	B4	– 04	41	Termes	Ter**mant**ia			
25	C4	– 03	41	Nu**mant**ia				
25	*unl*			Ne**mant**ourista				
46	D3	+ 16	39	Cla**mpet**ia	La**mpet**eia	A**mant**ia		
46	*unl*			A**mant**ia				
49	B3	+ 19	40	A**mant**ia				
54	C3	+ 20	39	Nekro**mant**eion				
58	B2	+ 21	37	Ery**mant**hos fl.				
58	B2	+ 21	37	Ery**mant**hos M.				
58	C3	+ 22	37	**Mant**houria				
58	*unl*			Ery**mant**hos				
58	*unl*			**Mant**hyrea				
62	*unl*			Na**mant**aloi?				
72	A2	+ 32	35	Aka**mant**on? M.				
72	A2	+ 32	35	Akamas Pr.	Aka**mant**is Pr.			
90	B4	+ 46	36	Matiane	**Mant**iane	Matienoi		

MEDIO- 'MIDDLE' (OI *mide*, W *mei-*)

AILR and PNPG Celtic Elements s.v. *medio-*; DLG s.v. *medios*; Lambert, '*Lugdunensis*', p. 247.

String MEDIO

Formally admissible (15 – as '27 *unl* Mediolon' duplicates '25 *unl* Mediolon')

8	E2	– 03	52	**Medio**lanum
9	*unl*	– 04	55	**Medio**nemeton
11	G3	+ 06	49	**Medio**matrici

[43] *Amantini* is derived < **Au-mant-* by Anreiter, *Die vorrömischen Namen Pannoniens*, pp. 28–29 (cf. review by Udolph, p. 133: *Am-ant-*). Even if this is right, the form is inadmissible as **Au-* would have remained in Celtic. The same applies to *Amantia*. In PNPG Celtic Elements s.v. *manto/u-*, however, *Amantinoi* is analysed with a unique prefix *a-* + *manto-*. On *Nemantourista* see VCIE, pp. 463–64 and 488, suggesting *Ne-mant-* (cf. Gorrochategui, 'Ptolemy's Aquitania and the Ebro valley', p. 149, and below, Ch. 8, n. 85).

11	B3	+01	49	**Mediol**anum Aulercorum	Eburovicum
14	H2	+02	46	**Medio**cantus	
14	E3	−01	45	**Mediol**anum	
14	H2	+02	46	**Mediol**anum	Stampensis
17	*unl*			***Mediol**anum	
17	C2	+04	45	**Mediol**anum	
18	B2	+04	47	[**Mediol**anum]	
22	*unl*	*+26*	*43*	**Mediol**anum	
24	*unl*	*−09*	*42*	**Medio**ga	
25	*unl*	*−03*	*40*	**Mediol**on	
27	*unl*			**Mediol**on	
39	E3	+09	45	**Mediol**an(i)um	
54	D4	+21	38	**Medio**n	

Note that the starred *Mediolanum* (17unl) does not really belong in the database (and is not in fact 'unlocated') as it is just one of many reconstructed examples of *Mediolanum* (e.g. Fabre, *Noms de lieux du Languedoc*, p. 49), in this case on the basis of a medieval *Meolano*, *Medulano,* modern *Méolans* (see Holder ii, 520, Rostaing, *Essai*, pp. 327–28, and Barruol, pp. 144 and 354, n. 1). An additional ancient *Mediolanion* (+16/48 ?) occurs in MS X of Ptolemy 2.11.15 (other MSS *Medoslanion* etc.). The *Atlas* also omits his *Mediolanion* (2.11.13) at +5/51. Both are included on **Map 4.7**.

Formally inadmissible (some or all clearly Latin/Greek)

22	*unl*			In **Medio**	
56	C3	+26	39	Poly**medion**	Palamedium
64	D2	+36	39	In **Medio**	
64	D3	+36	38	Symposion	In **Medio**?
67	G2	+38	37	In **Medio**	

MORI- 'SEA' (OI *MUIR*, W *MÔR*)

AILR and PNPG Celtic Elements s.v. *mori-*; GPN, pp. 232–33; DLG s.v. *mori*.

String MORI[44]

Formally admissible (5)

---

[44] Unfortunately this string leaves out *Vindomora*, mentioned in AILR and GPN. The *Atlas* does not include *Morimarusa*; see below, p. 186.

7	C3	– 04	48	Ar(e)**moric**a
8	C3	– 05	51	***Mori**dunum
8	*unl*	*– 04*	*50*	**Mori**dunum
9	D6	– 04	54	**Mori**kambe *Eischusis
11	B2	+ 01	50	**Mori**ni

Formally inadmissible

24	F1	– 06	43	**Memori**ana
62	F3	+ 31	39	**Amori**on
67	*unl*			**Commori**s Vicus

NANTU- 'VALLEY, WATER-COURSE' (W *NANT*)

GPN, p. 236; DLG s.v. *nantu-, nanto-* and p. 436 (cf. review by Billy, p. 282, and AILR Celtic Elements s.v. *nemo-*).

String NANT

Formally admissible (2 – as *Vernantes* is a ghost-form; see below):

18	D3	+ 06	46	**Nant**uates	
19	F2	+ 13	47	'Tar**nant**one'	
25	*unl*			Ver**nem**etis	Ver**nant**es

The source for *Vernemetis* is Venantius Fortunatus, *Carmina* 1.9, 'De basilica S. Vincenti Vernemetis', where the name is explained as meaning 'fanum ingens' in *Gallica lingua* (see *nemeto-* below). No variant *Vernantes* is given in the editions by Leo and Reydellet, nor would it agree with Fortunatus' etymology. It is clearly the *modern* name *Vernantes* (Maine-et-Loire), a distinct place first attested as *Vernemeta* in the Merovingian period (Nègre i, §2549; DLG, p. 234). An example of NANT, which could have been included in the *Atlas*, however, is *Loukounanta* (Procopius, *Buildings*, 4.4), in Trun (Trǎn), Bulgaria (+ 22/42).[45]

---

[45] Beševliev, p. 23; Orel, 'Thracian and Celtic', p. 5; Duridanov, 'Sprachspuren', p. 135; DLG s.v. *nantu-*.

Formally inadmissible

| 81 | *unl* | | **Danant** |
| 87 | *unl* | | Oinantheia |

NEMETO- 'SACRED GROVE' (OI NEMED, W NYFED)

AILR and PNPG Celtic Elements s.v. *nemeto-*; DLG s.v. *nemeton* (and p. 436); De Bernardo Stempel, 'Ptolemy's evidence for Germania Superior', p. 76.

String NEMET

Formally admissible (15 – as '16 *unl* Nemeturii' duplicates the next entry and '25 *unl* Vernemetis' duplicates the 14F4 entry)

8	D4	– 04	50	'Nemetotacio'	
8	F1	– 02	53	Aquae *Arnemetiae	
8	F2	– 02	52	'Vernemeto'	
9	*unl*	– 04	55	Medionemeton	
11	C2	+ 02	50	Nemetacum	Nemetocenna
11	C4	+ 02	48	*Nemetodurum	
11	H3	+ 07	49	Nemetes	
11	I3	+ 08	49	Noviomagus	Nemetae
14	F4	+ 00	44	Pompeiacum	Vernemetis
14	I3	+ 03	45	Augustonemetum	Civitas Arvernorum
16	*unl*			Nemeturii	
17	H5	+ 06	44	Nemeturii?	
19	G3	+ 14	46	'Tasinemeti'	
24	C3	– 09	41	Nemetatoi?	
24	D2	– 08	42	Nemetobriga	
25	*unl*			Vernemetis	Vernantes
63	*unl*	*+ 32*	*40*	Drynemeton	

On *Vernemetis* (in Venantius Fortunatus) see under *nantu-* above. The 25unl entry duplicates 14F4, where it is identified with *Pompeiacum* (identified with Caumont-sur-Garonne). *Vernemetis* seems in fact to have been near, but not identical with, *Pompeiacum*; see note in Reydellet's edition, p. 171.

See **Map 4.8.**

Formally inadmissible None

NERTO- 'STRENGTH' (OI *NERT*, W *NERTH*)

AILR and PNPG Celtic Elements s.v. *nerto-*; GPN, p. 237; DLG s.v. *nerto-*.

String NERT

Formally admissible (2 – as the coin-legend *Nertobis* is thought to refer to the *Nertobriga* at 25D4, cf. TIR K-30, p. 158)

25	D4	– 02	41	**Nert**obriga
25	*cn.*			**Nert**obis
26	D3	– 07	38	**Nert**obriga Concordia Iulia

On Ptolemy's *Nertereanes*, not in the *Atlas*, see below, Chapter 6, n. 87.

Formally inadmissible

38	*unl*			**Z**e**nert**is	
59	B3	+ 23	37	Agryle Hype**nert**hen	
59	C3	+ 23	37	Ankyle Hype**nert**hen	
59	C3	+ 23	37	Lamptrai Paraloi	Lamptrai Hype**nert**hen
59	C3	+ 23	37	Paiania Hype**nert**hen	
59	C2	+ 23	38	Pergase Hype**nert**hen	
59	C3	+ 23	37	Potamos Hype**nert**hen	

NEVIO-, NOVIO- 'NEW' (OI *NÚAE*, W *NEWYDD*)

AILR and PNPG Celtic Elements s.v. *neu(i)o-*, *nou(i)o-*; DLG s.v. *nouiios*.

String NEVIO, NOVIO, NOUIO, NOUO (no relevant forms found under string NEUIO, NEOUIO, NEVO, NOVO, NEOUO)[46]

---

[46] A string which might have been included is NOIO (cf. Lambert, '*Lugdunensis*', p. 247; De Bernardo Stempel, 'Ptolemy's evidence for Germania Superior', pp. 80 and 90; PNPG Comments s.n. *Nouiódounon*). In fact, however, in admissible forms this only occurs in compounds of *Noio-* + *dunum* or *magus* which I have already included under those elements. These *Noio-* names are included on Map 12.17 below. Note also 14H2 *Nogeomagus.

Formally admissible (18)[47]

7	G3	+00	48	**Novio**magus Lexoviorum			
8	G4	−01	50	**Novio**magus			
8	H3	+00	51	**Novio**magus			
10	B5	+05	51	Batavodurum	**Novio**magus	(Ulpia) **Novio**magus	Batavi
11	C3	+02	49	**Novio**magus			
11	D3	+03	49	**Novio**dunum?			
11	E3	+04	49	**Novio**magus			
11	F4	+05	48	**Novio**magus			
11	G3	+06	49	**Novio**magus Treverorum			
11	I3	+08	49	**Novio**magus	Nemetae		
14	E2	−01	46	**Novio**ritum			
14	E3	−01	45	**Novio**regum			
14	E3	−01	45	**Nouio**magos			
14	G1	+01	47	**Novio**dunum			
14	I1	+03	47	**Novio**dunum?	Nevirnum?	'Ebirno'	
18	D3	+06	46	Col. Iulia Equestris	**Novio**dunum		
20	C4	+15	45	**Nevio**dunum			
22	F3	+28	45	**Novio**dunum			

See **Map 12.17**.[48]

Formally inadmissible

67	H3	+38	36	Dabana	Tharrana	Man**nouo**rra	Davana
77	D1	+30	27	Nagos	**Nouo**i		
89	*unl*			Man**nouo**rra	Manneotai		

OCELO- 'PROMONTORY' (NOT IN INSULAR CELTIC; CF. OI *OCHAIR*, W *OCHR*)

AILR and PNPG Celtic Elements s.v. *ocelo*-; DLG s.v. *ocelo*-; Prósper, *Lenguas y religiones prerromanas*, pp. 107–18 and 509. See Chapter 3 above with maps.

String OCEL, OKEL

Formally admissible (15)

4	B3	+43	12	Akila	**Okel**is	Ocilia
4	*unl*			Pseud**okel**is		
8	H1	+00	53	**Okel**lou ? Akron		
9	*unl*			Cind**ocel**lum		

---

[47] *Novioritum* (14E2) seems in fact to be a reconstruction (cf. Holder ii, 793).
[48] This includes *Noio*- names, as noted in n. 46 above.

17	G3	+ 06	45	Graioceli?	
24	D4	− 08	40	Castellum Araocelum	
24	D4	− 08	40	**Ocel**um	
24	F3	− 06	41	**Ocel**um Duri	
24	F3	− 06	41	Arboukale	Alb**ocel**a[49]
24	*unl*	− 08	*41*	Castellum Louci**ocel**um	
24	*unl*	− 07	*40*	*****Ocel**um	
24	*unl*	− 08	*42*	**Okel**on	
24	*unl*	− 05	*43*	**Okel**a	Opsikella
24	*unl*	− 08	*42*	**Okel**on	
39	A3	+ 07	45	**Ocel**um	

Cindocellum (= **Cintocellum*?) may be in Scotland (PNRB, p. 308). *Tunnocelo* (ND), somewhere in north-west England, is omitted in the *Atlas*, which includes only 'Iuliocenon' (9unl) from the *Ravenna Cosmography*, on the basis of which an original **Itunocelum* is usually reconstructed (PNRB, p. 380; see above, p. 31).

Formally inadmissible None

OLI(:)NĀ 'BEND, ELBOW' (OI *UILEN*, W *ELIN*)

PNPG Possibly Celtic Elements s.v. {olina:-}; Luján, 'Ptolemy's *Callaecia*', p. 58; DLG s.v. *olina*; Lambert, '*Lugdunensis*', p. 218.

String Olin (case-sensitive)

Formally admissible (2)

| 7 | F3 | − 01 | 48 | **Olin**a fl. |
| 24 | *unl* | − 08 | *43* | **Olin**a |

Formally inadmissible None

PENNO- 'HEAD' (OI *CENN*, W *PEN*)

AILR and PNPG Celtic Elements and DLG s.v. *penno-*; cf. Gelling & Cole, *Landscape of Place-Names*, pp. 210–13.

---

[49] *Albocola* on Map 24 itself, evidently following CIL II 880, *Albocolensi*. CIL equates this with *Albocela* and *Arboukale*.

String PENN (no relevant forms found via string QUEN)

Formally admissible (7)

1	F2	+10	44	Ap(p)enninus M.	
8	E2	−03	52	**Penn**ocrucium	
18	D3	+06	46	**Penn**e Locos	
19	*unl*			A**penn**inus M.	
39	F5	+09	44	In Alpe **Penn**ino	
51	B3	+23	40	**Penn**ana	
75	*unl*			**Penn**e	

The unlocated *Apenninus M.* is in Raetia (Brenner/Brennero?). The first is the famous *Ap(p)enninus Mons* in Italy. It is popularly regarded as a *penn* name (e.g. Aubrey, cited above, p. 6); if so the formation would presumably be **ad-penn-* (as in PNPG). *Poeninus Mons* (17H2) derives not from Hannibal's *Poeni* (whence the conventional misspelling – *Penninus* is better), but probably from Celtic **penno-*, as noted already by Boxhorn, *Originum Gallicarum Liber*, p. 37.

Formally inadmissible

32	F4	+10	36	U**penna**	
65	C4	+29	36	*Or**peena***	Or**penna**

RATĀ, RATI- 'FERN' (OI *RAITH*, W *RHEDYN*) AND RĀTO-, RĀTA, RĀTE 'EARTHWORK' (OI *RÁ(I)TH*, W *BEDDROD*) (GROUPED TOGETHER AS THEY CANNOT ALWAYS BE DISTINGUISHED)

AILR and PNPG Celtic Elements s.vv. {rata:/i-} and {ra:to/a:-}; GPN, p. 241; DLG s.vv. *ratis* 'fougère' and *rate, ratis* 'muraille, rempart > fort' (cf. Lambert, '*Lugdunensis*', p. 250; De Bernardo Stempel, 'Ptolemy's evidence for Germania Superior', pp. 77–78 and 92).

String RATA, RATE, RATI, RATO, RATU, RATOU (and variants with RH)

Formally admissible (17 – as the two instances of *Ratakensioi* are duplicates)

6	B5	+69	22	Suarattra**ratae**	
6	*unl*			Rhagiraua	**Rati**ra
8	D3	−04	51	**Rato**stabios? fl.	
8	F2	−02	52	**Ratae**	
11	C3	+02	49	**Ratu**magus Silvanectum?	**Ratum**(...)?

11	H4	+ 07	48	Argentorate	
14	D1	− 02	47	*Ratiatum	
14	D2	− 02	46	Ratis Ins.	Arica
14	E3	− 01	45	Corterate	
15	E1	+ 05	44	Carpentorate	*Forum Neronis
17	E2	+ 05	45	*Brioratis	
21	E6	+ 22	43	Ratiaria	
21	*unl*			Ratakensioi	
22	*unl*			Ratakensioi	
25	*cn.*			Areikoratikos	Arekorata
58	*unl*	*+ 22*	*37*	Rhatiai	
65	C4	+ 29	36	Kibyratis	
87	K2	+ 36	45	Ilouraton	

The *Ratakensioi* were a people in north Dacia mentioned by Ptolemy (3.8.3), properly perhaps *Racatensii* according to Müller (p. 444).[50] The location of the place/ethnonym mentioned on the Celtiberian coin-legend (25 *cn.*) is uncertain: Villaronga, *Corpus Nummum Hispaniae*, p. 270, says it has been identified both with modern Ágreda (*Augustobriga*, Atlas 25D4 = −2/41) and with modern Argueda (area of Atlas 25D3 = −2/42). The former is rejected by TIR K-30, p. 51, which does not mention the latter. See discussion on p. 311 and **Map 12.18**.

Formally inadmissible (grouped according to vowel)

6	C4	+ 73	26	Oratae	
6	*unl*			Karatai	
11	H2	+ 07	50	Prata Aureliana	
12	E4	+ 11	48	Bratananium	
18	E3	+ 07	46	Col. Aventicum	Col. Pia Flavia
					Constans
					Emerita
					Helvetiorum
					Foederata
20	E2	+ 17	47	Quadrata	
20	*unl*			Quadrata	
21	D5	+ 21	44	Lederata	
27	A5	− 05	36	Aratispi	Rataspem
29	D1	− 02	35	Camarata?	
31	D4	+ 05	36	Fons Camerata?	
34	D2	+ 05	35	Thac(arata?)	
39	B3	+ 07	45	Quadrata	
39	*unl*			Quadrata	
42	C4	+ 12	42	Rostrata Villa	
42	*unl*			Sacrata	
46	*unl*			Crataeis fl.	

---

[50] Possibly connected with the *Rakatai* near Vienna (13B4 = + 16/48), TIR M-33, p. 71, which Holder ii, 1069, notes as the source of the Czech name for Austria, *Rakousy*. Holder quotes Ernault's suggestion of a connection with W *rhag*, i.e. 'those who oppose or stand in front'.

47	*unl*			Kragas M.	Kratas M.			
49	F1	+23	42	Spa**rata**				
54	*unl*			Marma**rata**				
59	A2	+23	38	Ke**rata** M.				
66	C1	+33	37	Ba**rata**				
68	C2	+36	35	*Maga**rata**richa				
83	C4	+37	27	Apataioi	A**rata**ei			
86	A3	+30	40	Ce**rata**e				
88	*unl*			Arsa**rata**				
91	*unl*			Gib**rata**	Gorbatha			
6	E4	+82	26	(H)Eorta	Eorta	Sageda	Sagala?	**Arate**?
14	E4	− 01	44	*Va**rate**do	'Vanitedo'			
16	*unl*			O**rate**lli				
20	*unl*			Ne**rate**				
22	C5	+25	43	Emporium Discodu**rate**rae				
25	F2	+00	43	Lactora	Lacto**rate**s			
30	H3	+04	36	Fe**rate**nses				
32	*unl*			Taga**rate**nsis Plebs				
33	B2	+08	35	Tur**rate**nses				
44	E2	+13	41	Fab**rate**ria Nova				
44	D2	+13	41	Fab**rate**ria Vetus				
44	F4	+14	40	Puteolanus Sinus	Crater			
46	D2	+16	39	Crathis fl.	**Crate**r fl.			
55	*unl*			Ake**rate**ion				
56	*unl*			Karseai	Karseis	Kerasai	Ke**rate**is	
58	C3	+22	37	Ga**rate**s fl.				
67	F2	+37	37	Epiphaneia ad Euph**rate**m				
67	F2	+37	37	Ourima	Antiochia ad Euph**rate**m	Arulis		
67	F2	+37	37	Zeugma	Seleukeia pros to Euph**rate**			
86	C3	+32	40	K**rate**ia	Flaviopolis	*Agrippeia?	K**rete**ia	
89	D1	+41	39	Autispa**rate**	Theodosiopolis			
93	E2	+48	31	Hithite fl.	Hudhud fl.	Kop**rate**s? fl.		
93	A2	+44	31	Euph**rate**s fl.	Arahtu fl.	Buranun fl.	Pu**rate**u fl.	
93	E1	+48	32	Sost**rate**	Shushtar			
4	*unl*			St**rati**oton				
14	G1	+01	47	Ce**rati**s				
17	F3	+05	45	Cularo	G**rati**anopolis			
23	C3	+29	45	G**rati**ana?				
24	E2	− 07	42	Soupe**rati**oi				
25	D4	− 02	41	A**rati**kos	A**rati**s			
27	A5	− 05	36	A**rati**spi	Rataspem			
31	G3	+07	36	Pa**rati**anis				
39	G3	+10	45	Pagus Far**rati**canus				
44	G3	+14	41	Ne**rati**i				
45	*unl*			In Hono**rati**anum				
54	D4	+21	38	St**rato**s	St**rati**ke			
58	*unl*			St**rati**e Ins.				
63	A4	+32	38	Praedia Quad**rati**ana				
66	C2	+33	37	Bo**rati**non M.				
71	*unl*			Theman	Saltus Hie**rati**kos			

74	D3	+ 30	30	Naucratis			
74	D3	+ 30	30	Naukratites Nomos			
86	D1	+ 33	42	Marsylla	Kallistratia?		
94	unl			Hieratis			
96	unl			Pratitae	Pantitae	Pantimathoi	
99	unl			Eukratidia			
4	unl			Eratonos Inss.			
4	unl			Strato			
9	E5	− 03	55	Castra Exploratorum			
22	unl			*Stratonis Turris			
25	H2	+ 02	43	Murato			
26	B3	− 09	38	Salacia (Imperatoria)	Municipium Salaciense		
27	A3	− 05	38	Epora	Epora Foederatorum		
47	E3	+ 14	37	Myttistraton			
51	unl			Stratonike(ia)			
52	E3	+ 29	40	*Pratomysia			
54	D4	+ 21	38	Stratos	Stratike		
56	F3	+ 27	39	Stratonicaea	Hadrianopolis		
58	B2	+ 21	37	Stratos			
60	D2	+ 25	35	Kairatos fl.			
61	G3	+ 28	37	Stratonikeia			
67	unl			Paratomos, Mon.			
68	A5	+ 35	34	Imperatoris Hadriani Augusti Definitio Silvarum			
68	C2	+ 36	35	*Telmenissos	Maratomyrton?		
69	A4	+ 34	32	Stratonos Pyrgos	Caesarea	Kaisareia Paralios	Cesarea Palestinae
74	unl			Ionon kai Karon stratopeda			
74	unl			Tyrion stratopeda			
75	unl			Stratonos			
87	unl			Stratoclia			
90	G4	+ 51	36	Straton fl.			
91	unl			Stratonicea			
6	unl			Souragana Phratou			
34	F3	+ 07	34	Ad Turres?	Paratouron		
60	unl			Marathousa	Moratousa		
77	unl			Damaratou			
79	unl			Pmoun Pisistratou			
4	unl			Sokratus			
11	unl			Bratuspantium			
15	C2	+ 04	43	*Varatunnum			
18	B3	+ 04	46	Desideratus, Mon.	Gurthonense Mon.		
21	unl			*Ducis Pratum			
45	unl			Fratuertium	Fratuentium		
47	E3	+ 14	37	Amestratus			
73	unl			Aratu			

Rīgo- 'king' (OI *rí*, W *rhi*)

AILR and PNPG Celtic Elements s.v. {ri:go-}; GPN, p. 248; DLG s.v. *rix* (and p. 437).

String RIG (excluding consonant + RIG, e.g. BRIG etc., despite GPN, p. 248 where *Dourotriges* is included) (RHIG not found)[51]

Formally admissible (18 – since the first two are duplicates)

5	*unl*			Sala**rig**a	
6	G5	+91	23	Sala**rig**a	
8	E1	– 03	53	**Rig**odounon?	
9	D5	– 04	55	Karbanto**rig**on?	
9	B5	– 06	55	Reri**g**onios Kolpos	
9	*unl*	*– 06*	*55*	Reri**g**onion	
11	G2	+06	50	Ico**rig**ium	
11	H2	+07	50	**Rig**omagus	
13	*unl*	*+ 17*	*50*	Boudo**rig**on	
14	E3	– 01	45	Bitu**rig**es Vivisci	
14	G1	+01	47	Bitu**rig**es Cubi	
14	H1	+02	47	Ava**ric**um	Biturigae
17	G4	+06	44	Catu**rig**es	
17	G4	+06	44	Catu**rig**omagus	
17	H5	+06	44	**Rig**omagus	
24	G1	– 05	43	Ava**rig**ini	
39	C3	+08	45	**Rig**omagus	
39	*unl*	*+09*	*44*	**Rig**onum fl.	
86	C3	+32	40	Gezato**rig**is	

For Ptolemy's *Boudorgis* (< **Boudorīgis* ?)[52] in Germania Magna (+15/50) see above under *boud-*. See also below, p. 246, on 42unl *Biturgia* (+11/43) in Italy (Ptolemy 3.1.43). The *Atlas* omits *Rigodulum* (Tacitus, *Historiae*, 4.71), now Riol east of Trier (+6/49) (Greule & Kleiber, 'Moseltal', p. 159). These three are included on **Map 4.9**.

---

[51] Some examples of RIC may be relevant, e.g. 14I3 **Ricomagus* (modern Riom); cf. Holder ii, 1188, for a variant in *Rigo-* not given in the *Atlas*. But this may have an element **rico-* 'furrow' (W *rhych*); see AILR and PNPG Celtic Elements s.v.

[52] An alternative analysis segments *Boudorgis* and *Koridorgis/Kondorgis* (Ptolemy 2.11.15) with 'Illyrian' *-dorgis*: see Schwarz, *Ortsnamen der Sudetenländer*, p. 20; Rasch, §§ IIAe and IVA (note also §XB on *Kasourgis* in Ptolemy 2.11.14). See also p. 186 below on *Bikourgion* (Ptolemy 2.11.14).

Formally inadmissible

5	D4	+ 79	11	Karige		
6	C3	+ 71	34	Arigaion	Acadira	Ariani
24	C3	– 09	41	Aquae Originae		
24	*unl*			Tourriga		
25	*unl*			Veriginae	Vereginae	
50	A2	+ 21	41	Erigon fl.		
56	G5	+ 28	38	*Tarigya		

Tourriga is better analysed *Tourr-ig-a* (cf. Luján, 'Ptolemy's *Callaecia*', p. 64) than *Tou-rrig-a* or *Tour-rig-a*. The '25 *unl*' entry derives from Venantius Fortunatus, *Carmina*, 1.19 'De *Vereginis* villa Burdegalensi', located on the *Garonna*. This relates to Baurech (*Bauregium*), dép. Gironde, according to Holder iii, 211; cf. Reydellet, *Venance Fortunat: poèmes*, i, 44, n. 85. There is no evidence in Leo's edition (p. 22) or Reydellet's (p. 44) for any variant with -*rig*-.

Ritu- 'ford' (W *rhyd*)

AILR and PNPG Celtic Elements s.v. *ritu*-; GPN, pp. 250–51; DLG s.v. *ritu*- 'gué' (cf. ibid., s.v. *ritu*-, *rito*-, 'course').

String RITU (RITOU, RHITU, RHITOU not found)[53]

Formally admissible (9)[54]

11	*unl*	+ 02	48	Anderitum	
11	*unl*	+ 01	49	Ritumagus	
14	C1	– 03	47	Darioritum	Veneti
14	E2	– 01	46	Novioritum	
14	G3	+ 01	45	Augustoritum	
14	I1	+ 03	47	'Bandritum'	
17	A4	+ 03	44	Anderitum	Civitas Gabalum
22	D5	+ 26	43	Abritus	
50	A3	+ 21	40	Begorritus L.	

---

[53] RITO might have been searched as well and would have produced, alongside irrelevant material, a number of relevant names: 8H4 *Anderidos/Anderelium/Anderitos* (+ 0/50); 9unl *Maporiton* and *Tadoriton* (southern Scotland); 12unl *Lokoriton* (+ 9/49?); 14E1 *Ouagoriton* (−1/48, cf. Lambert, '*Lugdunensis*', p. 248). Apart from *Maporiton* and *Tadoriton*, these are included on **Map 12.19**.

[54] *Novioritum* seems to be a reconstruction; see above under the first element.

Abritus could contain a prefix *ab-* (see KGP, p. 108, on *Ab-ritanor(um)*, cf. GPN, pp. 134 and 250), although a stem *abr-* (GPN, p. 431) is also possible, and see below, p. 258, n. 228. See **Map 12.19**.

Formally inadmissible

4	C2	+45	19	Cariati	Cariati	Cariat(h)	Chinati	Cyrmica	**Cyritu**ca
					(T)achoali	Tacitoali	Thacalin		
41	*unl*			**Tritu**rrita					
44	*unl*			Cominium **Ocritum**					

RUTU- 'MUD' (W *RHWD*)

AILR and PNPG Celtic Elements s.v. *rutu-*. See Chapter 3 above with maps.

String RUTU (RUTOU, ROUTOU, ROUTU not found, nor variants with RH)

Formally admissible (4)[55]

1	B4	−09	33	**Rutu**bis	
8	E2	−03	52	**Rutu**nium?	
8	I3	+01	51	**Rutu**piae	
16	E1	+07	44	Rotuba fl.	**Rutu**ba fl.

Formally inadmissible

32	D4	+09	36	Turris **Rutu**nda

SAG- 'SEEK' (OI *SAIGID*, W *HAEDDAF*) AND SAG-RO- 'STRONG' (OI *SÁR*, W *HAER*; CF. SEGO- BELOW) (GROUPED TOGETHER)

PNPG Celtic Elements s.v. *sag-* and AILR and PNPG Possibly Celtic Elements s.v. *sago-*; GPN, p. 251; DLG s.vv. *sag(i)-* and *sagro-*. Cf. Villar, *Indoeuropeos y no indoeuropeos*, pp. 312–13 and 384, and VCIE, pp. 267 and 472.

---

[55] See also Cousin, p. 459.

String SAG

Formally admissible (31)

3	*unl*		**Sag**anos fl.				
4	*unl*		**Sag**i(a)tta	**Sag**itha			
5	*unl*		**Sag**antion				
6	B5	+67 24	**Sag**apa Stoma				
6	E4	+82 27	(H)Eorta	Eorta	**Sag**eda	**Sag**ala?	Arate?
6	F4	+85 27	Chiroto**sag**i	Kirradai	Cirrabe Indi	Kirradia	Korouda Piladai
6	*unl*		Scythae	**Sag**ae	Sacae		
11	A4	+00 48	**Sag**ii				
14	G2	+01 46	*Vo**sag**um				
18	*unl*	*+06 47*	Lopo**sag**ium				
23	E1	+31 47	**Sag**aris fl.	Rhode fl.			
25	F2	+00 43	(Volcae) Tecto**sag**es	Tecto**sag**es	Tecto**sag**i		
25	G2	+01 43	Tolosa	Col. Iulia Tolosa	Civ. Tecto**sag**um	Tolosates	
25	H2	+02 43	Carcas(s)o	Col. Iulia	Carcasum Volcarum Tecto**sag**arum		
26	E5	− 06 36	**Sag**untia				
27	E2	− 01 39	**Sag**untum	Arse			
28	*unl*		Emporikos Kolpos	**Sag**igi Sinus			
40	C3	+12 44	Ostium **Sag**is				
42	G4	+14 42	**Sag**rus fl.				
46	D5	+16 38	**Sag**ra(s) fl.				
56	*unl*	*+27 39*	**Sag**ara				
62	*unl*	*+30 39*	**Sag**arenoi				
62	*unl*	*+29 38*	**Sag**arenoi?				
63	B1	+32 39	Tecto**sag**es				
65	E2	+30 37	**Sag**alassos				
86	C3	+32 40	Tekto**sag**es				
87	A3	+35 41	**Sag**ylion				
87	F1	+40 43	Sanigai	**Sag**inai			
89	F1	+43 39	Bagauna	'**Sag**ouana'	'Raugonia'		
90	*unl*		Bala**sag**an	Balasakan			
93	*unl*		**Sag**apenoi				

The *Aegosages* of Asia Minor (see below, p. 271) are omitted by the *Atlas* and are not included on **Map 12.28**.

Formally inadmissible

4	D2	+ 54	17	Abyssa		Abissagi
5	unl			Pasage		
6	A2	+ 64	37	Massagetai		
6	C3	+ 73	33	Arsagalitae	Orsaei	
6	C3	+ 71	34	Massaka	Masoga	Massaga
6	unl			Isagouros		
31	E3	+ 06	36	Am(p)saga fl.		
31	E4	+ 06	36	Caput Amsagae		
31	F4	+ 06	36	Caput Amsagae		
36	unl			Thapsagum		
60	A1	+ 23	35	Iousagoura? Ins.		
64	unl			Korsagaina		
94	D3	+ 53	30	Pasargadae	Batrakatash	Parsagada
94	unl			Pasagardai		

SAMARO- 'SUMMERY?' (CF. OI *SAM*, W *HAF*)

AILR and PNPG Celtic Elements s.v. {samaro/a:-}; GPN, p. 253; DLG s.v. *samo-*. See Chapter 3 with maps.

String SAMAR

Formally admissible (10)[56]

6	unl	*+ 73*	*33*	**Samar**ab(r)iae		
11	B2	+ 01	50	**Samar**a fl.		
11	C3	+ 02	49	**Samar**obriva Ambianorum		
24	unl	– 09	*43*	**Samar**ium		
26	unl	*– 04*	*38*	**Samar**iense Metallum		
69	B5	+ 35	32	**Samar**ia		
69	B5	+ 35	32	**Samar**ia	Sebaste	[*Gabinia]
69	unl	*+ 34*	*32*	Castra **Samar**itanorum		
75	unl	*+ 30*	*29*	**Samar**ia		
91	E3	+ 43	34	[**Samar**ra]	'Sumere'	

Formally inadmissible None

SEDO- 'SEAT' (OI *SAIDID*, W *GORSEDD*)

AILR Celtic Elements s.v. *sedo-*; GPN, p. 254.

String SED (excluding ES(S)ED, q.v.)

---

[56] On the last item, however, see above, p. 33, n. 54.

Note that this string excludes relevant names like *Camulossesa* (see *Camulo-* above) and *Demerosesa* (cf. PNRB, p. 296).

Formally admissible (15)

6	G2	+ 94	39	Isse**d**ones		
7	E2	− 02	49	Cose**d**ia	Constantia	
11	C4	+ 02	48	Metlo**sed**um	Mellodunum	
15	*unl*	*+ 04*	*43*	*Corio**ssed**um		
17	G5	+ 06	44	[**Sed**ena]		
17	G3	+ 06	45	Mello**sed**um		
18	E3	+ 07	46	*Sed**unum	**Sed**uni	
24	*unl*			Vicani Dercinoa**ssed**enses		
25	E4	− 01	41	(S)E**d**etani	Edetani	Edetania
27	E2	− 01	39	E**d**etania	Edetani	**Sed**etani?
60	F2	+ 26	35	**Sed**amnos? fl.		
66	A2	+ 32	37	*Sed**asa		
69	C5	+ 35	32	Salem	Salumias	**Sed**ima
87	E4	+ 39	40	**Sed**isca	Solonenica?	
88	*unl*			**Sed**ala		

Issedones could contain **In-* (cf. KGP, pp. 225–26). The *Dercinoassedenses* were somewhere in the territory of Clunia (i.e. Map 25B4 = −4/41); see Tovar, *Tarraconensis*, p. 370, citing a hospitality treaty between *Dercino-assedenses vicanii Cluniensium* and the people of *Termes* (25B4) printed by D'Ors, *Epigrafía jurídica*, p. 375. The reference for 27E2 should be Tovar, *Tarraconensis*, pp. 32–34 and 442–43, where the proposed identification of the *Sedetani* with the *Edetan(o)i* is discussed (see also TIR J-30, pp. 170–71, and K/J-31, pp. 143–44; García Alonso, *Península Ibérica*, pp. 475–76).[57]

Formally inadmissible

31		*unl*	**Tisedi**

Sᴇɢᴏ- 'ᴘᴏᴡᴇʀ; ʙᴏʟᴅ' (OI *seg*, W *hy*)

AILR and PNPG Celtic Elements s.v. *sego-*; GPN, pp. 256–57; DLG s.v. *sego-*; VCIE, pp. 276, 285–90 and 471–72. Anreiter, *Die vorrömischen Namen Pannoniens*, pp. 15, 124 and 202, traces the type *Segesta* to IE **seg-* 'sow', whereas Pokorny, IEW, p. 889, puts it under **seĝh-* with Celtic **sego-*.

---

[57] On the alternation between *Sed-* and *Ed-* here see De Bernardo Stempel, 'More on Ptolemy's evidence for Celtic Ireland', p. 102. (I do not accept that this makes it possible to connect *Étair* and *sedrom; the vowels and dentals are irreconcilable.) For a further example of *Issedones* see under *essedo-* above.

String SEG

Formally admissible (46)

8	C1	− 05	53	Seguntium				
8	G1	− 01	53	Segelocum				
9	F6	− 02	54	Segedunum				
11	E4	+ 04	48	Segessera				
11	H4	+ 07	48	Vosegus M.				
14	D1	− 02	47	Segora?				
14	D4	− 02	44	Segosa				
14	H1	+ 02	47	Segimovicus				
14	H4	+ 02	44	Segodunum	'Etodounon'	Civitas Rutenorum		
15	C1	+ 04	44	Segusio?				
15	E3	+ 05	43	Segobrigii				
16	A1	+ 05	44	Segustero				
17	C2	+ 04	45	Aquae Segetae				
17	C2	+ 04	45	Forum Segusiavorum	Segusiavi			
17	D4	+ 04	44	Segovellauni				
17	H4	+ 06	44	Segovii?				
17	I3	+ 07	45	Segusio	Segusini			
18	C2	+ 05	47	Segobodium?				
20	D4	+ 16	45	Segestica	Siscia			
24	C2	− 09	42	Assegonia				
24	G2	− 05	42	Segisama Iulia				
24	G2	− 05	42	Segisamo				
24	G4	− 05	40	Segovia				
24	H2	− 04	42	Segontia Paramika				
24	*unl*			Segisama Brasaca				
25	B3	− 04	42	Segesamunculum				
25	B4	− 04	41	Segortia Lanka				
25	C4	− 03	41	Segontia				
25	D3	− 02	42	Segia	Segla	Setia		
25	D4	− 02	41	Pagus Gallorum et Segardinenssium				
25	D4	− 02	41	Segeda	Begeda			
25	D4	− 02	41	Segontia				
26	D3	− 07	38	Segida	Restituta Iulia			
26	E4	− 06	37	Segida	Augurina			
26	*unl*	− *06*	*37*	Segovia				
27	C2	− 03	39	Segobriga				
27	D3	− 02	38	Segisa?				
32	F4	+ 10	36	Segermes				
33	*unl*	+ *09*	*35*	Seggo				
35	G2	+ 14	32	Sugolin	Seggera			
39	E5	+ 09	44	Segesta (Tigulliorum)	Tigullia			
47	B2	+ 12	38	Emporion Segestanon				
47	B3	+ 12	37	Aquae Segestanae	Aquae *Pacatianae	Aquae *Phimianae	Aquae *Pincianae
47	B3	+ 12	37	(S)Egesta	Egesta			
69	C3	+ 35	33	Segeira				
82	A3	+ 30	18	Segasa	Segusa			

24C2 *Assegonia* could contain *ad-seg-. 24unl *Segisama Brasaca* is given as the homeland of a legionary on CIL II 4157 but has not been identified (Tovar, *Tarraconensis*, p. 346; cf. OPEL iv, 208). 25cn. *Sekisanos* [recte *Sekisamos*] is etymologically the same but unidentified (TIR K-30, pp. 209–10). 25cn. *Sekaisa* is the same as 25D4 *Segeda* (see Gorrochategui, 'Ptolemy's Aquitania and the Ebro valley', p. 148) and 25cn. *Sekia* is the same as 25D3 *Segia* (TIR K-30, p. 207). For Ptolemy's *Segodounon* in Germania Magna (+ 8/50) see under *dūno-* above; it is included on **Map 12.25**.

Formally inadmissible

84	*unl*	Thys**seg**etae
88	*unl*	Mo**seg**a

Seno- 'old' (OI *sen*, W *hen*)

PNPG Celtic Elements s.v. *seno-*; DLG s.v. *senos*; De Bernardo Stempel, 'Ptolemy's Celtic Italy and Ireland', pp. 91, 94 and 104.

String SEN (excluding SENT, q.v.)

Formally admissible (24)

2	B3	− 08	52	**Sen**os fl.	
6	*unl*			**Sen**a	
7	B3	− 05	48	**Sen**a Ins.	Samnis Ins.
8	*unl*	*− 05*	*51*	Leuca fl.	(Leugo)**Sen**a fl.
11	C4	+ 02	48	**Sen**ones	
12	B4	+ 08	48	Vicus **Sen**ot(ensis)	
14	G1	+ 01	47	**Sen**aparia?	
17	D5	+ 04	44	**Sen**omagos	
20	B5	+ 14	44	**Sen**ia	
42	D1	+ 12	43	**Sen**ones	
42	E1	+ 13	43	**Sen**a fl.	
42	E1	+ 13	43	**Sen**a Gallica	
45	*unl*	*+ 17*	*40*	**Sen**um	
65	G4	+ 31	36	***Sen**nea?	
69	C4	+ 35	32	**Sen**nabris	Ginnabris
75	D3	+ 30	28	**Sen**okomis	
75	D3	+ 30	28	**Sen**ekeleu	
75	*unl*			**Sen**epsau	
75	*unl*			**Sen**epta	
75	*unl*			**Sen**nis	
77	*unl*			**Sen**amontai	
77	*unl*			**Sen**inebis	
77	*unl*			**Sen**is	
98	*unl*			Sina	**Sen**a

It has been suggested that *Sinomagi* (TP) at + 1/52 may belong with *seno-* (cf. PNRB, p. 456, and see s.v. *sito-* below), but is not included on **Map 12.20**; there was a quite distinct element *sīno-* (KPP, p. 53).

Formally inadmissible (some clearly Latin)

31	F4	+ 06	36	Fundus **Sen**eci(...)	
53	B2	+ 29	41	**Sen**ex Marinus	
63	B4	+ 32	38	***Sen**zousa	
77	D1	+ 30	27	**Sen**kyrkis	
77	D2	+ 30	27	**Sen**oabis	
77	F3	+ 31	26	Apa **Sen**outhou, Mon.	
77	*unl*			Seleslais	**Sen**aslais
77	*unl*			**Sen**atholthis	
77	*unl*			**Sen**berris	
80	inset	+ 32	23	Abaton	**Sen**met

SENTU- 'PATH' (OI *SÉT*, W *HYNT*)

AILR and PNPG Celtic Elements s.v. *sentu-*; DLG s.v. *sentu-*.

String SENT

Formally admissible (8)

9	D6	− 04	54	Gabro**sent**um
11	H2	+ 07	50	[**Sent**iacum]?
16	B2	+ 06	43	**Sent**ii
24	F4	− 06	40	**Sent**ice
42	D2	+ 12	43	**Sent**inum
44	*unl*	*+ 15*	*41*	**Sent**ianum
73	*unl*			**Sent**etes
75	*unl*			**Sent**o

Formally inadmissible

8	*unl*			Clau**sent**um
42	B3	+ 11	42	Vi**sent**ium
45	*unl*			Ur**sent**ini
46	D3	+ 16	39	Con**sent**ia
75	*unl*			**Sent**rempaei
80	B2	+ 32	25	T**sent**i

I assume that *Clausentum* (8unl) should be analysed *Claus-entum* (cf. *Claus-onna* > Clausonne and *Claus-etia* in France) rather than *Clau-sentum* (see PNRB, pp. 308–9 and 364–65; AILR Possibly Celtic Elements s.v. *clau-*).

SĪDO- 'SEAT, TUMULUS' (OI *síd*)

AILR and PNPG Celtic Elements s.v. {si:do-}.

String SID (omitting *Praesidium, Praesidae*)

Formally admissible (31 – since '42 *unl* Vesidia' duplicates the preceding entry)

3	*unl*			Kanasida		
3	*unl*			Sidodone		
6	*unl*			Silas fl.	Side fl.	
9	E6	− 03	54	Virosidum		
14	*unl*	*+01*	*44*	Vosidum		
18	B2	+ 04	47	Sidoloucum	Sidotoco	
26	E5	− 06	36	Asido	Asido Caesarina	
28	B5	− 06	34	Thamusida		
28	C5	− 06	34	Tocolosida		
41	*unl*	*+ 10*	*43*	Vesidia fl.		
42	*unl*			Vesidia fl.		
44	F3	+ 14	41	Sidicini		
44	F3	+ 14	41	Teanum Sidicinum		
45	D3	+ 16	40	Silvium	Sidis	
55	C3	+ 22	38	Side		
55	*unl*	*+ 23*	*38*	Sidous		
56	D4	+ 26	38	Sidoussa? Ins.		
58	E2	+ 23	37	Sidous		
58	E5	+ 23	36	Side		
59	*unl*	*+ 23*	*37*	Sidertos		
62	F2	+ 31	39	Konsidiana Choria		
65	B5	+ 29	36	Sidyma		
65	E5	+ 30	36	Siderous Pr.		
65	E5	+ 30	36	Siderous Limen	Posidarisous?	
65	F4	+ 31	36	Side		
66	D2	+ 33	37	*Sidamaria		
69	B2	+ 35	33	Sidon	Col. Aurelia Pia	
83	B4	+ 36	27	Sidenoi		
87	C3	+ 37	41	Polemonion	Side	Sidene
87	C4	+ 37	40	Sidenos fl.		
87	*unl*			Tzacher	Sideroun	
96	C2	+ 54	37	Sideris? fl.	Sarnios? fl.	

Asido could contain **ad-*. The above is an extensive but heterogeneous-looking list which I have not considered worth mapping.

Formally inadmissible

4	*unl*			Isidis Portus		
4	*unl*			Isidos ins.		
5	*unl*			Kassida		
6	A4	+64	25	Pasirae	Parsidai	Parsirai
18	B3	+04	46	Desideratus, Mon.	Gurthonense Mon.	
20	C5	+15	44	Sidrona		
22	B4	+24	44	Rusidava		
22	*unl*			Bassidina		
22	*unl*			Residina		
22	*unl*			Tamasidaua		
23	*unl*			Tamasidaua		
32	A4	+07	36	Vasidice?		
32	E3	+09	36	Thisiduo		
32	*unl*			Tisidium		
33	*unl*			Autipsida		
34	*unl*			Vasidice		
35	D1	+11	33	Pisida	Fisida	
42	*unl*			Usidicani		
46	*unl*			Besidiae		
51	A5	+23	39	Poseidonion Pr.	Posideum Pr.	
56	*unl*			Posidea		
59	B3	+23	37	Eiresidai		
60	*unl*			Prepsidai		
61	F3	+27	37	Si(b)de		
65	B4	+29	36	Kissidai? Pr.		
65	E2	+30	37	Seleucia	Claudioseleucia	Seleucia Sidera
65	E3	+30	37	Pisidia		
67	*unl*			Marcoupolis Thera	Gausitha	Charax Sidou
68	A2	+35	35	Posideion		
74	E2	+31	31	Isidos Polis tou Sebennytou		
77	*unl*			Alasideos		
77	*unl*			Isidorou		
78	*unl*			Isidis Ins.		
80	*unl*			Isidiou Oros		
81	*unl*			Sidopt		
84	*unl*			Topsidas fl.		
89	D1	+41	39	Tharsidarate		
89	D1	+41	39	Tharsidarate		
94	A5	+50	28	[Bushahr]	Antiocheia Persidos?	
94	B3	+51	30	Persides?	Susidae?	Pylae

SITO- 'LENGTH?' (OI *SITH-*, W *HYD*)[58]

AILR Celtic Elements s.v. *sito-*, following Jackson, 'On some Romano-British place-names', p. 58, on *Sitomago* (AI 480.1). Rivet & Smith (PNRB, p. 456), say that 'this appears to be a unique case of this word in ancient toponymy (compare perhaps for sense **litano-*)' and prefer *Sino-* as in TP. They may be correct, although see Lacroix, *Noms*, p. 114.

[58] Cf. Isaac, 'Welsh *byw*, *byd*, *hyd*'.

String Sit (case-sensitive)

Formally admissible (13), assuming -*tt*- is allowable

2	H2	+24	58	Sitones?				
5	*unl*			Sittokatis				
8	*unl*	+*01*	*52*	*Sitomagus				
18	*unl*	+*03*	*46*	Sitillia				
29	*unl*	−*02*	*35*	Sita Col.?				
32	*unl*			Sitipensis Plebs				
62	A3	+28	39	*Sittena?				
84	*unl*			Sittakenoi				
89	C3	+40	37	Si(t)ai	Siteon Chiphas			
91	F4	+44	33	Apolloniatis	Sittacene	Apollonia	Arbelitis	Palaestine
91	*unl*			Sittace				
94	B5	+51	28	Sitakos? fl.				
94	*unl*			Sitioganus				

In TP *Sitillia* is located between *Aquis Bormonis* and *Pocrinio* and the *Atlas* tentatively places both of these in square A3 of Map 18 (= +3/46).[59] I do not map these disparate *Sit(t)*- names, accepting that Rivet & Smith's view, quoted above, is probably correct.

Formally inadmissible

22		*unl*			'Sitioenta'
31		C4	+05	36	Sitifis
51		B4	+23	40	Sithonia
51		H1	+26	41	Sithones
51		*unl*			Sithone
75		D3	+30	28	Sitheus
89		*unl*			Sitrae
91		*unl*			Sitha

Tarvo- 'BULL' (OI *TARB*, W *TARW*)

AILR and PNPG Celtic Elements s.v. *taruo*-; GPN, pp. 262–63; DLG s.v. *taruos*; VCIE, p. 336.

[59] Weber, *Kommentar*, p. 60, tentatively emends to *Sicilia*. Holder ii, 1590, identifies *Sitillia* with Chizeuil, arr. Charolles, dép. Saône-et-Loire.

String TARV, TAROU (this string excludes, however, instances where the Celtic element may have been demetathesized or Latinized to *taur-*, cf. GPN, p. 261).

Formally admissible (4)

9	D2	− 04	58	*Tarou**edounon	Orkas Akra	
11	C2	+ 02	50	**Tarv**enna	Tarouanna	Tervanna
19	B3	+ 09	46	*Tarv**essedum		
40	C1	+ 12	45	**Tarv**isium		

Formally inadmissible

68	C2	+ 36	35	**Tarou**tia Emporon
75	D2	+ 30	29	Ibion Eikosipen**tarou**ron?
75	D3	+ 30	28	**Tarou**sebt
75	*unl*			**Tarou**thinou
84	D2	+ 38	46	Pa**tarou**e

Teut-/tout- 'people' (OI *túath*, W *tud*)

PNPG Celtic Elements s.v. *teuto-*, *touto-*, *teutono-*; GPN, p. 268; Evans, 'Celts and Germans', pp. 247–48; DLG s.v. *teuta*, *touta* (and p. 438).

String TEUT, TOUT

Formally admissible (9)

6	C3	+ 74	32	**Tout**apos? fl.
10	D4	+ 07	52	**Teut**oburgiensis? Saltus
10	E2	+ 08	54	**Teut**ones?
12	C3	+ 09	49	**Teut**oni
20	F4	+ 18	45	**Teut**oburgium
37	E2	+ 19	30	Maka**tout**ai
48	D2	+ 09	42	**Tout**elas Bomos
63	*unl*			Ambi**touti**
63	*unl*			**Tout**obodiaci

The last two are Galatian tribes (Pliny 5.146) which cannot be located exactly. For another possible *Touto-* name in Hispania see PNPG Comments s.n. *Tountóbriga*.

Formally inadmissible

10	*unl*			Siatout**anda**	
33	*unl*			Mo**tout**ourioi	
52	C4	+28	40	Mile**tout**eichos?	
56	E3	+27	39	**Teut**hrania	
56	E3	+27	39	**Teut**hras M.	
58	B1	+21	38	**Teut**heas fl.	
58	B2	+21	37	**Tout**hoa fl.	
58	C2	+22	37	**Teut**his	
58	C4	+22	36	**Teut**hrone	
58	*unl*			**Teut**hea	
61	F4	+27	36	**Teut**loussa Ins.	
86	D2	+33	41	Thymena	**Teut**hrania?
88	*unl*			San**tout**a	

The first of these is a ghost-name in Ptolemy 2.11.12, based on misunderstanding *sua tutanda* in Tacitus, *Annals*, 4.73 (see Müller's note).

Tɪɴᴄᴏ- 'ꜰɪʀᴍɴᴇss?' (OI *ᴛᴇ́ᴄ-, ᴛᴇ́ᴄᴀʀ*, W *ᴛᴇɪᴛʜɪ, ᴛʏɴɢʜᴀꜰ*)

AILR Celtic Elements s.v. *tinco-*; Evans, 'Nomina Celtica II', pp. 504–6; KPP, pp. 118–19.

String TINC (TINK not found)

Formally admissible (5)

14	G3	+01	45	Duro**tinc**um?	
14	H2	+02	46	**Tinc**ontium	**Tinc**ollo
17	G3	+06	45	Duro**tinc**um	Durotingum
20	B2	+14	47	Saba**tinc**a	
37	E2	+19	30	**Tinc**ausari	

Formally inadmissible None

Tʀᴇʙᴀ̄ 'ʜᴏᴍᴇ' (OI *ᴛʀᴇʙ*, W *ᴛʀᴇꜰ*)

AILR and PNPG Celtic Elements s.v. *trebo-*; Evans, 'Celts and Germans', p. 244; DLG s.v. *treb-*; cf. Prósper, *Lenguas y religiones prerromanas*, pp. 44 and 508.

String TREB

Formally admissible (17)[60]

8	F3	– 02	51	A**treb**ates	
11	C2	+ 02	50	A**treb**ates	
11	*unl*	*+ 02*	*50*	Fines A**treb**atum	
24	C1	– 09	43	Ar**t**abri	Arro**treb**ae
25	D3	– 02	42	Con**treb**ia Leucada	
25	D4	– 02	41	Con**treb**ia (Belaisca)	
39	E4	+ 09	44	Pagus Ambi**treb**ius	
39	F3	+ 09	45	**Treb**ia fl.	
42	D3	+ 12	42	**Treb**iae	
42	D4	+ 12	42	**Treb**ula Mutuesca	
43	D2	+ 12	41	**Treb**ula Suffenas	
44	D2	+ 13	41	**Treb**a	
44	F2	+ 14	41	'**Treb**ula'	
44	F3	+ 14	41	**Treb**ula Balli(ni)ensium	
44	*unl*	*+ 12*	*41*	**Treb**ium	
65	C5	+ 29	36	**Treb**endai	
65	D4	+ 30	36	**Treb**enna	

See **Map 4.10**.

Formally inadmissible None

Ux- 'HIGH' (OI *ós*, *ÚASAL*, W *UWCH, UCHEL*)

AILR and PNPG Celtic Elements s.v. {u:x-}; DLG s.vv. *uxamos, uxedios, uxellos* (cf. *oxso*-); MLH v/1, pp. 463–65; Hamp, 'Morphologic criteria', pp. 179–80; Isaac, 'Scotland', p. 202.

String Ux, Us, Oux, Ous (case-sensitive) (Ucs, Uks, Oucs, Ouks not found)

Formally admissible (19 – as the coin-legend *Usamus* probably refers to one or other of the two places called (*O*)*uxama*, TIR K-30, p. 249)[61]

6	E5	+ 82	22	**Oux**enton M.	
7	A3	– 06	48	**Ux**antis Ins.	A**x**anthos Ins.
8	E2	– 03	52	**Ux**acona	

---

[60] On the question whether *Arrotrebae* or *Artabri* is correct see García Alonso, *Península Ibérica*, pp. 141–42, and PNPG Comments s.n. *Ártabroi*.

[61] On *Ussubium* cf. AILR Possibly Celtic Elements s.v. *ussu-*. However, at the Munich workshop Prof. P. de Bernardo Stempel suggested *Uss-ubium* 'upper hill' (: OI *ub* 'point', a doubtful word, cf. LEIA s.v.).

9	E6	− 03	54	Uxelodu(nu)m		
9	*unl*	*− 04*	*54*	Uxela		
11	H2	+ 07	50	Usipetes		
14	F4	+ 00	44	Ussubium	Vesubio	
14	G3	+ 01	45	Userca		
14	H4	+ 02	44	Uxellodunum		
21	*unl*	*+ 18*	*48*	**Ous**kenon		
25	B3	− 04	42	**Oux**ama Barka		
25	B4	− 04	41	Uxama (Argaela)		
25	H2	+ 02	43	Usuerva	Husuerbas	Usuerna
25	*cn.*			Usamus		
33	G3	+ 10	34	Usil(l)a	Usula	
45	inset	+ 18	39	Uzentum	**Oux**enton	Augentum
42	*unl*			Usidicani		
48	A3	+ 08	39	Usel(l)is		
93	F1	+ 49	32	**Oux**ioi	Oxii	
94	*unl*			**Oux**ioi	Uxii	

On the forms of the name *Usipetes* see PNPG Comments s.n. *Ouispoi*. 21unl
Ouskenon (varr. *Oueskenon*, *Ouskainon*) is a *polis* of the Iazyges listed by
Ptolemy (3.7.2) at his long. 43° 15′, lat. 48° 20′. Since he places *Partiskon*,
which is at our long. 20° 10′, lat. 46° 20′ (Map 21C3), at his long. 45°, lat.
46° 40′, *Ouskenon* should be around our long. 18°, lat. 48°, or a little to the
east.[62] It has been suggested that the *Usidicani* (42unl) in Umbria (Pliny
3.114) should be restored to *Usdicani*, a name which recurs in Thrace; see
Zehnacker's edition, p. 239 (cf. Ptolemy, 3.11.6: *Ousdikêsikê*; CIL VI 32582:
a *civis Usdicensis* in Rome, perhaps from Thrace), Beševliev, pp. 76, 87 and
131, and Falileyev, '*Tylis*', p. 118.

See **Map 4.11.**

Formally inadmissible (omitting 9 examples of Greek *Ousia* 'estate' in
Cyprus and Egypt in the area of Maps 72 and 75)

1	F3	+ 14	37	Ustica Ins.	
25	*cn.*			Usekerte	
30	*unl*			Usar fl.	
44	G2	+ 14	41	Uscosium?	
49	C2	+ 20	41	Uscana	
69	B4	+ 35	32	Usha	
79	*unl*			Pmoun **Ous**ire	
84	*unl*			Uspe	
97	D2	+ 58	37	[Ustuva]	Astauene

[62] North or north-east of the Danube, of course. PNPG puts it at + 20/46. Strang, 'Lower
Danube region', calculated + 19.44/47.78. For *cen(n)* names see GPN, pp. 175–77.

Usekerte probably duplicates '25 *unl* Osicerda' (TIR K-30, p. 168; PNPG Comments s.n. *Osikérda* and Possibly Celtic Elements s.vv. {cerda:-} and *osi-*).

VELLAUNO- 'GOVERNOR' (OI *FOLLAIMNIGID?*)

PNPG Celtic Elements s.v. *uello-, uela-, uellauno-*; GPN, pp. 276–77; DLG s.v. *uellaunos*.

String VELLAUN, VELAUN, OUELAUN (cf. on *alauno-* above) (UELLAUN, UELAUN, OUELLAUN, OUELLAOUN, OUELAOUN not found)

Formally admissible (5 – as the two *Vellaunodunum* are duplicates; cf. under *dūno-* above):

8	G3	– 01	51	Catuvellauni
8	*unl*	– 03	50	Bolvelaunio
11	*unl*	+02	47	**Vellaun**odunum
14	*unl*	+02	47	**Vellaun**odunum
16	*unl*	+06	44	**Ouelaun**ioi
17	D4	+04	44	Sego**vellaun**i

See **Map 12.11**.

Formally inadmissible None

VENTĀ 'MARKET?' (W -*WENT*)[63]

AILR and PNPG Celtic Elements s.v. {uenta:-}; PNRB, pp. 262–65; Schumacher, *Primärverben*, p. 368.

String VENT, UENT (omitting examples of *Confluentes*), OUENT

---

[63] On W -*went*, as in *cadwent* and *Llinwent*, see Sims-Williams, 'Common Celtic, Gallo-Brittonic and Insular Celtic'. W *mynwent* 'graveyard', on the other hand, is a loan from Latin; for the syncope already in Latin note CIL XIII 659: MONMENT.

Formally admissible (8)

8	E3	− 03	51	**Vent**a			
8	F2	− 02	52	Banna**vent**a			
8	F3	− 02	51	**Vent**a			
8	I2	+ 01	52	**Vent**a			
9	D6	− 04	54	*Glanno**vent**a	Glannibanta		
11	D1	+ 03	51	*Ga**nuent**a?			
19	E3	+ 12	46	Tilia**vent**um (Maius) fl.	Tilia**vent**um Maius fl.	Tilia**vent**um Minus fl.	
26	F4	− 05	37	**Vent**ipo			

The river-name *Tiliaventum* (modern Tagliamento) is dubious, especially as the ancient spellings also have *b* and *m* (see Zehnacker's edition of Pliny Book 3, p. 250). It is included, however, on **Map 12.12**.

Formally inadmissible[64]

8	D2	− 04	52	**Louent**inon?			
8	D3	− 04	51	*A**vent**ius fl.			
8	*unl*			De**vent**ia Statio			
8	*unl*			*Der**vent**io fl.			
9	D6	− 04	54	Der**vent**io			
9	E6	− 03	54	Dor**vant**ium fl.	[Der**vent**io] fl.		
9	G6	− 01	54	Der**vent**io			
9	G7	− 01	53	[Der**vent**io] fl.			
15	D2	+ 04	43	Dr**uent**ia fl.			
18	E3	+ 07	46	Col. A**vent**icum	Col. Pia Flavia		
					Constans Emerita		
					Helvetiorum Foederata		
20	A4	+ 13	45	Pi**quent**um			
25	H4	+ 02	41	Col. Barcino	Col. Iulia Augusta	Paterna Fa**vent**ia	
26	*unl*			Fa**vent**ia	Vesci		
30	E3	+ 02	36	Casae Cal**vent**i?			
39	D4	+ 08	44	Io**vent**io Mons			
39	H3	+ 10	45	Bene**vent**um			
40	B3	+ 11	44	[Vicus A**vent**ia]			
40	B4	+ 11	44	Fa**vent**ia			
40	D1	+ 12	45	Li**quent**ia fl.			
40	D1	+ 12	45	Portus Li**quent**iae			
41	C1	+ 10	44	'A**vent**ia' fl.			
42	B1	+ 11	43	Cas**uent**illani			
42	C3	+ 12	42	Velzna	*Volsinii Veteres	Urbi**vent**us	
42	E2	+ 13	43	*Cl**uent**us fl.			
42	E3	+ 13	42	Tr**uent**us fl.			
42	F3	+ 13	42	Castrum Tr**uent**inum			
42	*unl*			Vis**uent**ani			

[64] Despite PNRB, p. 265, on *Beneventum*; cf. VCIE, p. 53, and Kitson, 'River-names', p. 80.

44	G2	+14	41	Terventum		
44	G3	+14	41	Beneventum	Maleventum	Benebentos
44	*unl*			Beneventanus Pagus		
44	*unl*			Carventum		
45	D3	+16	40	Casuentus fl.		
45	*unl*			Fratuertium	Fratuentium	

V̄ERBĀ 'COW, DEER' (OI *FERB(B)*)

AILR Celtic Elements s.v. *uerbo-*; cf. IEW, pp. 326 and 1170; NWÄI, pp. 77, n. 15, and 215; Vendryes, 'Latin *vervēx*'.

String VERB, UERB, OUERB

Formally admissible (6)

9	F7	− 02	53	**Verb**eia fl.	
11	D3	+ 03	49	**Verb**inum	Vironum
28	C5	− 06	34	**Ouerb**ikai	
31	*unl*	*+ 07*	*36*	**Verb**alis	
39	D2	+ 08	45	**Verb**anus L.	
65	D3	+ 30	37	***Ouerb**e	

On *Ouerbikai* (perhaps = *Ouer-bikai* however) see Chapter 10 below.

Formally inadmissible (see next entry)

25	H2	+ 02	43	Usuerva	Hus**uerb**as	Usuerna

VERNO- 'ALDER, SWAMP' (OI *FERN*, W *GWERN*)

AILR and PNPG Celtic Elements s.v. *uerno-*; PNRB, pp. 494–95; DLG s.v. *uerna*.

String VERN, UERN, OUERN

Formally admissible (9)

8	I3	+ 00	51	*Durovernum		
8	*unl*			**Vern**alis		
14	F1	+ 00	47	**Vern**aus	**Vern**adum?	
14	I3	+ 03	45	Augustonemetum	Civitas Ar**vern**orum	
14	*unl*	+ 01	44	Ale**vern**acum		
17	B2	+ 03	45	Ar**vern**i	Ar**vern**ia	
25	H2	+ 02	43	Usuerva	Husuerbas	Us**uern**a
25	G2	+ 01	43	**Vern**us Sol		
25	H3	+ 02	42	**Vern**odubrum fl.		

Vernalis was somewhere in south-west Britain (PNRB, p. 495). *Usuerna* is an error (Holder iii, 55, is correct in giving *Usuerua* as the reading of TP) and it is therefore omitted from **Map 12.13**.[65] *Vernus Sol*, attested only in AI 458.2 (*Verno Sole*), has been taken to be a Celtic–Latin hybrid (Nègre i, §5205), but Isaac's Celtic element *soli-* 'hall?, homestead?' (AILR Celtic Elements) is a possibility.

See **Map 12.13**.

Formally inadmissible[66]

2	B3	− 06	52	**Iouern**ikos Okeanos	Hibernikos Okeanos
2	B3	− 08	51	**Iouern**oi	
8	F2	− 02	52	'**Vern**emeto'	
14	F4	+ 00	44	Pompeiacum	**Vern**emetis
24	C3	− 09	41	Quar**quern**i	
24	D3	− 08	41	Aquae Quar**quern**ae	
25	*unl*			**Vern**emetis	**Vern**antes
44	D3	+ 13	41	Pri**vern**um	
44	E1	+ 13	42	*La**vern**ae	
44	F4	+ 14	40	A**vern**us L.	
44	*unl*			La**vern**ium	

VESU- 'EXCELLENT' (OI *FEB*, W *GWIW*)

AILR and PNPG Celtic Elements s.v. *uesu-*; DLG s.v. *uesu-*.

String VESU (UESU, UESOU, OUESU, OUESOU not found)

---

[65] The etymology of *Usuerua* is obscure, however; Dr G. R. Isaac suggested to me the bare possibility of **uts-swerwa* (cf. OI *serb*, W *chwerw*, 'bitter').
[66] On *Vernantes* see *nantu-* above.

Formally admissible (6)

14	F3	+ 00	45	**Vesu**nna	Petrucorii
14	F4	+ 00	44	Ussubium	**Vesu**bio
16	D1	+ 07	44	**Vesu**biani	
17	I4	+ 07	44	**Vesu**lus M.	
44	F4	+ 14	40	**Vesu**vius M.	
44	*unl*			'Maesulus' qui et '**Vesu**lus' M.	

The last (in Campania) may be due to confusion with Vesuvius according to *Map-by-Map Directory* i, 661.

Formally inadmissible None

VIC- 'FIGHT' (OI *FICHID*, W *AMYGAF*)

AILR and PNPG Celtic Elements s.v. *uic-*, *uico-*; GPN, p. 285; DLG s.v. *uic(o)-, -uices*.

String OUIK, VICA, VICE, VICI, VICO (VIKI, VIKE, OUICI, OUICE not found); VIC was not searched to avoid Latin *vicus*.[67]

Formally admissible (14)

8	D2	− 04	52	Ordo**vic**es	
9	E5	− 03	55	*Verco**vic**ium	
9	F6	− 02	54	Gabranto**uik**es	
9	F6	− 02	54	Longo**vic**ium	
9	G6	− 01	54	Gabranto**uik**on Kolpos	
9	*unl*	− 01	53	Delgo**vic**ia	
11	A4	+ 00	48	Eburo**vic**es	
14	C1	− 03	47	Herios fl.	**Vic**inonia fl.
14	F3	+ 00	45	Lemo**vic**es	
14	G2	+ 01	46	Cambio**vic**enses?	
24	*unl*	− 08	43	**Ouik**a	
25	C5	− 03	40	Erca**vic**a	
40	B1	+ 11	45	**Vic**etia	
86	*unl*	+ 33	40	'**Vic**iu'	

25unl *Ergaovia/Ergavcia* (*sic Map-by-Map Directory*) does not appear in the above list owing to the misprint (read *Ergaouika* with Ptolemy 2.6.66, cf. *Erguti* in Rav. 312.2). It is an unlocated place among the Vascones, different from 25C5 *Ercavica*; see Tovar, *Tarraconensis*, p. 397, Gorrochategui,

---

[67] Forms with BIC for VIC (cf. pp. 289–90 below) are not covered here. On names in *-vic(i)a*, which may be of different etymology, cf. GPN, p. 282, PNRB, p. 332, and PNPG Possibly Celtic Elements s.v. {u(o)ica:-}.

'Establishment and analysis', p. 162, PNPG Possibly Celtic Elements s.vv. {erca:-}, *erco-*; *erga-*, {erga:-}, *ergo-*; and {u(o)ica:-}, and VCIE, pp. 458–59. See **Map 4.12.**

Formally inadmissible

14	F1	+00	47	Na**vic**ellis	
15	*unl*			Ad **Vice**simum	
20	D3	+16	46	Ad **Vice**simum	
21	C5	+20	44	'No**vici**ani'	
24	*unl*			**Vica**ni Dercinoassedenses	
25	G2	+01	43	Ad **Vice**simum	
25	H3	+02	42	Ad **Vice**simum	
31	D4	+05	36	**C**ui**cul**	
33	*unl*			**Vico**ateriensis Plebs	
42	C4	+12	42	Ad **Vice**simum	
42	E4	+13	42	Aequi**cul**i	
45	B2	+15	41	Tri**vici** Villa?	
45	C4	+15	40	'**Vico** Mendicoleo'	Mendile(g)io
46	E2	+16	39	Ad **Vice**simum	
49	B2	+19	41	Olcinium	**Vici**nium
49	D1	+21	42	'**Vici**anum'	
89	E4	+42	36	**Vica**t?	

The *Vicinium* under 49B2 is better attested as *Olcinium* (cf. Zehnacker's edition of Pliny 3.144, p. 272) and 49D1 *'Vicianum'* is probably corrupt for *'Viclanum'* or similar (see TIR K-34, pp. 93 and 131, and below, p. 257).

VINDO- 'WHITE' (OI *FIND*, W *GWYN*)

AILR and PNPG Celtic Elements s.v. *uindo-*; DLG s.v. *uindos*.

String VIND, OUIND (UIND not found apart from OUIND)

Formally admissible (29)

6	D5	+75	22	**Ouind**ion M.	Lymodus? M.
8	A1	−07	53	Bou**ouind**a fl.	
8	E4	−03	50	**Vind**ocladia	
8	*unl*	*−02*	*51*	*****Vind**omium	
9	C5	−05	55	**Ouind**ogara Kolpos	
9	E6	−03	54	**Vind**olanda	
9	*unl*	*−07*	*54*	**Ouind**eris fl.	
9	F6	−02	54	**Vind**omora	

9	F6	− 02	54	**Vind**ovala		
11	A4	+ 00	48	**Ouind**inon	Subdinnum	Cenomani
12	D4	+ 10	48	Augusta **Vind**elicum	Aelia Augusta	
12	D4	+ 10	48	**Vind**elici		
13	B4	+ 16	48	Mun. **Vind**obona		
13	B4	+ 16	48	**Vind**obona		
14	B1	− 04	47	**Vind**ilis Ins.		
14	C1	− 03	47	**Vind**unit(t)a Ins.		
14	G1	+ 01	47	**Vind**ocinum		
14	I2	+ 03	46	*****Vind**iciacum		
15	D1	+ 04	44	**Vind**alium?		
15	E2	+ 05	43	**Vind**asca		
15	E2	+ 05	43	**Vind**elicus fl.	Soulgas fl.	
18	F2	+ 08	47	**Vind**onissa		
20	G2	+ 19	47	**Vind**onianus Vicus		
21	D7	+ 21	42	'**Vind**enis'		
24	*unl*	*− 06*	*42*	**Vind**ius M.		
25	B3	− 04	42	**Vind**eleia		
42	*unl*	*+ 12*	*43*	**Vind**enates		
62	H2	+ 32	39	Gordion	**Vind**ia?	
66	*unl*	*+ 33*	*36*	**Vind**emis		

Vindenates (CIL XI 4209), an Umbrian people, are *Vindinates* in Pliny 3.114 (see note on p. 239 of Zehnacker's edition). '*Vindenis*' (TP) is *Ouendenis* in Ptolemy 3.9.4 (cf. PNPG Comments s.n.), but *Vindinis* in Rav. 205.2 supports TP.

See **Map 4.13.**

Formally inadmissible None

Viro- 'MAN' (OI *FER*, W. *GŴR*)

AILR and PNPG Celtic Elements s.v. *uiro-*; GPN, p. 288; DLG s.v. *uiros* – some names may contain **wīro-* 'true' (cf. PNPG Possibly Celtic Elements s.v. {ui:ro-}).

String VIR, UIR, or OUIR plus vowel (note that this excludes the *Virdo fl.* in GPN, p. 288)

Formally admissible (18; or 17, as the coin-legend *Uirouias* may refer to *Virovesca*, TIR K-30, p. 247)

6	D4	+ 76	27	**Vir**ata
8	E2	− 03	52	*****Vir**oconium
9	D2	− 04	58	**Ouir**ouedroum Akron
9	E6	− 03	54	**Vir**osidum
11	D2	+ 03	50	**Vir**oviacum
11	D3	+ 03	49	**Vir**omandis

11	D3	+03	49	Augusta **Vir**omanduorum		
11	D3	+03	49	**Vir**omandui		
11	D3	+03	49	Verbinum		**Vir**onum
11	F3	+05	49	**Vir**iodunum		Veriodunum
15	C2	+04	43	*****Vir**innae?		
18	*unl*	*+06*	*46*	**Vir**omagus		Uromago
20	B3	+14	46	**Vir**unum		
25	B3	−04	42	**Vir**ovesca		
25	*cn.*			**Uir**ouias		
48	C2	+08	42	**Ouir**iballon Akron		
87	A4	+35	40	**Vir**asia		
88	C4	+44	40	Arma**ouir**a		

In the case of *Uromago* cf. GPN, p. 288, and AILR Celtic Elements s.v. {u:ro-}.

See **Map 4.14**.

Formally inadmissible

| 14 | I3 | +03 | 45 | S. **Quir**icus, Mon. | | |
| 27 | B4 | −04 | 37 | Iliberri | **Elvir**a | Municipium Florentinum |

Volco- 'HAWK?' (W GWALCH 'HAWK'? OR CF. OI FOLC 'WET (WEATHER)'?)

AILR and PNPG Possibly Celtic Elements s.v. *uolco-*; DLG s.v. *uolcos*; cf. Anreiter, *Die vorrömischen Namen Pannoniens*, p. 142 (on *Valco*); Rübekeil, pp. 92–108 and 414–20; Koch, 'Brân, Brennos', pp. 12–13.

String VOLC (UOLC, UOLK, VOLK, OUOLC, OUOLK not found)

Formally admissible (5)

15	B3	+03	43	Taurus	**Volc**arum Stagna	
15	B2	+03	43	**Volc**ae Arecomici		
25	H2	+02	43	Carcas(s)o	Col. Iulia	Carcasum **Volc**arum Tectosagarum
25	F2	+00	43	(**Volc**ae) Tectosages	Tectosages	Tectosagi
45	B3	+15	40	**Volc**ei		

Volgum at 20E3 (+17/46) may belong here (*Valco* in AI 233.3); see below, p. 210. The *Atlas* omits *Ouolkera* in Ptolemy 2.16.2, possibly identical with *Ad Turres* (20B4 = 14/45).[68]

---

[68] PNPG Comments s.n.

Formally inadmissible None

It seems wise to add a 'health warning' here: *It is not implied that all 'Celtic-looking' names listed as 'formally admissible' in this Chapter are in fact Celtic!*

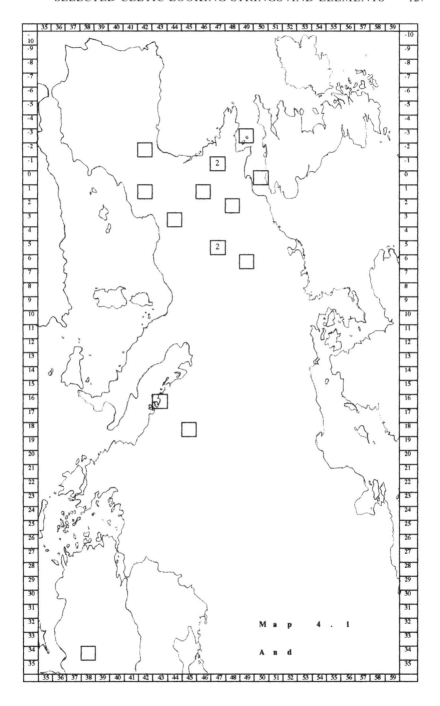

Map 4 . 1

And

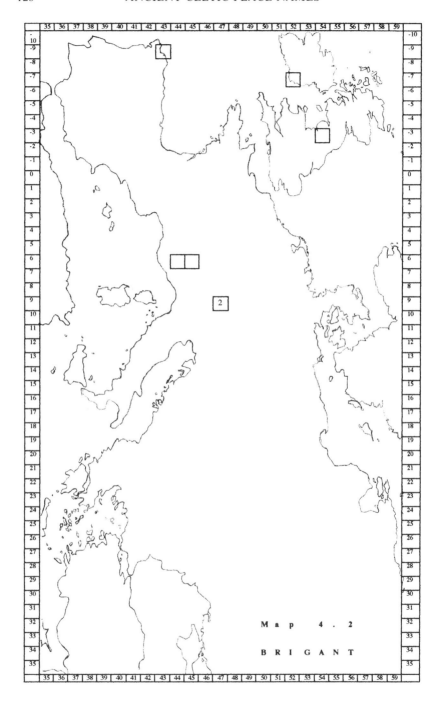

Map 4.2

BRIGANT

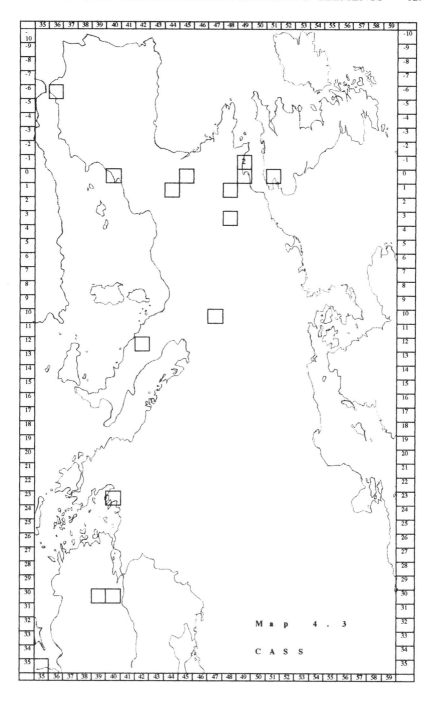

Map 4 . 3

C A S S

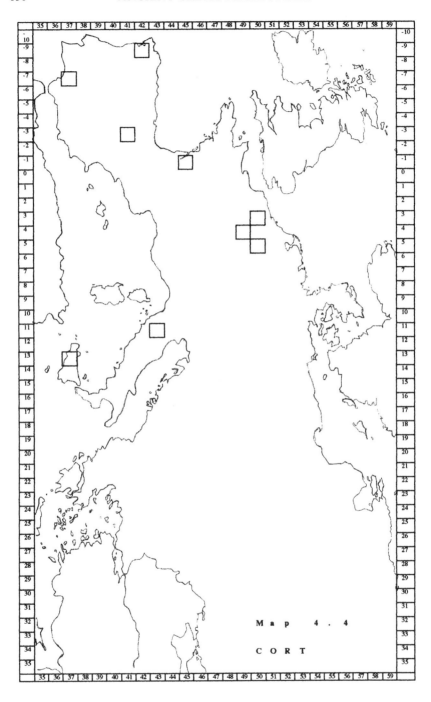

Map 4 . 4

CORT

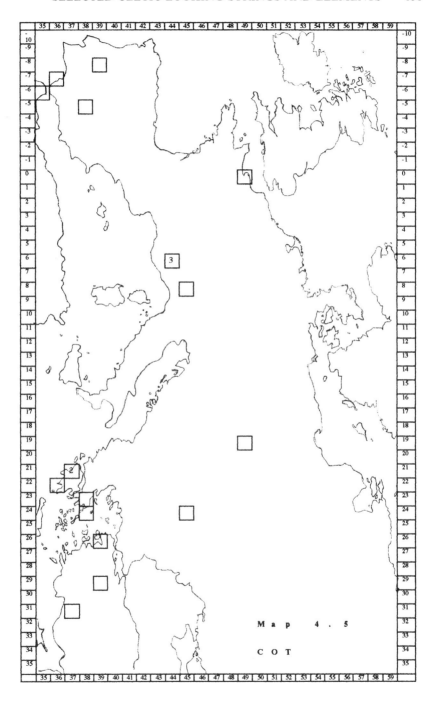

Map   4 . 5

C O T

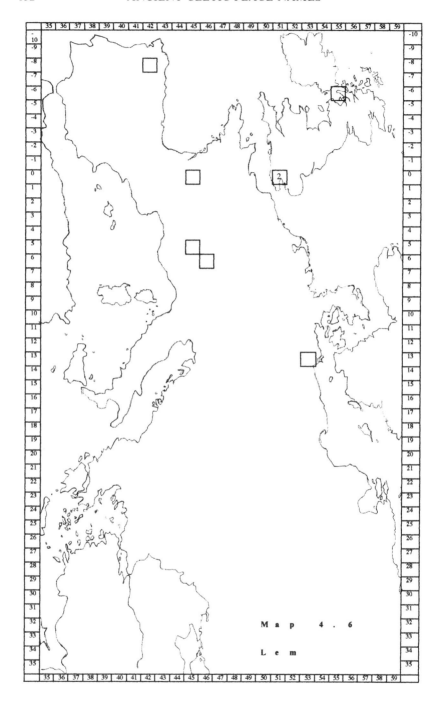

Map 4.6

Lem

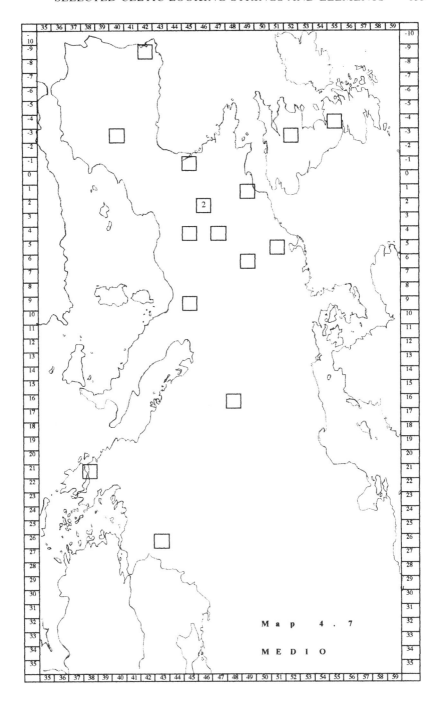

Map 4 . 7

M E D I O

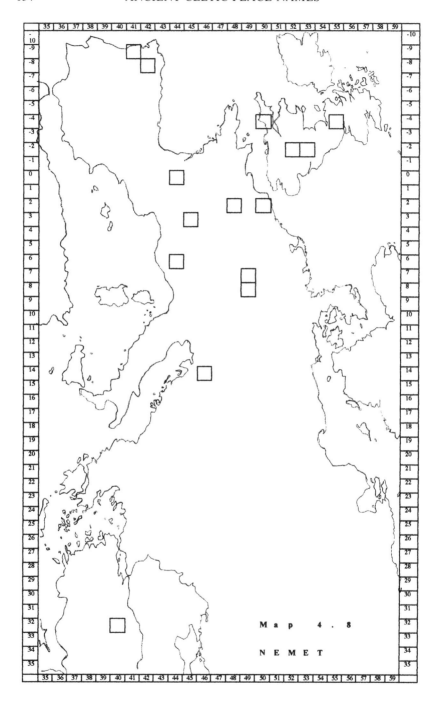

Map 4 . 8

N E M E T

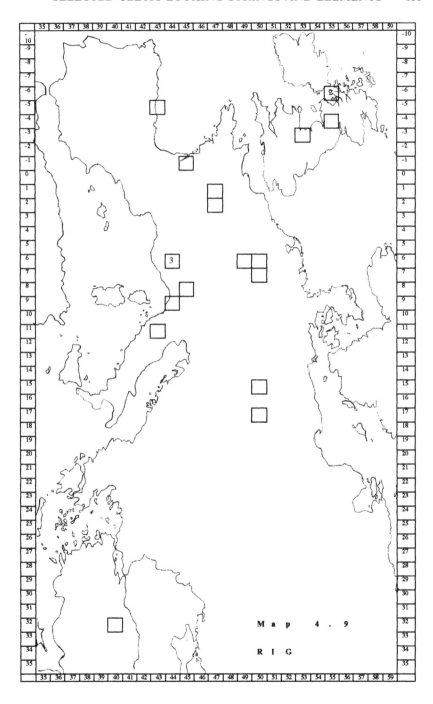

Map 4 . 9

R I G

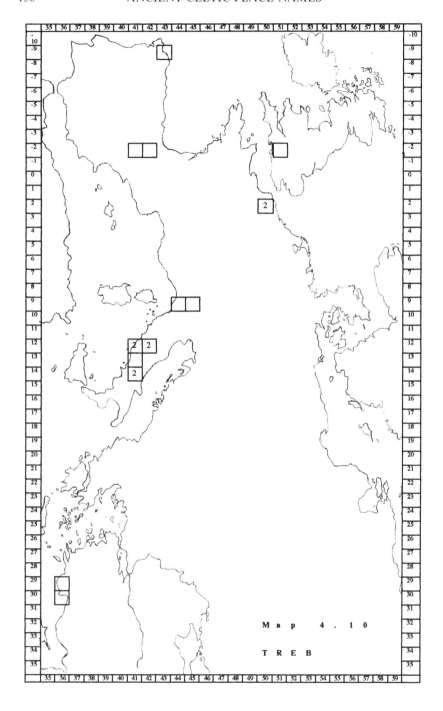

Map 4.10

TREB

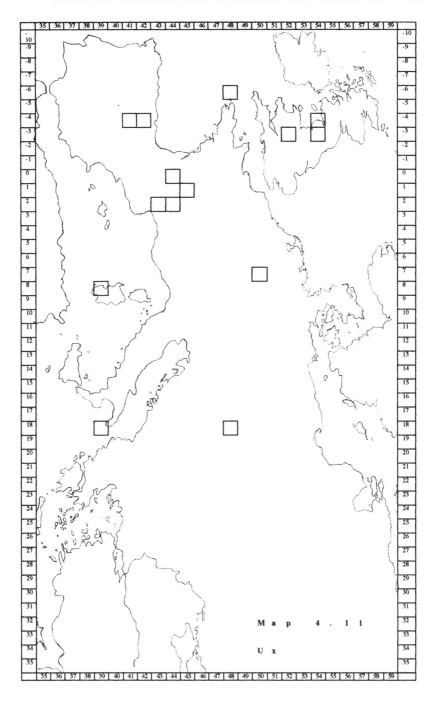

Map 4.11

Ux

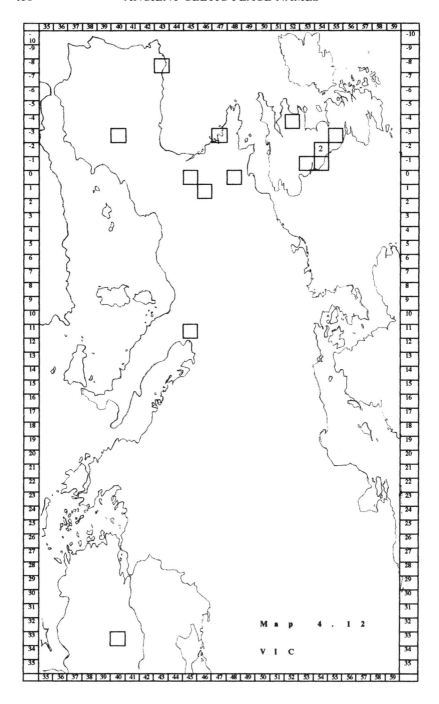

Map 4 . 12

V I C

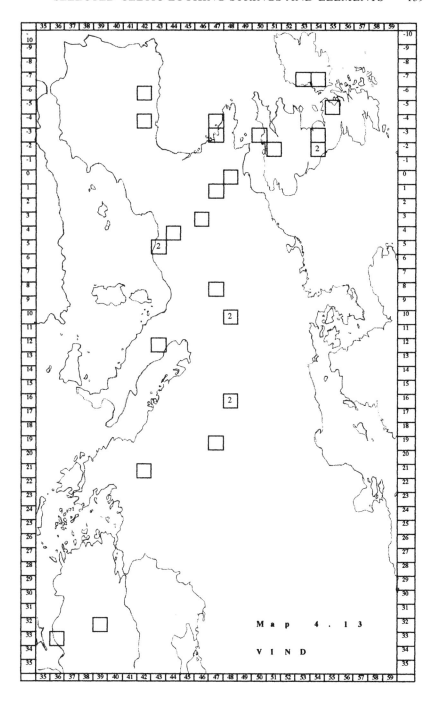

Map 4 . 1 3

V I N D

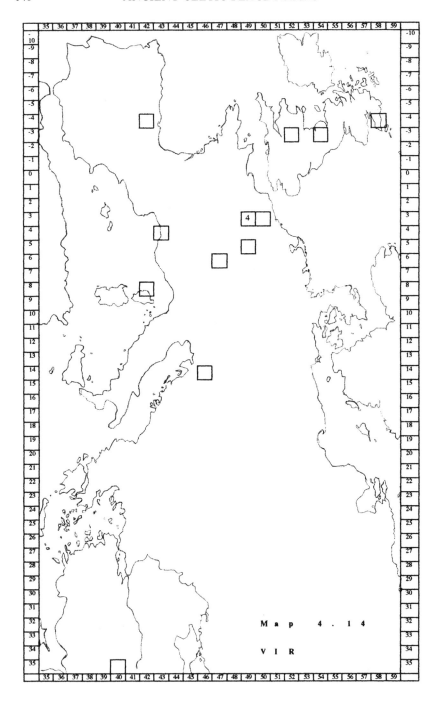

Map 4 . 14

V I R

THE DISTRIBUTION OF THE SELECTED CELTIC-LOOKING ELEMENTS

5.1 FORMALLY ADMISSIBLE DATA FROM CHAPTER 4

Eliminating the 'formally inadmissible' names, we are left with 1,212 lines of 'admissible' data in Chapter 4 above.[1] Of these we can eliminate 23 from further discussion (see Table 5.1) as being duplicates within the *Barrington* data (see Chapter 4).[2] The remaining data is sorted in Table 5.2 below by longitude and latitude, with the important exceptions that names south of latitude 35 and east of +35 longitude are omitted, as are names which

Table 5.1 Duplicates

21866	5	*unl*			Sala**riga**		
Fra.	14	*unl*	*+02*	*47*	Vellauno**dunum**		
Fra.	14	*unl*	*+02*	*47*	**Vellaun**odunum		
22479	16	*unl*			**Nemet**urii		
22824	22	*unl*			**Rata**kensioi		
Hisp.	24	*unl*			Ci**bilitan**i		
Hisp.	24	*unl*			Konto**bris**		
Hisp.	25	*cn.*			**Nert**obis		
Hisp.	25	*cn.*			**Uir**ouias		
Hisp.	25	*cn.*			**Us**amus		
Hisp.	25	*unl*			Verne**metis**	Vernantes	
Hisp.	25	*unl*			**Verne**metis	Vernantes	
Hisp.	26	*unl*			Ara**briga**		
Hisp.	26	*unl*			**Ebur**a Cerialis		
Hisp.	26	*unl*			**Lanc**ienses Transcudani		
Hisp.	26	*unl*			Lango**briga**		
Hisp.	26	*unl*			**Lango**briga		
Hisp.	26	*unl*			Tala**brica**	Tala**briga**?	Talabara?
Hisp.	27	*unl*			**Medio**lon		
23139	32	*unl*	*+07*	*36*	Au**durus** Fundus		
23314	35	*unl*			*****Amantes** (Gara**mantes**?)		
23609	42	*unl*			Ve**sid**ia fl.		
25874	62	*unl*			Petobr**ogen**		

---

[1] At the left in Tables 5.1 and 5.2 I include the APNI reference numbers; 'Fra.', 'Hisp.', 'Narb.' and 'Cors.' refer to additions to the APNI (see above, p. 19, n. 12).

[2] Note also that the six examples of *Vellaunodunum*, *Vernemetis* and *Langobriga* are the same three places respectively.

could not be located as closely as a single grid square (I will call these 'unlocatable names').[3] Table 5.2 forms the basis for Maps 5.1 and 5.2.

It will be noted that some places appear on more than one line of Table 5.2, for example when their name contains more than one relevant element (e.g. Caeto**briga**/**Caet**obriga) or when they bear more than one relevant name (e.g. **Alaun**a/**Litan**a). These places' grid references are placed in a box in Table 5.2 and are counted as single tokens on Maps 5.1 and 5.2. The grid references I have supplied for '*unl*' places are in *italics*.

Table 5.2 Celtic-looking names sorted by longitude and latitude

6920	26	A2	−10	39	**Ebur**obrittium			
6972	26	A2	−10	39	Iera**briga**	Lera**briga**		
7015	26	A2	−10	39	Londo**bris** Ins.			
6886	26	B4	−09	37	Cibi**litani**			
6994	26	B4	−09	37	Lac(c)o**briga**			
7039	26	B4	−09	37	Miro**briga**	Miro**briga** Celtica	Municipium Flavium Miro**brig**ensium	
Hisp.	26	*unl*	*−09*	*38*	Arco**briga**			
6828	26	B3	−09	38	Caeto**briga**			
6828	26	B3	−09	38	**Caet**obriga			
Hisp.	26	*unl*	*−09*	*38*	Meri**briga**	Mero**briga**		
Hisp.	24	*unl*	*−09*	*40*	Caeilo**brig**oi			
6007	24	C4	−09	40	Conim**briga**	Flavia Conim**briga**		
6058	24	C4	−09	40	Lango**briga**			
6058	24	C4	−09	40	**Lang**obriga			
6201	24	C4	−09	40	Tala**briga**			
Hisp.	24	*unl*	*−09*	*41*	Abourica	*Auo**briga**	Avo**brica**	Abo**brica**
Hisp.	24	*unl*	*−09*	*41*	Arco**briga**			
Hisp.	26	*unl*	*−09*	*41*	Avo**briga**	Abo**brica**		
Hisp.	24	*unl*	*−09*	*41*	Castellum Letio**bris**			
Hisp.	24	*unl*	*−09*	*41*	Elaeneo**briga**			
6104	24	C3	−09	41	**Nemet**atoi?			
6211	24	C3	−09	41	*Tongo**briga**	Tounto**briga**		
Hisp.	24	*unl*	*−09*	*41*	*Vala**briga**			
5924	24	C2	−09	42	As**seg**onia			
5953	24	C2	−09	42	**Brev**is			
6009	24	C2	−09	42	**Cort**icata Ins.			
6059	24	C2	−09	42	Lans**bric**a	Lais		
Hisp.	24	*unl*	*−09*	*42*	**Medio**ga			
Hisp.	24	*unl*	*−09*	*43*	Adro**brica**			
5921	24	C1	−09	43	Artabri	Arro**treb**ae		
5922	24	C1	−09	43	Arta**bris** Sinus	Megas Limen		
5979	24	C1	−09	43	Castellum Avilio**bris**			
6025	24	C1	−09	43	(Flavium) **Brigant**ium	**Brigant**ium	Portus Magnus?	

---

[3] All names in both categories will be considered in Chs. 6–10.

6137	24	C1	−09	43	Phlaouia Lam**bris**		
Hisp.	24	*unl*	*−09*	*43*	**Samar**ium		
Hisp.	26	*unl*	*−08*	*38*	Burrulo**briga**		
Hisp.	26	*unl*	−08	39	Deo**briga**		
Hisp.	26	*unl*	−08	39	**Deo**briga		
Hisp.	24	*unl*	−08	39	Kottaio**briga**		
Hisp.	24	*unl*	−08	39	**Kott**aiobriga		
Hisp.	26	*unl*	*−08*	*39*	Monto**brica**	Monto**briga**	Mundo**briga**
5978	24	D4	−08	40	Castellum Arao**cel**um		
6057	24	D4	−08	40	**Lanc**ienses Transcudani		
6070	24	D4	−08	40	Longo**briga**		
6084	24	D4	−08	40	Me(i)du**briga**		
6114	24	D4	−08	40	**Ocel**um		
Hisp.	24	*unl*	*−08*	*41*	Ara**briga**		
5916	24	D3	−08	41	Ara**brig**enses		
5964	24	D3	−08	41	Cala**dun**um		
5966	24	D3	−08	41	Calia**briga**	Cala**bria**	
Hisp.	24	*unl*	*−08*	*41*	Castellum Loucio**cel**um		
Hisp.	24	*unl*	*−08*	*42*	*Calu**briga**		
Hisp.	24	*unl*	*−08*	*42*	Castellum Tala**briga**		
Hisp.	24	*unl*	*−08*	*42*	**Kamb**aiton		
6050	24	D2	−08	42	Koilio**briga**		
6064	24	D2	−08	42	**Lem**avi		
6071	24	D2	−08	42	**Loug**ei		
6105	24	D2	−08	42	Nemeto**briga**		
6105	24	D2	−08	42	**Nemet**obriga		
Hisp.	24	*unl*	*−08*	*42*	**Okel**on		
Hisp.	24	*unl*	*−08*	*42*	**Okel**on		
Hisp.	24	*unl*	*−08*	*43*	**Olin**a		
Hisp.	24	*unl*	*−08*	*43*	**Ouik**a		
148	2	B3	−08	52	**Sen**os fl.		
6908	26	D5	−07	36	**Cot**inussa Ins.	Gaditana Ins.	
6993	26	D4	−07	37	**Kort**ikata		
7199	26	D4	−07	37	Turo**briga**		
7059	26	D3	−07	38	Nerto**briga** Concordia Iulia		
7059	26	D3	−07	38	**Nert**obriga Concordia Iulia		
7152	26	D3	−07	38	**Segid**a	Restituta Iulia	
Hisp.	26	*unl*	*−07*	*39*	Ebero**briga**		
7181	26	D2	−07	39	*Tongo**briga**		
6056	24	E4	−07	40	**Lanc**ienses Oppidani		
Hisp.	24	*unl*	*−07*	*40*	**Lank**ia Oppidana		
6091	24	E4	−07	40	Miro**briga**	Municipium Val(...)	
Hisp.	24	*unl*	*−07*	*40*	*Ocel**um**		
6006	24	E3	−07	41	**Comple**utica		
6075	24	E2	−07	42	**Lug**goni		
Hisp.	24	*unl*	*−07*	*43*	Castellum Ercorio**bris**		

1120	8	A2	−07	52	**Brigan**tes		
22234	8	*unl*	*−07*	*52*	**Doun**on		
1292	8	A2	−07	52	**Kori**ondoi		
1103	8	A1	−07	53	Bououinda fl.		
22342	9	*unl*	*−07*	*54*	**Ouind**eris fl.		
1563	9	A2	−07	58	**Dumn**a Ins.		
7511	28	C2	−06	35	**Cott**ae?	**Kot**es	Gytte
Hisp.	26	*Av*	*−06*	*36*	Argentarius M.	**Cass**ius M.	
6792	26	E5	−06	36	**Asido**	Asido	
						Caesarina	
6884	26	E5	−06	36	**Cet**aria		
7129	26	E5	−06	36	**Sagunt**ia		
Hisp.	26	*unl*	*−06*	*37*	Aria**ldunum**		
6846	26	E4	−06	37	**Carru**ca		
7153	26	E4	−06	37	**Seg**ida	Augurina	
Hisp.	26	*unl*	*−06*	*37*	**Seg**ovia		
6822	26	E3	−06	38	Bruto**briga**		
7038	26	E3	−06	38	Miro**briga**		
6794	26	E2	−06	39	Augusto**briga**		
6173	24	F4	−06	40	Sal**man**tica		
6190	24	F4	−06	40	**Sent**ice		
5908	24	F3	−06	41	Amallo**briga**	Abulo**brica**	
5918	24	F3	−06	41	Arboukale	Albo**cela**	
6115	24	F3	−06	41	**Ocel**um Duri		
Hisp.	24	*unl*	*−06*	*41*	Okto**douron**		
5954	24	F2	−06	42	**Brig**aecini		
5955	24	F2	−06	42	**Brig**aecium	**Brig**eco	
6055	24	F2	−06	42	**Lanc**ia	**Lanc**e	**Lanc**ienses
Hisp.	24	*unl*	*−06*	*42*	**Vind**ius M.		
6076	24	F1	−06	43	**Lug**goni		
Hisp.	24	*unl*	*−06*	*43*	**Lug**iso		
1046	7	A3	−06	48	**Uxant**is Ins.	**Axanthos** Ins.	
1605	9	B5	−06	55	**Lem**annonios		
					Kolpos		
22348	9	*unl*	*−06*	*55*	**Rerig**onion		
1651	9	B5	−06	55	**Rerig**onios		
					Kolpos		
1597	9	B3	−06	57	**Karn**onakai		
Hisp.	26	*unl*	*−05*	*37*	**Cet**urgi		
7212	26	F4	−05	37	**Vent**ipo		
Hisp.	26	*unl*	*−05*	*38*	**Kot**inai	Oleastron	
7286	27	A2	−05	39	Caesaro**briga**		
6081	24	G4	−05	40	**Mant**ua		
6188	24	G4	−05	40	**Seg**ovia		
6013	24	G2	−05	42	Desso**briga**		
6047	24	G2	−05	42	Iulio**briga**		
6052	24	G2	−05	42	Laco**briga**		
6185	24	G2	−05	42	**Seg**isama Iulia		
6186	24	G2	−05	42	**Seg**isamo		
5935	24	G1	−05	43	A**varig**ini		
6014	24	G1	−05	43	**Deval**es? fl.		
Hisp.	24	*unl*	*−05*	*43*	**Okel**a	Opsikella	
Hisp.	24	*unl*	*−05*	*43*	Tono**brica**	Teno**brica**?	
3130	14	A1	−05	47	**Corio**solites	**Corio**sopites	
1040	7	B3	−05	48	**Sen**a Ins.	**Samn**is Ins.	
1188	8	C4	−05	50	**Dumn**onii		

22248	8	*unl*	*−05*	*51*	Leuca fl.	(Leugo)**Sen**a fl.
1338	8	C3	−05	51	*Mori**dun**um	
1338	8	C3	−05	51	***Mori**dunum	
1402	8	C1	−05	53	**Segu**ntium	
1556	9	C5	−05	55	**Deou**a fl.	
22326	9	*unl*	−05	55	**Koria**	
1643	9	C5	−05	55	**Ouind**ogara Kolpos	
1516	9	C4	−05	56	**Bod**otria fl.	
1606	9	C4	−05	56	**Lind**on?	
22329	9	*unl*	*−05*	*56*	**Litan**omago	
22329	9	*unl*	*−05*	*56*	**Litan**omago	
7322	27	B4	−04	37	**Ebur**a	Cerialis
Hisp.	26	*unl*	*−04*	*38*	**Samar**iense Metallum	
6435	25	B5	−04	40	**Compl**utum	
6430	25	B4	−04	41	Col. **Clun**ia (Sulpicia)	
6665	25	B4	−04	41	Segortia **Lank**a	
6665	25	B4	−04	41	Segortia Lanka	
6726	25	B4	−04	41	**Ux**ama (Argaela)	
5952	24	H2	−04	42	**Brau**on?	
6012	24	H2	−04	42	Deo**brig**ula	
6012	24	H2	−04	42	**Deo**brigula	
6590	25	B3	−04	42	**Oux**ama Barka	
6661	25	B3	−04	42	**Sege**samunculum	
6187	24	H2	−04	42	**Seg**ontia Paramika	
6745	25	B3	−04	42	**Vind**eleia	
6746	25	B3	−04	42	**Vir**ovesca	
6468	25	B2	−04	43	Flavio**brig**a	Portus Amanum
6148	24	H1	−04	43	Portus Victoriae Iulio**brig**ensium	
3439	14	B1	−04	47	**Vind**ilis Ins.	
977	7	C3	−04	48	Ar(e)**moric**a	
22209	8	*unl*	*−04*	*50*	**Alaun**os fl.	
22228	8	*unl*	*−04*	*50*	*Derv**entio** fl.	
1275	8	D4	−04	50	**Isca**	
1279	8	D4	−04	50	**Iska** fl.	
22259	8	*unl*	*−04*	*50*	Mori**dunum**	
22259	8	*unl*	*−04*	*50*	**Mori**dunum	
1341	8	D4	−04	50	'**Nemet**otacio'	
1378	8	D3	−04	51	**Rato**stabios? fl.	
1119	8	D2	−04	52	**Brem**ia	
1361	8	D2	−04	52	Ordo**vices**	
1494	9	D6	−04	54	**Aball**ava	
1498	9	D6	−04	54	**Alaun**a	Alione
1558	9	D6	−04	54	**Derv**entio	
1577	9	D6	−04	54	**Gabr**osentum	
1577	9	D6	−04	54	Gabro**sent**um	
1579	9	D6	−04	54	*Glann**oventa**	Glannibanta
1616	9	D6	−04	54	**Mag**is?	
1623	9	D6	−04	54	Mori**kambe** *Eischusis	
1623	9	D6	−04	54	**Mori**kambe *Eischusis	
22355	9	*unl*	*−04*	*54*	**Uxel**a	

1514	9	D5	−04	55	**Blat**obulgium		
22300	9	*unl*	*−04*	*55*	Camulossesa		
					Praesidium		
1565	9	D5	−04	55	Karbant**orig**on?		
22336	9	*unl*	*−04*	*55*	**Medio**nemeton		
22336	9	*unl*	*−04*	*55*	Medio**nemet**on		
1497	9	D4	−04	56	**Alaun**a	Litana	
1497	9	D4	−04	56	Alauna	**Litan**a	
1510	9	D4	−04	56	**Bann**atia?		
1517	9	D4	−04	56	**Bod**otria?		
					Aestuarium		
1600	9	D2	−04	58	**Korn**aouioi	**Korn**abioi	**Korn**ouboi
1611	9	D2	−04	58	**Loug**oi		
1644	9	D2	−04	58	**Ouir**ouedroum		
					Akron		
1669	9	D2	−04	58	*****Tarou**e**doun**on	Orkas Akra	
1669	9	D2	−04	58	*****Tarou**edounon	Orkas Akra	
7432	27	C2	−03	39	Sego**brig**a		
7432	27	C2	−03	39	**Sego**briga		
Hisp.	25	*cn.*	*−03*	*39*	Seko**birik**es		
6461	25	C5	−03	40	Erca**vic**a		
Hisp.	25	*unl*	*−03*	*40*	**Medio**lon		
6290	25	C4	−03	41	Arco**brig**a		
6442	25	C4	−03	41	*****Cort**ona		
Hisp.	25	*unl*	*−03*	*41*	Mutu**durum**		
6663	25	C4	−03	41	**Seg**ontia		
6447	25	C3	−03	42	Deo**brig**a	Sobo**bric**a?	
6447	25	C3	−03	42	**Deo**briga	Sobobrica?	
6448	25	C2	−03	43	**Deou**a fl.		
3142	14	C1	−03	47	Dari**oritum**	Veneti	
3196	14	C1	−03	47	Herios fl.	**Vic**inonia fl.	
3441	14	C1	−03	47	**Vind**unit(t)a		
					Ins.		
1002	7	D3	−03	48	Fanum Martis	Civitas	**Corio**solitae
						Coriosolitum	
976	7	D2	−03	49	**And**ium? Ins.		
22220	8	*unl*	*−03*	*50*	**Bolvelaun**io		
22233	8	*unl*	*−03*	*50*	**Doun**ion		
1196	8	E4	−03	50	**Duro**triges		
1305	8	E4	−03	50	**Lind**inis		
1459	8	E4	−03	50	**Vind**ocladia		
1053	8	E3	−03	51	**Abon**a fl.		
1054	8	E3	−03	51	'**Abone**'		
22213	8	*unl*	*−03*	*51*	**Anicetis**		
1276	8	E3	−03	51	**Isca**		
1277	8	E3	−03	51	**Isca** fl.		
1452	8	E3	−03	51	**Vent**a		
1162	8	E2	−03	52	**Corn**ovii		
1333	8	E2	−03	52	**Medio**lanum		
1367	8	E2	−03	52	**Penn**ocrucium		
1389	8	E2	−03	52	**Rutun**ium?		
1447	8	E2	−03	52	Uxacona		
1460	8	E2	−03	52	*****Viro**conium		
1118	8	E1	−03	53	*****Brem**etenna-		
					cum		
					Veteranorum		
1160	8	E1	−03	53	**Condat**e		

1178	8	E1	−03	53	**Dev**a		
1382	8	E1	−03	53	Rigo**doun**on?		
1382	8	E1	−03	53	**Rig**odounon?		
1501	9	E6	−03	54	Alone?	**Alaun**a?	
1507	9	E6	−03	54	**Bann**a		
1520	9	E6	−03	54	**Brav**(o)niacum		
22298	9	*unl*	*−03*	*54*	**Brig**a		
1523	9	E6	−03	54	**Brig**antes		
1524	9	E6	−03	54	**Broc**avum		
1529	9	E6	−03	54	*****Camb**oglanna		
1547	9	E6	−03	54	*****Corio**sopitum	**Coria**	
1561	9	E6	−03	54	Dorvantium fl.	[**Derv**entio] fl.	
1614	9	E6	−03	54	**Lugu**valium		
1676	9	E6	−03	54	Uxelo**du**(nu)m		
1676	9	E6	−03	54	Uxelodu(nu)m		
1681	9	E6	−03	54	**Vind**olanda		
1685	9	E6	−03	54	Viro**sidum**		
1685	9	E6	−03	54	Viro**sidum**		
1521	9	E5	−03	55	**Brem**enium		
1525	9	E5	−03	55	*****Broc**olitia		
22304	9	*unl*	*−03*	*55*	**Corion**ototae		
1679	9	E5	−03	55	*****Verco**vicium		
1557	9	E3	−03	57	**Deou**a fl.		
22309	9	*unl*	*−03*	*57*	**Deou**ana		
23016	29	*unl*	*−02*	*35*	**Sit**a Col.?		
7431	27	D3	−02	38	**Seg**isa?		
6314	25	D4	−02	41	Augusto**brig**a	Augusto**brica**	
6438	25	D4	−02	41	Contre**bi**a (Belaisca)		
6568	25	D4	−02	41	Nerto**briga**		
6568	25	D4	−02	41	Nerto**briga**		
6592	25	D4	−02	41	Pagus Gallorum et **Seg**ardinenssium		
6660	25	D4	−02	41	**Seg**eda	Begeda	
6664	25	D4	−02	41	**Seg**ontia		
Hisp.	25	*cn.*	*−02*	*41*	**Alaun**		
6274	25	D3	−02	42	**And**elos		
6439	25	D3	−02	42	Contre**bi**a Leucada		
6662	25	D3	−02	42	**Seg**ia	**Seg**la	Setia
3369	14	D4	−02	44	**Seg**osa		
3326	14	D2	−02	46	**Rat**is Ins.	Arica	
3325	14	D1	−02	47	*****Rati**atum		
3368	14	D1	−02	47	**Seg**ora?		
994	7	E3	−02	48	**Condat**e Redonum	Civitas Riedonum	R(i)edones
975	7	E2	−02	49	**Alaun**a		
995	7	E2	−02	49	**Cori**allum		
996	7	E2	−02	49	Co**sed**ia	Constantia	
22221	8	*unl*	*−02*	*50*	**Brige**		
1078	8	F3	−02	51	Atre**ba**tes		
1193	8	F3	−02	51	Duro**corn**ovium		
1193	8	F3	−02	51	**Duro**cornovium		
1303	8	F3	−02	51	*****Leuco**magus		
1411	8	F3	−02	51	Sorvio**dun**um		
1453	8	F3	−02	51	**Vent**a		
22286	8	*unl*	*−02*	*51*	*****Vind**omium		

1061	8	F2	−02	52	**Alaun**a?		
1082	8	F2	−02	52	**Bann**aventa		
1082	8	F2	−02	52	Banna**venta**		
1300	8	F2	−02	52	*Leto**cetum**		
1329	8	F2	−02	52	Mandu**essedum**		
1329	8	F2	−02	52	**Mandu**essedum		
1377	8	F2	−02	52	**Ratae**		
1456	8	F2	−02	52	'Ver**nemeto**'		
1071	8	F1	−02	53	Aquae		
					*Arne**met**iae		
22299	9	*unl*	*−02*	*53*	**Camb**odunum		
22299	9	*unl*	*−02*	*53*	Cambo**dunum**		
1133	8	F1	−02	53	**Camul**odonum?		
1566	9	F7	−02	53	**Ebur**acum		
1678	9	F7	−02	53	**Verb**eia fl.		
1562	9	F6	−02	54	**Doun**on Kolpos		
1575	9	F6	−02	54	**Gabr**antouikes		
1575	9	F6	−02	54	Gabrant**ouikes**		
1610	9	F6	−02	54	Longo**vicium**		
22332	9	*unl*	*−02*	*54*	Lugu**nduno**		
22332	9	*unl*	*−02*	*54*	**Lugu**nduno		
1660	9	F6	−02	54	Sege**dunum**		
1660	9	F6	−02	54	Sege**dunum**		
1682	9	F6	−02	54	**Vind**omora		
1683	9	F6	−02	54	**Vind**ovala		
1499	9	F5	−02	55	**Alaun**a		
1500	9	F5	−02	55	**Alaun**a fl.		
Hisp.	27	*unl*	−01	38	**Ico**sitani		
7327	27	E2	−01	39	Edetania	Edetani	**Sed**etani?
7421	27	E2	−01	39	**Saguntum**	Arse	
6659	25	E4	−01	41	(S)**Ed**etani	Edetani	Edetania
3127	14	E4	−01	44	**Condat**is		
3050	14	E3	−01	45	**Bituriges**		
					Vivisci		
3124	14	E3	−01	45	**Condat**e		
3132	14	E3	−01	45	**Corter**ate		
3132	14	E3	−01	45	Corte**rate**		
3151	14	E3	−01	45	**Dumn**itonus		
3259	14	E3	−01	45	**Medio**lanum		
3290	14	E3	−01	45	Nouio**magos**		
3290	14	E3	−01	45	**Nouio**magos		
3294	14	E3	−01	45	**Novio**regum		
3372	14	E3	−01	45	'Sermanico**mago**'?		
3063	14	E2	−01	46	**Brig**iosum	**Brio**ssus	
3295	14	E2	−01	46	**Novio**ritum		
3295	14	E2	−01	46	Novio**ritum**		
3008	14	E1	−01	47	**And**ecavi		
3093	14	E1	−01	47	*Carn**ona**		
3209	14	E1	−01	47	Iulio**magus**	Civitas	
						Andecavorum	
3209	14	E1	−01	47	Iulio**magus**	Civitas	
						Andecavorum	
3331	14	E1	−01	47	Rob**rica**		
1019	7	F3	−01	48	Noio**doun**on		
					Diablintum		
1023	7	F3	−01	48	**Olin**a fl.		
981	7	F2	−01	49	Augusto**durum**	Baiocas	

984	7	F2	−01	49	Baiocasses	**Bod**iocasses	
984	7	F2	−01	49	Baio**casses**	Bodio**casses**	
1048	7	F2	−01	49	Vidu**casses**		
1355	8	G4	−01	50	Novio**magus**		
1355	8	G4	−01	50	**Novio**magus		
1142	8	G3	−01	51	**Catu**vellauni		
1142	8	G3	−01	51	Catu**vellauni**		
1192	8	G3	−01	51	Duro**cobriv**is		
1192	8	G3	−01	51	**Duro**cobrivis		
1190	8	G2	−01	52	Duro**brivae**		
1190	8	G2	−01	52	**Duro**brivae		
1198	8	G2	−01	52	**Duro**vigutum		
1293	8	G2	−01	52	Lacto**dor**um		
1331	8	G2	−01	52	Margi**dunum**		
1083	8	G1	−01	53	**Banno**vallum		
1155	8	G1	−01	53	Col. **Lind**um		
22307	9	*unl*	*−01*	53	Delgo**vici**a		
1560	9	G7	−01	53	[**Der**ventio] fl.		
1401	8	G1	−01	53	**Seg**elocum		
1559	9	G6	−01	54	**Der**ventio		
1576	9	G6	−01	54	**Gabr**antouikon Kolpos		
1576	9	G6	−01	54	Gabr**antouik**on Kolpos		
Hisp.	25	*Av*	*+ 00*	40	**Cass**ae Herronesi		
6393	25	F2	+ 00	43	Casino**magus**		
6534	25	F2	+ 00	43	Lug**dun**um Convenarum		
6534	25	F2	+ 00	43	**Lug**dunum Convenarum		
6748	25	F2	+ 00	43	(Volcae) Tecto**sages**	Tecto**sages**	Tecto**sagi**
6748	25	F2	+ 00	43	(**Vol**cae) Tecto**sages**	Tecto**sages**	Tecto**sagi**
3147	14	F4	+ 00	44	Dio**lind**um?		
3285	14	F4	+ 00	44	Nitio**brog**es		
3313	14	F4	+ 00	44	Pompeiacum	Ver**nemet**is	
3417	14	F4	+ 00	44	**Ussubium**	Vesubio	
3417	14	F4	+ 00	44	Ussubium	**Vesu**bio	
3096	14	F3	+ 00	45	**Cas(s)**inomagus		
3096	14	F3	+ 00	45	Cas(s)ino**magus**		
3219	14	F3	+ 00	45	**Lem**ovices		
3219	14	F3	+ 00	45	Lemo**vices**		
3429	14	F3	+ 00	45	**Vesu**nna	Petrucorii	
3200	14	F2	+ 00	46	Icio**dor**o		
3404	14	F2	+ 00	46	*Torno**magus**?		
3060	14	F1	+ 00	47	**Bric**ca		
3062	14	F1	+ 00	47	**Brig**gogalus		
3064	14	F1	+ 00	47	**Brio**treidis?**		
3077	14	F1	+ 00	47	Caesaro**dunum**	Civitas Turonorum	
3117	14	F1	+ 00	47	*Ciso**magus**		
3125	14	F1	+ 00	47	***Condat**e		
3242	14	F1	+ 00	47	*Manto**loma (g)um**		
3242	14	F1	+ 00	47	*Mant**oloma (g)um**		

3334	14	F1	+00	47	Rotomagus?			
3427	14	F1	+00	47	**Vern**aus	Vernadum?		
1964	11	A4	+00	48	**Conda**te			
2008	11	A4	+00	48	**Ebur**ovices			
2008	11	A4	+00	48	Eburo**vices**			
1018	7	G3	+00	48	Noio**doun**on	Nu Dionnum		
1020	7	G3	+00	48	Novio**magus** Lexoviorum			
1020	7	G3	+00	48	**Novio**magus Lexoviorum			
2249	11	A4	+00	48	**Ouind**inon	Subdinnum	Cenomani	
2302	11	A4	+00	48	Sagii			
22400	11	*unl*	*+00*	*49*	**Brevi**odurum			
22400	11	*unl*	*+00*	*49*	Brevio**durum**			
988	7	G2	+00	49	Cara**coti**cum			
2106	11	A3	+00	49	Iulio**bona**			
2399	11	A3	+00	49	Velio**cass**es			
1066	8	H4	+00	50	**Ander**idos	**Ander**elium	**Ander**itos	
1127	8	H3	+00	51	Caesaro**magus**			
22224	8	*unl*	*+00*	*51*	**Cass**i			
1153	8	H3	+00	51	Col. **Camulo**dunum			
1153	8	H3	+00	51	Col. Camulo**dunum**			
1191	8	H3	+00	51	Duro**brivae**			
1191	8	H3	+00	51	**Duro**brivae			
1195	8	H3	+00	51	**Duro**litum			
1197	8	I3	+00	51	*****Duro**vernum			
1197	8	I3	+00	51	*****Duro**vernum**			
1298	8	H3	+00	51	**Lem**ana fl.			
1356	8	H3	+00	51	Novio**magus**			
1356	8	H3	+00	51	**Novio**magus			
1374	8	I3	+00	51	Portus **Lem**anis			
1112	8	H2	+00	52	Brano**dunum**			
1131	8	H2	+00	52	'**Camb**orico'?			
1194	8	H2	+00	52	**Duro**liponte			
1358	8	H1	+00	53	**Okel**lou ? Akron			
6275	25	G3	+01	42	**Ando**sinoi			
6375	25	G2	+01	43	**Camb**olectri			
6680	25	G2	+01	43	Sosto**magus**	Sexto**magus**		
6705	25	G2	+01	43	Tolosa	Col. Iulia Tolosa	Civ. Tecto**sagum**	Tolosates
6739	25	G2	+01	43	**Vern**us Sol			
Fra.	14	*unl*	*+01*	*44*	Ale**vern**acum			
3097	14	G4	+01	44	**Cass**iaco			
3131	14	G4	+01	44	**Corn**ucio			
3148	14	G4	+01	44	**Div**ona	Civitas Cadurcorum		
Fra.	14	*unl*	*+01*	*44*	Vosi**dum**			
3029	14	G3	+01	45	Augusto**ritum**			
3065	14	G3	+01	45	**Briv**a (Curretia)			
3154	14	G3	+01	45	**Duro**tincum?			
3154	14	G3	+01	45	Duro**tincum**?			
3415	14	G3	+01	45	Userca			
3007	14	G2	+01	46	*****Ande**camulum			
3007	14	G2	+01	46	*Ande**camulum**			
3020	14	G2	+01	46	*****Argento**magus			

3053	14	G2	+01	46	**Blat**omagus			
3053	14	G2	+01	46	Blatomagus			
3080	14	G2	+01	46	**Camb**iovicenses?			
3080	14	G2	+01	46	Cambio**vice**nses?			
3119	14	G2	+01	46	Claudio**magus**			
3446	14	G2	+01	46	*Vo**sagum**			
3049	14	G1	+01	47	Bitu**riges** Cubi			
3181	14	G1	+01	47	**Gabr**is	*Gabrae		
3292	14	G1	+01	47	Novio**dunum**			
3292	14	G1	+01	47	**Novio**dunum			
3371	14	G1	+01	47	**Sen**aparia?			
3440	14	G1	+01	47	**Vind**ocinum			
1931	11	B4	+01	48	**Carn**utes			
1990	11	B4	+01	48	**Div**odurum?			
1990	11	B4	+01	48	Div**odurum**?			
1999	11	B4	+01	48	**Dun**ense Castrum			
2002	11	B4	+01	48	Duro**casses**			
2002	11	B4	+01	48	**Duro**casses			
2177	11	B3	+01	49	Mediolanum Aulercorum	**Ebur**ovicum		
2177	11	B3	+01	49	**Medio**lanum Aulercorum	Eburovicum		
22414	11	*unl*	*+01*	*49*	**Ritu**magus			
22414	11	*unl*	*+00*	*49*	Ritumagus			
2290	11	B3	+01	49	Roto**magus**			
2052	11	B2	+01	50	Gesoriacum	**Bon**onia		
2146	11	B2	+01	50	Linto**magus**?			
2199	11	B2	+01	50	**Mor**ini			
2321	11	B2	+01	50	**Samar**a fl.			
22235	8	*unl*	*+01*	*51*	**Dun**(...)			
373	8	I3	+01	51	Portus **Dubr**is			
1390	8	I3	+01	51	**Rutu**piae			
22269	8	*unl*	*+01*	*52*	*Sito**magus**			
22269	8	*unl*	*+01*	*52*	*Sit**o**magus			
1454	8	I2	+01	52	**Vent**a			
6492	25	H4	+02	41	**Ildur**o			
6658	25	H3	+02	42	Sebe**ndoun**on?	Besel**dun**um		
6738	25	H3	+02	42	Verno**dubr**um fl.			
6738	25	H3	+02	42	**Verno**dubrum fl.			
6376	25	H2	+02	43	**Camb**one			
6386	25	H2	+02	43	Carcas(s)o	Col. Iulia	Carcasum Volcarum Tectosagarum	
6386	25	H2	+02	43	Carcas(s)o	Col. Iulia	Carcasum **Volc**arum Tectosagarum	
6482	25	H2	+02	43	Hebromagus	**Ebur**omagus		
6482	25	H2	+02	43	Hebromagus	Eburo**magus**		
6725	25	H2	+02	43	**Us**uerva	Husuerbas	Usuerna	
6725	25	H2	+02	43	Usuerva	Husuerbas	Us**uern**a	
3090	14	H4	+02	44	Caranto**magus**			
3367	14	H4	+02	44	Sego**dun**um	'Etodounon'	Civitas Rutenorum	
3367	14	H4	+02	44	**Sego**dunum	'Etodounon'	Civitas Rutenorum	
3418	14	H4	+02	44	Uxello**dunum**			
3418	14	H4	+02	44	**Ux**ellodunum			

3159	14	H2	+02	45	Erno**dorum**		
2996	14	H2	+02	46	Acito**dunum**		
3013	14	H2	+02	46	Aquae Neri	*Nerio**magus**	
3081	14	H2	+02	46	**Camb**onum		
3146	14	H2	+02	46	**Derv**entum		
3168	14	H2	+02	46	*Exoli**dunum**		
3258	14	H2	+02	46	**Medio**cantus		
3260	14	H2	+02	46	**Medio**lanum	Stampensis	
3286	14	H2	+02	46	*Nogeo**magus**		
3401	14	H2	+02	46	**Tinc**ontium	**Tinc**ollo	
3033	14	H1	+02	47	Avaricum	Bitu**rigae**	
3066	14	H1	+02	47	**Briv**as		
3068	14	H1	+02	47	**Briv**odurum		
3068	14	H1	+02	47	Brivo**durum**		
22416	11	*unl*	*+02*	*47*	Vellauno**dunum**		
22416	11	*unl*	*+02*	*47*	**Vellauno**dunum		
3126	14	H1	+02	47	**Cond**ate		
3366	14	H1	+02	47	**Segim**ovicus		
22394	11	*unl*	*+02*	*48*	**Ander**itum		
22394	11	*unl*	*+02*	*48*	Ander**itum**		
1965	11	C4	+02	48	**Cond**ate		
2185	11	C4	+02	48	Metlosedum	Mello**dunum**	
2185	11	C4	+02	48	Metlo**sed**um	Mellodunum	
2217	11	C4	+02	48	*Nemeto**durum**		
2217	11	C4	+02	48	***Nemet**odurum		
22409	11	*unl*	*+02*	*48*	Petro**mant**ulum	Petrum Viaco	
2338	11	C4	+02	48	**Sen**ones		
1860	11	C3	+02	49	Augusto**magus**	Castrum de Silvanectis	
1904	11	C3	+02	49	**Briv**a Isarae		
1918	11	C3	+02	49	Caesaro**magus**		
2147	11	C3	+02	49	Litano**briga**?		
2147	11	C3	+02	49	**Litano**briga?		
2236	11	C3	+02	49	Novio**magus**		
2236	11	C3	+02	49	**Novio**magus		
2277	11	C3	+02	49	Ratu**magus** Silvanectum?	Ratum(...)?	
2277	11	C3	+02	49	**Ratu**magus Silvanectum?	**Ratum**(...)?	
2322	11	C3	+02	49	Samaro**briva** Ambianorum		
2322	11	C3	+02	49	**Samaro**briva Ambianorum		
1850	11	C2	+02	50	**Atreb**ates		
2005	11	C2	+02	50	**Duro**(i)coregum		
22405	11	*unl*	*+02*	*50*	Fines **Atreb**atum		
2215	11	C2	+02	50	**Nemet**acum	**Nemet**ocenna	
2363	11	C2	+02	50	**Tarv**enna	Tarouanna	Tervanna
7800	30	F3	+03	36	**Icos**ium		
23041	30	*unl*	*+03*	*36*	Tamariceto Praesidium		
3635	15	B3	+03	43	Taurus	**Volc**arum Stagna	
3662	15	B2	+03	43	**Volc**ae Arecomici		
3813	17	A4	+03	44	**Ander**itum	Civitas Gabalum	
3813	17	A4	+03	44	Ander**itum**	Civitas Gabalum	

3884	17	B4	+03	44	**Condat**e		
6436	25	I1	+03	44	**Condat**omagus?		
6436	25	I1	+03	44	Condato**magus**?		
3028	14	I3	+03	45	Augusto**nemet**um	Civitas Arvernorum	
3028	14	I3	+03	45	Augustonemetum	Civitas Arvernorum	
3823	17	B2	+03	45	**Arvern**i	**Arvern**ia	
3858	17	A3	+03	45	**Briv**as		
3843	17	A2	+03	45	*Bilio**magus**		
3201	14	I3	+03	45	*Icio**dor**um		
3935	17	B3	+03	45	Icid**mago**		
3329	14	I3	+03	45	*Rico**magus**		
22506	18	*unl*	*+03*	*46*	**Sit**illia		
3438	14	I2	+03	46	***Vind**iciacum		
4084	18	A2	+03	47	**Ab**allo		
3032	14	I1	+03	47	Autessio**durum**	Civitas Autissio**dor**ensis	
3040	14	I1	+03	47	'Band**ritum**'		
3293	14	I1	+03	47	Novio**dunum**?	Nevirnum?	'Ebirno'
3293	14	I1	+03	47	**Novio**dunum?	Nevirnum?	'Ebirno'
4116	18	A1	+03	48	Eburo**briga**		
4116	18	A1	+03	48	**Ebur**obriga		
2388	11	D4	+03	48	Tri**cass**es		
1858	11	D3	+03	49	Augusta Viro**mandu**orum		
1858	11	D3	+03	49	Augusta Vir**omanduorum**		
1941	11	D3	+03	49	**Catus**iacum?		
2235	11	D3	+03	49	Novio**dunum**?		
2235	11	D3	+03	49	**Novio**dunum?		
2403	11	D3	+03	49	**Verb**inum	Vironum	
2403	11	D3	+03	49	Verbinum	**Vir**onum	
2423	11	D3	+03	49	**Viro**mandis		
2424	11	D3	+03	49	Viro**mandui**		
2424	11	D3	+03	49	**Viro**mandui		
1975	11	D2	+03	50	**Cort**oriacum		
2006	11	D2	+03	50	**Dur**onum		
2425	11	D2	+03	50	**Vir**oviacum		
2045	11	D1	+03	51	*Gan**uent**a?		
8577	34	C2	+04	35	**Abann**ae?		
7376	27	inset	+04	39	**Mago**		
3460	15	C2	+04	43	*A**randun**um		
Narb.	15	*unl*	*+04*	*43*	*****Corio**ssedum		
Narb.	15	*unl*	*+04*	*43*	*Corio**ssedum**		
3660	15	C2	+04	43	*Virinnae?		
3483	15	C1	+04	44	*****Brig**innum?		
3989	17	D5	+04	44	Noio**magos**	Col. Augusta Tricastinorum	Tricastini
4039	17	D4	+04	44	Segovellauni		
4039	17	D4	+04	44	Sego**vellaun**i		
3626	15	C1	+04	44	**Segus**io?		
4042	17	D5	+04	44	Seno**magos**		
4042	17	D5	+04	44	**Seno**magos		
3656	15	D1	+04	44	**Vind**alium?		

3817	17	C2	+04	45	Aquae **Seg**etae	
3879	17	D2	+04	45	Col. **Lugdun**um	Col. Copia Claudia Augusta **Lugdun**um
3879	17	D2	+04	45	Col. **Lug**dunum	Col. Copia Claudia Augusta **Lug**dunum
3920	17	C2	+04	45	Forum **Seg**usiavorum	**Seg**usiavi
3956	17	C2	+04	45	**Lugdun**ensis	
3956	17	C2	+04	45	**Lug**dunensis	
3965	17	C2	+04	45	**Mediol**anum	
4096	18	B3	+04	46	Augusto**dun**um	
4009	17	C1	+04	46	Ro**dumn**a	
4140	18	B2	+04	47	**Mandub**ii	
4144	18	B2	+04	47	[**Mediol**anum]	
4168	18	B2	+04	47	**Sid**oloucum	**Sid**otoco
1859	11	E4	+04	48	Augusto**bon**a	
2003	11	E4	+04	48	**Duro**catalaunum	
2336	11	E4	+04	48	**Seg**essera	
2004	11	E3	+04	49	**Duro**cortorum	
2004	11	E3	+04	49	**Duro**cortorum	
2237	11	E3	+04	49	Novio**magus**	
2237	11	E3	+04	49	**Novio**magus	
1767	10	A4	+04	52	**Lugdun**um	
1767	10	A4	+04	52	**Lug**dunum	
3667	16	A2	+05	43	**Alaun**ium	
3497	15	F2	+05	43	**Catu**iacia	
3625	15	E3	+05	43	Sego**brig**ii	
3625	15	E3	+05	43	**Sego**brigii	
3657	15	E2	+05	43	**Vind**asca	
3658	15	E2	+05	43	**Vind**elicus fl.	Soulgas fl.
3860	17	F4	+05	44	**Camb**onum	
3492	15	E1	+05	44	Carpento**rate**	*Forum Neronis
3988	17	E5	+05	44	Noio**mag**os	
3761	16	A1	+05	44	**Seg**ustero	
3804	17	E3	+05	45	Allo**brog**es	
3857	17	E2	+05	45	*__Brio__ratis	
3857	17	E2	+05	45	*Brio**ratis**	
3885	17	F2	+05	45	**Condat**e	
3946	17	F2	+05	45	**Lem**incum	
4068	17	F2	+05	45	Venetoni**magus**	
159	18	C3	+05	46	Pons **Dubr**is	
4087	18	C2	+05	47	**And**ematunnum	
22395	11	*unl*	+05	47	**And**esina	
4106	18	C2	+05	47	Castrum **Divion**ense	*Dibio
4167	18	C2	+05	47	Sego**bod**ium?	
4167	18	C2	+05	47	**Sego**bodium?	
1940	11	F4	+05	48	**Catu**ricis	
2238	11	F4	+05	48	Novio**magus**	
2238	11	F4	+05	48	**Novio**magus	
2097	11	F3	+05	49	Iblio**durum**?	
2205	11	F3	+05	49	Moso**magus**	

2422	11	F3	+05	49	Virio**dunum**	Verio**dunum**		
2422	11	F3	+05	49	**Virio**dunum	Veriodunum		
1972	11	F2	+05	50	**Corio**vallum	Cortovallium		
1972	11	F2	+05	50	Coriovallum	**Cort**ovallium		
1702	10	B5	+05	51	Batavo**durum**	Noviomagus	(Ulpia) Noviomagus	Batavi
1702	10	B5	+05	51	Batavodurum	Novio**magus**	(Ulpia) Novio**magus**	Batavi
1702	10	B5	+05	51	Batavodurum	**Novio**magus	(Ulpia) **Novio**magus	Batavi
1939	11	F1	+05	51	**Catua**lium			
2370	11	F1	+05	51	Teu**durum**?			
7898	31	E4	+06	36	Castellum Arsaca**litan**um			
3687	16	C2	+06	43	*__Brig__omagus			
3687	16	C2	+06	43	*Brig**omagus**			
3762	16	B2	+06	43	**Sent**ii			
3806	17	H4	+06	44	Alpes **Cotti**ae			
3682	16	B1	+06	44	**Bod**iontici			
3855	17	H4	+06	44	**Brigant**io			
3856	17	H4	+06	44	**Brig**ianii			
3863	17	G4	+06	44	**Catur**iges			
3863	17	G4	+06	44	Catu**riges**			
3864	17	G4	+06	44	**Catu**rigomagus			
3864	17	G4	+06	44	Caturigo**magus**			
3864	17	G4	+06	44	Catu**rigo**magus			
3890	17	H5	+06	44	**Cotti** Regnum			
3902	17	H4	+06	44	Druantium	*Alpis **Cotti**a	Summae Alpes	Alpis Iulia
3905	17	G4	+06	44	Eburo**dunum**	Ebru**dunum**		
3905	17	G4	+06	44	**Ebur**odunum	Ebrudunum		
3936	17	G4	+06	44	Icto**durus**			
3986	17	H5	+06	44	**Nemet**urii?			
22481	16	*unl*	*+06*	*44*	**Ouelaun**ioi			
4007	17	H5	+06	44	Rigo**magus**			
4007	17	H5	+06	44	**Rigo**magus			
4040	17	H4	+06	44	**Seg**ovii?			
4038	17	G5	+06	44	[**Sed**ena]			
3854	17	G2	+06	45	**Brigant**io			
3904	17	G3	+06	45	**Duro**tincum	**Duro**tingum		
3904	17	G3	+06	45	Duro**tinc**um	Durotingum		
3932	17	G3	+06	45	Graio**celi**?			
3959	17	G2	+06	45	**Mant**ala			
3968	17	G3	+06	45	Mello**sedum**			
4036	17	H3	+06	45	Scingo**magus**			
4059	17	G3	+06	45	Ucennii	**Ikon**ioi		
4111	18	D3	+06	46	Col. Iulia Equestris	Novio**dunum**		
4111	18	D3	+06	46	Col. Iulia Equestris	**Novio**dunum		
4117	18	D3	+06	46	Eburo**dun**ensis L.			
4117	18	D3	+06	46	**Ebur**odunensis L.			
4118	18	D3	+06	46	Eburo**dunum**			
4118	18	D3	+06	46	**Ebur**odunum			
4133	18	D3	+06	46	**Lem**annus L.	Lausonius L.		
4146	18	D3	+06	46	Minno**dunum**	Minodum		
4150	18	D3	+06	46	**Nant**uates			
4155	18	D3	+06	46	**Penn**e Locos			

22511	18	*unl*	+06	46	V**romagus**	U**romago**
22511	18	*unl*	+06	46	**Viro**magus	U**romago**
4119	18	D2	+06	47	Epamanduo**durum**	
4119	18	D2	+06	47	Epa**mandu**oduram	
22504	18	*unl*	+06	47	Lopo**sagium**	
22509	18	*unl*	+06	47	Vetatu**duro**	
2412	11	G4	+06	48	Vicus **Bod**atius?	
1829	11	G3	+06	49	**And**ethanna	
1989	11	G3	+06	49	**Divo**durum	Mettis
1989	11	G3	+06	49	Divo**durum**	Mettis
2178	11	G3	+06	49	**Medio**matrici	
2239	11	G3	+06	49	Novio**magus** Treverorum	
2239	11	G3	+06	49	**Novio**magus Treverorum	
2413	11	G3	+06	49	Vicus Contio**magus**	
2007	11	G2	+06	50	**Ebur**ones	
2099	11	G2	+06	50	**Ico**rigium	
2099	11	G2	+06	50	Ico**rig**ium	
2165	11	G2	+06	50	Marco**magus**?	
2001	11	G1	+06	51	Durno**magus**	
23064	31	*unl*	+07	36	Au**durus**	
23068	31	*unl*	+07	36	Capraria	**Carr**aria?
23121	31	*unl*	+07	36	**Verb**alis	
3751	16	E1	+07	44	Rotuba fl.	**Rutu**ba fl.
3781	16	D1	+07	44	**Vesu**biani	
4074	17	I4	+07	44	**Vesu**lus M.	
3821	17	I2	+07	45	Are**brigium**	
9321	39	B3	+07	45	**Carr**eum Potentia	**Karr**ea
9407	39	A3	+07	45	**Ocel**um	
4041	17	I3	+07	45	**Segus**io	Segusini
3992	17	I1	+07	46	Octo**durus**	Forum Claudii Vallensium
4166	18	E3	+07	46	**Sed**unum	**Sed**uni
4105	18	E2	+07	47	**Camb**ete	
4165	18	E2	+07	47	Salo**durum**	
1840	11	H4	+07	48	Argento**rate**	
1905	11	H4	+07	48	**Broc**omagus	
1905	11	H4	+07	48	Broco**magus**	
2429	11	H4	+07	48	Vo**seg**us M.	
1899	11	I3	+07	49	Borbeto**magus**	
1998	11	H3	+07	49	**Dumn**issus	
2216	11	H3	+07	49	**Nemet**es	
1897	11	H2	+07	50	**Bod**obrica	
1897	11	H2	+07	50	Bodo**brica**	
1898	11	H2	+07	50	**Bonn**a	
2285	11	H2	+07	50	Rigo**magus**	
2285	11	H2	+07	50	**Rig**omagus	
2339	11	H2	+07	50	[**Senti**acum]?	
2395	11	H2	+07	50	**Usipet**es	
1793	10	D4	+07	52	**Teuto**burgiensis? Saltus	
1690	10	D2	+07	54	**Abal**us? Ins.	
11747	48	A3	+08	39	Moli**bod**es Ins.	
11802	48	A3	+08	39	U**sel**(l)is	
11691	48	A2	+08	40	**Corn**us	
11714	48	A2	+08	40	Giddi**litani**	

11737	48	A2	+08	40	**Korn**ensioi	
					'Aichilensioi'	
Cors.	48	C2	+08	42	**Ouir**iballon	
					Akron	
9380	39	D5	+08	44	**Lang**enses	
9310	39	C3	+08	45	**Bod**incus fl.	
9371	39	C3	+08	45	Industria	**Bod**incomagum?
9371	39	C3	+08	45	Industria	Bodinco**magum**?
9381	39	D3	+08	45	**Lang**obardi	
9437	39	C3	+08	45	Rigo**magus**	
9437	39	C3	+08	45	**Rig**omagus	
9483	39	D2	+08	45	**Verb**anus L.	
4241	19	A2	+08	47	*Brigo**bann**is	
4241	19	A2	+08	47	***Brig**obannis	
4311	19	A2	+08	47	Iulio**magus**	
4182	18	F2	+08	47	**Vind**onissa	
4444	19	A2	+08	47	Vitu**durum**	
2802	12	B4	+08	48	Vicus **Sen**ot(ensis)	
2738	12	B3	+08	49	*Salio**brig**a	
2643	12	B3	+08	49	Lopo**dunum**	
2240	11	I3	+08	49	**Novio**magus	Nemetae
2240	11	I3	+08	49	Novio**magus**	Nemetae
2240	11	I3	+08	49	Noviomagus	**Nemet**ae
1794	10	E2	+08	54	**Teut**ones?	
23246	33	*unl*	*+09*	*35*	**Seggo**	
8100	32	E4	+09	36	*Civitas Siva**litan**a	
8246	32	D4	+09	36	Pagus Assa**litan**us	
11739	48	B2	+09	40	'Lugu**idunec**'	Castra Felicia?
11739	48	B2	+09	40	'**Lugu**idunec'	Castra Felicia?
11770	48	B2	+09	40	Portus **Lugu**idonis	
Cors.	48	D2	+09	42	**Kloun**ion	
Cors.	48	D2	+09	42	**Mant**inon	
Cors.	48	D2	+09	42	**Tout**elas Bomos	
9309	39	F5	+09	44	**Bod**etia	
9369	39	F5	+09	44	In Alpe **Penn**ino	
9413	39	E4	+09	44	Pagus Ambi**trebi**us	
23473	39	*unl*	*+09*	*44*	**Rig**onum fl.	
9449	39	E5	+09	44	**Seg**esta	Tigullia
					(Tigulliorum)	
9332	39	E3	+09	45	'Comeli **magus**'	'Camelio**magus**'
9395	39	E3	+09	45	**Mediol**an(i)um	
9472	39	F3	+09	45	**Treb**ia fl.	
4407	19	B3	+09	46	*Tar**vessed**um	
4407	19	B3	+09	46	***Tar**vessedum	
4239	19	B2	+09	47	**Brigant**inus L.	Ven(non)etus L.
4240	19	B2	+09	47	**Brigant**ium	**Brigant**ii
4255	19	B2	+09	47	**Clun**ia	
4337	19	B2	+09	47	**Magi**a	
22426	12	*unl*	*+09*	*48*	Brago**durum**	
2773	12	C3	+09	49	**Teut**oni	
8286	32	F4	+10	36	**Seg**ermes	
23198	32	*unl*	*+10*	*36*	Voli**tana** Plebs	
23505	41	*unl*	*+10*	*43*	**Vesid**ia fl.	
23	1	F2	+10	44	A**p**(p)e**nn**inus M.	
9311	39	H2	+10	45	[**Brem**tonicum]	
9393	39	H3	+10	45	**Mant**ua	
4186	19	C2	+10	47	A**bod**iacum	

4246	19	C2	+10	47	**Camb**odunum				
4246	19	C2	+10	47	Cambo**dunum**				
22518	19	*unl*	*+10*	*47*	**Cass**iliacum				
2484	12	D4	+10	48	Augusta **Vind**elicum	Aelia Augusta			
2804	12	D4	+10	48	**Vind**elici				
1760	10	G3	+10	53	**Lang**obardi				
9810	42	B2	+11	43	**Cort**ona				
9546	40	A4	+11	44	Felsina	**Bon**onia			
9614	40	B1	+11	45	**Vice**tia				
2705	12	E4	+11	48	Parro**dunum**				
2795	12	E4	+11	48	Venaxamo**durum**				
11262	47	B3	+12	37	Aquae **Seg**estanae	Aquae *Pacatianae	Aquae *Phimianae	Aquae *Pincianae
11619	47	B3	+12	37	(S)**Eg**esta	Egesta			
11350	47	B2	+12	38	Emporion **Seg**estanon				
23681	44	*unl*	*+12*	*41*	**Cori**oli				
23796	44	*unl*	*+12*	*41*	**Treb**ium				
10329	43	D2	+12	41	**Treb**ula Suffenas				
23537	42	*unl*	*+12*	*42*	**Corn**etus Campus				
9843	42	C4	+12	42	Forum **Cass**ii				
10020	42	D3	+12	42	**Treb**iae				
10021	42	D4	+12	42	**Treb**ula Mutuesca				
9986	42	D1	+12	43	**Sen**ones				
9987	42	D2	+12	43	**Sent**inum				
23615	42	*unl*	*+12*	*43*	**Vind**enates				
9579	40	C3	+12	44	Ostium **Sag**is				
9608	40	C1	+12	45	**Tarv**isium				
4252	19	E3	+12	46	**Catu**brini				
4420	19	E3	+12	46	Tilia**ventum** (Maius) fl.	Tilia**ventum** Maius fl.	Tilia**ventum** Minus fl.	
4197	19	E2	+12	47	**Alaun**oi				
4220	19	E2	+12	47	Arto**briga**				
2755	12	F4	+12	48	Sorvio**durum**				
2553	12	F3	+12	49	**Gabr**eta? Hyle				
24085	47	*unl*	*+13*	*37*	**Kort**yga				
10669	44	D2	+13	41	**Treb**a				
9984	42	E1	+13	43	**Sen**a fl.				
9985	42	E1	+13	43	**Sen**a Gallica				
4199	19	F3	+13	46	Alpes **Carn**icae				
4247	19	F3	+13	46	**Carn**i				
4312	19	F3	+13	46	Iulium **Carn**icum				
4404	19	F2	+13	47	'**Tarn**antone'				
2504	12	G4	+13	48	Boio**durum**	Boiotro			
119	2	F3	+13	53	**Lem**ovii?				
10681	44	F4	+14	40	**Vesu**vius M.				
23684	44	*unl*	*+14*	*41*	**Duro**nia				
10640	44	F3	+14	41	**Sid**icini				
10660	44	F3	+14	41	Teanum **Sid**icinum				
10670	44	F2	+14	41	'**Treb**ula'				
10671	44	F3	+14	41	**Treb**ula Balli(ni)ensium				
9972	42	G4	+14	42	**Sagr**us fl.				
4804	20	B5	+14	44	**Sen**ia				
4684	20	B4	+14	45	**Loug**eon Helos				

4569	20	B3	+ 14	46	**Carn**ium		
4409	19	G3	+ 14	46	'Tasi**nemeti**'		
4864	20	B3	+ 14	46	**Vir**unum		
4636	20	B2	+ 14	47	'**Gabro**mago'		
4636	20	B2	+ 14	47	'Gabro**mago**'		
4783	20	B2	+ 14	47	Saba**tinca**		
22442	12	*unl*	*+ 14*	*49*	Maro**boud**on		
24100	47	*unl*	*+ 15*	*37*	**Mag**ea Fons		
10806	45	B3	+ 15	40	**Ebur**um		
11022	45	B3	+ 15	40	**Vol**cei		
23771	44	*unl*	*+ 15*	*41*	**Sent**ianum		
4723	20	C4	+ 15	45	Nevio**dunum**		
4723	20	C4	+ 15	45	**Nevio**dunum		
2516	12	I4	+ 15	48	**Cet**ium		
11173	46	D5	+ 16	38	**Sagr**a(s) fl.		
10979	45	D3	+ 16	40	Silvium	**Sid**is	
4503	20	D6	+ 16	43	**And**etrium		
4803	20	D4	+ 16	45	**Seg**estica	Siscia	
2850	13	B4	+ 16	48	**Carn**untum		
2857	13	B4	+ 16	48	Col. **Carn**untum	Col. Septimia Aurelia Antoniniana	
2885	13	B4	+ 16	48	**Ket**ion Oros		
2900	13	B4	+ 16	48	**Lang**obardi		
2919	13	B4	+ 16	48	Mun. Vindo**bona**		
2919	13	B4	+ 16	48	Mun. **Vind**obona		
2982	13	B4	+ 16	48	Vindo**bona**		
2982	13	B4	+ 16	48	**Vind**obona		
22463	13	*unl*	*+ 16*	*49*	Ebouro**dounon**		
22463	13	*unl*	*+ 16*	*49*	**Ebour**odounon		
22466	13	*unl*	+ 16	49	Melio**doun**on		
10861	45	G4	+ 17	40	**Mandur**ia	Mandonion	Amandrinum
23892	45	*unl*	*+ 17*	*40*	**Sen**um		
4527	20	E2	+ 17	47	Arra**bona**		
4527	20	E2	+ 17	47	**Arrabo**na		
22462	13	*unl*	*+ 17*	*50*	**Boud**origon		
22462	13	*unl*	*+ 17*	*50*	Boud**origon**		
125	2	G3	+ 17	52	**Lug**ii		
11011	45	inset	+ 18	39	Uzentum	**Oux**enton	Augentum
4504	20	F4	+ 18	45	**And**izetes		
4595	20	F4	+ 18	45	**Corn**acates		
4839	20	F4	+ 18	45	**Teut**oburgium		
22609	21	*unl*	*+ 18*	*46*	Cara**mant**esium Vicus		
4685	20	F3	+ 18	46	**Lug**io	Florentia	
4560	20	F2	+ 18	47	**Brig**etio		
4667	20	F2	+ 18	47	Kela**mant**ia		
22626	22	*unl*	*+ 18*	*48*	**Ous**kenon		
4596	20	G4	+ 19	45	**Corn**acum		
4863	20	G2	+ 19	47	**Vind**onianus Vicus		
2859	13	E3	+ 19	49	**Cot**ini		
12993	54	C4	+ 20	38	**Karn**os Ins.		
12861	54	C4	+ 20	38	A**carn**ania		
5295	21	C5	+ 20	44	Singi**dunum**		
5355	21	C5	+ 20	44	Tri**corn**(i)enses		
5356	21	C5	+ 20	44	Tri**corn**ium		

14413	58	B3	+21	37	**Karn**asion			
14447	58	B3	+21	37	**Koti**lion M.			
25185	58	*unl*	*+21*	*37*	**Koti**lon			
25208	58	*unl*	*+21*	*37*	**Lang**on			
13070	54	D4	+21	38	**Medi**on			
12040	50	A3	+21	40	Begor**ritus** L.			
12054	50	A4	+21	40	**Cambu**nii M.			
5380	21	D7	+21	42	'Vin**denis**'			
25153	58	*unl*	*+22*	*36*	**Karn**ion			
14448	58	D4	+22	36	**Koty**rta			
25152	58	*unl*	*+22*	*37*	**Karn**eates M.			
14414	58	C3	+22	37	**Karn**ion fl.			
25209	58	*unl*	*+22*	*37*	**Lank**ia			
14514	58	C2	+22	37	**Mant**ineia	Antigoneia		
25365	58	*unl*	*+22*	*37*	**Rhati**ai			
13650	55	C3	+22	38	**Side**			
5237	21	E6	+22	43	**Rati**aria			
4934	21	E5	+22	44	**Bon**onia			
14667	58	E5	+23	36	**Side**			
14790	59	A3	+23	37	**Boud**oron			
14790	59	A3	+23	37	Boud**oron**			
25181	58	*unl*	*+23*	*37*	**Korn**iata M.			
25505	59	*unl*	*+23*	*37*	**Side**rtos			
14669	58	E2	+23	37	**Sid**ous			
24567	55	*unl*	*+23*	*38*	**Boud**(e)ion	**Boud**(e)ia		
13313	55	E3	+23	38	**Boud**oros fl.			
13313	55	E3	+23	38	Boud**oros** fl.			
13473	55	F3	+23	38	**Koty**laion M.			
24759	55	*unl*	*+23*	*38*	**Sid**ous			
13426	55	F2	+23	39	**Iko**s			
12261	51	B4	+23	40	Ass(er)a?	Asseros	Cass**era**	
12411	51	B3	+23	40	**Penn**ana			
12393	51	B2	+23	41	Odo**mantes**	Odo**mant**ike		
15064	60	B2	+24	35	**Boud**roe Inss.			
15193	60	C2	+24	35	**Kori**on			
13472	55	G3	+24	38	**Koty**laion			
22756	22	*unl*	*+24*	*45*	**Kot**ensioi			
150	2	H2	+24	58	**Sit**ones?			
12380	51	F3	+25	40	Mesam**bria**			
12380	51	F3	+25	40	Mesam**bria**			
22936	23	*unl*	*+25*	*48*	**Karr**odounon			
22936	23	*unl*	*+25*	*48*	**Karr**o**doun**on			
15179	60	F2	+26	35	'**Ketia**'? Pr.			
15342	60	F2	+26	35	**Sed**amnos? fl.			
14126	56	D4	+26	38	**Sid**oussa? Ins.			
13945	56	D2	+26	39	**Koty**los M.			
5413	22	D5	+26	43	A**britus**			
22779	22	*unl*	*+26*	*43*	**Medio**lanum			
15530	61	E3	+27	37	Hali**carn**assus			
25660	61	*unl*	*+27*	*37*	Thym**bria**			
25660	61	*unl*	*+27*	*37*	Thym**bria**			
24854	56	*unl*	*+27*	*39*	**Kam**(br)e			
13917	56	E3	+27	39	**Ket**eios fl.			
24924	56	*unl*	*+27*	*39*	**Sag**ara			
5543	22	E6	+27	42	Mesem**bria**			
5543	22	E6	+27	42	Mesem**bria**			

5495	22	E4	+27	44	**Duro**storum			
15226	60	G3	+28	36	**Lind**os	**Lind**ia		
16047	62	A3	+28	39	*****Sitt**ena?			
12691	52	C2	+28	41	Sely(m)**bria**	Eudoxiopolis		
12691	52	C2	+28	41	Sely(m)**bria**	Eudoxiopolis		
5421	22	F3	+28	45	Alio**brix**			
5555	22	F3	+28	45	Novio**dun**um			
5555	22	F3	+28	45	**Novio**dunum			
16522	65	C4	+29	36	Kiby**ratis**			
16686	65	B5	+29	36	**Sid**yma			
16720	65	C5	+29	36	**Treb**endai			
15984	62	C4	+29	38	*****Lank**ena			
25721	62	*unl*	*+28*	*38*	**Bria**			
25721	62	*unl*	*+28*	*38*	**Bria**			
25891	62	*unl*	+29	38	**Sag**arenoi?			
15978	62	C3	+29	39	**Koti**aeion			
15988	62	C3	+29	39	**Mant**alos			
16685	65	E5	+30	36	**Sid**erous Limen	Posi**d**arisous?		
16684	65	E5	+30	36	**Sid**erous Pr.			
16721	65	D4	+30	36	**Treb**enna			
16667	65	E2	+30	37	**Sag**alassos			
16622	65	D3	+30	37	*****Ouerb**e			
15898	62	E4	+30	38	Beudos (Palaion)	**Boud**eia		
25771	62	*unl*	*+30*	*39*	**Kass**enoi			
25890	62	*unl*	*+30*	*39*	**Sag**arenoi			
12599	52	G3	+30	40	*****Kass**a			
16679	65	G4	+31	36	*****Senn**ea?			
16683	65	F4	+31	36	**Sid**e			
16382	65	D3	+30	37	**And**eda			
16543	65	G3	+31	37	**Kot**enna			
15976	62	F2	+31	39	K**onsid**iana			
					Choria			
5848	23	E1	+31	47	**Sag**aris fl.	Rhode fl.		
16805	66	B1	+32	37	Iconium	Claud**ic**onium	Col. Iulia	Col. Aelia
							Augusta	Hadriana
							Equestris?	Augusta
16830	66	A1	+32	37	**Korn**a?			
16898	66	A2	+32	37	*****Sed**asa			
15936	62	H2	+32	39	Gordion	**Vind**ia?		
16216	63	B1	+32	39	Tecto**sages**			
25956	63	*unl*	*+32*	*40*	**Drynemet**on			
19541	86	C3	+32	40	Gezat**origis**			
19603	86	C3	+32	40	**Mant**ineion			
19623	86	C3	+32	40	'Peto**brogen**'			
19643	86	C3	+32	40	Tekto**sages**			
26142	66	*unl*	*+33*	*36*	**Vind**emis			
16905	66	D2	+33	37	*****Sid**amaria			
16137	63	D1	+33	39	Eco**brogis**	Ecco**brig**a		
16137	63	D1	+33	39	Eco**brogis**	Eccobriga		
19556	86	D3	+33	40	**Ikot**arion?			
27146	86	*unl*	*+33*	*40*	'Viciu'			
19509	86	D2	+33	41	*****Bon**ita			
16103	63	F4	+34	38	**And**abalis			
16204	63	E4	+34	38	Sala**mbria**i	Sala**berin**a		
16204	63	E4	+34	38	Sala**mbria**i	Salaberina		
16132	63	F1	+34	39	**Corn**iaspa			

17178	68	A2	+35	35	**Cas(s)**ius M.	
16152	63	G3	+35	38	**Kamoul**ianai	Iustinianoupolis Nova
19994	87	A4	+35	40	**Vir**asia	
19944	87	A3	+35	41	**Sag**ylion	

5.2 THE DISTRIBUTION OF THE CELTIC-LOOKING NAMES IN TABLE 5.2 (MAPS 5.1 AND 5.2)

The figures on Map 5.1 give the number of tokens per square. (Italics are used for figures which include items listed as '*unl*' in Table 5.2.) Up to a point the figures speak for themselves. Celtic-looking elements are concentrated in the north-west. Their scarcity in Ireland and beyond the Rhine reflects the limitations of the ancient sources and the *Barrington* data. On the other hand their absence from the Pyrenees, south-eastern Spain and many parts of Italy, Greece, the Balkans, Asia Minor and Africa is very significant because those areas supply the majority of known ancient place-names.[4]

This is made clearer on Map 5.2, which presents the number of tokens on Map 5.1 as a proportion of the number of places with ancient toponym(s) in the square (using the figures from Map 2.2 in Chapter 2 above).[5] There is a slight statistical problem here. A square like −10/39 is straightforwardly 100% since '3' on Map 5.1 corresponds to the '3' on Map 2.2. On the other hand, a square like −5/56 has '*3*' on Map 5.1 (2 of these tokens being located in the *Atlas* and the third, *Litanomago*, being unlocated in the *Atlas*), but has only '2' on Map 2.2, which only enumerated 'located' toponyms. To avoid sums like '3 out of 2' tokens in such cases I have added the number of '*unl*' names in Table 5.2[6] to the figures in Map 2.2 before working out the percentages, in the case of square −5/56 for example, 3 divided by $(2 + 1) = 100\%$. Percentages worked out in this way are shown in *italics* on Map 5.2. This method is not perfect, since no allowance is made for the possibility that relevant '*unl*' names without Celtic-looking elements might be localizable after a great deal of extra research. Possibly a sophisticated statistical method might be used to take account of this possibility, but for the present purposes it seems sufficient to put the relevant figures in italics on Map 5.2 and emphasize that some of these italicized figures *may* exaggerate the proportion of Celtic-looking names.

---

[4] See Ch. 2 above, p. 21.

[5] Note that all percentages of .5 or less are rounded down. (There were no occurrences of .5% or less.)

[6] '*unl*' names includes the '*Av*' (Avienus) and '*cn.*' (coin-legend) names in Hispania. However, 25cn. *Alaun* at −2/41 is not counted as extra item in the calculations for Map 5.2 since it seems to be merely an alternative name for the located 25D4 *Allobo/Alauona* (see Ch. 4 above, s.v. *alaunā*).

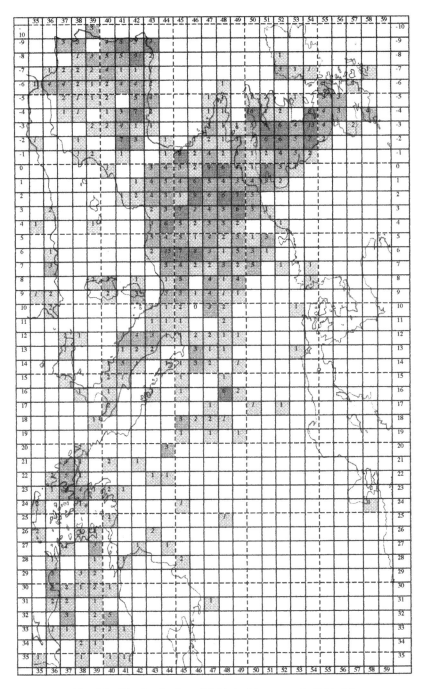

Map 5.1   The distribution of Celtic-looking names in Table 5.2

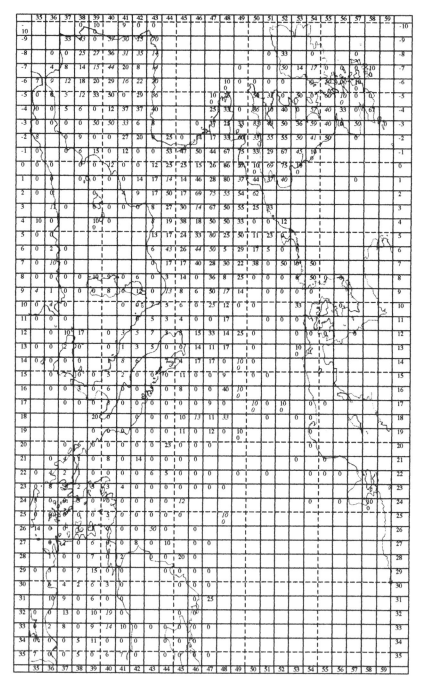

Map 5.2   The distribution of Celtic-looking names in Table 5.2 proportional to the number of known places

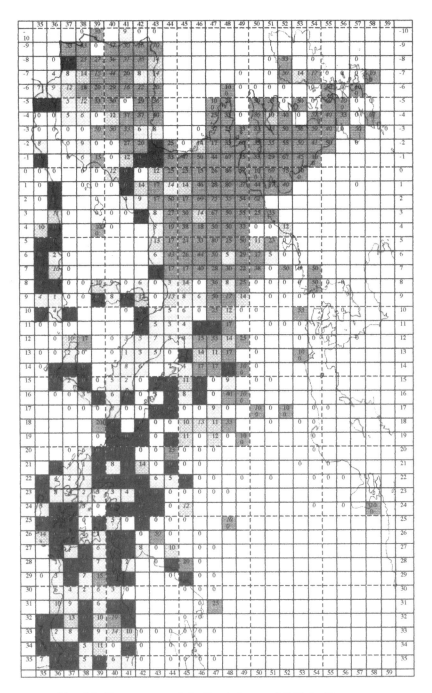

Map 5.3 The presence and significant absence of Celtic-looking names

Map 5.3 expresses the data in Map 5.2 more graphically by the use of shading. Squares with percentages of 15% and over have the darkest shading (but not black) and those with 10–14% and 1–9% are progressively lighter. Squares where ancient toponyms are attested on Map 2.2 but none contain our Celtic-looking elements are left white and are marked 0, unless *at least 10 named places* are known, in which case they are marked in black. The point here is that it is hardly significant when no Celtic-looking elements happen to occur in a square that only includes a few known names, whereas in areas where tens or even hundreds of names are attested the absence of Celtic-looking elements is highly significant. Thus black indicates *significant absence* of Celticity.

As we are dealing with small figures in many areas, it would be wrong to make deductions from individual percentages, especially in squares which are markedly different from their surroundings. Nevertheless, overall trends are immediately obvious. The north-western distribution of Celtic-looking elements in Map 5.1 is reinforced in Maps 5.2 and 5.3, as is the absence or rarity of Celtic-looking elements in most other areas. The darker (15% +) squares in Map 5.3 which are not in clusters are relatively few, and invite especial scrutiny to establish whether we are dealing with coincidences arising from very small numbers – numbers often as low as 1, as comparison with Map 5.1 reveals. Percentages between 1% and 14% occur in many areas, and it is tempting to disregard them as statistical 'noise' from elements which are merely Celtic-looking rather than Celtic; however, the presence of *clusters* of such lightly shaded areas, for instance in north Italy and Turkey, cautions one against discarding them.

The significant absence of Celtic-looking elements in most Mediterranean areas is indicated by the black squares. Where black squares adjoin shaded squares (e.g. in the Pyrenees and in Raetia) the data obviously needs to be scrutinized in detail 'on the ground', at a closer level of detail than one-degree squares (see Chapters 6–11 below).

5.3 CHECKING FOR NORTH-WESTERN BIAS

It may be wondered whether the north-western bias of the shading in Maps 5.1 and 5.3 reflects my own unconscious selection of Celtic elements from areas which I know best. To control this I have produced a map, Map 5.4, constructed in the same way as Map 5.1, on the basis of the elements in the anhydronyms in Pannonia which Anreiter categorizes as Celtic:[7]

---

[7] *Die vorrömischen Namen Pannoniens*, pp. 184–86.

Adnamantia
Bononia
Brigetio
Carrodun**um**
Cornacum
Matrica
Noviodun**um**
*Sing*idun**um**
Siscia
Vindobona
Cetius (Mons)
Belgites
Boii
Cornacates
Hercuniates
Latovici
*Scord*isci

The elements in **bold** here have already been included on my maps and those in *italics* are not regarded as Celtic by Anreiter. This leaves seven double underlined elements for which the evidence in the Barrington data can be collected via the following strings:

1. NAMANT

Adnamantia itself is not in the Barrington database, as the *Atlas* adopts the form *Annamatia* from the *Antonine Itinerary* (20F3 = +18/46). Hence there is only one example in the database:[8]

62	*unl*	+30	39	**Namant**aloi?

2. MATR

It is debated whether *Matrica* (like *Mediomatrici*) contains the Celtic word for 'mother' or one for 'material, wood', which would ultimately be related, as in Latin *mater, materies, materia*.[9] I therefore give all examples of the

<hr>

[8] On this see p. 272 below.
[9] Anreiter, *Die vorrömischen Namen Pannoniens*, pp. 169–70; IEW, p. 701. Cf. AILR and PNPG Possibly Celtic Elements s.v. matr-/{ma:tr-}.

string as formally admissible, even though some must be non-Celtic (the stem being pan-Indo-European):

4	*unl*			Mar(ae)u	**Matr**eu
6	*unl*			Maroga**matr**ae	
11	C4	+ 02	48	**Matr**ona fl.	
11	G3	+ 06	49	Medio**matr**ici	
17	H4	+ 06	44	**Matr**ona M.	
19	D2	+ 11	47	****Matr**eium	
20	E5	+ 17	44	Ad **Matr**icem	
20	F2	+ 18	47	**Matr**ica	
42	C4	+ 12	42	Vicus **Matr**ini	
42	F3	+ 13	42	**Matr**inus? fl.	
42	G3	+ 14	42	**Matr**inum	
44	*unl*	*+ 15*	41	Ad **Matr**em Magnam	
45	*unl*			Cama**latr**us	Cala**matr**us
60	C2	+ 24	35	Panto**matr**ion	Agrion
86	*unl*	*+ 33*	*40*	**Matr**ix	
91	*unl*			Bi**matr**a	

The unlocated examples from Maps 4, 6 and 91 are in Africa, India and Mesopotamia. The one from Map 45 may be in Lucania.

3. SISC (SISK IS NOT FOUND)[10]

14	G3	+ 01	45	****Sisc**iacum	
20	D4	+ 16	45	Segestica	**Sisc**ia
20	D4	+ 16	45	**Sisc**iani	

4. BELG[11]

8	E3	− 03	51	**Belg**ae		
11	G2	+ 06	50	**Belg**ica	**Belg**ae	
11	H3	+ 07	49	**Belg**inum		
20	*unl*			**Belg**ites		
25	*unl*	*− 01*	*41*	Begeda	**Belg**eda	Belikiom
91	*unl*			**Belg**ynaia		

The Pannonian *Belgites* (Map 20) are not located in the *Atlas*, the sole reference to them (Pliny 3.148) being geographically vague. The name from Map 91 is in Mesopotamia.

---

[10] Cf. PNPG Possibly Celtic Elements s.v. *sisco-*.
[11] Cf. Hamp, 'Morphology', p. 188.

5. Boi

The etymology and analysis of this Celtic stem is controversial. If *Boii* comes from IE *$g^w ow$-yo*-, Greek names in *Boio*- may ultimately be related at the Proto-Indo-European level.[12] In the following list of 'formally admissible' names I have not attempted to distinguish Celtic and non-Celtic ones:

12	G2	+ 13	50	**Boi**haemum	
12	G4	+ 13	48	**Boi**odurum	**Boi**otro
12	H2	+ 14	50	**Boi**i	
14	E4	− 01	44	**Boi**i	
14	I2	+ 03	46	**Boi**i?	
20	D2	+ 16	47	**Boi**i	
40	A3	+ 11	44	**Boi**(i)	
49	C3	+ 20	40	**Boi**oi	
49	C3	+ 20	40	**Boi**on M.	
55	C3	+ 22	38	**Boi**on	
56	*unl*	+ 26	38	**Boi**one	
58	E4	+ 23	36	**Boi**a(i)	Boea
58	*unl*	+ 23	36	**Boi**atikos Kolpos	
60	*unl*			**Boi**ai	
87	*unl*			**Boi**on	

60unl *Boiai* and 87 [inset] unl *Boion* belong in Crete and the east Crimea.

The following are formally inadmissible:

4	*unl*			Kol(o)**boi**		
5	inset			Nagadiba	Nagadiba Nesos	Nagadi**boi**
5	*unl*			Gali**boi**		
9	D2	− 04	58	Kornaouioi	Kornabioi	Kornou**boi**
35	*unl*			**Boi**n(ag?)		
36	*unl*			**Boi**n	**Boi**nag	
47	F4	+ 14	37	Eu**boi**a?		
48	D2	+ 09	42	Syr**boi**?		
50	A1	+ 21	41	Sto**boi**	Sto**boi**	
50	B3	+ 22	40	Eu**boi**a	Dausara	
54	*unl*			Eu**boi**a		
55	D1	+ 22	39	**Boi**be L.		
55	*unl*			**Boi**be		
55	*unl*			Eu**boi**a		
55	*unl*			Meli**boi**a		
55	*unl*			Meli**boi**a		
58	D2	+ 22	37	Eu**boi**a M.		
58	*unl*			**Boi**noa	Oinoe	
58	*unl*			Oinoe	**Boi**noa	
59	B1	+ 23	38	Eu**boi**cus Sinus		

---

[12] See below, p. 263.

60	C2	+ 24	35	**Boi**be			
61	*unl*			Om**boi**			
72	C2	+ 33	35	Keryn(e)ia	Keraunia	[Kir**boi**a]	Corinaeum?
80	B5	+ 32	24	Om**boi**			
85	E1	+ 47	46	Ser**boi**			
87	B4	+ 36	40	**Boi**nasa			

6. HERCUN, HERCYN (HERKUN, HERKYN NOT FOUND)[13]

| 12 | *unl* | *+ 11* | *50* | **Hercyn**ia Silva |
| 20 | E3 | + 17 | 46 | **Hercun**iates |

The *Hercynia Silva* is simply located north of the Danube in the *Atlas*. Since it was reputedly large, my grid reference is inevitably fairly arbitrary.

7. LATO

This Celtic stem probably occurs only in the name of the *Latobici*,[14] but the following seem formally admissible:

20	B4	+ 14	45	**Lato**bici	
20	B4	+ 14	45	Praetorium **Lato**bicorum	
27	B4	−04	36	Ossigi	Municipium **Lato**nium
32	H2	+ 11	37	**Lato**miae?	
60	E2	+ 25	35	**Lato**	
60	E2	+ 25	35	**Lato** pros Kamara	
80	B3	+ 32	25	Contra **Lato**polin	
80	B3	+ 32	25	**Lato**polis	

The following are formally inadmissible:

9	D5	−04	55	**Blato**bulgium		
14	G2	+ 01	46	**Blato**magus		
14	G1	+ 01	47	Ca**lato**nno		
34	D2	+ 05	35	Burgus Specu**lato**rius Antoninianus		
34	D2	+ 05	35	Burgus Specu**lato**rius Commodianus		
48	B1	+ 09	41	Tibula?	Tibou**lato**i	Portus *Tibulae?
60	E2	+ 25	35	Mi**lato**s		
48	D3	+ 09	41	Ba**lato**noi		

[13] Cf. DLG s.v. *ercunia*.
[14] Cf. GPN, p. 216; DLG s.v. *lato*- (on *lati*- cf. Blažek, 'Celtic–Anatolian isoglosses', pp. 126–27); PNPG Celtic Elements s.v. {la:to/i-}; KPP, pp. 52–55. The string *Lat*- is discussed by Villar, *Indoeuropeos y no indoeuropeos*, pp. 325–27.

Combining the 'formally admissible' data above with the 'formally admissible' data already given in Chapter 4 above for the elements *bon-*, *brig-* and *brigant, caito-, carr-, corno-, dūno-, novio-, vic-* and *vindo-*,[15] results in Map 5.4, showing the distribution of 'Pannonian Celtic-looking' elements. The background shading is repeated from Map 5.1. Although there are fewer names on Map 5.4 than Map 5.1, the overall distribution is very similar, confirming that the distribution in Map 5.1 is not distorted by a north-western bias in my initial choice of Celtic elements. The additional names in the south on Map 5.4 are due to occurrences of the strings BOI, LATO and MATR. No doubt they are due to non-Celtic languages possessing coincidental homonyms (e.g. Greek *Latom(e)ion* 'stone quarry') or cognates of similar shape.

I conclude that Maps 5.1 and 5.2 give a good impression of the relative distribution of Celtic toponymy, once account is taken of the statistical 'noise' arising from the mechanistic method which I employed to create them. This 'noise' – that is, patches of shading at unlikely places on the map – is the price paid for the use of an objective but crude method of assessing Celticity. In the following chapters, however, the data will be refined using a more traditional but subjective approach.

---

[15] Excluding the various duplicates already noted.

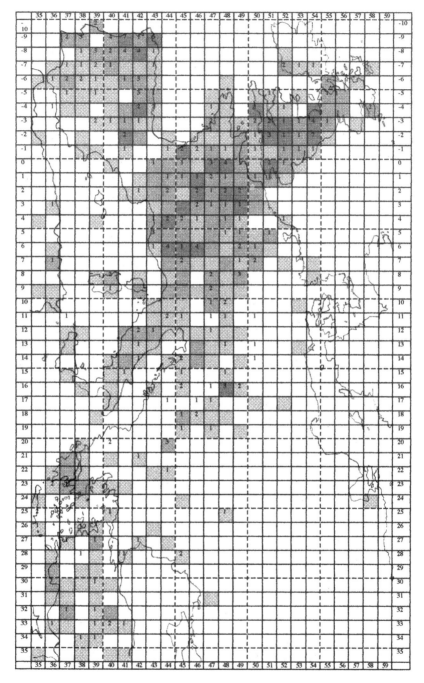

Map 5.4 The distribution of 'Pannonian Celtic-looking' names

6

THE EXTENT OF CELTIC NAMES, I:
NORTHERN EUROPE
(ABOVE 48 LATITUDE)

Chapters 6–9 examine the boundary between Celtic and non-Celtic names in more detail, where necessary discriminating between Celtic and quasi-Celtic names, and bringing in some further evidence where available, such as Celtic names missing from the *Atlas* and unlocatable Celtic-looking names whose general area is known. By 'unlocatable' names I mean 'unlocated' toponyms which were excluded from Table 5.2 in Chapter 5 because they could not be located to the accuracy of a single-degree square, unlike many of the other 'unlocated' toponyms in the *Atlas*'s *Map-by-Map Directory*.

The aim of these chapters is to establish the limits of Celtic toponymy, taking Maps 5.1–5.3 as a basis, but scrutinizing the data more closely where the Celticity of an area is in doubt. In each chapter I work from west to east. The level of detail and style of treatment varies from area to area. Chapter 6 covers northern Europe, Chapter 7 covers central Europe and Chapter 8 covers southern Europe, while Asia Minor is discussed in Chapter 9.

Each chapter contains a number of tables in which the names from the APNI are grouped in 1-degree squares. 'Celtic-looking' names from Table 2 in Chapter 5 are **bold** irrespective of whether they are genuinely Celtic. Probably Celtic names are <u>underlined</u>. Additional names mentioned in my discussion but not in the *Barrington* data are added between {curly brackets}, as are a few 'unlocated' names not previously adduced in Chapter 4, e.g. {12unl Bikourgion}. In squares without *any* Celtic names *all* the names are *italicized*.[1]

The maps in Chapter 6–9 cover most, though not all, of the areas covered in the tables. Four of the maps are relevant to more than one chapter: Maps 6.2 and 6.3 are relevant to Chapter 7 as well as to Chapter 6, and Maps 7.1 and 7.2 are relevant to Chapter 8 as well as to Chapter 7. The symbols on the maps indicate the location of the places named in the tables:

---

[1] These squares will therefore be unshaded in Map 11.1 in Ch. 11 below.

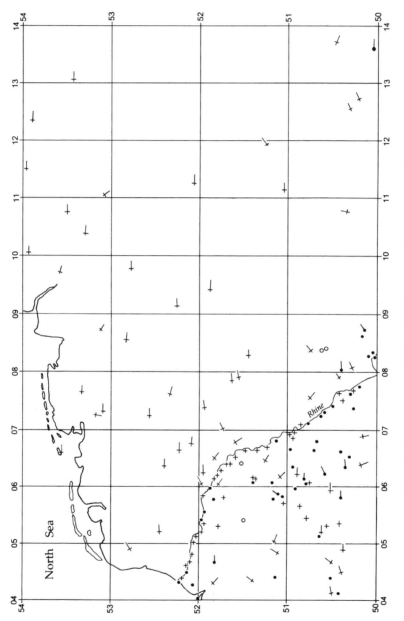

Map 6.1 The north-eastern limits of Celtic names, +4 to +14 (above lat. 50)

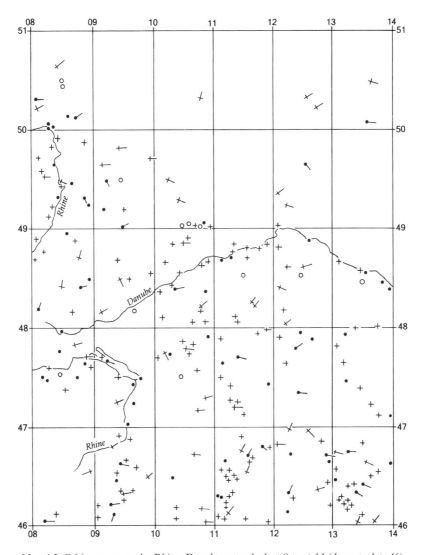

Map 6.2 Celtic names on the Rhine–Danube watershed, +8 to +14 (down to lat. 46)

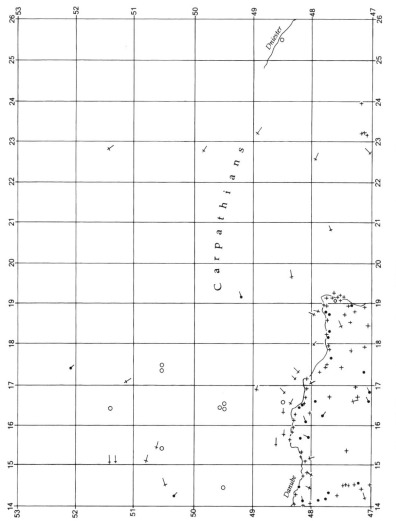

Map 6.3 The north-eastern limits of Celtic names, +14 to +26 (down to lat. 47)

circles = Celtic names, with solid circles for located names and open circles for 'unlocated' names (the latter generally placed in the middle of the relevant square)

crosses = non-Celtic names (located names only)

In the case of non-punctual features (such as rivers, lakes, mountain-ranges, islands, tribes and regions) the tail attached to the circle or cross indicates the direction in which the legend would run if it were given. It will be appreciated that legends and symbols could only be combined in a large work like the *Barrington Atlas*, to which reference should be made for more detail. The present maps cover larger areas than the *Atlas*'s maps and are intended to give a general impression of the linguistic geography.

The present chapter is fairly cursory; the aim is to establish the northern and north-eastern boundaries of Celtic toponymy. References to the maps in the *Atlas* are not given in the tables below, as the layout of the *Atlas* in this area is straightforward: nearly all the names discussed are on its Maps 7–13.

(a) From −10 to +1 longitude (above latitude 48)

This area covers Ireland, Britain and the northern French coast. Its Celticity is clear from my Maps 5.1–5.3, and is further borne out by the 'unlocatable' names in the data, that is, names in the tables in Chapter 4 which could not be located to a single degree square but which belong in the area of southern Britain and Ireland (*Atlas* Map 8) and northern Britain and Ireland (*Atlas* Map 9):[2]

8	*unl*	**Alaun**a
8	*unl*	**Deve**ntia Statio
8	*unl*	**Devi**onisso
8	*unl*	**Vern**alis
9	*unl*	A**tecotti**
9	*unl*	Cind**ocell**um
9	*unl*	**Eburo** *Castellum
9	*unl*	Ouak**omago**i

Further Celtic names could be added in Ireland by using Ptolemy, who is not fully exploited in the *Atlas*,[3] and in Britain and northern France by considering rarer elements,[4] but this not necessary here as the Celticity of the whole area is clear. That is not to say that there may not be unidentified

---

[2] There are no relevant unlocatable names in Map 7's area (either side of the English Channel).

[3] See Ch. 1, n. 18. Some Irish names appear on the *Atlas*'s Map 2.

[4] See PNRB and Gohil, *Ancient Celtic and Non-Celtic Place-Names*.

pockets of languages other than Celtic, Latin and Greek within it, for example Pictish in Scotland.[5]

Looking at the squares on the edges of the shaded Celtic-looking areas on Maps 5.1–5.3, the *Orcades insulae* (−3/59) can be regarded as Celtic,[6] but Ptolemy's *Taixalon akron* (−2/57) – *Taizalon* in the manuscripts – is presumably named from his *Taixaloi* tribe (−3/57), whose name 'cannot be said to be Celtic with any confidence' and is putatively non-Indo-European Pictish.[7] The '0%' square at −3/56 is merely the arbitrarily placed names *Britannia/Albion* (Atlas Map 2C2); in fact these are probably both Celtic names.[8] The '0%' at +1/57 is the arbitrarily placed *Germanicum Mare* (Map 2D2).

In the extreme north, off the edge of my maps, the *Atlas* has *Thule? Insulae* (−1/61 = 2C1) and *Hyperboreios/Douekalidonios Okeanos* (−7/62 = 2B1). The latter is probably Celtic.[9]

(b) From +2 to +7 longitude (above latitude 48)

Only the south-west of this area is solidly Celtic.[10] Elsewhere there is a transition to Germanic.

The 12% at +4/52 is solely due to the obviously Celtic **Lugdunum** (Katwijk) near the mouth of the Rhine (10A4), but another Celtic candidate in the same square is the ethnic name *Cananefates* (whence *Aurelium Cananefatium*, Voorburg), which Schrijver sees as a Celtic-Germanic hybrid, 'leek-lords' (cf. W. *cennin*).[11] There is also the probably Celtic *Matilo* (10A4).[12] The square below this (+4/51) has none of our selected Celtic-looking elements, but nevertheless its *Helinium* (10A5 = 11E1) is

---

[5] On Pictish names see Jackson, 'Pictish language', and Isaac, 'Scotland'. Greek names in Britain are discussed by Parsons, 'Classifying Ptolemy's English place-names' (but cf. caveat in the review of *Ptolemy* by Billy). On the controversial question of non-Celtic substrates in Ireland, compare, e.g. Schrijver, 'Non-Indo-European surviving in Ireland', with Isaac, 'Some Old Irish etymologies'.

[6] The name of the Orkneys is generally supposed to show Celtic loss of **p* (PNRB, p. 433; Isaac, 'Scotland'. p. 200). The favoured etymon is Celtic **orko-* 'pig(let)', OI *orc* (DLG and PNPG s.v. *orco-*), but there is also OI *orc* 'salmon' (LEIA s.vv.). A Celtic **orkā* 'pine' has also been proposed (Stalmaszczyk & Witczak, 'Celto-Slavic language connections'). Place-names in *Ork-* discussed below include *Orkelis, Orkatos, Orkistos* and *Orkaorkoi* (pp. 231, 239, 258, 270 and 273). Apart from 9D2 *Orkas akra* (opposite the *Orcades insulae*) and 42B4 *[Orcla]* in Italy, these are the only examples of the case-sensitive strings *Orc* and *Ork* (but not *Orch*) in the *Barrington* data. On *Orcus* as a personal name see Minkova, *Personal Names of the Latin Inscriptions of Bulgaria*, p. 223; cf. Holder ii, 869.

[7] Jackson, 'Pictish language', p. 136; PNRB, p. 464; Kitson, 'River-names', pp. 106–7. See discussion by Isaac, 'Scotland', p. 203, and PNPG Comments s.n. *Taiksáloi, Taízalon a.*

[8] Sims-Williams, 'Celtomania and Celtoscepticism', p. 20; Koch, 'Celts, Britons, and Gaels'.

[9] PNRB, pp. 44 and 338; Sims-Williams, 'Common Celtic'; De Bernardo Stempel, 'More on Ptolemy's evidence for Celtic Ireland', p. 98.

[10] No unlocatable names can be added from the area of Maps 10–12.

[11] Schrijver, 'De etymologie van de naam van de Cannenefaten', and 'Keltisch of niet', pp. 75–82; cf. Rübekeil, pp. 76–87 and 413; Falileyev & Isaac, 'Leeks and garlic'.

[12] GPN, p. 231; Toorians, *Keltisch en Germaans in de Nederlanden*, p. 104.

Celtic according to Schrijver (he compares Cornish *heyl* 'estuary')[13] and so, judging by its suffix, is its *Condacum?* (11E1), although this latter name is not attested early.[14] *Vacalus/Vahalis fl.* may also be Celtic.[15] On the other hand, the *Frisiavones* and *Sturii* in the same square have Germanic names,[16] emphasizing this as a Celtic–Germanic transition zone. In the next square down (+4/50 = 11E2) again has '0' for our selected Celtic-looking elements, but the *-acum* suffix appears in *Geminiacum* and *Vodgoriacum*,[17] and the other names are all obscure (*Aduatuci*,[18] *Condrusi*,[19] *Sabis? fl.*), apart from the Latin *Carbonaria Silva*.[20] The Celticity of this square depends on the *-acum* suffix.[21]

Moving a degree eastwards, +5/52 has '0%' for Celtic, although only 3 names occur, one of them being Latin – *Traiectum* (10B4) – and two, *Flevum L.* and *Fectio*, being Germanic.[22] At +5/51, besides the names in bold, *Carvo?* (10B5) may be Celtic,[23] and *Rhenus fl.* certainly is,[24] while Thurneysen entertained the idea that *Baetasii?* (11F1) was an opprobrious ethnonym (OI *baíth* 'foolish').[25] *Mediolanion* can be added from Ptolemy 2.11.13.[26] At

---

[13] 'Welsh *heledd, hêl*, Cornish **heyl*, "Latin" *helinium*, Dutch *hel-, zeelt*, and 'Keltisch of niet', pp. 72–75, seeing a precocious Brittonic type development from IE **selos* 'marsh' (as against **salia* in Padel, 'Cornish **heyl* "estuary"', and CPNE, pp. 127–28; for **salia* cf. Vennemann, 'Linguistic reconstruction', p. 220; Kitson, 'River-names', pp. 93–94). *Helinium* is much earlier than any evidence for /h-/ in Brittonic, and this is also rare in Gaulish (GPN, p. 397; McCone, *Towards a Relative Chronology*, p. 88). As *Helinium* is duplicated, there are in fact 6 places at +4/51 rather than the 7 of my Map 2.2.

[14] *Castrum nomine Condacum* and *Condacensi castro* in a tenth- or eleventh-century *Vita S. Reineldis*, and *Contheca* in 1147, cited by Gysseling, *Toponymisch Woordenboek*, i, 571, s.n. *Kontich*. It may derive from the personal name *Condus* (GPN, p. 337; LEIA C-196). On *-acum* names see Russell, 'Suffix', and for the Rhineland in particular Weisgerber, p. 351, and Kuhn, 'Die -acum-Namen am Rhein'.

[15] GPN, p. 476; Weisgerber, pp. 324 and 356; KPP, p. 302. Cf. Isaac, 'Scotland', p. 200, and PNPG Celtic Elements for *uac(c)o-* 'bent, curved' (cf. VCIE, pp. 75–78 and 123–25; KPP, p. 302). Germanic according to Reichert i, 747–48, and ii, 639. As *Mosa* has /o/ versus the */a/ of German *Maas*, it too may be Celtic (see PNPG Comments s.n.).

[16] Schönfeld, pp. 94–96 and 211; Svennung, p. 214.

[17] On the latter see AILR Possibly Celtic Elements s.vv. *d(o)go-*, *gorio-* and *uodo-*.

[18] Weisgerber, pp. 332, 336 and 354, n. 78; Kuhn, 'Die -acum-Namen am Rhein', pp. 392 and 394–95.

[19] Weisgerber, pp. 333 and 356; Toorians, *Keltisch en Germaans in de Nederlanden*, p. 73. Non-Germanic according to Reichert i, 226.

[20] Speculations in Holder, s.nn.

[21] Cf. p. 10 above and p. 302 below.

[22] Rasch, §VIb; Toorians, *Keltisch en Germaans in de Nederlanden*, pp. 98–99 and 103. Reichert i, 268 and 272, and ii, 506, has only *Flevum* as Germanic.

[23] Toorians, *Keltisch en Germaans in de Nederlanden*, pp. 95–96, comparing *Carvone* (TP) with *Carvium* at +6/51 below (both possibly Germanic according to Reichert i, 171, and ii, 490). Toorians makes a tentative case for the Celticity of *Levefanum?* (pp. 102–3).

[24] Stefan Zimmer in *RGermAlt*, s.n. *Rhein*; PNPG Celtic Elements s.v. {re:no-}. On *Rhenus* see also p. 200 below.

[25] Holder i, 327; non-Germanic according to Reichert i, 112.

[26] See Ch. 4 above, s.v. *medio-*.

+ 5/50 (11F2) *Arduenna Silva* is Celtic,[27] and *Perniciacum?/Pernaco* appears to contain the Celtic /a:ko/ suffix.[28]

A further degree to the east, the Celtic names at + 6/50 (11G2), in addition to those in bold, are *Aquae Granni* (alluding to a Celtic god),[29] *Belgica/Belgae*,[30] *Caerosi*,[31] *Sunuci*,[32] and the -*acum* names *Iuliacum*, *Tiberiacum?* and *Tolbiacum*. Celtic also appears securely at + 6/51 with **Durnomagus** on the Rhine (11G1), and *Carvium* may well be Celtic (cf. W *carw* 'stag'), though this has been debated.[33] *Blariacum* and *Mederiacum*[34] at the west of the square also give a slight Celtic tinge to a set of Latin, Germanic[35] or obscure[36] names. Note also a name in Ptolemy 2.11.14, missing in the *Atlas*: *Boudoris* (= Büderich).[37] Further north at this longitude Celtic disappears: the three ethnic names at + 6/52, *Tubantes* and the much later attested *Francia/Franci* and *Salii?* (10C4), are not Celtic,[38] and neither is the sole name at + 6/53, *Burcana Insula* (10C3).[39]

To the extreme north (+ 6/62), off the edge of all my maps, the *Atlas* has *Scadinavia/Skanza* (2E1).[40]

+ 7/50 is clearly Celtic: besides the names in bold (of which only **Usipetes** is doubtfully Celtic),[41] there are *Antunnacum* (with Celtic /a:ko/), *Cardena*,[42] and *Vosolvia/Bosolvia*.[43] There is no Celtic at + 7/51, although only four names are placed there, the Germanic ethnonyms *Bructeri* (10D5) and

---

[27] DLG s.v. *arduo-* .

[28] On *Paemani* cf. Reichert i, 539 (non-Germanic) and Sergent, 'Les premiers Celtes d'Anatolie', p. 333.

[29] DLG s.v. *grannos*; KPP, pp. 49 and 231–32.

[30] On *belg-* see Ch. 5 above, p. 168.

[31] DLG s.v. *caerac-*; Reichert i, 165.

[32] Schönfeld, s.n.; CIB, p. 202, n. 1241. Possibly Germanic according to Reichert i, 642, and ii, 617.

[33] Weisgerber, pp. 242–43, 352, 354, n. 80, 356–57 and 409, n. 46; DLG s.v. *caruos*. Cf. *Carvo* above. *Carvus* occurs as the name of a member of the Tungri: OPEL ii, 39.

[34] Kuhn, 'Die -acum-Namen am Rhein', pp. 392 and 395. The first is probably from a Celtic *Blar(i)us* (cf. DLG s.v. *blaros*).

[35] *Asciburgium, Burginatium, Quadriburgium*. See Weisgerber, pp. 347 and 351. On *Quadriburgium* cf. Anreiter, *Die vorrömischen Namen Pannoniens*, p. 138, n. 510 (perhaps worth mentioning here is Pokorny's etymology for W *caer* 'fort' < Latin *quadra* 'square', 'Some Celtic etymologies', p. 135). For *Tencteri* see Schönfeld s.n. and PNPG Comments s.n. *Tégkeroi*. On *Chamavi* see PNPG Comments s.n. *Khamauoi. Franci* in square + 6/51 is duplicated in + 6/52 in APNI.

[36] Weisgerber, pp. 354, n. 80 (*Calo, Novaesium*), 240, 269 and 335 (*Cugerni*, var. *Cuberni*), 354 (*Gelduba*), 330 (*Rura fl.*), 240 (*Sugambri*, cf. Map 6unl). On *Gelduba* cf. above, p. 5.

[37] See Ch. 4 above, s.v. *boud-*.

[38] Schönfeld, s.nn.; Weisgerber, p. 335. *Salii* is ambiguous. For a Celtic suggestion for *Tubantes* see PNPG Possibly Celtic Elements s.v. *tubo-*.

[39] Merely listed by Holder iii, 1001, but see DAG, pp. 889 and 921, G. Neumann in *RGermAlt* s.n. and Rübekeil, p. 381.

[40] On which see Svennung, pp. 51–56.

[41] Non-Germanic according to Reichert i, 739. Cf. Rübekeil, pp. 77 and 413.

[42] See above, Ch. 4, s.v. *carr-*.

[43] Weisgerber, p. 351.

Marsi (11H1)[44] and toponym *Caesia? Silva*[45] and the obscure *Lupia fl.* (11H1).[46] At +7/52 the two names are the Germanic ethnonym *(Ch)att-uarii* (10D4)[47] and the name which gave rise to the '50%' Celtic figure, **Teutoburgiensis? Saltus**, the Teutoburger Wald (10D4). As both elements are also attested in Germanic and *burg-* is not Celtic, the name must be classified as Germanic, at least in this area.[48] The next square to the north, +7/53, has two Germanic ethnonyms, *Ampsivarii* and *Chauci* and the obscure river-name *Amisia* (10D3), which underlies *Ampsivarii*.[49] In the final square northwards, +7/54, there are only two names, ***Abalus? Ins.** (the '50%' Celtic-looking item) and *Codanus? Sinus* (10D2). The latter is Germanic,[50] which leave *Abalus* very isolated. While it could be an instance of the Celtic 'apple' word, the stem is too widespread in north-western European languages for any confidence about this; and there is also the possibility of coincidence, since presumably unrelated names in *Abal-* are quite widespread in the ancient world, from Italy to India.[51]

---

[44] Schönfeld, s.nn.; Rübekeil, pp. 374–85.

[45] Heissi-Wald. Listed as Germanic by G. Neumann in *RGermAlt*, s.n. and Reichert i, 165, and ii, 489, and also by Holder i, 679, although at iii, 1036, he gives the personal name *Caesius* as 'auch celtisch'. A similar-looking name in Holder i, 685, *Caisada*, is probably not Celtic (see Gorrochategui, 'Ptolemy's Aquitania and the Ebro valley', pp. 148–49).

[46] Weisgerber, pp. 254, n. 48, and 329; Germanic according to Reichert i, 480, and ii, 564.

[47] Schönfeld, p. 131.

[48] Cf. GPN, pp. 266 and 268; Evans, 'Celts and Germans', pp. 247–48 (on *teut-*); Anreiter, *Die vorrömischen Namen Pannoniens*, pp. 137–38 and 185; AILR Comments s.n. *Teutiburgio*.

[49] Schönfeld, s.nn.; Holder i, 113 (s.n. *Amasias*), 133, and iii, 601; Svennung, p. 152; Rübekeil, pp. 323–27. *Amisia* (also *Amasia*), now Ems, has sometimes been labelled Celtic (see Schönfeld, p. 19; Chadwick, 'Some German river-names', p. 318, n. 2); it is Germanic according to Reichert i, 46, and ii, 460.

[50] Svennung, pp. 49–50 (non-Germanic according to Reichert i, 225).

[51] See Ch. 3 above. Svennung, p. 10, n. 3, notes that Kossinna tried to emend to *Sabalos* so as to connect *Abalus* (Pliny 37.35) with Ptolemy's *Sabalingioi* below.

	+4	+5	+6		+7	
54					*Abalus? Ins.* *Codanus? Sinus*	54
53			*Burcana Ins.*		*Amisia fl.* *Ampsivarii* *Chauci*	53
52	Albaniana Aurelium Cananefatium/ Forum Hadriani/ Cananefates Frisii Laurum **Lugdunum** Matilo Nigrum Pullum Praetorium Agrippinae	*Fectio* *Flevum L.* *Traiectum*	*Francia/* *Franci* *Salii?* *Tubantes*		*(Ch)Attuarii/* *Attuarii* **Teutoburgiensis? Saltus**	52
51	Helinium Condacum? Frisiavones Helinium fl. Mosa fl. Sturii Vacalus fl./ Vahalis fl.	**Batavodurum/** **Noviomagus/** **(Ulpia)** **Noviomagus/** Batavi Carvo? Castra Herculis? Grinnes Levefanum? Mannaricium Baetasii? **Catualium** Ceuclum Feresne? Rhenus fl. **Teudurum**? Toxiandria {Mediolanion}	Asciburgium Blariacum Burginatium Calo? Castra Vetera Col. Ulpia Traiana/ Tricensimae Cugerni **Durnomagus** Franci Gelduba Mederiacum	Novaesium Quadriburgium Rura fl. Sablones? Sugambri Tegula? Tencteri Carvium Chamavi Harenatium Drusiana Fossa {Boudoris}	*Bructeri* *Caesia? Silva* *Lupia fl.* *Marsi*	51
50	Aduatuci Carbonaria Silva Condrusi Geminiacum? Sabis? fl. Vodgoriacum	Amanium Arduenna Silva Atuatuca **Coriovallum/** **Cortovallium** Paemani/ Caemani Perniciacum?/ Pernaco Traiectus? Tungri Vervigium	Aquae Granni Ara Ubiorum/ Col. Claudia Ara Agrippinensium Belgica/Belgae Burungum? Caerosi Castellum Divitia **Eburones** **Icorigium** Iuliacum	Lesura fl. **Marcomagus?** Promea fl. Sunuci Tiberiacum? Tolbiacum Varnenum Ubii	Antunnacum **Bodobrica** **Bonna** Cardena Confluentes Contrua? Laugona? fl. Prata Aureliana **Rigomagus** Salisio **[Sentiacum]**? **Usipetes** Vosolvia/Bosolvia	50
	+4	+5	+6		+7	

(c) From +8 to +11 longitude (above latitude 48)

Square +8/48 (Map 11I4) is Celtic on account of *Sumelocenn-* whether or not **Senot-** is Celtic,[52] and *Abnoba* may also be Celtic.[53] +8/49 is '25%' on account of **Borbetomagus** (11I3), **Lopodunum**, **Noviomagus/Nemetae** and ***Saliobriga** (12B3),[54] and **Alisina fl.* seems to have a Celtic stem.[55] Further north the Celtic element continues in +8/50; this has none of our 'Celtic-looking' elements, but the ethnonym *Mattiaci* – and names derived from it (11I2) – appears Celtic,[56] as do *Mogontiacum* (11I2),[57] *Nida* (11I2 cf. W *Nedd*),[58] *Taunus M.*[59] and the river *Moenus* (11I2 cf. OI *moin* 'precious thing').[60] *Artaunon* (< Celtic **are* + *Taunos*) and *Segodounon* in Ptolemy 2.11.14 also belong here. In +8/51 the only name is the arbitrarily assigned *Germania /Barbaricum* (2E3).[61] +8/52 has only the Germanic *Angrivarii* (10E4)[62] and +8/53 only the etymologically controversial *Visurgis flumen*, now the Weser (10E3).[63] +8/54 has the Germanic **Teutones?** and *Angli* (10E2); it is '50%' on account of the first name, but this must be disregarded for the reasons noted under **Teutoburgiensis? Saltus** above.[64]

---

[52] GPN, pp. 177 and 258; CIB, p. 303, n. 63. For *Senot-* see Holder ii, 1500. *Agri Decumates* has been regarded as Celtic (Hind, '*Agri Decumates*'); cf. *decametos, decometos* 'tenth' in Marichal, *Les graffites*, p. 277. But see Rives, *Tacitus, Germania*, pp. 242–43.

[53] De Bernardo Stempel, 'Ptolemy's evidence for Germania Superior', p. 87; non-Germanic according to Reichert i, 8 (cf. ii, 451).

[54] On the whole region see Weisgerber. He notes that *Borbeto-* and *Lopo-* are obscure or non-Celtic (p. 352); but note personal names *Lopa* and *Lopus* cited as possibly Germanic by Reichert i, 476 and 479, and ii, 561 (cf. *lup-* in PNRB, p. 403?) and the suggestion in DLG s.v. *locu-* , and on *Borbeto-* see PNPG Celtic Elements and De Bernardo Stempel, 'Ptolemy's evidence for Germania Superior', p. 79. ***Saliobriga** ('Vic. Saliop', TIR M-32, p. 30) seems to be conjectured from '[Vi]cani Saliob...enses' in an inscription, whence 'VICUS SALIOB(rigensis?)' in Petit & Mangin, *Atlas des agglomérations secondaires*, no. 144.

[55] Cf. DLG s.v. *alisia*; Fabre, *Noms de lieux du Languedoc*, pp. 34–35; PNPG Celtic Elements s.v. *aliso-*; De Bernardo Stempel, 'Ptolemy's evidence for Germania Superior', p. 88. But *Al-is-* can be Germanic according to Reichert i, 36, and ii, 458, and cf. VCIE, pp. 435–36. On **Alisina fl.* (the Elsenz) see below, nn. 71 and 73.

[56] Cf. Schönfeld s.n.; GPN, p. 231; Weisgerber, pp. 346–48 and 351; Kuhn, 'Die -acum-Namen am Rhein', pp. 392 and 395; Rübekeil, pp. 63–73; Reichert i, 496–97; De Bernardo Stempel, 'Ptolemy's evidence for Germania Superior', p. 86; PNPG Celtic Elements s.v. *mat(t)u/i-*.

[57] Cf. GPN, p. 222; Weisgerber, pp. 351 and 355; Kuhn, 'Die -acum-Namen am Rhein', pp. 392 and 395; De Bernardo Stempel, 'Ptolemy's evidence for Germania Superior', p. 85; PNPG Celtic Elements s.v. *mogu-*. A personal name *Mogontinius* is attested; see OPEL s.n.

[58] Cf. Weisgerber, pp. 330 and 348, n. 48; Rasch, §VId (with non-Celtic parallels); PNRB, p. 425; Kitson, 'River-names', p. 94; Breeze, 'St Cuthbert, Bede, and the Niduari of Pictland'.

[59] On this and *Artaunon* see De Bernardo Stempel, 'Ptolemy's evidence for Germania Superior', pp. 86–87 and 90.

[60] Holder s.n.; Weisgerber, p. 329. Cf. LEIA M-36 and 59–60. On *Bucinobantes* see Rübekeil, pp. 170–80.

[61] On *Germani* cf. Weisgerber, pp. 240 and 337.

[62] Schönfeld s.n.; Rübekeil, pp. 350–57.

[63] Cf. Weisgerber, p. 70; Chadwick, 'Some German river-names', pp. 318 and 319, n. 1; Ekwall, *English River-Names*, p. 442 (cf. PNRB, p. 489); DLG, p. 323; Reichert i, 787, and ii, 654; IEW, p. 1134. Chadwick's Celtic explanation of *Wipper* is rejected by Ekwall, p. 443, and Udolph, *Namenkundliche Studien*, p. 79 (cf. GPN, p. 272, n. 3; DLG, p. 309).

[64] Cf. Svennung, p. 180.

North of these tribes are only the *Aviones* and *Sabalingioi?* at +8/55 (10E1) and *Chersonesos Kimbrike*[65] and *[Iutae]* at +8/56 (2E2), none of them Celtic-seeming.

One degree eastwards, at +9/48, the *Atlas* has only five names, none of them very Celtic-looking[66] – *Ad Lunam*, *Alba M.*, **Armisa fl.*, *Clarenna*,[67] and *Grinario (12C4) – and our '17%' is due to locating a sixth, **Bragodurum** (12unl) here. This **Bragodurum** (or *-dunum*) is mentioned only by Ptolemy (2.12.3), who places it *south* of the Danube, adjacent to *Drakouina* (perhaps Emerkingen).[68] In other words, it is near the very bottom of the +9/48 square through which the Danube runs – perhaps at Mengen (marked at 12C4).[69] The next square northwards, +9/49, has '14%' on Map 5.2 on account of **Teutoni**, which is no more likely to be Celtic than *Burgundiones* and *Hermunduri* (12C3).[70] Yet **Elantia fl.* (or, perhaps, **Elantis fl.*?) is very probably Celtic (: OI *elit* 'doe'),[71] **Murra fl.* may be,[72] and *Vicus Alisinensium* also looks Celtic.[73] 12unl *Lokoriton* (Ptolemy 2.11.14) belongs here and seems to be a name in Celtic *ritu-* 'ford'.[74] The next square northwards (+9/50) is blank, and then we have +9/51 with

---

[65] On *Cimbri* see Svennung, pp. 163–66, and GPN, pp. 438–40.

[66] Despite Reinecke, 'Die örtliche Bestimmung' (1925), who tended to label names like *Ad Lunam* as Celtic (p. 28) without any demonstration. The forest called *Louna* by Ptolemy 2.11.3 and 11 is cited as non-Germanic by Reichert i, 479; for it see p. 191 below (+17/48). TIR M-33, p. 54, and RGermAlt s.n. *Lunawald* connect it with Germanic *hlunja, Old Norse *hlynr*, 'maple'. Cf. Rasch, §VId.

[67] On the suffix *-enno* as possibly Celtic see Weisgerber, p. 321 (differently Rasch, §VCc). Cf. OI *clár* and the Welsh river-name *Clarach* (EANC, pp. 7–8)?

[68] *Map-by-Map Directory* i, 181; Emerkingen is at Map12C4. Cf. Müller's note, p. 282. *Brago-* is obscure; see PNPG Possibly Celtic Elements.

[69] See Reinecke, 'Die örtliche Bestimmung' (1924), p. 25; Kemkes et al., 'Spätbronzezeitliche und frührömische Wehranlagen auf dem "Berg" über Ennetach, Stadt Mengen, Kreis Sigmaringen'.

[70] All Germanic; see Schönfeld s.nn. Cf. on **Teutoburgiensis** and **Teutones** above.

[71] DLG, pp. 161 and 434; Sims-Williams, 'Development of the Indo-European voiced labiovelars', p. 226, n. 4; NWÄI, p. 83; VCIE, pp. 209–11. As noted by Pauly-Wissowa s.n. *Elant...*, TIR M-32, p. 14, and A. Schmid, *Das Flussgebiet des Neckar*, p. 24, n. 58, the name is incomplete and was deduced from a second-century inscription CIL XIII 6490 referring to *n(umerus) Brit(tonum) Elant([i?]ensium)*, perhaps connected with the river Elz. (An altar found in 1982 has the name in full, *Brittones Elantienses: L'Année Epigraphique*, 1986, no. 523.) As noted in CIL and by A. Schmid, a *villa* here was called *Alantia* in 773. W. P. Schmid, 'Alteuropäische Gewässernamen', p. 756, takes the *Al-* form to be primary, without mentioning the inscription *Elant....* Note that **Elantia fl.* is the Elz (east of the Neckar) as on Map 12C3, *not* the river Elsenz (west of the Neckar) as in the *Map-by-Map Directory* i, 172, which also gives *Alisina (12B3) for the Elsenz (p. 170), a name deduced from *c(ivitas) Alisin(ensis)* in CIL XIII 6482 (cf. TIR M-32, p. 14, and A. Schmid, *Das Flussgebiet des Neckar*, p. 23).

[72] It may show Celtic /rs/ > /rr/ by comparison with a *Mursa* in Pannonia; see Anreiter, *Die vorrömischen Namen Pannoniens*, p. 92, n. 374, and Rasch, §VIa.

[73] Presumably the same as the second-century *c(ivitas) Alisin(ensis)* in CIL XIII 6482, from which the name **Alisina fl.* (the Elsenz) at +8/49 above is deduced (see nn. 55 and 71 above).

[74] Above, p. 103, n. 53 (listed as Germanic by Reichert i, 476, and ii, 563, but 'lake ford' according to Rasch, §IIAf).

Melibokon? Oros (10F5) only, which is probably Germanic,[75] followed by a series of other names which are unlikely to be Celtic: + 9/52 *Cherusci* and *Dulgubnii?* (10F4),[76] + 9/53 *Albis fl.* (10F3) and + 9/54 *Saxones* and *Sigoulones?* (10F2).[77]

Celtic-looking names are absent from the 16 names[78] of + 10/48, with the exception of **Vindelici** and their city, **Augusta Vindelicum** (12D4), which account for the '12%'. This people dwelt south of the Danube. In the next square northwards (+ 10/49) there are 6 names: **Alcmona fl.*, *Biriciana*, *Iciniacum*, *Iuthungi*, *Mediana* and *Sablonetum* (12D3). Of these *Iciniacum* appears to be Celtic.[79] *Dêouona* in Ptolemy (2.11.14) may belong here and is clearly Celtic (Chapter 4 above, s.v. *dēvo-*), and the same applies to his *Kantioibis* and perhaps his *Rhiousiaoua* (2.11.15).[80] Further north, above the Roman *limes*, names of all sorts are rare, but there are no Celtic ones. At + 10/50 the *Thuringi* (12D2) are Germanic,[81] and at + 10/53 the **Langobardi**, *Reudigni* and *Suari(do)nes*[82] (10G3) all have satisfactory Germanic etymologies – the similarity of **Langobardi** (whence the '33%' figure) to Celtic **lang-* (and *bardos* 'poet'!) is of course fortuitous[83] – as do the *Dani* at + 10/56 (2F2).[84]

The 12 names[85] at + 11/48 do not seem to be *obviously* Celtic apart from the adjacent **Parrodunum** and **Venaxamodurum** (12E4), just below the

---

[75] IEW, p. 724. Cf. PNPG Comments s.n. According to Reichert i, 500, and ii, 484 and 571, it is possibly Germanic and possibly hybrid.

[76] Cf. Schönfeld, s.nn.

[77] Cf. ibid.

[78] *Aquileia, Augusta Vindelicum/Aelia Augusta, Caelius Mons, Guntia* (non-Germanic according to Reichert i, 415, but cf. ii, 530), *Licca fl., Losodica, Opia, Phoebiana, Piniana, *Raetovarii, Rapis?, Summuntorium, Vindelici, Virdo?* fl. (12D4), *Ad Novas, Rostrum Nemaviae* (19C1). *Licca* resembles OI *lecc*, W *llech* 'stone', but the modern form *Lech* and most ancient forms imply a single /k/ (cf. *Licates* at + 10/47 below) and this single /k/ is uncertainly attested in Celtic in this word although cf. DLG s.v. *lica, licca*, and De Bernardo Stempel, 'More on Ptolemy's evidence for Celtic Ireland', p. 99. Anreiter et al. 'Names of the Eastern Alpine region', pp. 131, 133 and 136, derive it from IE **(h₁)l(e)ik-* 'bend'; the full grade of this appear in W *llwyg* 'restiveness', IEW, pp. 309 and 669, and PNPG Possibly Celtic Elements s.v. *lico-*. *Rostrum Nemaviae* may be from the Celtic **nemo-* 'bending (river)' (cf. AILR Celtic Elements s.v.). *Virdo* may be Celtic (GPN, p. 125; DLG s.v. *uirido-*; on W *gwrdd* see Evans, '"gurdonicus"', p. 31, and Sims-Williams, 'Development of the Indo-European voiced labiovelars', p. 203).

[79] GPN, p. 352; cf. discussion of *Ico-* names s.v. in Ch. 4 above. *Mediana* is well paralleled in Celtic-speaking lands (Holder ii, 495–96), but also in Africa etc. (cf. Beševliev, p. 107, and Rasch, §1F).

[80] PNPG Comments s.n. *Kantioibis* and Possibly Celtic Elements s.v. *riuso-*. Müller, p. 274, suggests that *Rhiousiaoua* was near or identical with *Biriciana*.

[81] Schönfeld, s.n.

[82] That is, *Suarines*, var. *Suardones*, of Tacitus, *Germania*, 40.

[83] Despite Cousin, p. 420: 'bardes de la lance'.

[84] Schönfeld, s.nn.; Svennung, p. 147; Knobloch, 'Der Name der Langobarden'. *Reudo-* and *-igni* both occur in Celtic as well as Germanic: see CIB, p. 155, n. 921, and n. 189 below.

[85] *Abusina* (not included s.v. Celtic **abo-* in AILR Celtic Elements, cf. Rasch, §VId), **Ambra fl., Ambrae* (cf. Holder s.nn. and Rasch, §VIa – on Gaulish *ambe* cf. Stalmaszczyk & Witczak, 'Studies in Indo-European vocabulary', pp. 25–26, and DLG s.v.), *Bratananium, Celeusum, Germanicum, *Isaras fl.* (Holder compares Ir. *iar*, an adjective describing rivers, DIL s.v., and cf. PNPG Celtic Elements s.v. *iso-*), *Parrodunum, Vallatum, Venaxamodurum, Vetoniana, Vicus Scuttarensium* (12E4).

Danube in Vindelicia. However, Ptolemy's Danubian *Artobriga* in Vindel-
ica (2.12.4) may belong here as well, and be distinct from the place of the
same name at +12/47.[86] The gap to the north at +12/49 could perhaps be
filled by Ptolemy's *Nertereanes* (or *-oi*) and *Bibakon* (2.11.11 and 15), if the
former had Celtic **nerto-* and the latter had /a:/, and the gap at +11/50 by
his 12unl *Bikourgion* (2.11.14), although the case for the Celticity of these
names is weak.[87] Further north at +11/51 there are only the *Salas? fl.* and
the *Semnones* (12E1), who have a good Germanic etymology,[88] at +11/52
the *Kaloukones?* (10H4), whose name is of uncertain etymology (although
Celtic **calo-* 'call' is just possible),[89] and at +11/53 the Germanic *Farodini*
and *Suebi* (10H3).[90]

In his *Skandinavien bei Plinius und Ptolemaios* Svennung comments that
scholars have neglected sources other than Tacitus.[91] This is also true of the
Barrington Atlas. However, the only clearly *Celtic* name missing from the
Atlas and discussed by Svennung is Pliny's *Morimarusam . . . hoc est
mortuum mare* (4.95), referring to the sea between Denmark and Norway/
Sweden.[92] Unfortunately we do not know the location of the Celtic-
speaking mariners who coined the term. Pliny quotes Philemon as saying
that the name was used by the Cimbri (the probably Germanic-speaking
tribe from north Jutland). This people travelled very widely in Europe
before coming in contact with the Greeks, no doubt mixing with Celtic-
speakers at various stages (they had leaders with Celtic names).[93] Placing
the name on the map would probably not be a useful indication of the
extent of Celtic speech, seeing that we do not know where the Cimbri were
located when they started to use the name.

---

[86] PNPG Comments s.n.
[87] See ibid. s.nn.; also Reichert i, 521, and ii, 583, and Schönfeld, s.n. *Nertereani* (and *Nerthus*,
    'terra mater' in Tacitus, *Germania*, 40, cf. PNPG Celtic Elements s.v. *nerto-*). *Bikourgion* is
    non-Germanic according to Reichert i, 141. PNPG Comments notes that it might be for
    *Bitourgion (cf. below, p. 246, on 42unl *Biturgia*). Whether *Salas* (the Saale) can be Celtic
    has been debated: Chadwick, 'Some German river-names', p. 320, n. 4.
[88] Schönfeld, s.n.
[89] Cf. ibid. p. 59; TIR M-33, p. 47; AILR and PNPG Celtic Elements s.v. *calo-* (cf. PNPG
    Possibly Celtic Elements s.v. *callo-*); LEIA s.v. 2 *cailech*. Cf. Holder i, 705. The root occurs
    in many languages. Reichert i, 167, regards *Kaloukones* here (Ptolemy 2.11.10) as Germanic,
    but not the *Calucones* (Pliny 3.137) in the Alps (+9/46 below).
[90] Schönfeld, pp. 86 and 215. Gysseling, *Toponymisch Woordenboek*, i, 349, derives *Farodini*
    from Germanic **farud-* 'crossing, voyage' (cited by Gohil, *Ancient Celtic and Non-Celtic
    Place-Names*, p. 65).
[91] Svennung, p. 244. See also Bednarczuk, 'Ptolemy (III,5,8) Σούλωνες'.
[92] Svennung, pp. 12–13, 26–28, 42 and 78, and Tafel III; GPN, p. 233; DLG, p. 229; Falileyev,
    'Miscellanea Onomastica', §I.
[93] DAG, p. 905; GPN, p. 439, n. 4.

	+8		+9	+10	+11	
56	Chersonesos Kimbrike	[Iutae]		Dani		56
55	Aviones	Sabalingioi?				55
54	Angli	**Teutones?**	Saxones Sigoulones?			54
53	Visurgis fl.		Albis fl.	**Langobardi** Reudigni Suari(do)nes	Farodini Suebi	53
52	Angrivarii		Cherusci Dulgubnii?		Kaloukones?	52
51	Germania/ Barbaricum		Melibokon? Oros		Salas? fl. Semnones	51
50	Aquae Mattiacorum/ Mattiaci Bucinobantes Castellum Mattiacorum/ Mattiaci Chatti	Moenus fl. Mogontiacum Nida Taunus M. {Artaunon} {Segodounon}		Thuringi	{12unl Bikourgion}	50
49	Alta Ripa *Altiaia, **Borbetomagus** Buconica Nicer fl. **Noviomagus/** **Nemetae** Rouphiniana? Tabernae	Vicus Augustanus Vicus Iulius *Alisina fl. **Lopodunum** Med(...) *Saliobriga Suebi Nicretes	Burgundiones *Elantia fl. *Murra fl. **Teutoni** Vicus Alisinensium *Vicus Aurelianus Hermunduri {12unl Lokoriton}	*Alcmona fl. Biriciana Iciniacum Iuthungi Mediana Sablonetum {Dêouona} {Kantioibis} {Rhiousiaoua}	{Bibakon} {Nertereanes}	49
48	Abnob(ai)a Ore Aquae Saletio Vicus Bibiensium? Agri Decumates Alamanni	Arae Flaviae *Portus Saltus Sumelocennensis Sumelocenna **Vicus** **Senot(ensis)**	Ad Lunam Alba M. *Armisa fl. Clarenna *Grinario 12unl **Bragodurum**	Aquileia **Augusta** **Vindelicum/** Aelia Augusta Caelius Mons Guntia Licca fl. Losodica Opia Phoebiana Piniana *Raetovarii Rapis? Summuntorium **Vindelici** Virdo? fl. Ad Novas Rostrum Nemaviae	Abusina *Ambra fl. Ambrae Bratananium Celeusum Germanicum *Isaras fl. **Parrodunum** Vallatum? **Venaxamodurum** Vetoniana Vicus Scuttarensium {Artobriga}	48
	+8		+9	+10	+11	

(d) From +12 to +15 longitude (above latitude 48)

The 7 names at +12/48 (*Aenus fl.*,[94] *Cat(t)enates?*, *Iovisura*, *I(o)varus? fl.*, *Runicates?*,[95] *Sorviodurum*, *Turum*[96]) do not seem to be Celtic apart from **Sorviodurum** (12F4), which accounts for the '14%' on Map 5.2. We can add, however, Ptolemy's clearly Celtic *Karrodounon* (see Chapter 4 above, s.v. *carro-*). In the next square northwards, +12/49, the only probable Celtic name of the 4 (*Bac fl.*, *Gabreta? Hyle*, **Reganus fl.*, *Reginum/Castra Regina*[97]) is **Gabreta** (12F3), and this great forest seems to mark the limits of Celtic toponymy. Just to the north there are the apparently related names *Soudeta Ore* and *Soudianoi?* (12F2) at +12/50. The form *Soudianoi* is based on MS X of Ptolemy, and *Soudinoi* may be preferable. It has been suggested that **Sudini* is Celtic,[98] but this is not obvious (cf. *Soudinoi* at +24/54 below). Further north there are only the Germanic[99] *Varini* (10I3) at +12/53 and *(Ulme)Rugii* (10I2) at +12/54 (with the *Suebicum Mare* (2F3)), the Germanic[100] *Heruli?* (10I1) at +12/55 and *Suiones?* (2F2) at +12/57.

The Celticity of +13/48 is established by **Boiodurum/Boiotro** (12G4),[101] and supported by *Ioviacum?* and *Stanacum*,[102] although these *-acum* names could be creations of the Roman period, as *Batavi* must be (named after its garrison).[103] However, Ptolemy's Celtic *Gauauodouron* (2.13.3) belongs here (see Chapter 4 above, s.v. *duro-*). The others of the 6 names in this square are *Quintana* (12G4) and *Tergolape* (19F1). To the north are *Boihaemum* and the *Marcomanni* (12G2) at +13/50, the former semi-Celtic, from *Boii*, and the latter Germanic.[104] The +13/53 square appears as '100%' on account of the *Lemovii?* (2F3) alone, but it is very doubtful whether the *Le(:)mo-* element in their name is the Celtic word for 'elm' (unlike, for

---

[94] For a Celtic possibility see Anreiter et al., 'Names of the Eastern Alpine region', p. 129, AILR Comments s.n. *Ponte Aeni*, and PNPG Possibly Celtic Elements s.v. *eno-*.

[95] *Run-* vaguely recalls OI *rún* 'secret' but this stem is in any case also found in Germanic. See Holder ii, 1246–47; LEIA s.v. Superior sources have *Rhoukantioi* (Strabo) and *Rucinates* (Pliny): TIR M-33, p. 73.

[96] Cf. PNPG Possibly Celtic Elements s.v. {tura:-}, *turo-*.

[97] Possibly Celtic: see AILR Possibly Celtic Elements s.v. *rego-*.

[98] Schönfeld s.n., quoting Holder ii, 1654–55, and others. The comparison of *Sudeta* with OI *suide* 'sitting' is invalid as this had **o* (LEIA s.v. *said-*).

[99] Schönfeld s.nn. On *Uarini* (Celtic or Germanic), see PNPG Comments s.n. *Ouiroûnoi*. W *gwerin* 'folk' has been compared (DLG s.v. *uarina*).

[100] Schönfeld s.nn. *Eruli* and *Suiones*. On the latter see Svennung, pp. 57–61, 81–132 and 208–12; IEW, p. 882.

[101] For no obvious reason Anreiter, *Die vorrömischen Namen Pannoniens*, p. 156, n. 571, takes the first element to be a Celtic personal name *Boius*, related to the tribal name *Boii*. In view of *-durum* it is hardly the Germanic *Boio* (cf. Schönfeld s.n. and Reichert i,146). The late *Boiotro* form comes from Eugippius' *Vita Sancti Severini*.

[102] Russell, 'Suffix', p. 165.

[103] See above, p. 4.

[104] Anreiter, *Die vorrömischen Namen Pannoniens*, p. 157; Rasch, §IIIAd; Schwarz, *Ortsnamen der Sudetenländer*, p. 35; Svennung, p. 55; Schönfeld, p. 162. On *Boii* see below, p. 189.

example, *Lemovices* at Limoges in France). Even if *Lemovii* does contain the 'elm' word, it need not be Celtic, since this belongs to the 'vocabulaire du Nord-Ouest' in general.[105]

+14/48 has '0%' Celtic-looking elements, but one of its 10 names,[106] *Lauriacum* (12H4), has a Celtic suffix,[107] *[Druna] fl.* is perhaps cognate with OI *dron* 'firm',[108] and *Ovilava* may contain Celtic **ovi-* 'sheep' (this is not exclusively Celtic, however).[109] The next square northwards (+14/49) has no names on the Barrington map, but 12unl **Maroboudon** in Ptolemy (2.11.14) probably belongs around here,[110] hence the '100%' on Map 5.2. There are two names in the next square northwards (+14/50), the *Boii* and the *Marsigni?* (*sic leg.*) (12H2). The former are certainly Celtic and the latter are Germanic, although the suffix *-igni* is sometimes regarded as Celtic or Celticized.[111]

In +15/48 the 9% is due to **kaito-* in **Cetium** (12I4).[112] The other 10 names here[113] do not appear Celtic apart from *Tragisa(mus) fl.*[114] North of here, at +15/50, *Korkontoi* is obscure,[115] while *Ouandalike Ore* (12I2) is Germanic.[116] However, Ptolemy's Celtic-looking *Boudorgis* (2.11.14) can be added (Pardubice).[117] The final square northwards (+15/51) has *Vandali* (2G3) again and *Silingai?* (12I1) has a typically Germanic suffix.[118]

---

[105] DLG, p. 199, quoting Meillet. Reichert i, 461, and ii, 558, lists the name as Germanic. The *-vii* suffix is regarded as Germanic by Schönfeld, s.n. *Lemovii*.

[106] *Ad Iuvense?*, *Ad Mauros*, *Anisus fl.* (cf. Holder s.n. and Anreiter et al., 'Names of the Eastern Alpine region', p. 129, n. 53), *[Druna] fl.*, *'I(ve)ses' fl.*, *Lauriacum*, *Lentia* (cf. Holder s.n., Rasch, §IVC48, OPEL iii, 22, and Anreiter, *Die vorrömischen Namen Pannoniens*, p. 215, n. 749, also Reichert i, 461, on *Lentienses* at +8/47 below), *Lo(a)cus* [i.e. *Locus* or *Lacus*] *Felicis?*, *Ovilava*, *'Vetonianis'* (12H4).

[107] Russell, 'Suffix', p. 165.

[108] Holder i, 1330–31; LEIA D-201. The square brackets indicate that the river-name (now Traun, Austria) is reconstructed from *Truna* in 790 in TIR M-33, p. 35. Note, however, that the river Traun in Germany (+12/47) is actually attested as *Druna c.* 790 (*sic*) according to Reinecke, 'Die örtliche Bestimmung' (1925), pp. 36–37, which supports the reconstruction. For a different etymology see DLG s.v. *druna* and Kitson, 'River-names', p. 78.

[109] AILR Celtic Elements s.v. *oui(lo)-* and PNPG Comments s.n. *Abilouon*. Cf. Rasch, §VId.

[110] Following PNPG, *Germania Magna*; for various suggestions see TIR M-33, pp. 58–59. Cf. Rasch, §IIICb.

[111] Cf. Schönfeld, p. 164 (Gothic *marzjan* 'to anger'); Svennung, pp. 145–46; CIB, p. 155, n. 921 (see above on *Reudigni*). But Reichert i, 494 and 566, and ii, 595, lists *Marsigni* as non-Germanic and *Reudigni* as Germanic. On *Boii* see above, pp. 169 and 188.

[112] Anreiter, *Die vorrömischen Namen Pannoniens*, p. 164. See above, p. 29.

[113] *Ad Ponte(m) Ises*, *Ar(e)lapa fl.* and *Ar(e)lape* (contaminated by Celtic *Are-*, however, according to Anreiter et al., 'Names of the Eastern Alpine region', p. 116, cf. Rasch, §VIc), *Asturis?*, *Augustiana*, *Faviana*, **Kampoi*, *Namare* (cf. 24D1 *Namarini* in Spain, Tovar, *Tarraconensis*, p. 138, and VCIE, pp. 463–64), *Rugii*, *Tragisa(mus) fl.*

[114] TIR M-33, p. 83; Holder ii, 1901–2; Rasch, §VIa; DLG, p. 300 (OI *traig* 'foot'); Anreiter, *Breonen*, p. 139 (citing OI *tráig* 'ebb', with different ablaut, IEW, p. 1089). See also below, p. 256, on *Tragurium*.

[115] Possibly Germanic according to Reichert i, 226, and ii, 493.

[116] Schönfeld, pp. 66 and 256.

[117] PNPG, *Germania Magna*; see Ch. 4 above, s.vv. *boud-* and *rīgo-*.

[118] Schönfeld, p. 207; Svennung, p. 148; Reichert i, 610, and ii, 613.

	+12	+13	+14	+15	
57	*Suiones?*				57
56					56
55	*Heruli?*				55
54	*(Ulme) Rugii/* *Rugii* *Suebicum* *Mare*				54
53	*Varini*	***Lemovii?***			53
52					52
51				*Silingai?* *Vandali*	51
50	*Soudeta Ore* *Soudianoi?*	Boihaemum Marcomanni	Boii Marsingi? [sic]	Korkontoi Ouandalika Ore {Boudorgis}	50
49	Bac fl. **Gabreta? Hyle** *Reganus fl. Reginum/ Castra Regina		12unl **Maroboudon**		49
48	Aenus fl. Cat(t)enates? Iovisura Ivarus? fl./ Iovarus? fl. Runicates? **Sorviodurum** Turum {Karrodounon}	Batavi **Boiodurum/** **Boiotro** Ioviacum? Quintana Stanacum Tergolape {Gauauodouron}	Ad Iuvense? Ad Mauros Anisus fl. [Druna] fl. 'I(ve)ses' fl. Lauriacum Lentia Lo(a)cus Felicis? Ovilava 'Vetonianis'	Ad Ponte(m) Ises Ar(e)lapa fl. Ar(e)lape Asturis? Augustiana **Cetium** Faviana *Kampoi Namare Rugii Tragisa(mus) fl.	48
	+12	+13	+14	+15	

(e) From +16 to +19 longitude (above latitude 48)

+16/48 is as high as '40%' on Map 5.2 owing to the near duplication in the 6 names: **Carnuntum, Col. Carnuntum/Col. Septimia Aurelia Antoniniana, Ketion Oros** [cf. *Cetium* above], **Langobardi, Vindobona** and **Mun. Vindobona** (13B4). Of these **Langobardi** cannot be genuine Celtic (see above), and Anreiter regards **Carnuntum** as Pannonian rather than Celtic.[119] The other names in this square[120] do not appear obviously Celtic, although *Rakatai*,[121] *Marus flumen*[122] and *Comagena* could be.[123] *Mediolanion* can be added from MS X of Ptolemy.[124] North of here the *Atlas* is blank, but the '100%' at +16/49 is due to assigning 13unl **Ebourodounon** and 13unl **Meliodounon** to this square. *Ebouron* (Ptolemy 2.11.14) also belongs here.[125] At +16/51 Ptolemy's *Lougidounon* (2.11.13), not in the *Atlas*, is obviously Celtic and is probably to be connected with the *Lugii* marked just to the east.[126]

+17/48 has no Celtic names (*Baimoi, Gerulata, Laedavus fl., Louna Hyle*, 13C4),[127] and +17/49 is blank, but +17/50 has '100%' as a result of assigning 13unl **Boudorigon** to that square; Ptolemy's *Karrodounon* (2.11.14), now Krapkowice, also belongs here.[128] The square above (+17/51) is the (unless corrupt) non-Celtic *Ouiadoua? fl.* (2G3), that is *Viadua* (the Oder/Odra),[129] and at +17/52 are the **Lugii** (2G3), whose Celtic etymology is especially plausible in view of *Lougidounon* at +16/51.[130] Further north at +17/54 are the Germanic *Gothiscandza* and *Vidivarii* (2G3) and, at +17/55, the *Sarmaticus Oceanus*.

[119] Anreiter, *Die vorrömischen Namen Pannoniens*, pp. 47 and 189.

[120] *Aequinoctium, Ala Nova, Aquae, Cannabiaca?, Comagena, Marus fl., Quadi, Rakatai* (13B4). *Aquae* is merely duplicated under 20D1, so the total of names in the square is 14 rather than 15.

[121] See above, Ch. 4, n. 50.

[122] Compare the Celtic word for 'dead' (W. *marw* etc.) and *Morimarusa* above, p. 186. But cf. TIR M-33, p. 59, and Schwartz, *Ortsnamen der Sudetenländer*, pp. 20–22.

[123] Cf. AILR Celtic Elements s.v. *agi-*, {a:gi-}; Rasch, §VCd, also comparing the personal name *Comag(i)us* (cf. OPEL s.n.).

[124] See Ch. 4 above, s.v. *medio-*.

[125] See ibid. s.v. *eburo-*.

[126] Ahlqvist, 'Two ethnic names in Ptolemy'. See above, p. 86, s.v. *Lugu-*.

[127] *Baimoi* is Germanic according to Reichert i, 113, and ii, 475. A connection with the *Boii* has been suggested; cf. PNPG Comments s.nn. *Baîmoi, Bainokhaîmai*, and Schönfeld, s.n. *Baemi, Baenohaemae. Laedavus fl.* is a reconstruction (TIR M-33, p. 49; cf. Anreiter, *Die vorrömischen Namen Pannoniens*, pp. 246–47). On *Louna* see above, n. 66.

[128] See above, pp. 48 and 61.

[129] If emended to **Vidua* it would be a well-attested Celtic river-name (DLG s.v. *uidu-* 'arbre, bois'); see above, p. 27. This old suggestion is mentioned and rejected by Hubert, *Rise of the Celts*, p. 157. (Cf. fantastic speculations in Davies & Moorhouse, *Microcosm*, p. 43, quoted above, p. 7.) Reichert i, 774, lists *Ouiadou(a)* as non-Germanic and 'Old European'. Cf. Schwarz, *Ortsnamen der Sudetenländer*, pp. 26–27.

[130] Ahlqvist, 'Two ethnic names in Ptolemy'; cf. Schönfeld, s.n. The variation *Lugi(o)i*, *Lugiones* is discussed by Svennung, p. 214.

	+ 16	+ 17	+ 18	+ 19	
55		*Sarmaticus Oceanus*			55
54		*Gothiscandza Vidivarii*	*Ouenedikos Kolpos*	*Gepidi?*	54
53			*Vistula fl.*		53
52		**Lugii**			52
51	{Lougidounon}	*Ouiadoua? fl*	Sclaveni {Dounoi}		51
50		13unl **Boudorigon** {Karrodounon}			50
49	13unl **Ebourodounon** 13unl **Meliodounon** {Ebouron}			**Cotini**	49
48	Aequinoctium Ala Nova Aquae Cannabiaca? **Carnuntum Col. Carnuntum/ Col. Septimia Aurelia Antoniniana** Comagena **Ketion Oros Langobardi** Marus fl. **Mun. Vindobona** Quadi Rakatai **Vindobona** Aquae {Mediolanion}	*Baimoi Gerulata Laedavus fl. Louna Hyle*	Avares Laugaricio 21unl **Ouskenon** {21unl Bormanon}	*Osi*	48
	+ 16	+ 17	+ 18	+ 19	

+ 18/48 probably lies at the edge of Celtic territory, since + 18/47 just to the south includes the definitely Celtic **Brigetio** (20F2)[131] among other names.[132] The two names in the *Atlas* – *Avares* and *Laugaricio* (13D4) – are not Celtic,[133] but 21unl **Ouskenon**, which I have assigned here, could just possibly be a name in Celtic *Ux-*.[134] The adjacent name in Ptolemy 3.7.2 is 21unl *Bormanon*, which is arguably Celtic.[135] To the north, + 18/51 *Sclaveni* (13D1), + 18/53 *Vistula fl.* (2G3), + 18/54 *Ouenedikos Kolpos* (2G3; cf. *Venedi* below), are not Celtic, but *Dounoi* 'enclosures' in Ptolemy 2.11.10 (at + 18/51) obviously is – if this reading by Nobbe (MSS *(D)idounoi* etc.) is correct.[136]

+ 19/48 has only one name *Osi* (13E4), presumably Pannonian,[137] but we are still within Celtic territory here, as + 19/47 to the south includes the definitely Celtic **Vindonianus Vicus** (20G2)[138] and the only name at + 19/49 is the Celtic-looking **Cotini** (13E3), which can reasonably be agreed to be Celtic in view of Tacitus' comment on their *Gallica . . . lingua*.[139] North of this there is only one name, at + 19/54, the non-Celtic *Gepidi?* (2G3).[140]

(f) From + 20 to + 24 longitude (above latitude 48)

West of the **Cotini** there are few names north of latitude 48 in the *Atlas* and probably none of them are Celtic: + 20/54 the *Aestii* and *Venedi* (2H3);[141] + 21/53 the *Galindai* (2H3), + 21/55 the *Osioi?* (2H2);[142] + 22/49 the *Buri?*

---

[131] Anreiter, *Die vorrömischen Namen Pannoniens*, p. 162.

[132] See below, p. 211.

[133] See Rasch, §IIIAc, and Reichert ii, 6 on the latter.

[134] See Ch. 4 above, s.v. *ux-*.

[135] Ptolemy's reference is long. 43° 40′, lat. 48° 15′ (PNPG puts it and *Ouskenon* at + 20/46). On *borm-* see PNPG Celtic Elements s.v. *borbeto-* and Comments s.n. *Bórmanon*; GPN, pp. 154–56; DLG s.v. *boruo, bormo*; Rostaing, *Essai*, pp. 97–100; Sergent, 'Les premiers Celtes d'Anatolie', pp. 337–38; De Bernardo Stempel, 'Ptolemy's evidence for Germania Superior', pp. 79 and 90; and compare + 10/46 *Aquae Bormiae*, **Borma* (+ 6/43) and *Lucus Bormani* (+ 8/43) below, pp. 200, 244 and 246. In Thrace, on the other hand, *Bormiskos/Bromiskos* (51B3 = + 23/40) looks Greek (βρόμος/βόρμος 'oats'), but is Thracian according to Mihailov, 'Le suffixe *-sk-* en thrace', pp. 149–50. It must be stressed that *Aquae Bormiae* etc. are not certainly Celtic; Prósper, *Lenguas y religiones prerromanas*, pp. 329–31, and Villar, 'Celtic language', p. 254, argue strongly that they show a non-Celtic treatment of IE **gʷhor-mo-* 'warm'.

[136] Nobbe 2.11.18 and PNPG Comments s.n. See Ch. 4 above, s.v. *dūno-*.

[137] Schwarz, *Ortsnamen der Sudetenländer*, pp. 33–34; Anreiter, *Die vorrömischen Namen Pannoniens*, pp. 97–98. They spoke *Pannonica lingua*, like the *Aravisci/Eravisci* (Tacitus, *Germania*, 28 and 43).

[138] See below, p. 213. On the Celtic personal name *Vindonius* see CIB, p. 75.

[139] Tacitus, *Germania*, 43; Guyonvarc'h, 'Le nom des Cotini'; KPP, pp. 34 and 192; differently Anreiter, *Die vorrömischen Namen Pannoniens*, pp. 212–13. Tacitus says that they paid tribute and mined iron; see also below, p. 230, on the *Kotinai* of −5/38. Collis, *The Celts*, p. 190, associates them with the La Tène-ware using Puchov group of northern Slovakia.

[140] See Schönfeld, s.n. *Gipedae*.

[141] Schönfeld, pp. 273 and 280–81; Schmidt, 'Keltisch, Baltisch und Slavisch', p. 24.

[142] Schönfeld, p. 277 s.v. *Hosii*.

(13H3), +22/51 the *Gothi* (13H1),[143] +22/54 *Chronos fl.* (2H3), +22/55 *Roudon fl.* (2H2),[144] +22/56 the *Karbones*[145]and *Tourountes? fl.* (2H2); +23/ 48 *Karpates Oros* (1H1); +24/54 the *Soudinoi* (2H3), +24/56 *Chesinos fl.* (2H2), +24/58 **Sitones?** (2H2). The **Sitones** (var. *Sithones*) are vaguely located by Tacitus as living beyond the *Suiones*.[146] They are 'Celtic-looking' on account of the *Sito-* element (cf. OI *sith*, W *hyd* 'length'). But it is hardly likely that their name really is Celtic, in view of their remoteness from all other Celtic names (unless one were to try and make **sito-* refer to distance rather than length). Moreover, their name has a satisfactory Gemanic etymology, 'the side or coast people'.[147]

(g) +25 longitude, latitude 48

No names west of +24 longitude and north of latitude 48 are recorded in the *Atlas*. However, 23unl **Karrodounon** (Ptolemy 3.5.15) probably belongs here. It was on the river *Tyras* (Dniester) beside Dacia. The *Tyras* enters the area of Map 23 at +29/47 but rises far to the north-west (around +23/49), and clearly **Karrodounon** lay up-stream, north-west of the *Atlas*'s Map 23 (see Map 6.3 above). It is one of a string of places which Ptolemy places beside the *Tyras*. One of various tentative attempts to identify them is by Müller:

	long	lat.		long	lat.
Karródounon	49° 30′	48° 40′ = *Zalesozyky* [Zalischyky]		25° 44′	48° 39′
Maitó:nion	51°	48° 30′ = *Uszica*[148] [Stara Ushytsya]		27° 07′	48° 35′
Kle:pídaua	52° 30′	48° 40′ = *Iampol* [Yampil']		28° 18′	48° 15′
Ouibantauárion	53° 30′	48° 40′ = *Balta*		29° 37′	47° 46′
É:rakton	53° 50′	48° 40′ = *Rybnika*[149] [Rîbniţsa]		29° 00′	47° 46′

Since Ptolemy (3.8.4) assigns his co-ordinates 49° long./48° lat. to *Porolisson* in Dacia, which is really about 23° 09′ long. / 47° 12′ lat. (Moigrad-Jac, Map 1H1), his **Karrodounon** should be north-east of that, which suits Zalischyky or thereabouts reasonably well – this is why I

---

[143] Ibid. pp. 39 and 122–23.
[144] Or *Roubon*; cf. PNPG Comments s.n. *Rhoúbo:nos p.e.*
[145] Schönfeld, p. 275.
[146] *Germania* 45; see Rives's note, p. 321.
[147] On the etymology see Schönfeld, p. 279, and Svennung, p. 231. There were also *Sithones* in Thrace (Map 51H1 = +26/41); cf. Reichert i, 616.
[148] *Mogilew* [Mogilev/Mohyliv] according to Holder ii, 392.
[149] *Tiraspol* [on the Dniester] according to Holder i, 1457. *Eraktion* in the *Map-by-Map Directory* i, 364, is 'apparently a misprint' (PNPG Comments s.n. *É:rakton*).

assigned **Karrodounon** to +25/48 in Table 5.2.[150] Müller (p. 434) suggested that *Maitonion* and *Ouibantouarion* were also Celtic names, comparing *Matavonium* (= 16B3 *Matavo*) and *Argentovaria* (11H4) in Gaul, while admitting that *-ouarion* had been identified with Slavic *wari* 'habitation'.[151] **Karrodounon** at least is definitely Celtic and mirrors Ptolemy's place of the same name in Germania Magna (2.11.14), at Krapkowice in Poland (+17/50, not shown on Map 13C2).[152] These two names, with the Celtic-speaking **Cotini** between at +19/49, betray a Celtic presence north of the Carpathians, indicated also by the name **Lugii** (cf. Map 6.3 above).

Ptolemy mentions a couple of Celtic-looking mountains in European Sarmatia. *Alaunon oros* (3.5.5, around +30/50?) may recalls Celtic *Alauna* (see Chapter 4 above, s.v.), but is properly emended to *Alanon oros*, referring to the Scythian *Alanoi*, whom Ptolemy (3.5.7 and 9–10) calls *Alaunoi*.[153] *Bôdinon oros* (3.5.5, around +30/50?) recalls Celtic names in *Bo(u)d-* (see Chapter 4, s.v.) but is presumably to be connected with the *Bôdinoi* (3.5.10, around +29/47?), a Scythian people already discussed by Herodotus (4.109).[154]

[150] This is off the area covered in the *Atlas* – east of Maps 2 and 13 and north of Map 1. See also Pârvan, *Dacia*, p. 112 and map; Zubarev, 'The Roman roads between the Ister (Danube) and the Tyras (Dniester) in Claudius Ptolemaeus' description', map, p. 74. PNPG places it at '+24/49?' and Dr A. Falileyev informs me that it is usually equated with Kam''yanets'-Podil's'kyy (long. 48° 41'/lat. 26° 35') or its environs. Ptolemy's names are commonly correlated with La Tène material, for instance by Woźniak, 'Die östliche Randzone der Latènekultur', p. 384, Zirra, 'Eastern Celts of Romania', p. 10, and Teodor, 'Elemente Celtice', p. 46. For La Tène material and map see Cunliffe, *Ancient Celts*, pp. 175–76 and 307. The name of modern Halych (Galic) in the western Ukraine (long. 24° 44' / lat. 49° 07') is often derived from **Gālik-ja* 'Celts' city' (Andersen, 'Slavic and the Indo-European migrations', p. 48; Shchukin, 'Celts in eastern Europe', p. 202), but Dr Falileyev tells me that it is a common Slavic toponym meaning 'open space' (cf. *Galich* near Kostroma) and refers me to V. Neroznak, *Nazvanija drevnerusskich gorodov* (Moscow, 1983), pp. 56–57.

[151] GPN, p. 231 (*Matavonium* but not *Maitonion*, where the *ai* is a problem). Holder iii, 274, compares *Vibantavarion* with the Slavic(?) *Vibiônes* (Ptolemy 3.5.10), but Rübekeil, p. 395, connects it with a Germanic ethnonym **Vibant(a)varii*. For *-varia* cf. PNRB, p. 486; De Bernardo Stempel, 'Ptolemy's evidence for Germania Superior', pp. 78 and 92, García Alonso, 'Ptolemy and the expansion of Celtic language(s)', p. 140, and VCIE, pp. 480 and 489.

[152] Ch. 4 above, s.v. *carr-*.

[153] Placed at '+32/53?' in PNPG; see PNPG Comments s.nn. *Alaûnoi*, *Alaunoí* and *Alaûnon o*. Cf. *Alanoi* at 85B3 = +44/44 and Ptolemy 6.14.3 and 9 (ed. Humbach & Ziegler, i, 182 and 186, and ii, figs 33–34) and Stephen of Byzantium, cited by Müller, p. 420.

[154] PNPG Comments s.n. *Bo:dinòn o*. (I take all the grid references in this paragraph from PNPG); Müller, pp. 419–20, 427 and 431.

7

THE EXTENT OF CELTIC NAMES II:
CENTRAL EUROPE (LATITUDES 44–47)

In this chapter I examine the extent of Celtic names from central France in the west to the southern Ukraine in the east. References to the maps in the *Atlas* will be given in separate tables when the layout of the *Atlas* is complex, with many overlapping sheets. As in the previous chapter, *italics* are used in the tables of names to denote squares devoid of Celtic names, the names in **bold** are the 'Celtic-looking' names from Table 5.2 and underlining indicates probably Celtic names.

(a) From −5 to +7 longitude (above latitude 44 and below latitude 48)

This area covers central France, western Switzerland and the border of north-west Italy. Its Celticity is clear from Maps 5.1–5.3,[1] and need not be discussed further. This is not, of course, to claim that languages other than Celtic, Latin and Greek are absent.

(b) From +8 to +11 longitude (above latitude 44 and below latitude 48)

The following table shows how the grid squares relate to the *Atlas* maps.[2]

	+8	+9	+10	+11	
47	18F2	19B2	19C2	19D2	47
	19A2				
46	18F3	19B3	19C3	19D3	46
	19A3	39E1	39G1	39I1	
	39C1	39F1	39H1		
	39D1				
45	18F4	19B4	19C4	19D4	45
	19A4	39E2-3	39G2-3	39I2-3	
	39C2-3	39F2-3	39H2-3	40A1-2	
	39D2-3			40B1-2	

[1] There are no unlocatable 'Celtic-looking' names in the area of Barrington Maps 14, 17 and 18, apart from 17unl ***Mediolanum**, a starred form which does not really earn its place in the dataset (see Ch. 4 above, s.v. *medio-*), and 14unl **Antobroges** (see Ch. 4, s.v. *brog-*).

[2] Note also that 1F2 *Ap(p)enninus M.* is placed in +10/44. In the tables which follow I have *not* merged names from different maps into a single alphabetical sequence.

44	39C4-5	39E4-5	39G4-5	39I4-5	44
	39D4-5	39F4-5	39H4-5	40A3-4	
	16F1	41A1	41C1	40B3-4	
		41B1	41D1		
	+8	+9	+10	+11	

This area covers eastern Switzerland, western Austria and northern Italy. Its Celticity according to Maps 5.1–5.3 is more mixed, and the only unlocatable name omitted from Table 5.2 which can be added is '19unl **Apenn**inus M.', in Raetia (Brenner/Brennero?), the less famous mountain of this possibly Celtic name.[3] Maps 5.1–5.3 indicate the relatively limited Celtic element in the place-names here, but on closer inspection there is no square where it is wholly absent.

In the following tables the data from Table 5.2 is shown in bold. Without attempting an exhaustive analysis, these few Celtic-looking names can be supplemented by some additional Celtic names (underlined in the tables below):

+8/44 *Crixia*,[4] *Genua* (modern Genova),[5] *Album Ingaunum/Albingaunum* and *Ingauni*,[6] and perhaps *Tanarus fl.*[7]

+8/45   *Carbantia*,[8]   *Libicii*,[9] *Transpadana*,[10] *Vercellae*,[11] *Vertamocorii*,[12]   *Olonna   fl.*,[13]   *Votodrones*,[14]   *Cuttiae* (modern   Cozzo),[15]

[3] See Ch. 4 above s.v. *penno-*.

[4] AILR Celtic Elements s.v. *crixo-*.

[5] De Bernardo Stempel, 'Ptolemy's Celtic Italy and Ireland', pp. 87, 92 and 107; PNPG Celtic Elements s.v. {genua:}; Falileyev, review of DLG, p. 285. Cf. Anreiter et al., 'Names of the eastern Alpine region', p. 135; Lambert, '*Lugdunensis*', p. 238.

[6] De Bernardo Stempel, 'Additions to Ptolemy's evidence for Celtic Italy'.

[7] Cf. discussion of *Taneton* by De Bernardo Stempel, 'Ptolemy's Celtic Italy and Ireland', pp. 89, 92 and 105. Cf. Falileyev, 'Ptolemy revisited', pp. 86–87. De Bernardo Stempel, 'Additions to Ptolemy's evidence for Celtic Italy', suggests that *Dertona* could be a Celtic *Derk-t-ona*, but I would prefer to compare it with the presumably non-Celtic *Dertosa* in Spain; cf. Gorrochategui, 'Ptolemy's Aquitania and the Ebro valley', p. 147, and De Hoz, 'Narbonensis', p. 184.

[8] AILR Celtic Elements s.v. *carbanto-*.

[9] De Bernardo Stempel, 'Ptolemy's Celtic Italy and Ireland', pp. 90 and 106–7, suggesting **lubi-* > *libi-* (cf. DLG s.v.). *Libi-* occurs widely, including in areas where it is unlikely to be Celtic. Note 24C1 *Libyka fl.* (−9/43), 25G3 (+1/42) *Ioulia Libika* and 27C3 *Libiosa* (−3/38) in Spain, 15C2-3 *Libicii* and *Libica Ora* in France (+4/43), and 48A2 *Turris Libisonis* (+8/40) in Sardinia.

[10] On the river *Padus* (Po) see +11/45 below.

[11] De Bernardo Stempel, 'Ptolemy's Celtic Italy and Ireland', pp. 88, 94 and 105, and 'Additions to Ptolemy's evidence for Celtic Italy'; AILR and PNPG Possibly Celtic Elements s.v. {cella:-}. Cf. KPP, p. 179.

[12] DLG s.v. *uertamos*.

[13] Cf. DLG s.v. *ollos* and De Bernardo Stempel, 'Continental Celtic *ollo*', for forms with single *l*. (Cf. +9/45 *Ollius fl.* below.) 39unl *Latis fl.* may be Celtic and in this vicinity; see below, p. 240, n. 120.

[14] Delamarre, 'Gallo-Brittonica', pp. 125–26.

[15] De Bernardo Stempel, 'Ptolemy's Celtic Italy and Ireland', p. 95; and Ch. 4 above, s.v. *cot(t)-*. While the *Atlas* has only *Cuttiae* (39D3), some sources have *Cottiae* (TIR L-32, p. 58).

Novaria,[16]   *Ticinus*.[17] On the other hand, the **Langobardi** are false friends, as noted earlier.[18] On **Bodincus fl.** see +11/45 below.

+8/46 *Lepontii*.[19]

+8/47 *Aquae Helveticae*,[20]   *Tasg(a)etium*.[21] Ptolemy's *Drousomagos* (2.12.3) may belong here (see Chapter 4 s.v. *mag-*).

+9/44 *Litubium*,[22]   *Tigullia*,[23]   *Minerva Cabardiacensis* (/a:ko/ suffix),[24] *Saltus Bitunia(e)*,[25]   *Antion*,[26]   *Tarus fl.*,[27] and also **Boakias fl.* (39F5) and *Boacias* (41B1), assuming that *t* is read as in Ptolemy's spelling of the river (3.1.3: *Boaktou*) rather than *i* as in the *Antonine Itinerary*'s spelling of the town (293.5).[28] Dangerous though this line of argument is, note the similarity between *Ricina* on the Ligurian coast and Ptolemy's island of *Rikina* near Ireland (9A5).[29] *Veleia* may also be Celtic by association with *Veleia* in Spain (−3/42).

---

[16] De Bernardo Stempel, 'Ptolemy's Celtic Italy and Ireland', p. 94, and 'Additions to Ptolemy's evidence for Celtic Italy'.

[17] De Bernardo Stempel, 'Ptolemy's Celtic Italy and Ireland', pp. 95–96 and 105–7. She notes (p. 89, n. 9) that *Insubres* is obscure; for a suggestion see PNPG Celtic Elements s.v. *bero*, *br(o)-*.

[18] Above, p. 185.

[19] De Bernardo Stempel, 'Ptolemy's Celtic Italy and Ireland', pp. 91 and 105–7. Etruscan according to Hubschmied, 'Etruskische Ortsnamen in Rätien', p. 409. *Oskela* could be Celtic (DLG s.v. *oxso-*).

[20] On *Helvetii* see KGP, pp. 203–5, CIB, p. 130, De Bernardo Stempel, 'Ptolemy's evidence for Germania Superior', p. 74, PNPG Celtic Elements s.v. *eluo-*, and KPP, p. 232.

[21] GPN, p. 265; PNPG Celtic Elements s.v. *tasgo-*.

[22] For *Litu-* see DLG s.v. and GPN, pp. 217–18.

[23] De Bernardo Stempel, 'Ptolemy's Celtic Italy and Ireland', pp. 87, 94 and 106; Falileyev, review of DLG, p. 283.

[24] For this and other *-ācum* names around Veleia see Russell, 'Suffix', pp. 161–62.

[25] Cf. DLG s.v. *bitu-*.

[26] Cf. De Bernardo Stempel, 'Ptolemy's Celtic Italy and Ireland', pp. 89 and 111, on the *Antium* at +12/41; cf. DLG s.v. *anto-*. However, since I exclude the latter as being too isolated (below, p. 251, n. 181), this *Antion* should perhaps not count as Celtic either. Both names may belong to another Indo-European language.

[27] DLG s.v. *taro-*. But for problems with this element see review by Billy, p. 282. On the difficulty of classifying hydronyms in *Tar-* see GPN, p. 262 and n. 3, and García Alonso, 'Ptolemy and the expansion of Celtic language(s)', p. 137, n. 5, and cf. the 'Mediterranean' **TaR-* in Rostaing, *Essai*, pp. 266–68, and the 'Illyrian' *tar-* in Rasch, §IIAa.

[28] The *Atlas* follows TIR L-32, p. 36, and the editors of Ptolemy in preferring AI's *Boacias*. PNPG Comments s.n. *Boáktou*, notes **bou-ax-to-* 'place where cows are driven' as a Celtic etymology. Cf. De Bernardo Stempel, 'Ptolemy's Celtic Italy and Ireland', p. 87, n. 7.

[29] PNRB, p. 132; Toner, 'Identifying Ptolemy's Irish places and tribes', p. 79, n. 12; Weisgerber, p. 140, n. 151; CIB, p. 170, n. 1017; PNPG Celtic Elements s.v. *rico-* ('furrow'). Cf. *Helvia Ricina* below, p. 247. *Ricina* may be Latin, however. On Latin *ricinus* 'tick' and *rīcinus/rīcinium* 'head-dress' see IEW, pp. 335 and 1158, and DAG, p. 1339.

+9/45 *Gallianates* (cf. *Galli*), *Ticinum*,[30]   *Bergomum*,[31]   *Ollius fl.*,[32]   *Ad Padum* (cf. +11/45 below), *Cenomani*.[33]

+9/46 *Aneuniates*,[34] *Suanetes*,[35] *Larius/Comacinus L.*[36]

+9/47 *Ad Rhenum*.[37]

+10/44 *Ad Tarum* (cf. +9/44), *Tannetum*,[38] *Brixellum*,[39] *Mutina*.[40]

+10/45 *Brixia*,[41] **Bedriacum/Betriacum*,[42] *Cremona*,[43] *Belounoi*,[44] *Benacenses* and *Benacus L.*,[45] *Voberna*,[46] *Ari(o)lica/Arelica*,[47] *Verona*.[48] (Like *Verona*, **Mantua** has been regarded as Etruscan, but a Celtic etymology as for the *Mantua* in Spain has been defended by De Bernardo Stempel.)[49]

---

[30] De Bernardo Stempel, 'Ptolemy's Celtic Italy and Ireland', pp. 88, 95 and 105–7.

[31] Ibid. pp. 88, 92 and 106. Cf. AILR Celtic Elements s.v. *bergu-* and Falileyev, 'Ptolemy revisited', pp. 82–83.

[32] Cf. GPN, pp. 237–38.

[33] De Bernardo Stempel, 'Ptolemy's Celtic Italy and Ireland', pp. 91, 105 and 107; PNPG Celtic Elements s.v. *mano-* and Possibly Celtic Elements s.vv. *ceno-* and {ce:no-}. Lambert, '*Lugdunensis*', p. 225, rejects the equation with OI *cían*. *Leucerae/Leukon* could be Celtic, but the stem is widespread: PNPG Celtic Elements s.v. *leuco-*.

[34] Cf. Holder iii, 622, and DLG s.v. *aneunos*.

[35] Holder ii, 1649; DLG s.vv. *anatia* and *-uanos*.

[36] De Bernardo Stempel, 'Ptolemy's Celtic Italy and Ireland', pp. 95 and 106. AILR analyses the latter name with the (Celtic) /a:ko-/ suffix.

[37] On *Rhenus* see above, p. 179, and cf. +11/44 below. *Vennon(et)es* and *Ven(non)etus L.* are uncertainly Celtic cf. DLG s.v. *uenet-* and GPN, p. 279 and n. 3.

[38] See n. 7 above.

[39] De Bernardo Stempel, 'Ptolemy's Celtic Italy and Ireland', pp. 89, 92 and 106. Cf. PNPG Possibly Celtic Elements s.v. *brixo-*. Cf. Chapter 4 s.v. *brig-*, p. 53.

[40] De Bernardo Stempel, 'Ptolemy's Celtic Italy and Ireland', pp. 86, 89 and 105; Falileyev, 'Ptolemy revisited', p. 83, citing Greule & Kleiber, 'Moseltal', p. 161, on Müden (*Mudhena* in 1139). *Mutina* is considered Etruscan by Pallottino, *Saggi* ii, 723; Pfiffig, *Einfuhrung*, p. 92; Bonfante & Bonfante, *Etruscan Language*, p. 222. The much-forking *Gabellus fl.* (Pliny 3.118), notwithstanding the /e/, may belong with Celtic *gabalos* 'fork' (see DLG s.v. *gabalos*, VCIE, p. 459, and Grzega, s.vv. *gabalus* and **gabella*), but as this was borrowed into Latin, its occurrence in toponymy is of uncertain relevance for Celtic linguistic geography; cf. on *burgus* above, p. 4. On '*Aventia*' *fl.* (and +11/44 '*Vicus Aventia*') cf. DLG s.v. *auantia, auentia*, and De Bernardo Stempel, 'Ptolemy's evidence for Germania Superior', p. 82.

[41] De Bernardo Stempel, 'Ptolemy's Celtic Italy and Ireland', pp. 88, 92 and 106, and 'Additions to Ptolemy's evidence for Celtic Italy'. Cf. PNPG Possibly Celtic Elements s.v. *brixo-*.

[42] Russell, 'Suffix', pp. 162–63, noting that Juvenal has *Bebriaci*.

[43] De Bernardo Stempel, 'Ptolemy's Celtic Italy and Ireland', pp. 86, 88 and 105; AILR and PNPG Possibly Celtic Elements s.v. *cremo-*.

[44] Cf. De Bernardo Stempel, 'Ptolemy's Celtic Italy and Ireland', pp. 87 and 93. Cf. PNPG Comments, s.v. *Bekhounôn* and Possibly Celtic Elements s.vv. *bená-* and *benno-*.

[45] De Bernardo Stempel, 'Ptolemy's Celtic Italy and Ireland', pp. 87, 95 and 106; Russell, 'Suffix', pp. 162–63; PNPG Possibly Celtic Elements s.vv. *bená-* and *benno-*.

[46] Judging by its position, *Voberna* could be Celtic *Vo-* 'under' (cf. Weisgerber, p. 351) plus a cognate of either OI *bern* 'pass' or Breton *bern* 'heap of stones', but for a different explanation see DLG s.v. *vobera*. Are the **Vobenenses* in the same area connected despite the spelling?

[47] De Bernardo Stempel, 'More on Ptolemy's evidence for Celtic Ireland', p. 99.

[48] De Bernardo Stempel, 'Ptolemy's Celtic Italy and Ireland', pp. 86, 94, 105.

[49] Ibid. pp. 86, 88, 93 and 107; Delamarre, 'Gallo-Brittonica', p. 129. Cf. Pallottino, *Saggi*, ii, 721 and 724–25; Pfiffig, *Einführung*, p. 92; Bonfante & Bonfante, *Etruscan Language*, pp. 10 and 222.

Karraka (Ptolemy 3.1.28) in the Brixia region(?) may be Celtic.[50]

+ 10/46 *Aquae Bormiae*.[51]

+ 10/47 —[52]

+ 11/44   *Boi(i)*,[53] *Forum Gallorum*,[54] *Rhenus fl.*,[55] *Scultenna fl.*,[56] *Lingones*.[57]

+ 11/45 *Padus fl.*, according to De Bernardo Stempel's etymologies *k^wōd-ó-s* 'cutting river' or *k'wā-dó-s* 'swelling river'. On the other hand, Krahe, who stresses that *Padus* had a short /a/ metrically, would see it as cognate of the alternative name **Bodincus fl.** (+ 8/45). The latter, though 'Celtic-looking', is not really Celtic, but Ligurian according to Pliny.[58] Formally *Venetia* could be Celtic, but that is unlikely.[59]

+ 11/46 *Anaunion/Anauni*,[60] *Brixenetes?*,[61] *Burrus fl.*,[62] *Maiensis Statio*,[63] *Vervassium*.[64]

+ 11/47 *Cosuanetes*,[65] *Coveliacae?*,[66] **Mastiacum*.[67]

---

[50] See Ch. 4 above, s.v. *carr-*.

[51] On *Borm-* see p. 193, n. 135 above.

[52] Unless the *Genaunes* (*Genaunoi*) have a Celtic name, despite Anreiter et al., 'Names of the Eastern Alpine region', p. 135. Cf. on + 8/44 *Genua* above, and PNPG Comments s.n. *Benlaûnoi*. On **Abodiacum** see Ch. 4 above, s.v. *boud-/bodio-*. The suffix at least is Celtic. *Licates* derives from *Licca* at + 10/48 above.

[53] De Bernardo Stempel, 'Ptolemy's Celtic Italy and Ireland', p. 90. *Boiôn Gallôn* in Ptolemy 3.1.20.

[54] On the Celticity of the name *Galli* cf. above, p. 2, n. 5.

[55] Pliny 3.118 etc. Cf. De Bernardo Stempel, 'Tratti linguistici', p. 119, and 'Ptolemy's evidence for Germania Superior', pp. 84 and 90; LEIA s.v. *rían*; PNPG Celtic Elements s.v. {re:no-}.

[56] Holder ii, 1419. Holder's inclusion of *Anemo fl.* (i, 152) is very dubious.

[57] DLG and PNPG Possibly Celtic Elements s.v. *ling(o)-*; De Bernardo Stempel, 'Ptolemy's evidence for Germania Superior', pp. 75 and 89.

[58] De Bernardo Stempel, 'Ptolemy's Celtic Italy and Ireland', pp. 96 and 106, and 'Additions to Ptolemy's evidence for Celtic Italy'; Krahe, 'Zu einigen alten Gewässernamen'. See Pliny 3.122 and Zehnacker's note, p. 246.

[59] Tacitly rejected by De Bernardo Stempel, 'Ptolemy's Celtic Italy and Ireland', p. 87. Indo-European including Celtic according to Lambert, '*Lugdunensis*', pp. 232–33. It seems likely that the ethnonym *Veneti* was used independently by a number of Indo-European groups, only some of which were Celtic. For differing views see DLG s.v. *uenet-*, Bader, *Langues indo-européennes*, pp. 68–72, Loicq, 'Sur les peuples de nom "Vénète"', and VCIE, pp. 483 and 489, n. 515, with older literature in GPN, p. 279, n. 1.

[60] De Bernardo Stempel, 'Ptolemy's Celtic Italy and Ireland', pp. 88, 91 and 106; Delamarre, 'Gallo-Brittonica', pp. 126–27; PNPG Celtic Elements s.vv. *au-, auo-*, and Possibly Celtic Elements s.vv. *anauo-* and *ano-*.

[61] Presumably Celtic if *Brixia* and *Brixellum* above are Celtic. Some manuscripts of Pliny have *Brixentes* (3.137); see Zehnacker's edition, pp. 260 and 262, where they are identified with the *Briksantai* of Ptolemy 2.12.2.

[62] Cf. Sims-Williams, 'Degrees of Celticity', p. 10; KPP, p. 260.

[63] PNRB, pp. 406–7, with apparently mistaken equation with **Magia** at + 9/47 which is probably distinct.

[64] Cf. DLG s.vv. *uassos* and *uer(o)-*.

[65] Holder i, 1140; DLG s.vv. *anatia* and *-uanos*.

[66] If = *Co-veli-āc-* (Holder i, 1151, cf. iii, 140, 146 and 152), as pointed out by Dr A. Falileyev. It is from a personal name *Covelius* (related to *Covius, Covia*) according to Rasch, §IICa.

[67] *Mastiaco* (var. *Masciaco*) in AI 259.9; Russell, 'Suffix', p. 162. *Baio(u)arii* would be semi-Celtic if connected with *Boii* as sometimes argued; cf. Rübekeil, pp. 327–50.

	+8		+9		
47	Aquae Helveticae Tenedo/Wrzacha [!] **Vindonissa** Acronus L. Ad Fines ***Brigobannis**	**Iuliomagus** Lentienses Tasg(a)etium Turicum **Vitudurum** {Drousomagos}	Ad Rhenum Arbor Felix **Brigantinus L.**/ Ven(non)etus L. **Brigantium/** **Brigantii**	**Clunia** Constantia **Magia** Vennon(et)es	47
46	Oskela? Alpes Raeticae	Lepontii	Aneuniates Bergalei Bilitio Calucones Clavenna *Cunus Aureus Curia Lapidaria? Murus	Raetia/Raetii Ru(i)gusci Suanetes *Summus L. ***Tarvessedum** *Tinnetio Ceresius L. Larius/Comacinus L./ Comus L.	46
45	[Bugella] Pagus Agaminus [S. Iulianus] Ins. **Bodincus fl.** Carbantia/Ad Medias Cest(a)e Iadatini Industria/ **Bodincomagum?** Libicii **Rigomagus** Transpadana Vardagate/Vardacate Vercellae Vertamocorii Victumulae/Victimuli Insubres Montunates Olonna fl.	Plumbia Sebuinus Vicus Sibrium/ Castrum Insubrorum Subinates **Verbanus L.** Votodrones Agunia fl. Aliana Cuttiae Durriae Laevi **Langobardi** Laumellum Marici Novaria Retovium Sesites fl. Ticinus fl.	Addua fl. Argentea Ausuciates *Bromanenses [Comacina] Ins. Comum Eupilis L. Gallianates Lambrus fl. Leucerae/Leukon Licini Forum? Modicia Pagus *Fortunensis Ad IX Ad X Anamares/Anamari/ Anares Clastidium 'Comeli magus'/ 'Cameliomagus' Laus Pompeia	**Mediolan(i)um** Ticinum Tres Tabernae Anesiates Bergomum Ollius fl. Orumbovii/Orobii Parra Pons Aureoli Sarius fl. Tellegate Acerrae Ad Padum Ad Rota(s) Cenomani Clenna fl. *Forum Novum Lambrum Placentia **Trebia fl.**	45
44	Alba Pompeia Aquae Statiellae Hasta Statielli Tanarus fl. Canalicum Coeba Crixia Savo/Vicus Virginis? Vada Sabatia Dertona Forum Fulvii Valentinum Ioventio Mons Ir(i)a fl. Libarna	Liguria V(e)iturii Ad Figlinas/Falinis Ad Navalia Alba Docilia Fertor fl. Genua Hasta **Langenses** Porcibera fl./ Procibera/Porcifera Album Ingaunum/Albingaunum Gallinaria Ins. Ingauni Pullopice	Bobium Iria/Forum Iulii Iriensium Iria fl. Litubium **Pagus Ambitrebius** Pagus Luras Tidone fl. Ad Monilia/ Ad Munilia/ Ammonilia Ad Solaria 'Delphinis' Entella fl. Portus Delphini Ricina **Segesta** (Tigulliorum)/ Tigullia Tegulata Ad Fonteclos Florenti(ol)a Fundus Ancharianus Hadra fl. Minerva Cabardiacensis	Nure fl. Pagus Salutaris Saltus Berusetis Saltus Bitunia(e) [Sesterrio] fl. Veleia/Veleiates Antion *Boakias fl. **Bodetia** **In Alpe Pennino** Rubra Tarus fl. Apuani Arenaria? Ins. Boacias/[Boron] Macra fl. Portus Veneris Pullion 39unl **Rigonum fl.**	44

	+8	+9	

	+10		+11		
47	**Abodiacum** **Cambodunum** Damasia *Esco Estiones Focunates	*Foetes Genaunes Licates *Navoa Vemania 19unl **Cassiliacum**	Baio(u)arii Breuni Cosuanetes Coveliacae? Isinisca *Mastiacum	*Matreium *Parthanum/ *Tartenum Scarbia Teriolis Urusa? Veldidena	47
46	Aquae Bormiae Summus Vicus Tuliassi	Venostes Grebia Tublinates	Alpes Tridentinae Anaunion/Anauni [Appianum] Ausucum [Bauzanum] Brixenetes? Burrus fl. [Castrum Cimbra] Endidae [Enemase] Feltria/Felt(r)ini Isarci? Isarcus fl. Maiensis Statio	[Maletum] *Pons Drusi Sabiona Salurnis 'Sebatum' [Sermiana] 'Sublavione' [Tesana] Vervassium/ Anagnis *Vipitenum Trident(i)um Vettianus Fundus/ [Vitianum]	46
45	Brixia Camunni *Civitas Camunnorum Edrani Gennanates Sabini Sebinnus L. Tetellus Trump(i)lini *Vobenenses Bedriacum/ Betriacum Clesus fl./ Cleusis fl. Cremona Mella fl. *Minervium Pagus Farraticanus [Vulturina] Belounoi	Benacenses Benacus L. **[Bremtonicum]** Bretina Pagus Arusnatium/ Arusnates Stoeni? Vennum Voberna Ad Flexum/ Sermione Mansio Andes Ari(o)lica/Arelica Beneventum **Mantua** Mincius fl. Sirmio Verona {Karraka}	Ad Palatium At(h)esis fl. [Castrum Volaenes] Dripsinates Ligeris/Lagaris/ ['Lagare'] Retron fl. Sarnis Venetia Auraei Cadianum Hostilia Padus fl./Eridanus fl. Paludes Tartari Tartarus fl.	Acelum Astagus fl. Brinta? fl. *Duplavilis Misquilenses Plavis fl. Vicetia Ad Finem Aponus/Fons Aponi Ateste Mons Silicis Pagus Disaenius Patavium Togisonus? fl.	45
44	Ad Tarum Fidentia Forum Novum Incia fl. Parma Parma fl. Tannetum Forum Clodi? Gabellus fl./ *Secia fl./ *Secula fl.	Brixellum Campi Macri Mutina Pons *Seciae Regium Lepidum 'Aventia' fl. Auser fl. Frigidus fl. Friniates Luna Taberna Frigida **Ap(p)enninus M.**	Victoriolae Ad Medias Aemilia Boi(i) Colicaria Forum Gallorum Rhenus fl. Scultenna fl. Vicus Serninus Ad Idicem Felsina/**Bononia** Lavinius? fl. Silarus fl. Vatrenus fl.	[Feraria] Idex fl. Lingones [Vicus Aventia] Vicus Varianus Ad Silarum Ad Sinnium Anemo fl. Castellum Claterna [Claterna] fl. Faventia Forum Cornelii Sinnius fl. Vitis? fl.	44
	+10		+11		

(c) From +12 to +15 longitude (above latitude 44 and below latitude 48)

The following table shows how the grid squares relate to the *Atlas* maps.[68]

	+12	+13	+14	+15	
47	19E2	19F2	19G2		47
		20A2	20B2	20C2	
46	19E3	19F3	19G3		46
		20A3	20B3	20C3	
45	19E4	19F4	19G4		45
	40C1-2	20A4	20B4	20C4	
	40D1-2				
44	40C3-4	20A5	20B5	20C5	44
	40D3-4				
	+12	+13	+14	+15	

This area covers southern Austria, north-eastern Italy, Slovenia and western Croatia. Its Celticity according to Maps 5.1–5.3 is uneven, and no unlocatable Celtic-looking names omitted from Table 5.2 can be added to boost it. One can, however, add the Pannonian *Belgites* (20unl) mentioned by Pliny 3.148.[69] Maps 5.1–5.3 indicate the relatively limited Celtic element in the place-names here, and closer inspection indicates that they thin out and disappear in the south-west of the area. The absence of Celtic-looking names at +15/47 is not significant, as only one name is attested in this square, *Poidikon*.

In the following tables the data from Table 5.2 is shown in bold. Without attempting an exhaustive analysis, these few Celtic-looking names can be supplemented by some additional Celtic names (underlined in the tables below):

+12/44 **Butrium**,[70] *Ager Gallicus*,[71]   Padusa, Sacis ad Padum. For *Padus* as arguably Celtic see above. *Sacis* is to be equated with the river *Sagis* of **Ostium Sagis**, which, however, can only be regarded as possible example of Celtic **sag-* 'seek' in view of the occurrence of this root in other languages including Latin *sagio*.[72]

---

[68] Note also that 1F2 *(H)Adriaticum/Adriaticum/Superum Mare* is placed in +12/44.

[69] Anreiter, *Die vorrömischen Namen Pannoniens*, pp. 149–50. See above, Ch. 5, p. 168.

[70] De Bernardo Stempel, 'Ptolemy's Celtic Italy and Ireland', pp. 93, n. 16 and 106; PNPG Celtic Elements s.v. *boutro-*.

[71] For *Galli* see p. 2, n. 5 above.

[72] Cf. GPN, p. 251. For the *Sagis* see Nissen, *Italische Landeskunde*, i, 205, and ii, 214. Holder i, 366, suggested that *Bedesis fl.* might be Celtic (similarly Chevallier, *La romanisation de la Celtique du Pô*, i, 115), which may be correct, but see above, p. 24. **Neronia* contains a Sabine cognate of Celtic **nero-*, and *Ariminus fl.* and *Ariminum* are only possibly Celtic (see PNPG Celtic Elements s.vv. *nero-* and *mino-*). On *Ravenna* see PNPG Possibly Celtic Elements s.v. *rauo-*.

+ 12/45 *Meduacus* (related to the ethnonym Μεδόακοι, which is not included in the *Barrington* data).[73] Anreiter suggests that **Tarvisium** is a Celticization of a pre-Celtic *Taur-īsium.[74]

+ 12/46 *Ambilikoi*,[75] *Bellunum*,[76] '*Littamum*',[77] *Loncium?*.[78] It is unlikely that **Tiliaventum** really is Celtic.[79]

+ 12/47 *Ambisontes*.[80] The Celtic etymologies of *Bedaium and *Pons Aeni* are uncertain; the former is allowed here.[81] That of **Alaunoi** has been questioned, but **Artobriga** is obviously secure.[82]

+ 13/44 —

+ 13/45 *Varamos fl.*,[83] *Catali*.[84]

+ 13/46 *Ambidrauoi*,[85] *Santicum*.[86]

+ 13/47 '*Graviacis*', '*Laciacis*',[87] *Vocarium.[88] Notwithstanding evidence

---

[73] Russell, 'Suffix', pp. 161–62; DLG s.v. *medu-*; VCIE, p. 340.

[74] Anreiter, *Die vorrömischen Namen Pannoniens*, p. 141, n. 523.

[75] Celtic *ambi-* + pre-existing river-name: Anreiter et al., 'Names of the Eastern Alpine region', pp. 133 and 136.

[76] Uncertain: see De Bernardo Stempel, 'Ptolemy's Celtic Italy and Ireland', pp. 87 and 93, and PNPG Comments s.n. *Belôunon*.

[77] AILR Comments s.n. *Littamo. Aguntum* could be Celtic: cf. Anreiter et al., 'Names of the Eastern Alpine region', pp. 115–16 and 136; PNPG Celtic Elements s.v *agi-*, {a:gi-}.

[78] *Longion* in AI 279.6. Dr A. Falileyev suggests derivation from *longo-* 'ship' (see DLG s.v.).

[79] See above, Ch. 4, s.v. *venta*. It is not analysed as Celtic in PNPG.

[80] Anreiter et al., 'Names of the Eastern Alpine region', pp. 134 and 136; PNPG Celtic Elements s.v. *iso-*.

[81] Anreiter et al., 'Names of the Eastern Alpine region', pp. 117 and 129; AILR Comments s.nn. *Bidaio* and *Ponte Aeni*; PNPG Possibly Celtic Elements s.v. *eno-* and Comments s.n. *Bédakon*. On *Bed-* see also p. 24 above. On a river *Druna* in this area (not in the *Atlas*) see Ch. 6 above, p. 189, n. 108.

[82] Anreiter et al., 'Names of the Eastern Alpine region', pp. 117, 133 and 136. Cf. PNPG Comments s.nn. On the possibility that Ptolemy is referring to another *Artobriga* around + 11/48 see p. 186 above.

[83] PNRB, p. 486, misquoting *Varamus* in Pliny 3.126. Cf. AILR Celtic Elements s.v. *uaro-* and DLG s.v. *treuero-*. The root is not exclusively Celtic, however. *Alpes Venetae* is not counted as Celtic; see + 11/45 on *Venetia*. The alternative *Alpes Iuliae* has been thought to be a Latin reinterpretation of a Celtic name: DLG s.v. *iugo-*.

[84] On Celtic *catu-* in Venetic see DLG s.v. The *a* rather than *u* is a problem, but cf. forms in *Cata-* in GPN, pp. 172 and 174, and KGP, pp. 166–67.

[85] Celtic *ambi-* + 'Ancient European' river-name according to Anreiter et al., 'Names of the Eastern Alpine region', pp. 131 and 133. Cf. Anreiter, *Die vorrömischen Namen Pannoniens*, pp. 241–42.

[86] Uncertain. See Anreiter et al., 'Names of the Eastern Alpine region', pp. 126–27 and 136; Falileyev, 'Ptolemy revisited', p. 87; AILR Possibly Celtic Elements s.v. *santo-*; PNPG Comments s.n. *Siantikón*. Anreiter et al. doubt the Celticity of **Iulium Carnicum** etc. (pp. 120–22), but this is on the basis that **kar-n-* could have existed in Eastern Alpine Indo-European as well as Celtic. **Licus? fl.* may be Celtic: PNPG Possibly Celtic Elements s.v. *lico-* (cf. above, n. 75).

[87] Cf. DLG s.v. *graua* and Russell, 'Suffix', p. 165, listing the latter s.n. *Laciacum* and comparing a personal name *Lacius*.

[88] This form is based on TP; Ptolemy 2.13.3 implies *Vacorium*. Cf. PNPG Comments s.n. *Ouakórion* and Celtic Elements s.v. **uac(c)o-* ; Isaac, 'Scotland', p. 200 (cf. VCIE, pp. 75–78 and 123–25). Holder iii, 423 derives from *Voc-* but *Vo-* is also possible; cf. GPN, pp. 165 and 288, and Holder s.n. *Vocarus*.

for a prefix *Tar-* in Celtic,[89] it seems unlikely that **'Tarnantone'** should be analysed as Celtic *tar-nant-* in view of the proximity of *'Tarnasici'* (+ 14/46).[90]

+ 14/44 —. The absence of other Celtic names leaves **Senia** isolated; it could derive from some other dialect which retained IE **sen-* 'old'.[91] The Celticity of *Arba* (also *Arva*) is also very doubtful, as the IE stem **arw-* (cf. OI *arbor*, W *erw* 'acre') was widespread.[92]

+ 14/45 *Latobici* and *Praetorium Latobicorum*,[93] and *Longaticum*.[94] By contrast the similarity between **Lougeon Helos** and Celtic *Lugu-* is surely coincidental.[95] *Ouolkera* can be added from Ptolemy 2.16.2 (see Chapter 4 above, s.v. *volco-*).

+ 14/46 *Carvanca M.*,[96] *Matucaium*.[97] The Celtic etymology of **Virunum** is debatable.[98]

+ 14/47 *Ernolatia*,[99] *'Tutatio'*,[100] and perhaps *Monate*.[101] On the other hand, it is doubtful whether **Sabatinca** contains Celtic *tinco-*; it can also be segmented *Sab-at-inca*.[102]

+ 15/44 —. *Corinium* has naturally been compared to *Corinium* in Britain (Cirencester), but the Celticity of the latter is uncertain and the similarity may be accidental:[103] compare 72unl *Corinaeum* in Cyprus (p. 283 below).

---

[89] LEIA s.v. *tar*; KGP, p. 275. See also DLG, p. 436, with criticism by Billy in his review, p. 282.

[90] For this and similar names see Holder s.v. *Tarn-*; 'Illyrian' according to Rasch, §IVC8. On *Iuvavum* cf. Anreiter et al., 'Names of the Eastern Alpine region', pp. 123–24 and 136, and PNPG Comments s.n. *Klaudioúion*.

[91] Falileyev, '*Tylis*', pp. 116 and 128, describes *Senia* as 'at least consistent with Celtic' but probably indigenous, and quotes various opinions. Non-Celtic according to Rasch, §IE, who distinguishes it from a Celtic *Seniae vicus* near Trier (not in the *Atlas*).

[92] Cf. Holder i, 181; PNRB, p. 256; LEIA s.v. *arbor* 'céréale, blé'; Anreiter, *Die vorrömischen Namen Pannoniens*, p. 207. For a different etymology see Breeze, 'British-Latin place-names'.

[93] Anreiter, *Die vorrömischen Namen Pannoniens*, pp. 168–69 and 186; KPP, pp. 52–55. See above, Ch. 5, p. 170.

[94] DLG s.v. *longo-* and Delamarre, 'Gallo-Brittonica', pp. 121–23 (equating it semantically with *Nauportus*; cf. Šašel, 'Keltisches *portorium* in der Ostalpen').

[95] See GPN, p. 220, and Anreiter, *Die vorrömischen Namen Pannoniens*, pp. 244–45.

[96] DLG s.v. *caruos*.

[97] GPN, p. 231.

[98] GPN, p. 288; Anreiter et al., 'Names of the Eastern Alpine region', pp. 125–26; Anreiter, *Die vorrömischen Namen Pannoniens*, p. 136; AILR Celtic Elements s.v. *uiro-*.

[99] DLG and AILR Possibly Celtic Elements s.v. *erno-*.

[100] AILR Comments s.n. *Tutatione*.

[101] AILR Possibly Celtic Elements s.v. *mon-*.

[102] So AILR.

[103] PNRB, pp. 321–22; Coates et al., *Celtic Voices*, p. 299. The alleged Old Welsh equivalent is *Cair Ceri* (which has been compared with W *ceri* 'service-tree' – but is *ceri* from Late Latin *ceresia* 'cherry'?). The lack of /n/ makes this equation difficult (cf. CIB, p. 182, n. 1105) and *Ceri* may be an originally independent name (cf. Ekwall, *English River-Names*, p. 71, and EANC, pp. 132–33). PNPG, *Nes. Pret.*, derives *Korínion* from **coro-* (for which cf. GPN, p. 339, and DLG s.v.). Falileyev, '*Tylis*', p. 128, is non-committal. He is also sceptical (pp. 130–31) about Holder's inclusion of *Asseria* (Holder i, 248, cf. Anreiter, *Die vorrömischen Namen Pannoniens*, p. 96, n. 400), **Ausancalio* (i, 298), and *Nedinum* (ii, 697).

The same applies to the similarity between *Lissa Ins.* and Celtic **lissos* 'court'.[104]

+ 15/45 *Crucium.*[105] It has been suggested that 20unl *Bivium* = *Bibium* on the road from Senia to Siscia, may be Celtic, but it must surely be the Latin word for a fork in the road.[106]

+ 15/46 *Flavia Solva, Solva fl.*[107]

+ 15/47 —

[104] See below, p. 263, n. 238.

[105] Cf. DLG s.v. *crouco-*.

[106] AILR Celtic Elements s.v. *biuo-* 'alive'; Salway, 'Travel, *itineraria* and *tabellaria*', p. 28. Cf. Holder i, 415.

[107] Anreiter, *Die vorrömischen Namen Pannoniens*, pp. 218–19. AILR and PNPG Possibly Celtic Elements s.v. {celo-/a:-} notes *Celeia* (and *Albocela* in Spain, but for the latter see s.v. **ocelo-* in Ch. 4 above), but see Anreiter et al., 'Names of the Eastern Alpine region', pp. 122–23 and 136, and Anreiter, *Die vorrömischen Namen Pannoniens*, p. 51, n. 209.

	+12		+13		
47	**Alaunoi** *Albianum Ambisontes	<u>Artobriga</u> *<u>Bedaium</u> Pons Aeni	*Anisus Cucullae 'Graviacis' In Alpe 'In Murio'	Iuvavum 'Laciacis' **'Tarnantone'** *<u>Vocarium</u>	47
46	Aguntum <u>Ambilikoi</u> <u>Bellunum</u> **Catubrini** Ibligo Laianci 'Littamum' <u>Loncium?</u> Noricum/ Norici	Pagus Laebactium Reunia Saevates **Tiliaventum (Maius) fl./ Tiliaventum Maius fl./ Tiliaventum Minus fl.**	Ad Silanos Ad Trice(n)simum/ 'Viam Belloio' Aesontius fl/ Isontius fl. **Alpes Carnicae** Ambidrauoi [Artenia] **Carni** Forum Iulii [Glemona] **Iulium Carnicum**	'Larice' *Licus? fl. Meclaria Natiso fl. [Nemas] Osopus <u>Santicum</u> Statio Bilachiniensis Statio Plorucensis Statio Timaviensis Teurnia Dravus fl.	46
45	'Apicilia' Tergestinus Sinus Ad Cerasias Altinum Silis fl. **Tarvisium** Ad IX Ad XII/ <u>Meduacus Maior</u> Ad Portum Brundulum Fossis (H)Atria/Atria <u>Meduacus Maior fl.</u> <u>Meduacus Minor</u> <u>Meduacus Minor fl.</u>	<u>Ostium</u> Carbonaria Ostium Fossiones Ostium Philistina Portus Edronis Septem Maria [Torcellum] Ad Sanos [Equilum] [(H)Eraclia] Iulia Concordia Liquentia fl. Opitergium Portus Liquentiae Portus Reatinus Reatinum fl.	Ad Undecimum 1 Ad Undecimum 2 Alsa fl. Aquileia Avesica Castellum Pucinum Fons Timavi Gradus Pons Sonti Tergeste Timavus fl. <u>Varamos fl.</u> *Ad Fornulos Ad Ningum Aegida Alpes Iuliae/ Alpes Venetae Argao fl.	'Capris'/ Iustinopolis Cervaria Ins. <u>Catali</u> Fluvio Frigido/ Castra Formio fl. Frigidus fl. Histria/Histri Humagum Neapolis/ [Emoni(i)a] Ningum fl. Parentium Piquentum Piranum Ruginium 'Silvo' Siparis/Sapparis Ursaria Ins.	45
44	Atrianorum Paludes Augusta [Castrum Cumiacli] Corniculani *Hadriani/Radriani *Neronia/Naroma Ostium Caprasiae Ostium Eridanum/ Ostium Spineticum **Ostium Sagis** Ostium Volane <u>Sacis ad Padum</u> Septem Maria Spina Ad Novas Ad Rubiconem Ariminus fl./ Maricla fl. Bedesis fl.	<u>Butrium</u> Caesena Classis Compitum ad Confluentes Forum Livii Forum Popilii <u>Padusa</u> Ravenna Rubico fl. Sabis Sapis fl. Utens? fl. <u>Ager Gallicus</u> Aprusa fl. Ariminum (H)Adriaticum/ Adriaticum/ Superum Mare	*Fecusses/* *Secusses* *Mutila* *Nesactium* *Pola*	*Polaticum Pr.* *Polaticus Sinus* *Pullariae Inss.*	44
	+12		+13		

	+14		+15		
47	Ernolatia 'Tutatio' Ad Pontem **'Gabromago'** Monate *Murius fl.	Noreia **Sabatinca** Stiriate 'Surontio' 'Tartursanis' 'Viscellis'	Poidikon		47
46	Beliandrum 'Tarnasici' **'Tasinemeti'** Ad Nonum Ad Publicanos? Ad Quartodecimum [Albanta] fl. Atrans Candalicae **Carnium**	Carvanca M. Emona Iuenna Matucaium Praetentura Italiae et Alpium Saloca Taurisci **Virunum**	Ad Lotodos Ad Medias Celeia Colatio Flavia Solva Pannonia/ Pannonii	Poetovio Pultovia Ragando Solva fl. 'Upellis'	46
45	Acervo Ad Malum Ad Titulos? Ad Turres Albius M. Albona Alpes Delmaticae Arsia fl. Curicta Ins. Curicum Emona fl./ Nauportus fl. Flanaticus Sinus Flanona Fulfinium/ Fertinium	Iapudes In Alpe Iulia/ Ad Pirum Latobici Lauriana Longaticum **Lougeon Helos** Nauportus Ocra M. Praetorium Latobicorum Raparia Rundictes Tarsatica {Ouolkera}	Colapiani Colapis fl. Corcoras fl. Crucium Metulum	**Neviodunum** Romula Terponus Varciani {20unl Bibium/ Bivium}	45
44	*Apsarus* *Apsyrta Ins./* *Crepsa Ins.* *Apsyrtides Inss./* *Crepsi Inss.* *Arba* *Arba Ins.* *Cissa* *Crexa*	*Liburnia/* *Liburni* *Lopsica* *Mentorides Inss.* *Ortopla* *Portunata Ins.* **Senia** *Tedanius fl./* *Telavium fl.*	*Aenona* *Alveria* *Ancus* *Ansium* *Argyruntum* *Arupium* *Asseria* **Ausancalio* *Avendo* *Burnum* *Cissa Ins.*	*'Clambetis'* *Corinium* *Dalmatia* *Epidotium* *Iader* *Lissa Ins.* *Monetium* *Nedinum* *Raetinium?* *Sidrona* *Vegium*	44
	+14		+15		

(d) From +16 to +19 longitude (above latitude 44 and below latitude 48)

This area covers eastern Austria, eastern Croatia, Bosnia, western Hungary and western Serbia. In this and the following sections the relevant map references are given on the tables at the end of the sections. The Celticity of the area according to Maps 5.1–5.3 is uneven and no unlocatable 'Celtic-looking' names omitted from Table 5.2 can be added to boost it. Closer inspection confirms the continued absence of Celtic names from the south of the area. The absence of Celtic names in +19/46 is not significant, on the other hand, as only one name (*Iazyges*) belongs in this square, the west of the Great Hungarian Plain.

In the following tables the data from Table 5.2 is shown in bold. Without attempting an exhaustive analysis, these few Celtic-looking names can be supplemented by some additional Celtic names (underlined in the tables below):

+16/44 —[108]

+16/45 *Siscia* is Celtic according to Anreiter (cf. OI *seisc*, W *hesg* 'sedge'), although he does not regard the alternative name **Segestica** as Celtic.[109] *Breuci* is explained as 'grinders' by De Bernardo Stempel.[110]

+16/46 —[111]

+16/47 *Arrabo fl.*,[112] whence *Arabiates* (and **Arrabona** at +17/47), *Boii*,[113] and perhaps *'Muteno'*.[114]

+17/44 *Ad Matricem* (like *Matrica* at +18/47) is Celtic according to Anreiter;[115] though distant from the other names discussed in this section,

---

[108] Later scholarship has not followed the listing of *Salouia* (*Salvia*) as Celtic by Holder ii, 1332.

[109] Anreiter, *Die vorrömischen Namen Pannoniens*, pp. 124, 182 and 185 (cf. Udolph's review, p. 135); cf. AILR Comments s.n. *Sisciam* and PNPG Possibly Celtic Elements s.v. *sisco-*. Cf. above Ch. 4, s.v. *sego-*. *Ias(s)ii* might be compared with W *iâs* (Holder ii, 13–14), but see Anreiter, *Die vorrömischen Namen Pannoniens*, p. 68.

[110] 'Ptolemy's evidence for Germania Superior', p. 79. (Cf. IEW, p. 170; Anreiter, *Die vorrömischen Namen Pannoniens*, pp. 38–39.) Presumably, on this theory, the *Breuci* would have to be a Pannonian group with a Celtic name.

[111] Holder ii, 1297, lists *Sala*, but see Anreiter, *Die vorrömischen Namen Pannoniens*, p. 251.

[112] *Arabôn* etc. in some sources; see Anreiter et al., 'Names of the Eastern Alpine region', pp. 130 and 136; Anreiter, *Die vorrömischen Namen Pannoniens*, pp. 220–22; and Ch. 4 above, s.v. *abonā*.

[113] Anreiter, *Die vorrömischen Namen Pannoniens*, p. 157; KPP, pp. 222–23; cf. above, p. 169.

[114] Possibilities in Anreiter, *Die vorrömischen Namen Pannoniens*, p. 94 (cf. AILR Comments s.n.); cf. De Bernardo Stempel, on *Mutina* in Italy, cited above at +10/44.

[115] Anreiter, *Die vorrömischen Namen Pannoniens*, p. 170, n. 625 (cf. Ch. 5 above, p. 167). *Urbanus fl.* would have to be Celtic if *'Urbate'* at +17/45 were Celtic (AILR Comments s.n. and Possibly Celtic Elements s.v. *urbo-*, cf. GPN, p. 239), but see Anreiter, *Die vorrömischen Namen Pannoniens*, p. 259.

Ad Matricem could be connected with the apparently Celtic names in Dalmatia discussed in Chapter 8 below (those at + 16/43 = 20D6).
+ 17/45 *'Cardono'* (better *Karrodounon* as in Ptolemy).[116]
+ 17/46 *Hercuniates*,[117] and, in their territory, perhaps *Limusa*,[118] *'Silicenis'*,[119] and *Volgum* (better *Valco* as in AI).[120]
+ 17/47 *Moge(n)tiana*.[121]

+ 18/44 —
+ 18/45 Perhaps *'Leucono'?* and *'Vereis'*.[122] *'Bacuntius' fl.* (in Pliny 3.148) is regarded as an error for **Basant-* , which would agree with the modern name *Bosut*;[123] on the other hand, it is very tempting to follow Müller in connecting it with 21unl *Ouakontion* (= 20unl *Vacontium*) which Ptolemy (2.15.4) places in this vicinity.[124] The latter could be related, by a well-known Celtic dissimilation, to Celtic names like *Uocontii* (ethnonym) and *Uocontius/ Bocontius* (personal name).[125] While the **Cornacates** (whose name derives from the + 19/45 place **Cornacum**) are solidly Celtic, **Andizetes** is not a plausible example of Celtic **ande-* and **Teutoburgium** is unlikely to contain Celtic **teuto-* in view of the non-Celtic second element.[126]
+ 18/46 *Annamatia* (also *Adnamantia*),[127] and perhaps *Lussonium*.[128] *Sopianae* and *Tricciana* may be derived from Celtic personal names.[129] The

---

[116] Ibid. pp. 162–63. Cf. Anreiter et al., 'Names of the Eastern Alpine region', p. 122, n. 29, and above, Ch. 4, s.v. *carr-*.

[117] Anreiter, *Die vorrömischen Namen Pannoniens*, pp. 167 and 186, and Ch. 5 above, p. 170.

[118] Anreiter, *Die vorrömischen Namen Pannoniens*, p. 77, notes Celtic as a possibility only. His suggested Celtic etymology for '*Lentulis*' (pp. 214–15) is rejected in AILR Comments s.n.

[119] AILR Comments s.n. Cf. Anreiter, *Die vorrömischen Namen Pannoniens*, pp. 128–29.

[120] AILR Comments s.n. and Possibly Celtic Elements s.v. *uolco-*; Ch. 4 above, s.v. *volco-*. Cf. Anreiter, *Die vorrömischen Namen Pannoniens*, pp. 142 and 185.

[121] Ibid. pp. 196–97.

[122] AILR Celtic Elements s.v. *leuco-* and Comments s.n. *Vereis*. Anreiter, *Die vorrömischen Namen Pannoniens*, pp. 76–77, 144–46 and 185, treats them as Pannonian, but see review by Falileyev, p. 121, on *Leucono*.

[123] Anreiter, *Die vorrömischen Namen Pannoniens*, pp. 222–23. On the course of the Bosut see Zehnacker's edition of Pliny Book 3, p. 278.

[124] The *Map-by-Map Directory* i, 301 and 328, places it north of the Drava but, as Müller points out (p. 301), Ptolemy's latitude 46° 30′ is not reliable as he also assigns *Servitium* (20E4) to that latitude (2.15.4).

[125] DLG s.v. *uoconti*. However DLG and PNPG Celtic Elements s.v. *uac(c)o-* have a different explanation of *Vacontium*. Cf. VCIE, pp. 75–78 and 123–25.

[126] Anreiter, *Die vorrömischen Namen Pannoniens*, pp. 165, 31–32, and 137–38 respectively; also KPP, pp. 24–25, and AILR Comments s.n. *Teutiburgio*. *Magniana* could be Celtic (PNPG Celtic Elements s.v. *magno-*), but apart from Ptolemy all sources have *Marinianis* or similar (see TIR L-34, p. 78, and Anreiter, *Die vorrömischen Namen Pannoniens*, p. 195, n. 680).

[127] GPN, p. 235; Anreiter, *Die vorrömischen Namen Pannoniens*, p. 149 (cf. AILR Comments s.n. *Annamatio*); Ch. 5 above, p. 167.

[128] AILR Comments s.n. *Lussonium* and AILR and PNPG Possibly Celtic Elements s.v. *lusso-* (OI *lus* 'plants', W *llysiau*); differently Anreiter, *Die vorrömischen Namen Pannoniens*, pp. 80–81, comparing *Lussomana* (+ 18/47) which is less easy to see as Celtic.

[129] Anreiter, *Die vorrömischen Namen Pannoniens*, pp. 198–99 (cf. Mády, 'Zwei pannonische Ortsnamen').

Celticity of *Eravisci* and **Lugio** is uncertain, but I would accept the latter.[130] + 18/47 *Gardellaca/Cardabiaca*,[131] *Matrica*,[132] *Solva*.[133] **Kelamantia** (Ptolemy 2.11.15, var. *Kalamantia*) is a dubious example of Celtic *mant-*,[134] but **Brigetio** is securely Celtic.[135] '*Azao*' (AI) is *Anauon* in Ptolemy (2.11.15), a plausible Celtic name.[136]

+ 19/44 —[137]

+ 19/45 On *Bononia* (not in the *Atlas*) as an alternative name for *Malata* see Chapter 4, s.v. *bon-*.

+ 19/46 —

+ 19/47 —

(e) From + 20 to + 23 longitude (above latitude 44 and below latitude 48)

This area covers south-eastern Hungary, northern Serbia and western Romania. Its Celticity according to Maps 5.1–5.3 is slight and the only unlocatable Celtic-looking names omitted from Table 5.2 which can be added are 21unl **Rata**kensioi, somewhere in northern Dacia, and 22unl 'Zetnou**kort**ou' in Dacia Ripensis, neither likely to be a genuine Celtic name.[138] Maps 5.1–5.3 indicate that the Celtic element in the place-names here is very limited (and **Tricornium** and **Tricorn(i)enses** can perhaps be dismissed as Latin),[139] and closer inspection indicates that it is confined to the banks of the Danube, which dips down below the 44 latitude at + 23 longitude.[140]

---

[130] Anreiter, *Die vorrömischen Namen Pannoniens*, pp. 206–7 and 216–17. See also above, p. 191 on the *Lugii* at + 17/52. The *Eravisci/Aravisci* seem to have spoken *Pannonica lingua* (Tacitus, *Germania*, 28 and 43).

[131] Cf. Anreiter, *Die vorrömischen Namen Pannoniens*, p. 210. Not listed by Russell, 'Suffix'.

[132] Anreiter, *Die vorrömischen Namen Pannoniens*, pp. 169–70 and 185; cf. AILR Comments s.n. and *Ad Matricem* at + 17/44 above.

[133] Cf. Anreiter, *Die vorrömischen Namen Pannoniens*, pp. 218–19.

[134] On segmentation cf. Holder i, 883–84, Rasch, §VIc, and PNPG, *Germania Magna*.

[135] Anreiter, *Die vorrömischen Namen Pannoniens*, pp. 162 and 185.

[136] Cf. DLG s.v. *anauo-* and n. 60 above.

[137] Falileyev, '*Tylis*', p. 127, raised the possibility that *Savus fl.* might be Celtic (cf. Anreiter, *Die vorrömischen Namen Pannoniens*, p. 257). Map 21B5 includes the *Scordisci* twice, once as a 'Celtic-Illyrian' and once as a 'Pannonian' people. Cf. Mócsy, *Pannonia and Upper Moesia*, p. 5: 'the Scordisci were, of course, a group established by the Celts; in imperial times, however, their names were Illyrian (Pannonian), and some sources include them among the Thracians.' But against this see Papazoglu, pp. 271–389, esp. pp. 276, 346, n. 235, and 351, n. 250, regarding them as Celts. Anreiter, *Die vorrömischen Namen Pannoniens*, pp. 175–76, regards their name as Celtic on the grounds of preservation of IE **o*, but this only rules out 'Pannonian' (cf. review by Udolph, p. 135). The *-isci* suffix was not only Celtic; see NWÄI, p. 278, also Papazoglu, pp. 352–54, who argues that *Scordistai* is the older form and that *Scordisci* is a Celticization of it.

[138] See above Ch. 4, s.vv. *ratā* etc. and *corto-*.

[139] Duridanov, 'Sprachspuren', p. 132, n. 3. See, however, Papazoglu, p. 378.

[140] There thus are no Celtic names in this square, unless, with Müller, p. 443, and Holder ii, 1069, one emends Ptolemy's *Rhabôn* (3.8.2) to *Arabôn* (on which see Ch. 4 above, s.v. *abonā*).

	+16		+17		
47	20D2 Arabiates Arrabo fl. Bassiana Boii	'Muteno' Savaria Savarias fl. Scarbantia	20E2 Ad Flexum Ad Mures Ad Statuas? **Arrabona** Caesariana	Crispiana Duria fl. Moge(n)tiana Mursella Quadrata 'Stailuco'	47
46	20D3 *Ad Vicesimum* *Aquae Iasae* *Aqua Viva* *Curta* *Halicanum* *Iovia*	*'Piretis'* *Populi* *Pyrri* *Ramista* *Sala* *Sala fl.* *Sonista*	20E3 Hercuniates 'Lentulis' Limusa	'Mestrianis' Pelso L. 'Silicenis' Volgum	46
45	20D4 Ad Fines Ad Praetorium Alpes Ferreae Andautonia Breuci Ias(s)ii	Maezaei Oseriates **Segestica/** Siscia Sisciani Valdasus? fl. 'Varianis'	20E4 Aquae Balissae/ Municipium Iasorum 'Cardono'/Iovia 'Cocconis'	'Incero' Marsonia Serota Servitium 'Urbate'	45
44	20D5 *Clandate* *Ditiones* *Ninia* *Oeneus fl.* *Salvia*	*Salvium* *Sardeates* *Sarnade* *Splonum* *Ulcirus M.*	20E5 Ad Fines Ad Ladios Ad Matricem Aemate Apeva Baloie Bersellum Bistua Nova Castra Daesitiates	Indenea Ionnaria Leusaba Sapua Sapuates Sarute Stanecli Urbanus fl.	44
	+16		+17		

	+18		+19		
47	20F2 21A2 Azali 'Azao' **Brigetio** Campona Castra ad Herculem Crumerum Floriana? Gardellaca/ Cardabiaca	Gorsium/ Herculia Iasulones **Kelamantia** Lussomana? Matrica *Ponte Navata Solva Vetus Salina Cusus fl. *Granouas fl.	20G2 21B2 Aquincum Aquincum Castra Cirpi Contra Aquincum Transaquincum	Ulcisia Castra/Castra Constantia **Vindonianus** **Vicus** Contra Constantiam	47
46	20F3 21A3 Ad Latus Ad Statuas Alisca Alta Ripa Annamatia Contra Florentiam	Eravisci Intercisa Iovia **Lugio**/Florentia Lussonium Pinguis M. Sopianae Tricciana 21unl **Caramantesium** **Vicus**	20G3 21B3 *Iazyges*		46
45	20F4 21A4 Ad Basante Ad Labores? Ad Labores Pontis Ulcae/ 'Leutuoano' Ad Militare Ad Novas Albanum Altinum **Andizetes** Antiana Aureus M. 'Bacuntius' fl. Causilena Cibalae Cirtisa	**Cornacates** 'Donatianis'? Hiulca Palus/ Mursianus L. Iovalia 'Leucono'? 'Marinianis'/ Magniana Mursa Mursella/Mursa Minor/Mersella 'Picentino' Serena? 'Stravianis' **Teutoburgium** Ulca fl. 'Vereis' Metubarbis {21unl Ouakontion}	20G4 21B4 **Cornacum** Alma M./ Porphyriticus M. Amantini	Cuccium Cusum Malata/ {Bononia} Onagrinum Spaneta 'Ulmo'	45
44	20F5 21A5 *Bathinus fl.* *Hedum Castellum* *Daesitiatium* *'Saldis'* *[Salinae]*		20G5 21B5 *Ad Drinum* *Bassiana* *Budalia* *Domavium* *Dreinos fl.*	*Drinum Fl.* *Fossae* *Gensis/Gerd(...)* *Savus fl.* *Scordisci* *Scordisci* *Sirmium*	44
	+18		+19		

In the following tables the data from Table 5.2 is shown in bold. Without attempting an exhaustive analysis, these few Celtic-looking names can be supplemented by some additional Celtic names (underlined in the tables below):

+ 20/44 *Oktabon*.[141]
+ 20/45 *Rittium*.[142]

+ 21/44 '*Bao*',[143] *Viminacium*.[144] *Margus fl.* (and associated names) could be Celtic[145] but one cannot be sure in view of the occurrence of another *Margus fl.* in Asia, in *Margiana* (98C1) and various other *Marg-* names in Greece (*Margaia*, *Margala/Margana*, *Morgana/Margana*) and Asia;[146] some of these could contain Greek *margos* 'mad, rampant'.

At + 22/44, apart from **Bononia**, there are no certain Celtic names. *Timacus fl.* (*Timachus* in Pliny 3.149) does not necessarily have the Celtic /a:ko/ suffix,[147] and river-names in *Tim-* occur widely: compare *Timavus* in Venetia (19F4), *Timetos in Sicily (47F2) and *Timeles* in Lycia (65A2).

---

[141] For **octo-* see PNRB, p. 430, and Sims-Williams, 'Measuring Celticity', p. 282; for *-abôn* see Anreiter et al., 'Names of the Eastern Alpine region', p. 130 (cf. Ch. 4 above, s.v. *abonā*). The Celticity of the second element of **Singidunum** is defended by Anreiter, *Die vorrömischen Namen Pannoniens*, p. 178, n. 644, and Orel, 'Thracian and Celtic', p. 6.

[142] Holder ii, 1195; GPN, p. 251. Derivative of the distinctive Celtic **ritu-* 'ford' (< **pritu-*) or else **ritu-* 'course' (cf. DLG s.vv.). Anreiter, *Die vorrömischen Namen Pannoniens*, p. 116, explains *Rittium* differently.

[143] Cf. Papazoglu, p. 370, comparing Holder i, 343, for a (modern) name *Baon* in France. I would derive this form '*Bao*' (TIR L-34, p. 34), which does not deserve the inverted commas, from *bāgos 'beech', common in toponymy (cf. DLG s.v.; Anreiter, *Die vorrömischen Namen Pannoniens*, p. 75, n. 290).

[144] Holder iii, 320. Cf. García Alonso, 'On the Celticity of the Duero plateau', p. 45, and 'Ptolemy and the expansion of Celtic language(s)', pp. 138 and 148; Papazoglu, p. 368, n. 299. Not listed by Russell, 'Suffix', but marked with /a:/ in PNPG. On other names see Papazoglu, quoted above, p. 10.

[145] Compare Gaulish *marga* 'marl' in DLG s.v. *glisomarga*; AILR Celtic Elements s.v. *margi-*; Grzega, p. 202 (*margila/marga*). For various views see Schwarz, *Ortsnamen der Sudetenländer*, p. 22, Duridanov, 'Sprachspuren', p. 132, n. 3, and Papazoglu, p. 247. Another possibility is a connection with Latin *margo* 'border' (cf. Coates, 'Margidunum', a study criticized in AILR loc. cit.) or Gaulish *brog(i)* (DLG s.v.).

[146] See *Map-by-Map Directory*, Maps 5, 6, 58, 89 and 93, unlocated toponyms, s.nn.

[147] Modern Timok: TIR K-34, p. 125; L-34, p. 112; Müller, p. 454; Russell, 'Suffix', p. 165; Beševliev, p. 115; Duridanov, 'Thrakische und dakische Namen', p. 823; Mihailov, 'Le suffixe *-sk-* en thrace', p. 151. See below p. 257 on + 21/43 and + 22/43. *Taliata* (cf. GPN, p. 261, and PNPG Celtic Elements s.vv. {tala:-, tela:/o-}) and '*Gerulatis*' in the same square have been claimed as Celtic (cf. Holder s.nn; Duridanov, 'Sprachspuren', pp. 132 and 134).

	+20	+21	+22	+23	
47	21C2 *Pathissus fl./* *Tisia fl.*	21D2	21E2 *Limes Daciae* *Samus fl.*	21F2 *Certiae* *Largiana* *Porolissum* *Samum*	47
46	21C3 *Crisia fl.* *Maris(os) fl.* *Partiskon*	21D3 *Gilpil fl.* *Miliare fl.*	21E3 *Resculum*	21F3 *Alburnus Maior* *Ampelum* *Apulum/Apulenses* *Blandiana* *Brucla* *Napoca* *Optatiana* *Potaissa Salinae*	46
45	21C4 Acumincum <u>Rittium</u>	21D4 'Aizisis' *Arcidava* 'Berzobis' *Centum Putea* *Tibiskos fl.*	21E4 *Ad Pannonios* **Agnaviae/* *Acmonia* **Aquae* *Caput Bubali* *Dacia Drekon fl./* *Dric(c)a fl.* *Gaganae* 'Masclianis' *Micia* *Pons Augusti* *Tibiscum* *Ulpia Traiana* *Sarmizegetusa*	21F4 *Germisara* 'Petris' *(S)Acidava/Acidava* *Sarmizegetusa* *(Regia)*	45
44	21C5 Ad Sextum Ad Sextum Miliarem Altina *Aureus Mons Burgenae Idiminium 'Noviciani' <u>Oktabon</u> **Singidunum** Taurunum **Tricorn(i)enses** **Tricornium** Vinceia	21D5 Ad Nonum Ad Octavum Ad Scorfulas/ Ad Scrofulas Apus fl. <u>'Bao'</u> Castra Margensia Cuppae Idimum Iovis Pagus Lederata Margum Margus fl./ Brongos fl. Municipium Novae Picenses Pincus/ Punicum Pincus fl. <u>Viminacium</u>	21E5 Ad Aquas? Ad Mediam **Bononia** *Caput Bovis Clevora *Diana/Zanes Dierna/Tierua/Zerna Dorticum Drobeta Egeta 'Gerulatis' Moesi Phlorentiana Pontes Praetorium Taliata Timacus fl. Transdierna *Una	21F5 *Ad Mutrium/* *Amutrium* *Pelendava* *Rhabo fl.*	44
	+20	+21	+22	+23	

(f) From + 24 to + 27 longitude (above latitude 44 and below latitude 48)

This area covers central Romania. Its Celticity according to Maps 5.1–5.3 is scant, and the only unlocatable Celtic-looking names omitted from Table 5.2 which can be added are two forts listed by Procopius, 22unl **Bodas** on the Danube in Lower Moesia or Scythia and 22unl **Deoniana** in Moesia II, the latter of which at least is most unlikely to be Celtic.[148] It does not seem possible to add any more names, and **Kotensioi** (Ptolemy 3.8.3), which I have located rather approximately at + 24/45, cannot be regarded as a safe example of Celtic *cot(t)-*.[149] Even **Durostorum** is doubtful. The second element is obscure and the first has been claimed to have developed in Thracian from IE *g'her-* (cf. Greek χόρτος), while Rivet made the significant point that Celtic names with *Duro-* as the first element are confined to Belgica and Britain with the exception of the poorly transmitted *Durotincum* in the Alps which might be a 'rationalization' of a non-Celtic name; he suggested that **Durostorum** might be a 'secondary' name 'conferred by a Gaulish auxiliary unit before the establishment there of *Legio XI Claudia* in A.D. 106'.[150]

---

[148] See Ch. 4 above, s.vv. *boud-* and *dēvo-*. Βόδας has been regarded as Thracian, but Beševliev, p. 141, compares Celtic names like *Bodium* (reconstruction in Holder i, 459), *Segobodium* and *Bodiocasses*. He notes that Δεονιανα has been regarded as an error for *Leon(t)iana* (p. 140).

[149] TIR L-35, p. 80. They are not even listed in Holder and GPN, p. 187, and Falileyev, 'Place-names and ethnic groups in north-western Dacia', p. 35, instead compares Thraco-Dacian anthroponyms. He also rejects *Costoboci* (+ 27/47), but favours the (to my mind uncertain) linguistic Celticity of 21unl = 22unl *Anart(i)oi* (cf. 5unl *Anarta* in India) and 22unl *Teuriskoi* (cf. Bonfante, 'Il problema dei Taurisci e dei Carni', pp. 17–18, Mihailov, 'Le suffixe -sk- en thrace', pp. 152–53 and 160, n. 20, and NWÄI, p. 278) and of *Rhoukkonion* (Ptolemy 3.8.4).

[150] AILR and PNPG Possibly Celtic Elements s.v. *storo-*; Duridanov, 'Sprachspuren', p. 136; Falileyev, ''Ολόδορις', pp. 265–66; Rivet, 'Celtic names and Roman places', p. 13 and n. 30 (Poulter, 'Rural communities', p. 741, n. 7, gives the date as 116–17 AD); see further Falileyev, 'Tylis', pp. 111–12 and 124. Philipon, 'Le gaulois *dŭros*', p. 77, suggested that *Douro-* here is a Thracian cognate of the Gaulish word and of Greek names in *Thur-*; this is criticized by Vendryes, 'L'étymologie du gaulois *dumias*'. *Danuvius*, the Danube (in the same square) is *not* Celtic according to Anreiter, *Die vorrömischen Namen Pannoniens*, pp. 237–38. Certainly, its Celticity is unprovable; but see Lambert, '*Lugdunensis*', p. 218, and S. Zimmer in *RGermAlt.*, s.n. *Rhône*, on *Rhodanus fl.*, also KPP, pp. 55–56 and 228–29. Cf. Thurneysen, 'Etymologien', pp. 13–15, and PNPG Celtic Elements s.v. {da:nu-}.

	+24	+25	+26	+27	
47	22B1	22C1	22D1	22E1 23A1 *Costoboci* *Agathyrsoi*	47
46	22B2	22C2	22D2 *Angustia?* *Hierasos fl./* *Gerasus fl./* *Tiarantos? fl.*	22E2 23A2 *Carpi* *Piroboridava*	46
45	22B3 *Arutela/Alutela* *Buridava/* *Buridavenses *Caput Stenarum* *Castra Traiana* *Cedonia* *Pons Vetus* *Praetorium* 22unl **Kotensioi**	22C3 *Comidava/* *Cumidava* *Roxolani*	22D3	22E3 23A3	45
44	22B4 *Acidava* *Alutus fl.* *Pons Aluti* *Romula/Malva* *Rusidava*	22C4 *Getae*	22D4 *Nigrinianis/* *Candidiana* *Transmarisca*	22E4 23A4 Altinum Carsium **Durostorum** Flaviana Naparis? fl. Sacidava Sucidava Tegulitium Tropaeum Traiani Danuvius fl./Istros fl./ Hister fl.	44
	+24	+25	+26	+27	

(g) From + 28 to + 31 longitude (above latitude 44 and below latitude 48)

This area covers eastern Romania, Moldova and the southern Ukraine. Its Celticity according to Maps 5.1–5.3 is scant,[151] and + 31/47 **Sagaris fl.** should certainly be withdrawn, since the element **sag-* is widespread outside Celtic and the present name is quite isolated.[152] By contrast, at + 28/44 *Vicus 'Ver(gob)rittiani'* (near *Cius*, 22F4), if correctly reconstructed, contains the Gaulish word for a 'magistrate', *vergobretus*, first

---

[151] Note that 23unl **Karrodounon** (and other less clearly Celtic names in Ptolemy 3.5.15) do not in fact belong in the area of Map 23. See Ch. 6 above, p. 194.

[152] It is not included even by Holder. On rivers in *Sag-* see section (c) above on *Sagis*.

recorded by Caesar.[153]   This *vicus* was one of several quasi-municipal rural communities in the area electing their own magistrates, some of them incorporating Roman personal names in their names (*vicus Secundini*, etc.); all of them may be Roman creations of the early second century AD, partly involving resettlement of foreign peoples.[154]   One may suspect resettled Gauls here. Another *vicus* near Istria was 22unl *Dagis*, perhaps to be connected with Celtic **dago-* 'good' (OI *dag-*, W *da*).[155]   A river-name *Gabranus*, not in the Barrington data, can possibly be added here (see Chapter 4 above, s.v. *gabro-*).

In + 28/45 the well-known Celtic **Aliobrix** and **Noviodunum** can possibly be supplemented by *Arubium* (possibly comparable with Ptolemy's *Arouioi*, var. *Aroubioi*, in Gaul, 2.8.7) and by Ptolemy's ethnic name *Britolagai* (3.10.7), which has a suggestive minor variant *-galloi,* but should perhaps be emended to *-latai*).[156] *Dinogetia* (+ 28/45) is unlikely to be Celtic (: OI *dín* 'protection).[157]

[153]   The *vicus* is not noted by Holder iii, 213–14, or DLG s.v. *uergobretos, uercobretos* (and p. 438), but see Duridanov, 'Sprachspuren', p. 137, quoting the inscription as 'vicus Vergo[b]rittianus'. Doruţiu-Boilă, *Inscriptiones Scythiae Minoris*, v, pp. 137–38, no. 115, reads *vici Verg[o]/[b]rittiani*. In CIL III 12479, the reading was *vici Vero . . . . rtitiani* (both instance of *ti*, and the *ni*, ligatured), the bow after VER being taken as part of an O rather than a G. Duridanov points out (p. 134) that *Capidava* in the same square cannot be equated with the Celtic *Kapedounon* (Strabo 7.5.12) in Moesia Superior. On this unlocated place see Papazoglu, pp. 370–71.

[154]   Poulter, 'Rural communities', citing the name as 'vicus Vero[br?]ittiani' (pp. 730, 734 and 740).

[155]   Cf. DLG s.v. *dagos*. Note, however, Germanic names in *Dagi-* (LEIA s.v. *dag-*). TIR L-35, pp. 37, 66 and map Xg, suggests that it is the same as *Vicus Quintionis* (22F4); cf. Poulter, 'Rural communities', p. 739, where Δάγει χόρα and *Quintionis vicus* are both listed as near *Istria* but not equated.

[156]   Duridanov, 'Sprachspuren', p. 137 and n. 6; Holder i, 229 and 550; Falileyev, '*Tylis*', p. 113, and 'Celtic presence in Dobrudja'. With *Arouioi* cf. PNPG Celtic Elements s.v. *aruo-* and Comments s.n. Vendryes, in his review of Pârvan, *Dacia*, p. 335, accepted his comparison (p. 112) of 'le peuple des Britogalli ou Brigolati' with the Gaulish *Latobrigi*. On *brito-* see KGP, p. 156 and n. 3, GPN, p. 441, n. 5, and PNPG Celtic Elements s.v. *bret(t)o-, brito-*. On *-latai* cf. Blažek, 'Celtic-Anatolian Isoglosses', and Ch. 5 above, p. 170, on *lato-*. Note also VCIE, pp. 249 and 267, deriving *Braitolaion* in Lusitania from **brito-lag-yo-*.

[157]   Despite Delamarre, review of AILR, p. 262: 'Shelter-Wood'. See PNPG Possible Celtic Elements s.v. *dino-* and Falileyev, 'Zwischen Mythos und Fehler'.

	+28		+29	+30	+31	
47	22F1￼ 23B1		23C1￼ *Tyras fl.*	23D1￼ *Axiacae*￼ *Axiakes fl.*￼ *Crobyzi*	23E1￼ *Alazones*￼ *Hypanis fl.*￼ *Iazyges*￼ **Sagaris fl.**/￼ *Rhode fl.*	47
46	22F2￼ 23B2￼ *Pyretos fl.*￼ *Sarmatae*￼ *Thrakes*		23C2￼ *Macrocremni M.*￼ *Tagroi*￼ *Tyregetai*￼ 1I1￼ *Scythia*/￼ *Skythai*	23D2￼ *Hierasos fl.*￼ *Isiakon Limen*￼ *Istrianon Limen*￼ *Nikonion*￼ *Scopuli*￼ *Tyras*/*Ophioussa*	23E2￼ *Achilleios*￼ *Dromos*￼ *Borysthenes Ins.*/￼ *Thyora Ins.*￼ *Borysthenes*/￼ *Olbia*/￼ *Miletopolis*/￼ *Olbiopolis*￼ *Hieron Akron*￼ *Hylaeum Mare*￼ *Kallipidai*￼ *Mysaris Akra*￼ *Sangarius Sinus*	46
45	22F3￼ 23B3￼ *Aegyssus*￼ **Aliobrix**￼ <u>Arubium</u>￼ *Bastarnae*￼ <u>Britolagai</u>￼ *Dinogetia*￼ **Noviodunum**￼ *Thalamonium*￼ *Troesmis*￼ *Trog(l)odytae*		23C3￼ *Ad Stoma*￼ *Borion Stoma*￼ *Conopon*￼ *Diabasis*￼ *Eremia Geton*￼ *Gratiana?*￼ *Halmyris?*/￼ *Olymyria*/￼ *Salmorude?*￼ *Harpioi*￼ *Kalon Stoma*￼ *Narakon Stoma*￼ *Peuke Nesos*￼ *Pseudo Stoma*￼ *Psilon Stoma*/￼ *Thiagola*￼ *Salsovia*￼ *Sarmatica*￼ *Ta Antiphilou*	23D3￼ *Aepolium*￼ *Kremnisko*/￼ *Cremiscoe*￼ *Leuke Ins.*/￼ *Achilleos Nesos*/￼ *Achilleios*￼ *Dromos Ins.*/￼ *Phidonisi Ins.*	23E3	45
44	22F4￼ 23B4￼ *Argamum*￼ *Axiopolis*￼ *Beroe*￼ *Capidava*￼ *Cius*￼ *Histria*/*Istropolis*/￼ *(H)Istropolis*/*Istros*￼ *(L)Ibida*/*Ibida*￼ *Scythia Minor*￼ *Tomis*￼ *Vicus*￼ *Buteridavensis*￼ *Vicus Celeris*￼ *Vicus Clement(...)*￼ *Vicus Hi(...)*	Vicus Novus￼ Vicus Petrus￼ Vicus Quintionis￼ Vicus *Ramidava￼ Vicus *Scaptia￼ Vicus Scenopesis￼ Vicus Turris￼ *Mucaporis￼ Vicus￼ *Ulmetensium￼ Vicus Urb(...)￼ <u>Vicus</u>￼ <u>'Ver(gob)rittiani'</u>￼ Halmyris Limne￼ {22unl <u>Dagis</u>}￼ {<u>Gabranus fl.</u>}	23C4￼ *Hieron fl.*￼ *Peukes*/*Hieron*￼ *Stoma*	23D4	23E4	44
	+28		+29	+30	+31	

(h) From +32 to +35 longitude (above latitude 44 and below latitude 48)

This area covers the southern Ukraine. Its Celticity according to Maps 5.1–5.3 is non-existent and only one name looks as if it could be Celtic, *Siraci?* (+32/46), a tribe mentioned by Pliny (4.83) and Tacitus (*Annals* 12.15–16). If the *a* is long, the suffix is typically Celtic and the base could be Celtic **sīro-* 'long' (with its distinctively Celtic /iː/ < /eː/ cf. Latin *serus*),[158] but this may well be a coincidence, given the name's isolation from other Celtic toponyms. Perhaps we should rather compare the *Sirachoi/Sirakoi* (also *Sirakes*) further east, in East Asov (+39/44 = 84E4),[159] or *Sirakene* (+43/40 = 88B4) in Armenia. If the name *Siraci* really were Celtic, however, it might be a Celtic name referring to a 'distant' tribe (compare the suggestion on *Sitones* in Chapter 6 above, p. 194). A vaguely Celtic-looking name near the *Siraci* is 23unl *Erkabon* in the vicinity of Perekop (= *Taphros*, 23G2 = +33/46).[160]

---

[158] Russell, 'Suffix' (not mentioning this example); LEIA s.v. *sír*; AILR Celtic Elements s.v. {siːro-}. Other names with velar suffixes in the vicinity are 23unl *Tamyrake* and *Sarbakon*; PNPG places them at +32/45 and +32/46 and does not mark their /a/s as long.

[159] Strabo 11.2.1 (cf. 11.5.2 and 8, and n. on p. 174 of Lasserre's edition).

[160] Cf. PNPG Possibly Celtic Elements s.v. {ercaː-}, *erco-*.

	+32	+33	+34	+35	
47	23F1	23G1 *Acesinus? fl.*	23H1	23I1 84A1 *Gerros fl.*	47
46	23F2 *Borysthenes fl.* *Borysthenitai* *Enoecadioe* *Hippolaou* *Akra* *Hylaia/Abike* *Kephalonesos* *Panticapes? fl.* *Sardi* *Siraci?*	23G2 *Bykes fl.* *Bykes Limne* *Karkine?* *Karkinites/* *Hypakyris? fl./* *Pakyris* *Taphrioi* *Taphros/Taphrai*	23H2 *Coretus Sinus*	23I2 84A2 *Kremnoi* *Limnaioi*	46
45	23F3 *Kalos Limen?* *Karkinitis* *Kolpos*	23G3 *Basileioi/* *Basilikoi* *Kerkinitis?/* *Karkinitis/* *Koronitis* *Tamyrakes* *Kolpos* *Taurike Chersonesos*	23H3 *Satauci* *Torekkadai*	23I3 84A3 87I1-2 87J1-2 *Sapra Limne* *Satauci* *Theodosia/Ardabda* *(Heptatheos)/* *Theode(…)/* *Theudosia* *Kazeka*	45
44	23F4	23G4 *Chersonesos/Cherson/* *Heraclea* *Cherronesus/Megarike* *Kriou Metopon Pr.* *Palaia Chersonesos* *Parthenion?* *Akron* *Symbolon Limen* *Tauroi/* *Skythotauroi* *Tauroskythai/* *Skythotauroi* *Tracheia* *Chersonesos*	23H4 *Aloustou* *Phrourion* *Athenaion/* *Skythotauron* *Limen* *Charax* *Dory* *Gorzoubitai* *Lagyra* *Lampas* *Neapolis* *'Phrourion'*	23I4 84A4 87I3 87J3 *Istrianos fl.* *Korax Akron*	44
	+32	+33	+34	+35	

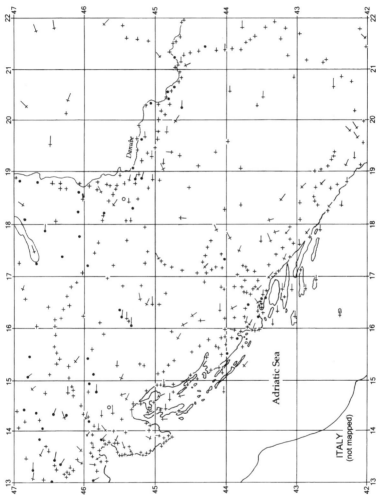

Map 7.1 Celtic names from the Adriatic to the Danube, +13 to +22 (down to lat. 42)

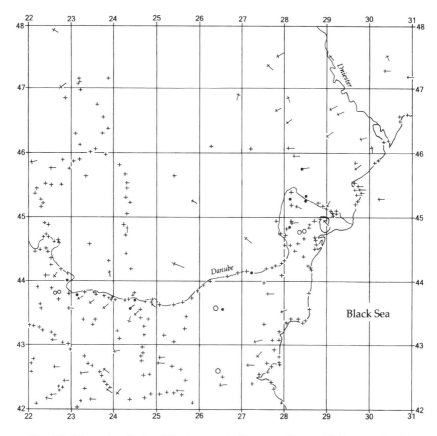

Map 7.2   The eastern limits of Celtic names in Europe, +22 to +31 (down to lat. 42)

8

THE EXTENT OF CELTIC NAMES, III:
SOUTHERN EUROPE
(LATITUDE 43 AND SOUTHWARDS)

In this chapter I examine the extent of Celtic names from Portugal in the west to the Black Sea in the east. As in the preceeding chapters, *italics* are used in the tables of names to denote squares devoid of Celtic names, names in **bold** are the 'Celtic-looking' names from Table 5.2 and underlining indicates other probably Celtic names.

(a) From −10 to −6 longitude (between latitudes 39 and 36)

This area covers southern Portugal and south-west Spain (for the north-west see (c) below). Its Celticity is uneven in Maps 5.1–5.3, especially in the south. There are four unlocatable Celtic-looking names omitted from Table 5.2 which belong in this general area (Map 26), but as none of them is known to belong in the areas which are blank on Maps 5.1–5.3, they do not alter the impression given by those maps:

26	*unl*	Bruto**briga**
26	*unl*	Esttle**dunum**
26	*unl*	Konto**bris**
26	*unl*	Per**briga**

The blank at −9/39 (26B2) could be due to the shortage of names in general in this square, only 6, but equally well it may be due to the non-Celticity of inland Lusitania. The 6 names are: *Aritium Praetorium*; *Collippo*; *Scallabis/Praesidium Iulium/Col. Scal(l)abitana*; *Sellium*; *Tagus fl.*; and *Tubucci/Tabucci/Tacubis*. Of these only the first (*Aritio Praetorio* in AI 418.8) looks as if it might be Celtic (< **are* + **ritu-* + **-io-* 'place facing the ford'), but, even if so, it is presumably named after *Aritium*,[1] one degree to the east (−8/39), possibly near a notable crossing of the river

---

[1] Ptolemy 2.5.6 (*Arition*) only (TIR J-29, p. 34), listed as Celtic, with hestitation, by García Alonso, 'Ptolemy and the expansion of Celtic language(s)', p. 143, and *Península Ibérica*, pp. 103–4; similarly PNPG segments *aro-* + *ito-* + *io*. The absence of *ritu-* from Iberia is an objection to my etymology; see Ch. 12, p. 311. *Aritio Praetorio* (AI 418.8) is *Aretio Pretorion* in Rav. 316.7 (TIR J-29, p. 34). *Ar(r)etium* in Etruria (modern Arezzo) would presumably be a distinct name (see n. 159 below). García Alonso also notes *Tagus fl.* as possibly Celtic (or *Alt-europäisch* or Lusitanian) and *Scallabis* as obscure but perhaps Celtic. For **tagu-* in Celtic cf. CIB, p. 86; Markey & Mees, 'Prestino', p. 147.

Tagus. The *Brutobriga* listed above was in Conventus Scallabitanus, but it is not known how close to Scallabis it was.[2]

South of latitude 39 (see tables below), the Celtic names thin out:

−10/38 has no Celtic names, unless *A(qua)bona/Equabona* is properly *Abona* (as in Rav. 306.19) or contains a Celtic **bona*.[3] There is, however, a shortage of places in general in this square (only 5).

−9/38 Perhaps *Salacia* (whence *Municipium Salaciense*) in addition to the three *briga* names.[4]

−9/37 Perhaps *Arandis/Aranni*[5] in addition to the two *briga* names.[6] On the other hand **Cibilitani** (Pliny 4.118, var. *Cilibitani*) is unlikely to be a genuine example of Celtic **litano-*; it has been derived from a hypothetical **Cibilis* (which is what is marked on Map 26B4 rather than **Cibilitani**) or **Cilipis*.[7]

−8/38 In addition to **Burrolobriga**,[8] perhaps *Ebora* but this is uncertain because at -7/36 *Ebora* is a variant of *Aipora* (coin-legend) and probably unrelated to Celtic **eburo-*.[9] *Anas fl.* may be Celtic or Latin (*anas* 'duck' > Spanish *ánade*).[10] I count neither as Celtic.

−8/37 —[11]

−8/36 —

−7/38 In addition to the secure *briga* and **sego-* names and *Celtica* in *Baeturia Celtica*, *Vama* is probably Celtic.[12]

−7/37 No Celtic names names apart from **Turobriga** and perhaps **Kortikata**,

---

[2] Curchin, *Magistrates*, pp. 169 and 272. It is said to have been founded by D. Junius Brutus (see below, p. 307, n. 7).

[3] See Chapter 4 above, s.v. **abonā*.

[4] AILR Celtic Elements s.v. *sal(o)-* .

[5] De Hoz, 'From Ptolemy to the ethnic and linguistic reality', p. 20; parallels in Holder i, 172 and iii, 649. See García Alonso, *Península Ibérica*, pp. 101–2: < **Are-randa*. The case rests more on **are* than **randa* as the latter was not Celtic in origin and was perhaps not borrowed early enough (cf. Sims-Williams, 'Welsh *Iâl*', pp. 62–63). For an alternative see PNPG Possibly Celtic Elements s.v. *arandi-*. Cf. p. 244 below on **Arandunum*. On names in *rand-* and *arand-* see also Lacroix, *Noms*, pp. 38–53.

[6] On **Lac(c)obriga** (*Lanco-* ?) and **Mirobriga** see Gorrochategui, 'Establishment and analysis', pp. 165–66; PNPG Possibly Celtic Elements s.v. *miro-*.

[7] TIR J-29, p. 63, and K-30, p. 96. An unlocated *Cilpe* is compared.

[8] AILR puts 26unl **Montobrica/Montobriga/Mundobriga** (near Arronches, Portugal?) in this square as well, whereas I have placed it in −8/39. Cf. Albertos, 'Los topónimos en *-briga*', no. 64.

[9] De Hoz, 'From Ptolemy to the ethnic and linguistic reality', p. 20 and n. 18. Cf. Ch. 4 above s.v. *eburo-*.

[10] PNRB, p. 249; DLG s.v. *ana*.

[11] De Hoz, 'From Ptolemy to the ethnic and linguistic reality', p. 20, n. 15, thinks the Celticity of *Arucci* improbable.

[12] García Alonso, 'On the Celticity of the Duero plateau', p. 30, n. 4; De Hoz, 'From Ptolemy to the ethnic and linguistic reality', p. 20 (in n. 15 he rejects *Curiga*); PNPG Possibly Celtic Elements s.v. {uama:-}; VCIE, pp. 278 and 333; Villar, 'Celtic language', pp. 259–61 and 267.

both at the north of the square if correctly located.[13] I would not dare connect *Tartessos/Tartessii* with Celtic **tartu-* 'thirst, dryness',[14] though that would suit the climate!

−7/36 Probably no Celtic names;[15] **Cotinussa Ins**. is completely isolated and thus unlikely to be an instance of Celtic *cot(t)-* 'old', since names in *Cot-* occur all over the ancient world.[16] On the other hand, there could be a connection with the possibly Celtic **Kotinai** at (b) below. Perhaps *Cotinus(s)a Insula* (Pliny 4.120) was a Celtic trading-station?[17]

−6/38 Besides the two *briga* names at the north of the square, we can probably add *Contosolia* in the same area.[18] 26unl *Rodacis* (Rav. 312.15), which could have the Celtic /a:ko/ suffix, will also belong at the north of the square if it was near *Metellinum* (Medellín).[19] *Artigi* cannot be connected with Celtic **arto-* 'bear' in view of the other names in *-tigi* in the area such as *Lastigi, Olontigi* and *Astigi*.[20]

−6/37 Apart from the securely Celtic **Segida** and 26unl **Segovia** on the river *Singilis*,[21] only the peculiarly named oppidum *Celti?* (Pliny 3.11), seemingly an ethnonym, can perhaps be added.[22] On the other hand, one Celtic-looking name should perhaps be withdrawn: **Carruca** can only tentatively be connected with Celtic **carr-* 'chariot' (cf. *Karraka* in Italy if that means 'town of the carts');[23] if it *is* connected it may be indirectly via Latin *carruca* 'coach, wheeled plough'.[24] An alternative Celtic comparison would be Welsh *carreg* 'stone' < **karrikā* and

---

[13] Cf. De Hoz, 'From Ptolemy to the ethnic and linguistic reality', pp. 19–20 (he lists them both as unlocated). The second may be from Latin *cortex*; see Ch. 4 above, s.v. *corto-*.

[14] LEIA s.v. *tart*; DLG s.v. *tartos*.

[15] De Hoz, 'From Ptolemy to the ethnic and linguistic reality', p. 20, nn. 15 and 18, rejects the Celticity of *Aipora/Ebora* and *Nabrissa*. On the former see Villar, *Indoeuropeos y no indoeuropeos*, pp. 101–2 and 117, and Ch. 4 above s.v. *eburo-*. *Iunonis Ins.* is listed in *Map-by-Map Directory* but not shown on Map 26.

[16] See list in Ch. 4 above s.v. **cot(t)-*.

[17] TIR J-29, pp. 71, 83 and 88 (*Potimusa* in Loeb edition, but usually emended to *Cotinusam*; cf. Mayhoff, p. 359). But both may derive from Greek *kotinos* 'olive tree'; García Alonso, *Península Ibérica*, p. 72.

[18] DLG s.v. *conto-* and p. 433. Cf. n. 31 below.

[19] The *Map-by-Map Directory* puts it between Rena and Medellín. However, TIR J-30, p. 278, places it between Lacipea and Turcalion and these are placed in the square to the north (26E2) in the *Barrington Atlas*. *Rodacis* is not listed by Russell, 'Suffix', p. 169, who stresses the difficulty of distinguishing /a:ko/ and /ako/ (p. 166). See Holder ii, 1201 for *Rodacis* and parallels, and García Alonso, 'Lenguas prerromanas', pp. 400 and 402.

[20] On *-tigi* names see section 12.3 below.

[21] Tovar, *Baetica*, pp. 113–14; TIR J-30, p. 299 and map.

[22] De Hoz, 'From Ptolemy to the ethnic and linguistic reality', pp. 20–21; AILR Possibly Celtic Elements s.v. *celti-*; GPN, pp. 332–33.

[23] GPN, p. 63, n. 2; De Bernardo Stempel, 'Ptolemy's Celtic Italy and Ireland', pp. 93–94. This may rather be cognate with W *carrog* 'torrent' (cf. LEIA C-43), which occurs as a place-name in Wales (see Lloyd-Jones, *Geirfa*, s.n. *Karrawc*).

[24] GPN, p. 63, n. 2.

carrog 'torrent' < **karrākā*, but these belong to a widespread and not peculiarly Celtic set of words in **kar(r)-* sometimes regarded as pre-Indo-European 'Ibero-Mediterranean' and sometimes as Indo-European.[25] **Arialdunum** (Pliny 3.10) and 26unl **Esttledunum**, which may be in the same Conventus Astigitanus,[26] are completely isolated from other *-dunum* names and De Hoz suspects that they 'conceal some non-Indo-European formation'.[27] An alternative would be to see an intrusive group of Celts (*Celti*?) behind them.[28] All the above places were on or near the lower reaches of *Singilis fl.*, which has sometimes been compared to *Singidunum* (Belgrade) and regarded as a Celtic name, but without much cogency.[29] (Compare rather −5/37 *Singili(a) Barba/Barla*, to the south-east, in a completely non-Celtic region.) 26unl *Kanaka* (Ptolemy 2.4.10) was somewhere in Conventus Hispalensis, but I omit it as we do not know its exact location, nor the quantity of its pre-velar *a*.[30]

−6/36 Possibly no Celtic names. *Carteia* could be Celtic,[31] but is very uncertain. In the absence of more obviously Celtic names, it is unlikely that **Asido** contains Celtic **sīdo-* or **Cetaria** Celtic **kaito-*.[32] Avienus' **Cassius Mons** (if it belongs here) is unlikely to be any more Celtic than *Cas(s)ius Mons* in Syria (68A2).[33] **Saguntia** (near **Asido**) is thus isolated and De Hoz rightly hesitates to label it Celtic, although it may well be.[34]

[25] LEIA C-42-43 and 225; GPN, p. 62, n. 2, and 163; Anreiter et al., 'Names of the Eastern Alpine region', p. 122; AILR and PNPG Possibly Celtic Elements s.v. *caro-*; KPP, pp. 158–59. See further on *Caraca* at -2/41 below.

[26] *Map-by-Map Directory* i, 434, citing Tovar, *Baetica*, p. 138.

[27] De Hoz, 'From Ptolemy to the ethnic and linguistic reality', pp. 20–21. **Arialdunum** could be syncopated from **Are-ialo-* (Sims-Williams, 'Welsh *Iâl*', p. 62). If so, note that *-ialo-* is distinctively both Gaulish and late.

[28] Villar, 'Celtic language', pp. 256–57 and 267–68, discusses the options of both early and late dates.

[29] Cousin, p. 469; DLG s.v *singi-* (the equation with Irish *séig(h)* 'falcon' is phonologically impossible); LEIA s.v. *seng* 'slender'. *Singi-* in *Singidunum* (Belgrade) is probably not Celtic; cf. Orel, 'Thracian and Celtic', p. 6, and Anreiter, *Die vorrömischen Namen Pannoniens*, pp. 178–79.

[30] Cf. n. 19 above. Cf. Holder i, 730. See maps in De Hoz, 'From Ptolemy to the ethnic and linguistic reality', pp. 26–27; TIR J-29, p. 52.

[31] Cf. on *Car(t)a* below, p. 237.

[32] On *Cetaria* see p. 29 above. De Hoz, 'From Ptolemy to the ethnic and linguistic reality', p. 20, n. 15, rejects *Arunda* as Celtic.

[33] See Ch. 4 above, s.v. *cassi-*.

[34] De Hoz, 'From Ptolemy to the ethnic and linguistic reality', pp. 20–21 and 28; Villar, *Indoeuropeos y no indoeuropeos*, pp. 312–13; PNPG Celtic Elements and Possibly Celtic Elements s.v. *sag(o)-*.

	−10	−9	−8	−7	−6	
38	26A3 *A(qua)* *bona/* *Equabona* *Barbarion* *Pr./* *Cepresicum* *Iugum* *Freiria* *Magnum Pr.* *Olisipo/* *Municipium* *Olisipo* *Felicitas* *Iulia*	26B3 **Caetobriga** *Calanta/ Calantica/ Calantum/ Calanatia Kal(l)ipous fl. Malateca Salacia (Imperatoria)/ Municipium Salaciense 26unl **Arcobriga** 26unl **Meribriga/ Merobriga**	26C3 Adrus fl. Anas fl./ Samus? fl. Ebora/ Municipium Ebora Liberalitas Iulia 26unl **Burrulobriga**	26D3 <u>Baeturia Celtica</u> Caspiana Contributa Iulia Ugultunia Curiga Emerita Augusta Evandria(na) Lacunis **Nertobriga** <u>**Concordia Iulia**</u> Perceiana/ Promptiana? Phornakis Plagiaria **Segida**/Restituta <u>Iulia Seria</u> Vama	26E3 Artigi Baedro Baeturia Turdulorum **Brutobriga** <u>Contosolia</u> Iulipa Mellaria Metellinum **Mirobriga** Municipium Flavium V(...) Regina {Rodacis}	**38**
37	26A4	26B4 Arandis/ <u>Aranni</u> **Cibilitani** Cuneus Ager **Lac(c)obriga** Metallum Vipascense/ Vipasca **Mirobriga/ Mirobriga Celtica/ Municipium Flavium Mirobrigensium** Patulus Portus Portus Hannibalis Sacrum Pr.	26C4 *Arucci (B)Aesuris/ Aesuris/Esuris Balsa Fines (Iulia) Myrtilis/ Myrtilis Ossonoba Ostium fl. Anae Pax Iulia/Pax Augusta/Col. Pacensis Praesidium Serpa Turduli 1B3 Lusitania*	26D4 Ad Rubras Anatolikon Stoma Caura Fodinae Hareni M. Herculis Ins. Iberos fl./Luxia fl. Ilip(ou)la Italica (I)Tucci/Tucci **Kortikata** Laelia/Caelia? Lastigi Ligustinus L. Maenuba Maenuba fl. *Marmorarius Pagus Olontigi Osset/Iulia Constantia O(sso)noba/ Onuba Aestuaria/ Olbia? Ostur Paisoula Tartessos/Tartessii **Turobriga** *Urium Urius fl.	26E4 Arva Astigi/Col. Augusta Firma Axati Baetis fl./ Certis fl./Perkes fl. Basilippo Callet/Callenses (Aeneanici) Canama/Canania Carbula Carmo **Carruca** Carula Celti?/Leptis? Detumo Hispalis/Col. Romula Ilipa Magna/ Ibylla/Ilipa Ilia Ilipula Minor/Ilipa Iporca Irni Lucurgentum Munda Munigua Naeva Obulcula Oducia Orippo Sal(pens)a **Segida**/Augurina Siarum/Fortunale Singilis fl./Silicense fl. Urso/Col. Genetiva Iulia Villo 26unl **Arialdunum** 26unl **Segovia**	**37**
	−10	−9	−8	−7	−6	

	−10	−9	−8	−7	−6	
36	26A5	26B5	26C5 *Cuneus Pr.*	26D5 *Ad Herculem* *Ad Pontem* *Ad Portum/Gaditanus* *Portus/MenestheosLimen?* *Aipora/Ebora* *Aphrodisias Ins./Erythea Ins./Iunonis* *Ins.* *Baetis Aestuaria* *Caepionis Monu./Scipionis Monu.* *Ceret* *Cimbii?* *Conobaria/Colobana* **Cotinussa Ins.**/ *Gaditana Ins.* *Curense Litus* *Gadeira/Gades/Col.* *Augusta Gaditana*/ *Urbs Iulia Gaditana* *Glaukou? Akra* *(H)Asta/Asta/Col. Hasta* *Regia/Ligystine?* *Herakleion* *Iunonis Ins.* *Iunonis Pr.* *Mercablum*/ *Merifabion* *Nabrissa* *Olbensis* *Pagus?* *Oleastrum* *L.Phosphoros*/ *Dianae Fanum*	26E5 *Acinippo* *Albus Portus* *Arunda* **Asido/Asido** **Caesarina** *B(a)elo*/ *Baldo*/ *Bardo* *Baelo fl.* *Baesippo* *Barbesula fl.* *Barbesula*/ *Barbariana?*/ *Bamaliana* *Bastouloi*/ *Poinoi*/ *Blastophoinikes* *Belleia? M.* *Besilus fl.* *Burdoga* *Calpe M.* *Cappa* *Caris(s)a/Carissa* *Aurelia* *Carteia/Calpe*/ *Karpessos/Kalpia*/ *Karp(e)ia* **Cetaria** *Cilpe*/ **Lacilbula?* *Erisane*/ *Arsa* *Ilipoula* *M.Iptuci* *Irippo?*/ *Serippo?* *Iulia Traducta*/ *Iulia Ioza*/ *Tingentera* *Kalath(ous)a*/ *Kaldouba* *Lacca* *Lacca fl.* *Lacippo* *Lascuta* *Lascutana* *Turris* *Mellaria* *Ocur(r)i* *O(no)ba* *Sabora* *Saepo* **Saguntia** *Salduba/Saltum/Saldo* *Saudo/Sandone* *Turirecina*/ *Regina/Col.* *Civium* *Romanorum* *Regina* *U(r)gia*/ *Caesaris* *Salutariensis*/ *Castrum Iulium* 28D1 *Heras? Ins.* *Columnae Herculis* 26Av *Argentarius M.*/ **Cassius M.**	36
	−10	−9	−8	−7	−6	

(b) From −5 to +2 longitude (between latitudes 39 and 36)

This area covers south-eastern Spain (for the north-east see (d) below).[35] Its Celticity is slight in Maps 5.1–5.3, especially to the south and east:[36]

−5/39 There is only the *-briga* name, *Toletum* being doubtfully Celtic.[37]

−5/38 *Solia* (deduced from inscriptions referring to *Sol(ienses)* and *Solenses*) may derive from the Celtic element **soli-* 'hall, homestead, habitation?' (cognate with German *Saal*) identified by Isaac.[38] *Epora* unlikely to be Celtic as Iberia was a mainly Q-Celtic area.[39] A more promising name is 26unl **Kotinai** (despite the *omega* rather than *omikron* in Strabo). This place, near which copper and gold were mined (Strabo 3.2.3: Κωτίνας), is vaguely located 'N[orth of] R. Guadalquivir in Turdetania?'.[40] As Strabo mentions *Kotinai* along with *Ilipa* (26E4) and *Sisapo* (27A3) among the mines in the mountain range north of the *Baitis* (Guadalquivir), it may lie at −6/37 or further north at −6/38 or north-west at −5/38; the gold and copper mines at Los Escoriales (−5/38 = 26F3)[41] would suit nicely, so I have placed it there. It may be an ethnonym used as a place-name, like *Celti* above (-6/37). It recalls the name of Tacitus' Celtic-speaking *Cotini* discussed above, p. 193. Curiously they too were mining folk.[42]

−5/37 In view of its non-Celtic termination **Ventipo** is hardly Celtic and **Ceturgi** is also dubious.[43]

−5/36 —[44]

---

[35] I omit the data from Africa below latitude 37 in the south-east of the area (Maps 27G-H5 and 30).

[36] There are no unlocatable examples of our Celtic-looking names in the *Barrington* data which belong in this general area (Map 27).

[37] Cf. PNPG Possibly Celtic Elements s.v. *tolo-*.

[38] AILR Celtic Elements s.v. *soli-*. TIR J-30, p. 305. A similar name, however, is *Contosolia* at −6/38 above (AI 444.5; TIR J-30, p. 153) and Isaac does not analyse this as containing his Celtic **soli-* but rather as *conto-* + *solo-* or *com-* + *toso-* + *olo-*; he does not include this in AILR Celtic Elements under his semantically uncertain **conto-* (there based on *Uo-cont-io-*), but see further DLG s.v. *conto-* 'hundred?'.

[39] AILR Comment s.n. Cf. *Aipora/Ebora* in n. 15 above.

[40] *Map-by-Map Directory* i, 435, citing Tovar, *Baetica*, p. 50. Cf. TIR J-30, p. 165. *Oleastron* (cf. TIR J-30, p. 254) is given as an alternative name in the *Atlas* because Tovar quotes Schulten's speculation that *Kotinai* was one of the places called *Oleastrum* (cf. Greek *kotinos* 'olive tree'). See García Alonso, *Península Ibérica*, p. 72.

[41] *Map-by-Map Directory* i, 421; TIR J-30, p. 175.

[42] Could there be a connection between the base **cott-* and mining operations? Compare the Welsh river-name *Cothi* (< **Cott-*) at the Roman goldmines at *Louentium*, Dolaucothi (EANC, pp. 134–35; PNRB, p. 400). But this may be a coincidence, for the 'bent' (> 'old') sense postulated for **cot(t)-* would suit *Cothi*; cf. PNPG Possibly Celtic Elements s.v. *cottaeo-*.

[43] See Ch. 3 above, p. 29. See Villar, *Indoeuropeos y no indoeuropeos*, *passim*, on *ipo* names, and García Moreno, 'Los topónimos en *-ippo-*'.

[44] *Malaca* is not included by Russell, 'Suffix', and AILR and PNPG, like VCIE, p. 61, leave the pre-velar /a/ short. *Cartima* could have Celtic **cart-* (cf. on *Carteia* and *Car(t)a*, pp. 227 and 237) but is uncertain. *Suel* is tentatively mentioned in PNPG Possibly Celtic Elements s.v. *suel-*.

−4/39 Ptolemy's *Barnakis* (2.6.56) belongs here and may be a Celtic /a:ko/ name.[45]

−4/38 **Samariense Metallum**, located here rather speculatively, is in any case doubtful in view of the widespread occurrence of *samar-* names.[46]

−4/37 **Ebura** (also called *Cerialis*) might seem safely Celtic, but the correct form is *Ebora*, a non-Celtic name represented by *Aipora/Ebora* at −7/36 .[47]

−4/36 —

−3/39 **Segobriga** and its derived ethnonym are the only Celtic names in this square.

−3/38 —[48]

−3/37 —[49]

−2/39 *Urbiaca* (AI 447.5) may belong here and is very probably Celtic.[50]

−2/38 **Segisa?** is the only obvious Celtic name here,[51] but *Contestania/Contestani* could perhaps be connected with the Gaulish personal name *Contessus*, *Conteddius*, and W *cynnes* 'warm'.[52] *Salika?* is probably Celtic ('willow').[53]

−2/37 *Eliocroca?*   may contain Celtic **croucā* 'hill',[54] which suits its

---

[45] On the location see TIR J-30, p. 105 ('-5/39?' in PNPG). It is not included by Russell, 'Suffix'. García Alonso, *Península Ibérica*, p. 323, favours Celtic. Cf. PNPG Possibly Celtic Elements s.v. *barno-*.

[46] See Ch. 3 above. *Laminium*, *Castulo* and *Oretani* are tentatively mentioned in PNPG Celtic Elements s.v. {la:mo-} and Possibly Celtic Elements s.vv. *casto-* and *oro-*.

[47] See Ch. 4 above, s.v. *eburo-*. *Tugia* is possibly Celtic < **togyā*; see AILR Comments s.n., comparing OI *tugae*. Cf. Celtiberian *togias* (Peñalba de Villestar), which Meid, *Celtiberian Inscriptions*, p. 37, translates 'covering, house, hall'; cf. MLH v/1, pp. 404–5; VCIE, pp. 92 and 260–61. Holder ii, 1980 equates *Tugia* with *Touía* in Ptolemy 2.6.58. *Calecula/Callicula* is doubtful: PNPG Possibly Celtic Elements s.v. *callo-* (cf. *Callet/Callenses* at −6/37 above).

[48] On *Libisosa* see Gorrochategui, 'Ptolemy's Aquitania and the Ebro valley', p. 147.

[49] *Ab(ou)la* is listed in DLG s.v. *abalo-*, but see the analysis *Ab-ula* in Villar, *Indoeuropeos y no indoeuropeos*, pp. 130–31, 154, 162, 274–75, 408 and 480, and VCIE, pp. 100, 102 and 106. *Tugiensis Saltus* stands or falls with *Tugia* at −4/37 above. 27unl *Orkelis* (Ptolemy 2.6.60, var. *Aorkelis*) may contain Celtic **orco-* (DLG s.v.); it was in the territory of Bastetania, and Tovar, *Tarraconensis*, p. 160, compares the modern name *Orce* east of Galera (as well as *Orkelis* in Thrace) – but it may be an error for *Ilorcis*. On **orco-* see above, p. 178, n. 6. See García Alonso, *Península Ibérica*, p. 361, and Villar, *Indoeuropeos y no indoeuropeos*, p. 384, who prefers to regard it as a variant of an Indo-European element *urc-*.

[50] Russell, 'Suffix', p. 169; AILR *ad loc.* and Possibly Celtic Elements s.v. *urbo-*. On the location see also TIR J-30, p. 348. The name *Attacum* (not in the *Barrington* data), mentioned by Russell, may be in this vicinity. See TIR J-30, p. 93 (PNPG s.n. *Attakon* (Ptolemy 2.6.57), has the old identification with Ateca (-2/41).) Cf. García Alonso, 'On the Celticity of the Duero plateau', p. 46; Gorrochategui, 'Ptolemy's Aquitania and the Ebro valley', pp. 145–46 and 148 (*Atta* + *co-*); Curchin, 'Five Celtic town-names', pp. 45–46 (*Atto/Atta* + *-acum*).

[51] Gorrochategui, 'Ptolemy's Aquitania and the Ebro valley', p. 148.

[52] Cf. DLG s.v. *contessos*. García Alonso, *Península Ibérica*, pp. 473–74, notes that Tovar (*Tarraconensis*, p. 31) rejected the Celtic etymology and regarded the Contestani as typically Iberian. PNPG segments as either *conto-* + *esto-* + *ano-* or *com-* + *testo-* + *ano-*.

[53] DLG s.v. *salico-*.

[54] DLG s.v. *crouco-* and AILR Comments s.n. ('hardly a certainty in this region'). The first element would probably be not **alio-* (AILR) but **elio-* 'abundance?', for which see KGP, pp. 203–5, and KPP, pp. 108 and 232. The reading *Eliocrora* in TIR J-30, p. 172, is not found in Cuntz's edition of AI 401.6.

situation, and, in view of its position on the coast, *Longuntica* is a good candidate for the native Celtic **longo-* 'ship' postulated by some scholars.[55]

−1/39 **Sedetani?** is uncertainly Celtic, not least because of doubts about the correct form of the name,[56] and **Saguntum** is also uncertain.[57]   In the same square *Sebelaci* (AI 400.1) is just possibly Celtic.[58]   But there are no obvious Celtic names on this longitude. *Saetabis* (here and at −1/38) is possibly related to OI *saeth*, W *hoed*, 'distress', but it may be Iberian.[59]
−1/38 the **Icositani**, a people mentioned by Pliny (3.19) as subordinate to *Ilici*, are presumably named from a place **Icosium* or similar and it is easier to compare this with *Icosium* on the facing African coast (+ 3/36 = 30F3) than the possible Celtic element **ico-*. Indeed, Pliny's 'in eam [i.e. colonia inmunis Ilici] contribuuntur Icositani' surely refers to the Algerian *Icosium*.[60]

There are no more Celtic names to the east. They are also absent from the toponymy of the Balearic Islands: *Baliares Inss./Gymnesiae Inss.*; **Bocchori*; *Capraria Ins./Capria Ins.*; *Guium?/Cinium*; *Iamo/Iamna*; **Mago**; *Palma*; *Pollentia*; *Sanisera*; **Tuci?*; *Hannibalis Ins.*; *Menariae Inss.*; *Tiquadra Ins.*[61] The similarity between **Mago** (+ 4/39) and Celtic **magos* is no doubt coincidental.[62]

---

[55] DLG s.v. and pp. 435–36; PNPG Possibly Celtic Elements s.v. *longo-*.
[56] See above, Ch. 4 s.v. *sedo-*.
[57] Cf. on -6/36 **Saguntia** above and PNPG Celtic Elements s.v. *sag-*.
[58] Russell, 'Suffix', p. 169. But see AILR *ad loc.* and Comments s.n. On the location cf. TIR J-30, p. 296. PNPG Possibly Celtic Elements s.v. *succo-*, *suco-* tentatively mentions *Sucro*.
[59] PNPG Celtic Elements s.v. *saeto-*. Cf. García Alonso, *Península Ibérica*, pp. 168 and 365.
[60] See Zehnacker's note, p. 135, and Tovar, *Tarraconensis*, p. 198. Cf. Ch. 4 above, s.v. *ico-*. *Alonis* is segmented with *alo-* in PNPG but not mentioned in Celtic Elements s.v. *alo-*.
[61] Map 27 inset. The last three are listed as 27unl.
[62] PNPG, *Hispania*, lists *Mago* as Phoenician. Cf. García Alonso, *Península Ibérica*, p. 425. It is generally believed to be named after Hannibal's brother.

	−5			−4		
39	26F2 27A2 **Caesarobriga**	Olcades? Toletum		27B2 (Ad)Murum/ Murum Alaba Alce(s)/Alea	Consabura/ Consabrum/ Kondabora Vicus Cuminarius {27unl Barnakis}	**39**
38	26F3 Solia 27A3 Carcuvium? Epora/ Epora Foederatorum Isturgi/ Municipium Triumphale Marianus M.	Sisapo?/ Saesapo/ Sisalo (S)Ucia/ Ucia/ Ouogia/ Setia/ S(i)tia/ Sutia 26unl **Kotinai/** Oleastron		27B3 *Ad Aras* *Ad DuoSolaria* *Ad Morum* *Ad Novlas* *Ad Turres* *Baecula?/* *Baikor* **Baesucci* *Cantigi* *Castulo/* *Caesarii* *Iuvenales*	*Castulonensis* *Saltus* *Edeba* *Ilugo* *Laminium* *Oretana Iuga* *Oretania/* *Oretani* *Oretum/Oria/* *Horetum* *26unl* **Samariense** **Metallum**	**38**
37	26F4 *Ad Aras* *Ad Decumum* *Corduba/Col.* *Patricia* *Ipagrum/* *Epagrum* *Lauro/* **Olaurum* *Munda fl.* *Ostippo* *Sabetanum* *Salsum fl.* *Singili(a)* *Barba/Barla* *Ulia(Fidentia)* *Urgapa?* **Ventipo** 27A4 *Abra* *Ad Gemellas?* *Ad Lucos* *Aiungi/* *Respublica* *Aiungitan(o)rum*	*Anticaria* *Ategua* **Batora* *Bora* *Calpurniana* *Castra* *Postumiana?* *Cisimbrium* *Igabrum/Egab-* *rum/Municipium* *Iulium* *Iliturgicola* *Ipolcobulcola/* *Municipium* *Polconensium* *Iponuba/Hippo* *Nova* **Ipsca/* *Municipium* *Contributum* *Ipscense*	*I(p)tuci/Col.* *Virtus Iulia* *Marruca* *Obulco/* *Municipium* *Pontificense* *Onuba* *Sacili/* *Municipium* *Martiale* **Sosontigi/* *Sosintigi* *Turdetania/* *Turdetani* *Ucubi/Col.* *Claritas* *Iulia Urgao/* *Vircao/* *Municipium* *Albense* *Urgauonense* *26unl* **Ceturgi**	27B4 *Acci/Col.* *Iulia* *Gemella* *Agatucci?/* *Acatucci* *Aurgi/* *Orongis/* *Auringis* *Bactara?* *Baebelo?* *Calecula/* *Callicula* **Ebura**/*Cerialis* *Fraxinum?* *Iliberri/Elvira/* *Municipium* *Florentinum* *Iliturgi/Forum* *Iulium*	*Ilurco* *Mentesa* *Bastia* *Ossigi/* *Municipium* *Latonium* *Salaria?/Col.* *Salariensis* *Solorius M.* *Tucci/Col.* *Augusta* *Gemella/* *Itukke* *Tugia* *Vergilia* *Viniolae?* *Vi(v)atia/* *Biatia* 1C3 *Baetica*	**37**
36	26F5 *Cilniana* *Iluro/Lauro?* *Nescania* *Salduba fl.* 27A5 *Aratispi/* *Rataspem*	*Ascua/* *Osqua* *Cartima* *Maenuba fl./* *Mainake fl.* *Maenuba/* *Menova/* *Maenoba*	*Mainake* *Malaca* *Malaca fl.* *Suel*	27B5 *Abdera/* *Abdara* *Caviclum?* *Selambina/* *Sel?* *Sexi/* *Saxetanum/* *Caesarea/* *Firmum* *Iulium*		**36**
	−5			−4		

	−3	−2	−1	+0	+1	
39	27C2 Ocules **Segobriga** Valeria 25cn. **Sekobirikes**	27D2 Ad Putea {27unl Urbiaca}	27E2 Ad Novlas Edeta/Leiria Edetania/ Edetani/ **Sedetani?** Portus Sucronis Saetabis **Saguntum**/Arse Sebelaci Sucro Sucro fl. Sucronensis Sinus Turia fl. Udiva? fl./Uduba fl. Valentia	27F2 Baliaricum Mare Colubraria? Ins.	27G2 Ebusus Ins.	39
38	27C3 Caput fl.Anae? Libisosa/ Colonia Forum Augustum Mariana Mentesa	27D3 Ad Palem? Asso Begastrum/ Bigastrum Contestania/ Contestani Fortuna Ilorci/ Ilourgeia Ilounon? Parietinae Salika? Saltigi **Segisa?**	27E3 Ad Aras Ad Ello? Ad Leones Ad Statuas? Ad Turres?/ Turres Saetab(...)? Alonis Ins. Alonis (I)Aspis/ Aspis Ilici/ Helike/ Ecclesia Elotana Ilicitanus Sinus IllikitanosLimen Lucentum/Akra Leuke?/Castrum Album? Saetabis? fl. Sorobis fl. Tader fl. 27unl **Icositani**	27F3 Dianium/ Hemeroskopeion Ferrarium Pr./ Tenebrium Pr. Planesia? Ins.	27G3 Colubraria Ins./Ophiussa Ins. Ebusus Pityussae Inss.	38
37	27C4 Ab(ou)la/ Al(a)ba Ad Morum Bastetania/ Bastetani/ Bastuli Basti Orospeda? M. *Tagili/ Respublica Tagilitana Tugiensis Saltus *Tutugi {27unl Orkelis}	27D4 Baria Eliocroca? Ficariensis Locus? Longuntica Spartarius? Campus	27E4 Carthago Nova/Col. Urbs Iulia/ Carthago Spartaria Saturni Pr./ Scombraria Pr. Scombraria Ins./ Hercules Ins. Thiar	27F4	27G4	37
36	27C5 Charidemos Pr. Murgi Portos Magnos TuranianaUrci? Urcitanus Sinus 1C3 Ibericum Mare/ Hibericum Mare	27D5	27E5	27F5	27G5	36
	−3	−2	−1	+0	+1	

(c) From −10 to −3 longitude (between latitudes 40 and 43)

This area covers northern Portugal and north-west Spain. Its Celticity is clear from Maps 5.1–5.3,[63] and is further borne out by the unlocatable names in the *Barrington* data which belong in this general area (mostly that of Map 24), even if not all of them are acceptable instances:

24	*unl*	Aliobr(i)o	
24	*unl*	Canibri	
24	*unl*	Carrinensis Ager	
24	*unl*	Lambriaca	
24	*unl*	Segisama Brasaca	
24	*unl*	Vicani Dercinoassedenses	
25	*cn.*	Areikoratikos	Arekorata

The low figures on the extreme west of the area are merely due to the shortage of toponyms of all sorts in squares that are mainly sea. Similarly, the absence of our Celtic-looking elements from −5/41 may well be coincidental, as there are only 6 names in that square, which lay within the territory of the Vaccaei: *Cauca*; *Gella/Tela*; *Nivaria*; *Pintia*; *Septimanca*; *Vaccaei* (24G3). Tentative Celtic etymologies have in fact been suggested for some of the 6, though without much conviction.[64] At −4/40 the relatively low percentage (12%) on Map 5.2 is due to only **Complutum** (25B5) being listed out of a total of 8 names: *Brittablo*; *Miaccum*; *Titulcia* (24H4); *Arriaca/Arentia*; *Caesada?/Cesaram*; *Complutum* (25B5); *Carac(c)a/Charakitanoi?*; *Tagonios fl.* (27B1). Of these, some sort of case can be made out for *Arriaca*, *Caesada* and *Carac(c)a* being Celtic.[65] The stem of *Brittablo* resembles Celtic names,[66] and the suffix of *Tagonios* (cf. *Tagus*) recalls the common Celtic *-onos*.

---

[63] See also García Alonso, 'On the Celticity of the Duero plateau', Gorrochategui, 'Ptolemy's Aquitania and the Ebro valley', and VCIE, pp. 429–91.

[64] Cf. García Alonso, 'On the Celticity of the Duero plateau', pp. 42 (*Pintia*) and 45 (*Gella-Tela-Tola* and *Cauca*), 'Ptolemy and the expansion of Celtic language(s)', p. 148, n. 26 (*Cauca*, cf. De Bernardo Stempel, 'More on Ptolemy's evidence for Celtic Ireland', p. 100), and *Península Ibérica*, p. 486. None of these is etymologized as Celtic in AILR and cf. PNPG Possibly Celtic Elements s.vv. {cauca:}, cauco-, and {gella:}. The Celticity of *Pint-* is rejected by Villar, 'Los antropónimos en *Pent-*, *Pint-*' (cf. DLG s.v. *pinpetos*, and Villar, *Indoeuropeos y no indoeuropeos*, pp. 439–40), and Prósper, *Lenguas y religiones prerromanas*, pp. 398 and 517.

[65] On the first see Russell, 'Suffix', p. 169. On *Caesada*, see García Alonso, *Península Ibérica*, pp. 330–31, and Gorrochategui, 'Ptolemy's Aquitania and the Ebro Valley', p. 148, and VCIE, pp. 179–80. *Carac(c)a* resembles *Karraka* in Italy, discussed above (p. 226) in connection with *Carruca* at −6/37.

[66] See above, p. 218. Cf. 26D5 *Mercablum* (−7/36).

(d) From −3 to +3 longitude (between latitudes 40 and 43)

This area covers north-east Spain, Andorra and south-west France. The unevenness of its Celticity is clear from Maps 5.1–5.3, and is not enhanced by the only 'Celtic-looking' name which could not be located to a single degree square but is assigned to the general area of Map 25:

25	*unl*	**Cott**ion

In fact *Cottion* does not certainly belong in our area; it may have been in the (Celtic) Auvergne.[67]

The extreme west of the area is securely Celtic, although further east the Celtic element is slight:

−3/43 In addition to **Deoua** fl., *Autrigones/Allotriges*.[68]

−3/42 In addition to **Deobriga/Sobobrica?**, *Alisanco*,[69] *Bele(g)ia/Veleia*,[70] *Berones*,[71] *Suessatium/Seustatio*,[72] **Tritium Magallum*,[73] and *Victoriacum*[74] are obvious additions. 25cn. *Uarakos* has a Celtic suffix and has been held to refer to *Vareia*, which may itself be Celtic.[75]

−3/41 In addition to the four names in bold, *Okilis*, if this is a variant of Celtic **ocel-*,[76] *Ouisontion*,[77] and **Voluca/Ouelouka*.[78]

−3/40 In addition to **Ercavica**[79] and **Mediolon**,[80] *Loutia/Lutiakos*.[81]

---

[67] See Ch. 4 above, s.v. *cot(t)-*.

[68] PNRB, p. 353; Gorrochategui, 'Establishment and analysis', p. 157 (who also sees *Neroua fl.* as Celtic, cf. PNPG Celtic Elements s.v. *neruo-*, and VCIE, pp. 465–66); Lambert, 'Lugdunensis', p. 239 (but cf. VCIE, pp. 441–43).

[69] On *Alis-* see p. 183 above. Simply Indo-European according to VCIE, pp. 435–36.

[70] Gorrochategui, 'Establishment and analysis', p. 160.

[71] PNPG Celtic Elements s.v. *bero-*, *br(o)-*. The Berones were *Keltoi* according to Strabo 3.4.5.

[72] DLG s.v. *suexs*; AILR s.n. and Comment s.n.; Gorrochategui, 'Establishment and analysis', p. 159. In Rav. 318.6 *eu* must be an error for *ue* (cf. TIR K-30, p. 215). PNPG segments *su-uesso/uesto-aso-io-* or *sueso-aso-io-*; cf. Possibly Celtic Elements s.vv. *suesso-*, *uesso-* and *uesto-*.

[73] Gorrochategui, 'Ptolemy's Aquitania and the Ebro valley', p. 146; García Alonso, 'Ptolemy and the expansion of Celtic language(s)', p. 149; PNPG Celtic Elements s.v. *tritio-*; VCIE, pp. 475–76. 25cn. *Titiakos* (Russell, 'Suffix', p. 168, Rubio Orecilla, 'Las formaciones secundarias', p. 585) may be the same *Tritium* (TIR K-30, p. 222). A similar unlocatable Celtiberian name is 25cn. *Titum* (TIR K-30, p. 223) and cf. 25cn. *Teitiakos* cited in n. 89.

[74] Not in Russell, 'Suffix'. This is not in TIR K-30 because it is not mentioned before its foundation in 581: Tovar, *Tarraconensis*, p. 376.

[75] TIR K-30, pp. 235–36; Russell, 'Suffix', p. 168; DLG s.v. *treuero-*; cf. García Alonso, 'Ptolemy and the expansion of Celtic language(s)', p. 149, and VCIE, pp. 480–81.

[76] For which see Ch. 3 above.

[77] Cf. DLG s.v. *uid-*.

[78] AILR s.n. *Voluce*; García Alonso, *Península Ibérica*, p. 307. *Numantia* cannot be labelled Celtic: see García Alonso, 'Ptolemy and the expansion of Celtic Language(s)', pp. 138 and 150.

[79] CIB, p. 161, n. 957; Gorrochategui, 'Establishment and analysis', p. 162. Cf. PNPG Possibly Celtic Elements s.vv. {erca:}, *erco-* and *erga-*, {erga:-}, *ergo-*; VCIE, pp. 458–59.

[80] Gorrochategui, 'Ptolemy's Aquitania and the Ebro valley', pp. 145–46. At −3/41 in PNPG.

[81] TIR K-30, pp. 144–45; DLG s.v. *luto-*; Russell, 'Suffix', pp. 166 and 168.

−2/43 —[82]

−2/42 Only perhaps *Car(t)a*,[83] apart from **Andelos**, **Contrebia Leucada** and **Segia**, and of these **Andelos** has also been analysed as Basque.[84] The Vascon 25unl *Nemantourista* probably belongs here, but may be Basque rather than Celtic.[85]

−2/41 In addition to the 7 names in bold, *Carae/Caraca* and *Caravis* may be Celtic,[86] also *Lousones*,[87] and the *Pagus Gallorum* associated with the **Segardenses** obviously refers to an intrusive settlement of Gauls (cf. *Forum Gallorum* and *Gallicum* below).[88] *Tertakom* (*sic!* for *Terkakom*) may be an /a:ko/ name.[89] *Voberca M.* may contain Celtic **wo* < **upo*.[90]

−2/40 —

−1/43 has no certain Celtic names, only the doubtful *Tarusates*.[91] *Medulla? fl.* could be assigned to Celtic or to some other Indo-European language.[92] It may be Latin *medulla* 'marrow'.

−1/42 *Suessetani*,[93] *Forum Gallorum*. In view of the presence of Gauls, could *Pertusa* be P-Celtic (W *perth*, OI *ceirt*)?[94] In such a context,

---

[82] *Tarbelli* etc. probably contain Basque *bel* rather than Celtic **tarb-*; see Gorrochategui, 'Ptolemy's Aquitania and the Ebro valley', p. 150, and AILR Comments s.n. *Terebellicis*. 25unl *Trition Touborikon*, which Ptolemy assigns to the Varduli, is Celtic (Gorrochategui, 'Ptolemy's Aquitania and the Ebro valley', p. 146; García Alonso, 'On the Celticity of the Duero plateau', p. 45; and n. 73 above), but it is not clear whether it belongs here or at −3/43 (see TIR K-30, p. 227).

[83] Cf. GPN, pp. 166–67, and DLG s.v. *carti-*, *carto-*.

[84] Gorrochategui, 'Ptolemy's Aquitania and the Ebro valley', p. 151, and 'Establishment and analysis', pp. 155 and 161. He also suggests a Basque explanation for *Beturri/Bitouris*. Differently VCIE, pp. 437 and 448–49.

[85] TIR K-30, p. 158; Gorrochategui, 'Ptolemy's Aquitania and the Ebro valley', p. 149, and 'Establishment and analysis', pp. 155 and 161; García Alonso, *Península Ibérica*, p. 389. Cf. above, p. 91, n. 43. VCIE, pp. 467–68, suggests that *Ologicus* is Celtic.

[86] Cf. AILR s.nn. and Comments s.nn. Curchin, 'Celticization and Romanization', p. 263, favours the 'rock' meaning, 'especially since Plutarch tells us that the Characitani lived in the side of a cliff'. Compare on **Carruca** at −6/37 above.

[87] Tovar, *Tarraconensis*, pp. 93–94. Cf. PNPG Possibly Celtic Elements s.v. *lusso-*.

[88] TIR K-30, pp. 121–22.

[89] Ibid. p. 221; Russell, 'Suffix', p. 168 (*TerCaCom*, gen. pl.; the second *t* of TIR and the *Atlas*'s *Tertakom* is a misprint for *k*, as pointed out by Dr G. R. Isaac.) I shall not refer otherwise to two similar names in the *Barrington* data, locatable only vaguely in Celtiberia: 25cn. *Okalakom* and 25cn. *Teitiakos* (TIR K-30, pp. 165 and 218; Russell, 'Suffix', p. 168).

[90] See Ch. 10 below, p. 287, n. 6.

[91] DLG s.v. *taro-*. But for problems with this element see above, Ch. 7, n. 27. *Venami* is possibly Celtic; cf. VCIE, pp. 482–83.

[92] Cf. Rasch, §IVC18/19; PNPG Celtic Elements s.v. *medu-;* De Hoz, 'Narbonensis', p. 178 and n. 42 on the *Medouloi*.

[93] DLG s.v. *suexs*; cf. PNPG Possibly Celtic Elements s.vv. *suesso-* and *uesso-*.

[94] Cf. AILR Comments s.n. *Parthano*. But it could be Latin *pertusus* 'pierced' as in *Petra Pertusa* at +12/43 below.

Iac(c)a may be compared with W *iach* 'healthy', with Gallo-Brittonic vocalism.[95]

−1/41 *Gallicum*. On **(S)Edetani** see above, p. 232. *Beleia* (Ptolemy 2.6.62) is a possible Celtic addition here (cf. −3/42 above).[96]

−1/40 —

+ 0/43 *Praemiacum?*, *Saviniago*, **Sexciacum?* (/a:ko/ names), **Maroialica*,[97] and *Onobrisates*.[98]

+ 0/42 —

+ 0/41 *Gallika Phlaouia* (cf. on *Gallicum* etc. above).[99] The river on which this stood, *Cinga* (modern Cinca), is not in the *Barrington* data, but can be added as probably Celtic.[100] 25unl *Kinna* (Ptolemy 2.6.71), which may belong here, may also be Celtic, though that is uncertain since *Cinna* is also a Latin (or possibly Etruscan) personal name.[101] *Soukkôsa*, a name in Ptolemy (2.6.67) but not in the *Atlas*, is uncertainly Celtic.[102]

+ 0/40 **Cassae Herronesi** (Avienus, *Ora Maritima*, line 491), referring to the Ebro delta (?), is isolated and so unlikely to contain Celtic **cassi-*; Schulten emended to *Onussae Cheronnesi* 'Onusa peninsula'.[103]

+ 1/43 In addition to **Vernus Sol** and other more obviously Celtic names in bold, *Blacinaco?*, *Fesciago*, *Galliaco*, **Pauliacum, Mon.*, *Satiago* (/a:ko/ names),[104] and *Granoialo*.[105]

---

[95] Gorrochategui, *Estudio*, p. 226, and 'Establishment and analysis', p. 162, and García Alonso, *Península Ibérica*, pp. 390–91, compare *Iac(c)a* with W *iach*. In oral discussion at the Madrid 'Ptolemy' workshop Prof. Peter Schrijver noted that the vocalism was not expected in Spain (see his *Studies in British Celtic Historical Phonology*, pp. 103–4, 108 and 464; DLG, pp. 185 and 434; cf. VCIE, pp. 266 and 460). The solution may be to associate the name with Gauls. The inhabitants were called *Iac(c)etani*: TIR K-30, p. 128. (But cf. PNPG Celtic Elements s.v. *ico-* and Possibly Celtic Elements s.v. {iacca:-}, *iacco-*.) Cf. *Catuiaca* and references s.v. *catu-* in Ch. 4 above, and DLG, pp. 432–34.

[96] García Alonso, *Península Ibérica*, pp. 369–70 and 477; PNPG and Celtic Elements s.v. *bell-*, *bello-*, *belo-*. (*Ebora* near here is dubious; see Ch. 4 above, n. 37.)

[97] This is based on 'Maroialicis . . . thermis' in Ausonius 18.31.242, probably 'hot springs of **Maroialum*'; cf. DLG s.vv. *ialon* and *maros* and Sims-Williams, 'Welsh *Iâl*', pp. 61–62.

[98] GPN, p. 371, n. 7. 'Ash- (i.e. spear-) breakers' is a tempting etymology. Cf. DLG s.v. *brista*.

[99] See Gorrochategui, 'Establishment and analysis', pp. 155 and 163, on these names as evidence of Gaulish influence.

[100] TIR K/J-31, p. 61 (where the possible association with Pliny's *Cincienses* (3.24) is noted); GPN, p. 178; cf. DLG s.v. *cinges* and p. 433.

[101] TIR K/J-31, p. 61; Gorrochategui, 'Establishment and analysis', p. 164 (cf. GPN, p. 176); Kajanto, *The Latin Cognomina*, pp. 42, 106–7 and 340. See below, pp. 275, 284 and 300, on *Kinna* in Galatia and Africa, and Falileyev, '*Tylis*', pp. 116 and 132, on *Kinna* in Illyricum.

[102] PNPG Possibly Celtic Elements s.v. *succo-*, *suco-*; García Alonso, *Península Ibérica*, p. 400. Cf. + 11/42 below.

[103] See Murphy's note, p. 65. For *Onusa* see TIR K/J-31, pp. 114–15. On the distinction between 25F4 *Otobesa/Etobesa* etc. and 27F1 *Etobesa* etc., see TIR K/J-31, p. 113, also K-30, p. 169.

[104] On *Sati-* names see Evans, 'Nomina Celtica I', and KPP, pp. 116–17. With *Ictium* perhaps cf. *Ictis* in PNRB, pp. 487–89. **Vernus Sol** is Latin according to AILR s.n., although cf. Comments s.n. and above, Ch. 4, s.v. *verno-*.

[105] DLG s.v. *grannos*; Sims-Williams, 'Welsh *Iâl*', p. 61. On *Tolosa* cf. De Hoz, 'Narbonensis', pp. 183–84, and PNPG Possibly Celtic Elements s.v. *tolo-*.

+1/42 —. **Andosinoi** probably belongs with Aquitanian *Andos(s)-*, not Celtic *ande-*,[106] and *Orgia* (recte *Orkia*?) and *Tarusco* are doubtfully Celtic.[107]

+1/41 —[108]

+2/43 *Birra fl.*,[109] *Lautrego*,[110] *Marciaco* (Celtic /a:ko/ suffix), *Petregontio*.[111] **Usuerva/Usuerna** seems unlikely to contain the Celtic element *Ux-*, on the other hand, and the reading *-uerna* rather than *-uerva* is incorrect.[112]

+2/42 The clearly Celtic names are **Vernodubrum fl.** (a tributary of *Birra fl.*) and **Sebendounon?/Beseldunum**, perhaps due to late Gaulish influence. Possibilities are *Cinniana* (if related to Celtic(?) *Kinna* at +0/41 above rather than the Latin personal names *Cinna* or *Cinnius*)[113] and *Col. Ruscino* and *Rouskinon fl.* if **ruska* is specifically Celtic, which seems unlikely.[114] *Alba fl.* could be Celtic, but the base is widespread.[115]

+2/41 Probably no Celtic names. **Ilduro** is unlikely to be a Celtic **duro**-name. The *Il-* is typical of Iberian names (such as *Iluro* nearby), and Gorrochategui suggests that *-o* was an Iberian ending (citing Iberian coin-legends including *ilturo*).[116] *Aquae Voconiae* recalls Celtic (*Vo-*) but the

---

[106] Cf. GPN, p. 139; Gorrochategui, *Estudio*, pp. 134–43 and 359.

[107] Gorrochategui, 'Establishment and analysis', p. 163; cf. GPN, p. 239, n. 8, DLG s.vv. *orco-* and *orget(o)-/orgeno-*, and PNPG Comments s.n. *O:rkía*. On *Tarusco* see +4/43 *Tarusco* below.

[108] *Bergistani/Bargousioi* may be Celtic, but IE *berg-* was widespread (AILR Celtic Elements s.v. *bergu-*; cf. DLG s.n. *bergusia*; Gorrochategui, 'Establishment and analysis', pp. 162–63). Gorrochategui (p. 164) notes the coincidental(?) similarity between *Lacetani* and *Lacobriga*, but we do not know if the element is Celtic. On *Tarraco* see Gorrochategui, 'Ptolemy's Aquitania and the Ebro valley', pp. 147 and 151, and VCIE, pp. 472–74. *Map-by-Map Directory* i, 409, puts 25cn. *Kaio*, which looks Celtic (CIB, p. 85), in the territory of the Cessetani, in which case it would belong here, but this localization is most uncertain (see TIR K/J-31, p. 95).

[109] Cf. W. *byr(r)*, fem. *ber(r)* 'short', OI *berr*, Gaulish *Birr(i)us* (LEIA B-42). *Albiga* is perhaps Celtic; cf. DLG s.v. *albos*.

[110] VCIE, p. 295. Not listed in DLG s.v. *lautron*. From Germanic *Leotricus* according to Nègre ii, §14849, s.n. *Lautrec*.

[111] Not listed in DLG s.v. *petuar(es)*, *petru-*, however. Cf., unconvincingly, Nègre ii, §15019, s.n. *Peyregoux*.

[112] See Ch. 4, s.vv. *ux-*, *verbā* and *verno-*.

[113] Gorrochategui, 'Establishment and analysis', p. 164; TIR K/J-31, p. 62; AILR Comments s.n.; *-ana* is not typically Celtic. On ***Besendunum** see Gorrochategui, 'Ptolemy's Aquitania and the Ebro valley', p. 149, and 'Establishment and analysis', p. 163, and Villar, 'Celtic language', pp. 256–57 and 267–68.

[114] De Hoz, 'Narbonensis', pp. 176–77 and 179, thinks it pre-Celtic; cf. AILR and PNPG Celtic Elements and DLG s.v. *ru(:)sca*; Grzega, pp. 223–24; Campanile, *Saggi*, pp. 285–86. Cf. AILR Comments s.n.

[115] DLG s.v. *albos*.

[116] 'Ptolemy's Aquitania and the Ebro valley', pp. 147–48. On *Egara* see ibid. p. 152. For *Il-* see section 12.3 below.

existence of a Celtic element *cono- is doubtful and the name may derive from a Latin name *Voconius*.[117]

+3/43 Besides the **Volcae**, *Luteva/Civ. Lutevensium*,[118] *Longostaletes*,[119] *Lattara*,[120] *Magalona*,[121] *Sextantio*,[122] and perhaps *Or(o)bis fl.*[123]

+3/42 —[124]

+3/41 —

(e) From +4 to +9 longitude (latitude 43)

This area covers a one-degree strip at the south of France and across the Italian border.[125] Its Celticity according to Maps 5.1–5.3 is fairly low, which at first sight seems to support the toponymists who minimize the Celtic contribution to the area,[126] but on closer inspection the number of Celtic names rises:

+4/43 *Libicii?* and *Libica Ora*,[127] *Nemausus*,[128] *Rhodanousia*,[129] *Gallicum Mare, Anatilii?*,[130] **Aramo?*,[131] *Cavares* (as 'people' and as 'confederation'),[132] *Ernaginum*,[133] *Glanum*,[134] *Col. Arelate/Col. Iulia Paterna Sext-*

---

[117] AILR Celtic Elements s.v.; Rostaing, *Essai*, pp. 452–53.

[118] DLG s.v. *luto-, luteuo-*.

[119] DLG s.vv. *longo-* and *nauson*; cf. KGP, p. 233.

[120] *Stagnum Latera* in Pliny 9.29, describing the marsh, now *l'étang de Lattes*, which supports the etymology in Holder ii, 150, and DLG s.v. *late*. See note in De Saint-Denis's edition, pp. 106–7. 39unl *Latis fl.* (TP), a tributary of the Po in appropriate terrain (around +8/45), may be etymologically related. Chevallier, *La romanisation de la Celtique du Pô*, i, 99, tentatively identified it with the Maira (+7/44).

[121] DLG s.v. *magalos*.

[122] DLG s.v. *sextan*; AILR Comments s.n. *Sextatione*; Rivet, *Gallia Narbonensis*, p. 170.

[123] DLG s.v. *orbios*; De Hoz, 'Narbonensis', pp. 176, n. 10, and 185, is sceptical. Perhaps add *Ledus fl.* (Dottin, *Langue gauloise*, p. 89).

[124] *Leucata Litus* could be Celtic, but the root is too widespread to be certain. *Sambroka fl.* is also uncertain (cf. GPN, p. 253, García Alonso, *Península Ibérica*, p. 180, and PNPG s.n. *Sambróka p.e.*).

[125] On this area see especially De Hoz, 'Narbonensis', who attempts to differentiate Gaulish and pre-Gaulish Celtic names. See also Rivet, *Gallia Narbonensis*, Barruol, esp. pp. 135–46, various essays in Garcia & Verdin (eds) *Territoires celtiques*, Garcia, *La Celtique méditerranéenne*, pp. 13–25, and De Hoz, 'Mediterranean frontier of the Celts'.

[126] Rostaing, *Essai*, pp. 315–40; Fabre, *Noms de lieux du Languedoc*, pp. 41–53 (more balanced than Rostaing); Billy, *Atlas Linguae Gallicae*, p. [i]; Vendryes, 'Note', p. 648. DLG, p. 10, n. 4 and *passim*, reacts against this. The identification of the Celticity of many inscriptions in southern Gaul (see RIG) has changed perceptions.

[127] See above, p. 197, on +8/45 *Libicii*.

[128] AILR and PNPG Celtic Elements s.v. *nemo-*.

[129] To be related to *Rhodanus fl.* (15D1), on which see Vendryes, 'Note', pp. 646–48, DLG s.v. *ro-*, Lambert, 'Lugdunensis', pp. 218 and 250, and S. Zimmer in *RGermAlt* s.n. Rhône.

[130] DLG s.v. *anatia*. Cf. 15unl **Anatilia*.

[131] Ibid. s.v. *aramo-*.

[132] Ibid. s.v. *cauaros*.

[133] Ibid. s.v. *erno-* and p. 434. Doubts are expressed by Isaac, AILR Possibly Celtic Elements s.v., and by De Hoz, 'Narbonensis', pp. 176, 181 and 185–86.

[134] DLG and AILR and PNPG Celtic Elements s.v. *glano-*, De Hoz, 'Narbonensis', p. 181.

	−3	−2		−1	
43	25C2 Autrigones/Allotriges **Deoua** fl. Neroua fl.	25D2 Aquae Terebellicae/Aquae Tarbellicae/Hydata Augousta (At)Uria fl./ Uria fl. Atur(r)us fl. Carasa Cocosates (Sexsignani) Imus Pyreneus	*Lapurdum* *Oiasso* *Oiasso* *Akron/Pyrenaei Pr.* *Summus Pyreneus* *Tarbelli* *(Quattuorsignani)* *Varduli*	25E2 *Aquitani/Novempopuli* **Atura/Vicus Iulii* *Bene(h)arnum* *Iluro/Ilurones* *Medulla? fl.* *Novum Oppidum* *Oscidates Montani* *Sotiates* *Tarusates/* *Latusates/* *Venarni/* *Venami/*Benarni*	43
42	25C3 Alba Alisanco Atiliana Barbariana Bele(g)ia/ Veleia Berones Carietes/Karistoi **Deobriga/Sobobrica?** Gebala Idoubeda M. Pelendones Suessatium/Seustatio *Tritium Magallum Tullonium/Toullika Vareia?{ = 25*cn.* Uarakos} Victoriacum	25D3 Alantone **Andelos** Aracaeli Beturri/Bitouris Calagurris (Nassica) Iulia Car(t)a	Cascantum **Contrebia** **Leucada** *Ilu(m)beris Ilurcis/Grac(ch)urris It(o)uris(s)a/Turissa Ologicus Pompelo **Segia/Segla/** Setia Vascones	25E3 Aspalluga Bourtina/Bortinae Calagurris *Fibularia Ebelinum Forum Gallorum Forum Ligneum Iac(c)a Osca/Urbs Victrix Pertusa Pyrenaei M. Suessetani Summus Pyreneus	42
41	25C4 **Arcobriga** Areva fl. **Cortona* Numantia Okilis Ouisontion Salo fl. **Segontia** Tittoi Vadavero M. **Voluca/* Ouelouka 25unl **Mutudurum**	25D4 Allobo/Alauona = 25*cn.* **Alaun** Aquae Bilbitanorum Aratikos/Aratis **Augustobriga/** **Augustobrica** Belloi Belsinon/*Balsio/ Bel(l)isone Bilbilis (Augusta) *Bursao/ Boursada Caius M. Carae/Caraca Caravis Carduae	Castra Aelia Chalybs fl. **Contrebia** **(Belaisca)** Lousones Manlianus Saltus **Nertobriga** Pagus Gallorum et **Segardinenssium** Platea **Segeda/** Begeda **Segontia** Sermonae Tertakom Turiaso Voberca M.	25E4 Auci/Arsi Caum Celsa/Col.Victrix Iulia Lepida Col. Caesaraugusta Gallicum Salduie/'Salduba' **(S)Edetani/Edetani/** **Edetania** Surdaones/ Sordones {Beleia}	41
40	25C5 **Ercavica** Loutia/Lutiakos 27C1 *Opta 25unl **Mediolon**	25D5 *Agiria* *Tourboletai*	27D1 *Lobetanoi*	25E5 *Ilercaones/* *Il(l)urgavonenses* *Lassira/Respublica* *Leserensis*	40
	−3	−2		−1	

	+0		+1		
43	25F2 Ad Sextum Aquae Convenarum Auscii Belsinum Besinum/ Vestianum? Bigorra Castrum Calagorris **Casinomagus** Egir(i)cius fl. Elimberrum/ 'Climberrum'/ Elimberrum Ausciorum Augusta	Elusa/Elusates/ Tasta Hungunverro Lactora/ Lactorates **Lugdunum** **Convenarum** *Maroialica Onobrisates Praemiacum? Saviniago *Sexciacum? *SparianumTarba/ TurbaVanesia Vicus Aquensis **(Volcae)** **Tectosages/** **Tectosages/** **Tectosagi**	25G2 Ad Iovem Ad Nonum Ad Vicesimum Agessinates Aquae Siccae *Badera Blacinaco? Bucconis **Cambolectri** Consoranni Elusio/ Elesiodulis Fesciago Fines Galliaco Granoialo	Ictium Mauringus *Pauliacum, Mon. *Sarnali Satiago **Sostomagus/** **Sextomagus** Tolosa/Col. Iulia Tolosa/ **Civ. Tectosagum/** Tolosates **Vernus Sol**	43
42	25F3 *Aerenosii* *Aquae* *Onesiorum/* *Onesiae* *Askerris*	*Boletum* *Convenae* *Labitulosa* *Onesi/* *Monesi* *Pyrenaeus* *Saltus*	25G3 *Aeso* **Andosinoi** *Cer(r)etani*	*Ioulia Libika* *Orgia* *Tarusco* *Urgellum*	42
41	25F4 Ad Novas Biclaro?/Biclara <u>Gallika Phlaouia</u> Iberi Ilerda/Iltirta Ilergetes/Ilourgetes/ Ilaraugatai/ Ilergaones/Regio Ilergetum Keresos	Mendiculeia Oleastrum Otobesa/Etobesa/ Otogesa Sicoris fl. Subi fl. Tolous/Telobis {Cinga} {25unl <u>Kinna</u>}	25G4 *(Ad) Fines/Fines* *Ad Septimum* *Decimum* *Antistiana* *Bergistani/* *Bargousioi* *Cessetania/* *CessetaniCol.* *Tarraco/* *Col. Iulia Urbs* *Triumphalis*	*Ies(s)os/* *Municipium* *Iessonensium* *Kissa/Cissis* *Lacetani* *Maius fl.* *Palfuriana* *Rubricatum fl.* *Setelsis* *Sigarra* *Stabulum* *Novum Subur?* *Tulcis fl.*	41
40	25F5 *Adeba* *Dertosa/Hibera Iulia* *Ilercavonia* *Indibilis/Intibilis*	*Sub Saltu* *Tria* *Capita* 27F1 *Etobesa/Etouissa?* *Ildum* 25Av. **Cassae Herronesi**	25G5 Hispanum/Ibericum Mare/(H)Ibericum Mare		40
	+0		+1		

	+2		+3		
43	25H2 Albiga Atax fl./Narbon? fl. Birra fl. Buxio Caborinio **Cambone** Carcas(s)o/Col. Iulia/ **Carcasum Volcarum** **Tectosagarum** [sic] Cedros Cerviano Col. Narbo Martius/Col. Iulia Paterna Claudia **Hebromagus/** **Eburomagus**	Lautrego Liviana Maleto? Marciaco Marcialio Marinio Murato Petregontio *Rubressus? L./Rubrensis? L. Semelingus Tricensimum **Usuerva/** Husuerbas/ **Usuerna**	25I2 Dehas 15A2-3 Arauris fl. Capraria Luteva/*Forum Neronis/Civ. Lutevensium Ad Ermum Agatha Araura/ Cessero Col. Baeterrae/Col. Victrix Iulia Paterna Elisykoi Liria? fl. Longostaletes Or(o)bis fl. Piscenae	15B2-3 Forum Domitii Lattara Ledus fl. Magalona Sextantio **Volcae** **Arecomici** Blasco Ins. Frontiana Mesua Setius M. Taurus/ **Volcarum** **Stagna**	43
42	25H3 Ad Centenarium/ Ad Centuriones Ad Pyrenaeum/ Summus Pyrenaeus Ad Stabulum Ad Vicesimum Alba fl. Atacini Cinniana/Cilniana Clodianus fl. Col. Ruscino Combusta Deciana	Ill(ib)erris/ Helena Indigetes/Indicetes Iuncaria Pompei Tropaea Rouskinon fl./ Tetus fl./Telis fl. Salsulae Fons Scalae Hannibalis? **Sebendounon?/** **Beseldunum** Septimania Sordonum Ora Ticis? fl./ Ticer fl. **Vernodubrum fl.**	25I3 *Caucholiberi* *Cervaria Pr.* *Emporiae/Emporion* *Indike* *Iovis? M.* *Leucata Litus* *Portus Veneris/* *Pyrenea Venus* *Pyrenaei Pr.* *R(h)oda/* *Rhode* *Sambroka fl.*		42
41	25H4 *Aquae Calidae* *Aquae Calidae?* *Aquae Voconiae* *Arnum fl.* *Arrago(na)* *Ausetani* *Auso/Ausa/* *Ausona* *Baetulo/* *Baitolo* *Baetulo fl.* *Blanda(e)* *Col.* *Barcino/Col.* *Iulia* *Augusta/* *Paterna Faventia*	*Egara* *Gerunda* **Ilduro** *Iluro* *Iovis M.* *Laeetania* *Lauro* *Praetorium?* *Rubricatum?* *Semproniana?* *Seterrae* *Turissa*	25I4 *Lounarion Akron*		41
	+2		+3		

anorum Arelate,[135]   *Traiectum Rhodani.*[136]   On the other hand, it seems unlikely that ***Virinnae?** contains Celtic **viro-*.[137]   **Arandunum** is deduced from an inscription referrring to *Arandunici,* and should perhaps be compared to names in *Arand-* rather than *-dunum.*[138]   *Tarusco* is very doubtful.[139]

+ 5/43   *Cabellio,*[140]   *Dexivates,*[141]   *Louerion M.,*[142]   *Tricores?,*[143]   *Gargarius.*[144]   A Celtic-looking name which might perhaps be added is '15unl *Sekoanos fl.*'; this entry is based on *Sêkoanos* (var. *Sikoanos*), given by Stephen of Byzantium as a city of the Massiliots, but thought to be the name of the river Arc or Touloubre.[145]

+ 6/43   *Sanitium,*[146]   *Suetrii,*[147]   *Verucini,*[148]   **Borma,*[149]   *Matavo,*[150]   *Vergunni.*[151]

---

[135] DLG s.vv. *are*(-) and *late* (and *sextan*?); De Hoz, 'Narbonensis', p. 181 Cf. PNPG Celtic Elements s.v. {la:to/i-}.

[136] For *Rhodanus* see n. 129 above. That *Druentia fl.* is Celtic is only a possibility; cf. PNPG Possibly Celtic Elements s.v. *dru-*; De Hoz, 'Narbonensis', pp. 177–78.

[137] The *Map-by-Map Directory* refers to CIL XII 3362 (an inscription VIRINN from Nîmes) and Rivet, *Gallia Narbonensis,* p. 170, for **Virinnae.* It is identified with modern *Védrines* (elsewhere < Latin *veterinae* 'pack-animals' according to Nègre i, §5704), but Rivet also records (pp. 173 and 179, n. 51) an identification with *Vézenobres.*

[138] Holder i, 172 and iii, 649. See above, n. 5.

[139] DLG s.v. *taro-*, but see review by Billy, p. 282, and above, Ch. 7, n. 27. 'Non-Celtic' according to De Hoz, 'Narbonensis', pp. 177, 179 and 185–86. Cf. + 1/42 *Tarusco* above.

[140] DLG s.v. *caballos*; Lambert, '*Lugdunensis*', p. 242; AILR Celtic Elements s.v. *cabello-*. Cf. Rostaing, *Essai,* p. 111. De Hoz, 'Narbonensis', p. 179, is doubtful. See also + 32/38 below, p. 274.

[141] DLG s.v. *dexsiuo-*.

[142] Ibid. s.v. *louernos* (with doubts).

[143] Barruol, p. 210. Cf. *Tricorii* in DLG s.vv. *budina, corios, tri-* and *uoconti.*

[144] DLG s.v. *gargo-*. A likely objection is that *Garg-* occurs in southern Italy (45C1 *Garganus M.*, 46unl *Garga* and *Garganus fl.*) and Asia Minor (p. 270 below). Cf. Rostaing, *Essai,* pp. 176–78; VCIE, pp. 242 and 267; Villar, 'Celtic language', p. 264.

[145] *Ethnikôn,* ed. Meineke, p. 562; *Map-by-Map Directory* i, 227, where these rivers are also identified with 15unl *Caenus fl.* – the Celtic etymology of the latter (: OI *caín*) is implicitly rejected by De Hoz, 'Narbonensis', p. 177, who regards it simply as 'probably IE'; cf. LEIA s.vv. *cain* and *caín.*

[146] De Bernardo Stempel, 'Ptolemy's Celtic Italy and Ireland', pp. 89, 92, 94 and 105. Cf. PNPG Possibly Celtic Elements s.v. *sani-*.

[147] DLG s.v. *etno-*; cf. also, however, *Su-etius* etc. in DLG s.vv. *etu-* and *su-*. On the *Suetri* see Zehnacker's edition of Pliny Book 3, pp. 151 and 264. Barruol, pp. 140 and 142, regards *Suelteri* (same square) as an ethnonym with the same Celtic(?) suffix *-eri*; the latter was not exclusively Celtic, however (cf. the Germanic *Tencteri* and *Bructeri* at + 6/51 and + 7/51 above). There is a problem in seeing *Suel-* as Celtic (see PNPG Possibly Celtic Elements s.v.). *Nerusii* is also doubtfully Celtic, as the stem is widespread (cf. PNPG Celtic Elements s.v. *nero-*).

[148] GPN, p. 124; DLG and PNPG s.v. *ueru-*.

[149] *Bormani* in Pliny 3.36. On *borm-* see above, p. 193.

[150] AILR Celtic Elements s.v. *matu/i-*; GPN, p. 231.

[151] A connection with W. *gwery*, OI *ferg*, is suggested in DLG s.v. *uergobretos*. For this root see also De Bernardo Stempel, 'Ptolemy's Celtic Italy and Ireland', p. 105. On *Forum Voconii* cf. on + 2/41 *Aquae Voconiae* above.

	+4	+5	+6	+7	+8	
43	15C2-3 Ambrussum *__Arandunum__ <u>Libicii?</u> <u>Narbonensis</u> <u>Nemausus</u> <u>Rhodanousia</u> *Varatunnum *__Virinnae?__ <u>Gallicum Mare</u> <u>Hispaniense? Ostium</u> <u>Libica Ora</u> <u>Metapinum? Ostium</u> 15D2-3 <u>Anatilii</u> *<u>Aramo?</u> <u>Avennio</u> Bellintum <u>Campi Lapidei</u> <u>Cavares</u> <u>Cavares</u> <u>Druentia fl.</u> <u>Ernaginum</u> <u>Glanum</u> Lettino Pons Aerarius Salluvii Tarusco Tedusia? Tericiae <u>Theline/Col.</u> <u>Arelate/Constantina/</u> <u>Col. Iulia</u> <u>Paterna</u> <u>Sextanorum</u> <u>Arelate</u> <u>Traiectum</u> <u>Rhodani</u> <u>Ugernum</u> Fossae Marianae? Fossae Marianae Gradus Massilitanorum Massalioticum? Ostium 15unl *__Coriossedum__	15E2-3 Ad Fines Albici Apta Iulia Cabellio <u>Col. Aquae</u> <u>Sextiae/Col. Iulia</u> Augusta Aquae Sextiae Dexivates <u>Louerion M.</u> <u>Orga Fons</u> *Pisavi Salyes __Vindasca__ __Vindelicus fl./__ <u>Soulgas fl.</u> Vulgientes Aemines Avatici Calcaria Solarium Dilis *Immadrae *Incarus Maritima Massalia/Massilia __Segobrigii__ <u>Stomalimne/</u> <u>Mastramela Stagnum</u> <u>Tricores?</u> 15F2-3 __Catuiacia__ <u>Carsicis</u> Citharista <u>Gargarius</u> <u>Tegulata</u> 16A2-3 __Alaunium__ *<u>Griselica</u> Reii Tritolii? Ad Turrem Camactulici? Salluvii Taurois/Tauroention Telo Martius	16B2-3 Alebaece Reiorum Apollinarium/ Apollinaris Reiorum/Reii Anteae Ligauni <u>Sanitium</u> __Sentii__ 'Stablo' Suetrii <u>Verucini?</u> <u>Alconis</u> Argenteus fl. *Borma <u>Forum</u> <u>Voconii</u> <u>Matavo</u> <u>Olbia</u> Pergantion Pomponiana? Stoechades Inss. Suelteri? 16C2-3 Ad Horrea Apron? fl. *__Brigomagus__ <u>Deciates</u> Glanate Nerusii Salinae <u>Vergunni</u> <u>Athenopolis</u> Col. Forum Iulii Heraclia Caccabaria Oxubii Sambracitanus Sinus	16D2-3 *Anao <u>Antipolis</u> *Avisio Cemenelum *Cuntinus <u>Herakles</u> Monoikos/ Portus Monoeci/ Monoikos Lero Ins. Lumo Navelis Nicaea Olivula Planasia Ins. /Lerina Ins. Tropaeum Augusti/ Alpium Tropaeum/ Alpis Summa/Alpis Maritima Vediantii <u>Vergoanum/</u> <u>Berconum</u> <u>Vintium</u> <u>Ligusticum</u> Mare 16E2 Alb(i)um Intimilium/ Albintimilium Costa Balenae Intemelii <u>Tavia fl.</u>	16F2 Lucus <u>Bormani</u> Portus Maurici	43
	+4	+5	+6	+7	+8	

+ 7/43 *Anao,[152] Cuntinus,[153] Vediantii,[154] Vintium,[155] Tavia fl.[156]

+ 8/43 Lucus Bormani.[157]

(f) From +9 to +15 longitude (between latitudes 42 and 43, omitting Corsica)

This area covers a two-degree strip across the Italian peninsula just north of Rome.[158] (Corsica is discussed separately below.) The Celtic-looking names are rare and in many cases probably due to coincidence.

+ 9/43 —

+ 10/43 **Vesidia fl.** cannot be considered seriously as an example of Celtic *sīd- in this context, even apart from semantic objections and the questionable segmentation Ve- rather than Ves-.

+ 10/42 —

+ 11/43 It has been tentatively suggested that Saena (Ptolemy's Σαινα, modern Siena) and **Cortona** are Celtic rather than Etruscan (Saena/Sena and Curtun), but this remains doubtful since they are so isolated from more obviously Celtic names.[159] One can compare 42unl **Cortuosa** in southern Etruria, which seems unlikely to be Celtic.[160] A definitely Celtic name in northern Etruria, if correctly transmitted, which cannot be localised precisely however, is 42unl Biturgia (Ptolemy 3.1.43) < *Biturīgiā.[161]

---

[152] DLG s.v. anauo-.

[153] Ibid. s.v. cuno- (tentatively).

[154] De Bernardo Stempel, 'Ptolemy's Celtic Italy and Ireland', pp. 89, 91 and 105; PNPG Comments s.n. Ouediantio:n and Possibly Celtic Elements s.v. uedio- and {ue:dio-}.

[155] De Bernardo Stempel, 'Ptolemy's Celtic Italy and Ireland', p. 89. (In 'Additions to Ptolemy's evidence' she compares Albintimelion; PNPG Celtic Elements s.v. uinto-.)

[156] So DLG s.v. tauo- (cf. Fabre, Noms de lieux du Languedoc, p. 44); but one might have expected *Tausia (cf. Isaac, 'Scotland', p. 204, s.n. Taoúa).

[157] On borm- see above, p. 193.

[158] See esp. De Bernardo Stempel, 'Ptolemy's Celtic Italy and Ireland'. Cf. Benozzo, review of Parsons & Sims-Williams (eds), Ptolemy, pp. 260–63.

[159] Cf. De Bernardo Stempel, 'Ptolemy's Celtic Italy and Ireland', pp. 87, 94 (Sena), and 87, 93, n. 15, 105 (Cortona); Pallottino, Saggi ii, 713–14, 720, 722 and 724; Bonfante & Bonfante, Etruscan Language, p. 222. Ar(r)etium resembles the Aritium in Spain (−8/39) discussed above, but had long vowels in Latin. It is possibly Etruscan: Pallottino, Saggi ii, 713, 717 and 725; Pfiffig, Einführung, p. 92; Bonfante & Bonfante, Etruscan Language, p. 222.

[160] See Ch. 4 above, s.v. cort-. The Hispanic *Cortona listed there is reconstructed from Cortonenses in Pliny 3.24; cf. Tovar, Tarraconensis, p. 410.

[161] De Bernardo Stempel, 'Ptolemy's Celtic Italy and Ireland', pp. 85, 92, 105, 107 and 111, and 'Additions to Ptolemy's evidence', p. 105. PNPG, Italia, and Holder iii, 875 put it at + 11/43 in the Cortona or Montevarchi region, which suits the references to Bituriza (TP) etc. in other sources (see Die Geographie des Ptolemaeus, ed. Cuntz, p. 160, and TP, ed. Weber, Segment III). Rav. 287.4 has Beturnis (var. Veturris in Guido, ibid. p. 125). De Bernardo Stempel places it much further south, in 'southern Tuscany'. She maintains that 'pretonic syncope in the Greek accented form accounts for Biturgía'. Cf. PNPG Comments s.n. Bitoúriges [= Bourges] on Bítourges in some Ptolemy MSS, and cf. Ch. 4 above s.v. rīgo- on Boudorgis. On Bituris among the Vascones see Gorrochategui, 'Establishment and analysis', p. 161, and above, p. 237, n. 84.

+ 11/42 *Succosa* and *Minio fl.* might be analysed as Celtic (compare *Soukkôsa* and *Minius fl.* in Hispania at + 0/41 above and at −9/42 = 24C2), but without any assurance.[162] In the case of *Graviscae*, a connection with Celtic *grawā 'sand' would suit a port, but this word is found throughout Italy and is probably non-Celtic in origin according to Campanile.[163]

+ 12/43 Besides **Senones, Sentinum**[164] and **Vindenates** (or *Vindinates*),[165] *Ager Gallicus* testifies to a Celtic presence in Umbria.[166] With regard to *Helvillum* see below on *Helvia*. The unlocatable 42unl **Usidicani** belongs in Umbria, but cannot be taken seriously as an example of Celtic *Ux-*.[167]

+ 12/42 There are no distinctively Celtic names here, notwithstanding the presence of a Gaulish inscription at *Tuder* (Todi).[168] The Celtic-looking **Trebiae** and **Trebula Mutuesca** are presumably Italic,[169] and **Cornetus Campus** no doubt belongs with *Corniculum* and *S. Cornelia, Mon.*, which we assigned to the 'inadmissible' category in Chapter 4 as being obviously Latin. Finally, **Forum Cassii** carries no weight even if the personal name *Cassius* has Celtic origins.[170]

+ 13/43 Apart from **Sena fl.** and **Sena Gallica**,[171] where the adjective *Gallica* supports the linguistic identification, there are only vague possibilities: *Cingulum* and **Cingulus M.* (ostensibly Latin, but cf. Celtic *cing-*);[172] *Helvia Ricina* and *Helvinus? fl.* (presumably Latin *helvus*, although compare Celtic names in *Helv-*).[173] *Matilica* is perhaps the only plausible Celtic addition.[174]

+ 13/42 *Aternus fl.* and *Matrinus? fl.* recall the Celtic words for 'father' and 'mother', but are quite isolated, hence De Bernardo Stempel comments that 'an Italic interpretation seems preferable'.[175] If there were a Celtic connection it might involve two peoples on the *Aternus* river: the *Marsi*,

---

[162] Cf. PNPG Possibly Celtic Elements s.v. *succo-*, *suco-* and Celtic Elements s.v. *mino-*.

[163] De Bernardo Stempel, 'Additions to Ptolemy's evidence'; cf. Campanile, *Saggi*, p. 284; DLG s.v. *graua*.

[164] De Bernardo Stempel, 'Ptolemy's Celtic Italy and Ireland', pp. 87, 89, 91, 93 and 105; DLG s.vv. *senos* and *sentu-*. But see Pallottino, *Saggi*, ii, 722, for *sentin-* in Etruscan.

[165] See Ch. 4 above, s.v. *vindo-*.

[166] Treating *Galli* as linguistically Celtic, as *passim* above; see p. 2.

[167] See Ch. 4 above, s.v. *ux-*.

[168] RIG II.1, no. E5. Cf. De Bernardo Stempel, 'Ptolemy's Celtic Italy and Ireland', p. 85.

[169] Cf. ibid. p. 89; DLG s.v. *treb-* , comparing cognates such as Oscan 'trííbúm ''domum, aedificium'' (*trēbom)'.

[170] See Ch. 4 above, s.v. *cassi-*.

[171] De Bernardo Stempel, 'Ptolemy's Celtic Italy and Ireland', pp. 87 and 94.

[172] LEIA s.v. *cingid*. Note also 42unl *Cingilia*.

[173] Cf. DLG and PNPG Celtic Elements s.v. *elu(o)-*; De Bernardo Stempel, 'Ptolemy's evidence for Germania Superior', p. 89; KPP, p. 232. Compare + 9/44 *Ricina* above, p. 198.

[174] Cf. DLG s.v. *matu-*, *mati-*; GPN, pp. 228–32.

[175] De Bernardo Stempel, 'Ptolemy's Celtic Italy and Ireland', pp. 89 and 111. Cf. LEIA s.v. *athir*.

	+9	+10	+11		
43	41B2-3 *Caprasia* *Ins.* *Urgo* *Ins./Gorgon* *Ins.*	41C2-3 *Fossae* *Papirianae* *Luca* *Pisae* *Portus Pisanus?* *Ad Fines* *Vada Volaterrana* 41D2-3 *Arnus fl.* *Hellana* *Pistoriae* *Valvata* *Caecina fl.* *Velathri/* *Volaterrae* 1F2 *Italia* 41*unl* **Vesidia fl.**	41E2-3 Ad Solaria Gallunianum 42A1-2 Anneianum Faesulae Florentia Mucella Saena	42B1-2 Ad Fines/ Ad Casas Caesarianas Casuentillani Etruria/Tuscia/ Rasna Mevaniola Sappinates? /Sapinia Tribus Ad Statuas Arretium Clusinus L. Clusium **Cortona** Manliana *Umbro fl. {42unl <u>Biturgia</u>}	43
42		41C4-5 *'Argoos Limen'* *Fuftuna/* *Populonium* *Ilva Ins./* *Aethalia Ins.* *Planasia Ins.* *Oglasa Ins.* 41D4-5 *Alma fl.* *Falesia* *Prilius L.* *Salebro?* *Vatl/* *Vetulonia* *Igilium* *Igilium Ins.*	41E4-5 *Prile fl.* *Telamon* *Umbro fl.* *Argentarius M.* *Artemisia Ins.* *Dianium Ins.* *Domitiana* *Incitaria?* *Portus* *Herculis* 42A3-4 *Albinia fl.* *Caletranus Ager* *Heba* *Osa fl.* *Rusellae* *Cosa* *Succosa*	42B3-4 *Aurinia/* *Saturnia* *Maternum* *Pallia fl.* *Suana* *Visentium* *Volsiniensis L.* *Volsinii* *Algae* *Aquae Tauri* *Armenta fl.* *Centum Cellae* *Forum Aurelii* *Graviscae* *Marta fl.* *Martanum* *Minio fl.* *[Orcla]* *Quintianum* *Rapinium* *Regis Villa/* *Regae* *Tarchna/* *Tarquinii* *Traianus?* *Tuscana* *Vulci* 44A1 *Castrum Novum* *Panapio/* *Punicum* *Pons Apollinis* *Pyrgi*	42
	+9	+10	+11		

	+12			+13		+14	
43	42C1-2 Crustumius fl. Monteferetra Pitinum Pisaurense Sarsina Sestinum Tifernum Mataurense Arna Perusia Tifernum Tiberinum Trasumennus L. Vettona	42D1-2 Ad Octavum <u>Ager Gallicus</u> Cales *Firmidianum Flaminia Forum Sempronii Intercisa/Petra Pertusa Metaurus fl. Nelurus fl. Pisaurum Pisaurus fl. Pitinum Mergens **Senones** Suasa	Umbria/Umbri Urvinum Mataurense Ad Aesim Asisium Attidium Clasius? fl. Helvillum Iguvium Nuceria Plestia Plestinus L. Prolaqueum **Sentinum** Tadinae Tinea fl. Tuficum 42unl **Vindenates**	42E1-2 Ad Aesim Aesis Fanum Fortunae Misus fl. Ostra **Sena fl.** <u>**Sena Gallica**</u> <u>Aesis fl.</u> Auximum Camerinum Cingulum *Cingulus M. *Cluentus fl. Cupra Montana Falerio Flusor fl. Helvia Ricina Matilica <u>Misco? fl.</u> Picenum	Planina Septempeda Tolentinum Trea Urbs Salvia 42F1-2 Ancon(a) Cunerum Pr. Numana Aspia fl. Castellum Firmanorum Cluana Cupra Maritima Firmum Picenum Helvinus? fl. Palmensis Ager Pausulae Potentia Tinna fl.		**43**
42	42C3-4 *Ameria* *Balneum Regis* *Clanis fl.* *Statonia* *Tuder* *Velzna/* **Volsinii* *Veteres/* *Urbiventus* *Ad Vicesimum* *Alsietinus L.* *Aqua Viva* *Aquae* *Apollinares* *Aquae* *Apollinares* *Novae* *Aquae Passeris* *Axia* *Baccanae* *Blera* *Ciminius L.* *Ciminius M.* *Falerii* *Falerii Veteres* *Falisci* *Ferentium* *Fescennium* ***Forum Cassii*** *Forum Clodii* *Horta* *Nar fl.* *Nepet* *Ocriculum* *Polimartium*	*Rostrata Villa* *Sabatinus L.* *Sorrina* *Sutrium* *Vadimonis L.* *Vicus Matrini* 42D3-4 *Carsulae* *Clitumnus fl.* *Fanum Fugitivi* *Fons Clitumni* *Forum Flaminii* *Fulginiae* *Hispellum* *Interamna* *Nahars* *Mevania* *Naharcer* *Nequinum/* *Narnia* *Sacraria* *Spoletium* ***Trebiae*** *Tres Tabernae* *Urvinum* *Hortense* *Velini L.* *Vespasiae* *Vicus Martis* *Avens fl.* *Capena* *Cures* *Eretum* *Farfarus fl.* */Fabaris fl.* *Forum Novum* *Himella fl.* *Lucus Feroniae* *Reate*	*Rosia Campus* *Sabini* *Sepernates?* *Soracte M.* *Tolenus fl.* ***Trebula*** ***Mutuesca*** *Velini L.* *Vicus Novus/* *Ad Novas* *Volusii* 43A1 *Caere/Kaisra/* *Agylla* 43B1 *Ad Gallinas* *Albas* *Careiae* *Veii* 43C1 *Corniculum* *Crustumerium* *Lamnae/Ad* *Lam(i)nas* *Nomentum* 43D1 *Aequi* *C. Maenius* *Bassus, Sep.* *Varia* 44B1 *Aquae* *Caeretanae* *S.Cornelia,* *Mon.* 44C1 *Digentia fl.* 42unl ***Cornetus*** ***Campus***	42E3-4 *Ad Aquas* *Ad Centesimum* *Badies* *Forum Decii* *Nemora* *Vacunae* *Nursia* *Phalacrinae/* *Falacrinae* *Tetricus M.* *Truentus fl.* *Aequiculi* *Alba Fucens* *Amiternum* *Aquae Cutiliae* *Aveia* *Cliternia* *Cutiliensis L.* *Fisternae* *Foruli* *Interocrium* *Paganica* *Pitinum* *Tiora Matiene* 42F3-4 *Albula fl.* **Aprutium* *Asculum* *Batinus? fl.* *Castrum* *Novum* *Castrum* *Truentinum* *Hatria*	*Interamnia* *Praetuttiorum* *Matrinus? fl.* *Praetuttii* *Tessuinus fl.* *Vomanus fl.* *Zerninus? fl.* *Aternus fl.* **Aufenginum* *Aufinum* *Caelanum* *Corfinium* *Cumara? fl.* *Furfo* **Hercules* *Curinus* **Incerulae* *Interpromium* *Marsi* *Paeligni* *Peltuinum* *Pinna* *Statulae* *Superaequum* *Tirinus fl.* *Vestini* 44D1 *Carsioli* 44E1 *Agellum* *Cerfennia* *Imeus M.* **Lavernae* *Marruvium* *Sulmo*	42G3-4 *Matrinum* *Anxanum* *Aternum* *Clocoris fl.* *Cluviae* *Marrucini* *Ortona* *Ostia Aterni* *Pallanum* ***Sagrus fl.*** 42H4 *Histonium* 44F1 *Carecini* *Infernates* *'Iovis Lareni'* *Iuvanum* **Pallanum* 44G1 *Buca*	**42**
	+12			+13		+14	

a name which recurs in Germania along with the ethnonym *Marsigni* (see pp. 181 and 189 above), and *Paeligni*, which recalls Celtic *-igni* names.[176] But no doubt this is a coincidence.

+ 14/42 **Sagrus fl.** looks Celtic (Gaulish *Sagro-*, OI *sár*, W *haer*),[177] but could be a cognate Indo-European formation – compare **Sagra(s) fl.** below, in the extreme south of Italy (+ 16/38).[178] On *Matrinum, Aternum* and *Ostia Aterni* see above (+ 13/42).

(g) Italian peninsula below latitude 42

The Celtic-looking names on Maps 5.1–5.3 are scarce, especially considering the hundreds of known toponyms, and are probably due to

44	*unl*	+ *12*	*41*	**Corio**li			
44	*unl*	+ *12*	*41*	**Treb**ium			
43	D2	+ *12*	*41*	**Treb**ula Suffenas			
44	D2	+ 13	41	**Treb**a			
44	*unl*	+ *14*	*41*	**Duro**nia			
44	F3	+ 14	41	**Sid**icini			
44	F3	+ 14	41	Teanum			
				Sidicinum			
44	F2	+ 14	41	'Trebula'			
44	F3	+ 14	41	**Treb**ula			
				Balli(ni)ensium			
44	*unl*	+ *15*	*41*	**Sent**ianum			
44	F4	+ 14	40	**Vesu**vius M.			
44	*unl*			'Maesulus' qui et			
				'Vesulus' M.			
45	B3	+ 15	40	**Ebur**um			
45	B3	+ 15	40	**Volc**ei			
45	D3	+ 16	40	Silvium	**Sid**is		
45	G4	+ 17	40	**Mand**uria	Mandonion	Amandrinum	
45	*unl*	+ *17*	*40*	**Sen**um			
45	inset	+ 18	39	Uzentum	**Oux**enton	Augentum	
46	D5	+ 16	38	**Sag**ra(s) fl.			
46	*unl*			**Aba**la			
47	B2	+ 12	38	Emporion			
				Segestanon			
47	B3	+ 12	37	Aquae	Aquae	Aquae	Aquae
				Segestanae	*Pacatianae	*Phimianae	*Pincianae
47	B3	+ 12	37	(S)**Eg**esta	Egesta		
47	*unl*	+ *13*	*37*	**Kort**yga			
47	*unl*	+ *15*	*37*	**Mag**ea Fons			
47	*unl*			**Cass**itana Massa			
47	*unl*			Kytattara	Enattara	**Ket**aria	

---

[176] CIB, p. 155, n. 921; DLG s.v. *pelignos*. It is uncertain whether the two names *Marsi* are ultimately related: Schönfeld, p. 164.

[177] LEIA s.v.; DLG s.v.

[178] On the wide distribution of *sag(a)ra* names see Villar, *Indoeuropeos y no indoeuropeos*, pp. 312–13.

coincidence or to the presence of Italic cognates of the rather restricted number of Celtic-looking elements in question (the strings TREB, SID and SEG dominate); compare for instance Latin *trabs*, Oscan *trííbúm* 'domum', Umbrian *tremnu* 'tabernaculo' with Old Welsh and Middle Irish *treb*, or Latin *seges, -etis*, with Middle Welsh *heaf* 'I sow').[179] The above list shows the Celtic-looking names from Table 5.2 arranged from north to south (the last seven are in Sicily), with four unlocatable ones interspersed at their approximate latitudes. No doubt they are all due to coincidence. The proximity of **Eburum** and **Volcei** is intriguing, but it would be a long shot to link these names with the brief fourth-century Celtic campaigns in central Italy (in Apulia and beside the *Mare Inferum*) mentioned by Livy (7.1.3 and 7.26.9).[180]

A search through all the toponyms of the area yields one or two names which could be interpreted as Celtic,[181] but none is really cogent.

(h) Corsica

The early names of Corsica are reported mainly by Ptolemy (3.2).[182]

+ 8/42 **Ouiriballon Akron** (3.2.3: var. *Ouêri-*, MS X) presumably takes its name from a tribe *Viriballoi, a plausibly Celtic name 'those of manly limbs?' (cf. *ballo-* 'limb' < **bal-no-*, OI *ball*, Gaulish *Ballo-*).[183]
+ 8/41 (*Matisa* may be Celtic.[184])

+ 9/43 —

---

[179] IEW, pp. 1090 and 887.

[180] For Apulia there is archaeological evidence at *Canusium* (45D2); cf. Hubert, *Greatness and Decline*, p. 12, and Vitali, 'Celts in Italy', p. 231. A general map of 'Sites de découvertes gauloises' is given by Grzega, Karte 1.

[181] De Bernardo Stempel, 'Ptolemy's Celtic Italy and Ireland', pp. 89 and 111, mentions *Antium* (43C4 = + 12/41).

[182] The lack of continuity between his names and later names is noted by Morrachini-Mazel & Boinard, *La Corse selon Ptolémée*. Tantalizing modern names in the west of the island are *Budiccie* (*Budicchie* or *Bodiccia* in 1615) by the river *Gravone*, ibid., pp. 35 and 53, n. 31 (cf. Celtic *boud-* in Ch. 4 above and DLG s.v. *graua* – but on the latter see Campanile, *Saggi*, p. 284). DLG s.v. *taro-* has a name not in the *Barrington* data: '*Tarauos* petit fleuve de Corse . . . = *Taravus* auj. *Tharaux* (Gard)' (cf. Nègre iii, §30002: Occitan *tarau* 'awl'), and De Bernardo Stempel, 'Additions to Ptolemy's evidence for Celtic Italy', adds the ethnonym *Taraben(i)oi* (+ 9/42). But for problems with this element **taro-* see above, Ch. 7, n. 27. Billy, *Atlas Linguae Gallicae*, includes Corsica in his database, as part of the French state, but Celtic toponyms there are below the threshold of 18 names per *département* on his overall map. The section 'Noms de lieux' by A. Blanchet in CAGR III (1933), pp. 23–24, is scanty. I have not seen Jehasse, 'La Corse antique d'après Ptolémée'. Corsica is not covered in PNPG. Its Celticity was pointed out independently by Prof. P. de Bernardo Stempel and myself in papers at the Munich 'Ptolemy' workshop.

[183] LEIA s.v.; Hamp, 'Morphology', pp. 187–88; DLG s.v.; GPN, pp. 147–48.

[184] De Bernardo Stempel, 'Additions to Ptolemy's evidence for Celtic Italy'.

	+8		+9		
43			48D1 *Sacrum Pr.*		43
42	48C2 Alouka Attiou Akron Chrysoun Oros Kaisias Aigialos Kasalos Kolpos Kerouinoi Kirkidios fl. **Ouriballon** **Akron** Ourkinion Palania	Rhion? Akron Rhoiton Oros Rhopikon Saone Sermigion Tilox Akron	48D2 Alalie/Aleria Attemidos Limen Asinkon Corsica/Kyrnos Ins. Gouola fl. Kanelate Keneston Kentourinon Kersounon Kilbensioi **Klounion** Likninoi?	Lourinon? Makrinoi **Mantinon** Mariana/Nikaia? Opinon/Opinoi Ouagon Akron Ouenikion Oulerios fl. Rhotanos fl. Syrboi? Talkinon Tarabenioi **Toutelas Bomos** Vanacini	42
41	48C3 *Agiation* *Ammodes* *Aigialos?* *Lokra fl.* *Matisa* *Pauka* *Tikarios fl.* *Titianoi* *Titianos Limen*	48A1 [SARDINIA] *Herculis Inss.*	48D3 Gallicum/Taphros Fretum Albiana Alista Balatonoi Favoni Portus Granianon Akron Hieron? fl. Koumasenoi? Marianon Marianon Akron Palla Phikaria Pitanos fl. Praesidium Rhoubra Soubasanoi Syrakousanos Limen	48B1 [SARDINIA] *Arktou Akra* *Cuniculariae Inss.* *Elefantaria* *Errebantion Akron/* *Erbentium* *Fossae? Ins.* *Ilva Ins.* *Phintonis Ins.* *Tibula?/Tiboulatoi/* *Portus *Tibulae?* *Turublum Minus* *Viniolae*	41
	+8		+9		

+9/42 **Mantinon** (*polis*) and **Klounion** (*polis*), together on the north coast (3.2.5), support each other's Celticity.[185] The tribe here was the *Vanacini* (3.2.7: *Ouanakinoi*), which may be a Celtic name.[186] From the facing mainland compare, for instance, the Gaulish personal name **Ouanaikos* at Nîmes (dative Ουαναικου) and a *Uanaius Uenic*[(or *Uenio*[ ) of the *Bodiontici* tribe of the Alpes Maritimae.[187] **Toutelas Bomos** 'the altar/cairn of Toutela', further down the east coast (3.2.5), is compared by Müller with 25unl *Tutela*, near Bilbilis in Spain,[188] and no doubt a Latin explanation (*tutela* 'guardian (deity?)') is preferable to Celtic. By contrast, in the interior *Ouenikion* (3.2.8) looks Celtic, 'place of **Venicos*'; compare Gaulish *ouenikoi* 'ceux du clan' and personal names *Venicius*, *Venic(i)a*, *Venico*, and Ptolemy's Irish ethnonym *Oueniknioi*.[189] *Likninoi?* recalls the Gaulish personal name *Licnos*.[190] *Rhotanos fl.* could be the same (Celtic) name as *Rhodanus* (the Rhône).[191] The **Vagoi* of *Ouagon Akron* (3.2.5: var. *Auagon* MS X) may be related to Latin *vagus* or *vāgio*, although the **wāg-* of Old Celtic *Vagna-* (OI *fán*, W *gwaun* 'valley') may be mentioned, and compare also *Vagoriton* in Gallia Lugdunensis (Ptolemy 2.8.7).[192]

+9/41 *Gallicum Fretum* (the channel between Corsica and Sardinia) may simply refer to the route to Gaul. (*Albiana* is only vaguely Celtic, as is *Granianon* (var. *Graniakon*) *Akron* in Ptolemy 3.2.5.)[193]

(i) Sardinia

+8/40 The names in **Corn-** are not likely to be Celtic rather than Italic and the **Giddilitani** presumably took their name from a **Giddilis* or similar, not from Celtic **litano-*.[194]

---

[185] In his note (p. 370) Müller compares *Clunia* in Spain. See also De Bernardo Stempel, 'Additions to Ptolemy's evidence for Celtic Italy'.

[186] Suggested by Dr A. Falileyev, comparing Gaulish names in *-uanos* (see DLG s.v.) such as *Cosuanates*.

[187] Lejeune, 'Compléments gallo-grecs: Nîmes G-524'; CIL III 8495; Holder iii, 98; OPEL iv, 146 and 154; Barruol, p. 385.

[188] Müller, p. 369; TIR K-30, p. 229 (Martial 4.55.16).

[189] Holder iii, 169; DLG s.v. *uenicos*; GPN, p. 278; De Bernardo Stempel, 'Ptolemy's Celtic Italy and Ireland', pp. 100–1, and 'Additions to Ptolemy's evidence for Celtic Italy'; CIB, p. 155, n. 921. It may be the same as *Enikoniai* in Strabo 5.2.7.

[190] RIG II/1 no. L-10; cf. *Licnos*, *-us*, in Holder ii, 211 (compared wrongly with Irish *lén* 'defeat; weakling'); this was independently suggested by P. de Bernardo Stempel at the Munich 'Ptolemy' workshop.

[191] For which see n. 129 above. Differently ('ligurisch') Holder ii, 1232; cf. Lambert, '*Lugdunensis*', p. 218. De Bernardo Stempel, 'Additions to Ptolemy's evidence for Celtic Italy', takes *Rhotanos* as Celtic, but compares the second element with OI *tanae* 'thin'.

[192] DLG s.v.; Holder iii, 84. On *Vagoriton* cf. PNPG Possibly Celtic Elements s.v. *uago-*.

[193] De Bernardo Stempel, 'Additions to Ptolemy's evidence for Celtic Italy'. She prefers the reading *Blatônoi* to *Balatinoi* (Ptolemy 3.2.7) and connects it with Celtic **blāto-* 'flour', for which see above Ch. 4, s.v.

[194] Bonello Lai, 'Il territorio dei *populi* e delle *civitates* indigene in Sardegna', pp. 169–73, treats *Giddilitani/Ciddilitani* as an indigenous name.

	+8		+9		
40	48A2 *Ad Herculem* *Ad Medias* *Ad Octavum* *Barbaria* *Bosa* *Buduntini* *Carbia* **Cornus** *Diabate? Ins.* *Erucium* *Eut(h)ychiani* *Fundus* *Cotronianus* **Giddilitani** *Gorditanum Pr.* *Gouroulis Nea?* *Gouroulis* *Palaia?* *Hafa?* *Hermaion Akron*	*Ilienses* *Korakensioi* **Kornensioi** **'Aichilensioi'** *Makopsisa* *Molaria* *Numisiae* *Nurac Sessar* *Nure* *Nymphaia Ins.* *Nymphaios* *Limen* *Patulcii* *Sardi Pelliti* *Sardinia Ins./* *Sardo Ins./* *Ichnoussa Ins.* *Temos fl.* *Turris* *Libisonis* *Sardoum Mare*	48B2 Aisaronensioi Augustae Balari Caput Tyrsi *Celesitani Coclearia Corsi *Cusinitani Fanum Carisi Fifenses Gemellae? Hermaia? Ins. Hydata Lesitana/Lesa Insani M./ Mainomena Ore *Kaidros fl.	Karensioi Kolymbarion Akron Loukouidonensioi **'Luguidunec'/** Castra Felicia? Nemus Sorabense/ Sorabile Nurritani Olbia Pheronia **Portus** **Luguidonis** Viniolae	40
39	48A3 *Aquae Calidae* *Neapolitanorum/* *Hydata* *Neapolitana* *Beronicenses* *Enosis Ins./* *Hierakon* *Nesos?* *Fundus* *Moddol(…)* *Hieros? fl.* *Hydata* *Hypsitana/Forum*	*Traiani* *Maltamonenses* *Maurousioi* *Metalla* **Molibodes Ins.** *Neapolis/* *Neapolitani* *Othoca* *Pacheia* *Akra* *Semilitenses* *Sulcensis Pr.* *Sulci(s)/* *Sulcitani* *Sulcis fl.* *Tharros* *Thyrsos fl.* **Usel(l)is** *Uticenses*	48B3 Alticienses Barbarikinoi Biora Caralis/Carales Caralitanum Pr./ Karalis Akra Custodia Rubriensis Ferraria	Ficaria Ins. Galillenses Karalitanos Kolpos Martenses Oualentia/ Valentini Patulcenses Campani Porticenses/ Korpikensioi *Rubrenses Saipros fl. Sarcapos Sikoulensioi Sulci(s)/ Solkitanoi	39
38	48A4 *Bitia* *Chersonesos Pr.*	*Herakleous?* *Limen* *Tegula*	48B4 Nora/ Norenses		38
	+8		+9		

+8/39 **Molibodes Ins.** is hardly Celtic. Inland, **Usel(l)is** is compared by Müller with *Ousil(l)a/Usula* on the facing coast of Africa (+10/34). He hints at a Punic connection and this is no doubt more likely than a comparison with Celtic *Uxela* in Britain, since Nora and other cities in Sardinia were Phoenician foundations.[195]

+8/38 —

+9/40 **Portus Luguidonis** (AI 79.6)[196] on the coast and, in the interior, **'Luguidunec'** (AI 81.7: var. *luguinec, lugudunec, lugudonec*), possibly also called *Castra Felicia* (Rav. 412.6 and 500.15), must be connected with Ptolemy's *Loukouidônênsioi* (3.3.6). Isaac comments : 'A connection with Celtic *Lugu-* seems inevitable, but a simple corruption of *Lugudunum* is too far fetched, especially in the light of Ptolemy's E[thnic] N[ame] . . . Perhaps *lugu-wid-on-* "one with the aspect of Lugus" (D[ivine] N[ame]? P[ersonal] N[ame]?).'[197]   Müller took a different line, suggesting Latin *lucus* plus the name of a divinity, perhaps *Felicius Viduus* who was culted in Sardinia.[198] If Müller is right about this, all plausible traces of Celtic in Sardinia disappear, unlike the case of Corsica.

+9/39 —

(j) From the Adriatic to the Black Sea, +15 to +29 longitude (between latitudes 42 and 43)

This area covers a two-degree strip across Croatia, Bosnia, Serbia and Montenegro, Romania and Bulgaria.[199] The Celtic-looking names shown in bold in the tables below are rare and partly due to coincidence. Nevertheless, there are some more or less plausible traces of Celtic both on the Dalmatian coast (to be connected with the *Corinium* at +15/44 discussed in Chapter 7 above?) and along the Danube when it dips below latitude 44 between longitudes 22 and 27. The Celtic names in Dalmatia, if genuine (I am not sure that they are), could presumably be due to movements down the coast or across the Adriatic.[200]

---

[195] Müller, p. 375, on 3.3.2; above, p. 117, s.v. *ux-*. On Nora see Zehnacker's edition of Pliny Book 3, p. 194.

[196] Cuntz's edition in fact reads *Portu Liguidonis*, but both AILR and *Atlas* have the spelling with *u*.

[197] AILR Comments s.n. *Portu Luguidonis*. (Sardinia is not covered in PNPG.) Ptolemy's *k* might be due to the influence of Greek *leuko-*. In the Munich 'Ptolemy' workshop P. de Bernardo Stempel suggested a comparison with the Old Irish personal name *Lugáed*, archaic gen. *Luguaedon*.

[198] Müller, pp. 379–80 and 383.

[199] The most important discussions of Celtic names in this area are by Falileyev, '*Tylis*', and Duridanov, '*Sprachspuren*'.

[200] Pliny 3.130 and 139 gives the impression that people like the *Varvarini* of *Varvaria* (+15/43) were distinct from (but presumably related to) the *Varvari* of northern Italy, but this is explained away as duplication in Zehnacker's notes, pp. 256 and 266.

+ 15/43 Perhaps *Arausa*[201] and *Blandona*.[202]

+ 15/42 —[203]

+ 16/43 Inland, **Andetrium** ('Ανδήτριον, 'Ανδνήριον, Ανδέκριον in Greek sources) is listed by Holder as Celtic, presumably on account of a resemblance to Celtic names in *Ande-* like *Anderit(i)um*, but the second element is obscure and an analysis *An-detrium* may be preferable;[204] a metathesis of **Anderit(i)on* (TP has *Andretio*) would also be possible. On the coast, *Tragurium* is also listed by Holder, and a connection with the Celtic root(s) **tra(:)g-* of OI *tráig*, W. *trai* 'ebb-tide', OI *traig* 'foot', Gallo-Latin *uertragus* 'hunting hound', is attractive.[205] Holder seems to have derived *Epetium*, which is also on the coast beside *Salona*, from P-Celtic **epo-* < **ek^w o-* 'horse',[206] and nearby *Pituntion* might be similarly classified and compared with W *pyd* 'danger' < **k^w ito-* 'what is looked out for'.[207] Names in *Pit-* are very widespread, however![208] The name of the *Manioi* (and cf. *Manios Kolpos*) recalls Gaulish *Cenomani* if that means 'far-going ones' (: W. *myn(e)d* 'go');[209] on the other hand, compare the *Melcumani* of + 18/43, which can hardly be Celtic, and *Maniai* in Arcadia in the Peloponnese (58unl).

+ 16/42 —

+ 17/43 —[210]

+ 17/42 —

+ 18/43 —

---

[201] Thurneysen, 'Etymologien', p. 13; Vendryes, 'Note', p. 646 (equivocal); LEIA s.v. *ara* 'tempe'; DLG s.v. *araus(i)o-*; Falileyev, '*Tylis*', p. 130 ('possibly but not necessarily Celtic').

[202] Cf. GPN, pp. 58–59; DLG s.v. *blando-* 'doux'. Falileyev, '*Tylis*', p. 131, and in his review of DLG, p. 284, is doubtful. Whether *Bland-* is Celtic is uncertain (it is 'auch lateinisch' even to Holder i, 446, cf. iii, 883–85, and García Alonso, *Península Ibérica*, p. 179); I did not count + 23/46 *Blandiana* in Dacia and + 2/41 *Blanda(e)* on the coast of Spain as Celtic above. Holder ii, 1396 includes *Scardona* but see Anreiter, *Die vorrömischen Namen Pannoniens*, pp. 175–76, and Falileyev, '*Tylis*', p. 129. On *Tit(i)us fl.* (cf. *Titos fl.* at -4/48 = 7C3) cf. Holder ii, 1862, KGP, pp. 278–79, and Falileyev, '*Tylis*', p. 128.

[203] *Korkyra Melaina* is in fact at + 16/42.

[204] Holder i, 147; cf. DLG s.v. *and-* ; Falileyev, '*Tylis*', p. 132.

[205] Holder ii, 1903 (not accepted by Falilyev, '*Tylis*', p. 133); references in LEIA s.vv; DLG s.v. *traget-*, and see on *Tragisa(mus) fl.* at + 15/48 in Ch. 6 above, p. 189. On the other hand compare *Tragos fl.* in Arcadia (58C2 = + 22/37) and *Tragion* a little further south in Messenia (58unl). *Salona* could come from Celtic **sal-* 'salt', but this IE root is widespread.

[206] Holder i, 1444; but Falileyev, '*Tylis*', p. 129, objects that this is unlikely in view of names like *Epidaurum* (+ 18/43).

[207] For this element (but not this example) see AILR and PNPG Celtic Elements s.v. *pito-*. It may occur in the Welsh promontory *Octapitarum* (Sims-Williams, 'Measuring Celticity', p. 282), although Pokorny (cited in PNRB, p. 430) derives this from an 'Illyrian' *pit* 'fir-tree' (Greek *pítus*, Albanian *piše*).

[208] See index to the *Atlas*.

[209] According to the etymology of De Bernardo Stempel, 'Ptolemy's Celtic Italy and Ireland', p. 91 (cf. Lambert, '*Lugdunensis*', p. 225, and PNPG Celtic Elements s.v. *mano-* and Possibly Celtic Elements s.v. *ceno-* and {ce:no-}). For forms in *-man* see GPN, p. 223, and DLG s.v. *manos*.

[210] *Novae* in the same area as the *Manioi* could be Celtic (see + 25/43 below).

+ 18/42 —
+ 19/43 —
+ 19/42 —
+ 20/43 —
+ 20/42 —[211]
+ 21/43 —. *Horreum Margi* cannot be counted as certainly Celtic (see on *Margus fl.* in Chapter 7 above, + 21/44) and *Timachi* is also unlikely to be Celtic.[212]

+ 21/42 —. **'Vindenis'** in the Latin sources is *Ouendenis* in Ptolemy (3.9.4).[213] The closest form among putative Celtic *windo-* names is **Vindenates** (or *Vindinates*) in Umbria (+ 12/43 above); however, Duridanov connects **'Vindenis'** with Albanian *vënd* 'place, country'.[214] The very next *polis* to *Ouendenis* in Ptolemy 3.9.4 is *Ouellanis*, which recalls Celtic names in *Vellauno-*; however, Müller equates this with *Beclano* and *Viciano* in the Latin sources (*'Vicianum'* in the *Atlas*), implying a non-Celtic **Veclano* or similar.[215]

+ 22/43 —. *Serdoi* has been regarded as Celtic, but this is questionable,[216] and **Ratiaria** probably derives from Latin *ratis* 'raft' rather than Celtic **ratis* 'fern' (which in any case entered Latin as a loanword), although compare 25H3 *Iuncaria* (+ 2/42) < Latin *iuncus* 'reed'.[217] *Remesiana* is sometimes related to the Celtic ethnonym *Remi*, but this remains uncertain.[218]

+ 22/42 Two unlocated names which can be added are 22unl *Kasibonon* and *Loukounanta* (see Chapter 4 s.vv. *bon-* (footnote) and *nantu-*). *Meldia* is

---

[211] If *Gabuleum* (*Gabuleo* in TP and *Gebulion* in Rav. 206.6) is connected with Celtic, it would probably be via Latin (cf. Grzega, p. 173; and above, Ch. 7, n. 40). It is an 'Illyrian' cognate of Gaulish *gabalos* according to Pokorny, cited in DLG s.v.; similarly Papazoglu, pp. 248 and 251. Cf. VCIE, p. 459.

[212] Named by Pliny (3.149) only, and clearly deriving from *Timac(h)us* at + 22/44 in Ch. 7 above (TIR L-34, p. 111); cf. *auxiliarii Timacenses* in ND, Or. IX 40, cited by Müller, p. 455, also *Timacum Maius* and *Timacum Minus* at + 22/43 (the /a/ is not marked as long in PNPG). Perhaps 'Triballian' according to Papazoglu, p. 71; other theories in Beševliev, p. 115, and Mihailov, 'Le suffixe *-sk-* en thrace', p. 151. Duridanov, 'Sprachspuren', p. 136, does not accept *Naissus*; cf. Papazoglu, pp. 248, 251 and 370.

[213] TIR K-34, p. 132; Papazoglu, pp. 201, n. 214, 250 and 251, n. 299.

[214] 'Thrakische und dakische Namen', p. 833. But *vënd* may be < **wen-ta*.

[215] Müller, p. 455; cf. TIR K-34, p. 131 (not mentioning Ptolemy) and Papazoglu, pp. 201, n. 214, and 250.

[216] Duridanov, 'Sprachspuren', p. 138; Falileyev, '*Tylis*', p. 118. The name of the (non-Celtic) *Triballi* (= *Triballoi* at + 21/42), first mentioned by Thucydides, might suggest OI *ball* 'limb' (cf. on + 8/42 **Ouiriballon Akron**, p. 251 above), and indeed the name was anciently associated with the Greek cognate *phallos*; however, the segmentation (*tri-* or *trib-*?) and language remain obscure; see Papazoglu, pp. 71–73, 81–86 and 664; Duridanov, 'Thrakische und dakische Namen', p. 836; De Bernardo Stempel, 'Ptolemy's evidence for Germania Superior', p. 76; Falileyev, '*Tylis*', p. 122. A curious parallel occurs in the Middle Irish *Bórama* (ed. Stokes, pp. 66–67) where a hill called *Tréball* is said to be named from 'three members', the penis and two testicles.

[217] Cf. DLG s.v. *ratis*; Grzega, p. 220. Duridanov, 'Sprachspuren', p. 132, n. 3, favours Latin (similarly PNPG Comments s.n. *Rhaitiaría Musôn*).

[218] Cf. Duridanov, 'Sprachspuren', pp. 132 and 136; DLG s.v. *remos*; Zimmer in *RGermAlt* s.n. *Remer*; Papazoglu, pp. 249 and 251; and Falileyev & Isaac, 'Remetodia', n. 13.

probably not Celtic.[219] *'Anausaro'* (TP) may contain a Celtic **anauo-*, but this is very uncertain.[220]

+23/43 *Remetodia* is probably Celtic, though it has also been regarded as Thracian.[221] *Regianum* could be Celtic, but is not distinctively so.[222]

+23/42 —. *Serdica* is unlikely to be Celtic (see +22/43 above) and the idea that *Burgaraca* has a Celtic suffix added to Latin *burgarii* is very hypothetical.[223]

+24/43 *Oescus fl.* and *Oescus*.[224]

+24/42 —[225]

+25/43 —[226]

+25/42 —

+26/43 Only **Mediolanum**[227] and allegedly **Abritus**.[228]

+26/42 A name which may belong here is 22unl *Orkelis* (Ptolemy 3.11.7) < **(p)orko-* 'pig(?)', although Müller suggests that it may be corrupt for **Orestis* and refer to *Hadrianoupolis* (51H1 = +26/41).[229]

+27/43 —

+27/42 —. **Mesembria** should be compared with +25/40 **Mesambria** and +28/41 **Sely(m)bria**,[230] also +50/28 *Mesambrie?* in Persia (94A5). With

---

[219] Duridanov, 'Sprachspuren', p. 138; AILR and PNPG Possibly Celtic Elements s.v. *meldo-*. Cf. Beševliev, p. 23; Lambert, '*Lugdunensis*', p. 228.

[220] TIR K-34, p. 15, and Papazoglu, p. 246; cf. DLG and PNPG Possibly Celtic Elements s.v. **anauo-* and comments on pp. 200 and 211 above on +11/46 *Anaunion* and +18/47 *Anauon*.

[221] Duridanov, 'Sprachspuren', p. 134; Falileyev & Isaac, 'Remetodia' (cf. GPN, p. 373, and DLG s.v. *remos*).

[222] PNPG Celtic Elements s.v. *rego(s)-*.

[223] Cf. Duridanov, 'Sprachspuren', p. 138; Beševliev, p. 20. See Ch. 12 on *burgus* names.

[224] Assuming o-grade of Celtic **(p)eisk-* 'fish' (see s.v. *iscā* in Ch. 4 above). However, Falileyev, '*Tylis*', p. 123, lists *Oiskos Triballon* as 'non-Celtic'. Cf. Falileyev, 'Celtic presence in Dobrudja'. Papazoglou, pp. 65–66 and 71, treats it as 'Triballian'. *Oitensioi?* may be Celtic: PNPG Possibly Celtic Elements s.v. *oeto-*.

[225] On *Lissas* (22unl) near Bessapara see n. 238 below.

[226] *Dimum* is *Diakon* in Ptolemy 3.10.5, which has been considered Celtic but seems to be a mere error (Falileyev, *Vostocnije Balkany na karte Ptolemeya*, and PNPG Comments s.n.). *Novae* (cf. *Novae* at +17/43) could be Celtic but is not distinctively so (Falileyev, '*Tylis*', p. 123), and the same goes for *Trimammium* (cf. AILR and PNPG Celtic Elements s.v. {mamma:-}).

[227] 'Between Trimammium [22C5] and Appiaria [22D5]' (*Map-by-Map Directory* i, 345). This is based on the order in which troops are listed in ND, Or. XL (p. 90). It could lie at +25/43.

[228] KGP, pp. 108–9, under *Ab-*. Cf. GPN, pp. 134 and 431. The literary sources vary between *t* and *tt* and have various vowels, but *Abrit-* is well supported epigraphically: Ivanov & Stojanov, *Abritus*, pp. 5–10.

[229] Duridanov, 'Sprachspuren', p. 139; Falileyev, '*Tylis*', pp. 113 and 119–20; DLG s.v. *orco-*; Müller, p. 482. (Tovar, *Tarraconensis*, p. 160, compares *Orkelis* in Spain, above, p. 231, n. 49.) Ptolemy places *Orkelis* 1 degree east and 20 minutes south of *Opisena*, which is tentatively identified in *Map-by-Map Directory* i, 345, with *Pizus* (22C6 = +25/42). *(H)adrianoupolis* was associated with the name of the Thracian tribe *Odrysai*, whence names like *Orestiada* for it: TIB-6, p. 161.

[230] See below, pp. 263 and 269.

	+ 15	+ 16	+ 17	+ 18	
43	20C6 Arausa Blandona Boulinoi Celadussae Inss. Colentum Ins. Diomedis Pr. Hyllis Pr. Scardona Tit(i)us fl. /Katarbates fl. Varvaria	20D6 Ad Dianam Adrion M. Aequum **Andetrium** Bova Ins. Brattia Ins. Bulsinius M. Delmatae Epetium Hylloi In Alperio Issa Ins. Manioi Manios Kolpos Nestoi Nestos fl./ Hippius fl. Olunta Ins./ Sollentia Ins. Oneum *Osinium Pelva Pharus Pharus Ins. Pituntium Pons Tiluri Promona Rider Salon fl. Salona Setovia Siculi Spalatum Synodion/Magnum Tambia Tauris Ins. Tilurium Tragurium 'Trono'	20E6 *Ad Libros* *Ad Turres* *Ardiaei/* *Vardaei* *'Aufustianis'* *Autariatae* *Bariduum* *Bathiatai* *Bigeste* *Biston?* *Bistua Vetus* *Delminium* *Deraemistae* *Deretini* *Diluntum* *In Monte* *Bulsinio* *'Laurento'* *Muccurum* *Naresii* *Naro fl.* *Narona* *Novae*	20F6 *Aquae S(…)* *Glinditiones* *Melcumani*	43
42	45 inset *Diomedeae Inss.* *Trimerus Ins.*	20D7 *Corcyra* *Nigra Ins.* *Diomedeae Inss.* *Korkyra Melaina* *Ladesta Ins.*	20E7 *Daorsi* *Elaphites Inss.* *Haemasi* *Melite Ins.* *Stagnum*	20F7 *'Ad Zizio'?* **Agruvium* *Anderva* *Asamum* *Enchelei* *Endirudini/Interphrourinoi?* *Epidaurum* *'Leusinio'* *Pardua* *Plana* *Pleraei* *Rhizon/Risinium* *Rhizonicus Sinus* *Salthua* 49A1 *Bouthoe*	42
	+ 15	+ 16	+ 17	+ 18	

	+19	+20	+21	+22	+23	
43	20G6 *Ris(…)* 21B6 **Malves(i)a* *S(…)*	21C6 *Cel(…)* *Celegeri* *Dard(…)* 1H2 *Moesia* *Superior*	21D6 *Ad Fines* *Ad Herculem* 'Cametas' *Dasmin(i)um/* *Praesidium* *Dasmini* *Gramrianae/* *Rampiana* *Hammeum* *Horreum* *Margi* *Naissus* *Praesidium* *Pompei* *Sarmates* *Timachi*	21E6 *Ballanstra* *Castra Martis* *Combustica* *Latina* *Mediana* **Radices* **Ratiaria** *Remesiana* *Romuliana* *Serdoi* *Timacum Maius* *Timacum Minus* 'Translitis' *Triballi* *Turres* 'Ulmo'	21F6 Almus Almus fl. Augusta fl. Cebrus Kebros fl. Montana Pomodiana/ Cumodina Remetodia Tautiomosis Vorovum Minor 22A5 Augustae Regianum Variana Vicus 'Bapeni'	43
42	49B1 *Ad Picaria(s)* *[Antibaris]* *Clausala fl.* *Doclea* *(H)Alata/* *Alata* *Labeatae* *Labeatis L.* *Meteon* *Pirustae* *Salluntum* *Scirtari* *Scodra* 'Varis'	49C1 *Creveni* *Dardania/* *Dardani* **Gabuleum* *Theranda*	21D7 *Iustiniana* *Prima* **'Vindenis'** 49D1 *Scupi* *Triballoi* *Ulpiana* 'Vicianum' *Vizi(…)*	21E7 *Ad Fines* *Meldia* 49E1 *Agrianes* 'Anausaro' Aquae? *Dentheletai* **Karistoron* *Laiaioi* Messapion M. *Pautalia* *Spinopara* *Tranupara* {22unl Kasibonon} {Loukounanta}	21F7 *Scretisca* *Serdica* 49F1 *Burgaraca* Dounax M. **Egerica* 'Extuomne' *Germania* *Helice* *Scaptopara* Skombros M. *Soneio* *Sparata* *Sportela* 22A6 *Succorum* *Angustiae*	42
	+19	+20	+21	+22	+23	

	+ 24	+ 25	+ 26	+ 27	+ 28	
43	**22B5** Ad Putea Asamus Asamus fl. Doriones Giridava Melta Oescus <u>Oescus fl.</u> <u>Oitensioi?</u> Pedonianis Pons Constantini Securisca Storgosia Sucidava Utus Utus fl. ValerianaVicus Longinopara Vicus Siamus Vicus Trullensium	**22C5** *Athrys fl./* *Iatros* *fl./Ieterus fl.* *Dimum/* *Dimenses* *Emporium* *Discoduraterae* *Emporium* *Piretensium* *Iatrus* *Nicopolis* *ad Istrum* *Novae* *Sexaginta Prista* *Trimammium*	**22D5** **Abritus** <u>Appiaria/</u> Appiarienses Tegris/Tegra 22unl <u>**Mediolanum**</u>	**22E5** *Erite/Ereta* *Krobyzoi* *'Locidae Regi'* *Marcianopolis* *Odessus* *Palmatis* *Pannissus* *Panysos fl.*	**22F5** *Bizone* *Callatis* *Dionysopolis* */Krounoi* *Gerania* *Karon Limen?* *Tirizis* *Tirizis Pr.*	43
42	**22B6** *Ad Radices* *Bessapara* *Bessi* *Diocletianopolis* *Moesia Inferior* *'Monte Haemo'* *Philippopolis/* *Trimontium* *Sernota* *Sostra* *Sub Radices* *Viamata*	**22C6** *Arzus* *Beroe/* *Augusta* *Traiana* *Carassura* *Celaletae* *Maiores* *Cillis?* *Haemus M.* *Parambole* *Pizus* *Pyrogeri* *Seuthopolis* *Tylis*	**22D6** Kabyle/ Diospolis/ Cabyleti Odrysae {22unl <u>Orkelis</u>}	**22E6** *Anchialus* *Apollonia* *Pontica/* *Sozopolis* *Aquae* *Calidae* *Aristaeum* *Aulaiouteichos/* *Agathopolis* *'Cazalet'?* *Chersonesos* *Deultum* *Haemi Pr.* *Koralloi* ***Mesembria*** *Naulochos/* *Templum* *Iovis?/* *Tetranaulochus* *Scatrae* *Sialetae*		42
	+ 24	+ 25	+ 26	+ 27	+ 28	

their /m/ rather than composition vowel,[231] these are not plausible Celtic compounds of Celtic *-bria* (whether < *-briga* or *-briva*). Since Strabo (7.6.1), **Mesembria** and **Sely(m)bria** have been supposed to contain a Thracian word *bria* 'polis', completely unrelated to the Celtic words.[232] Compare also **Thymbria** (61unl = +27/37) and **Salambriai** (63E4 = + 34/38) in Asia Minor (see Chapter 9 below). + 28/43 —[233]

(k) The Balkan peninsula below latitude 42, Greece and Crete

The Celtic-looking names on Maps 5.1–5.3 are scarce, especially considering the hundreds of known toponyms, and are probably due to coincidence or to the presence of cognates in Greek and other Indo-European languages of the rather restricted number of Celtic-looking strings in question (the strings BOUD, (-)BRIA, KARN, KOT and SID dominate).[234] The following list shows the Celtic-looking names arranged from north to south (there were no unlocatable ones omitted from Maps 5.1–5.3):

51	B2	+23	41	Odomantes	Odomantike	
52	C2	+28	41	Sely(m)**bria**	Eudoxiopolis	
52	C2	+28	41	Sely(m)**bria**	Eudoxiopolis	
50	A3	+21	40	Begor**ritus** L.		
50	A4	+21	40	**Camb**unii M.		
51	B4	+23	40	Ass(er)a?	Asseros	**Cass**era
51	B3	+23	40	**Penn**ana		
51	F3	+25	40	Mesam**bria**		
51	F3	+25	40	Mesam**bria**		
55	F2	+23	39	**Ikos**		
54	C4	+20	38	**Karn**os Ins.		
54	D4	+21	38	**Medion**		
55	C3	+22	38	**Side**		
55	*unl*	*+23*	*38*	**Boud**(e)ion	**Boud**(e)ia	
55	E3	+23	38	**Boudoros** fl.		
55	E3	+23	38	**Boudor**os fl.		
55	F3	+23	38	**Kot**ylaion M.		
55	*unl*	*+23*	*38*	**Sid**ous		
55	G3	+24	38	**Kot**ylaion		

[231] Although note *Conimbriga* (−9/40).
[232] On etymologies of *Mesembria* see Mihailov, *Inscriptiones Graecae in Bulgaria Repertae*, i, pp. 307–8, and Falileyev, *Vostocnije Balkany na karte Ptolemeya*. On *bria* see IEW, p. 1152, Katičić, *Ancient Languages of the Balkans,* p. 139, Duridanov, 'Sprachspuren', p. 133, n. 5, and Ch. 1 above, p. 14.
[233] *Callatis* is *Callacis* in AI 227.4, but that is clearly corrupt as the other sources have *t* (Holder i, 701 lists *Callatis* as Greek; cf. PNPG Possibly Celtic Elements s.v. *callo-*).
[234] On **Cambunii M.** and '**Ketia**'? **Pr.** see Ch. 3 above. **Ikos** can be compared with *Iconium* in Anatolia (p. 282 below), *Ikarion* in Attica (+23/38 = 55F4/58F1/59C2) and, in the Aegean, *Ikaros/Ikaria Ins.* (61C2) and *Ikarion Mare* (61C3). Note also 93E4 *E-kara/Icarus Ins.* in Kuwait!

58	B3	+21	37	**Karn**asion	
58	B3	+21	37	**Kot**ilion M.	
58	*unl*	*+21*	*37*	**Kot**ilon	
58	*unl*	*+21*	*37*	**Lang**on	
58	*unl*	*+22*	*37*	**Karn**eates M.	
58	C3	+22	37	**Karn**ion fl.	
58	*unl*	*+22*	*37*	**Lank**ia	
58	C2	+22	37	**Mant**ineia	Antigoneia
58	*unl*	*+22*	*37*	**Rhat**iai	
59	A3	+23	37	**Boud**oron	
59	A3	+23	37	Boudoron	
58	*unl*	*+23*	*37*	**Korn**iata M.	
59	*unl*	*+23*	*37*	**Sid**ertos	
58	E2	+23	37	**Sid**ous	
58	*unl*	*+22*	*36*	**Karn**ion	
58	D4	+22	36	**Kot**yrta	
58	E5	+23	36	**Side**	
60	G3	+28	36	**Lind**os	**Lind**ia
65	C4	+29	36	**Kib**y**ratis**	
65	B5	+29	36	**Sid**yma	
65	C5	+29	36	**Treb**endai	
60	B2	+24	35	**Boud**roe Inss.	
60	C2	+24	35	**Kor**ion	
60	F2	+26	35	'Ket**ia'? Pr.	
60	F2	+26	35	**Sed**amnos? fl.	

In Greece *Boud-* presumably derives from Greek *bous* 'cow'. Incidentally, the same must apply to *Boioi* and *Boion M.* (49C3 = +20/40) in Illyricum, *Boia(i)/Boea* (58E4 = +23/36) in Laconia, *Boion* (55C3 = +22/38) in Thessaly and *Boiai* (60unl) in Crete; if connected at all with the Celtic tribal name *Boii* it must be as cognate descendants of IE **g^wow-yo-s*.[235] *Karn-* appears to be widespread and not exclusively Celtic.[236] The string (-)BRIA (actually -MBRIA here) has been discussed *under* (j) above.[237] KOT- and SID- mostly occur in examples of Greek κοτυλ- 'hollow' and σιδ- 'pomegranate'. Overall, there seem to be no plausible traces of Celtic in the above list, nor in the other located and unlocated names from the area.[238]

---

[235] See Ch. 5 above, p. 169. Compare *Boione* (56unl) in Asia Minor and *Boion* (87 inset unl) in the Crimea. Cf. Katičić, *Ancient Languages of the Balkans*, p. 123; McCone, 'Werewolves', p. 11; Koch, 'Brân, Brennos', p. 13; Anreiter, *Die vorrömischen Namen Pannoniens*, p. 157, n. 578. An alternative etymology of *Boii* is 'cutters, slayers' (ibid. p. 157; AILR and PNPG Celtic Elements s.v. *boio-*; KPP, pp. 222–23). Multiple origin for names like *Boioi* is supposed by Schwarz, *Ortsnamen der Sudetenländer*, p. 35.

[236] Anreiter, *Die vorrömischen Namen Pannoniens*, p. 47, n. 191, citing Bonfante, 'Il problema dei Taurisci e dei Carni'. See Ch. 4 s.v. *carno-*.

[237] Above, p. 258.

[238] The same conclusion was reached by Dr E. R. Luján in the Madrid 'Ptolemy' workshop. DLG s.v. *lissos* (: W. *llys*, OI *less*) includes *Lissos* in Dalmatia (49B2 = +19/41). While the etymology seems not impossible here and in the case of *Lissas* (22unl = +24/42) in Moesia Inferior (AI 136.2), we must also compare *Lissos* in Crete (60A2), *Lissos fl.* in Sicily (47unl), *Lissa* in Lycia (65A4 = +28/36) and Africa (28unl, p. 284 below) and *Lissa Ins.* (20C5 = +15/44) in Dalmatia itself. *Lissos* may often be Greek. Cf. PNPG Possibly Celtic Elements s.v. *lisso-*.

A tantalizing exception in Macedonia is *Klitai* (50C3) at +22/40, which has
an attractive Celtic etymology (cf. OI *cleth*, ā-stem, f., 'concealment', Welsh
clyd 'shelter'),[239] and is only a few miles from a place called *Gallicum*
(identified as Philadelphiana in the *Atlas*).[240] This may well be a coincidence,
however, as there was another *Klitai* further south in Macedonia, near
Kassandreia (50D4 = +23/39),[241] and yet another near Bithynion (86B3 =
+31/40) in Asia Minor.[242]

[239] PNPG Celtic Elements s.v. {clita:-}, with reference to the *Klitai* in Ptolemy 5.1.3, not in the
Atlas but in the region of Bithynion (86B3 = +31/40). It is not in Zgusta. Note also DLG
s.v. *clitos*, *clita*, 'pillar'.

[240] This *Klitai* is first attested *c.* 200 BC and *Gallicum* appears in TP. See Papazoglou, *Villes de
Macédoine*, pp. 18–19, 175–76, 184–85, and 224–25, who also discusses the locations. She
notes that the origin of the name *Gallicum* is obscure (the form *Callicum* being preferred by
some and being said to be a 'Thracian' word for 'slime'), and that it is unclear whether it
derives from *Gallikos*, the medieval name of the river on which it must have stood (the
ancient *Echeidoros*), or vice versa.

[241] Livy 44.11.4 (*Clitas* (acc. pl.)), Ptolemy 3.12.35; not in the *Atlas* (unless = 50D4 *Kithas*, cf.
Müller, p. 516), but cited by Papazoglou, *Villes de Macédoine*, pp. 19, n. 26, and 185, n. 77.

[242] See above, n. 239.

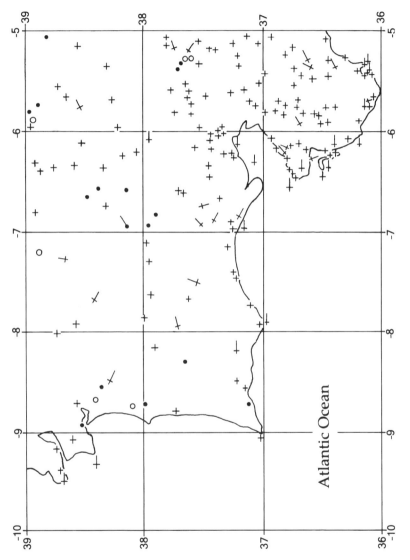

Map 8.1   The limits of Celtic names in south-western Iberia

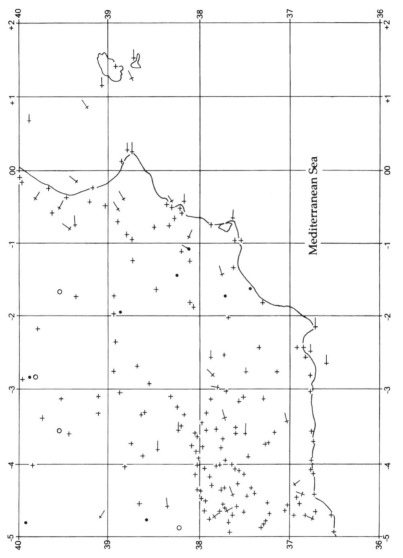

Map 8.2   The limits of Celtic names in south-eastern Iberia

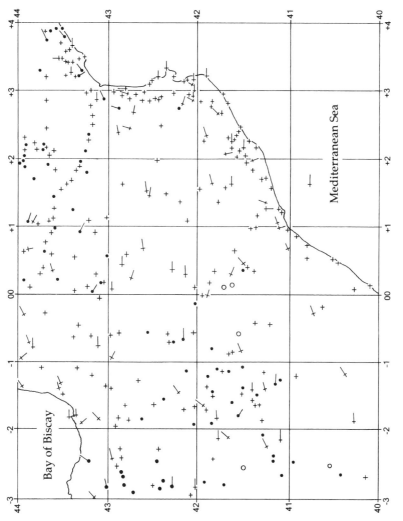

Map 8.3   The limits of Celtic names in north-eastern Iberia and the Pyrenees

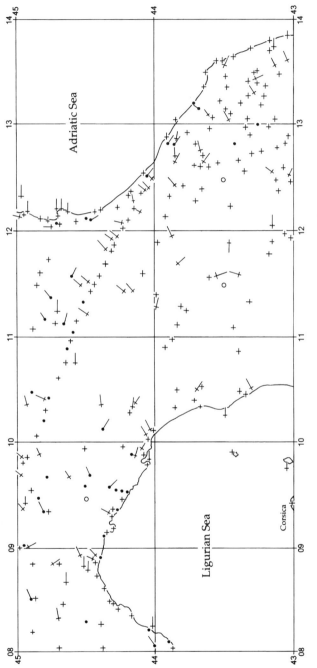

Map 8.4   The southern limits of Celtic names in Italy

9

THE EXTENT OF CELTIC NAMES, IV: ASIA MINOR (WEST OF LONGITUDE +35) WITH V: NOTE ON REMAINING AREAS AROUND THE MEDITERRANEAN (NORTH OF LATITUDE 35 AND WEST OF LONGITUDE +35)

As in the preceeding chapters, *italics* are used in the tables of names to denote squares devoid of Celtic names, names in **bold** are the 'Celtic-looking' names from Table 5.2 and underlining indicates probably Celtic names.

(a) Asia Minor west of longitude +29

The Celtic-looking names on Maps 5.1–5.3 are very scarce relative to the number of known toponyms, and as in Greece are probably due either to coincidence or to the presence of cognates in Greek and other Indo-European languages[1] of the rather restricted number of Celtic-looking strings in question (note that the strings (-)BRIA, KAMB, KARN, KET, KOT and SID reappear here).[2] The following list shows the Celtic-looking names arranged from north to south:

52	C2	+28	41	Sely(m)**bria**	Eudoxiopolis
56	D2	+26	39	**Kot**ylos M.	
56	*unl*	*+27*	*39*	**Kam**(br)e	
56	E3	+27	39	**Ket**eios fl.	
56	*unl*	*+27*	*39*	**Sag**ara	
62	A3	+28	39	***Sit**tena?	
56	D4	+26	38	**Sid**oussa? Ins.	
61	E3	+27	37	Hali**carn**assus	
61	*unl*	*+27*	*37*	Thym**bria**	

Sely(m)bria and **Thymbria** are not to be connected with Celtic *bri(g)a* or *bri(v)a*, as opposed perhaps to 'Thracian' *bria*, as discussed above.[3] **Thymbria** invites comparison with *Thymbras Pedion, Thymbrios fl.* and

---

[1] Cf. Luján, 'Galatian place names', p. 258.
[2] See preceding section. On **Kam(br)e** and **Keteios fl.** see Ch. 3 above.
[3] Above, p. 26, and see below on **Bria** at +29/38. Cf. Zgusta, p. 127.

Thymbra (all at 56C2 = +26/39) near Troy and 62unl *Thymbrion* in the vicinity of Tyriaion (62G5 = +31/38).[4]

In addition, there are a few names which might be regarded as Celtic if they appeared in Britain or Gaul but are hardly plausible here owing to their relative scarcity and the linguistic context provided by the majority of names: *Ambonium* (cf. Gaulish *ambe* 'river?');[5] *Gargara* and *Gargara Akron* (cf. OI *garg* 'ferocious');[6] *Samonion Pedion* (cf. Gaulish month-name *Samonios*, but also *Sam(m)onion Pr.* in Crete, Map 60F2!);[7] *Ollius fl.* (cf. W *oll*, OI *uile*, Gaulish *Ollo-* 'great, all');[8] *Boione* and *Boukolion* (resembling Celtic derivatives of the IE word for 'cow', but here presumably cognates in Greek, which shared the Celtic development of $*g^w > *b$);[9] *Kouara?* (cf. Gaulish *Co-* 'with' and *var-* 'water');[10] *Caunus* (cf. Gaulish personal name, but also Greek *kaunos* 'estate');[11] *Tragia* on the island of Naxos (cf. Gaulish names in *Trag-*);[12] *Samos* and *Samos Ins.* (cf. OI *sam*, W *haf*, 'summer');[13] *Gaison? fl.* and *Gaisonis L.* (cf. Gallo-Latin *gaesum* 'spear', OI *gae*, W *gwaew*);[14] *Orkatos* on the island of Kalymna (cf. OI *orc* 'pig').[15] In the following list they are interspersed with the names in bold repeated from above:

52	C2	+28	41	Sely(m)**bria**	Eudoxiopolis
56	unl	+27	40	Ambonium	
56	D2	+26	39	Gargara	
56	D2	+26	39	Gargara Akron	
56	C2	+26	39	Samonion Pedion	
56	unl	+26	39	Ollius fl.	
56	D2	+26	39	**Kot**ylos M.	
56	unl	+27	39	**Kam(br)**e	
56	E3	+27	39	**Ket**eios fl.	
56	unl	+27	39	**Sagara**	
62	A3	+28	39	*Sittena?	
56	unl	+26	38	Boione	
56	D4	+26	38	**Sid**oussa? Ins.	

---

[4] Ibid. p. 189. Cf. Freeman, *Galatian Language*, pp. 83 and 87, on the river *Tymbris/Tembris* at +30/39 below.

[5] DLG s.v.

[6] Ibid. s.v. *gargo-* and Ch. 8 above on +5/43 *Gargarius*. Zgusta, p. 134, thinks it Greek and onomatopoeic as in *gargarizô* 'gargle'.

[7] DLG s.v. Cf. Zgusta, p. 531.

[8] DLG s.v. *ollos*; De Bernardo Stempel, 'Continental Celtic *ollo*'.

[9] LEIA s.v. *buachail(l)*; cf. p. 263, n. 235 above on *Boione*.

[10] GPN, pp. 184–85, and DLG s.v. *treuero-*.

[11] DLG s.v. *counos* (cf. review by Billy, p. 281, and on Middle Irish *cúanna* see LEIA s.v. 1 *cúan*); CIB, pp. 85 and 199; Zgusta, p. 242. See also on *Kaunoi* in Mauretania below, Ch. 10.

[12] See Ch. 8, n. 205 above (with parallels in Arcadia etc.!).

[13] DLG s.v. *samo-*.

[14] DLG s.v. *gaiso-*.

[15] See DLG s.v. *orco-* and p. 178, n. 6 above, also below on *Orkistos* etc.

56	F5	+ 27	38	Boukolion
62	A4	+ 28	38	Kouara?
65	A4	+ 28	38	Caunus
61	*unl*	+ 25	37	Tragia
61	D2	+ 26	37	Samos
61	D2	+ 26	37	Samos Ins.
61	E2	+ 27	37	Gaison? fl.
61	*unl*	+ 27	37	Gaisonis L.
61	E3	+ 27	37	Hali**carn**assus
61	*unl*	+ 27	37	Thym**bria**
61	*unl*	+ 26	36	Orkatos

A clearly Celtic ethnonym, omitted in the *Barrington Atlas*, presumably because so transient, is that of the *Aegosages*, who crossed the Hellespont in 218 BC and settled briefly in the Troad. They laid siege to Ilium in 217/16 and were massacred soon afterwards.[16] Neither they nor any other of the Celts who passed through western Asia Minor seem to have left any certain trace in the toponymy, as we have seen.[17] It is hard to be convinced by Sergent's comparison of *Artace/Artake Ins.*, *Poimanenon* and *Dolionis* (all at 52B4 = + 27/40) with Celtic **artos* 'bear', with the *Paemani/Caemani* of Germania (+ 5/50) and with two places called *Dolus* in medieval France (modern *Déols* and *Dolus*).[18]

(b) Asia Minor between + 29° and + 36° and north of 38 latitude

In the following discussion and tables I omit the numerous names in the vicinity of the Bosphorus in squares + 29/41 and + 29/40. None of them has any Celtic appearance, with exception of *Bebrykes* (*Bebrúkôn* in some manuscripts of Ptolemy 5.1.13 (Nobbe's edition)), an ethnic name which has been derived from Celtic **bebros*, **bebrus*, 'beaver'.[19] While the comparison may be valid, the name does not have to be Celtic since the word occurs in various Indo-European languages.[20]

---

[16] Mitchell, *Anatolia*, i, 22; Tomaschitz, *Wanderungen*, pp. 175–79; Haywood, *Historical Atlas*, pp. 40–41; Freeman, *Galatian Language*, p. 65; DLG s.v. *sag(i)-*.

[17] At + 28/40 *Arganthoneion Mons* (52D3) has been regarded as Celtic (e.g. Sergent, 'Les premiers Celtes d'Anatolie', pp. 348 and 351; DLG s.v. *arganton*) but this is rejected by Weisgerber, 'Sprachreste', p. 159, n. 2.

[18] Sergent, 'Les premiers Celtes d'Anatolie', pp. 331 and 347–48; 332–33; and 335 respectively. On names in *Art-* cf. below, p. 286, n. 2. Nègre ii §§ 10863 and 14584 implausibly derives *Dolus* and *Déols* (Holder i, 1302) from respectively Roman and Germanic personal names, *Dolutius* and *Dodilus*. Better comparisons are W *dail* 'leaves, herbs' (cf. DLG s.v. *dola*) or W *dôl* 'meadow, valley'.

[19] DLG s.v. *bebros*, following Sergent, 'Les premiers Celtes d'Anatolie', pp. 346–47, who admits that the name is usually considered Thracian (p. 331). Cf. Müller, p. 800, note on line 6, and Katičić, *Ancient Languages of the Balkans*, p. 140.

[20] Duridanov, 'Thrakisch und dakische Namen', p. 829; IEW, p. 136; PNRB, p. 268; PNPG Possibly Celtic Elements s.v. *bebro-*.

+29/39 Besides **Mantalos**, at a major road intersection, which is recognized as a possibly Celtic name meaning 'road' (although Zgusta notes Greek *mandalos* 'doorbolt'),[21] and **Kotiaeion**, which is much less certain,[22] the ethnonym *Dagoutenoi* could perhaps contain Celtic *dago-* 'good'.[23]

+29/38 The Celtic-looking ***Lankena**[24] and **Sagarenoi?**[25] (distinct from the same ethnonym at +30/39 below) are very isolated and probably coincidental. Coincidence may also explain the similarity between *Bagis* and Gaulish **bagos* 'beech?'.[26] **Bria** is possibly another case of 'Thracian' *bria*.[27]

+30/41 —

+30/40 ***Kassa** is hardly Celtic,[28] and probably the same applies to:

+30/39 **Kassenoi**[29] and **Sagarenoi**.[30] *Tembris fl.* does not look Celtic, but the variant *Tembrogius* is well attested and appears Celtic or Celticized.[31] 62unl *Namantaloi?*, which appears Celtic, may also belong here.[32]

+30/38 *Beudos*/**Boudeia** is clearly non-Celtic.[33]

+31/41 —

+31/40 *Araunia* and *Balgatia* (also listed as 62unl *Valcaton*/*Balgatia*), both in the territory of the *Tolistobogii*, can perhaps be connected with the Old Welsh personal name *Araun*, Middle Welsh *Arawn*,[34] and with W

---

[21] DLG s.v. *mantalon* 'chemin'; Delamarre, 'Gallo-Brittonica', p. 128; Zgusta, pp. 29 and 366. Cf. *Map-by-Map Directory* ii, 972. See also 62unl *Mandalos* at +31/39 below.

[22] Zgusta, pp. 293–95, compares other place- and personal names in *Kot-* and Greek *kotos* 'grudge'.

[23] Not listed in GPN, pp. 188–89, nor DLG s.v. *dagos*. No etymology in Zgusta, pp. 146–47, who derives it from *Dagouta* in Ptolemy 5.2.13 (not in *Atlas*). Cf. p. 218 above on 22unl *Dagis* at +28/44, and Ch. 10 below on *Dagona* in eastern Anatolia.

[24] Better **Lanka*; see Zgusta, p. 330.

[25] Ibid. p. 524.

[26] Ibid. p. 113; DLG and PNPG Possibly Celtic Elements s.v.

[27] Zgusta, pp. 127–28 (under *Briana*, and comparing an unlocated *Briania* in Galatia).

[28] Ibid. p. 236. '*Cenon Gallicanon*'? (from AI 141.5) and *Gallos fl.* (cf. Müller's note, p. 801, on *Gallika*, Ptolemy 5.1.13) recall Latin *Gallus*, but on Greek *Gallos* see below, p. 273. Sergent, 'Les premiers Celtes d'Anatolie', pp. 345 and 357, suggested that the *Mariandunoi* (= 86A3 *Mariandynoi*) were Celtic.

[29] Zgusta, p. 236.

[30] Ibid. p. 524.

[31] Weisgerber, 'Sprachreste', p. 159; Zgusta, pp. 609–10; Mitchell, 'Population', p. 1059; Freeman, *Galatian Language*, pp. 80, 83 and 87.

[32] Not in GPN, p. 235. For the inscription ΝΑΜΑΝΤΑΛΟΝ, 'possibly ethnic of a village (Ναμαντανόν) [*sic*], in one of the churches of Alaca Asma in the region of Yazılıkaya (Map 62E3), see Haspels, *Highlands of Phrygia*, i, 328, and Zgusta, p. 419.

[33] Cf. *Boud(e)ia* in Greece, above p. 262, and Zgusta, p. 127. Note that *Aulutrene* is given twice in the *Map-by-Map Directory* for 62D5 but only once on the map.

[34] Cf. Schmidt, 'Sprachreste', p. 19, n. 18. No etymology in Zgusta, p. 88.

balch, OI *balc* 'proud' (although the *V*-variant is slightly troublesome) or with the name *Balgiaco* in a seventh-century French charter.[35] Ptolemy's region of *Bogdomanis* (situated below *Timonitis* = +31/41) belongs here and seems Celtic.[36] On the other hand, Ptolemy's *Klitai* (5.1.3), in the region of Bithynion, seems unlikely to be Celtic (cf. p. 264 above).

+31/39 While **Konsidiana Choria** is dubiously Celtic, *Tolastochora?* (also attested as *Toloscorio*) seems Celtic.[37] The *Trocnades* (whence the *Atlas*'s form **Trokna*) have been thought to have a Celtic name, although Weisgerber doubts this.[38] *Orkistos* may derive from Celtic *(*p*)*orko-* 'pig(?)'.[39] The same element may occur in 62unl *Orkaorkoi*, a people who lived in the vicinity.[40] Two names south-west of *Orkistos*, 62unl *Laginoi* and 62unl *Lagonia* invite comparison with Middle Irish *láigen* (f.) 'spear'.[41]

62unl *Mandalos*, in the western area of the *Trocnades*, may be a variant or Graecicized form of *Mantalos* 'road' (as at +29/39 above), or a derivative of *mandus* 'pony'.[42] Two further names, not in the *Barrington* data, which can be added here are [ ]*nobantenoi* and *Okondianoi*.[43] (*Gallos fl.* is not to be connected with *Gallus* 'Gaul' but with the homonymous Phrygian–Greek word for a priest of Cybele, as already stated by Pliny 5.147.)[44] The Celticity of *Germa* is very doubtful.[45]

+31/38 —

+32/41 —

---

[35] Cf. LEIA s.v. *balc*; Hamp, 'Morphology', p. 187; Zgusta, p. 115, citing Holder i, 336 (*Balgiacus*) and iii, 92 (*Valgas*, a Germanic(?) personal name).

[36] Ptolemy 5.1.3 (Müller, p. 800). Cf. PNPG Celtic Elements s.v. *mano-*, Possibly Celtic Elements s.v. *bogdo-* and Comments s.n., comparing *Robogdioi* in Ireland and *Mediobogdum* in Britain. See De Bernardo Stempel, 'More on Ptolemy's evidence for Celtic Ireland', p. 100.

[37] Freeman, *Galatian Language*, p. 87; Luján, 'Galatian place names', p. 259; cf. DLG s.v. *tolisto-* and PNPG Possibly Celtic Elements s.v. *tolasto-*, *tolisto-*.

[38] Freeman, *Galatian Language*, p. 76; Mitchell, *Anatolia*, i, 176; Zgusta, pp. 635–36; Weisgerber, 'Sprachreste', p. 159, n. 2. Perhaps compare the element **tro(u)g-*, **tro(u)c-* in GPN, pp. 381–82, and LEIA s.v. *trúag*, or PNPG Possibly Celtic Elements s.v. *trocmo-*.

[39] On this element in place-names see above, p. 178, n. 6. No etymology in Zgusta, p. 444.

[40] Mitchell, *Anatolia*, i, 54. Cf. Zgusta, p. 444.

[41] O'Rahilly, 'Mid. Ir. *lága*, *láige*. *lágan*, *láigen*'. But note **Lageina* at +31/38, as well as *Lagania* names at +32/39.

[42] For *nt* ~ *nd* cf. the personal name *Mandalonius* in DLG s.v. *mantalos*, unless this belongs s.v. *mandus* (as in GPN, p. 223). Cf. Zgusta, pp. 29 and 366.

[43] Mitchell, *Anatolia*, i, 50, n. 89, and 53; Freeman, *Galatian Language*, p. 66; Zgusta, p. 434.

[44] Kruta, *Celtes*, s.v. *Galli*. Cf. PNPG Comments s.n. *Gállika*.

[45] PNPG Comments s.n.; Luján, 'Galatian place names', p. 260; cf. Zgusta, pp. 135 and 138.

+ 32/40 Besides **Gezatorigis**,[46] **Mantineion, 'Petobrogen'** (recte *Ipetobrogen* ?),[47] **Tektosages**,[48] and (located here only approximately) **Drynemeton**,[49] add: **Artiknos* [recte *Chorion Artikniakon*],[50] *Bloukion*,[51] and **Ergobrotis* (also attested as *Erigobrogis*).[52] In this vicinity there may have been a place called **Souolibroga*.[53]

+ 32/39 Besides **Vindia?** (despite the question mark almost certainly located at Gordion)[54] and **Tectosages** again, add: *Tolistoagioi/Tolistobogioi*,[55] *Galatia* and *Gallograecia*,[56] *Gorbeus* (perhaps),[57] and *Orsologiakos/Rosolodiacus* (perhaps).[58]

+ 32/38 *Caballucome* could contain Gaulish *caballos* 'horse', but similar-looking forms are widespread, since *caballus* was current in Latin.[59] *Kongoustos/Congussus* appears to be a compound of Celtic **kom-* and **gustu-*, **gussu-* 'valour'.[60] (*Ouetissos/Ouetiston/Vetissus* is of uncertain Celticity.)[61]

+ 33/42 —

+ 33/41 **Bonita* is possibly Celtic, but isolated, and a Latin origin seems more likely (cf. Spanish *bonito* 'pretty'; 'striped tunny fish'??).[62] *Garios* on the coast is more likely to be connected with Greek *garos* 'fish(paste)' than OI *gáire* 'laugh' < **gārios*.[63] *Abonouteichos* ('wall of Abonos')

---

[46] Mitchell, *Anatolia*, i, 23 and 57. Genitive of a personal name **Gezatorix*.

[47] Freeman, *Galatian Language*, pp. 85–86; Müller, p. 802.

[48] Freeman, *Galatian Language*, pp. 67–69.

[49] Ibid. pp. 83–84; DLG s.v. *druid-* .

[50] Weisgerber, 'Sprachreste', p. 168; Freeman, *Galatian Language*, pp. 28 and 83.

[51] Zgusta, p. 491, citing Holder i, 452. Cf. W *blwch* 'bald', CPNE, p. 23. On the place itself see Mitchell, *Anatolia*, i, 53 and 55–57.

[52] Freeman, *Galatian Language*, p. 85 and n. 179; Zgusta, p. 171; DLG s.v. *brog(i)-*.

[53] Freeman, *Galatian Language*, pp. 79–80 (in his review, p. 358, Lambert translates this epithet of Zeus, *Swoli-broginos*, as 'du pays du soleil(?)'); Mitchell, *Anatolia*, i, 50, n. 89, 53 and 57. A possibly Celtic *Hêloua* in Ptolemy 5.4.4 is discussed in PNPG Comments s.n. *E:loúa* and Possibly Celtic Elements s.v. {elua:}, *eluo-*.

[54] Mitchell, *Anatolia*, i, 50 and 55, n. 114; Freeman, *Galatian Language*, p. 88; Zgusta, p. 459 (noting, however, a possible Anatolian parallel *Winda* or *Wenda*); DLG s.v. *uindos*; Luján, 'Galatian place names', p. 259.

[55] Freeman, *Galatian Language*, pp. 69–72; DLG and PNPG Possibly Celtic Elements s.v. *tolisto-*; Luján, 'Galatian place names', p. 256 and n. 14.

[56] Schmidt, 'Sprachreste', pp. 15–16.

[57] Luján, 'Galatian place names', p. 258 (noting variants in *Corb-*).

[58] Weisgerber, 'Sprachreste', pp. 159 and 168–69; Russell, 'Suffix', p. 165. But see PNPG Comments s.n. *Orsología*.

[59] Cf. DLG s.v.; Zgusta, p. 207. See on + 5/43 *Cabellio* above, p. 244.

[60] See respectively GPN, pp. 185–86, and DLG s.v. *gussu-*. Also noted by PNPG Comments s.n. *Kóggoustos* and Possibly Celtic Elements s.v. *gusto-*.

[61] Luján, 'Galatian place names', p. 261; Zgusta, pp. 458–59.

[62] Compare similar *Bon-* forms (some with omega) in Zgusta, pp. 124–25.

[63] Ibid. p. 134.

could be connected with Celtic *abonā 'river', but the gender is a problem.[64]

+ 33/40 Besides **Ikotarion?**[65] and perhaps **'Viciu'**, *Konkarztiakon is thought to be Celtic.[66] 86unl *Matrix* may be Celtic, as has been argued for *Matrica* in Pannonia and its cognates.[67]

+ 33/39 Besides **Ecobrogis/Eccobriga**,[68] *Mordiacus Mons*, the alternative name for *Magaba M.*, may have a Celtic suffix,[69] and *Kinna* is perhaps Celtic.[70] The Celtic name *Acitorigiaco* also belongs here.[71]

+ 33/38 A possible P-Celtic name here is *Perta*, corresponding to W *perth* 'bush, hedge' (cf. OI *ceirt*) or *perth (cf. OI *-cert* 'district'), although Zgusta also compares the Lycian personal names *Pertina*, *Pertinamuwa*.[72] Perta was one of the cities with a few residents bearing Celtic names.[73]

+ 34/42 —

+ 34/41 —

+ 34/40 —

+ 34/39 **Corniaspa**,[74] *Trokmoi* (also attested as *Trogmi*)[75] and *Taouion/Tabia* (also attested as *Tavium/Tavia*)[76] have all been regarded as Celtic.

[64] Ibid. pp. 42–43; PNPG Comments s.n. *Abó:nou theíkos.*

[65] Freeman, *Galatian Language*, p. 85; DLG s.v. *ico-*; Zgusta, p. 196.

[66] Mitchell, *Anatolia*, i, 50, n. 89, and 53 (note the variant forms).

[67] See Ch. 5 above, p. 167.

[68] Freeman, *Galatian Language*, pp. 84–85; AILR Comments s.nn. For similar alternations cf. PNPG Comments s.n. *Nitióbriges* (*Nitiobroges* being correct, RIG i, G-275).

[69] Cf. Mitchell, *Anatolia*, i, 54 and n. 108 (not in Russell, 'Suffix', p. 165). DLG s.v. *magalos* refers to '*Magala* montagne de Galatie'.

[70] See above, p. 238 on *Kinna* at + 0/41. See, however, Zgusta, pp. 265–66, for various *Kinn-* forms. Note that *Andraka/Andrapa* is rejected by Weisgerber, 'Sprachreste', pp. 159 and 169; cf. Zgusta, pp. 75–76.

[71] Weisgerber, 'Sprachreste', pp. 158–59 and 168–69; Freeman, *Galatian Language*, p. 83; DLG s.v. *acito-*; Russell, 'Suffix', p. 165. *Aspona* is Celtic according to Zgusta, p. 103, citing Holder i, 247–48; for *Aspaluca* etc., but none of these names is obviously Celtic and Holder himself labels *Aspaluca* in the Pyrenees (*Aspalluga* etc., AI 453.1) as Iberian. On the other hand, cf. **Corniaspa** at + 34/39 below.

[72] Cf. LEIA s.vv.; Zgusta, p. 487; PNPG Possibly Celtic Elements s.v. {perta:-}.

[73] Mitchell, 'Population', p. 1059.

[74] Zgusta, pp. 289–90. But *-asp-* is un-Celtic; cf. n. 71 above.

[75] Weisgerber, 'Sprachreste', p. 158, and Freeman, *Galatian Language*, pp. 73–76 (without etymology, but cf. on *Trocnades* at + 31/39 above, Zgusta, pp. 635–36, Luján, 'Galatian place names', p. 256, n. 16, and PNPG Possibly Celtic Elements s.v. *trocmo-*).

[76] DLG s.v. *tauo-* < *tauso-* (but see Isaac, 'Scotland', p. 204, for an objection); Zgusta, p. 599. On the form see also AILR Comments s.v. *Tavia*). Luján, 'Galatian place names', stresses the significance of the cuneiform parallel *Tawiniya* cited by Zgusta: 'This example provides salutary warning against excessive confidence when classifying as Celtic any given place name in Asia Minor' (pp. 256–57).

63unl *Stabiu*, a road-station west of *Taouion*, could tentatively be compared with OI *sab* 'stake' < **stabh-*.[77]

+34/38 **Andabalis** is isolated[78] and unlikely to contain Celtic *And-*, and **Salambriai**/*Salaberina* presumably belongs with the other non-Celtic names in *-mbria-*. Some scholars situate 63unl *Ouanota* near *Ouenasa* and regard it as Celtic, on the basis of Gregory of Nyssa's description of *Ouanôta* as a vernacular Galatian name (*Letters* 20.1),[79] but there seems no justification for this localization.

+35/42 —
+35/41 **Sagylion** is isolated[80] and unlikely to be Celtic since names in *sag-* are so widespread, and much the same applies to:
+35/40 **Virasia**.
+35/39 —
+35/38 **Kamoulianai** (also attested as *Kamoulia*) is counted as Celtic by Holder and Weisgerber, apparently rightly; Zgusta holds only its peripheral location against its Celticity, which raises the danger of a circular argument.[81]

In addition to the names already included there remain two unlocatable but obviously Celtic names from our collection of Celtic-looking names:

63	*unl*	Ambi**touti**
63	*unl*	**Toutobod**iaci?

Pliny 5.146 places these tribes in the vicinity of *Gordion*, along with 62unl *Voturi*, also a Celtic ethnonym;[82] they would be at about +31/39 or +32/39. Another Celtic-looking ethnonym in Galatia, 'probably

---

[77] LEIA s.v. Holder ii, 1629, lists a personal name *Stabius* from Adamclisi (Tropaeum Traiani in Moesia Inferior, 22E4 = +27/44) (CIL III 14214,1), but this may not be Celtic. On *Ratostabios* which Holder compares see Sims-Williams, 'Degrees of Celticity', p. 8, and 'Measuring Celticity', pp. 282–83, Russell, 'On reading Ptolemy', p. 187, and PNPG Comments s.n. *Rhatostathubíou p.e.*

[78] Zgusta, pp. 73 and 113, n. 109. [**Balbissa*] recalls OI *balb* 'dumb', but this is probably from Latin *balbus*: LEIA s.v. For *Balb-* see Zgusta, p. 114.

[79] Mitchell, *Anatolia*, i, 53, and 'Population', p. 1059, n. 25; Maraval (ed.), *Grégoire de Nysse: Lettres*, p. 259, n. 3. Zgusta, p. 455, rejects any identification with *Ouenasa* and doubts its Celticity. *Nyssa* is at +33/38 (63D3).

[80] Zgusta, p. 525, comparing the name of a mythical Scythian king *Sagylion*. *Andrapa* is doubted by Weisgerber, 'Sprachreste', pp. 159 and 169.

[81] Holder iii, 1067 (cf. personal name *Camulianus Camuli* at i, 724); Weisgerber, 'Sprachreste', p. 159; Zgusta, p. 220. Not in GPN, p. 161, nor DLG s.v. *camulos*.

[82] Freeman, *Galatian Language*, pp. 65, 73 and 77.

		+29			
41	52E2 52F2 53B2	53C2	(*names not* *noted here*)		41
40	52E3-4 52F3-4 53B3	53C3 62B1	(*names not* *noted here*)		40
39	62B2-3 Dagoutenoi Palox? [Akrokos]	*Aliana Kadoi Tiberioupolis? 62C2-3	Aizanoi Appia Epikteteis **Kotiaeion**	**Mantalos** Penkalas fl. Spore?	39
38	62B4-5 *Asteles fl.* *Bagis* *Hyllos fl.* **Kaualena* *Lyendos* *Temenouthyrai/* *Temeneia* *Atyochorion* *Blaundos/Mlaundos* *Dionysoupolis* *Hippourios fl.* *Hyrgaleis*	**Kagyetteia* *Mossyna* **Motaleia* *Motella/* *Metelloupolis* *Nais* **Saloudeia?* *Sindros fl.* **Thiounta* 62C4-5 *Akmonia* **Alia*	*Babdalai* *Dindymos M.* *Diokleia* *Dioskome/Diospolis* *Doiantos Pedion* *Eibeos* *Kleros Politike* **Lankena* *Moxeanoi* *Panasion* *Phrygia/Berecyntius* *Tractus/Berekyntes* *Traianoupolis*	*Fulvia/Eumeneia* *Glaukos fl.* **Homadena* *Klydros fl.* *Otrous* *Pentapolis* *Sebaste* 65B1 *Lounda* 65C1 *62unl* **Sagarenoi?** *62unl* **Bria**	38
		+29			

	+ 30				
41	52G2 *Desa *Morzapena	*Tenba Chelai Kalpas fl.	Kalpe Rhoe Thynias Ins./ Apollonia Ins./ Daphnousia Ins.	52H2 86A2 Mariandynus Sinus	41
40	52G3-4 *Baradendromia Boane/ Sunonensis L. Dekaton Kabia *Kalasyrta *Kassa *Leptoia *Prindea Sangarius fl. [Sophon] M.	Tarsos/Tarsia Terbos Trikomia 'Chogeae' *Eirakla *Kizoura *Mossynea *Oka Pithekas? fl. 'Protunica'	*Syllanta Tattaios 'Thateso' 52H3-4 Artemis *Ontoraita 86A3 Apsoda 'Cenon Gallicanon'? Ceratae	Dableis Doris Gallos fl. Hypios? M. Hypios fl. Iustiniani Pons Katapaspanas Mariandynoi	40
39	86A4 62D2-3 Hermos fl./ Bathys fl. Lamounia Marlakkou Kome Tembris fl./ {Tembrogius} *Thermae Privatae Trikomia? Aragokome	Araukome Arginousa *Birgena Eiokome Elaphoeis M. Iskome? Meiros Meiros Megale	Regio Ipsina et Moeteana *Soa *Tanaitena *Zemmeana Zingotos Kome 62E2-3 *Abouadeineita Dorylaion Midaion	Parthenios fl. *Serena Abboukome/ Apokome Malos Meter Arezastis Metropolis Nakoleia *Pontanena 62unl **Sagarenoi** 62unl **Kassenoi** 62unl Namantaloi?	39
38	62D4-5 Aquae Ger(...) Brouzos Kaystros fl. Kidyessos Agros Thermon Aulutrene Aulutrene Eukarpia Hierapolis Metropolitanus Campus *Polyntena Stektorion	62E4-5 Akroenos/ [Akroinos]/ Nikopolis Beudos (Palaion)/ **Boudeia** Dokimeion Doureios fl. *Etsyena Ipsos [Kedrea] Leontos Kome/ Leontos Thermon	Persis M. Prymnessos Synnada *Banboulena Hippophoras fl. *Karmena Metropolis *Oueiniata *Plouristreia/ Proureistreis Tymandos 65D1 Apamea/Kelainai/ Kibotos Apollonia/Mordiaion/ Sozopolis	Aporidos Come Aulutrena Aulutrene/ 'Aulocrene' L. Marsyas fl. Orgas fl. *Plinnena Rhotrini Fontes/ Aulutrene 65E1 Parlais/Col. Iulia Augusta Hadriana	38
	+ 30				

			+31		
41	86B2 *Acheron fl./* *Soonautes fl.* *Acherousias Pr.* *Dadybra* *Dia/Diospolis* *Elaios*	*Elaios fl.* *Heraclea* *Kales* *Kales fl.* **Kelesa*	*Krenides* *Ladon fl.* *Lilaios* *Lykos fl.* *Metroon/Aulia*	*Oxinas* *Oxinas fl./* *Kallichoros? fl.* *Psylla* *Sandarake* *Timonitis*	41
40	86B3 <u>Araunia</u> <u>Balgatia</u> Bithynion/ Claudiopolis/ Hadriana Dadastana Dadokome	Embolos Fines Gordioukome/ Iuliopolis *Hieronpotamon Hieros fl./ Siberis fl.	Kieros fl. Milia Modra Prusias ad Hypium/ Kieros Salon	Skopas fl. Sykeon 'Transmonte' {<u>Bogdomanis</u>}	40
39	62F2-3 Heptakometai **Konsidiana Choria** *Trokna <u>Amorion</u>	Knepelaos Lalandos Orkistos 62G2-3 (Col. Iulia Augusta Felix) Germa/ Germa	Dindymon M. Eudoxias? Gallos fl./Terias fl. Germia/Myriangeloi Goeleon	Pessinous/ Iustinianoupolis Spaleia Tolastochora? 62unl <u>Orkaorkoi</u> 62unl <u>Laginoi</u> 62unl <u>Lagonia</u> 62unl <u>Mandalos</u> {[ ]nobantenoi} {Okondianoi}	39
38	62F4-5 **Appolena* *Aurokra* *Phyteia* *Polybotos* *Alexandri Fontes/* *Midou Krene* *Anthios fl.* *Antiochia/* *Col. Caesarea*	*Gallos? fl.* *Paroreios* *Philomelion* *Tekmoreioi* *Tetrapolis* *62G4-5* *Arra*	*Klaneos?* **Selmena* **Azareis/*Ezareis* *Hadrianoupolis* *Karmeios? fl.* **Lageina* *Pissia* **Seilinda*	*Tyr(i)aion?* 65F1 *Anaboura* *Killanion Pedion/* *Cillanicus Tractus/* *Civitas Cillanensium*	38
			+31		

	+32		+33		
42			86D1 *Karambis* *Karambis Pr.*	*Marsylla/* *Kallistratia?* *Timolaion* *Zephyrion*	42
41	86C2 *Aigialos* *Amastris/* *Sesamos* *Billaios fl.* *Chele Pr.* *Cytorus M.* *Eryth(r)inoi* *Kaukones* *Kromna*	*Kytoros* *Meles fl.* *Mokata?* *Paphlagonia* *Parthenia* *Parthenios fl.* *Psilis fl./* *Papanios fl.* *Sora* *Tios/Tieion*	86D2 *Abonouteichos/* *Ionopolis* *Aiginetes fl.* *Amnias fl.* *Blaene* * ***Bonita***	*Garios* *Klimax* *Olgassys M.* *Thymena/* *Teuthrania?* *Ziporea*	41
40	86C3 Antoniopolis *Artiknos <u>Bloukion</u> <u>Carus Vicus</u> *Endeira *Ergobrotis <u>**Gezatorigis**</u> <u>Gordiane</u> Kaisareia/ Hadrianopolis/ Proseilemmene *Karza *Kimista Krateia/ Flaviopolis/ *Agrippeia?/ Kreteia	Krentios Legna 'Mandris' 'Manegordo' **Mantineion** <u>Mnizos</u> Modicus M. Peion/Peon **'Petobrogen'** <u>Potamia</u> 'Potomia Cepora' Prasmon **Tektosages** *Zeita 63unl **Drynemeton**	86D3 Anadynata Gangra/ Germanicopolis Halmyros fl. **Ikotarion?** Kalmizene Kandara?	Kimiata *Klossama *Kobara *Konkarztiakon Laziane Malos Xanthos fl. 86unl **'Viciu'** {86unl Matrix}	40
39	62H2-3 Gordion/**Vindia?** Lagania/ Anastasioupoli/ Lagantine 63A1-2 Modicus M. Olympus M. Papira Tolistoagioi/ <u>Tolistobogioi</u> <u>Axylon</u> Bagrum Myrikion/Therma	63B1-2 Ancyra *Androna/Andros/An- eros/Androsia Cenaxis Palus Delemna/Dilimnia <u>Galatia</u> <u>Gallograecia</u> <u>Gorbeus</u> <u>Orsologiakos/</u> <u>Rosolodiacus</u> **Tectosages** *Area *Orbana *Plomma	63C1-2 Bolecasgus Magaba M./ <u>Mordiacus M.</u> <u>Aliassum</u> Aspona Galea <u>Kinna</u>	63D1-2 **Ecobrogis/** **Eccobriga** <u>Sarmalius</u> Andraka/ Andrapa Cham(m)anene Parnassos {Acitorigiaco}	39
38	63A3-4 *Andeira *Keissia Ouetissos/ Ouetiston/Vetissus Proseilemmene *Aralla [Bardaetta] *Kindyria Laodikeia (Katakekaumene)/Clau- diolaodicea	*Pithoi Praedia Quadratiana *Zizima 63B3-4 Ekdaumaua/ Egdava/Gdanmaa Pegella *Pillitokome Caballucome <u>Kongoustos/</u> <u>Congussus</u> <u>Obizene</u> *Senzousa *Zemruta	63C3-4 Tatta L. *Anzoulada Comitanassus Perta 63D3-4 Nitazi/Nitalis	Nys(s)a Ozzala/Ozizal/ 'Iogola' Sadagolthina Garsauria/ Garsauritis Koropassos Ubinnaca	38
	+32		+33		

	+34		+35		
42	86E1 *Lepte Pr./* *Syrias Pr.*		86F1 *Armene* *Skopelos M.*	87A2 *Sinope/Sinopitis*	42
41	86E2 *Aiginetes* *Antikinolis* *Assyria* *Domanitis* *Euarchos fl./* *Euechos fl.*	*Kinolis* *Koloussa* *Pompeiopolis/* *Sebaste* *Potamoi* *Stephane*	86F2 *Kyptasia* *Ocherainos fl./* *Ochosbanes fl./* *Ochthomanes fl.* 87A3 *Andrapa/Neapolis/Neo-* *klaudiopolis* *Gadilon/Helega?/* *Gadilonitis* *Garzoubanthon/* *Orgibate*	*Halys fl.* *Karousa/* *Polichnion* *Kyptasia* *Pteria* **Sagylion** *Sarakene* *Zagora* *Zalekos fl.* *Zaliches/* *Leontopolis*	41
40	86E3 *Pimolisa* *Ximene?*		87A4 *Amaseia* *Babanomon* *Carissa/Garsi* *Chiliokomon* *Cromen* *Diakopa/Diakopene* *Euchaita* *Gazakene* *Iris fl.* *Kizari*	*Laodikeia* *Lithros? M.* *Pleuramis/* *'Ptemari'?* *Skotios* *Skylax fl.* *Thermai* *Phazemoniton/* *Phazemonitis* **Virasia** *Zela/Zelitis*	40
39	86E4 *Cappadox? fl.* 63E1-2 *Therma* *Trokmoi* Aquae Saravenae	*Saraouene* 63F1-2 **Corniaspa** Taouion/Tabia Sacoena *Soanda* 63unl Stabiu	63G1-2 *Pteria* *Basilika Therma* *Euaissa* 64A1-2 *Sibora/Foroba?/* *Sobara?*	64B1-2 *Agranai/Agriane* *Serm(o)usa/* *Sermouga* *Skylax fl.* *Cappadocia* *Eulepa/Aipoloi* *Saraouene*	39
38	63E3-4 *Argustana* *Asiana/Osiena* *Mo(u)rimene* *Arg(ai)os M./* *Argeiopolis M.* *Arianzos* *Borissos* *Caena* *Doara* *Garsaura/* *Col. Claudia* *Archelais/Koloneia* *Iustinianoupolis/* *Mokissos* *Kanotala* *Karbala* *[Koron]* *[Malandasa]* *Momasson* *Nandianulus/* *Nazianzos/Nadiandos* *Nora/Neroassos/* *Nanassos* **Salambriai/** *Salaberina*	*Tibernene* 63F3-4 *[Hagios Prokopios]* *Korama* *[Matiane]* *Ouenasa* *Salanda* *[Tamisos]* *Zoropassos* **Andabalis** *[*Balbissa]* *Chusa* *Dasmenda/* *[Dasmendron]* *Diokaisareia* *Limnai* *Malakopea* *Mataza* *Sasima* *Soandos* *[Sobesos]* *Villa Palmati* *Zeila*	63G3-4 **Kamoulianai/** Iustinianoupolis *Nova* *Kampai?* *Ochras* *Saccasena* *[Korama]* *Kyzistra* 64A3-4 *Archalla/Archelais* *Argaeus M.* *Mazaka* *Mazaka/Eusebeia/* *Caesarea*	64B3-4 *Anisa* *Arasaxa/Arathia* *Makelle* *Melas fl.* *Moutalaske* *Phlabianai* *Skandos* *Bagadania* *Cilicia* *[Kiskisos]*	38
	+34		+35		

towards Paphlagonia', is 63unl *Timoniacenses*, assuming an /a:ko/ suffix. The first part resembles *Timonitis* (86B2) in this area. Finally, Ptolemy 5.4.6 records three possibly Celtic names in the territory of the *Tectosages*: 63unl *Agrizama*, 63unl *Landosia* and 63unl *Ouinzela* (= Rav. 110.13 *Binzea*?).[83]

(c) Asia Minor between +29 and +35 longitude and south of latitude 38

The Celtic-looking names on Maps 5.1–5.3 are very scarce relative to the number of known toponyms and, as in western Asia Minor, are probably due to coincidence or to the presence of cognates in Greek and other Indo-European languages of the rather restricted number of Celtic-looking strings in question (SID and TREB account for 7 out of 17 'Celtic-looking' names). The following list shows the Celtic-looking names from Maps 5.1–

65	C2	+ 29	37	Anaua	Sanaos		
65	E2	+ 30	37	**Saga**lassos			
65	D3	+ 30	37	*****Ouerb**e			
65	D3	+ 30	37	**And**eda			
65	G3	+ 31	37	**Kot**enna			
65	G3	+ 31	37	Trogitis L.			
66	B1	+ 32	37	**Icon**ium	Claud**icon**ium	Col. Iulia Augusta Equestris?	Col. Aelia Hadriana Augusta
66	A1	+ 32	37	**Korn**a?			
66	A2	+ 32	37	*****Sed**asa			
66	D2	+ 33	37	*****Sid**amaria			
65	C4	+ 29	36	Kiby**ratis**			
65	B5	+ 29	36	**Sid**yma			
65	C5	+ 29	36	**Treb**endai			
65	E5	+ 30	36	**Sid**erous Limen	Pos**id**arisous?		
65	E5	+ 30	36	**Sid**erous Pr.			
65	D4	+ 30	36	**Treb**enna			
65	B5	+ 30	36	Kalaba(n)tia			
65	G4	+ 31	36	*****Senn**ea?			
65	F4	+ 31	36	**Sid**e			
66	*unl*	*+ 33*	*36*	**Vind**emis			

[83] Luján, 'Galatian place names', pp. 260–62; Zgusta, pp. 44, 329 and 460. Cf. PNPG Possibly Celtic Elements s.v. *lando-* and Comments s.n. *Ouinzela* (**Wind-io-elo-*). Not in DLG s.vv. *landa, agro-* and *uindos*. Zgusta comments (p. 460) that the existence of another *Ouinzela* in Pisidia (Ptolemy 5.5.7) is against the Celticity of the Tectosagan one. The Pisidian one is not in the Barrington data unless identical with 65E2 *Bindaios* (+ 30/37), which Zgusta compares.

5.3 arranged from north to south, but I have interpolated 3 other names which might be thought Celtic if they occurred in Britain or France: *Kalaba(n)tia*,[84] *Anaua*,[85] and *Trogitis L.*[86]

Probably none of these is Celtic.

V. NOTE ON REMAINING AREAS AROUND THE MEDITERRANEAN (NORTH OF LATITUDE 35 AND WEST OF LONGITUDE +35)

(a) Cyprus north of latitude 35

There are no relevant 'Celtic-looking' names in northern Cyprus, but 72unl *Corinaeum* (recorded by Pliny 5.130) may be mentioned and dismissed.[87] This may be a convenient place to cite the only 'Celtic-looking name' from southern Cyprus (omitted from Table 5.2 because south of latitude 35):

18026	72	C3	+ 33	34	**Korn**os?

(b) The Levant between latitudes 35 and 36, at longitude + 35

The only 'Celtic-looking' name from Table 5.2 is as follows:

68	A2	+ 35	35	**Cas(s)**ius M.

This is obviously unlikely to be Celtic,[88] and there are no other plausible Celtic names in the area. 68A3 *Gabala* (modern Jebele, + 35/35) is too isolated to be grouped with the European names in *Gabal-*.[89]

(c) Africa north of latitude 35

The Celtic-looking names from Table 5.2 are as follows, inserting two unlocatable items at their approximate positions:

---

[84] Superficially similar to names in *Cala-* in Hispania etc. and tribal names like *Atrebates* and *Trinobantes* in Britain (although these are to be segmented *Atreb-ates* and *Tri-nobantes*, PNRB, pp. 259–60 and 475–76; cf. Freeman, *Galatian Language*, p. 66, on *[ ]nobantenoi*, discussed above, p. 273). Zgusta, p. 214, derives it from Greek *kalabas* 'lizard'.

[85] Herodotus 7.30. Cf. *Anaua* in Britain and elsewhere (PNRB, pp. 249–50, with review by Sims-Williams, p. 93, and p. 211 above). The variant form, however, is *Sanaos* and the adjacent lake is *Sanaos L.* The original form was probably **Sanawa* and there are parallels for the loss of sigma. See Zgusta, pp. 72 and 533–34, and TIB-7, p. 371.

[86] Also listed in APNI (a rare duplication) at 66A2 (+ 32/37). Compare *Trokmoi/Trogmi* at + 34/39 above, but also *Trog(l)odytae* at + 28/45 above, p. 219.

[87] This recalls *Corinium* in Britain and Dalmatia (at + 15/44, p. 205 above) – but compare also the Macedonian word κορινᾶος 'bastard' (cited by Liddell & Scott).

[88] See on *Cassius M.* in Hispania, above, p. 227.

[89] DLG and PNPG Celtic Elements s.v. *gabalo(s)*. Cf. 90unl *Gabale* and other names listed as 'inadmissible' in Ch. 4 s.v. *abal-*, also VCIE, p. 459.

28	C2	−06	35	Cottae?	Kotes	Gytte
28	*unl*			Emporikos Kolpos	Sagigi Sinus	
29	*unl*	*−02*	*35*	Sita Col.?		
30	F3	+03	36	Icosium		
30	*unl*	*+03*	*36*	Tamariceto Praesidium		
34	C2	+04	35	Abannae?		
31	E4	+06	36	Castellum Arsacalitanum		
31	*unl*	*+07*	*36*	Audurus		
31	*unl*	*+07*	*36*	Capraria	Carraria?	
31	*unl*	*+07*	*36*	Verbalis		
32	E4	+09	36	*Civitas Sivalitana		
32	D4	+09	36	Pagus Assalitanus		
33	*unl*	*+09*	*35*	Seggo		
32	F4	+10	36	Segermes		
32	*unl*	*+10*	*36*	Volitana Plebs		
32	*unl*			Sitipensis Plebs		

These are probably all due to coincidence,[90] although Pliny's coupling of **Cottae** with 28unl *Lissa* as former *oppida* 'beyond the columns of Hercules' (5.2) may tantalize the Celticist.[91] The only other tempting name in the whole area is *Kinna M.* (Ptolemy 4.3.6, 32D2 = +9/37), since *Kinna* and *Cinniana* in Hispania and *Kinna* in Galatia have been tentatively regarded as Celtic;[92] but no doubt it contains the Latin personal name *Cinna* (for the formation compare *Cassius M.* at (b) above).

[90] On *Tamariceto* see Ch. 3 above.

[91] See Desanges, *Pline l'Ancien, Livre V, 1-46*, pp. 81–83. On *Liss-* names see above, p. 263, n. 238.

[92] See above, pp. 238, 239 and 275. Note also 91unl *Kinna* in Sittacene in Iraq (Ptolemy 6.1.6) and 94unl *Kinna* in Persia (Ptolemy 6.4.6). Is 31F3 *Celtianis* (+6/36) to be derived from Latin *celtis* 'African species of lotus'? The only name in *-acum* in Africa north of latitude 35 is *Armoniacum fl.* (32A3 = +7/36), *Armua* in Pliny 5.22; see Desanges's note, p. 203.

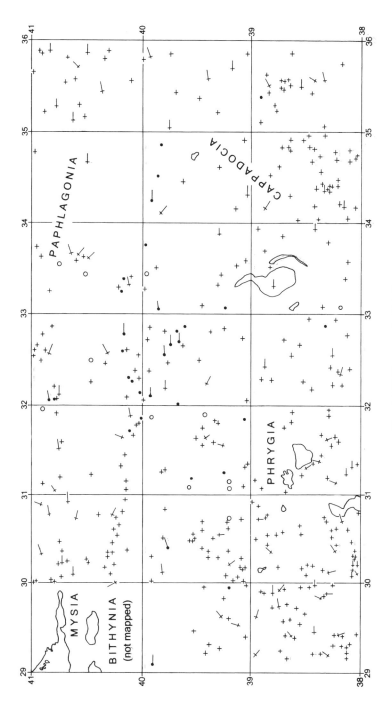

Map 9.1 Celtic names in Galatia

10

THE EXTENT OF CELTIC NAMES, VI: AFRICA AND ASIA (SOUTH OF LATITUDE 35 AND EAST OF LONGITUDE + 35)

(a) Africa south of latitude 35

The following are the 'Celtic-looking' names from outside the area covered in Table 5.2, with the addition of an unlocatable name at the end:

43	1	B4	− 09	33	Rutubis	
22992	28	unl	− 06	34	Ouobrix	
7567	28	C5	− 06	34	Ouerbikai	
7610	28	B5	− 06	34	Thamusida	
7612	28	C5	− 06	34	Tocolosida	
8565	33	G3	+ 10	34	Usil(l)a	Usula
8981	36	C5	+ 13	26	Fauces Garamanticae	
8984	36	C4	+ 13	27	Garamantes	
8894	35	G2	+ 14	32	Sugolin	Seggera
9085	37	E2	+ 19	30	Makatoutai	
9103	37	E2	+ 19	30	Tincausari	
9214	38	D1	+ 22	32	Ma(ra)ndis?	Arimantos Kome?
18182	73	E2	+ 27	31	Ladamantia	Leodamantium
26408	73	unl			Sentetes	

With the notable exceptions of **Ouobrix** and **Ouerbikai**, discussed below, and perhaps **Rutubis**, discussed in Chapter 3, none of these is plausibly Celtic. A tempting ethnonym which might be added is *Kaunoi* (28B5 = + 6/ 34), as their name would certainly be liable to interpretation as 'desirable ones' (: W *cun*, *Cun*, Middle Irish *cúanna*, Gaulish *Counos, Caunus*) if they lived in Europe.[1] Otherwise there seem to be no plausibly Celtic names in the rest of Africa.[2]

Ouobrix (28unl) was in a part of central Tingitana documented only by Ptolemy (4.1.7), who is agreed to have depended on information from

---

[1] DLG s.v. *counos* and above, p. 270, n. 11. Another possibility is W *cun*, OI *cúan* 'pack of wolves/dogs, host' (see LEIA s.v.). On the *Kaunoi* (Ptolemy 4.1.5) see Desanges, *Catalogue*, p. 32, Euzennat, 'Les Zegrenses', pp. 178–79, and Hamdoune, 'Ptolémée et la localisation des tribus', pp. 245, 251–52, 257 and 273–76.

[2] The only name in -*acum* south of latitude 35 is *Baracum?* (36D4 = + 14/27) from Pliny 5.37, probably modern Brak, on which see Desanges's note, pp. 407–8. *Artos Akron* (73E2 = + 27/31) is too isolated to be added to DLG s.v. *artos*. Rostaing, *Essai*, p. 62, proposed a 'Mediterranean' **art*-. On names in *Art*- see also Mihailov, 'Le suffixe -*sk*- en thrace', pp. 150–51.

before AD 110.[3] The name is identical with Celtic *Wo-brig-s, a compound meaning something like 'sub-hillfort' or 'place under the hill'. Both elements are distinctively Celtic. *Wo (OI fo 'under', W g(w)o- 'sub-, lesser') < IE *upo shows Celtic loss of IE *p and is well-attested in ancient Celtic names.[4] *brigs (OI brí 'hill', cf. W bre 'hill' < *brig-a) < IE *bhr̥g-s shows the typical Celtic treatment of syllabic *r as ri, and -brix and -briga place-names are very common, especially in Spain.[5] For the compound we can compare French places called Vouvr(a)y, which have been derived from *Vo-brig-io- 'unterhalb des Bergs, unter dem Berg, am Fuße des Berges', and also a (vicus) Vobergensis near Mainz and perhaps Voberca (now Bubierca) in Celtiberia.[6]

The current opinion is that Ptolemy's 'polis' was one of four places running from west to east in the direction of the valley of the Ouerrha (a tributary of the Sebou), an important line of communication between Morocco and Algeria: Baba–Pisciana–Ouobrix–Herpis.[7] Baba cannot be located,[8] but Pisciana (Vopiscianis in the Antonine Itinerary, Bobiscianis in the Ravenna Cosmography) is believed to be Sidi L'arbi Boujem'a, where the Roman road crosses the Sebou.[9] Since Ouobrix was only 20 minutes east and 5 minutes

---

[3] Berggren & Jones, Ptolemy's Geography, p. 23, n. 25; not later than the reign of Trajan (d. 117) according to Desanges, Catalogue, pp. 9–10. Müller suggested that Ouobrix might also have been mentioned as *Vobri by Mela, 3.107, in his list of the main inland urbes, which is corrupt in the only primary manuscript: gildauo dubritania. This idea has not been accepted by editors who emend to 'Gilda, Volubilis, Banasa' (Silberman (ed.), Pomponius Mela, Chorographie, pp. xlv, 95 and 323–24). Only Schmitt, Le Maroc d'après la 'Géographie' de Claude Ptolémée, p. 331, seems to take it seriously; his approach has not found favour with subsequent scholars. Hassan Limane and René Rebuffat, apud Akerraz et al., 'Nouvelles découvertes', pp. 315, n. 9, and 319, n. 30, note the possibility of emending Mela to read *Prisciana or *Vopiscianae (see n. 9 below).

[4] GPN, pp. 288–89; Weisgerber, p. 351; DLG s.v. uo-, uobera, uocaiton, etc..

[5] See Ch. 4 s.v.

[6] Greule, 'Keltisch *brig-', p. 202; Greule & Müller, 'Keltische Resistenzgebiete', pp. 248–53 (*voberetum is preferred in Nègre i, §4042, and DLG s.v. uobera); Weisgerber, pp. 344, 348 and 351, citing CIL XIII 6689 (the full-grade vocalism of berg might be due to Germanic influence, but not necessarily); Martial 1.49.14, cited in TIR K-30, p. 248, and VCIE, pp. 238, n. 234, and 344 (Voberca Mons in Atlas 25D4, but Martial simply says that it was a place for hunting). Vobesca in Holder iii, 423, is wrong.

[7] Ptolemy 4.1.7; Rebuffat, 'Au-delà des camps romains', pp. 496–99; Hamdoune, 'Ptolémée et la localisation des tribus', p. 269; eadem, 'Frontières théoriques', pp. 250–51. The Ouerrha is the river wrongly labelled Sububus (really the modern Sebou) in the Atlas at 28C5. The Ouerrha is a tributary of the Sebou.

[8] Desanges, Pline l'Ancien, Histoire Naturelle, Livre V, 1–46, pp. 92–93, argues for a site south of the Sebou and east of the axis Banasa–Volubilis.

[9] Marked on Atlas at 28C4; see Map-by-Map Directory i, 461 and 464, s.nn.; Euzennat, Le limes de Tingitane, pp. 57–58; Desanges, Pline l'Ancien, Histoire Naturelle, Livre V, 1–46, p. 92; Hamdoune, 'Ptolémée et la localisation des tribus', p. 269, n. 63; eadem, 'Frontières théoriques', pp. 239 and 251, n. 57; Akerraz et al., 'Nouvelles découvertes', pp. 275–76 and 296, no. MQ1, quoting an alternative identification with Souq Larb'a (Souk el Arba on Map 28C4). If the correct form was Pisciana (to be connected with piscis?), the form in Vo- could be contaminated by neighbouring *Vobrix. On the other hand, Vopiscus 'surviving twin' and

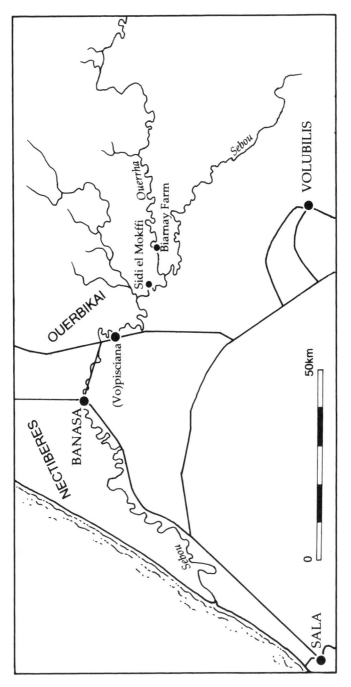

Map 10.1   Ancient Morocco

south of *Pisciana* according to Ptolemy,[10] I would guess that it is the Roman fort or watchtower at Sidi el Mokffi on the north bank of the Sebou, at the point where this navigable river first meets higher ground (28C5 = −6/34 in the *Atlas*); this is dated to the first century AD on the basis of its Hispanic pottery.[11] The name *Ouobrix* could refer to its position 'under' the hill behind it. The only other known ancient site in the vicinity is the Biarnay or Biarney farm (same grid square) on a hillock called M'Souïatt in the Ouerrha valley, 7 km from its confluence with the Sebou; this has been regarded as a possibly fortified Roman farm or watchtower of the first century AD,[12] and is thus another possible candidate.

Is the Celtic appearance of *Ouobrix* a coincidence? A sign that it may not be is Ptolemy's naming of an otherwise unknown people called **Ouerbikai** (4.1.5, var. *Ouerbikes*). This name has been explained either from Latin *vervex*, *vervix*, 'sheep', referring to pastoralists, or else as a corrupt doublet of Ptolemy's tribe *Oueroueis* (4.1.5, var. *Ouerougeis*), who are generally connected with the name of the river Ouerrha.[13] To the Celticist, however, *Ouerbikai/-es* looks like a Celtic ethnonym, either derived from **werb-* 'cow, deer' (cognate with *vervex*) plus an *-ik-* suffix (hence 'cattle people')[14] or, more likely, 'super-fighters', a compound of the common Celtic elements **wer* < **uper* (cf. Latin *super*) with Celtic loss of IE **p* and **wik-* 'fight' (cf. OI *fichid*). *Ver-* is frequent in Celtic personal names and place-names: an example in a Celtic ethnonym is *Ver-turiones* in Britain.[15] Celtic ethnonyms in *-vices* or *-vici* are very common, for example, *Eburovices*, *Gabrantouikes*, *Latovici*, *Lemovices* and *Ordovices*. Spellings with *beta* are to be expected in Greek sources and may also occur in Latin, as in *Latouici/Latobici*.[16] A Celtic personal name *Vervicius/Verbicius* is well attested.[17] A further Celtic

(once) *Vopiscianus* (CIL XIV 4242) are attested as Latin personal names (Kajanto, *The Latin Cognomina*, pp. 73, 75 and 295). GPN, p. 289, nn. 3 and 12, notes that *Vopiscus* has been regarded as Celtic. On Mela see n. 3 above.

[10] See map in Rebuffat, 'Au-delà des camps romains', p. 497.

[11] See Euzennat, *Le limes de Tingitane*, p. 58 and n. 73; Akerraz et al., 'Nouvelles découvertes', pp. 285, 309, 328 and 336, no. SN10: 'une éminence d'où la vue est très étendue sur la plaine et sur le confluent du Sebou et de l'Ouerrha' (p. 285).

[12] Euzennat, *Le limes de Tingitane*, p. 58 and n. 75; Akerraz et al., 'Nouvelles découvertes', pp. 244, 274, 309, 328 and 336, no. KW2. Hamdoune, 'Ptolémée et la localisation des tribus', p. 268, suggests that *Ouobrix* could be in the valley of the Ouerrha.

[13] Euzennat, 'Les Zegrenses', p. 177 and n. 12; idem, 'Les troubles de Maurétanie', p. 376; Desanges, *Catalogue*, p. 37; Hamdoune, 'Ptolémée et la localisation des tribus', pp. 249, 268–69 and 280; Rebuffat, 'Les tribus en Maurétanie Tingitane', pp. 24 and 36, n. 55. The latter adds, however: 'C'est donc à partir d'un radical WRW qu'on peut essayer de se lancer dans des comparaisons toponymiques' (p. 24, n. 8). On *vervex/vervix* see Vendryes, 'Latin *vervēx*'.

[14] See Ch. 4, s.v. *verbā*.

[15] GPN, pp. 279–80; KGP, pp. 290–92; PNRB, pp. 496–97 (corrected in my review).

[16] GPN, pp. 279–80 and 285; KGP, pp. 148 and 294–95 (for *vic-* names see Ch. 4 above, s.v.). For *Latobici* see Anreiter, *Die vorrömischen Namen Pannoniens*, pp. 168–69, KPP, pp. 52–55, and Ch. 5 above, p. 170.

[17] GPN, p. 285; KPP, p. 181. OPEL iv has 16 examples of *Vervicius, -a*, predominantly in Celtic areas, 1 each of *Vervecco* and *Vervecia*, and 2 of *Verbicius, -a* (both in Noricum).

possibility is that -bik- derives from the root *bhī- 'strike', as has been suggested in the case of *Latobici*.[18]

The location of Ptolemy's *Ouerbikai* varies in modern scholarship, owing to the confused way in which Ptolemy localized the peoples of Mauretania. Maurice Euzennat placed them just west of the confluence of the Sebou and Ouerrha in 1974,[19] but near the Loukkos north of Banasa in 1984,[20] and between the Sebou and Ouerrha, near the above-mentioned Biarnay farm, in his map (28C5) for the *Barrington Atlas*. The most penetrating discussion is due to Christine Hamdoune, who situates them just north of the Ouerrha where the higher ground begins, and she even assigns the 'polis' of *Ouobrix* to them, deducing that they were at least partly sedentary.[21]

I suggest that the name *Ouobrix* is due to these *Ouerbikai*. We can only guess why Celtic-speakers should be found in Morocco. Spain is the most likely place of origin and it may be significant that -brix names are common there.[22] The navigable river Sebou, which offered the Romans an easy entry from the Atlantic at the end of the first century BC,[23] could also have afforded passage to Celts from Spain. A definite hint of such contact is provided by the name of Ptolemy's *Nektiberes* (4.1.5). Müller suggested that they were Iberians transferred from Spain, perhaps from *Nertobriga* (if *Nekto-* were emended to *Nerto-*), in the same way as Hannibal is said by Polybius (3.33.10) to have transferred other populations from Spain to Libya.[24] Emendation is superfluous, as an element *Nekt-* is attested, as in the British personal name *Nectouelius* and arguably in the name of the *Silvanectes* (or *Sulbanectes*, etc.) in Gaul.[25] The name *Nektiberes* presumably means 'Iberians who are specifically **Nectes* or **Necti*' just as *Keltiberes* means 'Iberians who are specifically Celts'.[26] The *Nektiberes* are one of a group of four peoples whom Ptolemy places in the extreme south: *Nektiberes, Zegrensoi, Banioubai* and *Ouakouatai* (4.1.5). This is certainly erroneous, at least in part, because the *Zegrenses/Zegrensoi* ('below' the

---

[18] KPP, p. 54.

[19] 'Les Zegrenses', p. 181 (similarly, Desanges, *Catalogue*, pp. 37 and 261).

[20] 'Les troubles de Maurétanie', p. 377 (similarly Rebuffat, 'Au-delà des camps romains', p. 489).

[21] Hamdoune, 'Ptolémée et la localisation des tribus', pp. 268–69, 273, 280, 288, and map, p. 276. The localization is independent of her suggested link between the names *Ouobrix*, *Ouerbikai* and *Oueroueis*.

[22] See Ch. 4 above, s.v *brig-*.

[23] Hamdoune, 'Ptolémée et la localisation des tribus', p. 284.

[24] Müller, p. 586; Desanges, *Catalogue*, pp. 36–37. Celtic mercenaries were also used in Libya: Diodorus Siculus 20.64.2. Cf. Hamdoune, 'Ptolémée et la localisation des tribus', p. 260, who suggests that *Nektiberes* is a corruption of some name based on a Berber root NKTBR.

[25] Collingwood & Wright, *Roman Inscriptions of Britain*, i, no. 2142; CIB, p. 179; cf. Holder ii, 696. Various sources for the *Silvanectes* are cited in TIR M-30/31, p. 95; cf. Nègre i, §§ 2521–22, and Billy's review of Chaurand & Lebègue, *Noms de lieux de Picardie*, p. 335. (The latter took the first element to be Latin *silva*, p. 35.) For a different analysis see PNPG Celtic Elements s.v. *anecto-* and Comments s.n. *Soubánektoi*.

[26] Hoenigswald, 'Celtiberi'.

Nektiberes according to Ptolemy) and the *Banioubai* are known from other sources to belong to the region of Banasa; most scholars would move all four northwards.[27] Christine Hamdoune places the *Nektiberes* just north of Banasa, in the flood-plain of the Sebou.[28] If this is correct, as seems likely, we have another indication of Iberian penetration from the Atlantic in the area of *Ouobrix* and the *Ouerbikai/Ouerbikes*.

(b) From Egypt to the Levant

The 'Celtic-looking' names from this area are arranged approximately from west to east.[29] Some of them were discussed in Chapter 3 above. Probably none is Celtic.

26648	75	*unl*	*+30*	*29*	**Samar**ia		
18534	75	D3	+30	28	**Sen**ekeleu		
18535	75	D3	+30	28	**Sen**okomis		
19249	82	A3	+30	18	**Seg**asa	**Seg**usa	
19148	81	B3	+31	22	Forum **Camb**usis?		
19211	82	B3	+31	18	**Cort**um		
26612	75	*unl*			**Penn**e		
26653	75	*unl*			**Sen**epsau		
26654	75	*unl*			**Sen**epta		
26655	75	*unl*			**Senn**is		
26656	75	*unl*			**Sen**to		
26794	77	*unl*			**Sen**amontai		
26797	77	*unl*			**Sen**inebis		
26798	77	*unl*			**Sen**is		
19198	82	D4	+33	17	**Aba**le		
26265	69	*unl*	*+34*	*32*	Castra **Samar**itanorum		
17177	68	A4	+35	34	**Carn**e	**Karn**os	
17622	69	C3	+35	33	**Seg**eira		
17632	69	B2	+35	33	**Sid**on	Col. Aurelia Pia	
17612	69	C5	+35	32	Salem	Salumias	**Sed**ima
17613	69	B5	+35	32	**Samar**ia		
17614	69	B5	+35	32	**Samar**ia	Sebaste	[*Gabinia]
17627	69	C4	+35	32	**Senn**a**bris**	Ginna**bris**	
17854	71	B2	+35	31	Bethenna**bris**		
17217	68	B2	+36	35	**Kass**iotis		
17495	69	D4	+36	32	**Karn**aia	Astaroth?	

(c) The Pontic–Caspian region above latitude 44

---

[27] Rebuffat, 'Au-delà des camps romains', p. 489, leaves the *Nektiberes* in the south. Euzennat places them in the Rif near the Mediterranean, 'la Mer Ibérique dont ils évoquent le nom' ('Les Zegrenses', pp. 180–81, and 'Les troubles de Maurétanie', p. 378, n. 26; cf. *Map-by-Map Directory* i, 464).

[28] 'Ptolémée et la localisation des tribus', pp. 250–52, 256–61, and map, p. 276.

[29] Henceforth in lists of names from beyond the areas of Maps 5.1–5.3 I shall not normally attempt grid references for '*unl*' items unless worked out in earlier chapters.

Only five names in this area were collected in Chapter 4, and they are no doubt the result of coincidence:

27041	84	*unl*	*+ 38*	*47*	**Cet**ae	
27044	84	*unl*	*+ 38*	*47*	**Cot**obacchi	
27088	84	*unl*			**Sitt**akenoi	
27105	85	*unl*			Issedones	**Essed**ones
19678	87	K2	*+ 36*	*45*	Ilou**rat**on	

So slight a return from so large an area underlines that Celtic names are essentially absent here. The Sarmatian *Cetae* were a tribe and so unlikely to be an instance of Celtic **kaito-* 'wood',[30] and the *Cotobacchi*, mentioned with them by Pliny 6.19,[31] are more obviously connected with *Bacchus* than with Celtic **kot(t)o-*; given the appearance of the 'husbands of the Amazons' in Pliny's list, they may be mythical in any case. Similarly, 'the Issedones/Essedones, although somehow imagined in the region of the northern Caspian by Herodotus and others, seem to have no basis in fact and are therefore omitted' from the *Atlas* maps.[32] In any case, the oldest form is *Issedoi*, and *Issedones* and *Essedones* are later.[33] The *Sittakenoi* have a clearly non-Celtic name like the *Obidiakenoi* with whom Strabo (11.2.11) pairs them. By contrast, *Ilouraton* would certainly pass as Celtic in Gaul,[34] but is too isolated in the eastern Crimea to be taken very seriously.[35] Note also, on the far side of the Black Sea, 87unl *Matium* (an *oppidum* mentioned by Pliny, 6.12, probably in Colchis, that is, around 88A2 = +42/42), which recalls presumably Celtic names in *Mati-*; but it is probably the same as 87unl *Madia* (Ptolemy 5.9.5), which is less 'Celtic' and suggests that *Matium*'s Celtic look is coincidental.[36] Coincidences are bound to occur, and it is in fact surprising that the above list is so short. On Ptolemy's *Tektosakes*, sometimes located near the Urals, see (e) below.

(d) Eastern Asia Minor and adjacent areas in the rest of Asia above latitude 36

The 'Celtic-looking' names from this area are shown in the following table (with the unlocatable ones[37] grouped at the end).

[30] On *Cetae* see Ch. 3 above.
[31] Emended to *Costoboci* by Mayhoff, p. 436.
[32] *Map-by-Map Directory* ii, 1214.
[33] Pauly-Wissowa s.n. *Issedoi*. Cf. **Issedones** in China (6G2 = +94/39) below.
[34] Cf. GPN, pp. 354–56 and DLG s.v. *illio-*.
[35] See, however, Treister, 'Celts in the north Pontic area', Shchukin, 'Celts in eastern Europe', and map in Cunliffe, *Ancient Celts*, p. 307.
[36] See above, pp. 183 and 195. See Müller's notes, pp. 924–25. For names in *Mati-* much further east note 90A3 and B4 *Matiane* (+45/37 and +46/36). See also Zgusta, pp. 375–76, on *Mation* near Ephesus and in Crete.
[37] From the areas of Maps 64, 67, 87, 89–90 and 96–99.

16290	64	D2	+36	39	**Karn**alis	Komaralis	
26178	67	*unl*	*+36*	*36*	**Mag**ia Vicus		
17079	67	C4	+36	36	Oro**kass**ias Oros		
19936	87	C3	+37	41	Polemonion	**Side**	**Sid**ene
19873	87	C4	+37	40	**Kot**yora		
19954	87	C4	+37	40	**Sid**enos fl.		
16303	64	H4	+38	38	**Korn**e		
19951	87	E4	+39	40	**Sed**isca	Solonenica?	
20340	89	B1	+39	39	**Kori**aia?	Garine?	
19946	87	F1	+40	43	Sanigai	**Sag**inai	
20450	89	C3	+40	37	**Si(t)**ai	**Sit**eon Chiphas	
20090	88	A2	+42	42	**Kot**ais	Kytaia	
20218	89	F1	+43	39	Bagauna	'**Sag**ouana'	'Raugonia'
20025	88	C4	+44	40	Arma**ouir**a		
20342	89	G2	+44	38	**Kot**or(odz)		
20077	88	D3	+45	41	**Kamb**ysene		
20078	88	D3	+45	41	**Kamb**yses fl.		
27510	90	*unl*	*+46*	*37*	**Gabr**is		
21080	96	C2	+54	37	**Sid**eris? fl.	Sarnios? fl.	
795	6	G2	+94	39	**Issed**ones		
27267	87	*unl*			Tzacher	**Sid**eroun	
27434	89	*unl*			Odo**mant**is		
27503	90	*unl*			Bala**sag**an	Balasakan	
27803	98	*unl*			Sina	**Sen**a	

It is unlikely that any of these really are Celtic.[38] There are, however, a few plausible traces of Celtic east of Galatia in Armenia.

The name of *Sabrina flumen* (Map 64G1 = +38/39), now Karabudak in Turkey, a tributary of the Euphrates, is known from an inscription on a Roman bridge restored in AD 249/251.[39] The element *Sab-* occurs all over the ancient world, but the only other ancient example of the extension *Sab-r-* is the famous river *Sabrina* (Severn) in Britain, which can be compared with the river *Sabhrann* in Ireland and various English river-names and is presumably Celtic.[40] The Turkish *Sabrina* is in Armenia Minor, well beyond the area of Galatia. That it is more than a coincidence, however, is suggested by the name, *Skordiskos*, which Ptolemy gives to the mountain range immediately

---

[38] On *Kamb-* and *Gabris* see above, Ch. 3. The only other name which might be noted, apart from those mentioned below, is 89E1 *Andaga* (+42/39) in Armenia (cf. British *Andaga* 'Not good' or 'Very good', CIB, pp. 36, n. 84, 40, n. 111, and 211; differently Schrijver, 'Early Celtic diphthongization', p. 59).

[39] Bridge no. 5 on Map 64; Yorke, 'Inscriptions from Eastern Asia Minor', pp. 320–21; CIL III 13644. On the bridge see Mitford, 'Cappadocia and Armenia Minor', pp. 1184–85, 1212, 1219, and plate II.3.

[40] Sims-Williams, 'Degrees of Celticity', p. 8, and 'Measuring Celticity', pp. 270 and 283. For *Sab-* see VCIE, pp. 470–71. Cf. Isaac, 'Scotland', p. 209, n. 5, and PNPG Celtic Elements s.v. *sabro-* (< *samro-*); KPP, p. 281.

to the west (Map 64G1).[41] While this might be explained away,[42] the obvious explanation is that it was named after the famous Celtic tribe from the Balkans, the *Scordisci*.[43] Presumably an offshoot of them penetrated so far eastwards either overland through Galatia or across the Black Sea and down through Cappadocia.[44] If this is accepted, the Celtic appearance of two other names in the vicinity becomes explicable: *Dastracus M.* (64G1 = +38/ 39) and *Dagona* (89unl). *Dastracus M.* (Livy via Orosius 6.4.3: 'montem Dastracum') could contain the Celtic suffix /a:kos/, although an Iranian explanation is perhaps more likely.[45] A little to the east of *Scordiscus*, 89unl *Dagona*/*'Ad Dracones'* looks like a typically Celtic derivative of Celtic **dago-* 'good'.[46] Note also *Dagalasso* (87C4 = +37/40), although here Isaac rightly comments that 'the temptation to see a Celtic *Dago-* here should probably be resisted'.[47]

For *Sinoria* south-east of the Black Sea (+40/40), the *Atlas* gives the forms *Sinoria*/*Baiberdon* (87F4). Appian, *Mithridates* 101, however, calls it *Sinórêga phroúrion*, which has suggested a connection with *Sinorix*, father of the Galatian king Deiotarus who was also king of Armenia Minor and whose son was betrothed to the king of Armenia's daughter.[48] The name *Sinorix* (also found with *upsilon* in the first syllable) may be a variant of

---

[41] Ptolemy 5.6.7 (mapped by Mitford, 'Cappadocia and Armenia Minor', pp. 1214–15).

[42] Mitford's tentative equation in *Map-by-Map Directory* ii, 990, of *Scordiscus M.* with 'Sarmısak ("garlic") tepe?' implies that he connected the name with Greek *skord-* 'garlic' (if this is wrong his siting of the mountain may be too precise, especially as Ptolemy describes a much longer range). Müller (pp. 871–72) tried to emend *Skordiskos* to *Skoidiskos* or *Skoidissos* (cf. Papazoglu, p. 353, n. 258) which he then equated with *Skydises M.* (Map 87F4 = +40/40), which is too far east however (see Lasserre's edition of Strabo Book 11, p. 173). It might also be claimed that the mountain was called *scordiscus* 'saddle', perhaps because of its shape (on this word, not attested before the third century AD, and its connection with Scordiscan cavalry see Papazoglu, p. 452, and DAG, p. 1340).

[43] On them see above, p. 211, n. 137; it is not clear that their ethnic name is *linguistically* Celtic. Cf. Papazoglu, pp. 249 and 352–54, and Anreiter, cited in Ch. 5 above, p. 167.

[44] Papazoglu, p. 276, n. 14, notes that the (Galatian) *Tectosagi* and *Scordisci* have been considered to be related.

[45] Not in Russell, 'Suffix', p. 165. See note in Lasserre's edition of Strabo Book 12, p. 205; Pauly-Wissowa s.n. *Dasteira*; Magie, *Roman Rule in Asia Minor*, ii, 1222. 64unl *Dasteira* was identical or nearby, 87M4 = +38/40(?). There is no other example of the string DASTR in the *Barrington* data, but cf. the linguistically Iranian(?) 64unl *Dastarkon* (Zgusta, p. 156), which was on the river *Karmalas* (64C3 = +36/38) in Cappadocia (Strabo 12.2.5).

[46] But note that Ptolemy 5.6.20 has *omega* rather than the short Celtic *o* (Müller, p. 883, notes that TP has *Doganis*.) It is just to the east of *Scordiscus* on Mitford's Ptolemy-based map, 'Cappadocia and Armenia Minor', p. 1214. Isaac (AILR Comments s.n. *Ad Dracones*) suggests that *Dagona* could be a cult site of the Philistine god *Dagon*. The *Barrington Atlas* equates 89unl *Dagona* with *Ad Dracones* in AI, just west of Satala (89B1 = +39/40), but the equation seems unnecessary, and *Ad Dracones* seems too far north. Cf. Mitford's AI-based map, 'Cappadocia and Armenia Minor', p. 1216. The name *Ad Dracones* recurs in Africa (29E1 and 31unl).

[47] AILR Comments s.n. It may be an error for *Megalossos*; cf. Zgusta, p. 146. For other names in *dag-* see above, pp. 218 and 272.

[48] Pauly-Wissowa, IIIA (1927), 255; Mitchell, *Anatolia*, i, 36 and n. 105; Freeman, *Galatian Language*, pp. 83 and 86.

the attested *Senorix* or have a different first element;[49] in any case the vagaries of Greek spelling make a connection between Appian's form and the king's name quite plausible. Mitchell, however, raises the problem that it 'dates to a period before 63 B.C., when Deiotarus is not known to have any stake in Armenia Minor'.[50] The explanation may be that Appian's form is due to a folk-etymological reinterpretation, based on the knowledge that *Sinoria* was a Galatian fortress.

An unlocated Galatian fortress in Armenia mentioned only by Stephen of Byzantium is *Sintoion* (not in the *Atlas*), and this seems to bear a Celtic name based on *sentu-* 'path'.[51]

(e) Arabia to China

The following pages list the remaining 'Celtic-looking' names, arranged very approximately from west to east. Despite the large number of names here, they are a very small percentage of the total number of names and it is unlikely that any of them is genuinely Celtic.[52]

The one plausible name I would add is the Central Asian ethnonym *Tektosakes*, mentioned only by Ptolemy (6.14.9), an acceptable variant of the well-known Celtic *Tectosages*.[53]

As a compound, both elements of which are independently attested in combination with other Celtic elements, *Tectosages* can be regarded as a definitely Celtic ethnonym.[54] It is most probably related to Old Irish *techtaigidir* 'seeks to (re)establish a land claim' < **tekto-sag-*, and means

---

[49] KGP, pp. 268–69; GPN, p. 247; KPP, p. 53.

[50] Mitchell, *Anatolia*, i, 36, n. 105.

[51] Ibid., citing Honigmann, in Pauly-Wissowa IIIA (1927), 259 (who wrongly compared *Sinorix*); Freeman, *Galatian Language*, p. 86; DLG s.v. *sentu-*. Cf. Schmidt, 'Sprachreste', pp. 18–19.

[52] Many of them were selected for discussion in Ch. 3 above. **Ouindion M.** in India (Ptolemy 7.1.21 and 47), which looks tempting as a derivative of Celtic **windo-* 'white', is the Vindhya range. **Andomatis fl.** looks Celtic (cf. PNPG Celtic Elements s.v. *mat(t)u-/i-* on *Andomátounon* in Germania Superior, i.e. *Andematunnum* 18C2) but is Arrian's corruption of a Sanskrit name, *Dāmodara* (see *Map-by-Map Directory* i, 79). Names in *-acum* in Arabia include: 4unl *Novacum/Novata*, 4B2 *Caminacum* (+44/16), and 4C2 *Mari(a)ba/Barmalacum/Palmalac(h)um* (+45/15). In India 5D4 *Coliacum Pr.* (+79/10) is a corrupt form from Pliny 6.86 (see André's note, p. 116).

[53] See *Book 6*, ed. and transl. Humbach & Ziegler, i, 186, with variants. The spelling *-sakes* rather than *-sages* is insignificant. Müller prints *Tektosagai* in Galatia (5.4.6), but notes (p. 851) that the *editio princeps* had *Tektosakai*. Nobbe has *Tektosagai* there (his 5.4.8) but indexes them as *Tektosakai*. For the Gaulish *Tektosages* (2.10.6), the manuscripts are divided between *Tektosades* and *Tektosakes*; Cuntz, p. 57, prints the latter. A superficially similar Central Asian name is *Chirotosagi*, at 6F4 in the table below, from Pliny 6.64. Its first element is Sanskrit *Kirāta*, and André in his edition (p. 92) offers more than one Sanskrit explanation of the second, including an equation with the Iranian Sakas (cf. 6B4 *Sakai*, 6C2 *Sacae* and 6unl *Scythae/Sagae/Sacae*). Any attempt to explain away *Tektosakes* might take a similar route.

[54] For *-sag-* and *tecto-* see GPN, pp. 251 and 265–66; DLG and PNPG Celtic Elements s.vv. *sag(i)-* and *tecto-*. On the principle that compound names will be more securely Celtic than simple names see Sims-Williams, 'Five languages', pp. 34–35.

ID	Pg	Grid	Coord	No.	Name					
19311	83	B4	+36	27	**Sidenoi**					
19272	83	C5	+37	26	**Carrei**	Cariati				
27302	88	unl			**Kotomana**					
27326	88	unl			Sedala					
21397	3	unl			Anamis fl.	An(d)anis fl.				
21418	3	unl			Kanasida					
21439	3	unl			**Saganos fl.**					
21443	3	unl			**Sidodone**					
27633	91	unl			Mambri					
27673	91	unl			Sittace					
27749	93	unl			Ioukara	Iskara				
27768	93	unl			**Sagapenoi**					
Pers.	94	unl			**Derousiaioi**					
Pers.	94	unl			**Gabra**					
Pers.	94	unl			**Magoi**					
Pers.	94	unl			**Ouxioi**					
Pers.	94	unl			**Sitioganus**					
21529	4	unl			**Coria**	Boanum				
21530	4	unl			**Cornan**					
21544	4	unl			**Divitia**					
21656	4	unl			**Pseudokelis**					
21674	4	unl			**Sagi(a)tta**	Sagitha				
301	4	B2	+41	17	**Devade Inss.**					
20700	91	E3	+43	34	**[Samarra]**	'Sumere'				
291	4	B2	+43	16	Casani	Gasani	**Kassanitai**			
252	4	B3	+43	12	Akila	**Okelis**	Ocilia			
20625	91	F4	+44	33	Apolloniatis	Sittacene	Apollonia	Arbelitis	Palaestine	
27605	91	unl	+44	33	**Douros fl.**					
314	4	B2	+44	16	**Karna**	**Carnus**	**Karnana**			
20935	93	C3	+46	30	Dur-Yakin?	**Duru(m)?**				
21076	95	A3	+48	26	Gerra?	**Carra?**	Gerraioi	**Carrei**		
20918	93	F1	+49	32	**Ouxioi**	Oxii				
21005	94	B5	+51	28	Sitakos? fl.	Solis?				
706	6	A4	+63	25	Asthala		**Karmina? Ins.**	**Karmine Ins.**		
918	6	B5	+67	24	Sagapa Stoma				Nosala Ins.	
952	6	B5	+69	22	Suarattaratae					Nympharum Cubile

No.	Grid		Long.		Name					
450	D5	5	+71	08	**Cottonara**	Kottanarike				Piladai
522	D5	5	+71	08	**Kottiara**	Cotiara				
830	C3	6	+72	34	**Malamantos? fl.**					
19160	C2	81	+72	23	**Kortia**	Corte				
459	C4	5	+72	11	**Divae**					
22159	*unl*	6	+73	33	**Samarab(r)iae**					
965	C3	6	+74	32	**Toutapos? fl.**					
455	C3	5	+74	19	**Deopalli**					
876	D5	6	+75	22	**Ouindion M.**					
970	D4	6	+76	27	Virata	Lymodus? M.				
523	E3	5	+80	15	Kottis					
785	E4	6	+82	27	**(H)Eorta**	Eorta	Sageda	**Sagala?**	Arate?	
877	E5	6	+82	22	**Ouxenton M.**					
524	E3	5	+82	17	**Kottobora**					
659	E5	6	+84	24	**Abali**					
745	F4	6	+85	27	**Chirotosagi**	Kirradai	Cirrabe Indi	Kirradia	Korouda	
682	F5	6	+87	23	Andomatis fl.					
800	F5	6	+87	22	**Kambouson Stoma**					
798	G5	6	+90	22	**Kamberichon Stoma**					
922	G5	6	+91	23	Salariga					
21802	*unl*	5			Kassida					
21807	*unl*	5			**Ketaion Akron**					
21824	*unl*	5			**Mantitour**					
21865	*unl*	5			**Sagantion**					
21882	*unl*	5			**Sittokatis**					
21926	*unl*	6			Andiseni					
21974	*unl*	6			Bonis					
21975	*unl*	6			**Boudaia**					
21984	*unl*	6			Cartana	**Karnasa**	Tetrogonis			
22043	*unl*	6			**Karnasa**					
22053	*unl*	6			**Kottobara**					
22132	*unl*	6			Pharna**cotis** fl.					
22143	*unl*	6			Rhagiraua	**Ratira**				
22170	*unl*	6			Scythae	**Sagae**	Sacae			
22172	*unl*	6			Sena					
22178	*unl*	6			**Silas fl.**	Side fl.				

'possession seekers'.[55]   Such an appellation suits the predatory Celtic migrants described in Greek and Latin sources, and it is no surprise to find more than one group of *Tectosages* in Europe and Asia Minor: *Volcae Tectosages* in Bohemia or Moravia and in southern Gaul and *Tectosages* in Galatia around Ancyra. Caesar (*Gallic War* 6.24) thought that the Bohemian ones had emigrated from Gaul (most modern scholars suppose the reverse), and other ancient writers reported that the Gaulish *Tectosages* took part in the Celtic attack on Delphi in 279 BC, some returning to Toulouse and others emigrating permanently to Galatia.[56]   Much less known are the Central Asian *Tektosakes* mentioned only by Ptolemy (6.14.9).

The context in Ptolemy is important. He seems to have used and corrected a lost account of the Silk Road by Marinos of Tyre (*c.* AD 100), who in turn depended on a Macedonian merchant called Maes (Ptolemy 1.11–12).[57]   An important stopping place on this route was a so-called 'Stone Tower' (*Lithinos Pyrgos*), apparently in the Pamirs, which Ptolemy locates at his 135 longitude and 43 latitude (6.13.2).[58]   Due east of this 'Stone Tower', at his longitude 140 and latitude 43, was 'the base from which the merchants set out for Sera [China] and which is situated close to the Imaon [Himalaya] mountain range'; this was at the north-east corner of the land of the Sakai (6.13.1).[59]   According to Ptolemy, a branch of the Imaon mountains turned almost due north from this trading 'base' and extended to the 'Unknown Land' at his longitude 140 and latitude 63 (6.14.1 and 8).[60]   He presumably means the various mountains running through Kyrgyzstan, along the south-eastern border of Kazakhstan, and then intermittently up to the Siberian plateau and Arctic circle.[61]   On the western side of this northern branch of the

---

[55] Joseph, 'Origin of the Celtic denominatives in *-sag-', pp. 156–58.

[56] For the sources see Tomaschitz, *Wanderungen*, pp. 130–34, 145, 155–63 and 181; Rübekeil, pp. 92–101; Koch, 'Brân, Brennos', pp. 8–13. See *Atlas*, Maps 25F2 and 63B1; Haywood, *Historical Atlas*, pp. 36–37.

[57] Translation and discussion, with maps, in Berggren & Jones, *Ptolemy's Geography*, pp. 23–24, 71–74, 140–41 and 150–52.

[58] *Book 6*, ed. and transl. Humbach & Ziegler, i, 176–77, with maps in ii, figs 31–32.

[59] Compare maps in Humbach & Ziegler, ii, figs 31–32 and 34 (and p. 2, n. 2) with *Atlas* Map 6. Berggren & Jones, *Ptolemy's Geography*, p. 151 and 179, note noncommittally that Aurel Stein located the 'Stone Tower' near Daraut-Kurgan, Kyrgyzstan [+72/39] and the 'base' close to Irkeshtam, Kyrgyzstan, 'which is still a border post on the route to Kashi (Kashgar) in Xinjiang'. The *Atlas* (6D2) favours Tashkurgan (+75/37) for the *Lithinos Pyrgos*, while Rapin, 'L'incompréhensible Asie centrale', p. 218, places it near Osh (+72/40).

[60] See Humbach & Ziegler, ii, figs 31, 32, 34 and 35; Berggren & Jones, *Ptolemy's Geography*, pp. 140–41, maps 8A, B. Cf. Berthelot, *L'Asie ancienne centrale et sud-orientale d'après Ptolémée*, pp. 204–5 and fig. 6 facing p. 224 (note that he thought that the Stone Tower in Book 6 was not that of Book 1).

[61] Cf. Berggren & Jones, *Ptolemy's Geography*, pp. 173 and 180–81. Woźniak, 'Die östliche Randzone der Latenekultur', p. 384, thinks that Ptolemy means the Urals. These indeed run due north, but at longitude 60, which is incompatible with the rest of Ptolemy's text, unless he was combining very faulty data.

Imaon mountains, in 'Skythia', Ptolemy places the *Tektosakes* (6.14.9). He does not give exact locations for the 'Skythian' tribes, but the implication from the order in which he names them is that the *Tektosakes* were among the more northerly ones and closest to the Imaon mountains.[62] Since it is inconceivable that anything was known about people in Siberia, the *Tektosakes* should presumably be located in eastern Kazakhstan.

While *Tektosakes* could always represent some non-Celtic name, it is not inconceivable that there should be a Celtic people so far east. Since the Gaulish or Bohemian *Tectosages* are known to have gone as far as Turkey in their quest for land and possessions, another group could easily have followed the Silk Road east to 'the base from which the merchants set out for China' and then turned northwards into the mountains of Kazakhstan. Only archaeology or population genetics could confirm this.

---

[62] Cf. Humbach & Ziegler, ii, figs 34, 35, where positions at Ptolemy's latitudes 52–56 and his latitude 62 are suggested.

11

THE EXTENT OF CELTIC NAMES: SUMMARY

Map 11.1 summarizes the results of the preceding chapters. The figures, repeated from Map 5.2 in Chapter 5, give the number of places with Celtic-looking names (as listed in Table 5.2) expressed as a percentage of the number of places per square. The large unshaded area in the west has not been investigated in any detail in Chapters 6–8, since the Celtic element from Scotland to north-western Iberia was clear enough from the figures in Chapter 5 and has been taken for granted. Outside that area shading is used to indicate the squares which were classified as partly or wholly Celtic in the course of the more detailed examination in Chapters 6–9. In general that examination has confirmed the impression given in Map 5.2, but a few discrepancies, partly due to statistical factors, should be mentioned.

Map 11.1 indicates the extent of Celtic names by means of an outline round the main Celtic area and the three subsidiary areas north-west and south of the Black Sea. In many cases the Celticity of the frontier areas depends on a very few names, for example in Germania Magna, south-eastern Spain, Corsica, Sardinia, Dalmatia and Cappadocia, and if these were rejected the frontier would contract dramatically. All the relevant data is available in Chapters 6–9 for readers wishing to revise the map.

Thirty-nine squares, not indicated as Celtic in Maps 5.1–5.3, have been shaded in Map 11.1. The names now taken into account are listed in the following table. The second column shows the percentages from Map 5.2 and the third shows the total number of toponyms per square used in the calculation of those percentages (see p. 162 above). The new names contain strings not investigated in Chapter 4. Some, cited within curly brackets, are drawn from the *Barrington Atlas* lists of 'unlocated' names (marked *unl* in the table) or from sources not exploited in the *Atlas* (these are not marked *unl*). Full details and discussion of these names can be found in Chapters 6–9. Clearly, the Celticity of the new names is of variable quality; any reader disputing them can easily modify Map 11.1 on the basis of the following table.

1	0%	5	−04	39	{*unl* Barnakis}
2	0%	5	−02	37	Eliocroca; Longuntica
3	0%	1	−02	39	{*unl* Urbiaca}
4	0%	12	−01	42	Forum Gallorum; Iac(c)a; Pertusa; Suessetani
5	0%	13	+00	41	Gallika Phlaouia; {Cinga}; {*unl* Kinna}
6	0%	6	+04	50	Geminiacum; Vodgoriacum

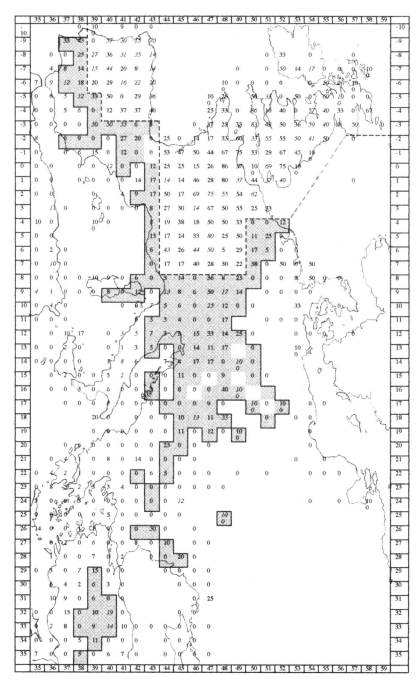

Map 11.1 Revised distribution of Celtic names in Europe and Asia Minor

7	0%	7	+04	51 Helinium (fl.); Condacum; Vacalus fl./Vahalis fl.
8	0%	21	+07	43 *Anao; *Cuntinus; Vediantii; Vintium; Tavia fl.
9	0%	2	+08	43 Lucus Bormani
10	0%	3	+08	46 Lepontii
11	0%	8	+08	50 Mattiaci (etc.); Moenus fl.; Mogontiacum; Nida; Taunus M.; {Artaunon}; {Segodounon}
12	0%	27	+09	41 Gallicum Fretum
13	0%	6	+10	46 Aquae Bormiae
14	0%	6	+10	49 Iciniacum; {Dêouona}; {Kantioibis}; {Rhiousiaoua}
15	0%	26	+11	46 Anaunion/Anauni; Brixenetes; Burrus fl.; Maiensis Statio; Vervassium
16	0%	12	+11	47 Cosuanetes; Coveliacae; *Mastiacum
17	0%	34	+13	45 Varamos fl.; Catali
18	0%	2	+13	50 Boihaemum
19	0%	10	+14	48 [Druna] fl.; Lauriacum
20	0%	2	+14	50 Boii
21	0%	10	+15	43 Arausa; Blandona
22	0%	34	+15	46 Flavia Solva; Solva fl.
23	0%	2	+15	50 {Boudorgis}
24	0%	11	+16	47 Arabiates; Arrabo fl.; Boii; 'Muteno'
25	–	–	+16	51 {Lougidounon}
26	0%	18	+17	44 Ad Matricem
27	0%	8	+17	45 'Cardono'
28	0%	7	+17	46 Hercuniates; Limusa; 'Silicenis'; Volgum
29	0%	1	+18	51 {Dounoi}
30	0%	2	+20	45 Rittium
31	0%	18	+21	44 'Bao'; Viminacium
32	0%	12	+22	42 {unl Kasibonon}; {Loukounanta}
33	0%	14	+23	43 Remetodia
34	0%	20	+24	43 Oescus; Oescus fl.
35	0%	2	+26	42 {unl Orkelis}
36	0%	24	+28	44 Vicus 'Ver(gob)rittiani'; {unl Dagis}; {Gabranus fl.}
37	0%	18	+31	40 Araunia; Balgatia; {Bogdomanis}
38	0%	19	+32	38 Kongoustos/Congussus
39	0%	11	+33	38 Perta

It will be seen that the Celticity of a number of squares depends solely on the possible presence of the Celtic /a:ko/ suffix (items 1, 3, 6), which is a weak indicator, especially when the stem to which it is attached is not Celtic.[1] In one case (12. *Gallicum Fretum*, between Corsica and Sardinia) the linguistic significance of *Gallicus* is obviously small, and in two cases (9 and 13) the Celticity depends on how the stem *Borm-* is classified, which is debated.[2]

In Map 11.1, a number of squares that were provisionally regarded as 'Celtic-looking' in Maps 5.1–5.3 are now unshaded as a result of the closer scrutiny in Chapters 6–9. The absence of shading in squares with percentages between 1 and 10 can be attributed without further discussion to the inevitable occurrence of Celtic-looking elements by mere coincidence. Percentages between 11% and 100% appear in 16 unshaded squares. They

---

[1] See above, p. 10.
[2] See above, p. 193, n. 135. Even granting that the theonyms *Bormo* etc. are linguistically Celtic, it is conceivable that the Celtic cult spread to non-Celtic-speaking areas.

are mostly due to the small number of names of all sorts in the squares in question. For example, +13/53 has '100%' but no shading because it was decided in Chapter 6 that the only place in this square, **Lemovii?**, was probably only 'Celtic-looking' rather than genuinely Celtic. The details for these 16 squares are summarized below; the second column gives the percentages and the third has the number of toponyms in the square that was used to calculate them.

1	15%	13	27	E2	−01	39	Edetania	Edetani	**Sed**etani?	
			27	E2	−01	39	**Sag**untum	Arse		
2	12%	8	25	*Av*	+00	40	**Cass**ae Herronesi			
3	11%	18	30	F3	+03	36	**Ic**osium			
			30	*unl*	+03	36	Tamar**iceto**			
							Praesidium			
4	100%	1	27	inset	+04	39	**Mag**o			
5	50%	2	10	D4	+07	52	**Teut**oburgiensis?			
							Saltus			
6	50%	2	10	D2	+07	54	**Abal*us? Ins.			
7	50%	2	10	E2	+08	54	**Teut**ones?			
8	33%	3	10	G3	+10	53	**Lang**obardi			
9	17%	6	47	B2	+12	38	Emporion			
							Seg**estan**on			
10	100%	1	2	F3	+13	53	**Lem**ovii?			
11	20%	5	45	inset	+18	39	Uzentum	**Oux**enton	Augentum	
12	14%	7	21	D7	+21	42	'**Vind**enis'			
13	12%	8	22	*unl*	+24	45	**Kot**ensioi			
14	14%	14	60	F2	+26	35	'**Ket**ia'? Pr.			
			60	F2	+26	35	**Sed**amnos? fl.			
15	25%	4	23	E1	+31	47	**Sag**aris fl.	Rhode fl.		
16	13%	23	66	B1	+32	37	**Ic**onium	Claud**icon**ium	Col. Iulia	Col. Aelia
									Augusta	Hadriana
									Equestris?	Augusta
			66	A1	+32	37	**Korn**a?			
			66	A2	+32	37	**Sed*asa			

Map 11.2 again indicates the extent of Celtic names by means of a line round the main Celtic area and the three subsidiary areas north-west and south of the Black Sea. Within the frontiers shown on Map 11.1 there were various blank squares. The lack of Celtic names in most of these squares may be due to their shortage of toponyms in general. In three cases, however, marked in black on Map 11.2, 10 or more toponyms are attested so the lack of Celtic names seems significant:

−2/43 and −1/43 *North-western Pyrenees and southern Aquitania.* This area is contiguous with the central Pyrenees, where the superficial Celtic element in square −1/42 (*Forum Gallorum, Iac(c)a, Pertusa* and *Suessetani*) seems to be due to secondary immigration from Gaul.[3] Square +0/42 has few

---

[3] See p. 237 above.

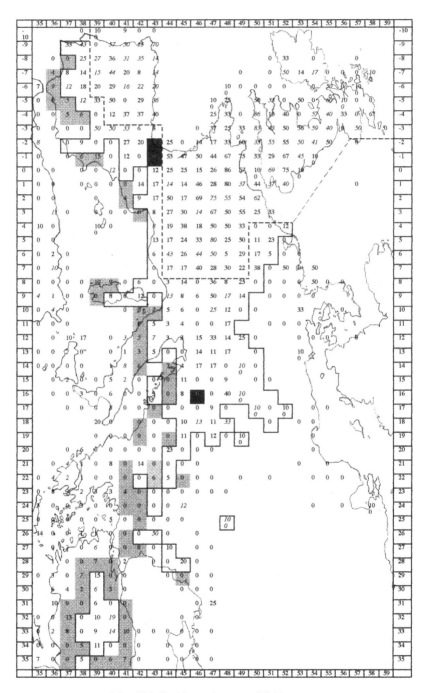

Map 11.2 Significant absences of Celtic names

names, but none of them is Celtic. In effect, then, there is a discontinuity between Celtic Gaul and Celtic Spain. This can be associated in part with the presence of Aquitanian (proto-Basque).[4]

+16/46 *North-western Pannonia*. The lack of Celtic names here may be a symptom of the superficiality of the Celticization of Pannonia; Anreiter points out that the Celtic toponyms, always in a minority, tend to be associated with places of economic and strategic importance.[5]

The question arises whether Celtic toponyms occurred beyond the frontiers marked on Map 11.2 but escaped recording. This is more plausible in areas where few names are recorded, such as Germany beyond the Rhine, than it is in well-documented areas like central Italy. On Map 11.2 darker shading marks the squares which were examined in Chapters 6–9 and found to contain 10 or more places with non-Celtic names. The frontier of Celtic names seems fairly secure at these squares, which are nearly all in the south. By contrast, in the north nothing excludes the hypothesis that Celtic names once joined *Lugii* (+17/52), *Dounoi* (+18/51), *Cotini* (+19/49) and *Karro-dounon* (+25/48?) in a great arc north of the Carpathians, and that they continued from *Karrodounon* south-east down the river Dniester to the Black Sea. Post-classical evidence would be needed to confirm this hypothesis, however.[6]

A final note of caution: there is no reason why the area of Celtic place-names must have been originally continuous; Celtic speakers may have passed through some areas too swiftly to affect their toponymy. The Celtic groups that eventually reached Galatia via Delphi illustrate this; they left no toponymic (or archaeological)[7] traces behind them in Greece. We must therefore resist the temptation to join up all the discrete areas on Map 11.2. For example, at longitude +25 there may have been a genuine discontinuity in Celtic toponymy along the Danube.[8]

[4] Cf. Gorrochategui, *Estudio*, and 'Lengua aquitana y lengua gala', and VCIE. For the equation of Aquitanian and Basque see Trask, *History of Basque*, pp. 398–403.

[5] Anreiter, *Die vorrömischen Namen Pannoniens*, p. 203, nn. 702–3. In the maps in KPP, pp. 347–49, the obviously Celtic *Belgites* (20unl) are fitted in at about +16/46, but they are not really localizable (see Anreiter, *Die vorrömischen Namen Pannoniens*, pp. 149–50). Some Celtic personal names occur in inscriptions in the north-west of this square, on the Norican border: *Eliomarus* at Rábagyarmat and *Adnamatus* at Jennersdorf (quoted in KPP, pp. 108 and 159, but not mapped on pp. 347–48).

[6] See Chapter 6, p. 195.

[7] Cunliffe, *Ancient Celts*, pp. 82 and 306, cited in Sims-Williams, 'Celtomania and Celtoscepticism', p. 31.

[8] On arguments about Celtic names along the Danube, see Papazoglu, cited above, p. 10. The *Atlas* marks *Tylis*, site of a well-known Celtic kingdom, at +25/42 (22C6); against this localization see Falileyev, '*Tylis*'.

12

PROSPECTS FOR FURTHER RESEARCH

12.1 CHRONOLOGICAL DIFFERENTIATION OF THE NAMES

This study has aimed to reveal the wide extent of Celtic place-names in the ancient world. Further research, of a different character, is needed to explain the historical context in which these names were first given.

One would like to know, for example, whether Celtic names were still spreading into new areas after they had become fossilized and overlaid by other linguistic strata in others. A real difficulty, however, is the relatively late date at which most Celtic names are attested, even around the Mediterranean where literacy first developed. For example, few of the Celtic names in the area of north Italy between latitudes 42 and 47 and longitudes +8 to +11 are mentioned in texts written before the first century BC, even though cities like *Mediolanum* (+9/45), *Cremona* and *Mantua* (+10/45), *Litubium* (+9/44) and *Bononia* (+11/44), are said by Livy and other sources to have been in existence in the fourth to second centuries BC.[1] In northern Europe, of course, very few names are attested before Caesar's conquests in the mid-first century BC, apart from a bare handful of names collected by early travellers like Pytheas and preserved by later writers such as Strabo and Avienus.[2]

Notwithstanding such problems, a careful comparison of Celtic names attested in, say, the first century BC with those attested in the fourth century AD might reveal significant developments. Perhaps some types of names would only appear in the later period. Allowances would have to be made for the differing nature of the sources; for example, Caesar and Livy would tend to mention major settlements whereas the later Itineraries would mention minor stopping places.

At present, however, we know little about changes in the popularity of different types of Celtic names. While it is easy to see what formations remained productive, such as the /a:ko/ suffix, which could be attached to Roman personal names,[3] it is harder to decide which ones were innovations and which were obsolescent. The fact that Caesar mentions no *-acus* names in Gaul may signify that this type of name (soon to be recorded by Tacitus and Pliny) was not yet current in his day, but it is hard to be sure.[4] In any

---

[1] See TIR L-32 s.nn. On these Celticity of these names see Chs. 7 and 8. Of these five, only *Mediolanum* is mentioned earlier than the first century BC, by Polybius 2.34.10–2.35.1.
[2] See Freeman, 'Earliest Greek sources'.
[3] Russell, 'Suffix'.
[4] Cf. ibid. pp. 143 and 151.

case, what is true of Gaul may not be true of other areas; ethnyms in -*akos* already occurred in Celtiberia in Caesar's time.[5]

Elements which were obviously productive in the Augustan period are those which were combined with *Augusto-*, *Caesaro-*, or *Iulio-*. In Gaul these are limited to *bona, dunum, durum, magus, nemetum* and *ritum*, and imperial names are not found with *briga* and *briva*.[6] It would be dangerous, however, to argue that *briga* and *briva* were no longer productive in Gaul; perhaps a hill or bridge was not considered worthy of the imperial name,[7] or perhaps the lack of examples is pure coincidence.

Another approach to the chronology of name-types is to see which ones are widely spread (these might be assumed to be early) and which ones are geographically more restricted (these might be assumed to be late). Thus the fact that Gaul and Britain have names in *briga, dunum* and *magus*, whereas only *briga* is typical of Iberia, has been taken to show that *briga* names 'appear to represent an early linguistic stage, before [Celtic] contacts with the British Isles'.[8] The implication is that only *briga* was in toponymic use at some early date (*c.* 750 BC, Piggott implied) and that *dunum* and *magus* came into use in central areas after some Celtic-speakers had crossed the Pyrenees. Such an interpretation is speculative, because we do not know what lexical items were current in prehistoric Common Celtic toponymy. It is possible that all three words existed only in the ordinary lexicon at first and became used in place-names in different areas independently and at different times. While Celtic-speakers in Iberia may have known all three words, as *words*, they perhaps chose to promote *brix/ briga* 'hill' (OI *brí*, W *bre*) to the status of 'hillfort, important place' and ceased, or never started, to use the others in toponymy. The evidence can thus re-interpreted in terms of dialect and fashion rather than chronology; the *dunum* names of Gaul are not necessarily a younger class than the *briga* names.

A useful caution is provided by Old English names in -*tun* (Modern English *town*). These are numerous and it would be easy to assume, by comparison with Scandinavian and Continental Germanic toponymy, that they belonged to an ancient layer of Germanic name-forming brought to Britain by the first Anglo-Saxon settlers in the fifth century. In fact, however, there is enough surviving documentation of seventh- and eighth-century English toponymy to make it virtually certain that names in -*tun* were only starting to come into fashion, at least for noteworthy places,

---

[5] Ibid. pp. 165–69.

[6] Bedon, 'Noms de villes hybrides', p. 39.

[7] In Spain *briga* occurs in several imperial names, as noted by Bedon (ibid. pp. 39, n. 15, and 46), but there it probably had a higher status, equivalent to *dunum* in Gaul (see below). On imperial names see further Rivet, 'Celtic names and Roman places', pp. 9–15. He quotes the opinion that *Brutobriga* in Spain was founded by D. Junius Brutus *c.* 133 BC and is thus the earliest known such hybrid (p. 4, n. 15; cf. Tovar, *Lusitanien*, p. 171). See also Ch. 1 above, p. 14, n. 66.

[8] Piggott, *Ancient Europe*, pp. 173–74, citing Rix, 'Zur Verbreitung'.

c. 730 AD.[9] It would thus be wrong to project a distribution map based on medieval place-names back into the sixth century, let alone earlier. In the same way, it is dangerous to use Celtic data on *briga* names from the first century BC and later as evidence of Celtic practice five or more centuries earlier.

Apart from these general problems, the detail of the distribution of names in *briga*, *dunum* and *magus* raises difficulties (see Maps 12.1–12.3). If *briga* names were part of Common Celtic toponymy, we might expect to find them all over the Celtic world, but there are gaps. There are only two in Britain and none in north Italy.[10] In the east the only secure example is *Aliobrix* (+28/45); *Ec(c)obriga* in Galatia (+33/39, TP and Rav.) is uncertain, as the *Antonine Itinerary* has *Ecobrogis*, and all the other places east of longitude +18 on Map 12.1 contain the element *bria* which is more likely to be Thracian *bria* than Celtic *bria* < *briga* in this region.[11] *Dunum* names are in fact rather more widespread than *briga* names, especially if the unlocated *Kapedounon* in Moesia Superior is taken into account. Even in Iberia there are *Sebendounon/Beseldunum* (+2/42), *Caladunum* (−8/41), *Arialdunum* (−6/37 ?) and an unlocatable *Esttledunum* nearby.[12] It might argued that these four rather obscure names are the remains of an old stratum of *dunum* names in Iberia which was eclipsed the productive *briga* stratum; alternatively, they could be relatively late intrusions.[13] By contrast, *magus* names have a very limited but concentrated distribution, especially as the two names in the south (+4/39 *Mago* and +15/37 *Magea Fons*) are irrelevant. Here we have a clear Gaulish and Insular[14] distribution which can be put together with similar distributions for some other elements discussed in 12.2 below.

The only other element for whose distribution an historical explanation has been advanced is *duro-* (see Map 12.4). Assuming that *Audurus (Fundus)*

---

[9] Cox, 'Place-names of the earliest English records', pp. 65–66; Gelling & Cole, *Landscape of Place-Names*, p. xx. For Continental evidence, see literature cited in Ch. 1, p. 13, n. 59.

[10] Although *Brixenetes* (+11/46), *Brixia* (+10/45) and *Brixellum* (+10/44) may be derivatives; see Chapter 4, s.v. *brig-* and PNPG Possibly Celtic Elements s.v. *brixo-*.

[11] See Ch. 8.

[12] See Ch. 4, s.v. *dūno-*. On *Arialdunum* see p. 227 above. A derivation of *Caladunum* from Greek *kala* 'logs', referring to a *murus gallicus*, is quoted by Billy, review of Parsons & Sims-Williams (ed.), *Ptolemy*, p. 314, but seems unlikely in view of the many names in *Cala-* in Iberia.

[13] Villar, 'Celtic language', pp. 256–57 and 267–68. See ibid. pp. 257–58 and 268 on *briga* names. If *Arialdunum* contains **ialo-* it may be late; see above, p. 227, n. 27.

[14] The lack of *magus* names in ancient sources for Ireland is probably due to the scarcity of sources not the scarcity of such names (a fraction of those from post-classical sources are marked on the eclectic maps by Rix and Piggott). Ptolemy's *Makolikon* (2.2.9) is unlikely to be relevant, as *magus* is not normally a first element. Incidentally, this name may disprove the intriguing observation that 'there are no compounds among the town-names in Ptolemy's Ireland' (De Bernardo Stempel, 'Ptolemy's Celtic Italy and Ireland', p. 102; she regarded this name as 'obscure' in n. 40, but now treats it as compound in 'More on Ptolemy's evidence for Celtic Ireland', p. 99). See also PNPG Possibly Celtic Elements s.vv. *lico-* and *maco-*.

in north Africa, *Duronia* in Italy and *Durostorum* on the eastern Danube are irrelevant,[15] the names are centred on Gaul and adjacent territories. Rivet argued that the subset with *Duro-* as the first element of a compound (e.g. *Durocortorum*, already in Caesar, *Gallic War* 6.44) was specifically 'Belgic' and that 'the most likely explanation of its appearance in Britain is the [Belgic] migration recorded by Caesar', the only case in Britain of the reverse compound being *Lactodorum*.[16] This 'Belgic' intepretation involves explaining away not only *Durostorum* but also *Durocasses* (+1/48) in the wrong part of Gaul as 'a tribal name and so irrelevant' (the same would presumably apply to −3/50 *Durotriges* in Britain),[17] and *Durotincum/Durotingum* (+6/45) as a 'rationalization' of a possibly Ligurian name (the same would presumably apply to +1/45 *Durotincum*).[18] Note also that according to Rivet himself there may have been a second **Durocornovium*, not in the *Atlas*, in Cornwall (Rav. *Purocoronavis*, *Purocoronains*),[19] which is rather far west to be 'Belgic'. Perhaps Rivet's case for 'Belgic' involves too much special pleading? On the other hand, the concentration of *Duro-* names in Britain seems to be more than coincidental, and a connection with the nearest part of the Continent seems plausible.

The southerly distribution of *duro-* names in Britain can perhaps be linked with the fact that no names containing *briva* occur further north than *Durobrivae* (Water Newton, Huntingdonshire), the most northern of the *duro-* names. Another place-name element, common in Gaul, which only appears in *southern* Britain is *ande-*; this only appears in *Anderidos/ Anderitos* on the Sussex coast (+0/50), a name twice paralleled by examples of *Anderitum* on the Continent.[20]

12.2 REGIONAL VARIATION IN NAMES

As can be seen from the maps in Chapter 4, some Celtic-looking elements occur all over the presumed Celtic areas of Europe and Asia Minor. Others are more restricted in distribution, however, and not simply because of the chance distributions that are bound to occur when small numbers are

---

[15] See Ch. 4 s.v. *duro-* and Ch. 7, p. 216. Of the names in Spain, *Ilduro* is clearly dubious; see Ch. 8 above, p. 239, and 12.2 (b) below.

[16] Rivet, 'Celtic names and Roman places', p. 13. Cf. Zupitza, 'Kelten und Gallier', pp. 17–18; Weisgerber, p. 44; PNRB, pp. 346–47.

[17] On which cf. Breeze, 'Not Durotriges but Durotrages'.

[18] Rivet, 'Celtic names and Roman places', pp. 14 and 13, n. 13 (citing Barruol, p. 138, on -*inc*-). For the other *Durotincum* (14G3 = (perhaps) Villejoubert, Cm. St-Denis-les-Murs), see RIG ii/2, no. L-75 (DVROTINCIO). AILR Celtic Elements sees the Celtic element *tinco-* in +2/46 *Tincontium* (14H2). For *Tinco-* as Celtic see above, Ch. 4 s.v.

[19] PNRB, p. 350.

[20] See Ch. 4 s.v. *ande-* and Map 4.1.

involved. The most striking regional variations are listed and mapped as follows.

(a) Elements confined to Britain and Gaul[21]

This is the largest group. The *magus* names discussed above belong here. See also (b) below on *rat-/rāt-* and *ritu-*. Other elements (see Maps 12.5–12.13) are:

banno- 'high; height' – rejecting *Abannae* in Africa.

brīuo-, brīuā 'bridge' – if *Brevis* in Iberia (−9/42) is rejected (as Latin?) and the various examples of *bria* in the east are otherwise explained, for example as Thracian *bria* 'polis' (cf. above on *briga*). The Austrian medieval name *Pons Prienne* (1254), now Perjen, suggests that the distribution went further south than on my map.[22] In Britain, as noted above, names containing *briva* occur no further north than *Durobrivae* (Water Newton, Huntingdonshire) and the word has no reflex in the later Brittonic languages, being superseded by *pont* from Latin – in fact Hamp regards Romano-British names like *Ad Pontem* and *Pontibus* as already semi-British.[23] What Celtic speakers in Iberia and the east called bridges and causeways remains obscure.[24]

catu- 'battle, army'.

condate 'confluence'. In Iberia *compl(e)ut-* seems to have been preferred (see Chapter 4, s.v.) and in Britain *condate* (in Cheshire) competed with the ancestor of W *cymer*, Breton *kemper*, OI *commar*, 'confluence', represented by *Combretovium* in Suffolk.[25] In general Latin *Confluentes* may have superseded Celtic terms.

corio- 'warband' (assuming that + 12/41 *Corioli* is irrelevant, p. 250 above).

dervo- 'oak'. This element is concentrated in Britain, but one name, *Derventum*, is in Gaul and is backed up by later derivatives.[26] A different ablaut form (not mapped) is arguably seen in southern Gaul in *Druentia fl.* (15D2 = +4/43), on which stood *Druantium* (17H4 = +6/44), and in *Drunemeton* (63unl *Drynemeton* = +32/40) in Galatia.[27]

vellauno- 'governor'.

ventā 'market?' – assuming that *Ventipo* in southern Spain, with its non-Celtic *-ipo* is irrelevant. If *Tiliaventum* in Austria/Italy is also irrelevant (see

---

[21] 'Gaul' may be used below in a broad sense, e.g. to include adjacent areas of Germania.

[22] Anreiter, *Breonen*, p. 138; DLG s.v. *briua*. PNRB, p. 347, notes that *briva* is 'abundantly documented in Gaulish ... rare in Iberia and seemingly unknown in the easterly Celtic regions'. Actually there are no examples from Iberia in Holder.

[23] '*Ad Pontem, Pontibus* as British'.

[24] Cf. Zimmer, '*A uo penn*', pp. 205–6.

[25] PNRB, pp. 313–16. Continental parallels to *cymer* in Holder i, 1071, and iii, 1259, and DLG s.v. *comberos*. There seems to be no ancient trace of **Adber-* or **Ab(b)er-* (Welsh *aber*).

[26] PNRB, pp. 333–34; Nègre i, §§ 2323–25; DLG s.v. *deruos*.

[27] Cf. DLG, pp. 141 and 149; Ch. 4 above, s.v. *nemeton*; PNPG Possibly Celtic Elements s.v. *dru-* (cf. Kitson, 'River-names', pp. 77–81 and 94); De Hoz, 'Narbonensis', pp. 177–78.

Chapter 4, s.v. *ventā*), the only ancient Continental example of the element is **Ganuenta* in the Netherlands.[28]

verno- 'alder, swamp'. In addition to the places mapped, there was 8unl *Vernalis* somewhere in south-west Britain.[29]

(b) Widespread elements absent from Iberia

This is the next largest group, and shows the distinctiveness of the Iberian peninsula rather better than the distribution of *dunum* names does. See Maps 12.14–12.20.

boud- 'victory' and *bodio-* 'yellow' (treated together since they are sometimes indistinguishable). The names mapped in Italy, Sardinia, Greece and Asia Minor are unlikely to be relevant, but the unlocatable names *Bodas* on the Danube in Lower Moesia or Scythia and *Toutobodiaci* in Galatia (see Chapter 4) suggest that these toponymic elements were pan-Celtic apart from Iberia.

carno- 'peak, cairn'. Whether the element *carn-* in all these toponyms is the same is doubtful; nevertheless, their absence from Iberia is striking.[30]

corno- 'horn'. The same applies to *corno-* which may in fact be etymologically related to *carno-*.

novio- 'new'. This is common in Gaul, but found also in south-east England, Pannonia and Scythia Minor, always with a restricted range of second elements, mostly *-dunum* and *-magus*. The absence from Iberia of any ***Noviobriga*, ***Neviobriga*, or the like is notable.

rat- 'fern' and *rāt-* 'earthwork' (treated together since they are sometimes indistinguishable). As the eastern examples are dubious,[31] these elements should perhaps be placed under (a) above, 'Elements confined to Britain and Gaul'. The only example of the string RAT in Iberia is the Celtiberian coin-legend *Areikoratikos/Arekorata* (25cn.), which is more naturally segmented *Are(i)-kor-at-ikos*.

ritu- 'ford'. This too should perhaps be placed under (a) above, since the eastern names *Abritus* (+26/43) and, more definitely, *Begorritus L.* (+21/40) are uncertain. The absence from ancient Iberia of both *briva* 'bridge' and *ritu* 'ford' is striking.[32]

---

[28] This form is deduced from an inscription to the goddess Nehalennia by 'Gimio Ganuent(ae?) cons(istens)' (TIR M-31, pp. 91–92). Toorians, *Keltisch en Germaans in de Nederlanden*, p. 114, takes the second element to be *venta* with Gan- < **genu-* 'mouth, river-mouth' (cf. DLG s.v. *genaua*). PNRB, pp. 263–64, say that there are no ancient Continental examples.

[29] I have not mapped *Usuerna*, as it is a misreading of *Usuerua*.

[30] VCIE, pp. 82, n. 224, and 85, notes only a theonym *Carneo* in Portugal.

[31] On *Ratiaria* (+22/43) and 21unl *Ratakensioi* see above, pp. 211 and 257.

[32] DLG s.v. *ritu-* mentions the etymology *Madrid* < **Mageto-ritum* or **Matu-ritum*. PNRB, p. 251, says that **ritu-* 'seems to be not known in N. Italy or Spain'. *Aritium* (−8/39) and *Aritium Praetorium* (−9/39) in Lusitania are uncertain examples; see Ch. 8 above, p. 224.

seno- 'old'. Possibly the synonymous *cot(t)-* was preferred in Iberia (see Chapter 4 s.v.)? The absence from Iberia of personal names in *Seno-* is also striking.[33]

Probably *duro-* is also rare or absent from Iberia, the two instances on Map 12.4 being dubious.[34] *Eburo-* may also be absent from Iberia (see (c) below).

(c) Widespread elements absent from the east

While the relative scarcity of Celtic toponyms in general may be a factor, the absence of the following is noteworthy (see Maps 12.21–25; *Ux-*, Map 4.11, may also belong here):

alaun- (meaning debated), found no further east than the *Alaunoi* of southern Germany.

dēvo-, dīvo- 'god'. The only unlocatable name in the east, omitted from the map, is *Deoniana* in Moesia II and this is unlikely to be Celtic.[35]

eburo- 'yew', found no further east than Ptolemy's *Ebourodounon* and *Ebouron* in the vicinity of Brno in the Czech Republic (+ 16/49). Owing to its position, the *Eburum* in southern Italy (+ 15/40), modern Eboli, seems unlikely to be Celtic, though Celticity cannot be ruled out.[36] *Ebura Cerialis* (−4/37) is shown on Map 12.23 but should properly be *Ebora*, a probably irrelevant name.[37]

Lugu- (divine name?), found no further east than *Lugio* in Hungary (Pannonia), which is moreover an uncertain instance.[38]

sego- 'power; bold', found no further east than *Segestica* in Pannonia (+ 16/ 45) – or no further east than *Segodounon* (+ 8/50), if names in *Segest-* are disassociated from *sego-*, which is plausible.[39]

(d) Widespread elements absent from Britain

It has already been noted (p. 309) that some elements only occur in *southern* Britain (*ande-, briva, duro-*). A few do not appear at all (see Maps 12.26–28):[40]

---

[33] KGP, pp. 266–67; OPEL iv, 67.

[34] Cf. VCIE, p. 348, noting TARVODVRESCA (ibid. pp. 303–5) as a possible exception.

[35] See Ch. 7 above, p. 216. The string *Dio-* (as in *Diolindum*) was not listed in Ch. 4, but I can find no *Dio-* names in the east that are plausibly Celtic.

[36] See Chapter 8, p. 251.

[37] See above, pp. 78 and 225.

[38] Non-Celtic explanation in Anreiter, *Die vorrömischen Namen Pannoniens*, pp. 216–17.

[39] See Ch. 4, s.v. *sego-*. I am assuming that *Seggo* and *Segermes* in Africa are irrelevant.

[40] I do not include *cot(t)-* 'old' among them, as the unlocatable *Atecotti* may have been British. *Cot(t)-* may in fact be absent from Gaul, since *Caracotinum* (Harfleur) is probably not an instance; on the other hand, 25unl *Cottion* may have been in Gaul. See Ch. 4, s.v. *cott-*, and Map 4.5. On *Cotini/Kotinai* see also Ch. 8, p. 230.

carro- 'cart, chariot'. This is absent from France as well and, if *Carruca* in Spain is otherwise explained,[41] *carro-* may be exclusively north-eastern. Possibly *carbanto-* was preferred in British and Gaulish toponymy, as in *Karbantorigon* in Britain (9D5 = −4/55), *Carpentorate* (15E1 = +5/44) in France and *Carbantia* (39C3 = +8/45) in north Italy. These are marked on Map 12.26 for comparison.

mant- 'path'. Possibly the synonym *sentu-* was preferred in Britain, as in *Gabrosentum* (−4/54).[42]

sag- 'seek' and *sag-ro-* 'strong'. Perhaps the absence of *sag-* in Britain is due to some confusion with *seg-* or even an ancient ablaut alternation? Thus we have *Seguntium* in Wales (−5/53) versus *Saguntia* and *Saguntum* in Spain (−6/36 and −1/39, cf. 5unl *Sagantion* in India), also *Vosegus M.* (+7/48)[43] and **Vosagum* (+1/46), in Germany and France.[44]

(e) Widespread element absent from Britain and Iberia

Only one well-attested element seems to come into this category: *bon-* 'base, foundation?'. This does not occur west of longitude 00 (see Map 12.29)

The overall impression given by the above data is that Gaul (broadly defined) and to some extent Britain (especially southern Britain) had the greatest variety of Celtic elements and that the peripheral areas in the east and especially in Iberia had the least variety. This agrees with Gorrochategui's impression:

> So far as the Celtic linguistic world is concerned, I have found a greater lexical richness in toponymy in Gaul than in Celtiberia, or even in Indo-European Hispania. Apart from frequency, I believe that we also see a greater vitality, since these elements are also freely used in the formation of Gallo-Roman hybrids. Comparing toponyms from the Roman period formed on the basis of Roman personal names, we find that in Hispania they are almost all compounds terminating in *-briga* (*Caesarobriga*, *Augustobriga*, *Iuliobriga* and *Flaviobriga*), with only one in *-olca* (*Octaviolca*), whereas in Gaul there is a much wider variation for such toponyms and the following among others are found: *Augustoritum*, *Augustonemetum*, *Augustodunum*, *Caesarodunum*, *Augustomagus*, *Iuliomagus*, *Augustodurum*.[45]

---

[41] See Ch. 8, p. 226.

[42] See Ch. 4, s.v. *sentu-*.

[43] *Vosegus* and *Vosagus* are both common in the sources for this range (the Vosges): Holder iii, 448.

[44] See remarks in Villar, *Indoeuropeos y no indoeuropeos*, pp. 312–13 and 384, VCIE, pp. 267 and 471–72, PNRB, p. 454, and PNPG Celtic Elements and Possibly Celtic Elements s.v. *sag(o)-* (< **sh₂g-*, zero-grade of **seh₂g-* 'follow a trail, seek').

[45] Gorrochategui, 'Ptolemy's Aquitania and the Ebro valley', pp. 149–50. He continues: 'to these must be added other combinations with *-bona*, *-ialos*, *-lanum*, *-briua*, and *–ratis*.' I have not found these with imperial names, apart from *-bona*.

Historical explanations for the above impressions are bound to be tentative. The lower frequency and vitality could be due to smaller Celtic-speaking populations, or to loss of contact with the more dynamic central regions, or to competition from pre-Celtic, non-Celtic or Graeco-Latin toponymy, or to a variety of such factors. It is also conceivable that areas like Galicia in the west and Galatia in the east preserve traces of fashions in Celtic place-names which are so early that we have difficulty in recognizing them as Celtic. Any assumption that areas with the greatest variety of Celtic names are the areas of the oldest Celtic speech should probably be resisted.

A further possible line of research would be to compare the distribution of different categories of Celtic names: hydronyms, oronyms, ethnonyms and so on. It is usually believed that the oldest names are likely to be those of rivers and mountains, so that these, when Celtic, may indicate the areas of the earliest settlement by Celtic-speakers.[46] Conversely, areas where Celtic river-names are much fewer than Celtic habitation-names, such as the eastern Danube basin or the Po basin,[47] might be argued to have been settled later.

12.3 RELATIONSHIP BETWEEN CELTIC AND NON-CELTIC NAMES

This study has operated with a simple distinction between Celtic and non-Celtic names, not even subdividing the latter into Latin and non-Latin. Obviously, more discrimination would lead to a more subtle linguistic geography. The same method that we have applied to Celtic elements could be applied to those other languages, and even to 'toponymic languages' deduced solely from place-names; this would help to clarify the frontiers between Celtic and other ancient languages.

Our method gives the best results with strings that are geographically quite defined. An example is given in Map 12.30. This shows the distribution in the *Barrington* data of the following strings:

TETRA

This is chosen to illustrate Greek, since this phonetic form of the Indo-European numeral 'four' is unique. The instances are as follows and clearly cover the area of Greek influence (75unl *Tetrathyron* was in Egypt and the places in maps 68 and 73 were in Syria and Libya):

---

[46] Hubert, *Rise of the Celts*, p. 151, used this argument in favour of a Celtic migration from Germany into Gaul, but his data seem untrustworthy. In general, distinguishing Celtic hydronyms and oronyms from merely Indo-European ones is difficult.

[47] Falileyev, 'Celtic presence in Dobrudja'; Chevallier, *La romanisation de la Celtique du Pô*, i, 113–15.

22	E6	+27	42	Naulochos	Templum Iovis?	**Tetra**naulochus
52	F3	+29	40	**Tetra**komia		
59	B3	+23	37	**Tetra**komoi		
59	C2	+23	38	**Tetra**polis		
62	F5	+31	38	**Tetra**polis		
62	*unl*	*+28*	*38*	**Tetra**pyrgia		
63	*unl*	*+32*	*38*	**Tetra**dion		
63	*unl*	*+33*	*38*	**Tetra**pyrgia		
65	E4	+30	36	**Tetra**pyrgia		
66	E2	+34	37	**Tetra**pyrgia?		
66	*unl*	*+34*	*37*	**Tetra**(pyrgia?)		
68	G2	+38	36	**Tetra**pyrgium		
73	C2	+25	32	Catabathmus Maior	Plynos Limen	**Tetra**pyrgia
75	*unl*			**Tetra**thyron		
86	*unl*	*+35*	*42*	**Tetra**kis		
87	L2	+36	45	**Tetra**xitai		

TIGI (as termination)

This string, which is possibly to be segmented *-t-igi* and regarded as a subtype of names in *-igi*,[48] is confined to southern Iberia:[49]

26	D4	−07	37	Las**tigi**	
26	D4	−07	37	Olon**tigi**	
26	E3	−06	38	Ar**tigi**	
26	E4	−06	37	As**tigi**	Col. Augusta Firma
26	*unl*			As**tigi** Vetus?	Eiskadia?
26	*unl*			Las**tigi**	
27	A4	−05	37	*Soson**tigi**	Sosin**tigi**
27	B3	−04	38	Can**tigi**	
27	D3	−02	38	Sal**tigi**	

DAVA/DAUA (as termination)

This string is predominantly found in the vicinity of Dacia,[50] except for *Cardava* in Arabia, *Egdava* in Anatolia,[51] and *Calcidava* in Armenia:

---

[48] Cf. Villar, *Indoeuropeos y no indoeuropeos*, p. 255.

[49] *Astigi Vetus* (cf. Ch. 4, n. 38, s.v. *iscā*) and *Lastigi* are not precisely locatable; see Tovar, *Baetica*, pp. 113, 138 and 167.

[50] Cf. Katačić, *Ancient Languages of the Balkans*, pp. 147–49 and 176; Duridanov, 'Thrakische und dakische Namen', p. 834; Anreiter, *Die vorrömischen Namen Pannoniens*, p. 179; Falileyev, '*Tylis*', p. 112. I ignore the string DABA, which adds nothing relevant. On the other hand, DEBA leads to 22unl *Moundeba*, *Scedeba* and *Zisnoudeba*.

[51] According to TIB-4, p. 166, a corrupt form in TP for *Ekdaumaua* (Ptolemy 5.4.8), that is *Gdanmaa*, *Gdammaua*; Zgusta, pp. 135–36, wrongly cites TP as *Ekdana*.

4	B2	+44	16	Car**dava**	Cardaba	
21	D4	+21	45	Arci**dava**		
21	F4	+23	45	(S)Aci**dava**	Aci**dava**	
21	F5	+23	44	Pelen**dava**		
21	*unl*			Doki**dava**		
21	*unl*	+23	46	Singi**dava**		
21	*unl*			Ziri**daua**		
22	B3	+24	45	Buri**dava**	*Buridavenses	
22	B4	+24	44	Aci**dava**		
22	B4	+24	44	Rusi**dava**		
22	B5	+24	43	Giri**dava**		
22	B5	+24	43	Suci**dava**		
22	C3	+25	45	Comi**dava**	Cumi**dava**	
22	E2	+27	46	Pirobori**dava**		
22	E4	+27	44	Saci**dava**		
22	E4	+27	44	Suci**dava**		
22	F4	+28	44	Capi**dava**		
22	F4	+28	44	Vicus *Rami**dava**		
22	*unl*	+25	*43*	Perbur**dava**		
22	*unl*			Daous**daua**		
22	*unl*			Tamasi**daua**		
22	*unl*			Zargi**daua**		
23	*unl*			Klepi**daua**		
23	*unl*			Tamasi**daua**		
23	*unl*			Zargi**daua**		
63	B3	+32	38	Ekdaumaua	Eg**dava**	Gdanmaa
89	D1	+41	39	Calci**dava**		

Apart from the locatable names shown on my map, 21unl *Dokidava* and *Ziridaua* were in western Dacia, *Daousdaua* was just south of the Danube in Moesia Superior and 22/23unl *Tamasidaua* and *Zargidaua* were in eastern Dacia, as was 23unl *Klepidaua* on the river Tyras (Dniester).[52]

PARA (as termination, excluding -*para* in Mediterranean island-names and -*ppara* which both have a quite distinct distribution)[53]

Some of the names in the following list are unlocated, but they are all in Thrace[54] except for *Lapara* and *Phousipara*, both in Melitine, Asia Minor.

---

[52] All are more or less tentatively marked on the map in Duridanov, 'Thrakische und dakische Namen', p. 838. See also PNPG Comments s.nn. *Tamasidaua* and *Zousídaua*. I only map the names in the *Atlas*; further names in -*daua* in Ptolemy are noted in PNPG at +23/46? (*Markódaua*), +24/47? (*Karsídaua, Patrídaua, Petródaua*), +24/46 (*Sándaua*), +26/46 (*Outídaua*), and +26/44 (*Nentídaua*). PNPG puts *Daoúsdaua* at +25/43.

[53] That is, excluding *Sippara, Souppara* and *Uzippara* in India and Africa, and the island-names *Lipara* and *Rhypara* near Sicily, Crete and Samos.

[54] See *Map-by-Map Directory* s.nn. (where it is noted that that the two places called *Beripara* may be the same). Cf. Duridanov, 'Thrakische und dakische Namen', pp. 820, 822, 825 and 838, who maps many of them. On the partition of -*dava* and -*para* cf. Brixhe & Panayotou, 'Le thrace', pp. 193–95.

22	B6	+ 24	42	Bessa**para**	
22	B5	+ 24	43	Vicus Longino**para**	
49	F1	+ 23	42	Scapto**para**	
49	E1	+ 22	42	Spino**para**	
49	E1	+ 22	42	Tranu**para**	
51	B1	+ 23	41	Ciropolis	Keir**para**
52	B2	+ 27	41	Dr(o)usi**para**	
64	E4	+ 37	38	[Lykandos]	[La**para**]
22	*unl*			Belaidi**para**	
22	*unl*			Be**para**	
22	*unl*			Beri**para**	
22	*unl*			Beri**para**	
22	*unl*			Bos**para**	
22	*unl*			Subzu**para**	
22	*unl*			Vicus Agata**para**	
50	*unl*			Tranu**para**	
50	*unl*			Za**para**	
64	*unl*			Eusimara	Phousi**para**?

BURG/BOURG

This string reflects a treatment of the syllabic resonant, contrasting with that in Celtic *brig-*, that is typical of Germanic and also of various East Alpine-Pannonian languages which are known only from onomastics.[55] The distribution of BURG/BOURG reflects this in part: the two unlocatable places called *Quadriburgium* on Maps 20 and 21 were both in Pannonia,[56] and note also that Ptolemy has a tribe of *Bourgiones* (3.5.8), somewhere in eastern Poland (+ 22/51?); they are not in the *Atlas* but I have added them on Map 12.30.[57] Yet, because Latin borrowed *burgus* 'watchtower, citadel' from one of these languages,[58] *Burgus* also turns up in place-names as far afield as Gaul (−1/45, Bourg-sur-Gironde), Numidia (+ 5/35) and Moesia Inferior (approx. + 26/42), while *Burgaraca* in Moesia Inferior has been thought to come from the Latin derivative *burgarii*,[59] and *Bourgousnoes* (Procopius, *Buildings*, 3.6.24) in Pontus presumably belongs here too. These Latin-based names have to be ignored in ordered to understand the distribution. (As of course does *Burgatha* in Israel.)

---

[55] Anreiter, *Die vorrömischen Namen Pannoniens*, pp. 11–12 and 41–42. Cf. Katačić, *Ancient Languages of the Balkans*, pp. 71–72.

[56] Anreiter, *Die vorrömischen Namen Pannoniens*, p. 138, n. 510. For the location of *Askibourgion Oros* and *Askibourgion* see *Map-by-Map Directory* i, 181 and 193, and PNPG. In *Map-by-Map Directory* i, 345, *Loukernariabourgou* is tentatively placed near *Lapidarias*, in turn located 'E Oescus, Dacia Ripensis', following Velkov, *Cities in Thrace and Dacia*, p. 92, who puts both near Utus (22B5).

[57] Location from PNPG. Cf. Müller, pp. 424–25.

[58] Anreiter, *Die vorrömischen Namen Pannoniens*, p. 41; DAG, p. 889.

[59] Duridanov, 'Sprachspuren', p. 138.

10	D4	+07	52	Teuto**burg**iensis? Saltus	
11	G1	+06	51	Asci**burg**ium	
11	G1	+06	51	**Burg**inatium	
11	G1	+06	51	Quadri**burg**ium	
12	C3	+09	49	**Burg**undiones	
12	*unl*	*+14*	*50*	Aski**bourg**ion Oros	
13	*unl*	*+16*	*50*	Aski**bourg**ion	
14	E3	−01	45	**Burg**us	
20	F4	+18	45	Teuto**burg**ium	
20	*unl*			Quadri**burg**ium	
21	C5	+20	44	**Burg**enae	
21	*unl*	*+18*	*47*	Comercium **Burg**us	
21	*unl*			Quadri**burg**ium	
22	*unl*	*+26*	*42*	'Orudisza ad **Burg**um'	
22	*unl*	*+24*	*43*	Loukernaria**bourg**ou	
34	D2	+05	35	**Burg**us Speculatorius Antoninianus	
34	D2	+05	35	**Burg**us Speculatorius Commodianus	
49	F1	+23	42	**Burg**araca	
69	A5	+34	32	**Burg**atha?	
87	E4	+39	40	Longini Fossatum	**Bourg**ousnoes

All the non-Celtic strings selected above give a clear pattern on Map 12.30, which can be readily interpreted in terms of a number of discrete languages. Some caution is needed, however. Where there is phonological evidence, there is no problem in distinguishing different languages, as in the case of *burg-* versus Celtic *brig-*. But does the use of different elements such as *-daua* versus *-para* necessarily indicate two languages, 'Dacian' and 'Thracian', rather than a dialectal(?) fashion within a single language? The answer is by no means obvious, hence a dispute on this point.[60] All the same, the discrete distributions of the strings on Map 12.30 can reasonably be understood in terms of linguistically meaningful isoglosses. This method could be extended to cover many other strings.

It is much harder to interpret the distribution of strings that appear over wide areas. A good example of such a widely found string is provided with names beginning *Il-* (see Map 12.31). All the examples from the *Barrington* data are listed below, grouped by longitude and latitude, with the unlocatable ones at the end. The two 24unl places duplicate the 27unl places of the same name and were somewhere in Carpetania (central Spain).[61] The other unlocatable names from *Atlas* Maps 25–27 were also in Spain. 44unl *Ilionenses* were an Italian people in Regio I, perhaps named from Troy.[62] 47unl *Ilaron* was a town in Sicily, 50unl *Ilion* was in

---

[60] See Brixhe & Panayotou, 'Le thrace', pp. 193–95; Falileyev, 'Celtic presence in Dobrudja'.
[61] Tovar, *Tarraconensis*, p. 234.
[62] See note on 3.64 in Zehnacker's edition of Pliny, p. 173.

Macedonia according to Stephen of Byzantium.[63] 48unl *Iloua Nesos* duplicates 48B1 *Ilva Ins.* The names on *Atlas* Maps 87 and 89, off my Map 12.31, were in the Crimea and Armenia.

26	D4	−07	37	Ilip(ou)la				
26	E4	−06	37	Ilipa Magna	Ibylla	Ilipa Ilia		
26	E4	−06	37	Ilipula Minor	Ilipa			
26	*Av.*	*−06*	*37*	Ileates				
26	E5	−06	36	Ilipoula M.				
27	A4	−05	37	Iliturgicola				
26	F5	−05	36	Iluro	Lauro?			
9	D2	−04	58	Ila fl.				
27	*unl*	*−04*	*39*	Ileosca				
27	B3	−04	38	Ilugo				
27	B4	−04	37	Iliberri	Elvira	Municipium Florentinum		
27	B4	−04	37	Iliturgi	Forum Iulium			
27	B4	−04	37	Ilurco				
25	D3	−02	42	*Ilu(m)beris				
25	D3	−02	42	Ilurcis	Grac(ch)urris			
27	D3	−02	38	Ilorci	Ilourgeia			
27	D3	−02	38	Ilounon?				
25	E2	−01	43	Iluro	Ilurones			
25	E5	−01	40	Ilercaones	Il(l)urgav- onenses			
27	E3	−01	38	Ilici	Helike	Ecclesia Elotana		
27	E3	−01	38	Ilicitanus Sinus				
27	E3	−01	38	Illikitanos Limen				
25	F4	+00	41	Ilerda	Iltirta			
25	F4	+00	41	Ilergetes	Ilourgetes	Ilaraugatai	Ilerga ones	Regio Ilergetum
25	F5	+00	40	Dertosa	Hibera Iulia Ilercavonia			
27	F1	+00	40	Ildum				
25	H3	+02	42	Ill(ib)erris	Helena			
25	H4	+02	41	Ilduro				
25	H4	+02	41	Iluro				
48	A2	+08	40	Ilienses				
48	B1	+09	41	Ilva Ins.				
41	C4	+10	42	Ilva Ins.	Aethalia Ins.			
49	B2	+19	41	Illyrii				
49	B3	+19	40	Illyricum				
54	C2	+20	39	Ilion?				
55	*unl*	*+22*	*39*	Iletia				
58	*unl*	*+22*	*36*	Ilios M.				
58	E3	+23	37	Eileoi	Ilei			
59	B3	+23	37	Ilissos fl.				
60	*unl*	*+24*	*35*	Ilattia				
51	F4	+25	40	Ilissos? fl.				
56	C2	+26	39	Ilieon Kome				
56	C2	+26	39	Ilium	Troia			

[63] *Ethnikôn*, ed. Meineke, p. 330 (Stephen lists various places of the same name).

56	unl	+ 26	39	*Ilbeita			
62	unl	+ 29	38	Ilouza			
66	C2	+ 33	37	Ilistra			
87	K2	+ 36	45	Ilouraton			
89	C2	+ 40	38	(E)Legerda	Legerda	Illyrisos	
24	unl			Ilarkouris			
24	unl			Ilourbida			
25	cn.			Iltirkesken			
25	cn.			Iltukoite			
26	unl			Ilipula Laus	Ilipoula Megale	Halo	Helo
27	unl			Ilarkouris			
27	unl			Ilourbida			
27	Av.			Ilerda			
44	unl			Ilionenses			
47	unl			Ilaron			
48	unl			Iloua Nesos			
50	unl			Ilion			

The *Il-* names are very common in Spain, where they form a coherent group, or perhaps two groups, one in the south and the other in the northeast.[64] But what about the *Il-* names elsewhere? Are any of the Mediterranean clusters related to the Iberian ones? It would be reckless to assume so. In fact, *Ilion* (Troy) is sometimes derived from an irrelevant *Wilu-sa-* in Anatolian.[65]

A similar problem arises with names containing the strings IPO and IPPO. These are concentrated in southern Spain, but there is a scatter of them all round the Mediterranean and beyond, probably by coincidence.[66] There is some overlap with the *Il-* names in southern Spain, but outside Spain there seems to be no significant correlation between IP(P)O and *Il-*; for example, IP(P)O is common in Africa, unlike *Il-*. In itself, the lack of correlation does not prove that the two strings do not belong to a single ancient Mediterranean language – after all, the distributions of DUN and BRIG are very different but both belong to the same language – but there is no positive reason to suppose that they do.

For information, the names containing IP(P)O in the *Barrington* data are listed below (but not mapped). I have weeded out names containing *-i-polis*, but not those containing *hippo*, since it is not at all clear where the boundary should be drawn between names containing Greek *hippos* and those like *Hippo Regius* for which other origins are assumed.[67]

---

[64] Cf. De Hoz, 'Narbonensis', pp. 182–83. The southern group is roughly coterminous with the -TIGI names.

[65] Bader, *Langues indo-européennes*, p. 10. Cf. Zgusta, p. 197.

[66] See map in Villar, *Indoeuropeos y no indoeuropeos*, p. 111, and further discussion by García Moreno, 'Los topónimos en -*ippo*-'.

[67] I have not attempted to supply grid references for 'unl' items. Tovar, *Tarraconensis*, p. 234, notes that 26unl *Dipo* below is *Hipo* in Livy.

5	C2			Poulipoula			
5	C3			Hippokoura			
5	*unl*			Hippokoura			
23	F2	+36	46	Hippolaou Akra			
26	A3	−10	38	Olisipo	Municipium Olisipo Felicitas Iulia		
26	B2	−09	39	Collippo			
26	B3	−09	38	Kal(l)ipous fl.			
26	D4	−07	37	Ilip(ou)la			
26	D5	−07	36	Aipora	Ebora		
26	E4	−06	37	Basilippo			
26	E4	−06	37	Iporca			
26	E4	−06	37	Orippo			
26	E5	−06	36	Acinippo			
26	E5	−06	36	Baesippo			
26	E5	−06	36	Ilipoula M.			
26	E5	−06	36	Irippo?	Serippo?		
26	E5	−06	36	Lacippo			
26	F4	−05	37	Ostippo			
26	F4	−05	37	Ventipo			
26	*unl*			Belippo	Besaro		
26	*unl*			Cedripo			
26	*unl*			Dipo			
26	*unl*			Ilipula Laus	Ilipoula Megale	Halo	Helo
26	*unl*			Ipora			
27	A4	−05	37	Ipolcobulcola	Municipium Polconensium		
27	A4	−05	37	Iponuba	Hippo Nova		
31	H3	+07	36	Hippo? Akra			
31	H3	+07	36	Hippo Regius			
32	E2	+09	37	Hippo Diarrhytus			
32	E2	+09	37	Hipponensis L.			
33	H1	+11	35	Alipota?	Gummi		
37	D2	+18	30	Hippou Akra			
38	D1	+22	32	Hippon			
46	D4	+16	38	Hipponion	Vibo Valentia		
46	D6	+16	37	Hipporum			
55	D4	+22	38	Hippotai?			
56	C5	+26	38	Hippoi Inss.			
56	*unl*			Hippoi			
56	*unl*			Hippokrorona			
58	C4	+22	36	Hippola			
59	*unl*			Hippotomadai			
60	B2	+24	35	Hippokoronion? M.			
60	*unl*			Hippoteia			
61	B5	+25	36	Hippouris Ins.			
62	B5	+25	36	Hippourios fl.			
62	E5	+30	38	Hippophoras fl.			
65	B4	+29	36	Hippoukome			
69	C4	+35	32	Hippos	Sousitha		
75	D3	+30	28	Hipponon	Phylake Hipponos		
83	B5	+36	26	Hippos Kome			
83	B5	+36	26	Hippos? Oros			
87	G2	+41	42	Hippos fl.			
87	H2	+42	42	Hippos? fl.			
94	*unl*			Hippophagoi			

The following obviously count as 'formally inadmissible':

8	F2	'Tripontio'				
8	H2	Duroliponte				
22	B6	Philippopolis	Trimontium			
24	F4	Ad Lippos	Appos			
35	C2	Tripolitana				
45	C1	Sipous	Sipontum			
47	G4	Epipolai				
50	D3	Kalindoia	Alindoia	Tripoiai		
50	unl	Kallipolitai				
50	unl	Philippoupolis				
50	unl	Tripoai				
51	H4	Kallipo(u)lis				
53	B3	Megale Ins.	Pityodes Ins.	Prinkipos Ins.		
54	C3	Tripolitai	Tripolissoi			
54	C4	Euripos?				
55	F4	Euripos				
58	unl	Dipoina(i)				
58	unl	Tripodiskos				
61	F3	Europos	Euromos	Philippoi	*Hyromos	*Kyromos
64	B2	Eulepa	Aipolioi			
64	D4	Arabissos	Tripotamos			
69	E4	Philippopolis				
86	D2	Ziporea				
87	F4	Psoron Limen	Hyssos	Sousarmia	Sousourmena	'Ysiporto'
87	G2	Astelephos fl.	Euripos fl.			

While few would disagree with the proposition that the wide distribution of names in *Il-* and *ip(p)o* is the result of coincidence, the so-called 'Old European river-names' are more controversial. Leaving aside arguments about whether they are Indo-European or non-Indo-European,[68] there is the even more fundamental problem of whether names beginning with such short sequences as *Al-* should be grouped together at all, given the likelihood of coincidence. For sake of comparison with Tovar's chronologically eclectic maps of 'Old European' river-names in *Al-*, *Sal-* and *Var-/Ver-*, also reproduced by Vennemann,[69] I list and map (Map 12.32) the river-names in the *Barrington* data that begin with these strings.[70] They are ordered by longitude, from

[68] Cf. Schmid, 'Alteuropäische Gewässernamen'; Vennemann, 'Linguistic reconstruction'; Kitson, 'River-names'.

[69] 'Linguistic reconstruction', pp. 219–20 and 222; Tovar, *Krahes alteuropäische Hydronymie*, pp. 36 and 38–39. Different points of view on 'Old European' are expressed by De Hoz, 'Narbonensis', p. 177, and Isaac, 'Scotland', p. 189, n. 1.

[70] Note that, unlike the Old Europeanists who draw on other toponyms conceivably derived from hydronyms, I use only names classified as *fl.* in APNI. This and the absence of medieval and modern data explains some of the disparities with Tovar's maps. I have omitted the following as being clearly of the wrong structure: 9F7 *Verbeia fl.*; 25H3 *Vernodubrum fl.*; 44unl *Ouerestis fl.*; 45unl *Vergellus fl.*; 87unl *Ouardanes fl.* Hence *Ver-* does not occur at all. 27unl *Salduba fl.* is omitted as a duplicate of 26F4.

Salsum in Morocco in the west to *Alibotra* (the Ganges)[71] in India in the east. (3unl *Salaros* was in western Asia.)

1a	C2	−10	30	Salsum? fl.	
28	A5	−07	34	Salat fl.	
24	F1	−06	43	Salia fl.	
26	F5	−05	36	Salduba fl.	
26	F4	−05	37	Salsum fl.	
9	C3	−05	57	Ouarar? fl.	
8	*unl*	*−04*	*50*	Alaunos fl.	
25	C4	−03	41	Salo fl.	
29	D1	−02	35	Salsum fl.	
9	F5	−02	55	Alauna fl.	
27	*Av.*	*−01*	*38*	Alebus fl.	
25	H3	+02	42	Alba fl.	
11	G3	+06	49	Alisontia fl.	
16	C1	+06	44	Varus fl.	
12	B3	+08	49	*Alisina fl.	
10	F3	+09	53	Albis fl.	
41	D4	+10	44	Alma fl.	
12	D3	+10	49	*Alcmona fl.	
42	A3	+11	42	Albinia fl.	
12	E1	+11	51	Salas? fl.	
43	C3	+12	42	Albunea fl.	
44	*unl*	*+12*	*41*	Allia fl.	
47	C3	+13	37	Alba fl.	
42	F3	+13	42	Albula fl.	
19	F4	+13	45	Varamos fl.	
20	B3	+14	46	[Albanta] fl.	
47	G4	+15	37	Alabon fl.	Alabis fl.
20	D6	+16	43	Salon fl.	
58	A2	+21	37	Alphe(i)os fl.	
58	*unl*	*+21*	*37*	Alisios fl.	Alesios fl.
21	F6	+23	43	Almus fl.	
56	C5	+26	38	Aleon? fl.	
56	*unl*	*+26*	*39*	Alabastros fl.	
62	*unl*	*+30*	*38*	Alandrus fl.	
88	C2	+44	42	Alontas fl.	
88	D3	+45	41	Alazonios fl.	
88	F3	+47	41	Albanos fl.	
6	*unl*	*+65*	*35*	Saleantes fl.	
6	E4	+84	25	Ganges fl.	Alibotra? fl.
3	*unl*			Salaros fl.	

Without doubt, 'Old Europeanists' would delete some of these on one ground or another (e.g. *Salsum* as Latin) and adjust Map 12.32 accordingly, presumably with close attention to morphological criteria. But even with adjustments, will the distribution of these strings be any more probative than those of *Il-* and *ip(p)o*? The contrast with the well-defined territories in Map 12.30 is striking. Clearly such material presents quite different challenges – ones which cannot be met in this book.

[71] Also listed as *Padus fl.* and *Phison fl.*

12.4 Synthesis with other disciplines

(a) Epigraphy

The place-name evidence discussed in this book covers a much greater area than the one from which we have continuous inscriptions in ancient Celtic languages such as Gaulish, Lepontic and Celtiberian;[72] presumably Celtic-speakers in this larger area were either illiterate or, later on, preferred to use Greek and Latin. The vernacular inscriptions are not found outside the area of the place-names, with the notable exception of the Gaulish inscription at *Tuder* (Todi) in southern Umbria (+12/42), which, as Lejeune says, could merely reflect the immigration of a single family from north of the Po.[73]

Celtic personal names are found in Latin inscriptions over a wide area, and their general distribution is consonant with that of the place-names. This is illustrated in Map 12.33, in which the backgound shading for place-names is repeated from Map 11.1. The figures give the numbers of Celtic compound names (the most recognizable type of personal name) in the Latin inscriptions covered in the *Onomastion Provinciarum Europae Latinarum* (OPEL).[74] This resource excludes Italy (apart from *Regiones IX–XI* = Gallia Cisalpina), Macedonia, Thracia and other southern and eastern provinces, but provides a massive sample (over 80,000 persons) for the northern and western provinces. Within these areas there is a good match between personal names and place-names once allowance is made for the probability, and in some cases certainty, that the rare persons with Celtic names commemorated in provinces such Dalmatia and Dacia were visiting legionaries or other incomers.[75] The scarcity of Celtic personal names north of the Rhine and Danube is inevitable, given the lack of inscriptions (except in Dacia), but their scarcity in the general area of Raetia is striking, since inscriptions are common if not abundant there. In fact, when the availability of inscriptions is taken into account, there is a marked separation between the two areas where the percentage of inscriptions with Celtic names is highest: Gaul and Germany in the west and Noricum and Pannonia in the east.[76] Needless to say, the occurrence of Celtic compound names must depend on complex sociological factors,

---

[72] See above, p. 3.

[73] RIG II.1, no. E5. Cf. De Bernardo Stempel, 'Ptolemy's Celtic Italy and Ireland', p. 85. Note a possible Celtic presence at *Biturgia*, perhaps at +11/43. See above, pp. 102 and 246, n. 161.

[74] These figures are provisional and derive from unpublished research conducted jointly with Dr M. E. Raybould. The approach is explained in Sims-Williams, 'Five languages', pp. 10–14 and 34–36, but the figures are different there, as only OPEL iii–iv was used.

[75] Sims-Williams, 'Five languages', pp. 13–14. The proportion of people with Celtic compound names whose foreign origin is specified is far higher in Dalmatia, Moesia and Dacia than elsewhere.

[76] Cf. map 3 in ibid. p. 13. For overall distribution of inscriptions see the fold-out map in OPEL i. OPEL seems relatively skimpy for Hispania.

and cannot be directly translated into numbers of Celtic-speakers.[77] Nevertheless, the similarity betweeen the distribution of Celtic place- and personal names is clearly non-random and deserves further investigation. An important consideration is that the inscriptions are centred on the first three centuries AD (the heyday of Latin epigraphy), whereas the Celtic toponymy shown as background shading on Map 12.33 is likely to have been established over a much longer period.

(b) History

The place-name evidence discussed in this book obviously invites comparison with evidence from ancient historians for the movements of 'Celts', 'Gauls', 'Galatians' and other peoples who are likely to have been what we would call Celtic-speakers. Thus the Celtic place-names in the Alps, north Italy and Asia Minor can naturally be associated with ancient historians' statements about Celtic migrations to the south and east.[78] Great caution is needed, however, because the ancient sources are often obscure or mutually inconsistent,[79] or, even more seriously, silent about population movements in many parts of Europe – not solely those in the north. It would be a mistake, therefore, to expect a complete correlation between recorded Celtic migrations and the place-names.

It is tempting to combine our distribution of place-names with the many modern maps which include dated arrows showing Celtic population movements. Unfortunately, however, the validity of such maps is in doubt.[80] A few of the problems can be listed:

1. Ancient authors are vague about dates. The Celtic arrival in Iberia, for instance, is hinted at but is nowhere dated,[81] and there is a serious disagreement between Livy's early date for the Celtic arrival in north Italy (c. 600) and the later date (c. 400) implied by other ancient historians. The most securely dated Celtic movements are the sack of Rome c. 387, the attack on Delphi in 279 and the invasion of Asia Minor in 278, but only the last of these three was likely to give rise to the permanent settlement that can be correlated with place-names.

2. When ancient authors refer to movements of Celtic or presumably Celtic peoples, we can rarely assume that the peoples in question were the *first* Celtic peoples to migrate to the area in question. The secondary movement of the *Belgae* across the English Channel to Britain is an obvious

---

[77] Sims-Williams, 'Five languages', pp. 14–15; KPP, pp. 326–27.
[78] Sources collected by Tomaschitz, *Wanderungen*.
[79] For example, on population movements in the Rhône–Alps region see Barruol, pp. 147–65.
[80] See esp. Collis, *The Celts*, pp. 93–128.
[81] Villar, 'Celtic language', gives a survey of views on Celtic arrival(s) in Iberia.

example, and the same applies to the minor movements of *Celtici* in Hispania mentioned by Strabo (3.3.5) and Pliny (3.13).[82]

3. Even when we know where to place one end of an arrow on the map, there can be uncertainty about its direction. For example, we do not really know where the Delphi expedition started from, nor where it retreated to: some sources suggest a retreat to Toulouse and others to a kingdom of *Tylis* near the Black Sea.[83] Again, some scholars, making a bold archaeological assumption, show the Gaulish settlers of north Italy starting from areas where La Tène styles flourished, while others, making a different assumption, follow Livy literally and make them start from the territories of the *Bituriges* and the other Gaulish tribes he names *as we find them located in later sources* (around Bourges and so on), trusting that the ethnic groups which remained in the homeland did not themselves move around in the meantime.[84] In general, there must be a suspicion that historians like Livy were sometimes simply making deductions from the identity of names between tribes in Gaul and in Italy (for example, *Senones* and *Lingones* in both countries).[85] Sometimes identity of name in the ancient world did mean identity of people, but there were notable exceptions (*Veneti* for instance),[86] and many ethnonyms like *Senones* 'old ones' are so obvious as to make polygenesis a plausible possibility. It is suspicious that modern scholars are happy to accept the ancient authors' statements when they fit in with modern theories (for example on the *Senones* emigrating to Italy), but are equally happy to reject the same authors' statements when they conflict with such theories, for example, Strabo's statement that the Boii emigrated to the Danube region after being expelled from Italy.[87] Obviously, toponymy is intimately connected with the spread of languages and their speakers, but generally it does not reveal the *direction* of the spread – witness the old arguments about whether the Celtic place-names of Germany were brought in by Celts moving east or left behind by Celts moving west.[88]

(c) Archaeology and population genetics

Finally, there is scope for comparing the place-name evidence with archaeological evidence, although that vast topic lies outside the scope of this book. It is hardly to be expected that any single 'Celtic' archaeological

---

[82] See ibid. pp. 246–48.

[83] Tomaschitz, *Wanderungen*, pp. 130–31; Mitchell, *Anatolia*, i, 13–14; *Tylis* is not identified; see Falileyev, '*Tylis*', and cf. above, p. 305, n. 8.

[84] See Collis, *The Celts*, pp. 62–63 and 97.

[85] Cf. map 'Linked names of peoples' in Collis, *The Celts*, p. 113.

[86] See above, Ch. 7, n. 59.

[87] See Collis, *The Celts*, pp. 115–17. Cf. above, p. 298.

[88] Hubert, *Rise of the Celts*, p. 151.

culture or artefact will always be found where there is evidence of Celtic speech, that is, from Portugal to Turkey and from Scotland to Italy; we know that some populations retain their languages while changing their habits of dress or warfare or burial, while other populations switch to new languages while retaining their material cultures and customs.[89] One must therefore agree with Collis, who is 'highly sceptical about how much archaeology can contribute' to linguistic geography. Nevertheless, as Collis himself notes, there may be occasions when archaeologists can identify intrusive cultures that can be correlated with intrusive Celtic-speakers.[90] The challenge is to see which archaeological–toponymic correlations are real and which ones are due to coincidental distribution patterns. The difficulty of dating the place-names adds to the problem. Chronology is still more of a problem in attempting to correlate ancient toponymic evidence with the modern evidence studied by population geneticists, whose use of the label 'Celtic' for biological phenomena has so far been superficial and ahistorical.[91] A convincing synthesis of language, archaeology and genetics may prove an impossible task, despite the obvious fact that all three reflect different aspects of human history. Eventually, however, it may be worth attempting.

[89] Cf. Sims-Williams, 'Celtomania and Celtoscepticism'.
[90] *The Celts*, p. 209; on p. 190 he correlates the Puchov La Tène style with Tacitus' Celtic-speaking Cotini. For works along such lines in Eastern Europe, see e.g. Shchukin, 'Celts in Eastern Europe', and Guštin, 'Die Kelten in Jugoslawien'.
[91] For examples, see Sims-Williams, 'Genetics, linguistics and prehistory'.

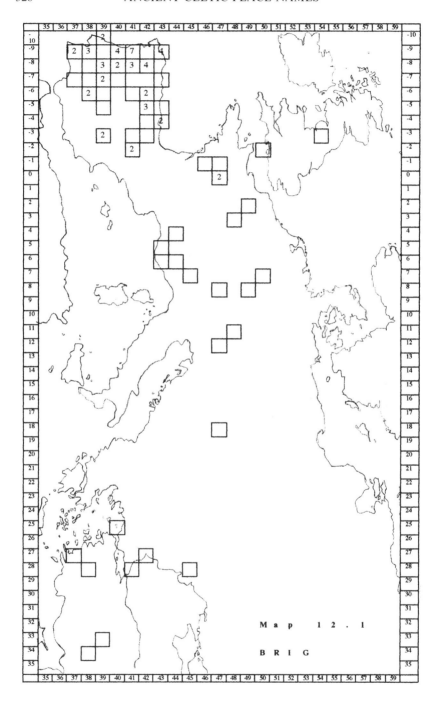

Map 12.1

BRIG

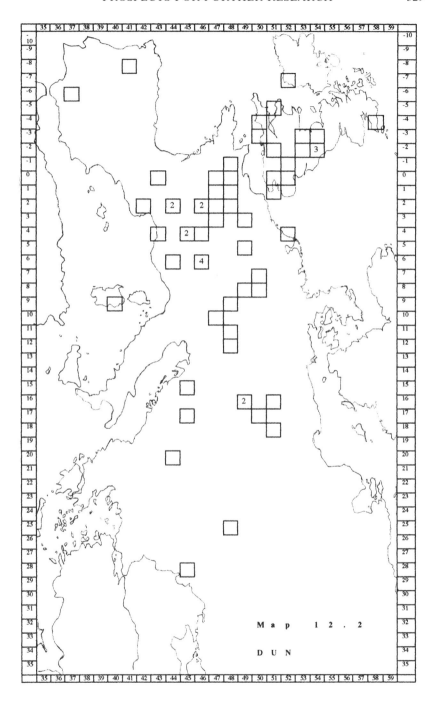

Map 12.2

DUN

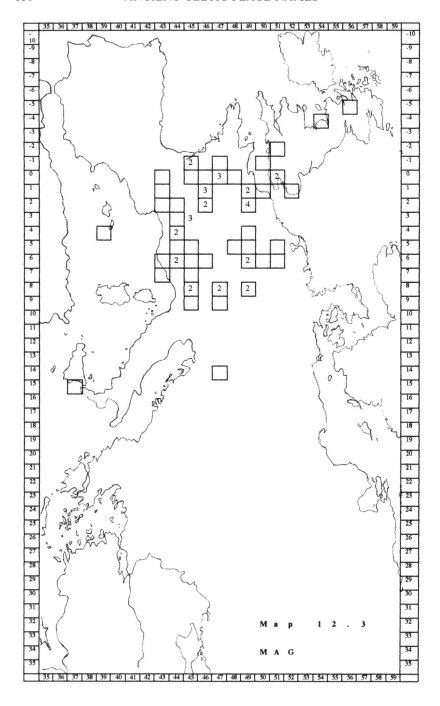

Map 12.3

MAG

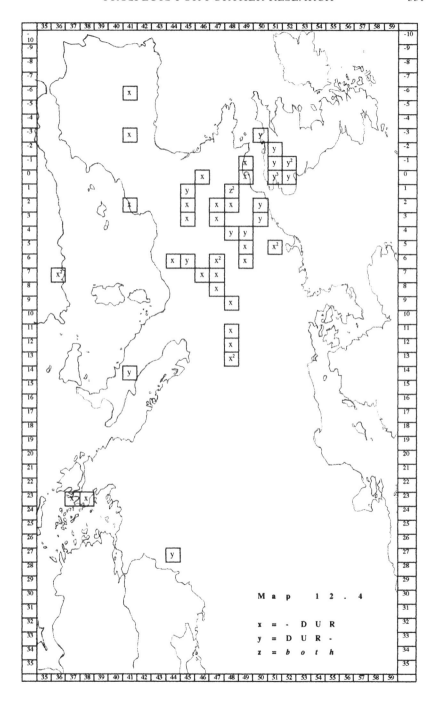

Map   1 2 . 4

x = - D U R
y = D U R -
z = b o t h

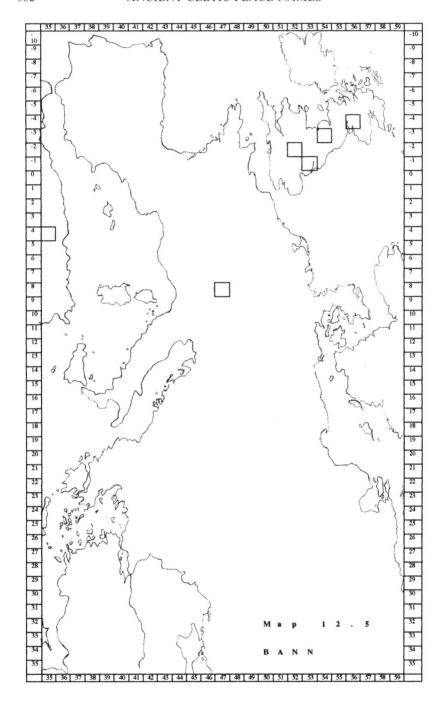

Map 12.5

BANN

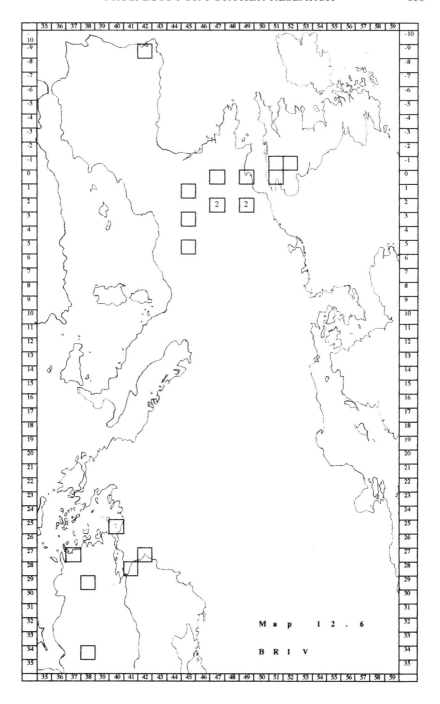

Map 12.6

BRIV

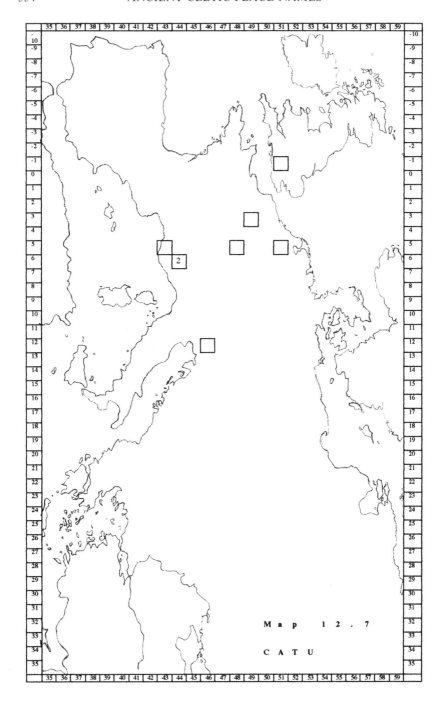

Map 12.7

CATU

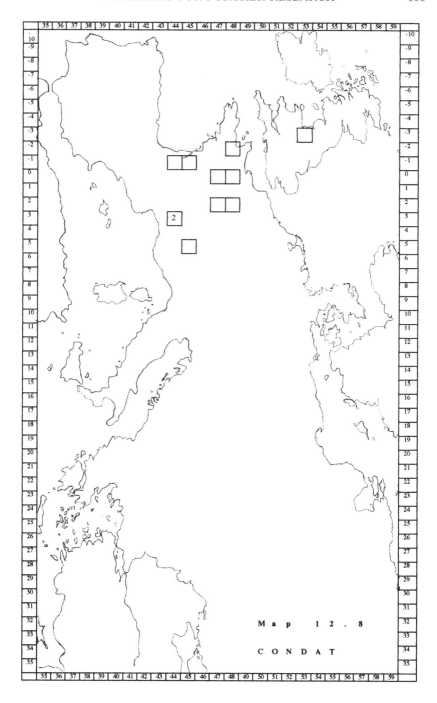

Map 1 2 . 8

C O N D A T

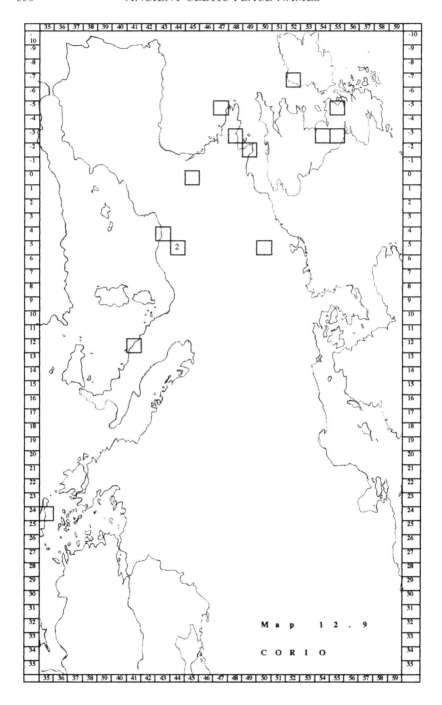

Map 12.9

CORIO

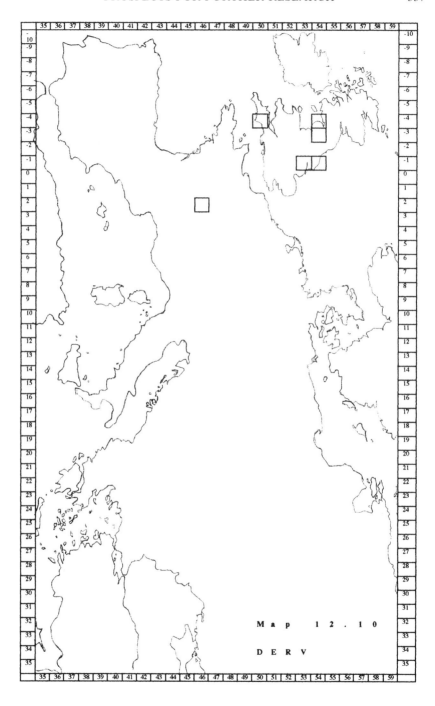

Map 12.10

DERV

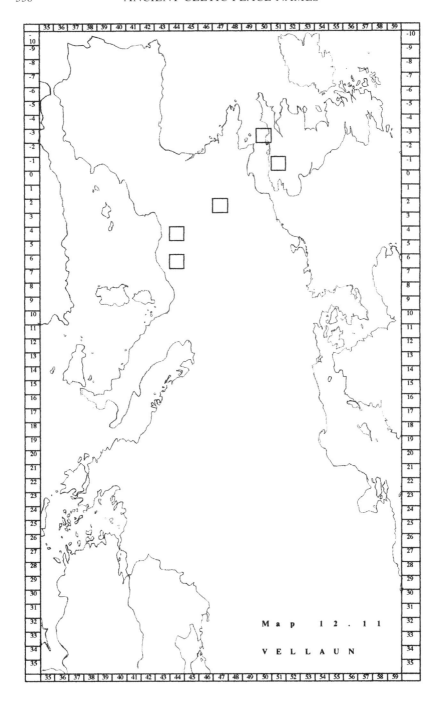

Map 12.11

VELLAUN

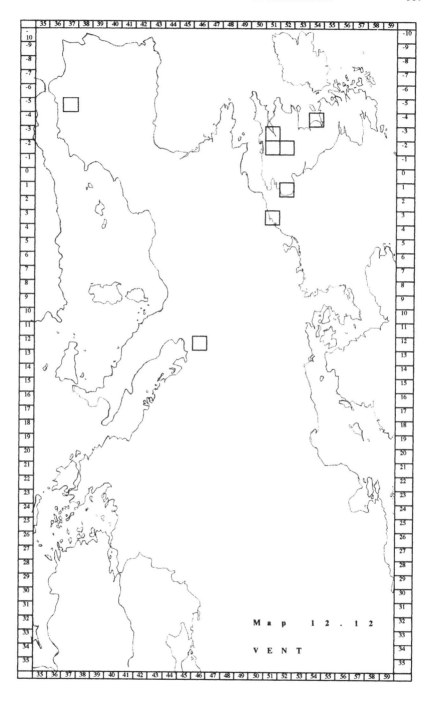

Map 12.12

VENT

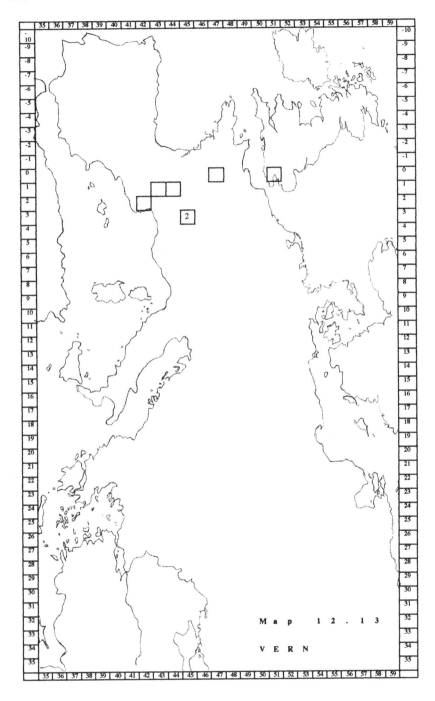

Map 12.13

VERN

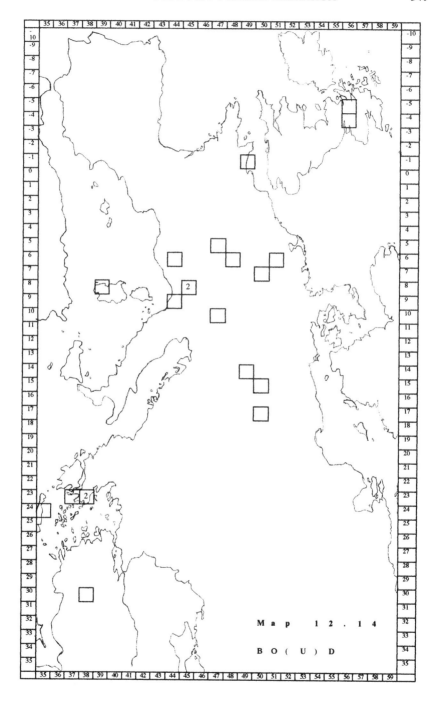

Map 12.14

BO (U) D

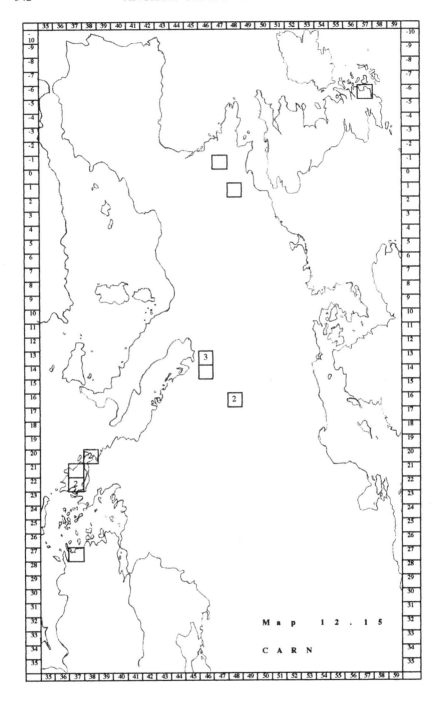

Map 12.15

CARN

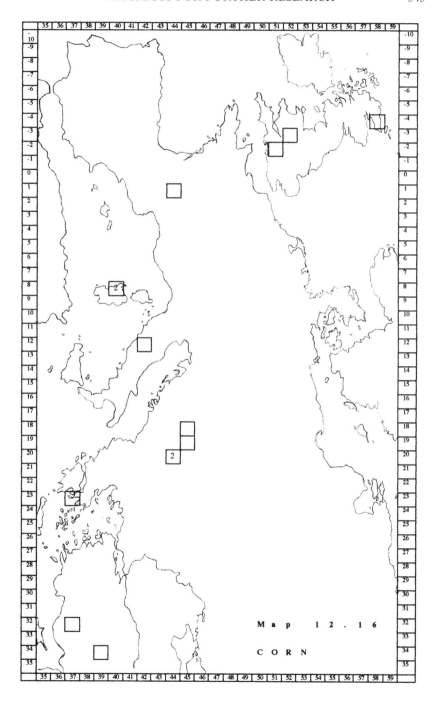

Map 12.16

CORN

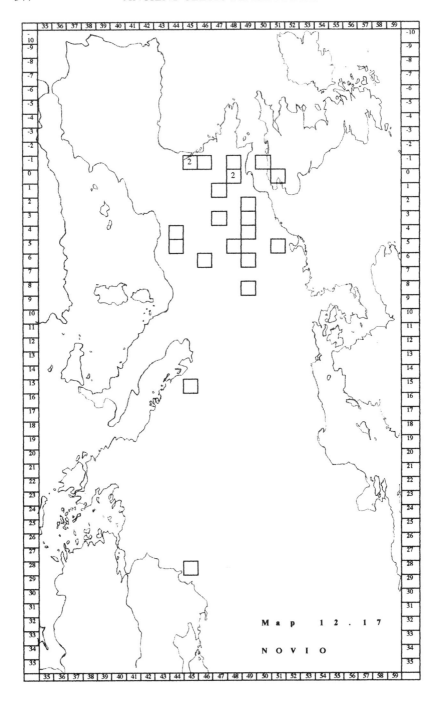

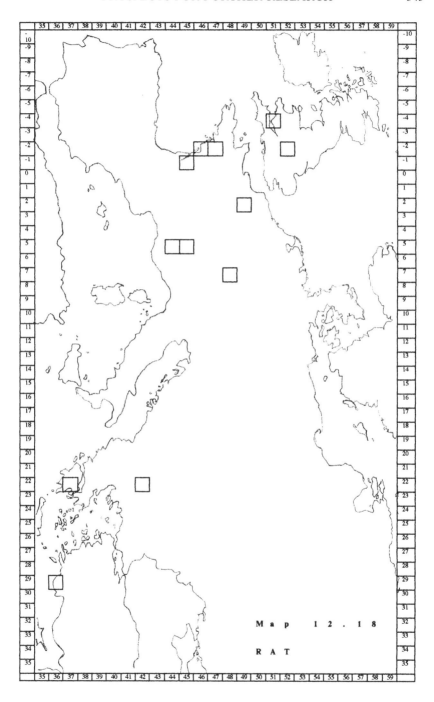

Map 12.18

RAT

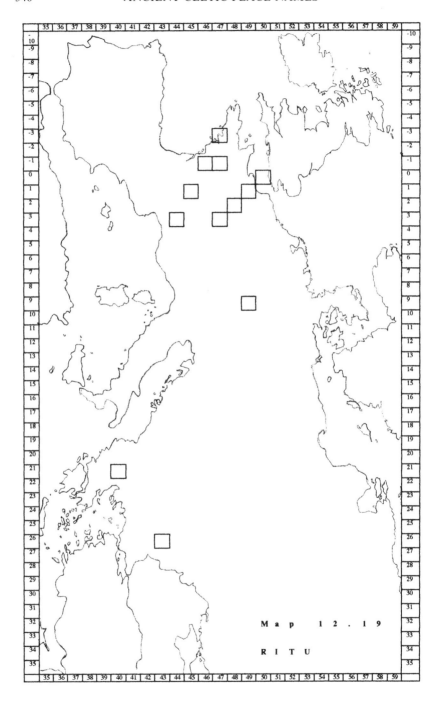

Map 12.19

RITU

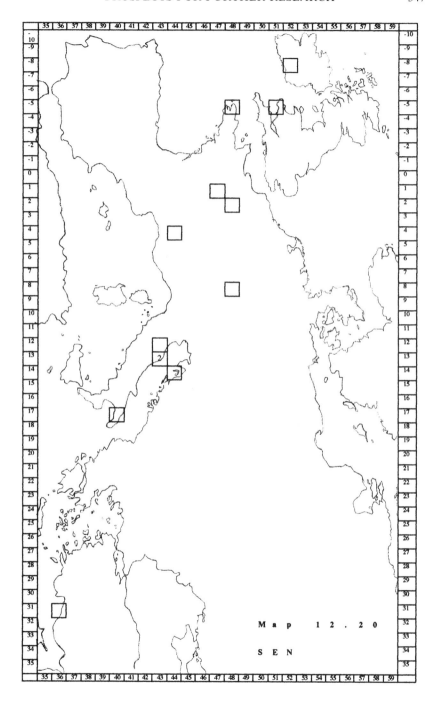

Map   1 2 . 2 0

S E N

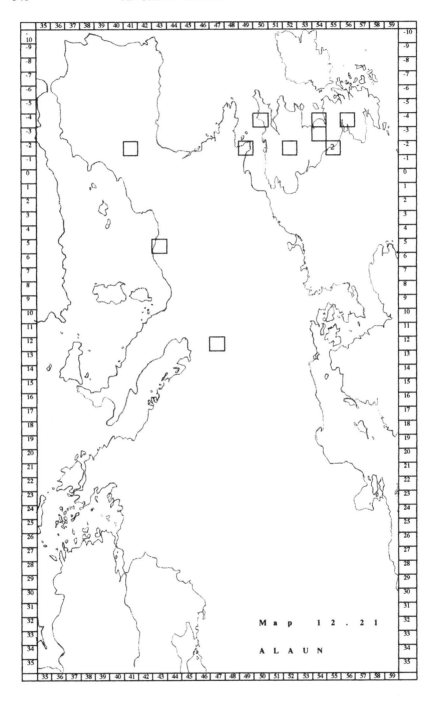

Map   1 2 . 2 1

A L A U N

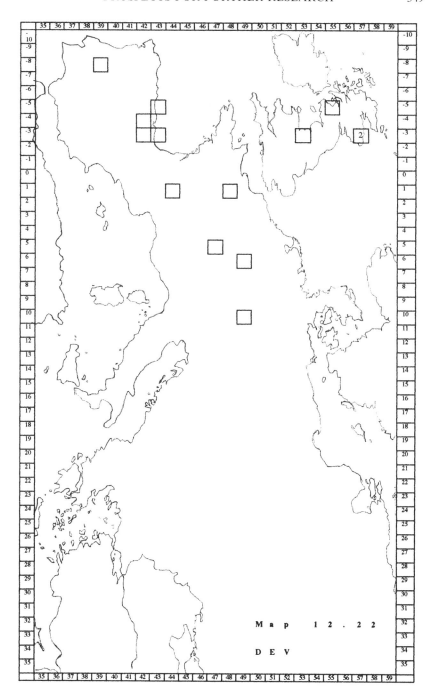

Map 1 2 . 2 2

D E V

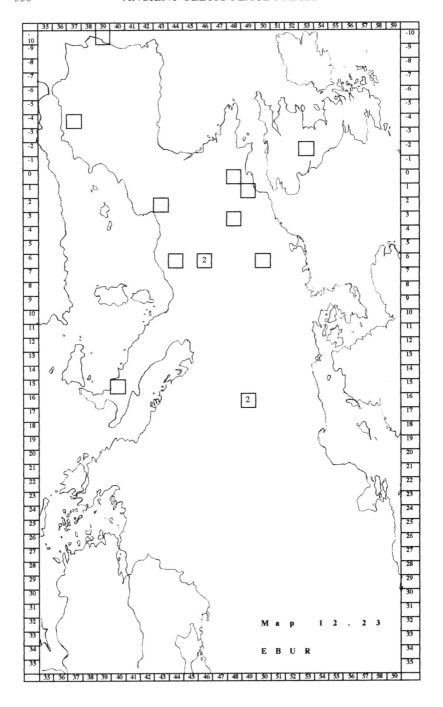

Map 12.23

EBUR

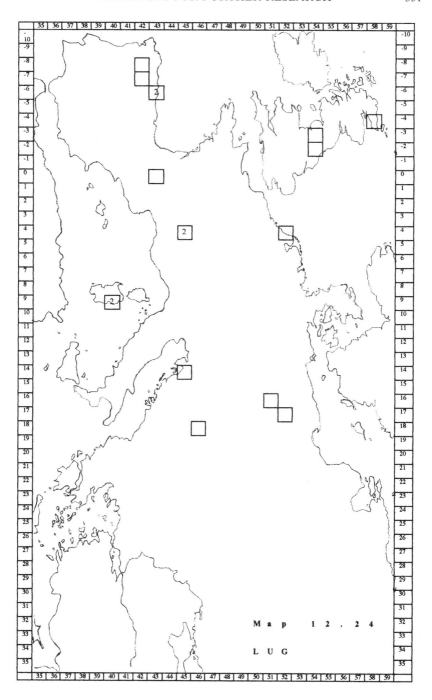

Map 12.24

LUG

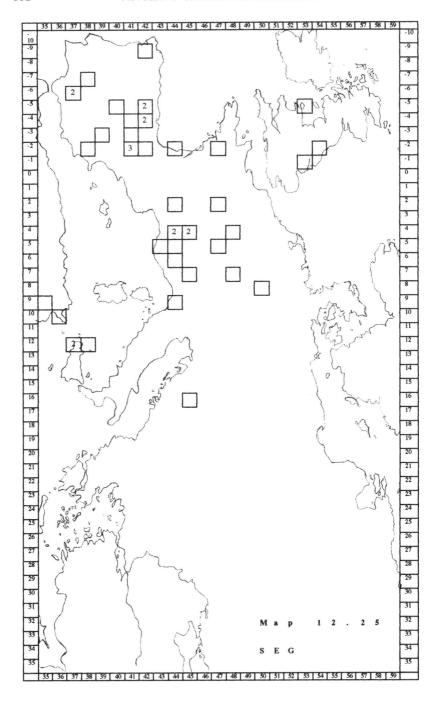

Map 1 2 . 2 5

S E G

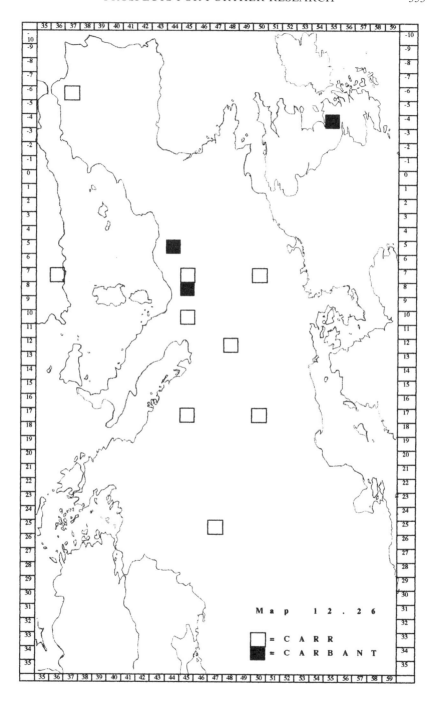

Map 12.26

□ = CARR
■ = CARBANT

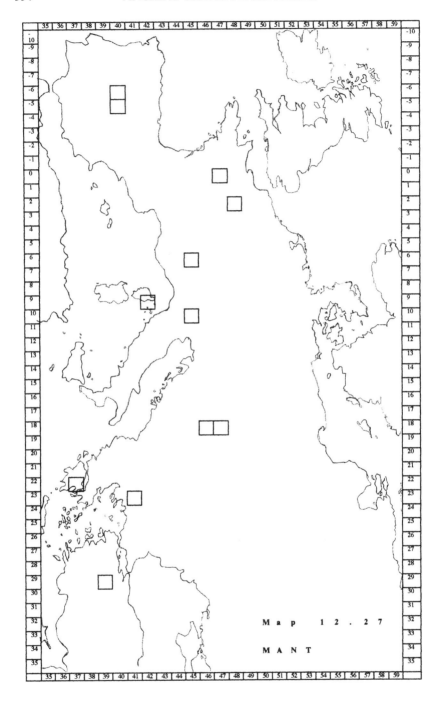

Map 12.27

MANT

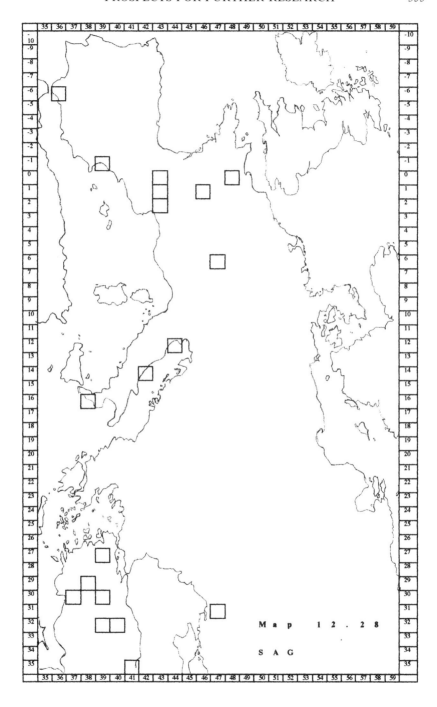

Map 1 2 . 2 8

S A G

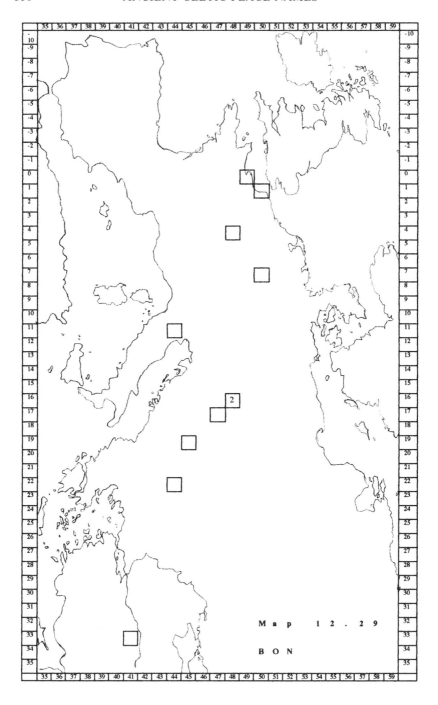

Map 12.29

BON

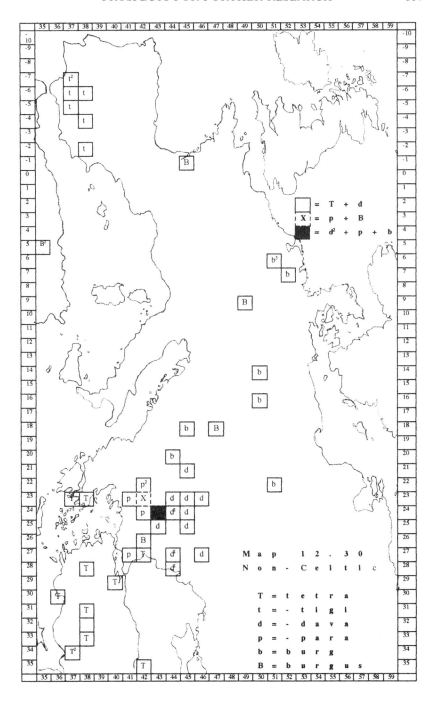

Map 12.30
Non-Celtic

T = tetra
t = -tigi
d = -dava
p = -para
b = burg
B = burgus

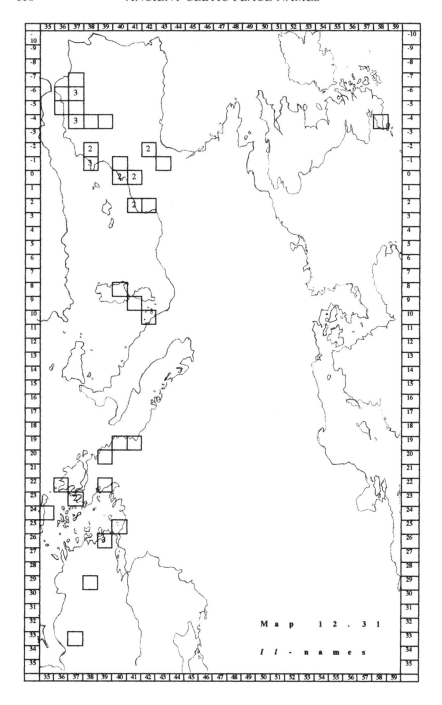

Map 12.31

ll-names

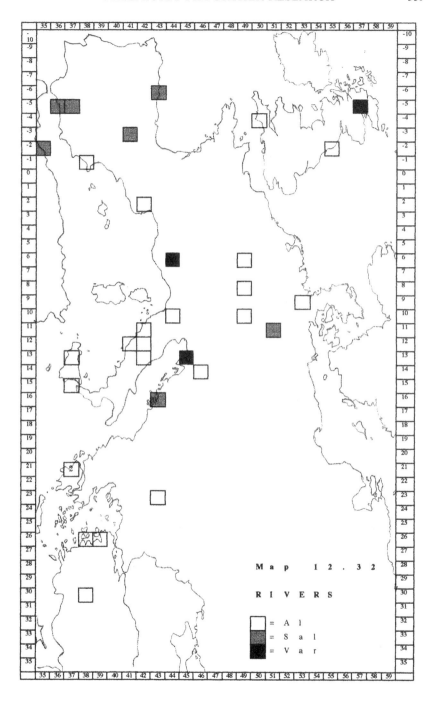

Map 12.32

RIVERS

= A l
= S a l
= V a r

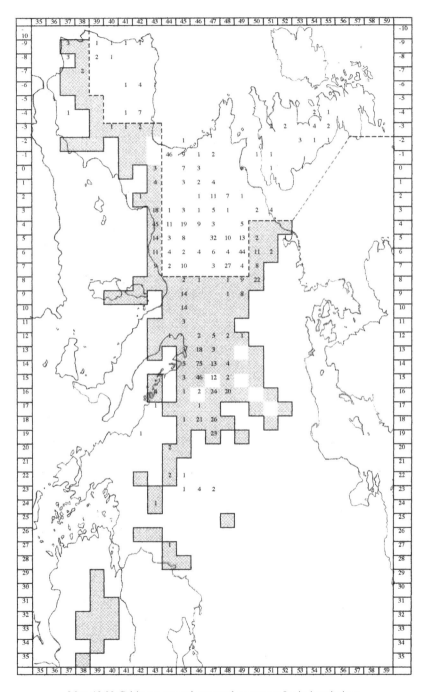

Map 12.33 Celtic compound personal names on Latin inscriptions

ABBREVIATIONS
AND BIBLIOGRAPHY

ABBREVIATIONS

General abbreviations

Av.	name from Avienus in *Map-by-Map Directory*. See above, p. 19.
AWMC	Ancient World Mapping Center, University of North Carolina, Chapel Hill
Civ.	*Civitas*; city, settlement
cn.	coin-legend in *Map-by-Map Directory*. See above, p. 19.
Col.	*Colonia*; colony
fl.	*flumen, fluvius*; river
IE	Indo-European, or Proto-Indo-European
Ins.	*Insula*; island
Inss.	*Insulae*; islands
L.	*Lacus*; lake
M.	*Mons, Montes*; mountain(s)
Mon.	*Monasterium*; monastery
Monu.	*Monumentum*; monument
Mun.	*Municipium*; city, settlement
OI	Old Irish
Pr.	*Promunturium*; cape, promontory
Sep.	*Sepulchrum, -a*; monuments(s), tomb(s)
unl	unlocated toponym in *Map-by-Map Directory*. See above, p. 19.
W	Welsh

Bibliographic abbreviations

AI   *Antonine Itinerary*. In Cuntz, Otto (ed.), 1929. *Itineraria Romana*, i, Leipzig.

AILR   Isaac, G. R., 2002. *The Antonine Itinerary Land Routes: Place-Names of Ancient Europe and Asia Minor. An Electronic Data Base with Etymological Analysis of the Celtic Name-Elements.* CD-ROM, Aberystwyth [re-issued as Appendix to PNPG].

ANRW   Temporini, Hildegard, & Wolfgang Haase (eds). *Aufstieg und Niedergang der römischen Welt*, Berlin, in progress.

APNI   AWMC Placename Inventory (see p. 19).

Atlas   Talbert, Richard J. A. (ed.), 2000. *The Barrington Atlas of the Greek and Roman World*, with 2-vol. *Map-by-Map Directory*, Princeton.

Avienus   Murphy, J. P. (ed.), 1977. *Rufus Festus Avienus: Ora Maritima*, Chicago.

Barruol   Barruol, Guy, 1999. *Les peuples préromains du sud-est de la Gaule: étude de géographie historique*, réimpression avec supplément, Paris.

BBCS   *Bulletin of the Board of Celtic Studies.*

Beševliev   Beševliev, Veselin, 1970. *Zur Deutung der Kastellnamen in Prokops Werk 'De Aedificiis'*, Amsterdam.

BzN   *Beiträge zur Namenforschung.*

CAG   Carte Archéologique de la Gaule, Paris, in progress.

CAGR   Carte Archéologique de la Gaule Romaine, Paris, in progress.

CIB   Sims-Williams, Patrick, 2003. *The Celtic Inscriptions of Britain: Phonology and Chronology, c. 400–1200*, Publications of the Philological Society, 37, Oxford.

CIL   Corpus Inscriptionum Latinarum, Berlin, in progress.

CMCS   *Cambrian* [up to 1993 *Cambridge*] *Medieval Celtic Studies.*

Cousin   Cousin, Georges, 1906. Additions au 'Alt-celtischer Sprachschatz' d'A. Holder. In *Études de géographie ancienne*, Paris, 346–489 [reprint in preparation, Aberystwyth].

CPNE	Padel, O. J., 1985. *Cornish Place-Name Elements*, Nottingham.
DAG	Whatmough, Joshua, 1970. *The Dialects of Ancient Gaul*, Cambridge, MA.
DIL	*Dictionary of the Irish Language*, 1913–76. Dublin.
DLG	Delamarre, Xavier, 2003. *Dictionnaire de la langue gauloise*, second edition, Paris.
EANC	Thomas, R. J., 1938. *Enwau Afonydd a Nentydd Cymru*, i, Cardiff.
ÉC	*Études celtiques.*
GPC	*Geiriadur Prifysgol Cymru: A Dictionary of the Welsh Language*, in progress.
GPN	Evans, D. Ellis, 1967. *Gaulish Personal Names*, Oxford.
Grzega	Grzega, Joachim, 2001. *Romania Gallica Cisalpina: Etymologisch-geolinguistische Studien zu den oberitalienisch-rätoromanischen Keltizismen*, Tübingen.
Holder	Holder, Alfred, 1896–1913. *Alt-celtischer Sprachschatz*, 3 vols, Leipzig.
IEW	Pokorny, Julius, 1959. *Indogermanisches etymologisches Wörterbuch*, i, Bern.
JEPNS	*Journal of the English Place-Name Society.*
KGP	Schmidt, Karl Horst, 1957. *Die Komposition in gallischen Personennamen*, Tübingen.
KPP	Meid, Wolfgang, 2005. *Keltische Personennamen in Pannonien*, Budapest.
LEIA	Vendryes, J., et al. *Lexique étymologique de l'irlandais ancien*, Dublin & Paris, in progress.
Liddell & Scott	Liddell, Henry George, & Robert Scott, 1968. *A Greek–English Lexicon, with a Supplement*, Oxford.
Map-by-Map Directory	See *Atlas.*
MLH v/1	Wodtko, Dagmar S., 2000. *Wörterbuch der keltiberischen Inschriften*, Vol. v, Part 1, of Untermann, Jürgen (ed.), *Monumenta Linguarum Hispanicarum*, Wiesbaden.
Müller	Müller, Carolus (ed.) 1883–1901. *Claudii Ptolemaei Geographia*, 2 parts with single pagination, Paris.
ND	Seeck, Otto (ed.), 1876. *Notitia Dignitatum*, Berlin.
Nègre	Nègre, Ernest, 1990–91. *Toponymie générale de la France*, 3 vols, Geneva.

NRO	*Nouvelle revue d'onomastique.*
NWÄI	De Bernardo Stempel, Patrizia, 1999. *Nominale Wortbildung des älteren Irischen*, Tübingen.
OPEL	Lőrincz, Barnabás, & Ferenc Redő (eds), 1994– 2002. *Onomasticon Provinciarum Europae Latinarum*, 4 vols, Budapest (vol. i) & Vienna (vols ii–iv).
Papazoglu	Papazoglu, Fanula, 1978. *The Central Balkan Tribes in Pre-Roman Times*, Amsterdam.
Pauly-Wissowa	Pauly, A., & G. Wissowa (eds), 1893–1978. *Real-Encyclopädie der klassischen Altertumswissenschaft*, Stuttgart.
Pliny	*Natural History.* Cited from edition by Mayhoff, except for Books 2 (Beaujeu), 3 (Zehnacker), 5 (Desanges), 6 (André & Filliozat), 9 (De Saint-Denis), 12 (Ernout) and 34 (Le Bonniec & de Santerre) (see Bibliography).
PNPG	Isaac, G. R., 2004. *Place-Names in Ptolemy's Geography: An Electronic Data Base with Etymological Analysis of the Celtic Name-Elements.* CD-ROM, Dept of Welsh, University of Wales, Aberystwyth.
PNRB	Rivet, A. L. F., & Colin Smith, 1979. *The Place-Names of Roman Britain*, London.
Ptolemy	Claudius Ptolemaeus, *Geography.* Unless Cuntz's edition is specified, Ptolemy is cited from Berggren & Jones for Book 1, Müller [see above] for Books 2–5, Humbach & Ziegler for Book 6, and Nobbe for Book 7.
Rasch	Rasch, Gerhard, 1950. *Die bei den antiken Autoren überlieferten geographischen Namen im Raum nördlich der Alpen vom linken Rheinufer bis zur pannonischen Grenze, ihre Bedeutung und sprachliche Herkunft*, Inaugural - Dissertation, Ruprecht-Karl-Universität, Heidelberg [new edition in preparation, Berlin, 2005].
Rav.	*Ravenna Cosmography.* In Schneetz, Joseph (ed.), 1990. *Itineraria Romana*, ii, *Ravennatis Anonymi Cosmographia et Guidonis Geographicae*, 1940, repr. with Index, Stuttgart.
RC	*Revue celtique.*
Reichert	Reichert, Hermann, 1987–90. *Lexikon der altgermanischen Namen*, 2 vols, Vienna.

RGermAlt	*Reallexikon der Germanischen Altertumskunde*, new edition, Berlin, in progress.
RIG	Recueil des Inscriptions Gauloises, Paris, in progress.
Rübekeil	Rübekeil, Ludwig, 2002. *Diachrone Studien zur Kontaktzone zwischen Kelten und Germanen*, Vienna.
SC	*Studia Celtica.*
Schönfeld	Schönfeld, M., 1965. *Wörterbuch der altgermanischen Personen- und Völkernamen*, repr. Heidelberg.
Svennung	Svennung, J., 1974. *Skandinavien bei Plinius und Ptolemaios*, Uppsala.
TIB	Tabula Imperii Byzantini.
TIB-4	Belke, Klaus, 1984. *Galatien und Lykaonien*, Vienna.
TIB-6	Soustal, Peter, 1991. *Thrakien*, Vienna.
TIB-7	Belke, Klaus, & Norbert Mersich, 1990. *Phrygien und Pisidien*, Vienna.
TIR	Tabula Imperii Romani (Union Académique Internationale).
TIR J-29	*Lisboa: Emerita, Scallabis, Pax Iulia, Gades*, Madrid, 1995.
TIR J-30	*Valencia: Corduba, Hispalis, Carthago Nova, Astigi*, Madrid, 2001.
TIR K-29	*Porto: Conimbriga, Bracara, Lucus, Asturica*, Madrid, 1991.
TIR K-30	*Madrid: Caesaraugusta, Clunia*, Madrid, 1993.
TIR K-34	*Naissus: Dyrrhachion—Scupi—Serdica—Thessalonike*, Ljubljana, 1976.
TIR K-35, I	*Philippi*, Athens, 1993.
TIR K/J-31	*Pyrénées Orientales—Baleares: Tarraco, Baliares*, Madrid, 1997.
TIR L-32	*Milano: Mediolanum—Aventicum—Brigantium*, Rome, 1966.
TIR L-33	*Trieste (Tergeste)*, Rome, 1961.
TIR L-34	*Budapest: Aquincum—Sarmizegetusa—Sirmium*, Budapest, 1968.
TIR L-35	*Bucarest: Romula—Durostorum—Tomis*, Bucarest, 1969.
TIR M-30/31	*Condate—Glevvm—Londinium—Lvtetia*, London, 1983.

TIR M-31	*Paris: Lutetia—Atvatuca—Ulpia, Noviomagus*, Paris, 1975.
TIR M-32	*Mainz*, Frankfurt, 1940.
TIR M-33	*Castra Regina, Vindobona, Carnuntum*, Prague, 1986.
TP	Weber, Ekkehard (ed.), 1976. *Tabula Peutingeriana, Codex Vindobonensis 324: Vollständige Faksimile Ausgabe im Originalformat*, Graz.
TPS	*Transactions of the Philological Society.*
VCIE	Villar, Francisco, & Blanca M. Prósper, 2005. *Vascos, Celtas e Indoeuropeos: Genes y Lenguas*, Salamanca.
VEPN	Parsons, David N., et al. (eds). *The Vocabulary of English Place-Names*, Nottingham, in progress.
Weisgerber	Weisgerber, Leo, 1969. *Rhenania Germano-Celtica*, Bonn.
ZCP	*Zeitschrift für celtische Philologie.*
Zgusta	Zgusta, Ladislav, 1984. *Kleinasiatische Ortsnamen*, Heidelberg.

BIBLIOGRAPHY

Adams, Colin, & Ray Laurence (eds), 2001. *Travel and Geography in the Roman Empire*, London.

Ahlqvist, Anders, 1975. Two ethnic names in Ptolemy. *BBCS* 26, 143–46.

Akerraz, Aomar, Véronique Brouquier-Reddé, Éliane Lenoir, Hasan Limane & René Rebuffat, 1995. Nouvelles découvertes dans le bassin du Sebou. In *Actes du VIe colloque international sur l'histoire et archéologie de l'Afrique du Nord, Pau, 1993*, ii, *Productions et exportations africaines. Actualités archéologiques*, Paris, 233–342.

Albertos Firmat, M.ª Lourdes, 1985. A propósito de algunas divinidades lusitanas. In Melena (ed.), *Symbolae Mitxelena*, i, 469–74.

Albertos Firmat, M.ª Lourdes, 1990. Los topónimos en *-briga* en Hispania. *Veleia* 7, 131–46.

Andersen, Henning (ed.), 2003. *Language Contacts in Prehistory: Studies in Stratigraphy*, Amsterdam.

Andersen, Henning, 2003. Slavic and the Indo-European migrations. In Andersen (ed.), *Language Contacts in Prehistory*, 45–76.

Andersson, Thorsten, 1991. The origin of the *tuna*-names reconsidered. In Wood, Ian, & Niels Lund (eds), *People and Places in Northern Europe 500–1600: Essays in Honour of Peter Hayes Sawyer*, Woodbridge, 197–204.

André, J., & Filliozat, J. (eds), 1980. *Pline l'Ancien: Histoire naturelle, livre VI, 2e partie*, Collection Budé, Paris.

Anreiter, Peter, 1997. *Breonen, Genaunen und Fokunaten: Vorrömisches Namengut in den Tiroler Alpen*, Innsbruck.

Anreiter, Peter, 2001. *Die vorrömischen Namen Pannoniens*, Budapest.

Anreiter, Peter, Marialuise Haslinger & Ulrike Roider, 2000. The names of the Eastern Alpine region mentioned in Ptolemy. In Parsons & Sims-Williams (eds), *Ptolemy*, 113–42.

Bader, Françoise (ed.), 1994. *Langues indo-européennes*, Paris.

Bammesberger, Alfred, & Theo Vennemann (eds), 2003. *Languages in Prehistoric Europe*, Heidelberg.

Beaujeu, Jean (ed.), 1950. *Pline l'Ancien: Histoire naturelle, livre II*, Collection Budé, Paris.

Bednarczuk, Leszek, 1999. Ptolemy (III,5,8) Σούλωνες: a Baltic name? In Eggers et al. (eds), *Florilegium Linguisticum*, 21–24.

Bedon, Robert, 1999. *Les villes des trois Gaules de César à Neron*, Paris.

Bedon, Robert, 2002. Hypothèses sur l'origine du nom antique d'Autun, *Augustodunum*, et sur les circonstances de sa formation. *Mémoires de la Société Éduenne* 56, 257–65.

Bedon, Robert, 2003. Les noms de villes hybrides en *Augusto-*, *Caesaro-* et *Iulio-* dans les Trois Gaules. In Defosse, Pol (ed.), *Hommages à Carl Deroux*, iii, *Histoire et épigraphie, Droit*, Collection Latomus 270, Brussels, 37–49.

Bejarano, Virgilio (ed.), 1987. *Hispania Antigua según Pomponio Mela, Plinio el Viejo y Claudio Ptolomeo*, Fontes Hispaniae Antiquae 7, Barcelona.

Benozzo, Francesco, 2002. Review of Parsons & Sims-Williams (eds), *Ptolemy*. *Studi celtici* 2, 258–65.

Berggren, J. Lennart, & Alexander Jones, 2000. *Ptolemy's Geography: An Annotated Translation of the Theoretical Chapters*, Princeton.

Berthelot, André, 1930. *L'Asie ancienne centrale et sud-orientale d'après Ptolémée*, Paris.

Billy, Pierre-Henri, 1986. Le toponyme *chambon*. In *Mélanges d'onomastique, linguistique et philologie offerts à Raymond Sindou*, i [Clermont-Ferrand?], 46–50.

Billy, Pierre-Henri, 1995. *Atlas Linguae Gallicae*, Hildesheim.

Billy, Pierre-Henri, 2000. Toponymie française et dialectologie gauloise. *NRO* 35/36, 87–104.

Billy, Pierre-Henri, 2001. Review of Chaurand & Lebègue, *Noms de lieux de Picardie*. *NRO* 37/38, 335–36.

Billy, Pierre-Henri, 2001. Review of Parsons & Sims-Williams (eds), *Ptolemy*. *NRO* 37/38, 313–15.

Billy, Pierre-Henri, 2002. Review of Grzega. *NRO* 39/40, 357–58.

Billy, Pierre-Henri, 2003. Review of DLG. *NRO* 41/42, 281–82.

Blažek, Václav, 2001. Celtic–Anatolian isoglosses. *ZCP* 52, 125–28.

Bonello Lai, Marcella, 1993. Il territorio dei *populi* e delle *civitates* indigene in Sardegna. In Mastino, Attilio (ed.), *La Tavola di Esterzili*, Sassari, 157–84.

Bonfante, Giuliano, 1939. Il problema dei Taurisci e dei Carni e l'entrata dei Galli in Italia. *Revue des études indo-européennes* 2, 16–23.

Bonfante, Giuliano, & Larissa Bonfante, 2002. *The Etruscan Language: An Introduction*, second edition, Manchester.

Boxhornius, Marcus Zuerius, 1654. *Originum Gallicarum Liber*, Amsterdam.

Breeze, Andrew, 2001. The British-Latin place-names *Arbeia*, *Corstopitum*, *Dictim*, and *Morbium*. *Durham Archaeological Journal* 16, 21–25.

Breeze, Andrew, 2003. Not Durotriges but Durotrages. *Notes & Queries for Somerset and Dorset* 35, 213–15.

Breeze, Andrew, 2003. St Cuthbert, Bede, and the Niduari of Pictland. *Northern History* 40, 365–68.

Brixhe, Claude, & Anna Panayotou, 1994. Le thrace. In Bader (ed.), *Langues indo-européennes*, 179–203.

Buchanan, George, 1584. *Rerum Scoticarum Historia*, Frankfurt.

Calderini, Aristide, & Sergio Daris, 1935–2003. *Dizionario dei nomi geografici e topografici dell'Egitto romano*, 5 vols + 2 supplements, Milan, Madrid, Bonn & Pisa.

Campanile, Enrico, 1999. *Saggi di linguistica comparativa e ricostruzione culturale*, Pisa & Rome.

Casson, Lionel (ed.), 1989. *The Periplus Maris Erythraei*, Princeton.

Casson, Lionel, 1995. The Greek and Latin sources for the southwestern coast of Arabia. *Arabian Archaeology and Epigraphy* 6, 214–21.

Chadwick, H. Munro, 1913. Some German river-names. In Quiggin, E. C. (ed.), *Essays and Studies Presented to William Ridgeway*, Cambridge, 315–22.

Chaurand, Jacques, & Maurice Lebègue, 2000. *Noms de lieux de Picardie*, Paris.

Chevallier, R., 1980. *La romanisation de la Celtique du Pô*, i, *Les données géographiques*, Paris.

Coates, Richard, 1980–81. Review of PNRB. *JEPNS* 13, 59–71.

Coates, Richard, 1981. Margidunum. *ZCP* 38, 255–68.

Coates, Richard, 2002. Review of Vennemann, 'Pre-Indo-European Toponyms'. *Nomina* 25, 160.

Coates, Richard, Andrew Breeze & David Horovitz, 2000. *Celtic Voices, English Places: Studies of the Celtic Impact on Place-Names in England*, Stamford.

Collingwood, R. G., & Wright, R. P. 1995. *The Roman Inscriptions of Britain*, i, new edition, Stroud.

Collis, John, 1999. George Buchanan and the Celts in Britain. In Black, Ronald, William Gillies & Roibeard Ó Maolalaigh (eds), *Celtic Connections: Proceedings of the 10th International Congress of Celtic Studies*, i, East Linton, 91–107.

Collis, John, 2003. *The Celts: Origins, Myths and Inventions*, Stroud.

Cox, Barrie, 1975–76. The place-names of the earliest English records. *JEPNS* 8, 12–66.

Cunliffe, Barry, 1997. *The Ancient Celts*, Oxford.

Cuntz, Otto (ed.), 1923. *Die Geographie des Ptolemaeus: Galliae, Germania, Raetia, Noricum, Pannoniae, Illyricum, Italia*, Berlin.

Curchin, Leonard A., 1990. *The Local Magistrates of Roman Spain*, Toronto.

Curchin, Leonard A., 1996. Five Celtic town-names in central Spain. *Habis* 27, 45–47.

Curchin, Leonard A., 1997. Celticization and Romanization of toponymy in central Spain. *Emerita* 65, 257–79.

Davies, Anna Morpurgo, 2000. Greek personal names and linguistic continuity. In Hornblower, Simon, & Elaine Matthews (eds), *Greek Personal Names: Their Value as Evidence*, Oxford, 15–39.

Davies, Norman, & Roger Moorhouse, 2003. *Microcosm: Portrait of a Central European City*, London.

Davillé, Louis, 1929. Le mot celtique 'cambo-' et ses dérivés en toponymie. *Revue des études anciennes* 31, 42–50.

Day, John V., 2001. *Indo-European Origins: The Anthropological Evidence*, Washington, DC.

De Alarcão, J., 1988. *Roman Portugal*, 2 vols, Warminster.

De Bernardo Stempel, Patrizia, 1987. *Die Vertretung der indogermanischen liquiden und nasalen Sonanten im Keltischen*, Innsbruck.

De Bernardo Stempel, Patrizia, 1995–96. Tratti linguistici comuni ad appellativi e toponimi di origine celtica in Italia. In Kremer, Dieter, & Alf Monjour (eds), *Studia ex hilaritate: mélanges de linguistique et d'onomastique sardes et romanes offerts à Heinz Jürgen Wolf*, Travaux de Linguistique et de Philologie 33/34, Strasbourg & Nancy, 109–36.

De Bernardo Stempel, Patrizia, 1995. Gaulish accentuation: results and outlook. In Eska et al. (eds), *Hispano-Gallo-Brittonica*, 16–32.

De Bernardo Stempel, Patrizia, 2000. Celtib. *karvo gortika* 'amicitiae favor', *rita* 'offrecida', *monima* 'recuerdo' y los formularios de las inscripciones celtibéricas. *Veleia* 17, 183–89.

De Bernardo Stempel, Patrizia, 2000. Ptolemy's Celtic Italy and Ireland: a linguistic analysis. In Parsons & Sims-Williams (eds), *Ptolemy*, 83–112.

De Bernardo Stempel, Patrizia, 2003. Continental Celtic *ollo* : Early Welsh (*h*)*ol*(*l*), *Olwen*, and *Culhwch*. *CMCS* 46, 119–27.

De Bernardo Stempel, Patrizia, 2003. Die sprachliche Analyse keltischer Theonyme ('Fontes Epigraphici Religionis Celticae ANtiquae'). *ZCP* 53, 41–69.

De Bernardo Stempel, Patrizia, 2005. Additions to Ptolemy's evidence for Celtic Italy. In De Hoz et al. (eds), *New Approaches*, 105–6.

De Bernardo Stempel, Patrizia, 2005. More on Ptolemy's evidence for Celtic Ireland. In De Hoz et al. (eds), *New Approaches*, 95–104.

De Bernardo Stempel, Patrizia, 2005. Ptolemy's evidence for Germania Superior. In De Hoz et al. (eds), *New Approaches*, 71–94.

De Hoz, Javier, 2000. From Ptolemy to the ethnic and linguistic reality: the case of south-west Spain and Portugal. In Parsons & Sims-Williams (eds), *Ptolemy*, 17–28.

De Hoz, Javier, 2001. Sobre algunos problemas del estudio de las lenguas paleohispánicas. *Paleohispanica* 1, 113–49.

De Hoz, Javier, 2005. Ptolemy and the linguistic history of the Narbonensis. In De Hoz et al. (eds), *New Approaches*, 173–88.

De Hoz, Javier (forthcoming). The Mediterranean frontier of the Celts and the advent of Celtic writing. In *Proceedings of the Twelfth International Congress of Celtic Studies, Aberystwyth*.

De Hoz, Javier, Eugenio R. Luján & Patrick Sims-Williams (eds), 2005. *New Approaches to Celtic Place-Names in Ptolemy's Geography*, Madrid.

De Saint-Denis, E. (ed.), 1955. *Pline l'Ancien: Histoire naturelle, livre IX*, Collection Budé, Paris.

Delamarre, Xavier, 2004. Gallo-Brittonica: transports, richesse et générosité chez les anciens Celtes. *ZCP* 54, 121–32.

Delamarre, Xavier, 2004. Review of AILR. *ZCP* 54, 261–63.

Desanges, Jehan, 1962. *Catalogue des tribus africaines de l'antiquité classique à l'ouest du Nil*, Dakar.

Desanges, Jehan (ed.), 1980. *Pline l'Ancien: Histoire naturelle, livre V, 1–46*, Collection Budé, Paris.

Dodgson, John McN., 1973. Place-names from *hām*, distinguished from *hamm* names, in relation to the settlement of Kent, Surrey and Sussex. *Anglo-Saxon England* 2, 1–50.

D'Ors, Alvaro, 1953. *Epigrafía jurídica de la España romana*, Madrid.

Doruţiu-Boilă, Emilia, 1980. *Inscriptiones Scythiae Minoris*, v, Bucharest.

Dottin, Georges, 1920. *La langue gauloise*, Paris.

Dumville, David, 1983. Ekiurid's *Celtica lingua*: an ethnological difficulty in *Waltharius*. *CMCS* 6, 87–93.

Duridanov, Ivan, 1995. Thrakische und dakische Namen. In Eichler et al. (eds), *Namenforschung*, i, 820–40.

Duridanov, Ivan, 1997. Keltische Sprachspuren in Thrakien und Mösien. *ZCP* 49/50, 130–42.

Eggers, Eckhard, et al. (eds), 1999. *Florilegium Linguisticum: Festschrift für Wolfgang P. Schmid*, Frankfurt am Main.

Eichler, Ernst, et al. (eds), 1995. *Namenforschung: Ein internationales Handbuch zur Onomastik*, i, Berlin.

Ekwall, Eilert, 1928. *English River-Names*, Oxford.

Elston, C. S., 1934. *The Earliest Relations between Celts and Germans*, London.

Ernout, A. (ed.), 1949. *Pline l'Ancien, Histoire naturelle, Livre XII*, Collection Budé, Paris.

Eska, Joseph F., R. Geraint Gruffydd & Nicolas Jacobs (eds), 1995. *Hispano-Gallo-Brittonica: Essays in Honour of D. Ellis Evans*, Cardiff.

Euzennat, Maurice, 1974. Les Zegrenses. In *Mélanges d'histoire ancienne offerts à William Seston*, Paris, 175–86.

Euzennat, Maurice, 1984. Les troubles de Maurétanie. *Comptes Rendus de l'Académie des Inscriptions et Belles-Lettres*, 372–91.

Euzennat, Maurice, 1989. *Le limes de Tingitane: la frontière méridionale*, Paris.

Evans, D. Ellis, 1966. 'gurdonicus' Supl. Sev. *Dial*. I.27.2. *SC* 1, 27–31.

Evans, D. Ellis, 1968–71. Nomina Celtica I: Catamantaloedis, Docnimarus, Satigenus. *ÉC* 12, 195–200.

Evans, D. Ellis, 1968–71. Nomina Celtica II: Duratius, Tincorix, ?Celt. *baido-, W. aladur. *ÉC* 12, 501–11.

Evans, D. Ellis, 1979. The labyrinth of Continental Celtic. *Proceedings of the British Academy* 65, 497–538.

Evans, D. Ellis, 1981. Celts and Germans. *BBCS* 29, 230–55.

Fabre, Paul, 1995. *Noms de lieux du Languedoc*, Paris.

Falileyev, Alexander, 2001. Ὀλοδόρις: Celtic or Thracian? *BzN* 36, 263–67.

Falileyev, Alexander, 2001. Galatian BEΔOPEI. *Münchener Studien zur Sprachwissenschaft* 61, 93–94.

Falileyev, Alexander, 2002. Ptolemy revisited, again. *CMCS* 43, 77–90.

Falileyev, Alexander, 2002. Review of Anreiter, *Die vorrömischen Namen Pannoniens. Acta Onomastica* 43, 119–24.

Falileyev, Alexander, 2003. Review of DLG. *Folia Linguistica Historica* 24, 281–93.

Falileyev, Alexander, 2003. Miscellanea Onomastica. *Indoeuropeïskoye yazykoznaniye i klasičeskaya filologiya* 7, 213–18.

Falileyev, Alexander, 2004. Place-names and ethnic groups in north-western Dacia: a case for Celtic. In *Thracians and Circumpontic World*, i, *Proceedings of the Ninth International Congress of Thracology, 2004*, Chişinău, 34–38.

Falileyev, Alexander, 2005. In search of Celtic *Tylis*: onomastic evidence. In De Hoz et al. (eds), *New Approaches*, 107–33.

Falileyev, Alexander, 2005. Celtic presence in Dobrudja: onomastic evidence. In *Ethnic Contacts and Cultural Exchanges North and West of the Black Sea: International Symposium 2005*, Iaşi, 291–303.

Falileyev, Alexander (forthcoming). *Vostocnije Balkany na karte Ptolemeya: Kritiko-bibliograficeskije razyskanija*, Munich.

Falileyev, Alexander (forthcoming). Zwischen Mythos und Fehler: Pseudo-keltische Ortsnamen auf der Balkanhalbinsel. In Birkhan, Helmut (ed.), *Viertes Symposium deutschsprachiger Keltologinnen und Keltologen, Linz 2005*.

Falileyev, Alexander, & G. R. Isaac 2003. Leeks and garlic: the Germanic ethnonym *Cannenefates*, Celtic **kasn-* and Slavic **kesn-. NOWELE* 42, 3–12.

Falileyev, Alexander, & G. R. Isaac 2005. Remetodia. *Acta Onomastica* 46 (forthcoming).

Fellows-Jensen, Gillian, 2000. John Aubrey, pioneer onomast? *Nomina* 23, 89–106.

Freeman, Philip, 1996. The earliest Greek sources on the Celts. *ÉC* 32, 11–48.

Freeman, Philip, 2001. *The Galatian Language*, Lewiston, Queenston & Lampeter.

Freeman, Philip, 2002. Who were the Atecotti? *Celtic Studies Association of North America Yearbook* 2, 111–14.

Garcia, Dominique, & Florence Verdin (eds), 2002. *Territoires celtiques: espaces ethniques et territoires des agglomérations protohistoriques d'Europe occidentale*, Paris.

Garcia, Dominique, 2004. *La Celtique méditerranéenne: habitats et sociétés en Languedoc et en Provence VIIIe–IIe siècles av. J.-C.*, Paris.

García Alonso, Juan Luis, 1992. On the Celticity of some Hispanic place names. *ÉC* 29, 191–201.

García Alonso, Juan Luis, 2000. On the Celticity of the Duero plateau: place-names in Ptolemy. In Parsons & Sims-Williams (eds), *Ptolemy*, 29–53.

García Alonso, Juan Luis, 2001. Lenguas prerromanas en el territorio de los Vetones a partir de la toponimia. In Villar & Fernández Álvarez (eds), *Religión, lengua y cultura*, 389–406.

García Alonso, Juan Luis, 2001. The place names of ancient Hispania and its linguistic layers. *SC* 35, 213–44.

García Alonso, Juan Luis, 2003. *La Península Ibérica en la Geografía de Claudio Ptolomeo*, Vitoria-Gasteiz.

García Alonso, Juan Luis, 2005. Ptolemy and the expansion of Celtic language(s) in Ancient Hispania. In De Hoz et al. (eds), *New Approaches*, 135–52.

García Moreno, Luis A., 2001. Los topónimos en *-ippo*: una reflexión etnográfica. In Villar & Fernández Álvarez (eds), *Religión, lengua y cultura*, 161–68.

Gelling, Margaret, 1978. *Signposts to the Past: Place-Names and the History of England*, London.

Gelling, Margaret, & Ann Cole, 2000. *The Landscape of Place-Names*, Stamford.

Gendron, Stéphane, 2003. *Les noms des lieux en France: essai de toponymie*, Paris.

Gohil, Ashwin E., 2005. *Ancient Celtic and Non-Celtic Place-Names of Northern Continental Europe: A Survey of Sources and Etymologies*. Unpublished Ph.D. Dissertation, University of Wales, Aberystwyth.

Gorrachategui, Joaquín, 1984. *Estudio sobre la onomástica indigena de Aquitania*, Vitoria-Gasteiz.

Gorrochategui, Joaquín, 1985. Lengua aquitana y lengua gala en la Aquitania etnográfica. In Melena (ed.), *Symbolae Mitxelena*, i, 613–28.

Gorrochategui, Joaquín, 1985–86. En torno a la clasificación del Lusitano. *Veleia* 2/3, 77–91.

Gorrochategui, Joaquín, 2000. Ptolemy's Aquitania and the Ebro valley. In Parsons & Sims-Williams (eds), *Ptolemy*, 143–57.

Gorrochategui, Joaquín, 2005. Establishment and analysis of Celtic toponyms in Aquitania and the Pyrenees. In De Hoz et al. (eds), *New Approaches*, 153–72.

Goukowsky, Paul (ed.), 1997. *Appien: Histoire romain*, ii, Collection Budé, Paris.

Greule, Albrecht, 2001. Keltisch **brig-* in der Toponymie Mitteleuropas. In Bentzinger, Rudolf, et al. (eds), *Sprachgeschichte, Dialektologie, Onomastik, Volkskunde*, Stuttgart, 197–205.

Greule, Albrecht, & Wolfgang Kleiber, 1999. Zur ältesten Sprachgeschichte im Moseltal (Mosella Romana). In Eggers et al. (eds), *Florilegium Linguisticum*, 155–77.

Greule, Albrecht, & Wulf Müller, 2002. Keltische Resistenzgebiete in der Germania und der Romania. *Onoma* 36, 245–54.

Guštin, Mitja, 1984. Die Kelten in Jugoslawien: Übersicht über das archäologische Fundgut. *Jahrbuch der Römisch-Germanischen Zentralmuseums Mainz* 31, 305–63.

Guyonvarc'h, Christian J., 1971. Le nom des Cotini. *Acta Archaeologica Carpathica* 12, 197–208.

Gwynn, Edward (ed.), 1924. *The Metrical Dindshenchas*, iv, Dublin.

Gysseling, Maurits, 1960. *Toponymisch Woordenboek van België, Nederland, Luxemburg, Noord-Frankrijk en West-Duitsland (vóór 1226)*, 2 vols, Brussels.

Halbherr, F., 1942. *Inscriptiones Creticae*, iii, ed. Margarita Guarducci, Rome.

Hamdoune, Christine, 1993. Ptolémée et la localisation des tribus de Tingitane. *Mélanges de l'École Française de Rome, Antiquité*, 105, i, 241–89.

Hamdoune, Christine, 1995. Frontières théoriques et réalité administrative: le cas de la Maurétanie Tingitane. In Rousselle, Aline (ed.), *Frontières terrestres, frontières célestes dans l'Antiquité*, Perpignan, 237–53.

Hamp, Eric P., 1966–67. Roman British *Rutupiae*, Gaulish *Rutuba*. *ÉC* 11, 413–14.

Hamp, Eric P., 1976. ʿΡουτύπιαι, *Rŭtŭpīnus* and morphological criteria. *BBCS* 26, 395–98.

Hamp, Eric P., 1982. On notable trees. *BBCS* 30, 42–44.

Hamp, Eric P., 1988. *Ad Pontem, Pontibus* as British. *BBCS* 35, 52.

Hamp, Eric P., 1988. *Bremenio* and Indo-European. *BBCS* 35, 53.

Hamp, Eric P., 1988. *Coria* and *Curia*. *BBCS* 35, 55.

Hamp, Eric P., 1989. Breton *dour zomm, leur zi*. *ÉC* 26, 64.

Hamp, Eric P., 1990. Briona AN(N)OKO(M)BOGIOS. *ÉC* 27, 180–81.

Hamp, Eric P., 1990. The morphology of Celtic **-sk-* adjectives. *ÉC* 27, 186–89.

Hamp, Eric P., 1991–92. British Celtic BRIGE and morphology. *SC* 26/27, 9–11.

Hamp, Eric P., 1991–92. Some toponyms of Roman Britain. *SC* 26/27, 15–20.

Hamp, Eric P., 1993. Morphologic criteria and evidence in Roman Britain. *Ériu* 44, 177–80.

Hamp, Eric P., 1997. Ὄκελον. *SC* 31, 276.

Hamp, Eric P., 2002. *llydan*. *SC* 36, 149–50.

Haspels, C. H. Emilie, 1971. *The Highlands of Phrygia: Sites and Monuments*, 2 vols, Princeton.

Haywood, John, 2001. *The Historical Atlas of the Celtic World*, London.

Hengst, Karlheinz, 2002. Eigennamen und Sprachkontakt in Osteuropa. Ein Modellfall: Der geographische Name *Samara*. *Onoma* 36, 41–90.

Herzfeld, Ernst, 1968. *The Persian Empire: Studies in Geography and Ethnography of the Ancient Near East*, Wiesbaden.

Hind, J. G. F., 1984. Whatever happened to the *Agri Decumates*? *Britannia* 15, 187–92.

Hoenigswald, Henry M., 1990. Celtiberi: a note. In Matonis, A. T. E., & Daniel F. Melia (eds), *Celtic Language, Celtic Culture: A Festschrift for Eric P. Hamp*, Van Nuys, CA, 13–15.

Hubert, Henri, 1934. *The Greatness and Decline of the Celts*, London.

Hubert, Henri, 1934. *The Rise of the Celts*, London.

Hubschmied, J. U., 1961. Etruskische Ortsnamen in Rätien. In Puchner, Karl (ed.), *VI. Internationaler Kongress für Namenforschung, 1958, Kongressberichte*, ii, Munich, 403–12.

Humbach, Helmut, & Susanne Ziegler (eds), 1998–2002. *Ptolemy: Geography, Book 6*, 2 parts, Wiesbaden.

Isaac, Graham R., 2002. Welsh *byw, byd, hyd*. *SC* 36, 145–47.

Isaac, Graham R., 2003. Some Old Irish etymologies, and some conclusions drawn from them. *Ériu* 53, 151–55.

Isaac, Graham R., 2005. Scotland. In De Hoz et al. (eds), *New Approaches*, 189–214.

Ivanov, Teofil, & Stojan Stojanov, 1985. *Abritus: Its History and Archaeology*, Razgrad.

Jackson, Kenneth H., 1947. On some Romano-British place-names. *Journal of Roman Studies* 37, 54–58.

Jackson, Kenneth H., 1980. The Pictish language. In Wainwright, F. T. (ed.), *The Problem of the Picts*, second edition, Perth, 129–66 and 173–76.

Jehasse, Jean, 1976. La Corse antique d'après Ptolémée. *Archeologia Corsa* 1, 143–70. [not seen]

Joseph, Lionel S., 1987. The origin of the Celtic denominatives in *-sag-. In Calvert Watkins (ed.), *Studies in Memory of Warren Cowgill*, Berlin, 113–59.

Kajanto, Iiro, 1965. *The Latin Cognomina*, Helsinki.

Katičić, Radoslav, 1976. *Ancient Languages of the Balkans*, i, The Hague.

Kemkes, Martin, Harald von der Osten-Woldenburg & Hartmann Reim, 1998. Spätbronzezeitliche und frührömische Wehranlagen auf dem 'Berg' über Ennetach, Stadt Mengen, Kreis Sigmaringen. *Archäologische Ausgrabungen in Baden-Württemberg*, 133–38.

Kitson, P. R., 1996. British and European river-names. *TPS* 94, 73–118.

Knobloch, Johann, 1985. Der Name der Langobarden. In Schützeichel, Rudolf (ed.), *Gießener Flurnamen-Kolloquium, 1984*, Heidelberg, 391–94.

Koch, John T., 1990. Brân, Brennos: an instance of early Gallo-Brittonic history and mythology. *CMCS* 20, 1–20.

Koch, John T., 2003. Celts, Britons, and Gaels: names, peoples, and identities. *Transactions of the Honourable Society of Cymmrodorion* 9, 41–56.

Krahe, Hans, 1963. Zu einigen alten Gewässernamen aus idg. *bhedh-. *BzN* 14, 180–86.

Kruta, Venceslas, 2000. *Les Celtes: histoire et dictionnaire*, Paris.

Kuhn, Hans, 1975. Die -acum-Namen am Rhein. *Rheinische Vierteljahrsblätter* 39, 391–95.

Lacroix, Jacques, 2003. *Les noms d'origine gauloise: la Gaule des combats*, Paris.

Lambert, Pierre-Yves, 1990. Welsh *Caswallawn*: the fate of British *au*. In Bammesberger, Alfred, & Alfred Wollmann (eds), *Britain 400–600: Language and History*, Heidelberg, 203–15.

Lambert, Pierre-Yves, 1994. *La langue gauloise*, Paris.

Lambert, Pierre-Yves, 1995. Préverbes gaulois suffixés en *-io-*: ambio-, ario-, cantio-. *ÉC* 31, 115–21.

Lambert, Pierre-Yves, 1997. Gaulois tardif et latin vulgaire. *ZCP* 49/50, 396–413.

Lambert, Pierre-Yves, 2000. Remarks on Gaulish place-names in Ptolemy. In Parsons & Sims-Williams (eds), *Ptolemy*, 159–68.

Lambert, Pierre-Yves, 2003. Review of Freeman, *Galatian Language*. *ÉC* 35, 358–59.

Lambert, Pierre-Yves, 2005. The place-names of *Lugdunensis* [Λουγδουνησία] (Ptolemy II 8). In De Hoz et al. (eds), *New Approaches*, 215–51.

Lasserre, François (ed.), 1966. *Strabon, Géographie*, ii, *Livres III et IV*, Collection Budé, Paris.

Lasserre, François (ed.), 1975. *Strabon, Géographie*, viii, *Livre XI*, Collection Budé, Paris.

Lasserre, François (ed.), 1981. *Strabon, Géographie*, ix, *Livre XII*, Collection Budé, Paris.

Le Bonniec, H., & Gallet de Santerre, H. (eds), 1953. *Pline l'Ancien, Histoire naturelle, Livre XXXIV*, Collection Budé, Paris.

Lejeune, Michel, 1990. Compléments gallo-grecs: Nîmes G-524. *ÉC* 27, 175–76.

Leo, F. (ed.), 1881. *Venanti Fortunati Opera Poetica*, Monumenta Germaniae Historica, Auctores Antiquissimi, 4/1, Berlin.

Lewis, Charlton T., & Charles Short, 1879. *A Latin Dictionary*, Oxford.

Lloyd-Jones, J., 1931–63. *Geirfa Barddoniaeth Gynnar Gymraeg*, 2 vols, Cardiff.

Loicq, Jean, 2003. Sur les peuples de nom 'Vénète' ou assimilé dans l'occident européen. *ÉC* 35, 133–65.

Loth, J., 1897. Bretons insulaires en Irlande. *RC* 18, 304–9.

Luján, Eugenio R., 2000. Ptolemy's *Callaecia* and the language(s) of the *Callaeci*. In Parsons & Sims-Williams (eds), *Ptolemy*, 55–72.

Luján, Eugenio R., 2005. The Galatian place names in Ptolemy and the methodological problems of dealing with Celtic linguistic evidence in Asia Minor. In De Hoz et al. (eds), *New Approaches*, 253–65.

MacQueen, John, 1990. The Renaissance in Scotland. In Williams, Glanmor, & Robert Owen Jones (eds), *The Celts and the Renaissance: Proceedings of the Eighth International Congress of Celtic Studies*, Cardiff, 41–56.

Mády, Z., 1966. Zwei pannonische Ortsnamen. *Acta Antiqua Academiae Scientiarum Hungaricae* 14, 197–210.

Magie, David, 1950. *Roman Rule in Asia Minor*, 2 vols, Princeton.

Maier, Bernhard, 1996. Is Lug to be identified with Mercury (*Bell. Gall.* VI 17, 1)? New suggestions on an old problem. *Ériu* 47, 127–35.

Maier, Bernhard, 1997. Zu den keltischen Namen von Carlisle und Colchester. *BzN* N.F. 32, 281–85.

Manni, Eugenio, 1981. *Geografia fisica e politica della Sicilia antica*, Rome.

Maraval, Pierre (ed.), 1990. *Grégoire de Nysse: Lettres*, Sources Chrétiennes 363, Paris.

Marichal, Robert, 1988. *Les graffites de la Graufesenque*, Paris.

Markey, Thomas L., & Bernard Mees, 2003. Prestino, patrimony and the Plinys. *ZCP* 53, 116–67.

Marks, Jonathan, 2002. *What it Means to be 98% Chimpanzee: Apes, People, and their Genes*, Berkeley & Los Angeles.

Mayhoff, Carolus (ed.), 1967. *C. Plinii Secundi Naturalis Historiae Libri XXXVII*, i, *Libri I–VI*, Stuttgart.

McCone, Kim R., 1986. Werewolves, cyclopes, *díberga*, and *fíanna*: juvenile deliquency in early Ireland. *CMCS* 12, 1–22.

McCone, Kim R., 1996. *Towards a Relative Chronology of Ancient and Medieval Celtic Sound Change*, Maynooth.

McCrindle, J. W., 1877. *Ancient India as Described by Megisthenês and Arrian*, Calcutta, Bombay & London.

M'Charek, Amade, 2005. *The Human Genome Diversity Project: An Ethnography of Scientific Practice*, Cambridge.

McManus, Damian, 1991. *A Guide to Ogam*, Maynooth.

Mees, Bernard, 2003. Stratum and shadow: a genealogy of stratigraphy theories from the Indo-European West. In Andersen (ed.), *Language Contacts in Prehistory*, 11–44.

Meid, Wolfgang, 1994. *Celtiberian Inscriptions*, Budapest.

Meillet, A., 1925, *La méthode comparative en linguistique historique*, Oslo.

Meineke, A. (ed.), 1849. *Stephanos Byzantinii: Ethnikôn*, Berlin.

Melena, José L. (ed.), 1985. *Symbolae Ludovico Mitxelena Septuagenario Oblatae*, 2 vols, Vitoria-Gasteiz.

Meyers, Eric M. (ed.), 1997. *Oxford Encyclopedia of Archaeology in the Near East*, 5 vols, New York & Oxford.

Mihailov, Georgi, 1970. *Inscriptiones Graecae in Bulgaria Repertae*, i, Sofia.

Mihailov, Georgi, 1987. Le suffixe *-sk-* en thrace. *Linguistique balkanique* 30, 147–62.

Minkova, Milena, 2000. *The Personal Names of the Latin Inscriptions in Bulgaria*, Frankfurt am Main.

Mitchell, Stephen, 1980. Population and the land in Roman Galatia. *ANRW* II.7.2, 1053–61.

Mitchell, Stephen, 1993. *Anatolia: Land, Men, and Gods in Asia Minor*, i, *The Celts in Anatolia and the Impact of Roman Rule*, Oxford.

Mitford, Timothy B., 1980. Cappadocia and Armenia Minor: historical setting of the *limes*. *ANRW* II.7.2, 1169–1228.

Mócsy, András, 1974. *Pannonia and Upper Moesia*, London.

Mócsy, András, 1983. *A római név mint társadalomtörténeti forrás*, Budapest.

Moore, John H., 1995. The End of a Paradigm. *Current Anthropology* 36, 530–31.

Morrachini-Mazel, G., & R. Boinard 1989. *La Corse selon Ptolémée*, Cahier Corsica 128/129/130, Bastia.

Murphy, J. P. (ed.), 1977. *Rufus Festus Avienus: Ora Maritima*, Chicago.

Nenci, G., & G. Vallet (eds), 1977–. *Bibliografia topografica della colonizzazione greca in Italia e nelle isole tirreniche*, Pisa & Rome.

Nichols, Johanna, 1996. The comparative method as heuristic. In Durie, Mark, & Malcolm Ross (eds), *The Comparative Method Reviewed: Regularity and Irregularity in Language Change*, New York & Oxford, 39–71.

Nissen, Heinrich, 1883–1902. *Italische Landeskunde*, 2 vols, Berlin.

Nobbe, Carolus Fridericus Augustus (ed.), 1843. *Claudii Ptolemaei Geographia*, 3 vols, Leipzig.

Nussbaum, Alan J., 1986. *Head and Horn in Indo-European*, Berlin.

Oakley, S. P., 1995. *The Hill-Forts of the Samnites*, London.

O'Rahilly, Thomas F., 1942. Mid. Ir. *lága, láige. lágan, láigen*. *Ériu* 13, 152–53.

O'Rahilly, Thomas F., 1946. *Early Irish History and Mythology*, Dublin.

Orel, Vladimir E., 1987. Thracian and Celtic. *BBCS* 34, 1–9.

Oswald, Felix, 1931. *Index of Potters' Stamps on Terra Sigillata*, East Bridgford.

Padel, Oliver, 1979–80. Cornish **heyl* 'estuary'. *SC* 14/15, 240–45.

Pallottino, Massimo, 1979. *Saggi di Antichità*, ii, Rome.

Papazoglou, Fanoula, 1988. *Les villes de Macédoine à l'époque romaine*, École Française d'Athènes, Bulletin de Correspondance Hellénique, Supplément 16, Athens & Paris.

Parsons, David N., 2000. Classifying Ptolemy's English place-names. In Parsons & Sims-Williams (eds), *Ptolemy*, 169–78.

Parsons, David N., & Patrick Sims-Williams (eds), 2000. *Ptolemy: Towards a Linguistic Atlas of the Earliest Celtic Place-Names of Europe. Papers from a Workshop, Sponsored by the British Academy, in the Department of Welsh, University of Wales, Aberystwyth*, Aberystwyth.

Pârvan, Vasile, 1928. *Dacia*, Cambridge.

Petit, Jean-Paul, & Michel Mangin (eds), 1994. *Atlas des agglomérations secondaires de la Gaule Belgique et des Germanies*, Paris.

Pfiffig, Ambros Josef, 1972. *Einführung in die Etruskologie*, Darmstadt.

Philipon, E., 1909. Le gaulois *dūros*. *RC* 30, 73–77.

Piggott, Stuart, 1951. William Camden and the *Britannia*. *Proceedings of the British Academy* 37, 199–217.

Piggott, Stuart, 1965. *Ancient Europe*, Edinburgh.

Pokorny, J., 1950. Some Celtic etymologies. *Journal of Celtic Studies* 1, 129–35.

Potts, D. T., 1990. *The Arabian Gulf in Antiquity*, 2 vols, Oxford.

Poulter, A. G., 1980. Rural communities (vici and komai) and their role in the organization of the *limes* of Moesia Inferior. In Hanson, W. S., & L. J. F. Keppie (eds), *Roman Frontier Studies 1979*, iii, British Archaeological Reports, International Series, 71(iii), Oxford, 729–44.

Priese, Karl-Heinz, 1984. Orte des mittleren Niltals in der Überlieferung bis zum Ende des christlichen Mittelalters. In Hitze, Fritz (ed.), *Meroitistische Forschungen 1980*, Meroitica, 7, Berlin, 484–97.

Prósper, Blanca María, 2002. *Lenguas y religiones prerromanas del occidente de la Península Ibérica*, Salamanca.

Quentel, P., 1962. Le nom de Brest. *Revue internationale d'onomastique* 14, 88–92.

Radt, Wolfgang, 1999. *Pergamon*, second edition, Köln.

Ramat, Anna Giacolone, & Paolo Ramat (eds), 1998. *The Indo-European Languages*, London.

Rance, Philip, 2001. Attacotti, Déisi and Magnus Maximus: the case for Irish federates in Late Roman Britain. *Britannia* 32, 243–70.

Rapin, Claude, 1998. L'incompréhensible Asie centrale de la carte de Ptolémée: propositions pour un décodage. *Bulletin of the Asia Institute* 12, 201–25.

Rebuffat, René, 1982. Au-delà des camps romains d'Afrique mineure: renseignement, contrôle, pénétration. *ANRW* II.10.2, 474–513.

Rebuffat, René, 2001. Les tribus en Maurétanie Tingitane. *Antiquités africaines* 37, 23–44.

Reinecke, Paul, 1924; 1925; 1926. Die örtliche Bestimmung der antiken geographischen Namen für das rechtrheinische Bayern. *Der bayerische Vorgeschichtsfreund* 4, 17–48; 5, 17–48; 6, 17–44.

Reydellet, Marc (ed.), 1994. *Venance Fortunat: poèmes*, i, *Livres I–IV*, Collection Budé, Paris.

Reynolds, L. D. (ed.), 1983. *Texts and Transmission*, Oxford.

Rives, J. B., 1999. *Tacitus: Germania*, Oxford.

Rivet, A. L. F., 1980. Celtic names and Roman places. *Britannia* 11, 1–19.

Rivet, A. L. F., 1988. *Gallia Narbonensis*, London.

Rix, Helmut, 1954. Zur Verbreitung und Chronologie einiger keltischer Orstnamentypen. In *Festschrift für Peter Goessler*, Stuttgart, 99–107.

Robert, Louis, 1962. *Villes d'Asie Mineure*, second edition, Paris.

Robin, Christian Julien, 1995. La Tihāma yéménite avant l'Islam: notes d'histoire et de géographie historique. *Arabian Archaeology and Epigraphy* 6, 222–35.

Rostaing, Charles, 1950. *Essai sur la toponymie de la Provence*, Paris.

Rubio Orecilla, Francisco J., 2001. Las formaciones secundarias en -*ko*- del Celtibérico. In Villar & Fernández Álvarez (eds), *Religión, lengua y cultura*, 581–94.

Russell, Paul, 1988. The suffix -*āko*- in Continental Celtic. *ÉC* 25, 131–73.

Russell, Paul, 1995. Brittonic words in Irish glossaries. In Eska et al. (eds), *Hispano-Gallo-Brittonica*, 166–82.

Russell, Paul, 2000. On reading Ptolemy: some methodological considerations. In Parsons & Sims-Williams (eds), *Ptolemy*, 179–88.

Salway, Benet, 2001. Travel, *itineraria* and *tabellaria*. In Adams & Lawrence (eds), *Travel and Geography*, 22–66.

Schmid, Anneliese, 1962. *Das Flussgebiet des Neckar*, Wiesbaden.

Schmid, Wolfgang P., 1995. Alteuropäische Gewässernamen. In Eichler et al. (eds), *Namenforschung*, i, 756–62.

Schmidt, K. H., 2003. Review of Parsons & Sims-Williams (eds), *Ptolemy. ZCP* 53, 274–76.

Schmidt, Karl Horst, 1985. Keltisch, Baltisch und Slavisch. In Melena (ed.), *Symbolae Mitxelena*, i, 23–29.

Schmidt, Karl Horst, 1994. Galatische Sprachreste. In Schwertheim, Elmar (ed.), *Forschungen in Galatien*, Bonn, 15–28.

Schmitt, Paul, 1973. *Le Maroc d'après la 'Géographie' de Claude Ptolémée*, Tours.

Schoff, Wilfred H. (ed.), 1914. *Parthian Stations by Isidore of Charax: An Account of the Overland Trade Route between the Levant and India in the First Century B.C.*, Philadelphia.

Schrijver, Peter, 1995. De etymologie van de naam van de Cannenefaten. *Amsterdamer Beiträge zur älteren Germanistik* 41, 13–22.

Schrijver, Peter, 1995. *Studies in British Celtic Historical Phonology*, Amsterdam.

Schrijver, Peter, 1995. Welsh *heledd, hêl*, Cornish **heyl*, 'Latin' *helinium*, Dutch *hel-, zeelt.* *NOWELE* 26, 31–42.

Schrijver, Peter, 2000. Keltisch of niet: twee namen en een verdacht accent. In Hofman, Rijcklof, Bernadette Smelik & Lauran Toorians (eds), *Kelten in Nederland*, Utrecht & Münster, 69–87.

Schrijver, Peter, 2000. Non-Indo-European surviving in Ireland in the first millennium AD. *Ériu* 51, 195–99.

Schrijver, Peter, 2005. Early Celtic diphthongization and the Celtic–Latin interface. In De Hoz et al. (eds), *New Approaches*, 55–67.

Schulten, A., 1955–57. *Iberische Landeskunde*, 2 vols, Baden-Baden.

Schumacher, Stefan, 2004. *Die keltischen Primärverben*, Innsbruck.

Schwarz, Ernst, 1961. *Die Ortsnamen der Sudetenländer als Geschichtsquelle*, Munich.

Sergent, Bernard, 1988. Les premiers Celtes d'Anatolie. *Revue des études anciennes* 90, 329–58.

Shaw, Francis, 1956. The background to *Grammatica Celtica. Celtica* 3, 1–16.

Shchukin, Mark, 1995. The Celts in eastern Europe. *Oxford Journal of Archaeology* 14, 201–27.

Silberman, A. (ed.), 1988. *Pomponius Mela: Chorographie*, Collection Budé, Paris.

Sims-Williams, Patrick, 1980–82. The development of the Indo-European voiced labiovelars in Celtic. *BBCS* 29, 201–229 and 690.

Sims-Williams, Patrick, 1982. Review of PNRB. *CMCS* 4, 90–93.

Sims-Williams, Patrick, 1998. Celtomania and Celtoscepticism. *CMCS* 36, 1–35.

Sims-Williams, Patrick, 1998. Genetics, linguistics, and prehistory: thinking big and thinking straight. *Antiquity* 72, 505–27.

Sims-Williams, Patrick, 1998. The Celtic languages. In Ramat & Ramat (eds), *The Indo-European Languages*, 345–79.

Sims-Williams, Patrick, 2000. Degrees of Celticity in Ptolemy's names: examples from Wales. In Parsons & Sims-Williams (eds), *Ptolemy*, 1–15.

Sims-Williams, Patrick, 2002. The five languages of Wales in the pre-Norman inscriptions. *CMCS* 44, 1–36.

Sims-Williams, Patrick, 2004. Review of Day, *Indo-European Origins. Kratylos* 49, 39–43.

Sims-Williams, Patrick, 2005. Measuring Celticity from Wales to the Orient. In De Hoz et al. (eds), *New Approaches*, 267–87.

Sims-Williams, Patrick, 2005. Welsh *Iâl*, Gaulish names in *Ial-* and *-ialo-*, and the god Ialonus. *CMCS* 49, 57–72.

Sims-Williams, Patrick (forthcoming). Common Celtic, Gallo-Brittonic and Insular Celtic. In Lambert, Pierre-Yves, & Georges-Jean Pinault (eds), *Gaulois et celtique continental: Colloque international 1998*, Paris.

Skála, Emil, 2002. Die Ortsnamen von Böhmen, Mähren und Schlesien als Geschichtsquelle. *Bohemia* 43, 385–411.

Smith, A. H., 1956. *English Place-Name Elements*, 2 vols, Cambridge.

Smith, Colin, 1980. The survival of Romano-British toponymy. *Nomina* 4, 27–40.

Sprenger, A., 1875. *Die alte Geographie Arabiens als Grundlage der Entwicklungsgeschichte des Semitismus*, Bern.

Stalmaszczyk, Piotr, & Krzysztof Tomasz Witczak, 1993. Studies in Indo-European vocabulary. *Indogermanische Forschungen* 98, 24–39.

Stalmaszczyk, Piotr, & Krzysztof Tomasz Witczak, 1995. Celto-Slavic language connections: new evidence for Celtic lexical influence upon Proto-Slavic. *Linguistica Baltica* 4, 225–32.

Stokes, Whitley, 1891–93. On the Bodleian fragment of Cormac's Glossary. *TPS*, 149–206.

Stokes, Whitley (ed.), 1892. The Borama. *RC* 13, 32–124 and 299–300.

Strang, Alastair (unpublished). Ptolemy's geography of the Lower Danube region, or, analysing Ptolemy's Ninth Map of Europe. [Typescript, based on part of his Ph.D. thesis, *Ptolemy's Geography Reappraised*, University of Nottingham, 1994.]

Šašel, Jaroslav, 1966. Keltisches *portorium* in den Ostalpen (zu Plin. n. h. III 128). In *Corolla Memoriae Erich Swoboda Dedicata*, Graz & Köln, 198–204.

Talbert, Richard J. A., 2003. Barrington Atlas of the Greek and Roman World: the cartographic fundamentals in retrospect. *Cartographic Perspectives* 46, 4–27 and 72–76.

Talbert, Richard, & Kai Brodersen (eds), 2004. *Space in the Roman World: Its Perception and Presentation*, Münster.

Teodor, Silvia, 1988. Elemente celtice pe teritoriul est-carpatic al României. *Arheologia Moldovei* 12, 33–51.

Thurneysen, Rudolf, 1891. Review of Holder, *Alt-celtischer Sprachschatz*, Lieferung 1. *Literaturblatt für germanische und romanische Philologie* 12/7, 242–44.

Thurneysen, Rudolf, 1932. Etymologien. *Zeitschrift für vergleichende Sprachforschung* 59, 13–16.

Thurneysen, Rudolf, 1991–95. *Gesammelte Schriften*, 3 vols, Tübingen.

Tomaschitz, Kurt, 2002. *Die Wanderungen der Kelten in der antiken literarischen Überlieferung*, Vienna.

Toner, Gregory, 2000. Identifying Ptolemy's Irish places and tribes. In Parsons & Sims-Williams (eds), *Ptolemy*, 73–82.

Toorians, Lauran, 2000. *Keltisch en Germaans in de Nederlanden*, Mémoires de la Société Belge d'Études Celtiques 13, Brussels.

Tovar, Antonio, 1974. *Iberische Landeskunde*, i, *Baetica*, Baden-Baden.

Tovar, Antonio, 1976. *Iberische Landeskunde*, ii, *Lusitanien*, Baden-Baden.

Tovar, Antonio, 1977. *Krahes alteuropäische Hydronymie und die westindogermanischen Sprachen*, Heidelberg.

Tovar, Antonio, 1982. The god *Lugus* in Spain. *BBCS* 29, 591–99.

Tovar, Antonio, 1989. *Iberische Landeskunde*, iii, *Tarraconensis*, Baden-Baden.

Trask, R. L., 1997. *The History of Basque*, London.

Treister, Michail J., 1993. The Celts in the north Pontic area: a reassessment. *Antiquity* 67, 789–804.

Udolph, Jürgen, 1994. *Namenkundliche Studien zum Germanenproblem*, Berlin.

Udolph, Jürgen, 2004. Review of Anreiter, *Die vorrömischen Namen Pannoniens*. *Kratylos* 49, 132–37.

Valesius, Hadrianus, 1675. *Notitia Galliarum*, Paris.

Velkov, V., 1977. *Cities in Thrace and Dacia in Late Antiquity*, Amsterdam.

Vendryes, J., 1903. Latin *vervēx* (*vervīx*), irlandais *ferb*. *Mémoires de la Société de Linguistique de Paris* 12, 40–42.

Vendryes, J., 1912. L'étymologie du gaulois *dumias*. *RC* 33, 463–66.

Vendryes, J., 1929. Review of Ekwall, *English River-Names*. *RC* 46, 336–37.

Vendryes, J., 1929. Review of Pârvan, *Dacia*. *RC* 46, 334–36.

Vendryes, J., 1955. Note sur la toponymie celtique. In *Recueil de travaux offert à M. Clovis Brunel*, ii, Paris, 641–50.

Vennemann, Theo, 1994. Linguistic reconstruction in the context of European prehistory. *TPS* 92, 215–84.

Vennemann, Theo, 1998. Pre-Indo-European toponyms in central and Western Europe: *Bid-*/*Bed-* and *Pit-* names. In Nicolaisen, W. F. H. (ed.), *Proceedings of the XIXth International Congress of Onomastic Sciences, Aberdeen, 1996*, ii, Aberdeen, 359–63.

Villar, Francisco, 1994. Los antropónimos en *Pent-*, *Pint-* y las lenguas indoeuropeas prerromanas de la Península Ibérica. In Bielmeier, Roland, & Reinhard Stempel (eds), *Indogermanica et Caucasica: Festschrift für Karl Horst Schmidt*, Berlin, 234–64.

Villar, Francisco, 1995. *Estudios de Celtibérico y de toponimia prerromana*, Salamanca.

Villar, Francisco, 2000. *Indoeuropeos y no indoeuropeos en la Hispania Prerromana*, Salamanca.

Villar, Francisco, 2004. The Celtic language of the Iberian peninsula. In Baldi, Philip, & Pietro U. Dini (eds), *Studies in Baltic and Indo-European Linguistics in Honor of William R. Schmalstieg*, Amsterdam, 243–73.

Villar, Francisco, & M.ª Pilar Fernández Álvarez (eds), 2001. *Religión, lengua y cultura prerromanas de Hispania*, Salamanca.

Villaronga, Leandre, 1994. *Corpus Nummum Hispaniae ante Augusti Aetatem*, Madrid.

Vitali, Daniele, 1991. The Celts in Italy. In Moscati, Sabatino (ed.), *The Celts*, London, 220–35.

Watkins, Calvert, 1994. *Selected Writings*, ii, Innsbruck.

Watkins, Calvert, 1998. Proto-Indo-European: comparison and reconstruction. In Ramat & Ramat (eds), *The Indo-European Languages*, 25–73.

Weber, Ekkehard, 1976. *Tabula Peutingeriana, Codex Vindobonensis 324: Kommentar*, Graz.

Weisgerber, Leo, 1931. Galatische Sprachreste. In *Natalicium Johannes Geffcken zum 70. Geburtstag*, Heidelberg, 151–75.

Whittaker, C. R., 1994. *Frontiers of the Roman Empire*, Baltimore.

Wilkinson, John Garth, 2004. **Lanum* and *Lugudunum*: full lune, and light on an unkempt wraith. *Nomina* 27, 71–89.

Wirth, Gerhard, & Oskar von Hinüber (ed.), 1985. *Arrian: der Alexanderzug, Indische Geschichte*, Munich & Zurich.

Witzel, Michael, 1987. On the localisation of Vedic texts and schools. In Pollet, Gilbert (ed.), *India and the Ancient World: History, Trade and Culture before AD 650*, Leuven, 173–213.

Wodtko, Dagmar S., 2003. Review of Parsons & Sims-Williams (eds), *Ptolemy*. *Kratylos* 48, 232–34.

Woodard, Roger D. (ed.), 2004. *The Cambridge Encyclopaedia of the World's Ancient Languages*, Cambridge.

Woźniak, Zenon, 1976. Die östliche Randzone der Latènekultur. *Germania* 54, 382–402.

Yorke, V. W., 1898. Inscriptions from eastern Asia Minor. *Journal of Hellenic Studies* 18, 306–27.

Zehnacker, Hubert (ed.), 1998. *Pline l'Ancien: Histoire naturelle, livre III*, Collection Budé, Paris.

Zimmer, Stefan, 2003. *A uo penn bit pont*: aspects of leadership in Celtic and Indo-European. *ZCP* 53, 202–29.

Zirra, Vlad, 1976. The eastern Celts of Romania. *Journal of Indo-European Studies* 4, 1–41.

Zubarev, V. G., 1999. The Roman roads between the Ister (Danube) and the Tyras (Dniester) in Claudius Ptolemaeus' description. *Vestnik Drevnei Istorii* 1999, Part 3, 67–76.

Zupitza, E., 1902–3. Kelten und Gallier. *ZCP* 4, 1–22.

INDEX OF PLACE-NAMES